THE ENGLISH LEGAL SYSTEM

THE ENGLISH LEGAL SYSTEM

Seventeenth Edition

2016–2017

Gary Slapper, LLB (UCL), LLM (UCL), PhD (LSE), PGCE (Law) (Manc)

Global Professor, New York University; Director, New York University, London; Door Tenant, 36 Bedford Row; Visiting Professor of Law, The Chinese University of Hong Kong, and The Open University, UK

David Kelly, BA, BA (Law), PhD

Previously Principal Lecturer in Law, Staffordshire University

Routledge
Taylor & Francis Group

LONDON AND NEW YORK

Seventeenth edition published 2016
by Routledge
2 Park Square, Milton Park, Abingdon, Oxon, OX14 4RN

and by Routledge
711 Third Avenue, New York, NY 10017

Routledge is an imprint of the Taylor & Francis Group, an informa business

First edition published by Cavendish 1994
Sixteenth edition published by Routledge 2015

British Library Cataloguing in Publication Data
A catalogue record for this book is available from the British Library

Library of Congress Cataloging-in-Publication Data
A catalog record for this title has been requested

ISBN: 978-1-138-94444-2 (hbk)
ISBN: 978-1-138-94445-9 (pbk)
ISBN: 978-1-315-67189-5 (ebk)

Typeset in Simoncini Garamond
by Apex CoVantage, LLC

Printed and bound by CPI Group (UK) Ltd, Croydon, CR0 4YY

CONTENTS

PREFACE

In a law lecture delivered on 25 October 1758, William Blackstone described law as 'this most useful and most rational branch of learning'. With the growth and pervasion of law in the succeeding two and a half centuries, the importance of legal study has risen accordingly.

Law permeates into every cell of social life. It governs everything from the embryo to exhumation. It governs the air we breathe, the food and drink that we consume, our travel, sexuality, family relationships, property, the world of sport, science, employment, business, education, health, everything from neighbour disputes to war. Taken together, the set of institutions, processes, laws and personnel that provide the apparatus through which law works, and the matrix of rules that control them, are known as the legal system.

This system has evolved over a long time. Today it contains elements that are very old, such as the coroners' courts, which have an 800-year history, and elements that are very new, such as electronic law reports and judges using laptops and tablets.

A good comprehension of the English legal system requires knowledge and skill in a number of disciplines. The system itself is the result of developments in law, economy and politics, sociological change and the theories which feed all these bodies of knowledge. This book aims to assist students of the English legal system in the achievement of a good understanding of the law, and of its institutions and processes. We aim to set the legal system in a social context, and to present a range of relevant critical views.

Being proficient in this subject also means being familiar with contemporary changes and proposed changes, and this new edition has been comprehensively revised and updated to take these into account.

Since the sixteenth edition of this book, the changes to the English legal system have been many and varied. We have included in the text a wide range of legislative, common law, constitutional and European developments that have occurred in the last year.

We are once again very grateful to all those who advanced suggestions for improvement of the book since the previous edition; many of those suggestions have been implemented in this edition.

Gary Slapper
David Kelly
22 January 2016

THE ENGLISH LEGAL SYSTEM – AN OVERVIEW

This book is about the English legal system. It is helpful to note, right at the very beginning, that the system was never designed in full at one point. It is over a thousand years old and it has evolved over that time.

Even some of the elements within the system which appear to run all the way through, such as the monarchy, have changed considerably over the centuries. Monarchs in the tenth century, for example, did not rule over the whole of what would be today seen as the UK, and their powers were not limited by conventions as they are in modern times.

It is also important to note that the system has not come to a stop today. It is still growing and developing and always will do. At one time in the long history of the legal system, there was no democratic parliament to make law, but now there is. At one time, law could be declared by the monarch, but now that is impossible.

For a long time before the twentieth century there was no organised system of appeals in criminal cases but today there is such a system. In its early stages of development, the legal system had no organised law reporting so, in law courts, previous cases were analysed only in an oral way with lawyers and judges giving accounts of previous cases from memory, whereas today we have libraries full of voluminous law reports and all major decisions published in full online. Indeed, communications technology is completely altering the way the system works by allowing for new relationships between lawyers and their clients to exist in an electronic sphere. Precedents (previous cases which are relevant to the one in dispute) from all around the world can be consulted instantly in court using a computer, and mobile telephony can be used to summon witnesses to legal cases.

The pen and parchment allowed law to work in one particular way; the printing press meant law could be developed to a higher level of sophistication; the prevalence of the typewriter and photocopying facilities changed things further; and the internet and mobile telephony take law into a different sphere. It is clear that the story has not stopped here and that law will continue to develop in relation to technology.

Law, though, is also affected by the politics and the economy that surround it. New laws affecting the way the legal system works can be passed by one parliament but subsequently repealed when a different group of politicians gain power and want to change the legal system in accordance with their political views. In this textbook we aim not only to explain the law and mechanisms of the legal system but to situate those changes in the context of such matters as *how the law came to be what it is* and *what social, economic and political issues arise from the legal system.*

In *Chapter 1* we examine the different approaches to legal study and the way that this book engages with such study. We also examine basic questions affecting the study of the legal system such as what is meant by law and how law can be classified according to different criteria.

In *Chapter 2* we examine the rule of law and human rights. These are very important ideas at the centre of the modern legal system. They are always in the thinking of lawyers, judges, legislators and civil servants and quite often they are ideas which are explicitly part of legal discussions. In its briefest form, the 'rule of law' is the idea that everyone is governed by the existing law, that no one is above it, and that random or capricious decisions in law courts are undesirable. The rule of law refers to an idea by which people are governed by rules, not by the whim of rulers.

The story of 'human rights' is a long one whose origins can be traced back many centuries, but such rights were systematically enshrined in documents by the United Nations and in Europe only from the middle of the last century. Since then they have become democratically implanted in many countries such as the UK. They cover basic unalterable rights, such as that no one should be tortured, and other rights such as the right to freedom of expression, which can only be taken away where there is a compelling need under such criteria that it is in the interests of a democracy.

In *Chapter 3* we examine various types of legislation as sources of law. In general language, people speak about 'the law' as if it were one single thing, but in fact there are various sorts of law, including law that we follow from being a member of the European Union, legislation direct from the UK Parliament, and the judicial decisions of the higher level courts in the UK. Legislation is a prodigious source of modern law. In recent times, Parliament has been making about 25 new Acts a year.

In *Chapter 4* we examine case decisions as a source of law. The higher courts – in particular the Court of Appeal and the Supreme Court – produce a large annual output of decisions that become part of English law. In *Chapter 5*, we examine the third main source of law in the English legal system: law from both the European Union and the European Court of Human Rights.

In *Chapters 6* and *7* we examine the civil courts and the civil process. In general terms 'civil law' means the law which governs the relationship *between* organisations like companies, and *between* individuals and organisations, and *between* individuals. This is different from the criminal process and courts, which we look at in *Chapters 9, 10*, and *11*, where one of the parties is the state and that party is prosecuting an individual or organisation for committing a crime.

In one sense, the civil courts and civil process are sub-compartments of the English legal system. It is, though, not quite as straightforward as that. It is not the case that the buildings and the people who work in the civil side of law are entirely separate from the people and buildings concerned with the criminal side of the system. Some judges and lawyers, and some of the court and governmental buildings, deal with both civil and criminal matters. The civil courts have their own system of procedures and rules and their own special set of court orders and remedies. Typically, for example, a litigant in the civil process wishes to have an award of damages to compensate them for some harm or loss, or an order (an injunction) to stop someone from doing something legally wrong.

In *Chapter 8* we examine the Family Courts and Process, a hugely important part of the system that deals with marriage, divorce, cohabitation, disputes between parents over the upbringing of their children, financial support for children upon separation or divorce, local authority powers to protect children and adoption.

In *Chapters 9*, *10* and *11* we examine the Criminal Courts and criminal process. Prosecutions for crimes are brought by the state against individuals or groups of individuals or organisations such as companies. To be convicted of a crime is a serious matter and, where the crime is a serious one, conviction can result in a life-changing sentence for the convict. Of all prosecutions brought each year, of which there are over 1.5 million, 98 per cent are carried out in magistrates' courts, with the remainder being held as trials before a jury in Crown Courts.

The state is mighty and powerful and highly resourced, whereas the individual is comparatively weak and poorly resourced. So, over time, rules about what evidence can be heard in court have evolved to prevent the state getting a conviction where the evidence would not sustain a fair conviction. No one, for example, can be convicted on the basis of a confession alone – there must be other credible evidence against them. That rule is to prevent confessions being extracted from suspects by improper means. Today, there are debates about whether defendants in criminal trials have too many rights; we examine these issues in these chapters.

In *Chapter 12* we examine the judiciary. Much of modern law comes from democratically passed legislation but these laws will often be given clear meaning only once they are interpreted and applied by judges in law courts (we examine the rule of statutory interpretation in *Chapter 3*). So, as the judiciary plays such a critically important role in 'making law', it becomes very important to analyse and evaluate this body of people, this legal institution. In this chapter we examine the constitutional role of the judiciary and such issues as how judges are selected and trained, and how their conduct is regulated.

In *Chapter 13* we examine the role of judicial reasoning and politics. The scientific study of how judges arrive at the judgments in cases is of momentous importance because it is through that route that so much of English law is made real.

In *Chapter 14* we examine the jury. The system of the jury trial has ancient origins and has been an indispensable part of the English legal system ever since. It is now replicated in over 50 countries of the Commonwealth and is, according to one theory, the most important element in a legal system that guarantees against the tyranny of the state.

In *Chapter 15* we examine arbitration, tribunal adjudication and alternative dispute resolution. Going through the law courts to resolve a civil dispute or family law dispute is almost always a very long, expensive and confrontational event. There is considerable doubt about whether that approach is the best one in all cases. In this chapter we look at the alternative mechanisms to standard law court hearings. These began as adventurous innovations on the outskirts of the legal system, but their success in various ways has given them a progressively larger and more important role within the legal system. Arbitration, tribunal adjudication and alternative dispute resolution are now a central part of the legal system.

In *Chapter 16* we examine legal services. For most citizens the legal system's main manifestation is through its lawyers. This chapter examines and evaluates the systems through which legal advice and representation in court are provided. We examine the different types of lawyer, such as solicitors and barristers, and the changing structure of legal services. Recently we have moved into an era where lawyers can be involved in offering legal services in businesses which combine with other professionals such as accountants, and where commercial companies (even supermarkets) can own law firms.

In *Chapter 17* we examine the funding of legal services. Most citizens, of course, do not know any more about the law than they know about chemistry or medicine. It is therefore problematic if they have to try to defend themselves against a criminal or civil action without a lawyer. How should legal services be provided to people who could not otherwise afford to pay for a lawyer? In this chapter we examine the rules of the legal aid system and its changing features in the light of the economic and political environment. In 1950, 85 per cent of the English population was covered by the legal aid system, whereas by 2014 the proportion of people covered had fallen to 25 per cent. The significance and consequences of access to law are covered in this chapter.

ACKNOWLEDGEMENTS

We owe immeasurable gratitude to many people for the work and expertise that contributed to this book. We owe a particular debt to Suzanne, Hannah, Emily, Charlotte, Jane and Michael for their patience and support, again, while we researched, read and wrote.

We have again greatly benefited from the encouragement and sustained, meticulous professionalism of Fiona Briden at Routledge. Her thoughtful approach to guiding the redesign of this book has been superb. We are very grateful to Emily Wells at Routledge for her excellent management of the editorial process, and to Karen Davies for her expertise on the diagrams. We are greatly indebted to Marie Roberts at Apex CoVantage for her marvellous project management and vigilant professionalism, and to Jackie Day for expertly managing the production at Routledge once again. The book benefited greatly from the superbly punctilious copy-editing of Janelle Bowman. We owe great thanks again to the outstanding professionalism of solicitor Vicki Scoble in civil process, the legal professions and civil law. The work of Michael Coley, rising star of the bar, on the criminal process, and the civil and criminal courts, has been outstanding. We are indebted to Professor Dame Hazel Genn QC, Carolyn Bracknell, Christopher Donnellan QC, Ben Fitzpatrick, Alisdair Smith, Professor Michael Furmston, HH Judge Lynn Tayton QC and John Cooper QC. We are greatly indebted for the magnificent work of Natasha Phillips, Editor-in-Chief of the *Encyclopaedia on Family and The Law*, on Family Courts and Process.

Others have offered uplifting encouragement, observations and assistance, or have stimulated our thinking in a helpful way. Thanks are thus due to Doreen and Ivor Slapper, Clifford, Maxine, Pav, Anish, the late Raie Schwartz, David and Julie Whight, Professor Robert Reiner, Hugh McLaughlan, Eric Sneddon, Abigail Carr, Robert Zimmerman, Carol Howells, Professor Sir Jeffrey Jowell QC, Professor Ian Dennis, Professor Matthew Weait, Professor Tony Lentin, Frances Thomas, Alison Morris, Patrick Whight, Alaric Best, Malcolm Park, Sheriff Andrew M Cubie, Frances Gibb, Legal Editor of *The Times*, Sir Stephen Sedley and The Rt Hon The Lord Woolf.

Guide to using the book

The English Legal System contains a number of features designed to support and reinforce your learning. This Guided Tour shows you how to make the most of your textbook by illustrating each of the features used by the authors.

Chapter introductions

These introductions are a brief overview of the core themes and issues you will encounter in each chapter.

1.1 INTRODUCTION

There are a number of possible approach or formalistic approach. This approach legal universe as the object of study. It is specific rules, both substantive and pro law and which regulate social activity. T that study is restricted to the sphere of to which the legal rules are applied. Ir

Diagrams

Visual learners are catered for via a series of diagrams and tables, which help facilitate the understanding of concepts and interrelationships within key topics.

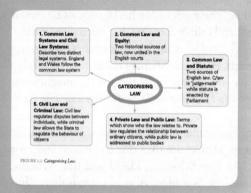

1. Common Law Systems and Civil Law Systems: Describe two distinct legal systems. England and Wales follow the common law system

2. Common Law and Equity: Two historical sources of law, now united in the English courts

3. Common Law and Statute: Two sources of English law. C/law is 'judge-made' while statute is enacted by Parliament

CATEGORISING LAW

5. Civil Law and Criminal Law: Civil law regulates disputes between individuals, while criminal law allows the State to regulate the behaviour of citizens

4. Private Law and Public Law: Terms which show who the law relates to. Private law regulates the relationship between ordinary citizens, while public law is addressed to public bodies

FIGURE 1.1 *Categorising Law.*

Chapter summaries

The essential points and concepts covered in each chapter are distilled into concise summaries at the end of each chapter in order to provide you with an at-a-glance reference point for each topic.

CHAPTER SUMMARY: LAW AND LEGA

THE STUDY OF LAW

The study of law is not just a matter of learning the law is about learning a mass inform the work of the good student.

Food for thought

Key questions are included at the end of each chapter to inform further study and to help deepen your understanding of important topics.

FOOD FOR THOUGHT

1. When asked to think of a law, m
    public form of law, criminal law.
    aspect of law and one that doe:
    elements of the law do. Most pe
    law impinging on them, but i

Further reading and useful websites

Selected further reading and useful websites are included at the end of each chapter to provide a pathway for further study.

FURTHER READING

Barnett, H, *Constitutional and Administrative I*
Bradney, A *et al, How to Study Law*, 7th edn, 2
Clinch, P, *Using a Law Library*, 2nd edn, 2001,
Mansfield, M, *Memoirs of a Radical Lawyer*, Bl
Slapper, G, and Kelly, D, *Questions and Answe*
Routledge
Susskind, R, *The End of Lawyers?*, 2009, Oxfo:

Companion website

Signposts to relevant material available on the book's popular companion website are included at the end of each chapter.

COMPANION WEBSITE

Now visit the companion website to:

- listen to Gary Slapper's audio introduction
- test your understanding of the key terms u:
- revise and consolidate your understanding bank of multiple choice questions;
- view and follow all of the links to the Usef
- keep up to date with the very latest develo:

Guide to the companion website

www.routledge.com/cw/slapper

'One of the best sets of online resources I have ever seen.' *Richard Lee, Senior Lecturer, Manchester Metropolitan University*

For lecturers

Visit *The English Legal System*'s companion website to discover a comprehensive range of resources designed to enhance the teaching and learning experience for both students and lecturers.

A free suite of exclusive resources developed to help you to teach the English legal system.

Testbank

Download a fully customisable bank of questions which test your students' understanding of the English legal system. These can be migrated to your university's Visual Learning Environment so that they can be customised and used to track student progress.

Diagrams

Use diagrams from the text in your own lecture presentations with our PowerPoint slides.

For students

Audio Introduction to The English Legal System.

Listen to Gary Slapper describe the authors' aims and intentions in his audio introduction to *The English Legal System.*

Legal skills guide

Improve your essential legal skills with our practical guides to Mooting, Negotiation, Finding Legal Information, Legal Writing and more.

Multiple choice questions

Test your understanding of the English legal system with more than 200 online questions, each including hints, commentary and links back to the textbook.

Glossary terms and flashcards

Search over 100 essential legal terms in our handy online Glossary or check your knowledge with our interactive flashcards.

LIST OF FIGURES

TABLE OF CASES

TABLE OF STATUTORY INSTRUMENTS

TABLE OF EUROPEAN LEGISLATION

LIST OF ABBREVIATIONS

ABH	actual bodily harm
ABS	alternative business structures
ACAS	Advisory, Conciliation and Arbitration Service
ACLEC	Advisory Committee on Legal Education and Conduct
ACSL	average custodial sentence length
ADR	alternative dispute resolution
AEO	attachment of earnings orders
AJF	Administrative Justice Forum
AJTC	Administrative Justice and Tribunals Council
ASBO	Anti-social Behaviour Order
ATE	After-The-Event
BCAT	Bar Course Aptitude Test
BME	black and minority ethnic
BPTC	Bar Practice Training Course
BSB	Bar Standards Board
CAB	Citizens Advice Bureau
Cafcass	Children and Family Court Advisory and Support Service
CBO	Criminal Behaviour Order
CC	Competition Commission
CCRC	Criminal Cases Review Commission
CCS	Consumer Complaints Service
CDS	Criminal Defence Service
CFAs	conditional fee arrangements
CILEx	Chartered Institute of Legal Executives
CJA	Criminal Justice Area
CJC	Civil Justice Council
CJEU	Court of Justice of the European Union
CJR	Civil Justice Review
CJSSS	*Criminal Justice: Simple, Speedy, Summary*
CLA	Civil Legal Aid
CLAD	Civil Legal Advice
CLS	Community Legal Service
CLSP	Community Legal Service Partnership
CMP	closed material procedure
CNR	cell nuclear replacement
COREPER	Committee of Permanent Representatives

CPD	continuing professional development
CPR	Civil Procedure Rules
CPS	Crown Prosecution Service
CRAR	Commercial Rent Arrears Recovery
CRASBO	Criminal Anti-social Behaviour Order
CSEW	Crime Survey for England and Wales
DCA	Department for Constitutional Affairs
DPA	Deferred Prosecution Agreement
DPP	Director of Public Prosecutions
EAT	Employment Appeal Tribunal
EC	European Community
ECF	Exceptional Cases Funding Scheme
ECHR	European Convention on Human Rights
ECJ	European Court of Justice
ECOFIN	economic and financial matters
ECtHR	European Court of Human Rights
EEC	European Economic Community
EMS	European Monetary System
EMU	European Monetary Union
EPA	Ending Power of Attorney
EVEL	English Votes for English Laws
FDAC	Family Drug and Alcohol Court
FGM	female genital mutilation
FSA	Financial Services Authority
FTA	failed to appear
GAD	Government Actuary's Department
GAR	guaranteed annuity rate
GCHQ	Government Communications Headquarters
GM	genetically modified
GRC	General Regulatory Chamber
GRO	General Register Office for England and Wales
HCA	Higher Court Advocates
HFEA	Human Fertilisation and Embryology Authority
HMCS	Her Majesty's Courts Service
HMCTS	Her Majesty's Courts and Tribunals Service
HMRC	Her Majesty's Revenue and Customs
ICAEW	Institute of Chartered Accountants in England and Wales
IPC	Investigatory Powers Commissioner
IPPs	Indeterminate Sentences for Public Protection
IPS	ILEX Professional Standards
IPSA	Independent Parliamentary Standards Authority
ISIL	Islamic State of Iraq and the Levant
JAC	Judicial Appointments Commission
JC	Judicial College
JCIO	Judicial Conduct Investigations Office

JO	Judicial Office
JP	Justice of the Peace
JSB	Judicial Studies Board
KPI	key performance indicators
LAA	Legal Aid Agency
LCD	Lord Chancellor's Department
LCF	Law Centres' Federation
LCS	Legal Complaints Service
LDP	Legal Disciplinary Practice
LETR	Legal Education and Training Review
LIP	litigant in person
LLP	limited liability partnership
LO	Legal Ombudsman
LPA	Lasting Power of Attorney
LPC	Legal Practice Course
LSB	Legal Services Board
LSC	Legal Services Commission
LSET	Legal services, education and training
LSO	Legal Services Ombudsman
MDP	multidisciplinary practices
MEP	Member of the European Parliament
MFR	minimum funding requirement
MIAM	Mediation Information and Assessment Meeting
MNP	multinational partnership
MoJ	Ministry of Justice
MRO	medical reporting organisation
NASS	National Asylum Support Service
NFIB	National Fraud Intelligence Bureau
NJPS	New Judicial Pension Scheme
NPO	Norwich Pharmacal order
NSPCC	National Society for the Prevention of Cruelty to Children
OFR	outcomes-focused regulation
OFT	Office of Fair Trading
OJC	Office for Judicial Complaints
OLC	Office for Legal Complaints
OOCD	out-of-court disposal of criminal offences
PAP	pre-action protocol
PC	practising certificate (solicitors)
PCA	Parliamentary Commissioner for Administration
PDS	Public Defender Service
PEP	profit per equity partner
PNC	Police National Computer
QBD	Queen's Bench Division
QC	Queen's Counsel
RTA	road traffic accidents

RUC	Royal Ulster Constabulary
SCPO	Serious Crime Prevention Order
SDT	Solicitors' Disciplinary Tribunal
SEC	Social Entitlement Chamber
SFO	Serious Fraud Office
SI	Statutory Instrument
SIAC	Special Immigration Appeals Commission
SRA	Solicitors Regulation Authority
SRL	self-represented litigants
STV	single transferable vote
TEU	Treaty on European Union
TFEU	Treaty on the Functioning of the European Union
TPIMs	terrorism prevention and investigation measures
TSI	Trading Standards Institute
UNCITRAL	United Nations Commission on International Trade Law
UT	Upper Tribunal
VHCC	very high cost cases
VOO	Violent Offender Order

LAW AND LEGAL STUDY 1

There are a number of possible approaches to the study of law. One such is the traditional or formalistic approach. This approach to law is posited on the existence of a discrete legal universe as the object of study. It is concerned with establishing a knowledge of the specific rules, both substantive and procedural, which derive from statute and common law and which regulate social activity. The essential point in relation to this approach is that study is restricted to the sphere of the legal without reference to the social activity to which the legal rules are applied. In the past, most traditional law courses and the majority of law textbooks adopted this 'black letter' approach. Their object was the provision of information on what the current rules and principles of law were, and how to use those rules and principles to solve what were, by definition, legal problems. Traditionally, English legal system courses have focused attention on the institutions of the law, predominantly the courts, in which legal rules and principles are put into operation, and here too the underlying assumption has been as to the closed nature of the legal world – its distinctiveness and separateness from normal everyday activity. This book continues that tradition to a degree, but also recognises, and has tried to accommodate, the dissatisfaction with such an approach that has been increasingly evident among law teachers and examiners in this area. To that end, the authors have tried not simply to produce a purely expository text, but have attempted to introduce an element of critical awareness and assessment into the areas considered. Potential examination candidates should appreciate that it is just such critical, analytical thought that distinguishes the good student from the mundane one.

Additionally, however, this book goes further than traditional texts on the English legal system by directly questioning the claims to distinctiveness made by, and on behalf of, the legal system and considering law as a socio-political institution. It is the view of the authors that the legal system cannot be studied without a consideration of the values that law reflects and supports, and again, students should be aware that it is in such areas that the truly first-class students demonstrate their awareness and ability.

1.2   THE NATURE OF LAW

One of the most obvious and most central characteristics of all societies is that they must possess some degree of order to permit the members to interact over a sustained period of time. Different societies, however, have different forms of order. Some societies are highly regimented with strictly enforced social rules, whereas others continue to function in what outsiders might consider a very unstructured manner with apparently few strict rules being enforced (see Roberts 1979).

Order is therefore necessary, but the form through which order is maintained is certainly not universal, as many anthropological studies have shown (see Mansell 2015).

In our society, law plays an important part in the creation and maintenance of social order. We must be aware, however, that law as we know it is not the only means of creating order. Even in our society, order is not solely dependent on law, but also involves questions of a more general moral and political character. This book is not concerned with providing a general explanation of the form of order. It is concerned more particularly with describing and explaining the key institutional aspects of that particular form of order that is *legal* order.

The most obvious way in which law contributes to the maintenance of social order is the way in which it deals with disorder or conflict. This book, therefore, is particularly concerned with the institutions and procedures, both civil and criminal, through which law operates to ensure a particular form of social order by dealing with various conflicts when they arise.

Law is a *formal* mechanism of social control and, as such, it is essential that the student of law be fully aware of the nature of that formal structure. There are, however, other aspects to law that are less immediately apparent, but of no less importance, such as the inescapable political nature of law. Some textbooks focus more on this particular aspect of law than others, and these differences become evident in the particular approach adopted by the authors. The approach favoured by this book is to recognise that studying the English legal system is not just about learning legal rules, but is also about considering a social institution of fundamental importance.

1.2.1   LAW AND MORALITY

There is an ongoing debate about the relationship between law and morality and as to what exactly that relationship is or should be. Should all laws accord with a moral code, and, if so, which one? Can laws be detached from moral arguments? Many of the issues in this debate are implicit in much of what follows in the text, but the authors believe that, in spite of claims to the contrary, there is no simple causal relationship of dependency or determination, either way, between morality and law. We would rather approach both morality and law as ideological, in that they are manifestations of, and seek to explain and justify, particular social and economic relationships. This essentially materialist approach, to a degree, explains the tensions between the competing ideologies of law and morality and explains why they sometimes conflict and why they change, albeit asynchronously, as underlying social relations change.

Law and morality

At first sight it might appear that law and morality are inextricably linked. There at least appears to be a similarity of vocabulary in that both law and morality tend to see relationships in terms of rights and duties, and much of law's ideological justification comes from the claim that it is essentially moral. However, that is not necessarily the case and much modern law is of a highly technical nature (such as rules of evidence or procedure), dealing with issues that have very little, if any, impact on issues of morality as such. Opinions about the relationship between law and morality diverge between two schools of thought:

- One side adopts a 'natural law' approach which claims that law must be moral in order to be law, and that 'immoral law' is a contradiction in terms. Natural lawyers usually base their ideas of law on underlying religious beliefs and texts which are in the very literal sense sacrosanct, but this is not a necessity and opposition to specific law may be based on pure reason or political ideas.

- The other side can be characterised as 'legal positivists'. They argue that law has no necessary basis in morality and that it is simply impossible to assess law in terms of morality.

These issues feed into debates as to what is connoted by the rule of law, which will be considered in some detail in Chapter 2 of this text.

The legal enforcement of morality: The Hart v Devlin debate

This aspect of the law and morality debate may be reduced to the question: does the law have a responsibility to enforce a moral code, even where the alleged immorality takes place in private between consenting adults? Consider this example: in Britain there are over two million cohabiting gay couples. Homosexual sex was legalised in 1967 (for 21-year-olds, lowered to 18-year-olds in 1994), and consensual heterosexual anal intercourse was decriminalised by s 143 of the Criminal Justice and Public Order Act 1994. In British legal debate the moral issue was fought out in the 1960s by Lord Devlin and Professor HLA Hart. Devlin argued that 'the suppression of vice is as much the law's business as the suppression of subversive activities'. A shared morality, he argued, is the cement of society, without which there would be aggregates of individuals but no society. Hart argued that people should not be forced to adopt one morality for its own sake. He repudiated the claim that the loosening of moral bonds is the first stage of social disintegration, saying that there was no more evidence for that proposition than there was for Emperor Justinian's statement that homosexuality was the cause of earthquakes.

In any event it might be said that Hart 'won' the debate in the sense that it was his influence that led to the passing of the 1960s legislation liberalising the law on abortion, prostitution and homosexuality, and abolishing capital punishment. However, such issues can still arise – as was seen in the *Brown* case, considered later, and the ongoing issue of the 'rights' relating to assisted suicide as considered in *R (on the application of Purdy) v Director of Public Prosecutions* (2009).

The morality of the law maker

One particular aspect of the debate that will be repeatedly highlighted in what follows is the way in which certain individuals, particularly judges, have the power not just to make and mould law, but to make and mould law in line with their own ideologies, i.e. their individual values, attitudes and prejudices – in other words, their moralities.

> Morality *vis à vis* the law constitutes an external environment which interacts with the lawmaking process, not because law makers are blessed with divine insight into the 'general will', but rather because laws tend to be based on value – loaded information which percolates to the law-makers (*whose own individual values have a disproportionate influence upon the process*) (L Bloom-Cooper and G Drewry, *Law and Morality* (1976), p. xiv).

This issue is central to the Royal College of Nursing case considered in Chapter 3 and on the companion website at: www.routledge.com/cw/slapper.

1.3   CATEGORIES OF LAW

There are various ways of categorising law, which initially tend to confuse the non-lawyer and the new student of law. What follows will set out these categorisations in their usual dual form, while at the same time trying to overcome the confusion inherent in such duality. It is impossible to avoid the confusing repetition of the same terms to mean different things and, indeed, the purpose of this section is to make sure that students are aware of the fact that the same words can have different meanings, depending upon the context in which they are used.

1.3.1   COMMON LAW AND CIVIL LAW

In this particular juxtaposition, these terms are used to distinguish two distinct legal systems and approaches to law. The use of the term 'common law' in this context refers to all those legal systems that have adopted the historic English legal system. Foremost among these is, of course, the United States, but many other Commonwealth and former Commonwealth countries retain a common law system. The term 'civil law' refers to those other jurisdictions that have adopted the European continental system of law derived essentially from ancient Roman law, but owing much to the Germanic tradition.

The usual distinction to be made between the two systems is that the common law system tends to be case-centred and hence judge-centred, allowing scope for a discretionary, *ad hoc*, pragmatic approach to the particular problems that appear before the courts, whereas the civil law system tends to be a codified body of general abstract principles which control the exercise of judicial discretion. In reality, both of these views are

1. **Common Law Systems and Civil Law Systems:** Describe two distinct legal systems. England and Wales follow the common law system

2. **Common Law and Equity:** Two historical sources of law, now united in the English courts

3. **Common Law and Statute:** Two sources of English law. C/law is 'judge-made' while statute is enacted by Parliament

CATEGORISING LAW

5. **Civil Law and Criminal Law:** Civil law regulates disputes between individuals, while criminal law allows the state to regulate the behaviour of citizens

4. **Private Law and Public Law:** Terms which show who the law relates to. Private law regulates the relationship between ordinary citizens, while public law is addressed to public bodies

FIGURE 1.1 *Categorising Law.*

extremes, with the former overemphasising the extent to which the common law judge can impose their discretion and the latter underestimating the extent to which continental judges have the power to exercise judicial discretion. It is perhaps worth mentioning at this point that the Court of Justice of the European Union (CJEU), established, in theory, on civil law principles, is in practice increasingly recognising the benefits of establishing a body of case law.

It has to be recognised, and indeed the English courts do so, that, although the CJEU is not bound by the operation of the doctrine of *stare decisis* (see below, 4.2) it still does not decide individual cases on an *ad hoc* basis and, therefore, in the light of a perfectly clear decision of the CJEU, national courts will be reluctant to refer similar cases to its jurisdiction. Thus, after the ECJ, as it was then referred to, decided in *Grant v South West Trains Ltd* (1998) that Community law, now referred to as Union law, did not cover discrimination on grounds of sexual orientation, the High Court withdrew a similar reference in *R v Secretary of State for Defence ex p Perkins (No 2)* (1998) (see below, 5.3, for a detailed consideration of the CJEU).

1.3.2 COMMON LAW AND EQUITY

In this particular juxtaposition, the terms refer to a particular division within the English legal system.

The common law has been romantically and inaccurately described as the law of the common people of England. In fact, the common law emerged as the product of a particular struggle for political power. Prior to the Norman Conquest of England in 1066, there was no unitary, national legal system. The emergence of the common law represents the imposition of such a unitary system under the auspices and control of a centralised power in the form of a sovereign king; in that respect, it represented the assertion and affirmation of that central sovereign power.

Traditionally, much play is made about the circuit of judges travelling round the country establishing the 'King's peace' and, in so doing, selecting the best local customs and making them the basis of the law of England in a piecemeal but totally altruistic procedure. The reality of this process was that the judges were asserting the authority of the central state and its legal forms and institutions over the disparate and fragmented state and legal forms of the earlier feudal period. Thus, the common law was common *to* all in application, but certainly was not common *from* all. (The contemporary meaning and relevance and operation of the common law will be considered in more detail later in this chapter and in Chapter 3.)

By the end of the thirteenth century, the central authority had established its precedence at least partly through the establishment of the common law. Originally, courts had been no more than an adjunct of the King's Council, the *Curia Regis*, but gradually the common law courts began to take on a distinct institutional existence in the form of the Courts of Exchequer, Common Pleas and King's Bench. With this institutional autonomy, however, there developed an institutional sclerosis, typified by a reluctance to deal with matters that were not, or could not be, processed in the proper *form of action*. Such a refusal to deal with substantive injustices because they did not fall within the particular parameters of procedural and formal constraints, by necessity, led to injustice and the need to remedy the perceived weaknesses in the common law system. The response was the development of *equity*.

Plaintiffs unable to gain access to the three common law courts might directly appeal to the sovereign, and such pleas would be passed for consideration and decision to the Lord Chancellor, who acted as the king's conscience. As the common law courts became more formalistic and more inaccessible, pleas to the Chancellor correspondingly increased and eventually this resulted in the emergence of a specific court constituted to deliver 'equitable' or 'fair' decisions in cases that the common law courts declined to deal with. As had happened with the common law, the decisions of the Courts of Equity established principles that were used to decide later cases, so it should not be thought that the use of equity meant that judges had discretion to decide cases on the basis of their personal idea of what was just in each case.

The division between the common law courts and the Courts of Equity continued until they were eventually combined by the Judicature Acts (JdA) 1873–75. Prior to this legislation, it was essential for a party to raise an action in the appropriate court – for example, the courts of law would not implement equitable principles; the Acts, however, provided that every court had the power and the duty to decide cases in line with common law and equity, with the latter being paramount in the final analysis.

Some would say that, as equity was never anything other than a gloss on common law, it is perhaps appropriate, if not ironic, that now both systems have been effectively subsumed under the one term: common law.

Common law remedies are available as of right. Remedies in equity are discretionary: in other words, they are awarded at the will of the court and depend on the behaviour and situation of the party claiming such remedies. This means that, in effect, the court does not have to award an equitable remedy where it considers that the conduct of the party seeking such an award has been such that the party does not deserve it (*D & C Builders v Rees* (1965)).

1.3.3 COMMON LAW AND STATUTE LAW

This particular conjunction follows on from the immediately preceding section, in that the common law here refers to the substantive law and procedural rules that have been created by the judiciary through the decisions in the cases they have heard. Statute law, on the other hand, refers to law that has been created by Parliament in the form of legislation. Although there has been a significant increase in statute law in the twentieth and twenty-first centuries, the courts still have an important role to play in creating and operating law generally and in determining the operation of legislation in particular. The relationship of this pair of concepts is of central importance and is considered in more detail in Chapters 3 and 4.

1.3.4 PRIVATE LAW AND PUBLIC LAW

Private law deals with relations between individuals with which the state is not directly concerned or involved in. Public law, on the other hand, relates to the interrelationship of the state and the general population, in which the state itself is a participant. Somewhat confusingly, under the English legal system the state can enter into private law relationship with individuals, so the term public law is more accurately restricted to those aspects where the state is acting in a public capacity.

There are two different ways of understanding the division between private and public law. At one level, the division relates specifically to actions of the state and its functionaries vis-à-vis the individual citizen, and the legal manner in which, and form of law through which, such relationships are regulated: public law. In the nineteenth century, it was at least possible to claim, as AV Dicey did, that under the common law there was no such thing as public law in this distinct administrative sense and that the powers of the state with regard to individuals were governed by the ordinary law of the land, operating through the normal courts. Whether such a claim was accurate or not when it was made – and it is unlikely – there certainly can be no doubt now that public law constitutes a distinct and growing area of law in its own right. The growth of public law in this sense has mirrored the growth and increased activity of the contemporary state, and has seen its role as seeking to regulate such activity. The crucial role of judicial review in relation to public law will be considered in some detail in section 13.5, and the content and impact of the Human Rights Act 1998 will be considered in Chapter 2.

There is, however, a second aspect to the division between private and public law. One corollary of the divide is that matters located within the private sphere are seen as purely a matter for individuals themselves to regulate, without the interference of the state, whose role is limited to the provision of the forum for deciding contentious issues and mechanisms for the enforcement of such decisions. Matters within the public sphere, however, are seen as issues relating to the interest of the state and general public, and as such are to be protected and prosecuted by the state. It can be seen, therefore, that the category to which any dispute is allocated is of crucial importance to how it is dealt with. Contract may be thought of as the classic example of private law, but the extent to which this purely private legal area has been subjected to the regulation of public law, in such areas as consumer protection, should not be underestimated. Equally, the most obvious example of public law in this context would be criminal law. Feminists have argued, however, that the allocation of domestic matters to the sphere of private law has led to a denial of a general interest in the treatment and protection of women. By defining domestic matters as private, the state and its functionaries have denied women access to its power to protect themselves from abuse. In doing so, it is suggested that, in fact, such categorisation has reflected and maintained the social domination of men over women.

1.3.5 CIVIL LAW AND CRIMINAL LAW

Civil law is a form of private law and involves the relationships between individual citizens. It is the legal mechanism through which individuals can assert claims against others and have those rights adjudicated and enforced. The purpose of civil law is to settle disputes between individuals and to provide remedies; it is not concerned with punishment as such. The role of the state in relation to civil law is to establish the general framework of legal rules and to provide the legal institutions to operate those rights, but the activation of the civil law is strictly a matter for the individuals concerned. Contract, tort and property law are generally aspects of civil law.

Criminal law, on the other hand, is an aspect of public law and relates to conduct which the state considers with disapproval and which it seeks to control and/or eradicate. Criminal law involves the *enforcement* of particular forms of behaviour, and the state, as the representative of society, acts positively to ensure compliance. Thus, criminal cases are brought by the state in the name of the Crown and cases are reported in the form of *Regina v . . .* (*Regina* is simply Latin for 'queen' and case references are usually abbreviated to *R v . . .*) whereas civil cases are referred to by the names of the parties involved in the dispute, for example, *Smith v Jones*. In criminal law, a prosecutor prosecutes a defendant (or 'the accused'). In civil law, a claimant sues (or 'brings a claim against') a defendant.

In distinguishing between criminal and civil actions, it has to be remembered that the same event may give rise to both. For example, where the driver of a car injures someone through their reckless driving, they will be liable to be prosecuted under the Road Traffic legislation, but at the same time, they will also be responsible to the injured party in the civil law relating to the tort of negligence.

Standard of proof
A crucial distinction between criminal and civil law is the level of proof required in the different types of cases. In the criminal case, the prosecution is required to prove that the defendant is guilty beyond reasonable doubt, whereas in a civil case, the degree of proof is much lower and has only to be on the balance of probabilities. This difference in the level of proof raises the possibility of someone being able to succeed in a civil case, although there may not be sufficient evidence for a criminal prosecution. Indeed,

this strategy has been used successfully in a number of cases against the police where the Crown Prosecution Service (CPS) has considered there to be insufficient evidence to support a criminal conviction for assault. A successful civil action may even put pressure on the CPS to reconsider its previous decision not to prosecute (see, further, below, 11.2, for an examination of the CPS). In June 2009, relatives of the victims of the Omagh bombing in Northern Ireland, which killed 29 people in 1998, won the right to take a civil case against members of the Real IRA, following the failure of a criminal prosecution to secure any convictions. In approving the action the judge in the case held that there was overwhelming evidence against four members of the terrorist group in relation to the atrocity. A subsequent criminal charge against one of the four was withdrawn in February 2016.

Burden of proof

It is essential not to confuse the standard of proof with the burden of proof. The latter refers to the need for the person making an allegation, be it the prosecution in a criminal case or the claimant in a civil case, to prove the facts of the case. In certain circumstances, once the prosecution/claimant has demonstrated certain facts, the burden of proof may shift to the defendant/respondent to provide evidence to prove their lack of culpability. The reverse burden of proof may be either *legal* or *evidential*, which in practice indicates the degree of evidence they have to provide in order to meet the burden they are under.

It should also be noted that the distinction between civil and criminal responsibility is further blurred in cases involving what may be described as hybrid offences. These are situations where a court awards a civil order against an individual, but with the attached sanction that any breach of the order will be subject to punishment as a criminal offence. As examples of this procedure may be cited the Protection from Harassment Act (PfHA) 1997 and the provision for the making of Anti-social behaviour orders available under s 1(1) of the Crime and Disorder Act 1998. Both of these provisions are of considerable interest and deserve some attention in their own right.

The Protection from Harassment Act was introduced as a measure to deal with 'stalking', the harassment of individuals by people continuously following them, and allowed the victim of harassment to get a court order to prevent the stalking. Stalking was made a fully-fledged criminal activity under s 111 of the Protection of Freedoms Act (PFA) 2012. Sub-section (1) inserted a new s 2A into the PfHA 1997 under which a person was guilty of the criminal offence of stalking if they pursued a course of conduct in breach of the prohibition on harassment in s 1(1) of the PHA 1997, and that course of conduct itself amounted to stalking.

Additionally, sub-section (2) inserted a new s 4A into the PfHA 1997 introducing the offence of stalking involving fear of violence or serious alarm or distress. A person will be guilty of that offence where they pursue a course of conduct amounting to stalking which causes another to fear, on at least two occasions, that violence will be used against them or it causes the victim serious alarm or distress that has a substantial adverse effect on their usual day-to-day activities.

Interestingly a new s 2A(3) provides a non-exhaustive list of examples of behaviour that are associated with stalking which includes such actions as 'following a person' and 'watching or spying on a person'.

The House of Lords answered the questions as follows:

(1)   Proceedings for an anti-social behaviour order were civil under domestic law. In support of this conclusion the court relied on a number of factors. First, the Crown Prosecution Service was not involved in applications for the making of such an order as they were in criminal proceedings. Second, there was no need to show *mens rea*, or the guilty mind required to establish criminal liability. Thirdly, the issuing of the ASBO was not a penalty as such, as would be the outcome of a criminal case. As the House found no contrary cases in the European Court of Human Rights it concluded that ASBO procedures could not be seen to be criminal for the purposes of Art 6 of the Human Rights Act 1998.

(2)   Following on from the first determination, that the proceedings were civil in nature, the Civil Evidence Act 1995 and the Magistrates' Courts (Hearsay Evidence in Civil Proceedings) Rules 1999 permitted the introduction of hearsay evidence. However, as regards the weight given to such evidence, that depended on the facts of each case, but its cumulative effect could be sufficient to support the issuing of the order.

(3)   As regards the issue of the standard of proof, however, the House held that *the criminal standard should be applied*. For the purposes of s 1(1)(a) of the Crime and Disorder Act, it would suffice for the magistrates *'to be sure'* that the defendant had acted in an anti-social manner. In the words of Lord Steyn:

> [the magistrates] must in all cases under section 1 apply the criminal standard . . . it will be sufficient for the magistrates, when applying section 1(1) (a) to be sure that the defendant has acted in an anti-social manner, that is to say in a manner which caused or was likely to cause harassment, alarm, or distress to one or more persons not of the same household as himself.

As with many of the previous government's initiatives, the ASBO and its related orders did not find favour with the coalition government and in July 2010 the Home Secretary, Theresa May, announced her wish to see ASBOs replaced by simpler sanctions that would be easier to obtain and to enforce and that, where possible, 'should be rehabilitating and restorative, rather than criminalising and coercive'. Subsequently in May 2012, the Home Office published a White Paper, *Putting victims first: more effective responses to anti-social behaviour*, which set out the government's proposals to replace the then 19 existing powers with six new ones, and giving victims a say in how agencies tackle anti-social behaviour. Those proposals were enacted in the Anti-social Behaviour, Crime and Policing Act 2014.

Anti-social Behaviour, Crime and Policing Act (ABCP) 2014

In addition to reducing the 19 distinct anti-social behaviour orders to just six, the Act also introduced the concept of a 'community trigger' to ensure that the public had the power to demand that appropriate authorities take action in the event of a complaint about anti-social behaviour accompanied by a provision to allow for the implementation of 'community remedies'.

Section 2 of the Act defines anti-social behaviour as conduct:

(i)   that has caused, or is likely to cause, harassment, alarm or distress to any person,

(ii)   capable of causing nuisance or annoyance to a person in relation to that person's occupation of residential premises, or

(iii)   capable of causing housing-related nuisance or annoyance to any person.

What actually amounts to anti-social behaviour is not defined in specific terms, but the sort of behaviour that is subject to this form of control includes, although it is not limited to:

- harassment of residents or passers-by;
- verbal abuse;
- vandalism;
- nuisance;
- smoking or drinking alcohol while under age;
- drug or alcohol abuse;
- begging;
- prostitution;
- kerb-crawling;
- and since October 2014, failing to control invasive plants such as Japanese knotweed.

An application for an ASBO is not made by individuals who are subjected to the anti-social behaviour, for the obvious reason that they might be subjected to further victimisation. It is the function of local authorities, police forces, including the British Transport Police, and registered social landlords to collect the evidence and put it to the courts.

Injunction to prevent anti-social behaviour (ss 1–21)

This action replaces a number of civil orders and injunctions including ASBOs and Anti-social Behaviour Injunctions. An injunction may be made against a person aged 10 or over if the court is satisfied, on the balance of probabilities (the civil standard of proof), that the person has engaged in, or is threatening to engage in, anti-social behaviour and that it is just and convenient to grant the injunction. There is no minimum or maximum term for an injunction for adults but in the case of under 18s, the maximum term is 12 months. The fact that the injunction can be issued on the civil rather than the criminal standard of proof, effectively obviates the decision of the House of Lords in the *McCann* case.

Such orders can only be issued if the offender has been given a written warning that the notice will be issued if their conduct doesn't change and that they have been given enough time to have reasonably made those changes, and yet have chosen not to do so.

It is a criminal offence not to comply with a community protection notice.

Public spaces protection order (ss 59–75)

A public spaces protection order is an order that identifies the public place and prohibits specified things being done in the restricted area and/or requires specified things to be done by persons carrying on specified activities in that area. The order may not last for more than three years and the local authority must consult with the chief police officer and the local policing body before issuing the order.

Failure to comply with a public spaces protection order is a criminal offence.

Closure of premises

A police officer of at least the rank of inspector, or a local authority, may issue a closure notice if satisfied on reasonable grounds that the use of particular premises has:

(i)   resulted, or is likely soon to result, in nuisance to members of the public, or

(ii)   there has been or is likely soon to be disorder near those premises associated with the use of those premises, and

(iii)   the notice is necessary to prevent the nuisance or disorder from continuing, recurring or occurring.

A closure notice prohibits access to the premises for a period specified in the notice up to a maximum three months and may prohibit access by all persons except those specified, at all times and in all circumstances.

Whenever a closure notice is issued an application can be made to a magistrates' court for a closure order. This can be made by a constable or the local authority and must be heard by the magistrates' court not later than 48 hours after service of the closure notice.

The community trigger

The community trigger is intended as a means of recourse for those victims of anti-social behaviour who consider that there has not been an appropriate response to their complaints about such behaviour. The Act incorporates a mechanism for victims of persistent anti-social behaviour to request that relevant bodies, local authorities, the police, health providers and providers of social housing, undertake a case review involving a consideration of what action has previously been taken, and collectively deciding whether any further action could be taken in regard to the issue. An individual, community or business can make an application for a case review, and the relevant bodies are required to carry out a case review if the threshold is met. The Act provides that the threshold should be set no higher than three complaints, but agencies may choose to set a lower threshold.

The body which carries out a review must inform the applicant of the outcome of the review and any recommendations made. It must also publish annually how many triggers have been activated and how many case reviews have been carried out.

The community remedy document

A community remedy document contains a list of appropriate remedial actions to be carried out by a person who has been found liable for anti-social behaviour or has committed a minor criminal offence to be dealt with without court proceedings.

This provision looks to provide for the victim of low-level crime or anti-social behaviour to have a say in deciding the punishment imposed on, or actions required to be carried out by, offenders where they are dealt with without a formal court hearing. Among other things, such actions could include paying compensation to victims, repairing any damage caused or engaging in mediation to resolve ongoing disputes.

In order to ensure that the community remedy does not become the modern pillory or stocks, the local policing body is required to ensure that the actions in the community remedy document are reasonable and proportionate.

ASBO statistics

The most recent statistics available relate to the period 1 April 1999 to 31 December 2013, available at: https://www.gov.uk/government/statistics/anti-social-behaviour-order-statistics-england-and-wales-2013

In relation to ASBOs issued, the statistics reveal that:

- During the period covered, a total of 24,427 ASBOs were issued. The highest number of ASBOs issued in any calendar year was 4,122 in 2005, since when there was a year-on-year fall in the number issued. However, in 2013, 1,349 ASBOs were issued, a 2 per cent increase from the 1,329 ASBOs issued in 2012.
- Since 1 June 2000, 86 per cent of ASBOs have been issued to males, 20,836 as against 3,487 issued to females (Table 2).
- Since 2004, more ASBOs have been issued following conviction for a criminal offence rather than following a simple application. Thus in 2013, 65 per cent of ASBOs were issued following a conviction for a criminal offence (Table 3).

As regards breaches of ASBOs, the statistics show that:

- There have been a total of 70,770 separate breaches of ASBOs during the period covered. However, it should be noted that individual ASBOs tend to be breached on numerous occasions, on average five times (Table 10).
- The breach rate (by year of issue) shows that on average 29 per cent of ASBOs are breached within the year of issue.
- Immediate custodial sentences were given to 7,503 offenders for breaches of ASBOs with an average custodial sentence length of five months (Table 13).

Assessment of the ASBO regime

While the new procedure may seem initially to offer a welcome additional protection to the innocent individual, it has to be recognised that such advantage is achieved in effect by criminalising what was, and remains, in other circumstances non-criminal behaviour, and deciding its applicability on the basis of the lower civil law burden of proof.

In a joint letter to *The Observer* newspaper in October 2013, the children's commissioner Dr Maggie Atkinson and a number of others claimed that the new procedure will 'punish children over the age of 10 simply for being children' by widening the definition of anti-social behaviour and reducing the burden of proof so sharply that the effect could be to 'outlaw everyday activities' such as skateboarding or ball games. As they stated:

> We acknowledge that antisocial behaviour can blight the lives of individuals and communities, but this bill is not the answer. It promotes intolerance of youth, is a blow for civil liberties and will damage children's relationship with the police.

Anti-social behaviour orders have been subject to much criticism for the way they have been used in an attempt to define wider social problems as problems merely relating to social order. Of particular concern is the way that they and related orders are used to deal with political protestors, those suffering from mental health problems and young people generally.

As one commentator has put it:

> The reality is that ASBOs are being used far beyond their initial remit of dealing with vandals and nuisance neighbours. Behaviour that is overtly non-criminal is being criminalised and society's vulnerable groups are being targeted. Increasingly it is behaviour that is different rather than 'antisocial' that is being penalised. The form such punishment takes is perhaps of even greater concern because ASBOs effectively bypass criminal law and operate within their own shadow legal system. In effect, we no longer need to break the law to go to jail. In this sense they typify a growing abandonment of the rule of law   (Max Rowlands, ECLN Essays no 9: 'The state of ASBO Britain – the rise of intolerance').

A further example of the relationship between criminal law and civil law may be seen in the courts' power to make an order for the confiscation of a person's property under the Proceeds of Crime Act 2002 (see below, 2.5.1.1).

Private prosecutions

It should not be forgotten that although prosecution of criminal offences is usually the prerogative of the state, it remains open to the private individual to initiate a private prosecution in relation to a criminal offence. It has to be remembered, however, that even in the private prosecution, the test of the burden of proof remains the criminal one requiring the facts to be proved beyond reasonable doubt. An example of the problems inherent in such private actions can be seen in the case of Stephen Lawrence, the young black man who was gratuitously stabbed to death by a gang of white racists while standing at a bus stop in London. Although there was strong suspicion, and indeed evidence, against particular individuals, the CPS declined to press charges against them on the basis of insufficiency of evidence. When the lawyers of the Lawrence family mounted a private prosecution against the suspects, the action failed for want of sufficient evidence to convict. As a consequence of the failure of the private prosecution, the rule against double jeopardy meant that the accused could not be retried for the same offence at any time in the future, even if the police subsequently acquired sufficient new evidence to support a conviction. The report of the Macpherson Inquiry into the manner in which the Metropolitan Police dealt with the Stephen Lawrence case gained much publicity for its finding of 'institutional racism' within the service, but it also made a clear recommendation that the removal of the rule against double jeopardy be considered. Subsequently, a Law Commission report recommended the removal of the double jeopardy rule and provision to remove it, under particular circumstances and subject to strict regulation, was contained in ss 75–79 of the Criminal Justice Act 2003.

In September 2010 two men, Gary Dobson and David Norris, were arrested for the murder of Stephen Lawrence. Dobson had been one of the people originally charged in the private prosecution, but the Court of Appeal held that there was sufficient new scientific evidence to justify a retrial under the Criminal Justice Act 2003. Following another review of the scientific evidence, and the discovery of new and substantial evidence, Dobson and Norris were prosecuted in 2011 and convicted of Stephen Lawrence's murder (3 January 2012).

In considering the relationship between civil law and criminal law, it is sometimes thought that criminal law is the more important in maintaining social order, but it is at least arguable that, in reality, the reverse is the case. For the most part, people come into contact with the criminal law infrequently, whereas everyone is continuously involved with civil law, even if it is only the use of contract law to make some purchase. The criminal law of theft, for example, may be seen as simply the cutting edge of the wider and more fundamental rights established by general property law. In any case, there remains the fact that civil and criminal law each has its own distinct legal system. The nature of these systems will be considered in detail in later chapters. The structure of the civil courts is considered in Chapter 6 and that of the criminal courts in Chapter 9.

1.4 APPROACHES TO LAW AND LEGAL STUDY

There are a number of possible approaches to the study of law, each of which has its own implications for how law is understood, located and studied.

1.4.1 BLACK LETTER LAW

The first is the traditional/formalistic approach. This 'black letter' approach to law, as it is commonly referred to, is posited on the existence of a discrete legal universe as the object of study. Such an approach is clearly manifested in the phrase 'the law is the law'. (In a lecture given more than 20 years ago I facetiously cited this statement as coming from the Fat Controller in the Thomas the Tank Engine books. It is with some amazement that I now find that there are posts on the internet making the same point.)

At their starkest, black letter law and legal formalism assume and claim to operate a form of mechanistic jurisprudence in which legal decisions are reached by means of marshalling and applying the appropriate legal rules. However, the nature and source of those rules appear as an unquestioned and unquestionable given, being derived from authoritative legal sources, again through the application of the correct rules of jurisprudential analysis and exegesis by those skilled in the arcane arts of legal hermeneutics. To simplify, the operation of legal formalism depends upon the application of legal rules by impartial experts to particular facts in order to derive inescapable and hence unquestionable outcomes, those outcomes being merely the result of the logical application of the rules.

This formalistic approach has a crucial impact on the way in which law is understood, taught and studied. As law is understood as being about purely legal rules, so legal study becomes seen as acquiring not just the knowledge of those rules but also the acquisition of the distinctly legal skills needed to derive and apply, not to say manipulate, those rules. Thus, the study of law is seen as establishing a knowledge of the specific legal rules that regulate social activity without reference to the social activity to which the legal rules are applied. However, as well as learning the law in the foregoing sense as simply a body of rules and principles and techniques to be mastered, it is important to learn something *about* law. The reason for this, and the justification for the approach adopted in this book, is that law cannot be examined merely in its own terms, for it amounts to considerably more than just the trade of lawyers.

1.4.2 CONTEXTUALISM

The second approach to the study of law is the contextualist approach. This is by far the most common approach to law in modern academic institutions, and the intention behind it is to recognise that law is a *social* phenomenon and operates within a social context. Society requires particular tasks to be undertaken, be it the maintenance of order or the regulation of economic activity, and it is the function of law to perform those tasks.

The move from the black letter approach to the contextualist one involves an important shift in emphasis. No longer is law seen as simply a matter to be explained and justified in its own terms. It no longer constitutes its own discrete universe, but is analysed, and perhaps more importantly it can actually be assessed, within its socio-economic context, and its performance can be evaluated in relation to the supposed purposes within that socio-economic context.

1.4.3   CRITICAL LEGAL THEORY

The contextualist approach may therefore be seen as an advance on the sterile legalism of the black letter approach to the extent that it takes cognisance of, and seeks to accommodate human behaviour within, the real world. I would suggest, however, that there is still one major shortcoming in its approach. True, it seeks to place law in its context, but what exactly is the context into which law is to be fitted? In our particular society the context is, and without any pejorative overtones, advanced capitalism. The difficulty with the contextualist approach is that it tends to take that particular context for granted: as a given, the assumed, unproblematic, and to that extent unquestioned, background in relation to which law has to operate. To that extent the concern of the contextualist is still the *legal* regulation of particular behaviour, without any great detailed consideration of the actual behaviour to which the legal rules are addressed.

It is only a third type of approach to the study of law that attempts to remedy that shortcoming in the contextualist approach; that third type of approach, and the one espoused by this particular text, is the critical/theoretical approach to law. From this perspective, not only is law in context an object of study, but equally, if not more essentially, the context within which law functions is itself an object of study. Neither law nor its social context is taken for granted, and the actual social relations and activity to which law is applied are examined in order to try to account for the existence of law in the first place.

In our society, as has been stated previously, law appears to, and does, play an important part in the creation and maintenance of social order, its centrality being typified in the very phrase 'law and order', with its underlying suggestion that the two go together, with the latter, order, depending on the existence of the former, law. We must be aware, however, that law, as we know it, is not the only means of creating order. (Even in our society, order is not solely dependent on law, and we are not continuously having recourse to the courts in order to solve our problems.)

Critical legal study is concerned with seeking a general explanation of the form of order, but more particularly it is concerned with a search for the explanation of why our society has developed its particular form of *legal* order. In stressing the contribution that law makes to determining what we accept as order in our society, we are implicitly asserting the point that there can be no single universal idea of order, but rather that there are different versions of order. The version operating in our society, an order essentially shaped by law, is but one specific type of order; it is both culturally and historically specific to our present society.

Whichever approach one adopts to legal study – and each is valid within its own terms – will depend not just upon the individual student's approach and the ideological framework they operate within, but also the area of law that the student wishes to research. Some projects may be open to a merely expository analysis, while others, by the very nature of the subject, will demand a more critical analysis and explanation.

1.5   SKILLS

At the centre of any law student's course will be the law library, although, increasingly, paper-based resources are being supported by internet and other electronic sources. As well as general academic skills, law students need to develop particular skills relating to the finding and reading of legal texts. They are also required to develop the specific skills of writing legal essays and answering problem questions. The online Legal Skills Guide website that supports this text encourages the development of such skills; see www. routledge.com/cw/slapper.

CHAPTER SUMMARY: LAW AND LEGAL STUDY

THE STUDY OF LAW

The study of law is not just a matter of learning rules. It is a general misconception that learning the law is about learning a mass of legal rules. Critical, analytical thought should inform the work of the good student.

THE NATURE OF LAW

Legal systems are particular ways of establishing and maintaining social order. Law is a formal mechanism of social control. Studying the English legal system involves considering a fundamental institution in our society.

CATEGORIES OF LAW

Law may be categorised in a number of ways, although the various categories are not mutually exclusive.

Common law and civil law relate to distinct legal systems. The English legal system is a common law one, as opposed to Continental systems, which are based on civil law.

Common law and equity distinguish the two historical sources and systems of English law. Common law emerged in the process of establishing a single legal system throughout the country. Equity was developed later to soften the formal rigour of the common law. The two systems are now united, but in the final analysis, equity should prevail.

Common law and statute relate to the source of law. Common law is judge-made; statute law is produced by Parliament.

Private law and public law relate to whom the law is addressed. Private law relates to individual citizens, whereas public law relates to institutions of government.

Civil law and criminal law distinguish between law, the purpose of which is to facilitate the interaction of individuals, and law that is aimed at enforcing particular standards of behaviour.

APPROACHES TO LEGAL STUDY
Students of law can adopt a number of distinct approaches to legal study. Prominent among these are the traditional 'black letter' approach, the more evaluative 'contextualist' approach or the more radical 'critical legal studies' approach.

SKILLS
This textbook is supported by a Legal Skills Guide that can be found at www.routledge.com/cw/slapper. There you can improve the skills you'll need to be a successful law student, and ultimately a successful lawyer.

FOOD FOR THOUGHT

1   When asked to think of a law, most people immediately think of that archetypal public form of law, criminal law. However, although important, that is only one aspect of law and one that does not affect most people in the way that other elements of the law do. Most people can go through a day without the criminal law impinging on them, but it is almost certain that they will enter into contractual relationships, even if it is only riding on a bus or buying a sandwich. Equally the private law of property structures our society and is essential to its operation. Consider what other areas of law have an impact on how our society functions. If you are studying for a law degree, think of all the legal subjects you might possibly study.

2   Consider the relationship between law and morality. Is there any underpinning moral basis to law?

3   Consider the relationship of law and society and the following questions:
     Does law exist independently of society?
     Does law create society or does society create law?
     Is law simply a matter of legal rules and legal reasoning?
     What does law actually do?

4   Consider the roles of a law student, lawyer, judge:
     What essential skills are required to perform these roles satisfactorily?
     Do these skills differ, and if so, why?

FURTHER READING

Barnett, H, *Constitutional and Administrative Law*, 11th edn, 2015, Abingdon: Routledge
Bradney, A *et al*, *How to Study Law*, 7th edn, 2014, London: Sweet & Maxwell
Clinch, P, *Using a Law Library*, 2nd edn, 2001, London: Blackstone
Fitzpatrick, P (ed), *Dangerous Supplements*, 1991, London: Pluto
Mansfield, M, *Memoirs of a Radical Lawyer*, 2009, London: Bloomsbury

Slapper, G, and Kelly, D, *Questions and Answers on the English Legal System*, 2013 & 2014, Abingdon: Routledge

Susskind, R, *The End of Lawyers?*, 2009, Oxford: OUP

SOCIAL AND LEGAL ORDER

Mansell, W, *A Critical Introduction to Law*, 4th edn, 2015, London: Cavendish Publishing

Roberts, S, *Order and Dispute*, 1979, Harmondsworth: Penguin

LEGAL LANGUAGE

Friedman, L, 'On interpretation of laws' (1988) 11(3) Ratio Juris 252

Goodrich, P, *Reading the Law*, 1986, Oxford: Basil Blackwell

Jackson, B, *Making Sense in Law*, 1995, London: Deborah Charles

USEFUL WEBSITES

The constant impingement of legal issues on all aspects of social and individual life should be tracked and explored at:

www.bbc.co.uk
www.theguardian.com
www.independent.co.uk
www.ft.com
www.justice.gov.uk
The official website of the Ministry of Justice.

COMPANION WEBSITE

Now visit the companion website to:

- listen to Gary Slapper's audio introduction to the English legal system;
- test your understanding of the key terms using our Flashcard Glossary;
- revise and consolidate your understanding of 'Law and legal study' using our bank of multiple choice questions;
- view and follow all of the links to the Useful Websites above;
- keep up to date with the very latest developments in the law from the Student Law Review;
- access the supporting Legal Skills Guide, with guidance, exercises and activities across eight key skills from legal writing and research to understanding and using cases and statutes.

www.routledge.com/cw/slapper

THE RULE OF LAW AND HUMAN RIGHTS

2

This chapter considers two concepts that are not always, or indeed usually, dealt with in English Legal System textbooks: the two interrelated concepts are 'the rule of law' and 'human rights'. However, it is the contention of the authors that ideas about the rule of law and human rights are, and always should have been, at the core of our understanding and assessment of any, and certainly our own, legal system, and further that they are assuming a more apparent and increased centrality and importance in relation to its operation and justification. However, it has to be recognised from the outset that any consideration of the specific ideas inherent in these general concepts cannot be approached satisfactorily from the purely 'black letter' legal perspective, but must engage the student in a related consideration of the socio-political context from which they derive and to which they relate and on which they operate. Further, the concepts themselves are fluid and, as will be seen, different commentators have adopted widely varying approaches to them.

2.2 THE RULE OF LAW

The 'rule of law' represents a symbolic ideal against which proponents of widely divergent political persuasions measure and criticise the shortcomings of contemporary state practice. This varied recourse to the rule of law is, of course, only possible because of the lack of precision in the actual meaning of the concept; its meaning tends to change over time and, as will be seen below, to change in direct correspondence with the beliefs of those who claim its support and claim, in turn, to support it. It is undeniable that the form and content of law and legal procedure have changed substantially in the course of the twentieth and twenty-first centuries. It is usual to explain such changes as being a consequence of the way in which, and the increased extent to which, the modern state intervenes in everyday life, be it economic or social. As the state increasingly took over the regulation of many areas of social activity, it delegated wide-ranging discretionary powers to various people and bodies in an attempt to ensure the successful implementation of its policies. The assumption and delegation of such power on the part of the state brought it into potential conflict with previous understandings of the rule of law, which had entailed a strictly limited ambit of state activity. The impact of this on the understanding and operation of the principle of the rule of law and its implications in relation to the judiciary are traced out below and will be returned to in Chapter 12.

Some might consider that it is not appropriate to have a section such as this in a textbook on the English legal system and that its proper place would be in a text on constitutional law or legal theory. However, it is essential to appreciate the central importance of the concept of the rule of law to the whole structure and operation of the English legal system. The fundamental nature of the concept of the rule of law is and always has been central, although perhaps implicit, in all the aspects of the legal system that are considered in this text. However, the Constitutional Reform Act (CRA) 2005 has for the first time recognised this centrality in the form of a statutory provision. As s 1 of the Act simply and clearly states, it does not adversely affect:

(a)   the existing constitutional principle of the rule of law, or

(b)   the Lord Chancellor's existing constitutional role in relation to that principle.

This very point was taken up by the former most senior judge in the House of Lords, the late Lord Bingham, whose speech on the issue will be considered in detail below.

As has been stated, although the idea of the rule of law is difficult to give a substantive definition of, that has not prevented a number of legal and social theorists from attempting to do just that. However, as will be seen and as has already been hinted at, the various explanations of what is, or should be, understood by the concept differ considerably and are different in accord with the socio-political approach adopted by the individual writers.

2.2.1 AV DICEY

According to AV Dicey in *An Introduction to the Study of the Law of the Constitution* (1885), the UK had no such thing as administrative law as distinct from the ordinary law of the land. Whether he was correct or not when he expressed this opinion – and there are substantial grounds for doubting the accuracy of his claim even at the time he made it – it can no longer be denied that there is now a large area of law that can be properly called administrative, that is, related to the pursuit and application of particular state policies, usually within a framework of statutory powers.

According to the notoriously chauvinistic Dicey, the rule of law was one of the key features that distinguished the English constitution from its Continental counterparts. Whereas foreigners were subject to the exercise of arbitrary power, the Englishman was secure within the protection of the rule of law. Dicey suggested the existence of three distinct elements, which together created the rule of law as he understood it:

An absence of arbitrary power on the part of the state: the extent of the state's power, and the way in which it exercises such power, is limited and controlled by law. Such control is aimed at preventing the state from acquiring and using wide discretionary powers, for, as Dicey correctly recognised, the problem with discretion is that it can be exercised in an arbitrary manner, and that above all else is to be feared, at least as Dicey would have us believe.

Equality before the law: the fact that no person is above the law, irrespective of rank or class. This was linked with the fact that functionaries of the state are subject to the same law and legal procedures as private citizens.

Supremacy of ordinary law: the fact that the English constitution was the outcome of the ordinary law of the land and was based on the provision of remedies by the courts rather than on the declaration of rights in the form of a written constitution.

It is essential to recognise that Dicey was writing at a particular historical period but, perhaps more importantly, he was writing from a particular political perspective that saw the maintenance of *individual* property and *individual* freedom to use that property as one chose as paramount. He was opposed to any increase in state activity in the pursuit of collective interests. In analysing Dicey's version of the rule of law, it can be seen that it venerated *formal* equality at the expense of *substantive* equality. In other words, he thought that the law and the state should be blind to the real concrete differences that exist between people, in terms of wealth or power or connection, and should treat them all the same, as possessors of *abstract* rights and duties.

There is an unaddressed, and certainly unresolved, tension in Dicey's work. The rule of law was only one of two fundamental elements of the English polity; the other was parliamentary sovereignty. Where, however, the government controls the legislative process, the sovereignty of parliament is reduced to the undisputed supremacy of central government. The tension arises from the fact that, whereas the rule of law was aimed at controlling arbitrary power, parliament could, within this constitutional structure, make provision for the granting of such arbitrary power by passing appropriate legislation.

This tension between the rule of law and parliamentary sovereignty is peculiar to the British version of liberal government. Where similar versions of government emerged on the Continent, and particularly in Germany, the power of the legislature was itself subject to the rule of law. This subordinate relationship of state to law is encapsulated in the concept of the *Rechtsstaat*.

This idea of the *Rechtsstaat* meant that the state itself was controlled by notions of law, which limited its sphere of legitimate activity. Broadly speaking, the state was required to institute general law and could not make laws aimed at particular people.

The fact that this strong *Rechtsstaat* version of the rule of law never existed in England reflects its particular history. The revolutionary struggles of the seventeenth century had delivered effective control of the English state machinery to the bourgeois class, who exercised that power through parliament. After the seventeenth century, the English bourgeoisie was never faced with a threatening state against which it had to protect itself; it effectively was the state. On the Continent, this was not the case and the emergent bourgeoisie had to assert its power against, and safeguard itself from, the power of a state machinery that it did not control. The development of *Rechtsstaat* theory as a means of limiting the power of the state can be seen as one of the ways in which the Continental bourgeoisie attempted to safeguard its position. In England, however, there was not the same need in the eighteenth and nineteenth centuries for the bourgeoisie to protect itself behind a *Rechtsstaat* version of the rule of law. In England, those who benefited from the enactment and implementation of general laws as required by *Rechtsstaat* theory – the middle classes – also effectively controlled parliament and could benefit just as well from its particular enactments. Thus, in terms of nineteenth-century England, as Franz Neumann stated, the doctrines of parliamentary sovereignty and the rule of law were not antagonistic, but complementary.

2.2.2 FA VON HAYEK

FA von Hayek followed Dicey in seeing the essential component of the rule of law as being the absence of arbitrary power in the hands of the state. As Hayek expressed it in his book *The Road to Serfdom* (1944):

> Stripped of all technicalities the Rule of Law means that government in all its actions is bound by rules fixed and announced beforehand.

Hayek, however, went further than Dicey in setting out the form and, at least in a negative way, the content that legal rules had to comply with in order for them to be considered as compatible with the rule of law. As Hayek expressed it:

> The Rule of Law implies limits on the scope of legislation, it restricts it to the kind of general rules known as formal law; and excludes legislation directly aimed at particular people.

This means that law should not be particular in content or application, but should be general in nature, applying to all and benefiting none in particular. Nor should law be aimed at achieving particular goals: its function is to set the boundaries of personal action, not to dictate the course of such action.

Hayek was a severe critic of the interventionist state in all its guises, from the fascist right wing to the authoritarian left wing and encompassing the contemporary welfare state in the middle. His criticism was founded on two bases:

Efficiency: from the microeconomic perspective – and Hayek was an economist – only the person concerned can fully know all the circumstances of their situation. The state cannot wholly understand any individual's situation and should, therefore, as a matter of efficiency leave it to the individuals concerned to make their own decisions about what they want or how they choose to achieve what they want, so long as it is achieved in a legal way.

Morality: from this perspective, to the extent that the state leaves the individual less room to make individual decisions, it reduces their freedom.

It is apparent, and not surprising considering his Austrian background, that Hayek adopted a *Rechtsstaat* view of the rule of law. He believed that the meaning of the rule of law, as it was currently understood in contemporary English jurisprudence, represented a narrowing from its original meaning, which he believed had more in common with *Rechtsstaat* than it presently did. As he pointed out, the ultimate conclusion of the current weaker version of the rule of law was that, so long as the actions of the state were duly authorised by legislation, any such act was lawful, and thus a claim to the preservation of the rule of law could be maintained. It should be noted that Hayek did not suggest at any time that rules enacted in other than a general form are not laws; they are legal, as long as they are enacted through the appropriate and proper mechanisms; they simply are not in accordance with the rule of law as he understood that principle.

Hayek disapproved of the change he claimed to have seen in the meaning of the rule of law. It is clear, however, that, as with Dicey, his views on law and the meaning of the rule of law were informed by a particular political perspective. It is equally clear that what he regretted most was the replacement of a free market economy by a planned economy, regulated by an interventionist state. The contemporary state no longer simply provided a legal framework for the conduct of economic activity, but was actively involved in the direct coordination and regulation of economic activity in the pursuit of the goals that it set. This had a profound effect on the form of law. Clearly stated and fixed general laws were replaced by open-textured discretionary legislation. Also, whereas the Diceyan version of the rule of law had operated in terms of abstract rights and duties, formal equality and formal justice, the new version addressed concrete issues and addressed questions of substantive equality and justice.

Hayek's views in relation to law and economics were extremely influential on conservative political thinking in the last quarter of the twentieth century and, in particular, on the Conservative government of Margaret Thatcher, which was elected in 1979 with the overt policy of reducing the impact and influence of the central state on economic activity and individuals. Thatcher was famous/infamous for, among other things, her declaration that there was no such thing as society, 'only individuals and families'.

2.2.3 EP THOMPSON

The rule of law is a mixture of implied promise and convenient vagueness. It is vagueness at the core of the concept that permits the general idea of the rule of law to be appropriated by people with apparently irreconcilable political agendas in support of their particular political positions. So far, consideration has been given to Dicey and Hayek, two theorists on the right of the political spectrum who saw themselves as proponents and defenders of the rule of law; however, a similar claim can be made from the left. The case in point is EP Thompson, a Marxist historian, who also saw the rule of law as a protection against, and under attack from, the encroaching power of the modern state.

Thompson shared Hayek's distrust of the encroachments of the modern state and he was equally critical of the extent to which the contemporary state intervened in the day-to-day lives of its citizens. From Thompson's perspective, however, the problem arose not so much from the fact that the state was undermining the operation of the market economy, but from the way in which the state used its control over the legislative process to undermine civil liberties in the pursuit of its own concept of public interest.

In *Whigs and Hunters* (1975), a study of the manipulation of law by the landed classes in the eighteenth century, Thompson concluded that the rule of law is not just a necessary means of limiting the potential abuse of power, but that:

> ... the Rule of Law, itself, the imposing of effective inhibitions upon power and the defence of the citizen from power's all-intrusive claims, seems to me an unqualified human good.

In reaching such a conclusion, Thompson clearly concurs with Hayek's view that there is more to the rule of law than the requirement that law be processed through the appropriate legal institutions. He too argued that the core meaning of the rule of law involved more than mere procedural propriety and suggested that the other essential element is the way, and the extent to which, it places limits on the exercise of state power.

2.2.4 JOSEPH RAZ

Some legal philosophers have recognised the need for state intervention in contemporary society and have provided ways of understanding the rule of law as a means of controlling discretion without attempting to eradicate it completely. Joseph Raz ('The Rule of Law and its virtue' (1977) 93 LQR 195), for example, recognised the need for the government of men as well as laws, and that the pursuit of social goals may require the enactment of particular, as well as general, laws. Indeed, he suggested that it would be impossible in practical terms for law to consist solely of general rules. Raz even criticised Hayek for disguising a political argument as a legal one in order to attack policies of which he did not approve. Yet, at the same time, Raz also saw the rule of law as essentially a negative value, acting to minimise the danger that could follow the exercise of discretionary power in an arbitrary way. In that respect, of seeking to control the exercise of discretion, he shares common ground with Thompson, Hayek and Dicey.

Raz claimed that the basic requirement from which the wider idea of the rule of law emerged is the requirement that the law must be capable of guiding the individual's behaviour. He stated some of the most important principles that may be derived from this general idea:

> Laws should be prospective rather than retroactive. People cannot be guided by or expected to obey laws that have not as yet been introduced. Laws should also be open and clear to enable people to understand them and guide their actions in line with them.

Laws should be stable and should not be changed too frequently as this might lead to confusion as to what was actually covered by the law.

There should be clear rules and procedures for making laws.

The independence of the judiciary has to be guaranteed to ensure that they are free to decide cases in line with the law and not in response to any external pressure.

The principles of natural justice should be observed, requiring an open and fair hearing to be given to all parties to proceedings.

The courts should have the power to review the way in which the other principles are implemented to ensure that they are being operated as demanded by the rule of law.

The courts should be easily accessible as they remain at the heart of the idea of making discretion subject to legal control.

The discretion of the crime preventing agencies should not be allowed to pervert the law.

It is evident that Raz saw the rule of law being complied with if the procedural rules of law-making were complied with, subject to a number of safeguards. It is of no little interest that Raz saw the courts as having an essential part to play in his version of the rule of law. This point will be considered further in section 13.5 in relation to judicial review.

2.2.5 ROBERTO UNGER

In *Law and Modern Society* (1976), the American critical legal theorist Roberto Unger set out a typology of social order, one category of which is essentially the rule of law system. Unger distinguished this form of social order from others on the basis of two particular and unique characteristics. The first of these is *autonomy*: the fact that law has its own sphere of authority and operates independently within that sphere without reference to any external controlling factor. Unger distinguished four distinct aspects of legal autonomy, which may be enumerated as follows:

substantive autonomy: this refers to the fact that law is not explicable in other, non-legal terms. To use the tautological cliché – the law is the law. In other words, law is self-referential, it is not about something else; it cannot be reduced to the level of a mere means to an end, it is an end in itself;

institutional autonomy: this refers to the fact that the legal institutions such as the courts are separate from other state institutions and are highlighted in the fundamental principle of judicial independence;

> *methodological autonomy*: this refers to the fact that law has, or at least lays claim to having, its own distinct form of reasoning and justifications for its decisions;
>
> *occupational autonomy*: this refers to the fact that access to law is not immediate, but is gained through the legal professions, who act as gatekeepers and who exercise a large degree of independent control over the working of the legal system.

The second distinguishing feature of legal order, according to Unger, is its *generality*: the fact that it applies to all people without personal or class favouritism. Everyone is equal under the law and is treated in the same manner.

In putting forward this typology of social order, Unger recognised the advantages inherent in a rule of law system over a system that operates on the basis of arbitrary power, but he was ultimately sceptical as to the reality of the equality that such a system supports and questioned its future continuation. The point of major interest for this book, however, is the way in which each of the four distinct areas of supposed autonomy is increasingly being challenged and undermined, as will be considered at the end of the next section.

2.2.6 MAX WEBER

Unger saw the development of the rule of law as a product of Western capitalist society and, in highlighting the distinct nature of the form of law under that system, he may be seen as following the German sociologist Max Weber. Weber's general goal was to examine and explain the structure and development of Western capitalist society. In so doing, he was concerned with those unique aspects of that society which distinguished it from other social formations. One such distinguishing characteristic was the form of law that he characterised as a formally rational system, which prefigured Unger's notion of legal autonomy (see Weber, *Wirtschaft und Gesellschaft* (trans 1968)).

Weber's autonomous legal system was accompanied by a state that limited itself to establishing a clear framework of social order and left individuals to determine their own destinies in a free market system. In the course of the twentieth century, however, the move from a free market to a basically planned economy, with the state playing an active part in economic activity, brought about a major change in both the form and function of law.

2.2.7 THE RULE OF LAW AND THE CONTEMPORARY FORM OF LAW

While the state remained apart from civil society, its functions could be restricted within a limited sphere of activity circumscribed within the doctrine of the rule of law. However, as the state became increasingly involved in actually regulating economic activity, the form of law had by necessity to change. To deal with problems as and when they arose, the state had to assume discretionary powers rather than be governed by fixed predetermined rules. Such discretion, however, is antithetical to the traditional idea of the rule of law, which was posited on the fact of limiting the state's discretion. Thus emerged the tension between the rule of law and the requirements of regulating social activity that FA von Hayek, for one, saw as a fundamental change for the worse in our society.

With specific regard to the effect of this change on law's previous autonomy, there is clear agreement among academic writers that there has been a fundamental alteration in the nature of law. Whereas legislation previously took the form of fixed and precisely stated rules, now legislation tends be open-textured and to grant wide discretionary powers to particular state functionaries, resulting in a corresponding reduction in the power of the courts to control such activity. The courts have resisted this process to a degree, through the expansion of the procedure for judicial review, but their role in the area relating to administration remains at best questionable. The growth of delegated legislation, in which parliament simply passes enabling Acts, empowering ministers of state to make regulations, as they consider necessary, is a prime example of this process (considered in detail in section 3.5). In addition, once made, such regulations tend not to be general but highly particular, even technocratic, in their detail.

The increased use of tribunals with the participation of non-legal experts rather than courts to decide disputes, with the underlying implication that the law is not capable of resolving the problem adequately, also represents a diminishment in law's previous power, as does the use of planning procedures as opposed to fixed rules of law in determining decisions. (Tribunals will be considered in Chapter 15.)

Legislation also increasingly pursues substantive justice rather than merely limiting itself to the provision of formal justice as required under the rule of law. As an example of this, consumer law may be cited: thus, in the Consumer Rights Act 2015, contract terms are to be evaluated on the basis of fairness and, under the Consumer Credit Act 1974, agreements may be rejected on the basis of their being extortionate or unconscionable. Such provisions actually override the market assumptions as to formal equality in an endeavour to provide a measure of substantive justice.

All the foregoing examples of a change can be characterised as involving a change from 'law as end in itself' to 'law as means to an end'. In Weberian terms, this change in law represents a change from *formal rationality*, in which law determined outcomes to problems stated in the form of legal terms through the application of abstract legal concepts and principles, to a system of *substantive rationality*, where law is simply a mechanism to achieve a goal set outside of law.

In other words, law is no longer seen as completely autonomous as it once was. Increasingly, it is seen as merely instrumental in the achievement of some wider purpose, which the state, acting as the embodiment of the general interest, sets. Paradoxically, as will be seen later, even when the law attempts to intervene in this process, as it does through judicial review, it does so in a way that undermines its autonomy and reveals it to be simply another aspect of political activity.

The return to a more Hayekian, free-market-based economy and polity since the election of the Thatcher Conservative government in 1979, and its continuation by all other governments, of whatever persuasion, since then has certainly changed the rhetoric and ideology about the relationship of the individual and the state. It can hardly be denied that the pursuit of essentially cost-cutting measures, by the previous coalition and present Conservative governments, in response to the economic imperatives of a perceived economic imbalance, has had a significant, not to say damaging, impact on the operation of the legal system. Indeed some have gone so far as to suggest that by treating the legal system in the same way as any other emanation of state provision it has undermined not only the independence of law and the legal system but also its own commitment to the rules of law as established in s 1 of the CRA 2005.

2.3   THE RULE OF LAW AND THE JUDICIARY

The commentators considered above came from a variety of academic backgrounds, but the essential practical importance of the concept of the rule of law was highlighted in a speech delivered by the former most senior Law Lord, the late Lord Bingham of Cornhill, in November 2006 under the deceptively simple title 'The Rule of Law' (the sixth *Sir David Williams Lecture* delivered at the Centre for Public Law at the University of Cambridge).

As has already been indicated, the Constitutional Reform Act (CRA) 2005 provides, in s 1, that the Act does not adversely affect 'the existing constitutional principle of the rule of law' or 'the Lord Chancellor's existing constitutional role in relation to that principle'. That provision is further reflected in the oath to be taken by Lord Chancellors under s 17(1) of the Act, to respect the rule of law and defend the independence of the judiciary. However, as Lord Bingham pointed out, the Act does not actually define what is meant by the rule of law, or indeed the Lord Chancellor's role in relation to it. He also recognised the difficulty in fixing a single meaning or in fact any substantive content to the principle, citing various different academic references to it, some of which have been considered above, but nonetheless he felt it appropriate to offer his own understanding of the rule of law.

In Lord Bingham's view, the authors of the 2005 Act apparently also recognised the difficulty of formulating a succinct and accurate definition suitable for inclusion in a statute, and consequently left the task of definition to the courts, if and when the occasion arose. The importance of such a task of definition cannot be underestimated, for it places an essential duty on, and considerable power in the hands of, the judiciary. If, as the CRA recognises, the rule of law is an existing constitutional principle, then the judges will be required to construe statutes in relation to that principle in such a way as to ensure that they do not infringe that constitutional principle. A further implication of the CRA is that the Lord Chancellor's conduct, in relation to role and duty to the rule of law, would be open to judicial review, were they to be challenged in that regard. As the rule of law already is an existing constitutional principle of the UK and one that may be more contentious in the future, it becomes imperative to attempt to define what it actually means. It is this task that Lord Bingham sets himself in the lecture under consideration and he suggests that at its core is the idea that 'all persons and authorities within the state, whether public or private, should be bound by and entitled to the benefit of laws publicly and prospectively promulgated and publicly administered in the courts'.

Bingham rests his basic understanding on John Locke's dictum that 'Wherever law ends, tyranny begins'. Yet, even in that regard, he demurs by admitting that in some proceedings justice can only be done if they are *not* dealt with in public.

However, the main importance is the detail that Lord Bingham introduces through his consideration of the eight implications, or sub-rules, that he holds are particular aspects of the general principle of the rule of law. These sub-rules are:

- The law must be accessible and so far as possible intelligible, clear and predictable.

The reasoning behind this requirement is that if everyone is bound by the law they must be able without undue difficulty to find out what it is, even if that means taking advice from their lawyers. Equally the response should be sufficiently clear that a course of action can be based on it. However, for this to be achieved, there has to be an end to what Lord Bingham refers to as the 'legislative hyperactivity which appears to have become a permanent feature of our governance'. This excessive legislation, exacerbated by baffling parliamentary draftsmanship, is particularly problematic in relation to the 'torrent of criminal legislation', not all of which is 'readily intelligible'.

However, Lord Bingham does not leave his fellow judges in doubt about their responsibilities in the creation of legal uncertainty and criticises 'the length, complexity and sometimes prolixity of modern common law judgments, particularly at the highest level'. However, on consideration he rejects the supposed benefit of single opinion decisions in the House of Lords, with only one judgment and four decisions in agreement with that, in favour of multiple judgments 'where the well-considered committee of five or more, can bring to bear a diversity of professional and jurisdictional experience which is valuable in shaping the law'.

As Lord Bingham saw it, the benefit of multiple decisions in shaping the law was, however, subject to the three caveats:

(i) whatever the diversity of opinion the judges should recognise a duty, not always observed, to try *to ensure that there is a clear majority ratio*. Without that, no one can know what the law is until Parliament or a later case lays down a clear rule.

(ii) excessive innovation and adventurism by judges had to be avoided. Without challenging the value or legitimacy of judicial development of the law, taken to extremes, such judicial creativity can itself destroy the rule of law.

(iii) all these points apply with redoubled force in the criminal field with the conclusion that judges should create new offences or widen existing offences so as to make punishable conduct that was not previously subject to punishment.

- Questions of legal right and liability should ordinarily be resolved by application of the law and not the exercise of discretion.

Lord Bingham does not share Dicey's complete antipathy to the exercise of discretion, and cites immigration law as an example where it has been advantageous. Nonetheless he does believe that the essential truth of Dicey's insight stands and that 'the broader and more loosely-textured a discretion is, *whether conferred on an official or a judge,* the greater the scope for subjectivity and hence for arbitrariness, which is the antithesis of the rule of law'. However, he is satisfied that the need for discretion to be narrowly defined, and its exercise to be capable of reasoned justification, are requirements which UK law almost always satisfies.

- The laws of the land should apply equally to all, save to the extent that objective differences justify differentiation.

However, if the law is to apply to all, then governments should also accept the converse, that the rule of law does not allow for any distinction between British nationals and others. Unfortunately, the second part of the reciprocal link did not appear to have been considered when Parliament passed Part 4 of the Anti-terrorism, Crime and Security Act 2001, which was held to be incompatible with the Human Rights Act in the *Belmarsh* cases (see 2.5.2).

- The law must afford adequate protection of fundamental human rights.

This sub-rule goes beyond the formalistic approaches of both Dicey and Raz to insist that the rule of law does in fact connote a substantive content, although Lord Bingham is less certain as to the particular detail of that content. In response to Raz he states:

> A state which savagely repressed or persecuted sections of its people could not in my view be regarded as observing the rule of law, even if the transport of the persecuted minority to the concentration camp or the compulsory exposure of female children on the mountainside were the subject of detailed laws duly enacted and scrupulously observed. So to hold would, I think, be to strip the existing constitutional principle affirmed by section 1 of the 2005 Act of much of its virtue and infringe the fundamental compact which, as I shall suggest at the end, underpins the rule of law.

But he also recognises that this is a difficult area and that there is not even a standard of human rights universally agreed among 'so-called' civilised nations. However, although he admits to this element of vagueness about the content of this sub-rule, he maintains that 'within a given state there will ordinarily be a measure of agreement on where the lines are to be drawn, and in the last resort (subject in this country to statute) the courts are there to draw them'.

Consequently, the rule of law must require the legal protection of such human rights as are recognised in that society.

- Means must be provided for resolving, without prohibitive cost or inordinate delay, bona fide civil disputes which the parties themselves are unable to resolve.

As a corollary of the principle that everyone is bound by and entitled to the benefit of the law is the requirement that people should be able, in the last resort, to go to court to have their rights and liabilities determined. In stating this sub-rule Lord Bingham makes it clear that he is not seeking to undermine arbitration, which he sees as supremely important, rather he is looking to support the provisions of a properly funded legal aid scheme, the demise of which he clearly regrets, as may be seen from the following:

> Whether conditional fees, various pro bono schemes and small claims procedures have filled the gap left by this curtailment I do not myself know. Perhaps they have, and advice and help are still available to those of modest means who deserve it. But I have a fear that tabloid tales of practitioners milking the criminal legal aid fund of millions, and more general distrust of lawyers and their rewards, may have enabled a valuable guarantee of social justice to wither unlamented.

Lord Bingham is equally concerned about the fact that successive governments have insisted that the civil courts, judicial salaries usually aside, should be self-financing: the cost of running the courts being covered by fees recovered from litigants. The danger with such an approach is that the cost of going to court in order to get redress may preclude some people from gaining access to the legal system.

- Ministers and public officers at all levels must exercise the powers conferred on them reasonably, in good faith, for the purpose for which the powers were conferred and without exceeding the limits of such powers.

As Lord Bingham saw it:

> The historic role of the courts has of course been to check excesses of executive power, a role greatly expanded in recent years due to the increased complexity of government and the greater willingness of the public to challenge governmental (in the broadest sense) decisions. Even under our constitution the separation of powers is crucial in guaranteeing the integrity of the courts' performance of this role.

This judicial role has of course been met through judicial review.

However, Lord Bingham is conscious, and unarguably so it would appear, of a shift away from the traditional relationship of the courts and the executive, under which the convention was that ministers, however critical of a judicial decision, and exercising their right to appeal against it or, in the last resort, legislate to reverse it retrospectively, did not engage in any public attack on the judiciary. In a muted, although nonetheless threatening, rejoinder to the present government Lord Bingham states his view that:

> This convention appears to have worn a little thin in recent times, as I think unfortunately, since if ministers make what are understood to be public attacks on judges, *the judges may be provoked to make similar criticisms of ministers*, and the rule of law is not, in my view, well served by public dispute between two arms of the state.

- Adjudicative procedures provided by the state should be fair.

The rule of law would seem to require no less. The general arguments in favour of open hearings are familiar, summed up on this side of the Atlantic by the dictum that justice must manifestly and undoubtedly be seen to be done and on the American side by the observation that 'Democracies die behind closed doors'.

While he sees application of this sub-rule to ordinary civil processes to be largely unproblematic, he does recognise that there is more scope for difficulty where a person faces adverse consequences as a result of what he is thought or said to have done or not done, whether in the context of a formal criminal charge or in other contexts such as deportation, precautionary detention, recall to prison or refusal of parole. The question in those circumstances is what does fairness ordinarily require? Lord Bingham's first response to the question is that, first and foremost, decisions must be taken by adjudicators who are:

> independent and impartial: independent in the sense that they are free to decide on the legal and factual merits of a case as they see it, free of any extraneous influence or pressure, and impartial in the sense that they are, so far as humanly possible, open-minded, unbiased by any personal interest or partisan allegiance of any kind.

But additionally a second element is involved, which relates to the presumption that any issue should not be finally decided against a person until they have had an adequate opportunity for their response to the allegation to be heard. In effect this means that:

> a person potentially subject to any liability or penalty should be adequately informed of what is said against him; that the accuser should make adequate disclosure of material helpful to the other party or damaging to itself; that where the interests of a party cannot be adequately protected without the

benefit of professional help which the party cannot afford, public assistance should so far as practicable be afforded; that a party accused should have an adequate opportunity to prepare his answer to what is said against him; and that the innocence of a defendant charged with criminal conduct should be presumed until guilt is proved.

In the context of criminal law this raises two pertinent issues:

(i)   *Disclosure.* This relates to material in the possession of the prosecutor, which they are for reasons of public interest unwilling to disclose to the defence. As the law stands at present, material need not be disclosed if in no way helpful to the defence; if helpful to the point where the defence would be significantly prejudiced by non-disclosure, the prosecutor must either disclose the material or abandon the prosecution.

(ii)   *Reverse burden of proof.* Some statutory offences place a reverse burden on the defendant; i.e. the defendant has to show that they did not commit the offence alleged. In Lord Bingham's opinion such reversals in the normal burden of proof are 'not in themselves objectionable, but may be so if the burden is one which a defendant, even if innocent, may in practice be unable to discharge'.

However, of much more concern to Lord Bingham in this regard was the increase in the instances, outside the strictly criminal sphere, in which Parliament has provided that the full case against a person, put before the adjudicator as a basis for decision, should not be disclosed to that person or indeed to their legal representative. One example of this procedure is of course the non-derogation control orders issued under the Prevention of Terrorism Act 2005. A further inroad in relation to this issue is to be found in the provisions of the Justice and Security Act 2013 (see p 73). In his Rule of Law lecture he expressed the view that:

Any process which denies knowledge to a person effectively, if not actually, accused of what is relied on against him, and thus denies him a fair opportunity to rebut it, must arouse acute disquiet. But these categories reflect the undoubted danger of disclosing some kinds of highly sensitive information, and they have been clearly identified and regulated by Parliament, which has judged the departure to be necessary and attempted to limit its extent.

In *SSHD v E* (2007) he was required to provide a practical consideration of and decision in relation to the concerns raised above.

●   The existing principle of the rule of law requires compliance by the state with its obligations in international law.

This particular section of Lord Bingham's lecture is interesting for the indirect way in which he examines the involvement of the UK in the ongoing war in Iraq while, as he said, 'not for obvious reasons touch[ing] on the vexed question whether Britain's involvement in the 2003 war on Iraq was in breach of international law and thus, if this sub-rule is sound, of the rule of law'.

The way he achieved this was through a comparison between the procedures followed in 2003 and those followed at the time of the Suez invasion of 1956. While he concluded that the comparison suggests that over the period the rule of law has gained ground in the UK, it also allowed him to make some pointed comments in relation to the way the current war was initiated. In this regard he considered the different roles assumed by the law officers in both situations, and while he welcomed the involvement of the Attorney General in providing legal advice to the government, he raised doubts about to whom the Attorney General ultimately owed his duty – the government, as the then Attorney General had seen it, or the public at large, which Lord Bingham, personally, appears to support, as is evident from the following passage (the role of the Attorney General will be considered further in section 12.3.2):

> There seems to me to be room to question whether the ordinary rules of client privilege, appropriate enough in other circumstances, should apply to a law officer's opinion on the lawfulness of war: it is not unrealistic in my view to regard the public, those who are to fight and perhaps die, rather than the government, as the client . . . [a]nd the case for full, contemporaneous, disclosure seems to me even stronger when the Attorney General is a peer, not susceptible to direct questioning in the elected chamber.

In conclusion Lord Bingham correlated the rule of law with a democratic society based on

> an unspoken but fundamental bargain between the individual and the state, the governed and the governor, by which both sacrifice a measure of the freedom and power which they would otherwise enjoy. The individual living in society implicitly accepts that he or she cannot exercise the unbridled freedom enjoyed by Adam in the Garden of Eden, before the creation of Eve, and accepts the constraints imposed by laws properly made because of the benefits which, on balance, they confer. The state for its part accepts that it may not do, at home or abroad, all that it has the power to do but only that which laws binding upon it authorise it to do. If correct, this conclusion is reassuring to all of us who, in any capacity, devote our professional lives to the service of the law. For it means that we are not, as we are sometimes seen, mere custodians of a body of arid prescriptive rules but are, with others, the guardians of an all but sacred flame which animates and enlightens the society in which we live

– a true Lockean view of the rule of law if there ever was one.

Inherent in Lord Bingham's speech is a tension between the judges and the other elements in the constitution – the executive/government and Parliament – with Lord Bingham seeing the role of the judges as protecting the society from unlawful inroads into its liberties and rights. This tension has been heightened by the enactment of the Human Rights Act 1998, to be considered in the following section; however, before that can be done it is necessary to examine the concept of the separation of powers and related concepts such as parliamentary sovereignty and judicial independence. Although the idea of the separation of powers can be traced back to ancient Greek philosophy, it was advocated in early modern times by the English philosopher Locke and the later French philosopher Montesquieu, and found its practical expression in the constitution of the United States. The idea of the separation of powers is posited on the existence of three distinct functions of government (the legislative, executive and judicial functions) and the conviction that these functions should be kept apart in order to prevent the centralisation of too much power. Establishing the appropriate relationship between the actions of the state and the legal control over those actions crucially involves a consideration of whether there is any absolute limit on the authority of the government of the day. Answering that question inevitably involves an examination of the general constitutional structure of the UK and, in particular, the interrelationship of two doctrines: parliamentary sovereignty and judicial independence. It also requires an understanding of the role of judicial review and the effect of the Human Rights Act 1998, and has caused no little friction between the judiciary and the executive, especially in the person of the Home Secretary.

There is, in any case, high judicial authority for claiming that the separation of powers is an essential element in the constitution of the UK (see *R v Hinds* (1979), p 212, in which Lord Diplock, while considering the nature of different Commonwealth constitutions in a Privy Council case, stated that 'It is taken for granted that the basic principle of the separation of powers will apply . . .'). In any case, the point of considering the doctrine at this juncture is simply to highlight the distinction and relationship between the executive and the judiciary and to indicate the possibility of conflict between the two elements of the constitution. This relationship assumes crucial importance if one accepts, as some have suggested, that it is no longer possible to distinguish the executive from the legislature as, through its control of its majority in the House of Commons, the executive (that is, the government) can legislate as it wishes and in so doing, can provide the most arbitrary of party political decisions with the form of legality. The question to be considered here is to what extent the judiciary can legitimately oppose the wishes of the government expressed in the form of legislation, or to what extent they can interfere with the pursuit of those wishes. As will be seen below, the power of the judiciary in relation to legislative provisions has been greatly enhanced by the passage of the Human Rights Act 1998.

The separation of powers and the Constitutional Reform Act 2005
The details of this major constitutional reform Act will be considered in detail in due course, but it cannot be denied that the force that drove the government to introduce

the Act was an understanding of the imperatives of the separation of powers and the wish to regularise the constitution of the United Kingdom within that framework. Consequently, the anomalous position of the Lord Chancellor, who was a member of all three branches of the political structure, was to be resolved and the House of Lords, as the supreme court, was to be removed from its location within the legislative body.

2.3.2 PARLIAMENTARY SOVEREIGNTY

As a consequence of the victory of the parliamentary forces in the English revolutionary struggles of the seventeenth century, Parliament became the sovereign power in the land. The independence of the judiciary was secured, however, in the Act of Settlement 1701. The centrality of the independence of the judges and the legal system from direct control or interference from the state in the newly established constitution was emphasised in the writing of John Locke, who saw it as one of the essential reasons for, and justifications of, the social contract on which the social structure was assumed to be based. It is generally accepted that the inspiration for Montesquieu's *Spirit of Law* (*De L'Esprit des Lois*) was the English constitution, but if that is truly the case, then his doctrine of the separation of powers was based on a misunderstanding of that constitution, as it failed to take account of the express *superiority of parliament* in all matters, including its relationship with the judiciary and the legal system.

It is interesting that previous conservative thinkers have suggested that the whole concept of parliamentary sovereignty is itself a product of the self-denying ordinance of the common law. Consequently, they suggested that it was open to a subsequent, more robust, judiciary, confident in its own position and powers within the developing constitution, to reassert its equality with the other two elements of the polity. Just such an approach may be recognised as implicit in a number of the judgments of the augmented nine-person House of Lords in *Jackson v HM Attorney General* (2005). The case concerned the use of the Parliament Acts to pass legislation banning hunting with dogs, and in that respect it will be considered in detail in section 3.3, but in doing so it by necessity raised, without the requirement to deal definitively with, the essential constitutional question as to the relationship of the courts and parliament. While the majority of the judges, at the least, express reservations as to the power of the House of Commons under the Parliament Acts, the most overtly challenging statement can be seen in the judgment of Lord Steyn. His view of parliamentary sovereignty may be deduced from the following passage, in which he considers the argument of the Attorney General that the application of the Parliament Acts effectively is subject to no limitation:

> If the Attorney General is right the 1949 Act could also be used to introduce oppressive and wholly undemocratic legislation . . . The classic account given by Dicey of the doctrine of the supremacy of Parliament, pure and absolute as it was, can now be seen to be out of place in the modern United Kingdom.

> Nevertheless, the supremacy of Parliament is still the *general* principle of our constitution. It is a construct of the common law. The judges created this principle. If that is so, it is not unthinkable that circumstances could arise where the courts may have to qualify a principle established on a different hypothesis of constitutionalism. In exceptional circumstances involving an attempt to abolish judicial review or the ordinary role of the courts, the Appellate Committee of the House of Lords or a new Supreme Court may have to consider whether this is a constitutional fundamental which even a sovereign Parliament acting at the behest of a complaisant House of Commons cannot abolish.

Lord Steyn's reasoning was subsequently questioned, and the traditional view of parliamentary sovereignty was reasserted by the former Master of the Rolls and current President of the Supreme Court, Lord Neuberger, in his Weedon Lecture in April 2011. As he put it:

> Ultimately, it might be said that Lord Steyn's point that the courts had invented Parliamentary sovereignty and could therefore remove or qualify it involves an intellectual sleight of hand: Parliamentary sovereignty *was acknowledged* rather than *bestowed* by the courts. They acknowledged what had been clearly established by civil war, the Glorious Revolution of 1688, the Bill of Rights 1689 and the Act of Settlement 1701   (emphasis added).

Lord Neuberger went on:

> [Parliament] can, if it chooses, and clearly and expressly states that it is so doing, enact legislation which is contrary to the rule of law . . . neither the Convention nor the Human Rights Act goes nowhere near to imposing a limit on Parliamentary legal sovereignty.
>
> It is true that membership of the Convention imposes obligations on the state to ensure that judgments of the Strasbourg court are implemented, but those obligations are in international law, not domestic law. And, ultimately, the implementation of a Strasbourg, or indeed a domestic court judgment is a matter for Parliament. If it chose not to implement a Strasbourg judgment, it might place the United Kingdom in breach of its treaty obligations, but as a matter of domestic law there would be nothing objectionable in such a course. It would be a political decision, with which the courts could not interfere.

European Union Act 2011

In September 2011, Parliament passed the European Union Act 2011. The main purpose of the Act was to make provision for the application of the post-Lisbon treaties. However, s 18 of the Act, for the first time, places the common law principle of parliamentary sovereignty on a statutory footing and states that all EU law takes effect in the UK only by virtue of the will of Parliament, as provided in the European Communities Act (ECA) 1972. The issue of parliamentary sovereignty in relation to the European Union will be considered in section 5.1.1.

R (Evans) v Attorney General (2015)

This case raises issues in relation to the interrelationship of the rule of law, the power of the judiciary and parliamentary sovereignty. Evans, a *Guardian* journalist, had made a request under the Freedom of Information Act (FOI) 2000 for the release of correspondence between Prince Charles and various government ministers. As some of the letters related to environmental issues, a request was also made under the Environmental Information Regulations (EIR) 2004. Initially the request was refused, but was eventually approved after a six-day hearing before the Administrative Appeals Chamber of the Upper Tribunal. The government departments concerned did not appeal the UT decision, but on 16 October 2012 the Attorney General issued a certificate under section 53(2) FOIA 2000 and regulation 18(6) EIR 2004 stating that he had, on 'reasonable grounds', formed the opinion that the departments were entitled to refuse disclosure of the letters. Among his justifications for his action was 'the potential damage that disclosure would do to the principle of the Prince of Wales' political neutrality, which could seriously undermine the Prince's ability to fulfil his duties when he becomes King'. Evans's challenge to the issue of the certificate was ultimately decided by the Supreme Court, which decided by a majority of five to two that the certificate was unlawful under the 2000 Act (the court also decided by 6 to 1 that the certificate was contrary to EU law).

Lord Neuberger, with whom Lords Kerr and Reid agreed, concluded that 'reasonable grounds' could not mean that the Attorney General could issue a certificate merely because he would have reached a different conclusion to the Upper Tribunal.

> A statutory provision which entitles a member of the executive (whether a Government Minister or the Attorney General) to overrule a decision of the judiciary merely because he does not agree with it would not merely be unique in the laws of the United Kingdom. It would cut across two constitutional principles which are also fundamental components of the rule of law. First, . . . it is a basic principle that a decision of a court is binding as between the parties, and cannot be ignored or set aside by anyone including (indeed it may fairly be said, least of all) the executive. Secondly, it is also fundamental to the rule of law that decisions and actions of the executive are, . . . reviewable by the court at the suit of an interested citizen   (paras 51–52).

These passages may be seen as Lord Neuberger's clarion call for the rights of the rule of law and the common law power of the judiciary in the face of executive and legislative power. However, his judgment actually rested on the unreasonable nature of the Attorney General's decision in the circumstances of the case. In so doing it may be said to recognise the pre-eminence of parliamentary sovereignty: for he recognises that properly constructed legislation can supersede either the final authority of judicial decisions or the requirement of judicial review, or indeed both.

Perhaps after all there is not so great a distance between Lord Neuberger's stance and the apparently contrary one expressed by Lord Hughes that:

> The rule of law is of the first importance. But it is an integral part of the rule of law that courts give effect to Parliamentary intention. The rule of law is not the same as a rule that courts must always prevail, no matter what the statute says   (para 154).

2.3.3 JUDICIAL INDEPENDENCE

The exact meaning of 'judicial independence' became a matter of debate when some members and ex-members of the senior judiciary suggested that the former Conservative Lord Chancellor, Lord Mackay of Clashfern, had adopted a too-restrictive interpretation of the term, which had reduced it to the mere absence of interference by the executive in the trial of individual cases. They asserted the right of the legal system to operate independently, as an autonomous system apart from the general control of the state, with the judiciary controlling its operation, or at least being free from the dictates and strictures of central control.

According to Lord Mackay, in the first of his series of Hamlyn lectures entitled 'The Administration of Justice' (1994):

> The fact that the executive and judiciary meet in the person of the Lord Chancellor should symbolise what I believe is necessary for the administration of justice in a country like ours, namely, a realisation that both the judiciary and the executive are parts of the total government of the country with functions that are distinct but which must work together in a proper relationship if the country is to be properly governed . . . It seems more likely that the interests of the judiciary in matters within the concerns covered by the Treasury are more likely to be advanced if they can be pursued within government by a person with a lifetime of work in law and an understanding of the needs and concerns of the judiciary and who has responsibility as Head of the Judiciary, than if they were to be left within government as the responsibility of a minister with no such connection with the judiciary.

The tension inherent in the relationship between the courts and the executive government took on a more fundamental constitutional aspect with the passing of the Human
Rights Act 1998. By means of that Act, the courts were given the right to subject the
actions and operations of the executive and, indeed, all public authorities to the gaze and
control of the law, in such a way as to prevent the executive from abusing its power. If the
Human Rights Act represented a shift in constitutional power towards the judiciary, the
Act was nonetheless sensitive to maintain the doctrine of parliamentary sovereignty. In
the United States, with its written constitution, the judiciary in the form of the Supreme
Court has the power to declare the Acts of the legislature unconstitutional and consequently invalid. No such power was extended to the UK courts under the Human Rights
Act, although some commentators saw the Human Rights Act as eventually leading to a
similar outcome in the UK. Such tension was further heightened when, in June 2003, the
government announced its intention to radically alter the constitution, and the judges'
role within it, at an apparent single stroke by the expedient of removing the role of Lord
Chancellor.

Given the judiciary's suspicion of Lord Mackay as Lord Chancellor, it is not a little ironic that the government's announcement of its intention to abolish the position of
Lord Chancellor was met by strong judicial reaction, in language very similar to that used
by that former holder of the office. The judges, supported by many parliamentarians and
commentators, made it absolutely clear that they thought that their independence would
best be protected by a strong, legally qualified, champion within the cabinet. Such a
role had been performed by the Lord Chancellor. Consequently, the judiciary generally
regretted, not to say resisted, the abolition of the office as originally provided for in the
Constitutional Reform Bill 2003. Although such resistance succeeded in retaining the
office of the Lord Chancellor, its functions were greatly reduced and s 2 of the Constitutional Reform Act of 2005 provides that the holder of the office should be 'qualified
by experience', which need not include legal experience. Neither will the holder of the
office necessarily sit in the House of Lords. However, in recognition of the sensitivities of
the judiciary, s 3 of the Act, for the first time, places a legal duty on government ministers
to uphold the independence of the judiciary and specifically bars them from trying to
influence judicial decisions through any special access to judges.

When Gordon Brown replaced Tony Blair as Prime Minister in the summer of
2007, the resulting Cabinet reshuffle resulted in the abolition of the Department for
Constitutional Affairs and its being replaced by a new Justice Ministry headed by Jack
Straw, who also replaced Lord Falconer as Lord Chancellor, although remaining a member of the House of Commons. The new ministry, which is ultimately responsible for
looking after the interests of the judiciary and courts, also assumed responsibility for the
prison service, which caused the judges great concern as they feared that their allocation from the joint ministerial budget would be under pressure from the ever-expanding
prison budget.

Following the General Election of 2010, the new coalition Justice Minister was
the extremely experienced MP Kenneth Clarke QC, although his experience did not
save him from being replaced in the Cabinet reshuffle in September 2012. The replacement was Chris Grayling, who is the first non-lawyer to hold the office of Lord Chancellor. The current Lord Chancellor is Michael Gove, another non-lawyer.

The need for separation of legislative, executive and judicial powers: acts as a 'check' on the potential for arbitrary government. This is known as 'the separation of powers'. It facilitates the 'rule of law'.

Supported by **the 'rule of law':**
- requires that all people and organisations be subject to law, and no one is above the law.
- enshrined in legislation for the first time by the *Constitutional Reform Act 2005*

Examples of overlap between powers:
- **Prime Minister:** member of the executive (Cabinet) and of the legislature (Parliament)
- **Lord Chancellor:** no longer head of the judiciary (since the *Constitutional Reform Act 2005*) but still a member of the executive (Cabinet) and the legislature (Government)
- **Monarch:** has a *legislative* function (provision of Royal Assent to bills), an *executive* function (appointing Government Ministers) and a *judicial* function (courts are the monarch's courts. judges are the monarch's judges and criminal prosecutions are brought in the name of the sovereign)

Examples of distinctions between powers:
- **Independence of the judiciary:** Now enshrined in legislation by means of the *Constitutional Reform Act 2005 (CRA).* In particular, *s 3(1)* provides that 'The Lord Chancellor, other Ministers of the Crown and all with responsibility for matters relating to the judiciary or otherwise to the administration of justice must uphold the continued independence of the judiciary'.
- **Creation of a Supreme Court:** CRA established a new, independent, Supreme Court, separate from the House of Lords with its own independent appointments system, its own staff, budget and accommodation. Justices of the Supreme Court are no longer allowed to sit as members of the House of Lords.
- **Judicial Review of the acts of the Executive by the judiciary:** While the courts enforce the will of Parliament by giving effect to its legislative acts, they retain the right to review activities of the Executive by means of Judicial Review.
- **The Human Rights Act** has gone some way to ensure that basic rights cannot be removed by the state and are actionable in the courts.

FIGURE 2.1 *The Rule of Law.*

2.4   HUMAN RIGHTS DISCOURSE AND THE RULE OF LAW

In an article published in the *London Review of Books* and *The Guardian* newspaper in May 1995, three years before the enactment of the Human Rights Act, the High Court judge, as he then was, Sir Stephen Sedley, made explicit the links and tensions between the doctrine of the rule of law and the relationship of the courts and the executive, and the implications for the use of judicial review as a means of controlling the exercise of executive power. In his view:

> Our agenda for the 21st century is not necessarily confined to choice between a 'rights instrument' interpreted by a judiciary with a long record of illiberal adjudication, and rejection of any rights instrument in favour of

Parliamentary government. The better government becomes, the less scope there will be for judicial review of it.

But, for the foreseeable future, we have a problem: how to ensure that as a society we are governed within a law which has internalised the notion of fundamental human rights. Although this means adopting the Rule of law, like democracy, as a higher-order principle, we do have the social consensus which alone can accord it that primacy. And, if in our own society the Rule of law is to mean much, *it must at least mean that it is the obligation of the courts to articulate and uphold the ground rules of ethical social existence which we dignify as fundamental human rights* . . . There is a potential tension between the principle of democratic government and the principle of equality before the law . . . The notion that the prime function of human rights and indeed the Rule of law is to protect the weak against the strong is not mere sentimentality. It is the child of an era of history in which equality of treatment and opportunity has become perceived . . . as an unqualified good, and of a significant recognition that you do not achieve equality merely by proclaiming it . . . fundamental human rights to be real, have to steer towards outcomes which invert those inequalities of power that mock the principle of equality before the law.

Such talk of fundamental human rights denies the absolute sovereignty of parliament in its recognition of areas that are beyond the legitimate exercise of state power. It also recognises, however, that notions of the rule of law cannot be satisfied by the provision of merely formal equality as Dicey and Hayek would have it and previous legal safeguards would have provided. For Sedley, the rule of law clearly imports, and is based on, ideas of substantive equality that market systems and legal formalism cannot provide and in fact undermine. His version of the rule of law clearly involves a reconsideration of the relationship of the executive and the judiciary, and involves the latter in a further reconsideration of their own previous beliefs and functions.

2.5 THE HUMAN RIGHTS ACT 1998

As is evident in the quotation from Sir Stephen Sedley above, some judges, at least, saw their role in maintaining the rule of law as providing protection for fundamental human rights. In attempting to achieve this end, they faced a particular problem in relation to the way in which the unwritten English constitution was understood, and was understood to operate. The freedom of individual action in English law was not based on ideas of positive human rights which could not be taken away, but on negative liberties: that is, individual subjects were entitled to do whatever was not forbidden by the law. This was particularly problematic when it was linked to the doctrine of the sovereignty of parliament, which, in effect, meant that parliament was free to restrict, or indeed remove, individual liberties at any time merely by passing the necessary legislation.

It is generally accepted that the courts developed the procedure of judicial review, as an aspect of the rule of law, in an attempt to protect individuals from the excesses of an over-powerful executive (see below, 13.5, for a detailed consideration). But, in so doing, they were limited in what they could achieve by the very nature of the procedure available to them. They could not directly question the laws produced by parliament on the basis of substance, as constitutional courts in other systems could, but were restricted essentially to questioning the formal or procedural proprieties of such legislation. There was, however, an alternative forum capable of challenging the substance of English law, and one that was based on the assumption of positive rights rather than negative liberties. That forum was the European Court of Human Rights (ECtHR).

It has to be established and emphasised from the outset that the substance of this section has absolutely nothing to do with the European Union as such; the Council of Europe is a completely distinct organisation and, although membership of the two organisations overlap, they are not the same. The Council of Europe is concerned not with economic matters, but with the protection of civil rights and freedoms (the nature of these institutions and the operation of the ECtHR will be considered in detail in Chapter 15).

The UK was one of the initial signatories to the European Convention on Human Rights and Fundamental Freedoms (hereafter the ECHR) in 1950, which was instituted in post-war Europe as a means of establishing and enforcing essential human rights. In 1966, the UK recognised the power of the European Commission on Human Rights to hear complaints from individual UK citizens and, at the same time, recognised the authority of the ECtHR to adjudicate in such matters. It did not, however, at that time incorporate the ECHR into UK law.

The consequence of non-incorporation was that the Convention could not be directly enforced in English courts. In *R v Secretary of State for the Home Department ex p Brind* (1991), the Court of Appeal decided that ministerial directives did not have to be construed in line with the ECHR, as that would be tantamount to introducing the ECHR into English law without the necessary legislation. UK citizens were therefore in the position of having to pursue rights, which the state endorsed, in an external forum rather than through their own court system and, in addition, having to exhaust the domestic judicial procedure before they could gain access to that external forum. Such a situation was extremely unsatisfactory, and not just for complainants under the ECHR. Many members of the judiciary, including the then Lord Chief Justice Lord Bingham, were in favour of incorporation, not merely on general moral grounds, but equally on the ground that they resented having to make decisions in line with UK law which they knew full well would be overturned on appeal to the European Court. Equally, there was some discontent that the decisions in the European Court were being taken, and its general jurisprudence was being developed, without the direct input of the UK legal system. The courts, however, were not completely bound to decide cases in presumed ignorance of the ECHR, and did what they could to make decisions in line with it. For example, where domestic statutes were enacted to fulfil ECHR obligations, the courts could, of course, construe the meaning of the statute in the light of the ECHR. It was also possible that, due to the relationship of the ECHR with European Community (as it then was) law, the courts could find themselves applying the former in considering the latter.

More indirectly, however, where the common law was uncertain, unclear or incomplete, the courts ruled, wherever possible, in a manner which conformed with the ECHR or, where statute was found to be ambiguous, they presumed that parliament intended to legislate in conformity with the UK's international obligations under the ECHR. As the late Lord Bingham put it:

> In these ways, the Convention made a clandestine entry into British law by the back door, being forbidden to enter by the front (Earl Grey Memorial Lecture, 1998).

Even allowing for this degree of judicial manoeuvring, the situation still remained unsatisfactory. Pressure groups did agitate for the incorporation of the ECHR into the UK legal system, but when in 1995 a Private Member's Bill moving for incorporation was introduced in the House of Lords, the Home Office minister, Lady Blatch, expressed the then Conservative government's view that such incorporation was 'undesirable and unnecessary, both in principle and practice'. The Labour opposition, however, was committed to the incorporation of the ECHR into UK law and, when it gained office in 1997, it immediately set about the process of incorporation. This process resulted in the Human Rights Act (HRA) 1998.

Rights provided under the European Convention on Human Rights

The Articles incorporated into UK law, and listed in Sched 1 to the Act, cover the following matters:

- the right to life. Article 2 states that 'Everyone's right to life shall be protected by law';

- prohibition of torture. Article 3 actually provides that 'No one shall be subjected to torture or to inhuman or degrading treatment or punishment';

- prohibition of slavery and forced labour (Art 4);

- the right to liberty and security. After stating the general right, Art 5 is mainly concerned with the conditions under which individuals can lawfully be deprived of their liberty;

- the right to a fair trial. Article 6 provides that 'everyone is entitled to a fair and public hearing within a reasonable time by an independent and impartial tribunal established by law';

- the general prohibition of the enactment of retrospective criminal offences. Article 7 does, however, recognise the *post hoc* criminalisation of previous behaviour where it is 'criminal according to the general principles of law recognised by civilised nations';

- the right to respect for private and family life. Article 8 extends this right to cover a person's home and their correspondence;

- freedom of thought, conscience and religion (Art 9);

- freedom of expression. Article 10 extends the right to include 'freedom . . . to receive and impart information and ideas without interference by public authority and regardless of frontiers';

- freedom of assembly and association. Article 11 specifically includes the right to form and join trade unions;

- the right to marry (Art 12);

- prohibition of discrimination in relation to the enjoyment of the rights and freedoms set forth in the convention (Art 14);

- the right to peaceful enjoyment of possessions and protection of property (Art 1 of Protocol 1);

- the right to education (subject to a UK reservation (Art 2 of Protocol 1));

- the right to free elections (Art 3 of Protocol 1);

- the right not to be subjected to the death penalty (Arts 1 and 2 of Protocol 6).

The rights listed can be relied on by any person, non-governmental organisation or group of individuals. Importantly, they also apply, where appropriate, to companies that are incorporated entities and hence legal persons. However, they cannot be relied on by governmental organisations, such as local authorities.

The nature of rights under the act, proportionality and derogation

The rights listed above are not all seen in the same way. Some are absolute and inalienable and cannot be interfered with by the state. Others are merely contingent and are subject to derogation, that is, signatory states can opt out of them in particular circumstances. The ECtHR also recognises the concept of 'a margin of appreciation', which allows for countries to deal with particular problems in the context of their own internal circumstances (see below, 5.4). The absolute rights are those provided for in Arts 2, 3, 4, 7 and 14. All the others are subject to potential limitations. In particular, the rights provided for under Arts 8, 9, 10 and 11 are subject to legal restrictions such as are:

> . . . necessary in a democratic society in the interests of national security or public safety, for the prevention of crime, for the protection of health or morals or the protection of the rights and freedoms of others   (Art 11(2)).

The UK entered such a derogation in relation to the extended detention of terrorist suspects without charge, under the Prevention of Terrorism (Temporary Provisions) Act 1989, subsequently replaced and extended by the Terrorism Act 2000. Those powers had been held to be contrary to Art 5 of the Convention by the ECtHR in *Brogan v UK* (1989). The UK also entered a derogation with regard to the Anti-terrorism, Crime and Security Act 2001, which was enacted in response to the attack on the World Trade

Center building in New York on 11 September of that year. The Act allowed for the detention without trial of foreign citizens suspected of being involved in terrorist activity (see, further, below, 2.5.2).

In deciding the legality of any derogation, courts are required not just to be convinced that there is a need for the derogation, but they must also be sure that the state's action has been proportionate to that need. In other words, the state must not overreact to a perceived problem by removing more rights than is necessary to effect the solution.

In the Supreme Court decision *Bank Mellat (Appellant) v Her Majesty's Treasury (Respondent) (No. 2)* (2013) Lord Reed set out the determinant issues in relation to proportionality regarding any particular measure relating to the Human Rights Act. These were:

(1)   whether the objective of the measure is sufficiently important to justify the limitation of a protected right,

(2)   whether the measure is rationally connected to the objective,

(3)   whether a less intrusive measure could have been used without unacceptably compromising the achievement of the objective, and

(4)   whether, balancing the severity of the measure's effects on the rights of the persons to whom it applies against the importance of the objective, to the extent that the measure will contribute to its achievement, the former outweighs the latter. . . . In essence, the question at step four is whether the impact of the rights infringement is disproportionate to the likely benefit of the impugned measure.

With further regard to the possibility of derogation, s 19 of the 1998 Act requires a minister, responsible for the passage of any Bill through parliament, either to make a written declaration that it is compatible with the Convention or, alternatively, to declare that although it may not be compatible, it is still the government's wish to proceed with it.

The structure of the Human Rights Act

The HRA has profound implications for the operation of the English legal system. However, to understand the structure of the HRA, it is essential to be aware of the nature of the changes introduced by the Act, especially in the apparent passing of fundamental powers to the judiciary. Under the doctrine of parliamentary sovereignty, the legislature could pass such laws as it saw fit, even to the extent of removing the rights of its citizens. The 1998 Act reflects a move towards the entrenchment of rights recognised under the Convention, but, given the sensitivity of the relationship between the elected parliament and the unelected judiciary, it has been thought expedient to minimise the change in the constitutional relationship of parliament and the judiciary.

Section 2 of the Act requires future courts to take into account any previous decision of the ECtHR. This provision impacts on the operation of the doctrine of precedent within the English legal system, as it effectively sanctions the overruling of any previous English authority that was in conflict with a decision of the ECtHR.

However, in *Price v Leeds City Council* (2006), the House of Lords held that where there were contradictory rulings from it and the European Court of Human Rights, English courts were required to follow the ruling of the House of Lords. The case is considered in detail at 4.4.

Section 3 requires all legislation to be read, so far as possible, to give effect to the rights provided under the Convention. As will be seen, this section provides the courts with new and extended powers of interpretation. It also has the potential to invalidate previously accepted interpretations of statutes that were made, by necessity, without recourse to the Convention (see *Mendoza v Ghaidan* (2002)).

Section 4 empowers the courts to issue a declaration of incompatibility where any piece of primary legislation is found to conflict with the rights provided under the ECHR. This has the effect that the courts cannot invalidate primary legislation, essentially Acts of Parliament but also Orders in Council, which are found to be incompatible; they can only make a declaration of such incompatibility, and leave it to the legislature to remedy the situation through new legislation. Section 10 provides for the provision of remedial legislation through a fast-track procedure, which gives a minister of the Crown the power to alter such primary legislation by way of statutory instrument.

Section 5 requires the Crown to be given notice where a court considers issuing a declaration of incompatibility and the appropriate government minister is entitled to be made a party to the case.

Section 6 declares it unlawful for any public authority to act in a way that is incompatible with the ECHR, and consequently the Human Rights Act does not *directly* impose duties on private individuals or companies unless they are performing public functions. Whether or not a private company is performing a public function can prove problematic; there are instances where they would clearly be considered as doing so: such as privatised utility companies providing essential services, or if a private company were to provide prison facilities then clearly it would be operating as a public authority. However, at the other end of an uncertain spectrum, it has been held that, where a local authority fulfils its statutory duty to arrange the provision of care and accommodation for an elderly person through the use of a private care home, the functions performed by the care home are not to be considered as of a public nature. At least that was the decision of the House of Lords by a majority of three to two in *YL v Birmingham City Council* (2007), a surprisingly conservative decision, and one that met with much dismay, given that there was the expectation that the public authority test would be applied generously.

Section 6(3), however, *indirectly* introduces the possibility of horizontal effect into private relationships. As s 6(3)(a) specifically states that courts and tribunals are public authorities they must therefore act in accordance with the Convention. The consequence of this is that although the HRA does not introduce new causes of action between private individuals, the courts, as public authorities, are required to recognise and give effect to their Convention rights in any action that can be raised.

In *R v (on the application of Al-Skeini) v Secretary of State for Defence* (2007), which related to the conduct of the armed forces in Iraq, the House of Lords held that s 6 applies to a public body even if it is acting outside the United Kingdom territory, as long as it is acting within the jurisdiction of the United Kingdom, and jurisdiction depends upon control of the relevant location.

Where a public authority is acting under the instructions of some primary legislation, which is itself incompatible with the ECHR, the public authority will not be liable under s 6.

Section 7 allows the 'victim of the unlawful act' to bring proceedings against the public authority in breach. However, this is interpreted in such a way as to permit relations of the actual victim to initiate proceedings.

Section 8 empowers the court to grant such relief or remedy against the public authority in breach of the Act as it considers just and appropriate.

Where a public authority is acting under the instructions of some primary legislation, which is itself incompatible with the ECHR, the public authority will not be liable under s 6.

Section 19 of the Act requires that the minister responsible for the passage of any Bill through parliament must make a written statement that the provisions of the Bill are compatible with ECHR rights. Alternatively, the minister may make a statement that the Bill does not comply with ECHR rights, but that the government nonetheless intends to proceed with it.

Reactions to the introduction of the HRA have been broadly welcoming, but some important criticisms have been raised. First, the ECHR is a rather old document and does not address some of the issues that contemporary citizens might consider as equally fundamental to those rights actually contained in the document. For example, it is silent on the rights to substantive equality relating to such issues as welfare and access to resources. Also, the actual provisions of the ECHR are uncertain in the extent of their application, or perhaps more crucially in the area where they can be derogated from, and at least to a degree they are contradictory. The most obvious difficulty arises from the need to reconcile Art 8's right to respect for private and family life with Art 10's freedom of expression. Newspaper editors have expressed their concern in relation to this particular issue, and fear the development, at the hands of the court, of an overly limiting law of privacy that would prevent investigative journalism. This leads to a further difficulty – the potential politicisation, together with a significant enhancement in the power, of the judiciary. Consideration of this issue will be postponed until some cases involving the HRA have been examined.

Perhaps the most serious criticism of the HRA was the fact that the government did not see fit to establish a Human Rights Commission to publicise and facilitate the operation of its procedures. Many saw the setting up of such a body as a necessary step in raising human rights awareness and assisting individuals, who might otherwise be unable to use the Act, to enforce their rights.

2.5.1   JUDICIAL INTERPRETATION AND APPLICATION OF THE HUMAN RIGHTS ACT

Before and subsequent to the coming into effect in England of the HRA on 2 October 2000, the newspapers were full of dire warnings as to the damaging effect that the Act would have on accepted legal principles and practices. However, an examination of some of the earliest cases to reach the higher courts may serve to dispel such a view.

Although the HRA was enacted in 1998, it did not come into force generally until October 2000. The reason for the substantial delay was the need to train all members of the judiciary, from the highest Law Lord to the humblest magistrate, in the consequences and implications of the new Act. However, the Act was in force before that date in Scotland as a consequence of the devolution legislation, the Scotland Act, which specifically applied the provisions of the HRA to the Scottish Parliament and executive. It is for that reason that the earliest cases under the Human Rights provisions were heard in the Scottish courts.

2.5.1.1 Restriction of non-absolute rights and proportionality

Road Traffic Act 1988

In *Brown v Stott* (2001), the claimant had been arrested at a supermarket on suspicion of the theft of a bottle of gin. When the police officers noticed that she smelled of alcohol, they asked her how she had travelled to the store. Brown replied that she had driven and pointed out her car in the supermarket car park. Later, at the police station, the police used their powers under s 172(2)(a) of the Road Traffic Act 1988 to require her to say who had been driving her car at about 2.30 pm, that is, at the time when she would have travelled in it to the supermarket. Brown admitted that she had been driving. After a positive breath test, Brown was charged with drink-driving, but appealed to the Scottish High Court of Justiciary for a declaration that the case could not go ahead on the grounds that her admission, as required under s 172, was contrary to the right to a fair trial under Art 6 of the ECHR.

In February 2000, the High Court of Justiciary supported her claim on the basis that the right to silence and the right not to incriminate oneself at trial would be worthless if an accused person did not enjoy a right of silence in the course of the criminal investigation leading to the court proceedings. If this were not the case, then the police could require an accused person to provide an incriminating answer which subsequently could be used in evidence against them at their trial. Consequently, the use of evidence obtained under s 172 of the Road Traffic Act 1988 infringed Brown's rights under Art 6(1).

Even before the HRA was in operation in England, the Scottish case was followed by a similar ruling in Birmingham Crown Court in July 2000.

The implication of these decisions was extremely serious, not just in relation to drink-driving offences, but also in relation to fines following the capture of speeding cars by traffic cameras. As can be appreciated, the film merely identifies the car; it is s 172 of the Road Traffic Act that actually requires the compulsory identification of the driver. If *Brown v Stott* stated the law accurately, then the control of speeding cars and drink-driving was in a parlous state.

However, on 5 December 2000, the Privy Council reversed the judgment of the Scottish appeal court in *Brown*. The Privy Council reached its decision on the grounds that the jurisprudence of the ECtHR, established through previous cases, had clearly established that while the overall fairness of a criminal trial could not be compromised, the constituent rights contained in Art 6 of the ECHR were not themselves absolute and could be restricted in certain limited conditions. Consequently, it was possible for individual states to introduce limited qualification of those rights, so long as they were aimed at 'a clear public objective' and were 'proportionate to the situation' under consideration. The ECHR had to be read as balancing community rights with individual rights. With specific regard to the Road Traffic Act, the objective to be attained was the prevention of injury and death from the misuse of cars, and s 172 was not a disproportionate response to that objective.

Subsequently, in a majority decision in *O'Halloran v UK* (2007), the European Court of Human Rights approved the use of s 172 in order to require owners to reveal who had been driving cars caught on speed cameras.

See also the related decision of the House of Lords in *Sheldrake v Director of Public Prosecutions* (2004), which concerned s 5(2) of the Road Traffic Act 1988 relating to the offence of being in charge of a vehicle after consuming excess alcohol. The court held that s 5(2) did not require the prosecution to prove that the defendant was likely to drive while intoxicated. Rather, the effect of s 5(2) was to allow the defendant to escape liability if they could prove, on a balance of probabilities, that there was no likelihood of their driving in their intoxicated condition. The House accepted that this interpretation of s 5(2) infringed the presumption of innocence and introduced a reverse burden of proof, but it considered that such a provision was neither arbitrary nor did it go beyond what was reasonably necessary, given the need to protect the public from the potentially lethal consequences of drink-driving. As Lord Bingham explained the matter:

> The defendant has a full opportunity to show that there was no likelihood of his driving, a matter so closely conditioned by his own knowledge and state of mind at the material time as to make it much more appropriate for him to prove on the balance of probabilities that he would not have been likely to drive than for the prosecutor to prove, beyond reasonable doubt, that he would. I do not think that imposition of a legal burden went beyond what was necessary.

Confiscation cases

Prior to the Proceeds of Crime Act 2002, a number of Acts of Parliament allowed for the property of individuals to be confiscated where it was assumed that such assets were the result of criminal activity. That legislation included the Criminal Justice Act 1988, as amended by the Proceeds of Crime Act 1995, the Drug Trafficking Act 1994 and the Terrorism Act 2000.

In allowing the court to make such an assumption, the Acts reversed the usual burden of proof to the extent that the person against whom the powers are used is required to demonstrate, on the balance of probabilities, that their assets are not the product of criminal activity. Section 1(1) of the Proceeds of Crime (Scotland) Act 1995 also allows for individuals' assets to be confiscated on the basis of similar assumptions.

In October 2000, in *McIntosh v AG for Scotland*, it was argued that the assumption made under s 3(2) of the 1995 Act displaced the presumption of innocence in Art 6(2) of the ECHR and hence was unlawful. McIntosh had been convicted for supplying heroin and the Crown had applied for a confiscation order under the 1995 Act. The Crown submitted that, since confiscation orders did not constitute a separate criminal offence, Art 6(2) of the Convention could not grant him the presumption of innocence in respect of such an action.

The High Court of Justiciary, Lord Kirkwood dissenting, approved McIntosh's submission and issued a declaration to that effect and, in so doing, threatened the efficacy of the whole confiscation policy.

In December 2000, the Court of Appeal in England, sitting with Lord Chief Justice Woolf on the panel, had the opportunity to consider the effect of the HRA on the assumptions relating to confiscation powers in the case of *R v Benjafield and Others* (2001). In the Court of Appeal's opinion, the express reversal of the burden of proof in confiscation proceedings amounted to a substantial interference with the normal presumption of innocence. However, it held that parliament had adequately balanced the defendant's interests against the public interest and cited the fact that the question of confiscation only arose after conviction and that the court should not make a confiscation order when there was a serious risk of injustice. It also considered that the court's role in the appeal procedure ensured that there was no unfairness to the individual concerned. As in the Privy Council's decision in *Brown*, the Court of Appeal held that where the discretion given to the court and prosecution was properly exercised, it was justifiable as a reasonable and proportionate response to a substantial public interest. In so doing, it declined to apply the High Court of Justiciary's decision in *McIntosh*, preferring the approach of the Privy Council in *Brown*.

When the further appeal in the *McIntosh* case came before the Privy Council in February 2001, the decision of the Scottish appeal court was unanimously overturned on two grounds:

- the confiscation order was not by way of a criminal action and therefore the assumptions were not in contravention of Art 6(2). An application for a confiscation order did not, of itself, lay a criminal charge against the convicted defendant. Although the court could assume that such a defendant had been involved in drug trafficking, there were no statutory assumptions as to a defendant's guilt for drug-trafficking offences;

- in addition, and more generally, Art 6(2) was not an absolute right and therefore, following *Brown*, could justifiably be encroached upon by the proportionate enactment of a democratically elected Parliament in the pursuit of its anti-crime policy.

In reaching this decision, the Privy Council expressly approved the Court of Appeal's decision in *R v Benjafield*.

Subsequently, in *Phillips v UK*, decided in July 2001, the ECtHR concurred with the decision of the Privy Council in *McIntosh* by holding, by a majority of five to two, that the confiscation procedure under the Drug Trafficking Act 1994 was not contrary to European Convention rights and, unanimously, that in any event the provisions of the Act represented a proportionate response to the problem under consideration.

Finally, when *R v Benjafield* came on appeal to the House of Lords, it felt comfortable in following the decisions and reasoning in both *McIntosh* and *Phillips*. At the same time, the House of Lords also applied that reasoning to confiscation procedure under the Criminal Justice Act 1988 in *R v Rezvi* (2002).

The courts' power to make confiscation orders was extended under the Proceeds of Crime Act (PCA) 2002, which came into full effect in March 2003.

2.5.1.2   Judicial interpretation of statutes under s 3 of the HRA

R v A (2001)

It has long been a matter of concern that in cases where rape has been alleged, the common defence strategy employed by lawyers has been to attempt to attack the credibility of the woman making the accusation. Judges had the discretion to allow questioning of the woman as to her sexual history where this was felt to be relevant, and in all too many cases this discretion was exercised in a way that allowed defence counsel to abuse and humiliate women accusers. Section 41 of the Youth Justice and Criminal Evidence Act (YJCEA) 1999 placed the court under a restriction that seriously limited evidence that could be raised in cross-examination of a sexual relationship between a complainant and an accused. Under s 41(3) of the 1999 Act, such evidence was limited to sexual behaviour 'at or about the same time' as the event giving rise to the charge that was 'so similar' in nature that it could not be explained as a coincidence.

In *R v A*, the defendant in a case of alleged rape claimed that the provisions of the YJCEA 1999 were contrary to Art 6 of the ECHR to the extent that they prevented him from putting forward a full and complete defence. In reaching its decision, the House of Lords emphasised the need to protect women from humiliating cross-examination and prejudicial but valueless evidence in respect of their previous sex lives; it nonetheless held that the restrictions in s 41 of the 1999 Act were *prima facie* capable of preventing an accused from putting forward relevant evidence that could be crucial to his defence.

However, rather than make a declaration of incompatibility, the House of Lords preferred to make use of s 3 of the HRA to allow s 41 of the YJCEA 1999 to be read as permitting the admission of evidence or questioning relating to a relevant issue in the case where it was considered necessary by the trial judge to make the trial fair. The test of admissibility of evidence of previous sexual relations between an accused and a complainant under s 41(3) of the 1999 Act was whether the evidence was so relevant to the issue of consent that to exclude it would be to endanger the fairness of the trial under Art 6 of the ECHR. Where the line is to be drawn is left to the judgment of trial judges. In reaching its decision, the House of Lords was well aware that its interpretation of s 41 did a violence to its actual meaning, but it nonetheless felt it within its power so to do. The words of Lord Steyn are illustrative of this process:

> In my view section 3 requires the court to subordinate the niceties of the language of section 41(3)(c), and in particular the touchstone of coincidence, to broader considerations of relevance judged by logical and common sense

THE HUMAN RIGHTS ACT 1998

> criteria of time and circumstances. After all, it is realistic to proceed on the basis that the legislature would not, if alerted to the problem, have wished to deny the right to an accused to put forward a full and complete defence by advancing truly probative material. It is therefore possible under section 3 to read section 41, and in particular section 41(3)(c), as subject to the implied provision that evidence or questioning which is required to ensure a fair trial under Article 6 of the Convention should not be treated as inadmissible.

In this way, the House of Lords restored judicial discretion as to what can be raised in cross-examination in rape cases. It is to be hoped, sincerely but without much conviction on the basis of past history, that it is a discretion that will be exercised sparingly and sympathetically.

Re S (2002)

In *Re S*, the Court of Appeal used s 3 of the HRA in such a way as to create new guidelines for the operation of the Children Act 1989, which increased the courts' powers to intervene in the interests of children taken into care under the Act. This extension of the courts' powers in the pursuit of the improved treatment of such children was achieved by reading the Act in such a way as to allow the courts increased discretion to make interim rather than final care orders, and to establish what were referred to as 'starred milestones' within a child's care plan. If such starred milestones were not achieved within a reasonable time, then the courts could be approached to deliver fresh directions. In effect, what the Court of Appeal was doing was setting up a new, and more active, regime of court supervision in care cases.

The House of Lords, however, although sympathetic to the aims of the Court of Appeal, felt that it had exceeded its powers of interpretation under s 3 of the HRA and, in its exercise of judicial creativity, it had usurped the function of parliament.

Lord Nicholls explained the operation of s 3:

> The Human Rights Act reserves the amendment of primary legislation to Parliament. By this means the Act seeks to preserve parliamentary sovereignty. The Act maintains the constitutional boundary. Interpretation of statutes is a matter for the courts; the enactment of statutes are matters for Parliament . . . [but that any interpretation which] departs substantially from a fundamental feature of an Act of Parliament is likely to have crossed the boundary between interpretation and amendment.

Unfortunately, the Court of Appeal had overstepped that boundary.

Mendoza v Ghaidan (2002)

In *Mendoza v Ghaidan* (2002), the Court of Appeal used s 3 to extend the rights of same-sex partners to inherit a statutory tenancy under the Rent Act 1977. In *Fitzpatrick v Sterling*

Housing Association Ltd (1999), the House of Lords had extended the rights of such individuals to inherit the lesser assured tenancy by including them within the deceased person's family. It declined to allow them to inherit statutory tenancies, however, on the grounds that they could not be considered to be the wife or husband of the deceased as the Act required. In *Mendoza*, the Court of Appeal held that the Rent Act, as it had been construed by the House of Lords in *Fitzpatrick*, was incompatible with Art 14 of the ECHR on the grounds of its discriminatory treatment of surviving same-sex partners. The court, however, decided that the failing could be remedied by reading the words 'as his or her wife or husband' in the Act as meaning 'as if they were his or her wife or husband'. *Mendoza* is of particular interest in the fact that it shows how the HRA can permit lower courts to avoid previous and otherwise binding decisions of the House of Lords. It also clearly shows the extent to which s 3 increases the powers of the judiciary in relation to statutory interpretation.

In spite of this potential increased power, the House of Lords found itself unable to use s 3 in *Bellinger v Bellinger* (2003). The case related to the rights of transsexuals and the court found itself unable, or at least unwilling, to interpret s 11(c) of the Matrimonial Causes Act 1973 in such a way as to allow a male to female transsexual to be treated in law as a female. Nonetheless, the court did issue a declaration of incompatibility (see below for explanation).

2.5.1.3   Declarations of incompatibility under s 4 of the HRA

As has been stated previously, the courts are not able to declare primary legislation invalid, but, as an alternative, they may make a declaration that the legislation in question is not compatible with the rights provided by the ECHR.

The first declaration of incompatibility was actually issued in *R v (1) Mental Health Review Tribunal, North & East London Region (2) Secretary of State for Health ex p H* in March 2001. In that case, the Court of Appeal held that ss 72 and 73 of the Mental Health Act 1983 were incompatible with Art 5(1) and (4) of the ECHR inasmuch as they reversed the normal burden of proof, by requiring the detained person to show that they should not be detained rather than the authorities to show that they should be detained.

R v Secretary of State for the Environment, Transport and the Regions ex p Holding & Barnes plc and others (2001)

In this case, the House of Lords overturned an earlier decision of the Administrative Court that had called into question the operation of the planning system under the Town and Country Planning Act 1990. Under the Act, the ultimate arbiter in relation to planning decisions was the Secretary of State. The Administrative Court held that, as a member of the executive, determining policy, the Secretary of State should not be involved in the quasi-judicial task of deciding applications. It followed, therefore, that the operation of the planning system was contrary to the right to a fair hearing by an independent tribunal as provided for under Art 6 of the ECHR.

In overturning that decision, the House of Lords unanimously decided that the planning process was human rights compatible. In their Lordships' view, the possibility of judicial review was sufficient to ensure compliance with Art 6(1) of the ECHR, even though it could only remedy procedural rather than substantive deficiencies.

Indeed, their Lordships showed some displeasure at the manner in which Art 6 had been deployed in an attempt to undermine the democratically elected Secretary of State by seeking to pass the power to make policy decisions from him to the courts. Both Lords Slynn and Hoffmann quoted the words of the European Commission in *ISKCON v UK* (1994) with approval:

> It is not the role of Article 6 of the Convention to give access to a level of jurisdiction which can substitute its opinion for that of the administrative authorities on questions of expediency and where the courts do not refuse to examine any of the points raised . . .

Even more pointedly, Lord Hoffmann commented that:

> The Human Rights Act 1998 was no doubt intended to strengthen the rule of law but not to inaugurate the rule of lawyers.

The politics of the Human Rights Act

Historically, the Conservative Party argued against the enactment of the Human Rights Act (HRA) by the Labour government in 1998, on the grounds that it diminished the power of parliament and gave too much power to the unelected judiciary. In October 2009, in an article in the tabloid paper *The Sun*, the leader of the then opposition party, David Cameron, reaffirmed the Conservative Party's opposition to the HRA and promised that, if elected, he would replace it with a British Bill of Rights. However, subsequently, in 2010, on forming a coalition government with the Liberal Democrat Party, which was committed to the HRA, Cameron appeared to drop any proposals to repeal the Act

Nonetheless, rumblings of discontent continued to emanate from some parts of the Tory party. Thus in October 2011, at the Conservative Party annual conference, the Home Secretary, Theresa May, reasserted her party's antagonism to the HRA, stating that it 'had to go'. In her notorious 'catgate' speech she justified the attack on the Act as follows:

> We all know the stories about the Human Rights Act. The violent drug dealer who cannot be sent home because his daughter – for whom he pays no maintenance – lives here. The robber who cannot be removed because he has a girlfriend. The illegal immigrant who cannot be deported because – *and I am not making this up* – he has a pet cat.

Regrettably for the Home Secretary and the truth, an examination of the transcripts of the case in point revealed that ownership of a cat was not actually the ground for refusing the deportation order and her claims were ridiculed as laughable by the then Justice Secretary Ken Clarke. Clarke subsequently had to apologise and was subsequently replaced by Chris Grayling, who, while in opposition – and like his leader David Cameron – famously announced that he was in favour of tearing up the HRA and replacing it with a British document.

At the Conservative Party annual conference in September 2013, Theresa May reasserted her attack on the Human Rights Act and even went as far as accusing the judiciary of using their powers under the Act 'to put the law on the side of foreign criminals instead of the public'. She further promised that her party's next manifesto would promise to scrap 'Labour's'[sic] Human Rights Act and that 'if leaving the European Convention is what it takes to fix our human rights laws, that is what we should do.'

Given what had been stated previously, and no doubt as a way of reasserting its right of centre credentials in the face of the challenge from UKIP, it was not unexpected that at the Conservative Party conference of 2014 various statements were made by May, Grayling and Cameron that they were prepared to withdraw from the European Convention on Human Rights (ECHR) after the upcoming election in 2015. In Cameron's words:

> So at long last, with a Conservative government after the next election, this country will have a new British Bill of Rights, to be passed in our parliament, rooted in our values. And as for Labour's Human Rights Act? We will scrap it, once and for all.

Following the conference, an eight-page strategy paper, entitled Protecting Human Rights in the UK, was published by Grayling. The document proposed that the text of the original convention would be written into UK law, that UK courts would no longer be required to 'take into account' ECtHR decisions, together with provisions that would have the effect that the rulings of the ECtHR would not have legal effect in the UK without the consent of parliament. As he put it: 'Effectively, turning Strasbourg [sic] into an advisory body.'

A Constitution Society and UK Constitutional Law Association paper, '"Common Sense" or Confusion? The Human Rights Act and the Conservative Party' by Dimelow and Young (http://www.consoc.org.uk/) provides an interesting assessment of the proposals before the actual election in May 2015. However, following the victory of the Conservative Party in that election, the previous statements and proposals were discounted as pre-election hyperbole, when the subsequent Queen's Speech on the opening of the new parliamentary session made only passing reference to the Human Rights Act.

Nonetheless, in October 2015, an 'exclusive' (i.e. strategically leaked) article in *The Independent* newspaper reported that the government was planning to 'fast-track' a British Bill of Rights into UK law. It was stated that the Bill would be worded to clearly indicate that the UK would not be withdrawing from the *European Convention on Human Rights* and its provisions would mirror those of the Convention. The report claimed that a 12-week consultation would be initiated before the end of 2015, following which the Bill would proceed straight to the House of Commons, without a preliminary Green or White Paper.

It was immediately clear that the government was anxious to avoid the ECHR issue becoming entangled with the referendum on the UK's continued membership of the EU, due to take place by June 2016, but few commentators shared the optimism of the government as regards the likelihood of the Bill securing an unobstructed passage, given the number of potential hazards in its way. Among these, in no particular order of danger, may be cited the government's slender 12-vote majority in the House of Commons and the stated opposition of some of its own members to the proposal, its overall lack of a majority in an antagonistic House of Lords, the stated opposition of the Scottish Parliament with its now overwhelmingly strong representation at Westminster, and the fact that the Human Rights Act was an integral part to the intergovernmental Good Friday agreement which saw the establishment of the current settlement in Northern Ireland.

2.5.2 HUMAN RIGHTS AND ANTI-TERRORISM LEGISLATION

It is almost commonplace that the recognition of human rights is most sorely tested when those claiming the protection of those rights might not otherwise meet with sympathetic treatment. Thus it is the argument of those who would repeal the Human Rights Act that it is used as a block on the pursuit of substantive law and order by shyster lawyers who recognise its utility as a means of protecting the rights of criminals, prisoners, illegal immigrants and other supposedly blameworthy or morally dubious individuals at the expense of the rights of the good, and no doubt God-fearing (in a non-Islamic way), moral majority. However, it is precisely the universality and non-contingent nature of human rights, the fact that they are, or at least should be, an attribute of every person, irrespective of status, class, race, gender, religion or political belief, that provides the foundation for the very theory of human rights. It might also be said that the extent to which the universality of human rights is recognised and applied to even 'the undeserving' is the test of the very humanity of a society and its legal system.

What follows requires a consideration of perhaps the most essential tension between the courts, in their recognition and application of human rights, and the state in its desire to protect what it perceives as the public interest through controlling those it considers a threat to that public interest: a tension between judiciary and legislature, and perhaps one that prefigures future tension between the fairly recently established Supreme Court and parliament.

Anti-terrorism, Crime and Security Act 2001

Following the terrorist attack on the World Trade Center on 11 September 2001, the UK parliament introduced the Anti-terrorism, Crime and Security Act (ACSA) 2001. This Act allowed for the detention, without charge, of non-UK citizens suspected of terrorist activities, but who could not be repatriated to their own countries because of fear for their well-being.

Protection of human rights in the UK:
- **The Human Rights Act 1998 (HRA)**: introduces into UK law rights contained in the **European Convention on Human Rights and Fundamental Freedoms (ECHR)**
- The **European Union Charter of Fundamental Rights** enshrines certain rights, many of which are also found in the ECHR, into EU and UK law (*see Chapter 5*)

The European Convention on Human Rights and Fundamental Freedoms (ECHR):
- International treaty, taking effect in 1953 to protect human rights and fundamental freedoms in Europe following World War II
- While the UK played a pivotal role in its creation, and is a signatory, the ECHR was not incorporated into UK law. In 1966 individuals were given the right to petition the **European Court of Human Rights (ECtHR)**
- **HRA 1998** entered into force in 2000, giving effect to the ECHR and allowing individuals to enforce ECHR rights in national courts

Enforcement of human rights in the UK

The Human Rights Act 1998:
- creates a domestic means of protecting rights by
  (i) requiring **public bodies** to comply with the **ECHR**, and
  (ii) obliging **national courts** to interpret national law in a manner compatible with the ECHR, in so far as it is possible to do so. Higher courts may also issue a *'Declaration of Incompatibility'* should UK statute conflict with the ECHR. However, Parliament cannot be compelled to amend the law
- When enacting a new statute, the minister responsible issues a **statement** as to whether the Bill is compatible or incompatible with the ECHR (the government may proceed with the Bill in either circumstance)

Interplay between national courts and the ECtHR:
- Statistics demonstrate that UK national courts and the ECtHR rarely disagree, with less than 2 per cent of cases finding a violation by a UK public body, which, it can be argued, is due to the high quality of UK court judgments
- While certain sections of the media may portray the ECtHR as unilaterally imposing its will on domestic courts, the two have demonstrated a willingness to engage in dialogue
- Where cases have been successfully brought before the ECtHR, many have resulted in significant milestones in protection of human rights

Enforcing rights under the ECHR:
- ECHR rights are only enforceable vertically (i.e. against a **public body** and not an individual)
- An individual who believes his rights have been breached may bring an action before a national court. (Remedy is usually a declaration of rights but can include compensation.)
- Where all national remedies have been exhausted, or there is no real prospect of achieving anything other than a declaration of incompatibility, it may be possible to bring a case before the **ECtHR** if that Court considers the case to be admissible. A final appeal may be available to the ECtHR's Grand Chamber
- As the ECHR has not been incorporated into UK law, UK courts are under a duty to do no more than 'take into account' (**s 2 HRA**) judgments of the ECtHR, while the government has discretion on how to remedy a breach, although its record on implementation has been described as 'exemplary'

FIGURE 2.2 *Enforcement of Human Rights in the UK.*

Such a provision was clearly contrary to Art 5 of the ECHR. Consequently, the government was required to enter a derogation from the Convention by virtue of the Human Rights Act 1998 (Designated Derogation) Order 2001, the justification for the derogation being that the prospect of terrorism following 11 September 2001 threatened the life of the nation.

SIAC hearings and special advocates

The Special Immigration Appeals Commission (SIAC) was empowered under the ACSA 2001 to hear appeals in relation to decisions taken under it. The SIAC originally had been established by the Special Immigration Appeals Commission Act 1997 in response to a decision of the ECtHR in *Chahal v UK* (1997), in relation to the political deportations. Hearings before the SIAC are conducted on both an open basis and a closed basis. In the former, anyone can attend, but in the latter, which deal with matters of state security, not only the public but also the detained persons and their lawyers are excluded and therefore have no access to, let alone the possibility of challenging, the evidence used against them. In closed session, the detainees are represented by special advocates who are lawyers with clearance to access secret and security documents. These special advocates are neither appointed by the people they represent, nor are they at liberty to divulge any information to them. (See, further, Justice and Security Act 2013 p 73)

The Belmarsh cases

This title refers to a number of cases that focused on the issues of the compatibility of ACSA 2001 with the European Convention on Human Rights and the compliance with the convention of orders made under its auspices.

A v Secretary of State for the Home Department (SIAC and the Court of Appeal) (2002)

In July 2002, the SIAC held that the ACSA 2001 was not in compliance with the anti-discriminatory provisions of Art 14 of the Convention to the extent that it treated non-nationals differently from UK nationals.

The then Home Secretary, David Blunkett, attacked the SIAC decision and it was subsequently overturned by the Court of Appeal. According to the Court of Appeal, the case concerned an example of what is referred to as the 'area of due deference' within which the courts will 'defer on democratic grounds to the considered opinion of the elected body or person whose actual decision is said to be incompatible with the Convention'. As the Home Secretary was better qualified than the courts to decide what action had to be taken to safeguard national security, the courts should not intervene.

The approach of the Court of Appeal in this case was reminiscent of the quiescent attitude of previous courts when faced with the exercise of executive power. Perhaps the classic example of such subservience is to be found in *Liversidge v Anderson* (1942) in which a majority of the House of Lords approved the power of the Home Secretary to imprison a person without trial under wartime defence regulations. Lord Atkin, in the minority, famously railed against the granting of such uncontrolled power to the Home Secretary and accused his fellow members of the House of Lords of being '. . . more executive-minded than the executive'.

A v Secretary of State for the Home Department (House of Lords) (2004)

Somewhat surprisingly a further appeal to the House of Lords resulted in a crushing judgment against the Act and an undisguised and unmitigated rebuke to the government and its anti-terrorism policies. The strength of the decision was almost startling, especially in the light of the previously more accommodating decisions of the Court of Appeal in relation to state policy. The case was heard by a panel of nine Law Lords, Lord Steyn having stood down from the appeal because he had previously expressed the view that the derogation was unjustified, and it was decided by a majority of eight to one, only Lord Walker dissenting, that the ACSA was incompatible with the provisions of the ECHR.

Although the House of Lords recognised the deference due to the government and parliament and accepted that the government had been entitled to conclude that there was a public emergency, it nonetheless concluded that the response to the perceived threat had been disproportionate and incompatible with the rights under the ECHR.

The House pointed out the illogicality at the heart of the Act for, if the potential threat to the security of the UK *by UK nationals* suspected of being al-Qaida terrorists could be addressed without infringing their right to personal liberty, then why could not similar measures be used to deal with any threat presented by *foreign nationals*.

The House of Lords also held that ss 21 and 23 of the Act were disproportionate for the general reason that the provisions did not rationally address the threat to the security of the UK presented by al-Qaida terrorists.

As a result, the House of Lords decided that s 23 of the ACSA was incompatible with Art 5 and Art 14 of the ECHR and appropriately quashed the Derogation Order 2001, as it was secondary rather than primary legislation.

While the preceding report of *A v Secretary of State for the Home Department* provides an objective account of the House of Lords' decision, it does little to reflect the intensity of feeling expressed in the individual judgments of those involved in the case, which can only be appreciated through the words of the judges involved. While the leading judgment of Lord Bingham, the senior Law Lord, was delivered in measured, if critical, terms, it cannot but be recognised that some of the other members of the judicial panel expressed themselves in such florid language as to lay themselves open to the accusation of 'showboating' – an expression used to indicate a mixture of self- and over-indulgence.

The most patently (over-)rhetorical judgment was delivered by Lord Hoffmann, of which the following quotation is merely one example:

> 95. . . . Of course the government has a duty to protect the lives and property of its citizens. But that is a duty which it owes all the time and which it must discharge without destroying our constitutional freedoms. There may be some nations too fragile or fissiparous to withstand a serious act of violence. But that is not the case in the United Kingdom. When Milton urged the government of his day not to censor the press even in time of civil war, he said:
>
> > 'Lords and Commons of England, consider what nation it is whereof ye are, and whereof ye are the governors'

96. This is a nation which has been tested in adversity, which has survived physical destruction and catastrophic loss of life. I do not underestimate the ability of fanatical groups of terrorists to kill and destroy, but they do not threaten the life of the nation. Whether we would survive Hitler hung in the balance, but there is no doubt that we shall survive Al-Qa'ida.

However, perhaps the most overtly political speech was that of Lord Scott, which contained the following passages:

142. . . . The making of such a declaration [of incompatibility] will not, however, affect in the least the validity under domestic law of the impugned statutory provision. *The import of such a declaration is political not legal.*

154. . . . The Secretary of State is unfortunate in the timing of the judicial examination in these proceedings of the 'public emergency' that he postulates. It is certainly true that the judiciary must in general defer to the executive's assessment of what constitutes a threat to national security or to 'the life of the nation'. But judicial memories are no shorter than those of the public and the public have not forgotten the faulty intelligence assessments on the basis of which United Kingdom forces were sent to take part, and are still taking part, in the hostilities in Iraq.

155. . . . Indefinite imprisonment in consequence of a denunciation on grounds that are not disclosed and made by a person whose identity cannot be disclosed is the stuff of nightmares, associated whether accurately or inaccurately with France before and during the Revolution, with Soviet Russia in the Stalinist era and now associated, as a result of section 23 of the 2001 Act, with the United Kingdom (emphasis added).

It is significant to note that these speeches were delivered before the murderous bombings in London on 7 July 2005, or perhaps the rhetorical flourishes might have been more controlled. In any event, the House of Lords' decision, in what has become known as the *Belmarsh* case, represented a general exercise in judicial activism in relation to the executive power, but its declaration of incompatibility together with the quashing of the derogation order left the government with a particular problem: whether it would be able to renew the provisions of the ACSA in March 2005, as was required by the Act itself. When it became apparent that there was no such possibility, the government introduced new procedures for dealing with suspected terrorists under the Prevention of Terrorism Act 2005 (PTA 2005).

Prevention of Terrorism Act 2005 and control orders
The Act as eventually passed dealt with one of the shortcomings of the ACSA by widening the provisions of the previous legislation to control all terrorist-related activity,

irrespective of nationality or indeed the particular cause the terrorists supported. But perhaps even more essentially, it did not attempt to continue the detention without trial regime under the ACSA, which was replaced with a new system of 'control orders'. These control orders were to be of two distinct types; derogating and non-derogating in relation to the ECHR.

Derogating control orders

As its title suggests, this type of control order required derogation from ECHR because it deprived the person affected of their liberty by requiring them to remain in a particular place at all times. It was equivalent to house arrest and consequently it clearly infringes the person's rights under Art 5 of the ECHR. In the event no derogation orders were ever sought.

Non-derogating control orders

This type of control order allowed the Home Secretary to impose a range of controls over people's activities from a ban on the use of mobile phones or the internet, to control of the movement of the individuals including the imposition of curfews and the use of tagging for the purposes of monitoring those curfews.

The 2005 Act retained the role of the *special advocate*, who was expected to support the interests of the suspect in regard to material that neither the accused nor his chosen legal representatives were allowed access to.

Any breach of a control order, without reasonable excuse, was a criminal offence punishable on indictment by imprisonment of up to five years.

The legal effect of non-derogation control orders issued under the PTA 2005 were considered by the House of Lords in a series of related appeals, the decisions in which were delivered in three judgments at the end of October 2007.

The maximum length of control orders

In the first, *Secretary of State for the Home Department v JJ and others* (2007), the issue was whether an order imposing an 18-hour curfew, coupled with other restrictions on the activities of those subject to the orders, amounted to deprivation of liberty and consequently were contrary to Art 5 of the ECHR. In deciding the question, the court recognised the distinction between the *unqualified* right to liberty and the *qualified* rights of freedom of movement, communication and association provided under the ECHR as previously expressed by the ECtHR.

The general effect of the particular control orders in question were summarised by the Court of Appeal in para 4 of its judgment as follows:

> The obligations imposed by the control orders are set out in annex I to Sullivan J's judgment. They are essentially identical. Each respondent is required to remain within his 'residence' at all times, save for a period of six hours between 10 am and 4 pm. In the case of GG the specified residence is a

one-bedroom flat provided by the local authority in which he lived before his detention. In the case of the other five respondents the specified residences are one-bedroom flats provided by the National Asylum Support Service. During the curfew period the respondents are confined in their small flats and are not even allowed into the common parts of the buildings in which these flats are situated. Visitors must be authorised by the Home Office, to which name, address, date of birth and photographic identity must be supplied. The residences are subject to spot searches by the police. During the six hours when they are permitted to leave their residences, the respondents are confined to restricted urban areas, the largest of which is 72 square kilometres. These deliberately do not extend, save in the case of GG, to any area in which they lived before. Each area contains a mosque, a hospital, primary health care facilities, shops and entertainment and sporting facilities. The respondents are prohibited from meeting anyone by pre-arrangement who has not been given the same Home Office clearance as a visitor to the residence.

In addition, the controlled persons were required to wear an electronic tag and to report to a monitoring company on first leaving their flat after a curfew period and on returning to it before a curfew period. They were forbidden to use or possess any communications equipment of any kind except for one fixed telephone line in their flat maintained by the monitoring company. They were at liberty to attend a mosque of their choice if it was in their permitted area and approved in advance by the Home Office. A request by JJ to study English at a college outside his area was refused.

At first instance Sullivan J held that the cumulative effect of the obligations placed on the respondents went far beyond the mere restriction of liberty, recognised as potentially legitimate by the ECtHR, and was such as to deprive them of their liberty in breach of Art 5 of the Convention. As a result, Sullivan J held that the Secretary of State had had no power to make an order that was incompatible with Art 5 of the ECHR and any such purported order had to be treated as a nullity and totally ineffective.

Sullivan J's decision was subsequently approved by the Court of Appeal and, on further appeal to the House of Lords, it was decided by a majority of three to two that neither the judge at first instance nor the Court of Appeal had erred in their legal reasoning and the House of Lords expressly approved their rulings. In the view of the House, the effect of the 18-hour curfew, coupled with the effective exclusion of social visitors meant that the men subject to the control orders were practically in solitary confinement for an indefinite duration. Further, the House of Lords confirmed that as the control orders were a nullity, the defects in them could not be cured by the court simply amending the content of the provisions as was argued for by the Secretary of State.

Of the majority of the House of Lords who held that the control orders amounted to a deprivation of liberty, Lord Bingham and Baroness Hale were content simply to hold that the 18-hour curfew was contrary to Art 5 without considering the possibility of an alternative period that would count as merely a restriction on, rather than a deprivation of, liberty and hence be lawful. However, Lord Brown suggested that a 16-hour curfew period would be an acceptable limit.

The second of the linked cases, *Secretary of State for the Home Department v MB & AF* (2007) also concerned the issues considered in *JJ* and on this occasion the House of Lords unanimously held that a curfew of 14 hours with related restrictions did not amount to a deprivation of liberty. Consequently, if 14 hours did not count as a deprivation of liberty on the basis of *AF*, and 18 hours did amount to such a deprivation as in *JJ*, then Lord Brown's 16 hours appeared to be the appropriate time limit for curfews under PTA 2005 control orders.

However, in *Secretary of State for the Home Department v AP* (2010), which concerned someone subject to a control order confined to a flat for 16 hours a day in a Midlands town 150 miles away from his family in London, Lord Brown subsequently clarified/retracted his original suggestion.

In *AP* the Supreme Court unanimously decided that conditions that might be proportionate restrictions upon Art 8 rights to respect for private and family life can 'tip the balance' in relation to Art 5, which guarantees the right to liberty and security. In other words, the court should take account of the *effect* of any restrictions in deciding whether a control order amounts to a deprivation of liberty. However, in the leading judgment Lord Brown stated that:

> I nevertheless remain of the view that for a control order with a 16-hour curfew (*a fortiori* one with a 14-hour curfew) to be struck down as involving a deprivation of liberty, the other conditions imposed would have to be *unusually destructive* of the life the controlee might otherwise have been living   (emphasis added).

The use of torture to extract evidence

After release from Guantanamo Bay, former detainees brought civil claims against UK ministers and intelligence agencies, alleging that the authorities had been complicit in their unlawful imprisonment and the abuse they received while in captivity. Initially, the High Court allowed the possibility of the state raising a defence to the civil action based on evidence that could not be openly disclosed to the claimants. However, the Court of Appeal forcefully rejected such a possibility as being a fundamental breach of the common law.

A v Secretary of State for the Home Department (2005)

During the hearing relating to the appeals against their detention under the provisions of ACSA in October 2003, SIAC stated that the fact that evidence against the detainees had, or might have been, obtained through torture inflicted by foreign officials, but without the complicity of the British authorities, could be used in determining the outcome of the cases. SIAC held that *while the use of torture might affect the weight to be given to the evidence, its source did not render it legally inadmissible.*

On appeal the Court of Appeal confirmed the approach previously taken by SIAC, holding by a majority that it would be contrary to the exercise of the statutory power and unrealistic to expect the Home Secretary to investigate each statement relied on, in order to determine whether it had been produced as a result of torture.

Subsequently a seven-strong panel of the House of Lords heard a further appeal on two issues. The first related to the question as to whether evidence produced through torture could be used in any circumstances. The second related to the burden of proof in relation to showing whether or not torture had been used to produce the evidence in question.

In relation to the first issue, the House was unanimous in its disapproval of the previous approaches of SIAC and the Court of Appeal. It was clear under the common law and under international law that no evidence obtained as a result of torture could be used, even if the torture was conducted by another state, without the complicity of the United Kingdom authorities. While parliament might have the power to approve the use of torture evidence, it had not done so through ACSA. This general view is encapsulated in the words of Lord Bingham at para 52:

> . . . it would of course be within the power of a sovereign Parliament (in breach of international law) to confer power on SIAC to receive third-party torture evidence. But the English common law has regarded torture and its fruits with abhorrence for over 500 years, and that abhorrence is now shared by over 140 countries which have acceded to the Torture Convention. I am startled, even a little dismayed, at the suggestion (and the acceptance by the Court of Appeal majority) that this deeply-rooted tradition and an international obligation solemnly and explicitly undertaken can be overridden by a statute and a procedural rule which make no mention of torture at all.

However, as to the second issue the House of Lords divided 4:3, with the majority holding that SIAC should only *not* admit evidence if it concluded, on a balance of probabilities that it was obtained by torture. If SIAC was in doubt as to whether the evidence was obtained by torture, then it should admit it, but it should bear its doubt in mind when evaluating the evidence.

On the other hand, a strongly argued minority opinion held that SIAC should refuse to admit evidence if it was unable to conclude that there was not a real risk that the evidence had been obtained by torture. *If it was in doubt whether the evidence had been procured by torture, then the commission should exclude the evidence.*

The majority did, however, state that the individual defendant would not be expected to shoulder the entire burden of demonstrating that a particular piece of evidence stated to justify their certification and detention was obtained by torture. According to Lord Hope, the defendant would only be required to raise the issue that the information used against them might have come from a country suspected of practising torture, after which the task of assessing the matter would be passed to SIAC itself.

Lord Rodger, rather naïvely, described how 'those in the relevant department who were preparing a case for a SIAC hearing would sift through the material, *on the look-out for anything that might suggest torture had been used*', and as he later pointed out (para 143, emphasis added):

> The Home Secretary accepted that he was under a duty to put any such material before the Commission. *With the aid of the relevant intelligence services, doubtless as much as possible will be done.* And SIAC itself will wish to take an active role in suggesting possible lines of inquiry.

Consequently defendants could rest assured, confident in the understanding that those who were seeking to have them detained would do everything in their power to ensure that the evidence against them was free from any taint of torture. Perhaps Lord Bingham deserves the final cutting comment on the flawed reasoning of the majority in the House of Lords:

> My noble and learned friend Lord Hope proposes, in paragraph 121 of his opinion, the following test: is it *established*, by means of such diligent enquiries into the sources that it is practicable to carry out and on a balance of probabilities, that the information relied on by the Secretary of State *was* obtained under torture? This is a test which, in the real world, can never be satisfied. The foreign torturer does not boast of his trade. The security services, as the Secretary of State has made clear, do not wish to imperil their relations with regimes where torture is practised. The special advocates have no means or resources to investigate. The detainee is in the dark. It is inconsistent with the most rudimentary notions of fairness to blindfold a man and then impose a standard which only the sighted could hope to meet. *The result will be that, despite the universal abhorrence expressed for torture and its fruits, evidence procured by torture will be laid before SIAC because its source will not have been 'established'* (at para 59, emphasis added).

The Terrorism Prevention and Investigation Measures Act 2011

In January 2011 the Home Secretary announced the government's intention with regard to the future of the control order regime, after some reportedly tense negotiations with her coalition partners in the Liberal Democrat party. The generally accepted assessment of the proposals was that they were a political compromise, which did little to live up to promises of the previous rhetorical claims as to a more liberal regime, with some commentators referring to the proposal as 'control order lite'.

The subsequent Terrorism Prevention and Investigation Measures Act 2011 included the following provisions:

- the new laws are permanent, doing away with the requirement for parliament to renew them on an annual basis;
- the replacement for the control order regime are to be known as Terrorism Prevention and Investigation Measures (TPIMs);
- there will be a two-year limitation on TPIMs, but they may be extended if new information emerges that leads the Home Secretary to believe that the person is still a danger;
- the Secretary of State must now have 'reasonable grounds to believe' rather than 'reasonable grounds to suspect' that a person may pose a terrorist threat;
- the Secretary of State is required to seek the court's permission before imposing the measures, except in the most urgent cases where the notice must be referred immediately to the court for confirmation;
- the previous curfew requirements were replaced by 'overnight residence' requirements;
- electronic tagging and restrictions on travel were retained;
- greater access to the internet, phones and personal meetings is allowed.

Nonetheless, the Terrorism Prevention and Investigation Measures Act 2011 retains the power to relocate individuals to another part of the country without consent under powers for the Secretary of State to impose enhanced TPIM notices. This, essentially emergency, power may only be used when Parliament is not in session, i.e. between the dissolution of a Parliament and the first Queen's Speech of the next Parliament.

Protection of Freedoms Act 2012
This Act relaxed a number of provisions introduced by the previous government. Among other measures (it has 121 sections and 10 schedules), the Act:

- introduced a new regime for police 'stop and searches' under the Terrorism Act 2000;
- reduced the maximum pre-charge detention period under the Terrorism Act from 28 to 14 days;

The Justice and Security Act 2013
The embarrassment suffered by the government as a result of the consideration of sensitive security-related material in open court in actions taken against it by former prisoners imprisoned by the United States at Guantanamo Bay fostered its determination to prevent such embarrassment in the future. The result was a Justice and Security Green Paper issued in October 2011, which allowed a relatively short time for consultation, closing in January 2012. Although the Green Paper was subject to much criticism, rather than

issue a White Paper to allow further consideration, the government preferred to publish its Justice and Security Bill in May 2012 which subsequently became an Act in 2013.

The Act has three purposes:

- the oversight of the Security Service, the Secret Intelligence Service, the Government Communications Headquarters and other activities relating to intelligence or security matters;
- the provision for closed material procedure in relation to certain civil proceedings;
- the prevention of making certain court orders for the disclosure of sensitive information; and for connected purposes.

Part 2 of the Act contains the most immediately controversial material, in that s 6 makes provision to enable the Secretary of State to apply to the court for a 'closed material procedure' (CMP) in certain civil proceedings in the courts. This is essentially an extension to other civil courts of the procedure previously considered in relation to SIAC under which the detained person and their legal representatives are prevented from hearing, and of course challenging, evidence presented to the court in their absence. Section 9 similarly allows for the appointment of special advocates to protect the interest of the detained person (see p 65). The minister triggers the process by deciding that a closed material procedure is needed, and applying to the judge, who decides whether to allow it or not. The judge *must* grant the application if one of the parties to the proceedings would be required to disclose material in the proceedings and the disclosure would be damaging to national security.

It has been suggested by supporters of the CMP that it will improve accountability and oversight on the ground that it will actually allow highly sensitive intelligence information to be heard in private as opposed to being completely excluded under a public interest immunity certificate, as is the case at present.

Section 17 relates to what are known as Norwich Pharmacal orders (NPOs). Such court orders apply in civil proceedings where one party seeks the disclosure of information from another party in order to identify the proper defendant, support their case or establish their defence to an action (*Norwich Pharmacal Co. & Others v Customs and Excise Commissioners* (1974)). The essential point, however, is that the involvement of the party required to provide the information may well be completely innocent, but nonetheless they are still required to supply the information, where it is deemed necessary in the interests of justice. It was on the basis of such a Norwich Pharmacal order that Binyam Mohamed, the leading Guantanamo Bay claimant, had gained access to the documents required to support his action against the UK security services.

Section 17 requires that a court may not order the disclosure of information sought if the information is sensitive information.

What is covered by the term 'sensitive information' is defined in sub-section 17(3) as information:

(a)   held by an intelligence service;

(b)   obtained from, or held on behalf of, an intelligence service;

(c)   derived in whole or part from information obtained from, or held on behalf of, an intelligence service;

(d)   relating to an intelligence service; or

(e)   specified or described in a certificate issued by the Secretary of State, in relation to the proceedings, as information which should not [be] ordered to disclose[d].

Such a provision goes a very long way to completely emasculating the operation of Norwich Pharmacal orders in matters relating to state security, much, one can only imagine, to the great delight of the government and the security services.

In considering the potential effect of what is now s 1[7], Fiona de Londras of University College Dublin School of Law commented:

> It is true that the certification is subject to review (s 1[8]), and it is quite possible that the courts would impose a demanding standard on the government to justify any decision ruling that certain information is sensitive, but that notwithstanding, section 1[7] is difficult to describe as anything but an affront. Its purpose is unquestioningly to ensure yet another avenue towards discovering the depth and breadth of the UK's involvement in what might charitably be called unsavoury activities is blocked.
>
> Even if the certification process – itself a stunning provision of quasi-judicial power to a government minister – were to disappear in the legislative process (and I don't believe it will), the remainder of section 1[4] is still a matter of extreme concern   (http://www.guardian.co.uk/law/2012/may/29/justice-security-section-13).

The collapse of Syria, the emergence of ISIL and ongoing instability in Iraq led to the enactment of the Counter-terrorism and Security Act 2015. The Act contains provisions aimed at disrupting those intending to join the fighting by:

● providing the police with a temporary power to seize a passport at the border from individuals of concern;

● creating a Temporary Exclusion Order that will control the return to the UK of a British citizen suspected of involvement in terrorist activity abroad;

● enhancing border security by toughening transport security arrangements around passenger data, including 'no fly' lists and screening measures;

● enhancing existing TPIMs, including the introduction of stronger locational constraints and a power requiring individuals to attend meetings with the authorities as part of their ongoing management.

CHAPTER SUMMARY: THE RULE OF LAW AND HUMAN RIGHTS

Various writers have different understandings of what the concept actually means, but see it essentially as involving a control of arbitrary power – Dicey, Hayek, Thompson, Raz, Unger and Weber.

The essential question is whether the UK is still governed under the rule of law, and of course the conclusion depends on the original understanding of the rule of law: Hayek and Thompson would have said not; Raz would say it was. Sir Stephen Sedley has a view as to the continued operation of the rule of law, which is based on substantive equality and challenges previous legal thought. Current judicial thought may be taken from the detailed consideration of the rule of law provided by the late Lord Bingham.

SEPARATION OF POWERS

The judges and the executive in the separation of powers have distinct but interrelated roles in the constitution. The question arises as to the extent to which the courts can act to control the activities of the executive through the operation of judicial review. The position of the Lord Chancellor as judge and member of the government has been questioned by many, including the current government.

THE HUMAN RIGHTS ACT 1998

The HRA incorporates the ECHR into domestic UK law. The Articles of the ECHR cover the following matters:

the right to life (Art 2);

prohibition of torture (Art 3);

prohibition of slavery and forced labour (Art 4);

the right to liberty and security (Art 5);

the right to a fair trial (Art 6);

the general prohibition of the enactment of retrospective criminal offences (Art 7);

the right to respect for private and family life (Art 8);

freedom of thought, conscience and religion (Art 9);

freedom of expression (Art 10);

freedom of assembly and association (Art 11);

the right to marry (Art 12);

prohibition of discrimination (Art 14).

The incorporation of the ECHR into UK law means that UK courts must decide cases in line with the above Articles. This has the potential to create friction between the judiciary and the executive/legislature.

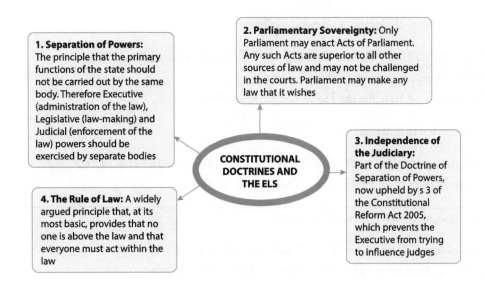

1. Separation of Powers:
The principle that the primary functions of the state should not be carried out by the same body. Therefore Executive (administration of the law), Legislative (law-making) and Judicial (enforcement of the law) powers should be exercised by separate bodies

2. Parliamentary Sovereignty: Only Parliament may enact Acts of Parliament. Any such Acts are superior to all other sources of law and may not be challenged in the courts. Parliament may make any law that it wishes

CONSTITUTIONAL DOCTRINES AND THE ELS

3. Independence of the Judiciary: Part of the Doctrine of Separation of Powers, now upheld by s 3 of the Constitutional Reform Act 2005, which prevents the Executive from trying to influence judges

4. The Rule of Law: A widely argued principle that, at its most basic, provides that no one is above the law and that everyone must act within the law

FIGURE 2.3 *Constitutional Doctrines and the English Legal System.*

THE STRUCTURE OF THE HUMAN RIGHTS ACT 1998

Section 2 requires future courts to take into account any previous decision of the ECtHR.

Section 3 requires all legislation to be read so far as possible to give effect to the rights provided under the Convention.

Section 4 empowers the courts to issue a declaration of incompatibility where any piece of primary legislation is found to conflict with the rights provided under the Convention.

Section 6 declares it unlawful for any public authority to act in a way that is incompatible with the Convention.

Section 7 allows the 'victim of the unlawful act' to bring proceedings against the public authority in breach.

Section 8 empowers the court to grant such relief or remedy against the public authority in breach of the Act as it considers just and appropriate.

Section 10 provides for fast-track remedial legislation where an Act of Parliament has been declared incompatible with Convention rights.

Section 19 of the Act requires that the minister responsible for the passage of any Bill through Parliament must make a written statement as to whether its provisions are compatible with Convention rights.

CASES DECIDED UNDER THE HUMAN RIGHTS ACT 1998

Cases relating to s 3 powers:

R v A (2001);

Re S (2002);

Mendoza v Ghaidan (2003).

Cases relating to declarations of incompatibility:

R v (1) Mental Health Review Tribunal, North & East London Region (2001);
Wilson v Secretary of State for Trade and Industry (2003);
A v Secretary of State for the Home Department (2004).

Cases relating to sentencing:

R v Secretary of State for the Home Department ex p Anderson and Taylor (2002);
A v Secretary of State for the Home Department (2005).

Cases relating to anti-terrorism legislation:

A v Secretary of State for the Home Department (2002) & (2004);
Secretary of State for the Home Department v JJ and others (2007);
Secretary of State for the Home Department v AP (2010);
Secretary of State for the Home Department v MB & AF (2007);
Al Rawi & Ors v Security Service & Ors (2010);
A v Secretary of State for the Home Department (2005);
Mohamed, R (on the application of) v Secretary of State for Foreign & Commonwealth Affairs 1 & 2 (2010).

FOOD FOR THOUGHT

1   Consider what exactly is meant by the rule of law. Is it simply a matter of legal rules or does it connote something else? For example, Nazi Germany was notoriously legalistic, but were the legal rules it introduced and applied really the outcome of the rule of law?

2   Consider the distinction between the form and substance of the law. Is law 'right' simply because it has been introduced in the appropriate manner? If not, what grounds are there for criticising such law?

3   Consider the nature of human rights. What are they exactly and where do they come from? Would people have no human rights if there were no formal legal provisions, such as the Human Rights Act, recognising them?

4   Is it ever justifiable to torture suspects to acquire information? If not, why not? If it is, what limits can/should be placed on its use and who should regulate its use?

5   Some commentators and politicians complain that the Human Rights Act has increased the power of the judges. To what extent is this correct, and if it is correct, how has that been achieved, and is it a matter to be concerned about?

6   Human rights are currently politically controversial, with many members of the Conservative Party actively seeking the repeal and replacement of the Human Rights Act with a purely domestic Bill of Rights. To what extent is this proposal welcome, or feasible, in the current political/social context?

FURTHER READING

Anti-Social Behaviour Orders: Analysis of the First Six Years, 2004, London: National Association of Probation Officers

Bennion, F, 'A naked usurpation?' (1999) 149 NLJ 421

Bingham, T (Lord), 'The Way We Live Now: Human Rights in the New Millennium', Earl Grey Memorial Lecture [1998] 1 Web JCLI

Bingham, T (Lord), *The Rule of Law*, 2010, London: Allen Lane

Dicey, AV, *Introduction to the Law of the Constitution*, 1885, London: Macmillan

Feldman, D, 'The Human Rights Act and constitutional principles' (1999) 19(2) JLS, June

Fenwick, H, *Civil Liberties and Human Rights*, 4th edn, 2007, Abingdon: Routledge-Cavendish

Fenwick, H, Masterman, R and Phillipson, G (eds), *Judicial Reasoning under the UK Human Rights Act*, 2011, Cambridge: CUP

Fine, R, *Democracy and the Rule of Law*, 1984, London: Pluto

Hayek, FA von, *The Road to Serfdom*, 1944, London: Routledge

Hill, C, *Liberty Against the Law*, 1996, Harmondsworth: Penguin

Horowitz, MJ, 'The Rule of Law: an unqualified good?' (1977) 86 Yale LJ 561

Kairys, D (ed), *The Politics of Law: A Progressive Critique*, 1990, London: Pantheon

Kavanagh, A, 'Judging the judges under the Human Rights Act: deference, disillusionment and the "war on terror"' [2009] PL 287–304

Keating, D, 'Upholding the Rule of Law' (1999) 149 NLJ 533

Laws, J (Sir), 'Law and democracy' [1995] PL 72

Locke, J, *The Treatises of Government*, 1988, Cambridge: CUP

Raz, J, 'The Rule of Law and its virtue' (1977) 93 LQR 195

Rozenberg, J, 'Upholding the Rule of Law' (2009) 106(6) Law Soc Gazette 8

Sedley, S (Sir), *Freedom, Law and Justice*, 1998, Hamlyn Lectures, London: Sweet & Maxwell

Sedley, S (Sir), 'Human rights: a 21st century agenda' [1995] PL 386

Steiner, H and Alston, P, *International Human Rights in Context*, 3rd edn, 2007, Oxford: OUP

Steyn (Lord), 'Civil liberties in modern Britain' [2009] PL 228–36

Thompson, A, 'Taking the right seriously: the case of FA Hayek', in Fitzpatrick, P (ed), *Dangerous Supplements*, 1991, London: Pluto

Thompson, E, *Whigs and Hunters*, 1975, Harmondsworth: Penguin

Wadham, J, 'Rights and responsibilities' (2009) 106(39) Law Soc Gazette 8

Young A, 'R (Evans) v Attorney General – the Anisminic of the 21st Century?', UK Const L Blog (31 March 2015) (available at http://ukconstitutionallaw.org)

Young, J, 'The politics of the Human Rights Act' (1999) 26(1) JLS 27

Zander, M, 'The Prevention of Terrorism Act 2005' (2005) 155 NLJ 438

USEFUL WEBSITES

http://ukconstitutionallaw.org
The United Kingdom Constitutional Law Association (UKCLA) is the UK's national body of constitutional law scholars affiliated to the International Association of Constitutional Law. Its object is to 'encourage and promote the advancement of knowledge relating to United Kingdom constitutional law (broadly defined) and the study of constitutions generally'.

http://www.coe.int/en/
The Council of Europe site – it includes all the decisions of the Commission on Human Rights, the Court of Human Rights and the Committee of Ministers back to 1951.

www.equalityhumanrights.com
The official website for the Equality and Human Rights Commission.

www.lse.ac.uk/collections/LSEPublicLecturesAndEvents/pdf/20060222-Goldsmith.pdf
An online transcript of 'Government and the Rule of Law in the Modern Age', a lecture given in 2006 by The Rt Hon Lord Goldsmith QC, Attorney General.

COMPANION WEBSITE

Now visit the companion website to:

- test your understanding of the key terms using our Flashcard Glossary;
- revise and consolidate your knowledge of 'The rule of law and human rights' using our Multiple Choice Question testbank;
- view all of the links to the Useful Websites above.

www.routledge.com/cw/slapper

SOURCES OF LAW: LEGISLATION

3

3.1 INTRODUCTION

This and the following two chapters consider where law comes from and where students of law have to look to find it. As was stated in Chapter 1, in civil law systems one only has to look in the appropriate code to find the law relating to that area. However, in a common law system one has not only to look at the legislation, both primary and secondary, made by parliament, but one also has to look in the cases for the judicial statement that actually constitute that common law. Nor should it be forgotten that much of English law is now a restatement of the law of the European Union.

3.2 EUROPEAN UNION

Ever since the UK joined the European Economic Community, now the European Union, it has progressively, but effectively, passed the power to create laws that have effect in this country to the wider European institutions. In effect, regarding Union matters, the UK's legislative, executive and judicial powers are now controlled by, and can only be operated within, the framework of European Union (EU) law. It is essential, therefore, even in a text that is primarily concerned with the English legal system, that the contemporary law student is aware of the operation of the legislative processes of the EU. Chapter 5 of this book will consider the EU and its institutions in some detail; the remainder of this chapter will concentrate on internal sources of law.

3.3 PRIMARY LEGISLATION

If the institutions of the EU are sovereign within its boundaries, then within the more limited boundaries of the UK, the sovereign power to make law lies with parliament. Under UK constitutional law, it is recognised that parliament has the power to enact, revoke or alter such, and any, law as it sees fit. Even the Human Rights Act (HRA) 1998 reaffirms this fact in its recognition of the power of parliament to make primary legislation that is incompatible with the rights provided under the European Convention on Human Rights (ECHR). Whether this will remain the case in the future is, however, a moot point. Coupled with this wide power is the convention that no one parliament can bind its successors in such a way as to limit their absolute legislative powers.

This absolute power is a consequence of the historical struggle between parliament and the Stuart monarchy in the seventeenth century. In its conflict with the Crown, Parliament claimed the power of making law as its sole right. In so doing, Parliament curtailed the royal prerogative and limited the monarchy to a purely formal role in the legislative procedure. In this struggle for ultimate power, the courts sided with Parliament and, in return, Parliament recognised the independence of the courts from its control. Prerogative powers still exist and remain important, but are now mainly exercised by the government in the name of the Crown, rather than by the Crown itself. Some of the general prerogative powers are extremely important, such as the declaration of war and the power to issue, refuse or withdraw passport facilities, but others are less so, such as powers connected with prepaid postage stamps.

Although we still refer to our legal system as a common law system, and although the courts still have an important role to play in the interpretation of statutes, it has to be recognised that legislation is the predominant method of law-making in contemporary times. It is necessary, therefore, to have some knowledge of the workings of the legislative process.

3.3.1 THE PRE-PARLIAMENTARY PROCESS

Any consideration of the legislative process must be placed in the context of the political nature of Parliament. Most statutes are the outcome of the policy decisions taken by government, and the actual policies pursued will of course depend upon the political persuasion and imperatives of the government of the day. Thus, a great deal of law creation and reform can be seen as the implementation of party political policies.

For example, previous Labour governments introduced considerable constitutional reform as proposed in its manifestos. Thus, the Scottish Parliament and the Welsh Assembly have been instituted and many hereditary peers have been removed from the House of Lords. As the election in May 2010 resulted in no one party having an overall majority of Members of Parliament, the government had to be formed by a coalition of the larger Conservative and smaller Liberal Democrat parties. As the basis for this coming together, the parties had to fashion a compromise programme, rather than insist on pursuing their individual manifesto promises. This generated some disquiet among some people who voted for a particular party on the basis of a specific manifesto promise, only to see that promise subsequently denied. This was particularly the case with some Liberal Democrat voters who expressed anger when their party subsequently supported an increase in university fees, in spite of its pre-election promise not to do so.

The establishment of the coalition government in 2010 clearly involved an increase in fissile tendencies, as the government faced not only the difficulty of controlling members of more than one party, but the much harder task of holding together two discrete memberships with sometimes incompatible political views. In response to this perceived potential difficulty one of the first decisions taken by the coalition was to introduce the constitutionally controversial Fixed-term Parliaments Act 2011. The stated purpose of this Act was to provide for five-year fixed-term parliaments. As a result, the date of the next General Election will be 7 May 2020. The Act does allow the Prime Minister some leeway to alter the date by up to two months before or after that date. It also provides only two ways in which an election can be triggered before the end of the five-year term:

- if a motion of no confidence was passed and no alternative government was found;
- if a motion for an early General Election was agreed either by at least two-thirds of the House or without division.

The 2015 General Election resulted, somewhat surprisingly, in an outright Conservative majority, when they secured 330 of the possible 650 seats. As, by convention, the government is drawn from the party controlling a majority in the House of Commons, it can effectively decide what policies it wishes to implement and trust to its majority to ensure that its proposals become law. Accusations have been made that when governments have substantial majorities, they are able to operate without taking into account the consideration of their own party members, let alone the views of opposition members. It is claimed that their control over the day-to-day procedure of the House of Commons, backed with their majority voting power, effectively reduces the role of Parliament to that of merely rubber-stamping their proposals.

The government generates most of the legislation that finds its way into the statute book, but individual Members of Parliament may also propose legislation in the form of Private Member's Bills.

There are in fact three ways in which an individual Member of Parliament can propose legislation:

- through the ballot procedure, by means of which 20 backbench Members get the right to propose legislation on the 10 or so Fridays in each parliamentary Session specifically set aside to consider such proposals;
- under Standing Order 39, which permits any Member to present a Bill after the 20 balloted Bills have been presented;
- under Standing Rule 13, the 10-minute rule procedure, which allows a Member to make a speech of up to 10 minutes in length in favour of introducing a particular piece of legislation.

Of these procedures, only the first has any real chance of success and even then success will depend on securing a high place in the ballot and on the actual proposal not being too contentious. Examples of this include the Abortion Act 1967, which was introduced as a Private Member's Bill to liberalise the provision of abortion, and the various attempts that have subsequently been made by Private Member's Bills to restrict the original provision. In relation to particular reforms, external pressure groups or interested parties may very often be the original moving force behind them. When individual

Members of Parliament are fortunate enough to find themselves at the top of the ballot for Private Member's Bills, they may well also find themselves the focus of attention from such pressure groups proffering pre-packaged law reform proposals in their own particular areas of interest.

The decision as to which government Bills are to be placed before Parliament in any Session is under the effective control of two Cabinet committees:

- the *Future Legislation Committee* determines which Bills will be presented to Parliament in the *following* parliamentary Session;
- the *Legislation Committee* is responsible for the legislative programme conducted in the *immediate* parliamentary Session. It is the responsibility of this Committee to draw up the legislative programme announced in the Queen's Speech, delivered at the opening of the parliamentary Session.

Green Papers are consultation documents issued by the government, which set out and invite comments from interested parties on particular proposals for legislation. After considering any response, the government may publish a second document in the form of a White Paper, in which it sets out its firm proposals for legislation.

The publication of draft Bills is a third way through which pre-legislative consultation and scrutiny can take place. In recent years it has become common for government departments to issue such draft Bills to allow for consultation and for more detailed scrutiny of the proposed text to take place before the Bill is formally introduced into the legislative process. Such draft Bills are made available on the UK Parliament website and are examined either by select committees in the House of Commons or in the House of Lords or by a joint committee of both Houses of Parliament.

3.3.2 THE LEGISLATIVE PROCESS

Parliament consists of three distinct elements: the House of Commons with 650 directly elected members; the House of Lords with 826 unelected members; and the monarch.

Before any legislative proposal, known at that stage as a Bill, can become an Act of Parliament, it must proceed through, and be approved by, both Houses of Parliament and must receive the Royal Assent. The ultimate location of power, however, is the House of Commons, which has the authority of being a democratically elected institution.

A Bill must be given three readings in both the House of Commons and the House of Lords before it can be presented for the Royal Assent. It is possible to commence the procedure in either House, although money Bills must be placed before the Commons in the first instance.

When a Bill is introduced in the Commons, it undergoes five distinct procedures:

- *First reading*. This is purely a formal procedure in which its title is read and a date set for its second reading.
- *Second reading*. At this stage, the general principles of the Bill are subject to extensive debate. The second reading is the critical point in the process of a

Bill. At the end, a vote may be taken on its merits and, if it is approved, it is likely that it will eventually find a place in the statute book.

- *Committee stage.* After its second reading, the Bill is passed to a standing committee whose job it is to consider the provisions of the Bill in detail, clause by clause. The committee has the power to amend it in such a way as to ensure that it conforms with the general approval given by the House at its second reading. Very occasionally, a Bill may be passed to a special standing committee which considers the issues involved before going through the Bill in the usual way as a normal standing committee. Also, the whole House may consider certain Bills at committee stage. In general, these are Bills of constitutional importance, such as the House of Lords Bill, which proposed the reformation of the Upper House in 1999. Other Bills that need to be passed very quickly and certain financial measures, including at least part of each year's Finance Bill, are also considered by the committee of the whole House.

- *Report stage.* At this point, the standing committee reports the Bill back to the House for consideration of any amendments made during the committee stage.

- *Third reading.* Further debate may take place during this stage, but it is restricted to matters relating to the content of the Bill; questions relating to the general principles of the Bill cannot be raised.

When a Bill has completed all these stages, it is passed to the House of Lords for its consideration. After consideration by the Lords, the Bill is passed back to the Commons, which must then consider any amendments to the Bill that might have been introduced by the Lords. Where one House refuses to agree to the amendments made by the other, Bills can be repeatedly passed between them but, as Bills must usually complete their process within the life of a particular parliamentary Session, a failure to reach agreement within that period might lead to the total loss of the Bill. However, in 1998, the House of Commons Modernisation Committee agreed that, in defined circumstances and subject to certain safeguards, government Bills should be able to be carried over from one Session to the next, in the same way that Private and Hybrid Bills may be. The first Bill to be treated in this way was the Financial Services and Markets Bill 1998–99, which the House agreed to carry over into the 1999–2000 Session after a debate on 25 October 1999. The effect was to stay proceedings on the Bill in standing committee at the end of the 1998–99 Session and to carry it over into the next Session, when the committee resumed at the point in the Bill it had previously reached. In October 2004, a contested vote in the Commons made the carry-over process a permanent Standing Order of the House.

English Votes for English Laws (EVEL)

On 22 October 2015, a vote in the House of Commons agreed to alter its standing orders in order to introduce new legislative procedures for enacting Bills, or provisions in Bills, that apply only to England. Under the new procedure, English MPs, sitting as an English Grand Committee, will be able to block legislation deemed to solely affect England, although the Bill would ultimately be subject to a full vote of the House of Commons.

Introduction: *Most new legislation is introduced by the government as a result of policy decisions. However, legislation can be introduced by a Member of Parliament (MP) or peer (a member of the House of Lords). For the sake of simplicity, this flowchart concentrates on legislation introduced by the government, but a similar process will be followed for legislation introduced by others.*

Consultation stages: *Allow the opportunity for interested parties to provide their comments on legislative proposals. While the following stages are commonly employed, and provide an opportunity to influence future legislation, they are optional:*

(i) **White Paper:** *sets out proposals for change; interested parties are consulted. As a result:*
(ii) **Green Paper:** *a consultation paper may be issued.*

Draft Bill prepared: *undertaken by specialist lawyers. Allows for further scrutiny of proposals.*

Passage of a Bill: *The following stages are a requirement if a Bill is to become law:*

(i) **First Reading:** *comprises a formal introduction. Long title of Bill will be read out but no opportunity for debate is provided. Completion of this stage allows a Bill to be printed.*
(ii) **Second Reading:** *MPs discuss the main principles of a Bill. MPs may vote at the end of this stage, particularly if a Bill is controversial.*
(iii) **Committee stage:** *Bill is considered by a committee of MPs. Amendments may be proposed and voted on.*
(iv) **Report stage:** *Bill, with amendments or changes, is 'reported' to the House. All MPs can review the amended Bill. Those not involved at the previous stage may suggest further changes.*
(v) **Third reading:** *MPs debate and vote on the Bill in its final form.*

Transfer to the House of Lords: *If a Bill begins in the House of Commons – and is approved – it is then sent to the House of Lords, where it goes through the same stages. If the Lords make changes to a Bill, it returns to the Commons for MPs to consider any amendments. Both the Commons and Lords must agree on the final Bill before it can become law. If the Bill is a Finance Bill, the legislation can be passed after a year even if the House of Lords is opposed to it.*

Royal Assent: *Results in a 'Bill' becoming an 'Act':*

Once approval has been obtained from both the Commons and Lords, the Bill will require the approval of the monarch – called 'Royal Assent'. The monarch provides approval on the advice of ministers. Once assent has been provided, the Bill then becomes law (on a specified date) and is described as an **Act of Parliament.**

FIGURE 3.1 *The Legislative Process.*

The change was justified as a way of addressing the so-called West Lothian Question, the position where English MPs cannot vote on matters which have been devolved to other parts of the UK, but Scottish, Welsh and Northern Ireland MPs can vote on those same matters when the UK Parliament is legislating solely for England.

The policy paper supporting the proposed changes explained the procedure thus:

- When a bill has been introduced in the Commons, the Speaker will certify whether the Bill, or parts of it, should be subject to the new process.

- Once the Speaker has certified a Bill, it continues to second reading and committee stage as normal.

- Any Bills that the Speaker has certified as England-only in their entirety will be considered by only English MPs at committee stage. The membership of this committee will reflect the numbers of MPs that parties have in England. After this the Bill continues to report stage as normal.

- For Bills containing English or English and Welsh provisions, there is then a process for gaining the consent of English or English and Welsh MPs. A legislative Grand Committee considers a consent motion for any clauses that the Speaker has certified as English or English and Welsh only. This is a new stage which will allow all English or English and Welsh MPs either to consent to or to veto those clauses.

- If clauses of the Bill are vetoed by the legislative Grand Committee, there is a reconsideration stage when further amendments can be made, to enable compromises to be reached. The whole House can participate in this stage, which is, in effect, a second report stage for disputed parts of the Bill. This is followed by a second legislative Grand Committee at which all English or English and Welsh MPs are asked to consent to the amendments made by the whole House. If no agreement is reached at this point, the disputed parts of the Bill fall.

- Following report stage and any consent motions, the Bill continues to third reading, in which now all MPs can participate. It then progresses to the House of Lords. If there are any consequential amendments to the rest of the Bill required as a result of disputed parts of the Bill falling, there will be an additional stage before third reading to allow this.

The legislative process in the House of Lords is unchanged.

The alteration to the standing orders of the House was criticised for politicising the position of the Speaker, as that person would be in the position of having to adjudicate from which votes Scottish MPs should be excluded. However, the strongest opposition from both Labour and Scottish National opposition parties was on the grounds that the EVEL procedure undermined the equality of all Members of Parliament and that, in any event, it was no more than a device aimed primarily at securing future Conservative control over laws operating in England in the event of a Labour/SNP alliance majority in the UK.

The Parliament Acts

Given the need for legislation to be approved in both Houses of Parliament, it can be seen that the House of Lords has considerable power in the passage of legislation. However, the fact that it was never a democratically accountable institution, together with the fact that until 2005 it had an in-built Conservative Party majority reflecting its previous hereditary composition, meant that its legislative powers had to be curtailed. Until the early years of the twentieth century, the House of Lords retained its full power to prevent the passage of legislation. However, Lloyd-George's Liberal budget of 1909 brought the old system to breaking point when the House of Lords originally refused to pass it. Although the budget was eventually passed after a General Election in 1910, a second election was held on the issue of reform of the House of Lords. As a result of the Liberal victory the Parliament Act of 1911 was introduced, which removed the House of Lords' power to veto a Bill. As a matter of interest, the 1911 Act also reduced the maximum lifespan of a Parliament from seven years to its current five years and specifically retained the House of Lords' power to block any attempt to prolong the lifetime of a parliament. The Parliament Act of 1911 reduced the power of the Lords to delay a Bill by up to two years. In 1949 the Parliament Act of that year further reduced the Lords' delaying powers to one year, but it is significant that the 1949 Act was itself only introduced through the use of the previous Parliament Act of 1911.

Since 1949 the delaying powers of the House of Lords have been as follows:

- a 'Money Bill', that is, one containing only financial provisions, can be enacted without the approval of the House of Lords after a delay of one month;
- any other Bill can be delayed by one year.

Only four substantive Acts have been passed into law without the consent of the House of Lords:

- the War Crimes Act 1991
- the European Parliamentary Elections Act 1999
- the Sexual Offences (Amendment) Act 2000
- the Hunting Act 2004.

The last piece of legislation, the Hunting Act, was introduced to prohibit the hunting of mammals with dogs and was particularly designed to outlaw the tradition of fox-hunting.

However, of essential importance in relation to this Act was that the use of the Parliament Act 1949 to pass it, in the face of the refusal of the House of Lords, gave rise to a consideration of the legality of the Act itself in *Jackson v HM Attorney General* (2005).

Jackson v HM Attorney General (2005)

The appellants argued that the 1949 Act was itself invalid on the basis that it did not receive the consent of the House of Lords, and the Parliament Act 1911 did not permit an Act such as the 1949 Act to be enacted without the consent of the House of Lords. Thus, although the Hunting Act gave rise to the case, the essential underlying issue related to the validity of the 1949 Act, which in turn depended on the effect of the 1911 Parliament Act. As Lord Bingham put it, 'The merits and demerits of the Hunting Act, on which opinion is sharply divided, have no bearing on the legal issue which the House, sitting judicially, must resolve.'

In its reading of the Parliament Acts, the Court of Appeal concluded that under the 1911 Act the House of Commons had the power to make a 'relatively modest and straightforward amendment'. The Court of Appeal went on to conclude that the Parliament Act of 1949 was within that ambit, as an example of a 'relatively modest' amendment, as was the Hunting Act. However, the Court of Appeal raised doubts as to the power of the House of Commons, acting without the agreement of the House of Lords, to make changes 'of a fundamentally different nature to the relationship between the House of Lords and the Commons from those which the 1911 Act had made'. Thus the Court of Appeal raised the fundamental constitutional question relating to the ultimate power of the House of Commons.

Once again an augmented nine-member panel of the House of Lords was required to deal with these fundamental constitutional issues. In doing so, the House of Lords unanimously held that the reasoning of the Court of Appeal could not be sustained. In reaching that conclusion the House of Lords rejected the argument that the Parliament Act of 1911 was an exercise in the *delegation* of powers from Parliament to the House of Commons, which could not later be used to extend those powers. Rather, as Lord Bingham stated:

> The overall object of the 1911 Act was not to delegate power: it was to restrict, subject to compliance with the specified statutory conditions, the power of the Lords to defeat measures supported by a majority of the Commons . . .

The House of Lords, however, did differ in their assessment of the extent of the power extended to the House of Commons under the Parliament Acts. It is clear that a majority of the House of Lords were of the view that the House of Commons could use the powers given to it under the Parliament Acts to force through such legislation as it wished, but a number of the judges were of the view that the Commons could not extend its own lifetime through such a procedure, as that would be in direct contradiction to the provisions of the Parliament Act 1911. Also, as has been pointed out at 2.3.2, although the decision in *Jackson* exemplifies the traditional deference of the courts to the supremacy of laws of Parliament, the possibility of future changes in the relationship between the two institutions was at least hinted at in the judgment of Lord Steyn.

The Royal Assent is required before any Bill can become law. There is no constitutional rule requiring the monarch to assent to any Act passed by Parliament. There is, however, a convention to that effect, and refusal to grant the Royal Assent to legislation passed by Parliament would place the constitutional position of the monarchy in jeopardy. The procedural nature of the Royal Assent was highlighted by the Royal Assent Act 1967, which reduced the process of acquiring Royal Assent to a formal reading out of the short title of any Act in both Houses of Parliament.

An Act of Parliament comes into effect on the date of the Royal Assent, unless there is any provision to the contrary in the Act itself. It is quite common either for the Act to contain a commencement date for some time in the future, or for it to give the appropriate Secretary of State the power to give effect to its provisions at some future time by issuing statutory instruments. The Secretary of State is not required to bring the provisions into effect and it is not uncommon for some parts of Acts to be repealed before they are ever in force.

An example of this is the massive, and hugely complex, Criminal Justice Act (CJA) 2003. As yet, not all of its provisions have come into effect, and full implementation will only take place over an extended timescale, if at all. One instance of this, which raises a number of issues that will be considered further in various sections of this book, relates to the provisions of s 43 of the CJA, which provides for the prosecution of certain serious and complex fraud cases to be conducted without a jury. Unusually, by virtue of s 330(5) of the CJA, any statutory instrument seeking to bring s 43 into force required an affirmative resolution of both Houses of Parliament. Following the failure of the Jubilee extension fraud cases the government announced its intention to implement s 43, and to that end a draft commencement order was produced. However, in July 2007 the House of Lords effectively killed off a Fraud (Trials without a Jury) Bill by postponing its consideration for six months and subsequently it never re-appeared. Eventually s 113 of the Protection of Freedoms Act 2012 repealed s 43 of the CJA.

Another example of this failure to implement legislative provisions may be seen in the Equality Act 2010, one of the last pieces of legislation passed by the previous Labour government. Although the coalition Home Secretary and Minister for Women and Equalities brought most of the provisions into effect through commencement orders, she let it be known that she would not do so with all its provisions and certainly not s 1 of the Act, which *imposed a duty on public bodies* to have due regard when making strategic decisions to reducing the inequalities of outcome that result from socio-economic disadvantage. In response, critics accused her of rendering the Act 'virtually toothless'.

3.3.2.1 Parliamentary reform

The 1997 Labour government was elected on the promise of the fundamental reform of the House of Lords, which it saw as undemocratic and unrepresentative. After establishing a Royal Commission, the government embarked on a two-stage process of reform. The first stage of reform was achieved through the House of Lords Act 1999, which removed the right of the majority of hereditary peers to sit in the House of Lords. The second stage of reform was set out, towards the end of 2001, in a White Paper entitled 'Completing the Reform'.

The most controversial aspect of the White Paper was the relatively small proportion of directly elected members it proposed, especially when compared with the large proportion of members who would be nominated rather than elected. The government, faced with much criticism, even from its own MPs, set up a joint committee of both Houses of Parliament to consider the course of future reform. Somewhat surprisingly, that committee made no recommendation and merely listed seven possible options for determining the membership of a reformed House of Lords. The options were:

- a fully appointed house;
- a fully elected house;

- 80 per cent appointed, 20 per cent elected;
- 80 per cent elected, 20 per cent appointed;
- 60 per cent appointed, 40 per cent elected;
- 60 per cent elected, 40 per cent appointed;
- 50 per cent appointed, 50 per cent elected.

Even more surprisingly, in February 2003, the House of Commons voted against all of the options and thus failed to approve any of them. The closest vote, for an 80 per cent elected house, fell narrowly by 284 votes against to 281 in favour.

It should be noted that the House of Lords no longer has a majority of members taking the Conservative Party whip. It remains to be seen whether the difficulties suffered by the government in attempting to pass the Tax Credit Regulations 2015 (see below, 3.5.4.1) will result in any specific reform proposals, but it remains the case that the House of Lords, at least as presently constituted, appears to be untenable in the long term: the fact that it only has some 400 places to sit means that it can only function if most of its members do not attend.

On coming to power in 2010 the Conservative/Liberal Democrat coalition passed the Conservative-inspired Parliamentary Voting System and Constituencies Act (PVSCA) 2011, which provided for a future reduction in the number of MPs to 600 while equalising the numerical size of constituencies. The Act, at the behest of the Liberal Democrats, also provided for a referendum on an alternative voting system, which was subsequently rejected in May 2011.

The coalition government's policy on reform of the House of Lords faced the initial problem of combining the two parties' manifesto proposals, the Conservatives preferring a 'mainly elected' second chamber and the Liberal Democrats a 'fully elected' second chamber. In May 2011 the government published a White Paper and draft Bill containing proposals for a smaller, reformed House of Lords. The draft Bill provided for:

- the powers of the reformed House of Lords to remain the same;
- the reformed House to be limited to 300 members, each eligible for a single term of 15 years;
- elections to use the single transferable vote (STV), electing a third of members each time with elections normally taking place at the same time as General Elections;
- multi-member electoral districts, to be drawn up independently based on national and county boundaries;
- a continuation of the presence of Bishops of the Church of England in the House of Lords, but reducing their number from 26 to 12;
- a transition staggered over the course of three electoral cycles.

Crucially, the draft Bill proposed a reformed House of Lords with 80 per cent of elected members (240), with the remaining 20 per cent (60 members) appointed independently to sit as cross-benchers.

However, in July 2012, 91 Conservative MPs effectively killed off any possibility of the reform Bill being passed by aligning, and voting, with the Labour Party against a 'programme motion' which would have set a timetable for debate on the measure. Without such a limit on debate there was no real chance of the Bill being passed and Nick Clegg, the Liberal Democrat leader and deputy prime minister, who had been pushing for the reform, had to recognise defeat and effectively withdraw the Bill.

The proposed reduction in the number of MPs was included in the Conservative Party's pre-election manifesto in 2015, but Prime Minister Cameron was subsequently placed under pressure not to implement the policy by a number of his own MPs who feared for their positions in any such reduction. In any event, the PVSCA 2011 remains on the statute book, perhaps to be implemented at a later date.

3.3.3 THE DRAFTING OF LEGISLATION

In 1975, in response to criticisms of the language and style of legislation, the Renton Committee on the Preparation of Legislation (Cmnd 6053) examined the form in which legislation was presented. Representations were made to the Committee by a variety of people ranging from the judiciary to the lay public. The Committee divided complaints about statutes into four main headings relating to:

- obscurity of language used;
- over-elaboration of provisions;
- illogicality of structure;
- confusion arising from the amendment of existing provisions.

It was suggested that the drafters of legislation tended to adopt a stylised archaic legalism in their language and employed a grammatical structure that was too complex and convoluted to be clear, certainly to the layperson and even, on occasion, to legal experts. These criticisms, however, have to be considered in the context of the whole process of drafting legislation and weighed against the various other purposes to be achieved by statutes. The actual drafting of legislation is the work of parliamentary counsel to the Treasury, who specialise in this task. The first duty of the drafters must be to give effect to the intention of the department instructing them, and to do so in as clear and precise a manner as is possible. These aims, however, have to be achieved under pressure, and sometimes extreme pressure, of time. An insight into the various difficulties faced in drafting legislation was provided by a former parliamentary draftsman, Francis Bennion, in an article entitled 'Statute law obscurity and drafting parameters' ((1978) British JLS 235). He listed nine specific parameters which the drafter of legislation had to take into account. These parameters are as follows:

- *Legal effectiveness.* This is the need for the drafters to translate the political wishes of those instructing them into appropriate legal language and form.

- *Procedural legitimacy*. This refers to the fact that the legislation must conform with certain formal requirements if it is to be enacted. For example, it is a requirement that Acts be divided into clauses, and Bills not assuming this form would not be considered by Parliament.

- *Timeliness*. This refers to the requirement for legislation to be drawn up within particularly pressing time constraints. The effect of such pressure can be poorly drafted and defective provisions.

- *Certainty*. It is of the utmost importance that the law be clearly set down so that individuals can know its scope and effect and can guide their actions within its provisions. The very nature of language, however, tends to act against this desire for certainty. In pursuit of certainty, the temptation for the person drafting the legislation is to produce extremely long and complex sentences consisting of a series of limiting and refining sub-clauses. This process in turn, however, tends merely to increase the obscurity of meaning.

- *Comprehensibility*. Ideally, legislation should be comprehensible to the layperson, but given the complex nature of the situation that the legislature is dealing with, such an ideal is probably beyond attainment in practice. Nonetheless, legislative provisions certainly should be open to the comprehension of the Members of Parliament who are asked to vote on them, and they certainly should not be beyond the comprehension of the legal profession who have to construe them for their clients. Unfortunately, some legislation fails on both these counts.

- *Acceptability*. This refers to the fact that legislation is expected to be couched in uncontentious language and using a traditional prose style.

- *Brevity*. This refers to the fact that legislative provisions should be as short as is compatible with the attainment of the legislative purpose. The search for brevity in legislation can run counter to the wish for certainty in, and acceptability of, the language used.

- *Debatability*. This refers to the fact that legislation is supposed to be structured in such a way as to permit it, and the policies that lie behind it, to be debated in parliament.

- *Legal compatibility*. This refers to the need for any new provision to fit in with already existing provisions. Where the new provision alters or repeals existing provisions, it is expected that such effect should be clearly indicated.

A consideration of these various desired characteristics shows that they are not necessarily compatible; indeed, some of them, such as the desire for clarity and brevity, may well be contradictory. The point remains that those people charged with the responsibility for drafting legislation should always bear the above factors in mind when producing draft legislation, but if one principle is to be pursued above others, it is surely the need for clarity of expression and meaning.

3.3.4 TYPES OF LEGISLATION

Legislation can be categorised in a number of ways. For example, distinctions can be drawn between the following:

- *Public Acts*, which relate to matters affecting the general public. These can be further subdivided into either government Bills or Private Member's Bills.

- *Private Acts*, on the other hand, relate to the powers and interests of particular individuals or institutions, although the provision of statutory powers to particular institutions can have a major effect on the general public. For example, companies may be given the power to appropriate private property through compulsory purchase orders.

- *Enabling legislation* gives power to a particular person or body to oversee the production of the specific details required for the implementation of the general purposes stated in the parent Act. These specifics are achieved through the enactment of statutory instruments. (See below, 3.5, for a consideration of delegated legislation.)

Acts of Parliament can also be distinguished on the basis of the function they are designed to carry out. Some are *unprecedented* and cover new areas of activity previously not governed by legal rules, but other Acts are aimed at *rationalising* or *amending* existing legislative provisions.

- *Consolidating legislation* is designed to bring together provisions previously contained in a number of different Acts, without actually altering them. The Companies Act of 1985 was an example of a consolidating Act. It brought together provisions contained in numerous amending Acts that had been introduced since the previous consolidation Act of 1948. The new Companies Act 2006 also consolidated some previous legislation passed since the 1985 Act, but as it also contains previous common law provisions it may also be seen as an example of the next category.

- *Codifying legislation* seeks not just to bring existing statutory provisions under one Act, but also looks to give statutory expression to common law rules. The classic examples of such legislation are the Partnership Act of 1890 and the Sale of Goods Act 1893 (now 1979).

- *Amending legislation* is designed to alter some existing legal provision. Amendment of an existing legislative provision can take two forms:

    (i)   a *textual amendment* is one where the new provision substitutes new words for existing ones in a legislative text or introduces completely new words into that text. Altering legislation by means of textual amendment has one major drawback, in that the new provisions make very little sense on their own, without the contextual reference of the original provision they are designed to alter;

interpretative role of the judge should include, where necessary, the power to look beyond the words of statute in pursuit of the reason for its enactment, and that meaning should be construed in the light of that purpose and so as to give it effect. This purposive approach is typical of civil law systems. In these jurisdictions, legislation tends to set out general principles and leaves the fine details to be filled in later by the judges who are expected to make decisions in the furtherance of those general principles.

European Union (EU) legislation tends to be drafted in the continental, civil law manner. Its detailed effect, therefore, can only be determined on the basis of a purposive approach to its interpretation. This requirement, however, runs counter to the literal approach that is the dominant approach in the English system. The need to interpret such legislation, however, has forced a change in that approach in relation to EU legislation and even with respect to domestic legislation designed to implement Community/ Union legislation. Thus, in *Pickstone v Freemans plc* (1988), the House of Lords held that it was permissible, and indeed necessary, for the court *to read words into* inadequate domestic legislation in order to give effect to EU law in relation to provisions relating to equal pay for work of equal value. (For a similar approach, see also the House of Lords' decision in *Litster v Forth Dry Dock* (1989) and the decision in *Three Rivers DC v Bank of England (No 2)* (1996), considered below at 3.4.4.2.)

In *Usdaw v Ethel Austin Limited (In Administration)* and *Usdaw v WW Realisation 1 Limited and Others* (2013), the Employment Appeal Tribunal (EAT) concluded that s 188(1) of the Trade Union and Labour Relations (Consolidation) Act (TULRA) 1992 did not properly implement the UK's obligations in Art 1(a) of the European Union Collective Redundancies Directive 98/59 EC of 20 July 1998. By virtue of s 188, employers are required to engage in collective consultation when proposing to make 20 or more employees redundant at one establishment within a period of 90 days or less. The ground of contention was whether 'one establishment' meant one specific location, i.e. one shop for example, or whether it referred to more than one of the employer's locations. At first instance the Employment Tribunals found that each shop was an 'establishment' and so only those employees who worked in shops with 20 or more employees were entitled to protective awards in breach of the consultancy provision. Consequently, those employees working in smaller stores (around 4,400 in total) were not entitled to the protection of the consultancy provision. On appeal, the EAT held that s 188 of TULRA did not give full effect to the original directive, which, in the tribunal's opinion, was to be operated by counting individual establishments together as a single entity. Accordingly, it held that, in order to give effect to the directive, s 188 must be *read without the words* 'at one establishment'. On further appeal, the Court of Appeal referred the case to the Court of Justice for the European Union for final determination under Art 267 of the Treaty on the Functioning of the European Union (see p 197).

In April 2015 the CJEU confirmed the earlier opinion of the Advocate General that employers were not required to aggregate dismissals in all establishments, merely those in individual establishments.

It has to be recognised that for some time there has been a move away from the over-reliance on the literal approach to statutory interpretation to a more purposive approach. As Lord Griffiths put it in *Pepper v Hart* [1993] 1 All ER 42 at 50:

> The days have long passed when the court adopted a strict constructionist view of interpretation which required them to adopt the literal meaning of the language. The courts now adopt a purposive approach which seeks to give effect to the true purpose of legislation and are prepared to look at much extraneous material that bears on the background against which the legislation was enacted.

Such a shift has been necessitated, to no little degree, by the need for the courts to consider matters that were not within the original contemplation of Parliament at the time when the legislation was passed, but which have since been brought into play by the effect of technological advances. As Lord Steyn in *R (Quintavalle) v Secretary of State for Health* [2003] 2 All ER 113 at 123 put it:

> The pendulum has swung towards purposive methods of construction. This change was not initiated by the teleological approach of European Community jurisprudence, and the influence of European legal culture generally, but it has been accelerated by European ideas . . .

That process may be traced through a number of controversial cases starting with *Royal College of Nursing of the United Kingdom v Department of Health and Social Security* (1981) (considered in detail at 3.4.3). In his minority judgment Lord Wilberforce, in that case, had expressed the view that ([1981] AC 800 at 822):

> In interpreting an Act of Parliament it is proper, and indeed necessary, to have regard to the state of affairs existing, and known by Parliament to be existing, at the time. It is a fair presumption that Parliament's policy or intention is directed to that state of affairs. Leaving aside cases of omission by inadvertence . . . *when a new state of affairs, or a fresh set of facts bearing on policy, comes into existence, the courts have to consider whether they fall within the Parliamentary intention. They may be held to do so, if they fall within the same genus of facts as those to which the expressed policy has been formulated. They may also be held to do so if there can be detected a clear*

> *purpose in the legislation which can only be fulfilled if the extension is made.*
> How liberally these principles may be applied must depend upon the nature
> of the enactment, and the strictness or otherwise of the words in which it
> has been expressed . . . In any event there is one course which the courts
> cannot take, under the law of this country; they cannot fill gaps; they cannot
> by asking the question 'What would Parliament have done in this current
> case – not being one in contemplation – if the facts had been before it?'
> attempt themselves to supply the answer, if the answer is not to be found in
> the terms of the Act itself   (emphasis added).

In other words, Lord Wilberforce thought that legislation *may not* be construed so as to
cover new states of affairs, if the new construction required the court to fill gaps, or to
ask what Parliament would have done in relation to situations that it could not have had
any knowledge of, and hence were outside the ambit of the actual text of the legislation.

However, the court *could* use a purposive reading to extend the law to new situations where one of two things applied:

(i)   the genus of subject matter encompassed the new subject matter; or

(ii)   parliament's purpose was clear and an extended reading was necessary to give
         effect to it.

Given that Lord Wilberforce actually decided that the *Royal College of Nursing* case
was not one in which the court should use the purposive approach, it is perhaps not a
little ironic that his exposition of the appropriate circumstances under which the courts
can adopt a purposive approach has been generally accepted, and, in many cases, used
to extend the application of statutes in a way that he himself might very well not have
agreed with.

In *R (Quintavalle) v Secretary of State for Health* (2003) the courts were asked to
declare whether embryos created by cell nuclear replacement (CNR), a form of human
cloning involving a human egg and a cell from a donor's body, were regulated under the
Human Fertilisation and Embryology Act (HFE) 1990, which had been passed at a time
when embryos were only ever created by fertilisation of an egg by a sperm. Section 1(1)(a)
of the Act defines embryos as 'a live human embryo where fertilisation is complete'.

An organisation opposed to cloning and embryo experimentation, the Pro-Life
Alliance, contested a statement from the government that therapeutic cloning research
was permitted under the HFE Act 1990, subject to licensing by the regulatory authority, the Human Fertilisation and Embryology Authority (HFEA). The Alliance sought a
declaration that the authority had no power to license such research on the grounds that
an embryo created by cell nuclear replacement did not fall within the statutory definition of 'embryo'. The argument for the Alliance was that as cloned embryos created by
CNR were never fertilised, as commonly understood, they could not be subject to the
Act and, more importantly for them, the HFEA could not have any authority to license
any such activity.

At first instance the declaration sought by the Alliance was granted 'with some reluctance', the judge saying that the government's argument to have the statute take account of new technology involved 'an impermissible rewriting and extension of the definition'. However, the Court of Appeal set aside the declaration, which decision the House of Lords subsequently confirmed, holding that the purposive interpretation argued for by the government did *not* require the court to assume the mantle of legislator. In so doing both Lord Bingham and Lord Steyn referred to the importance of a purposive approach in enabling the courts to give effect to the intention of Parliament in areas where legislative provisions need to be considered in the context of rapid scientific and technological change.

In deciding *Quintavalle*, the House of Lords based its decision on Lord Wilberforce's comments in the *Royal College of Nursing* case, which in the opinion of Lord Bingham 'may now be treated as authoritative'. In so doing the House of Lords held that embryos created by CNR, notwithstanding the fact that they were unfertilised, were within the same '*genus of facts*' as embryos created naturally or fertilised *in vitro*. In putting Lord Wilberforce's proposition into operation, the House of Lords held that CNR organisms were, in essence, sufficiently like other embryos to be considered as belonging to the same '*genus of facts*'. Parliament could not rationally have been assumed to have intended to exclude such embryos from the regulation; consequently, the fact of fertilisation was not to be treated as integral to the s 1 definition. As a result, they were subject to the control of the HFE Act 1990 and the HFEA could authorise research using such embryos.

In reaching his decision, Lord Bingham considered the purpose and procedure of statutory interpretation and concluded that ([2003] 2 All ER 113 at 118):

> The basic task of the court is to ascertain and give effect to the true meaning of what Parliament has said in the enactment to be construed. But that is not to say that attention should be confined and a literal interpretation given to the particular provisions which give rise to difficulty. Such an approach not only encourages immense prolixity in drafting, since the draftsman will feel obliged to provide expressly for every contingency which may possibly arise. It may also (under the banner of loyalty to the will of Parliament) lead to the frustration of that will, because undue concentration on the minutiae of the enactment may lead the court to neglect the purpose which Parliament intended to achieve when it enacted the statute . . . The court's task, within the permissible bounds of interpretation, is to give effect to Parliament's purpose. So the controversial provisions should be read in the context of the statute as a whole, and the statute as a whole *should be read in the historical context of the situation which led to its enactment* (emphasis added).

With regard to the specific question of whether words in statutes should retain their original meaning, or whether they may be interpreted in the light of contemporary social factors, Lord Bingham concluded that legislation is akin to a living text, the meaning of which speaks differently as the social context in which it speaks changes. In his view (at 118):

> There is, I think, no inconsistency between the rule that statutory language retains the meaning it had when Parliament used it and the rule that a statute is always speaking . . . The meaning of 'cruel and unusual punishments' has not changed over the years since 1689, but many punishments which were not then thought to fall within that category would now be held to do so.

The impact of the preference for the purposive approach over the literal one may be seen in *R v Z and others* (2005) in which four men were charged with being members of a proscribed organisation contrary to s 11(1) of the Terrorism Act 2000. Schedule 2 of the Act listed the organisations proscribed under the Act. It referred to the IRA but did not specifically mention the 'Real IRA', which the men were allegedly members of. At first instance the judge found no case to answer, but following a reference by the Attorney General for Northern Ireland, the Northern Ireland Court of Appeal disagreed, concluding that it was the intention of the legislature to include the 'Real IRA' within the term 'the IRA' and that the legislation therefore had to be construed in such a way as to include that organisation.

In the House of Lords, counsel for the accused argued that the task of the court was 'to interpret the provision which parliament has enacted and not to give effect to an inferred intention of parliament not fairly to be derived from the language of the statute'. The House of Lords rejected that argument, holding that the historical context of the legislation was of fundamental importance. It decided that all the Westminster and Stormont statutes were directed towards the elimination of Irish-related terrorism and that the general approach in legislation had been to proscribe the IRA, using that title as a blanket description that 'embraced all emanations, manifestations and representations of the IRA, whatever their relationship to each other'.

The effect of *Pepper v Hart* (1993), permitting access to *Hansard*, will be considered at 3.4.4.2 below, but for the moment, it is still the case that the judges remain subject to the established rules of interpretation of which there are three primary rules of statutory interpretation, together with a variety of other secondary aids to construction.

3.4.3 RULES OF INTERPRETATION

In spite of the content of the preceding section, it is still necessary to consider the traditional and essentially literally based approaches to statutory interpretation. What follows in this and the following two sections should be read within the context of the Human Rights Act (HRA) 1998, which requires all legislation to be construed in such a way as, if at all possible, to bring it within the ambit of the European Convention on

Human Rights (ECHR). The effect of this requirement is to provide the judiciary with powers of interpretation much wider than those afforded to them by the more traditional rules of interpretation, as can be seen from *R v A* (2001), considered above at 2.5.1.2. However, to quote Lord Steyn further in this particular context ([2001] 3 All ER 1 at 16):

> . . . the interpretative obligation under section 3 of the 1998 Act is a strong one. It applies even if there is no ambiguity in the language in the sense of the language being capable of two different meanings . . . [s]ection 3 places a duty on the court to strive to find a possible interpretation compatible with Convention rights. Under ordinary methods of interpretation a court may depart from the language of the statute to avoid absurd consequences: section 3 goes much further. Undoubtedly, a court must always look for a contextual and purposive interpretation: section 3 is more radical in its effect . . . In accordance with the will of Parliament as reflected in section 3 it will sometimes be necessary to adopt an interpretation which linguistically may appear strained.
>
> The techniques to be used will not only involve the reading down of express language in a statute but also the implication of provisions. A declaration of incompatibility is a measure of last resort. It must be avoided unless it is plainly impossible to do so.

Nonetheless, where the HRA is not involved, the courts still have to interpret legislative provisions. The three traditional rules of statutory interpretation are as follows:

1   *The literal rule*

Under this rule, the judge is required to consider what the legislation actually says rather than considering what it might mean. In order to achieve this end, the judge should give words in legislation their literal meaning – that is, their plain, ordinary, everyday meaning – even if the effect of this is to produce what might be considered an otherwise unjust or undesirable outcome. The literal rule appears at first sight to be the least problematic method of interpreting legislation. Under this rule, the courts most obviously appear to be recognising their limitations by following the wishes of Parliament as expressed in the words of the legislation under consideration. When, however, the difficulties of assigning a fixed and unchallengeable meaning to any word is recalled, the use of the literal rule becomes less uncontroversial. A consideration of the cases reveals examples where the literal rule has been used as a justification for what otherwise might appear as partial judgments on the part of the court concerned in the case.

Inland Revenue Commissioners v Hinchy (1960) concerned s 25(3) of the Income Tax Act 1952, which stated that any taxpayer who did not complete their tax return was subject to a fixed penalty of £20 plus *treble the tax which he ought to be charged under the Act.* The question that had to be decided was whether the additional element of the penalty should be based on the total amount that should have been paid, or merely the unpaid portion of that total. The House of Lords adopted a literal interpretation of the statute and held that any taxpayer in default should have to pay triple their original tax bill.

In *R v Goodwin* (2005) the rider/driver of a jet-ski in the sea off Weymouth, crashed into another jet-ski, causing serious injuries to the rider/driver of the other machine.

The defendant was prosecuted under s 58 of the Merchant Shipping Act 1995, which makes it an offence for 'the master of . . . a United Kingdom ship' negligently to do any act which causes or is likely to cause serious injury to any person. Section 313 of the Act defines a ship as including every description of vessel 'used in navigation'. At first instance it was decided that a jet-ski was a ship for the purposes of the Merchant Shipping Act 1995 and as a result the defendant pleaded guilty.

On appeal, however, the Court of Appeal quashed his conviction, deciding that a jet-ski is not 'used in navigation' for the purpose of travel from one place to another and as s 58 only applies to sea-going ships and the jet-ski was used only within the port of Weymouth, it could not really be described as 'sea-going'.

A further problem with regard to the literal rule, relating to the difficulty judges face in determining the literal meaning of even the commonest of terms, can be seen in *R v Maginnis* (1987). The defendant had been charged under the Misuse of Drugs Act 1971, with having drugs in his possession and *with intent to supply them*. He claimed that, as he had intended to return the drugs to a friend who had left them in his car, he could not be guilty of *supplying* as charged. In this case, the judges, from first instance, through the Court of Appeal to the House of Lords, disagreed as to the literal meaning of the common word 'supply'. Even in the House of Lords, Lord Goff, in his dissenting judgment, was able to cite a dictionary definition to support his interpretation of the word. It is tempting to suggest that the majority of judges in the House of Lords operated in a totally disingenuous way by justifying their decision on the literal interpretation of the law while, at the same time, fixing on a non-literal meaning for the word under consideration. In actual fact, in *R v Maginnis*, each of the meanings for 'supply' proposed by the various judges could be supported by dictionary entries. That fact, however, only highlights the essential weakness of the literal rule, which is that it wrongly assumes that there is such a thing as a single, uncontentious, literal understanding of words. While *R v Maginnis* concerned the meaning of 'supply', *Attorney General's Reference (No 1 of 1988)* (1989) concerned the meaning of 'obtained' in s 1(3) of the Company Securities (Insider Dealing) Act 1985, since replaced by the Criminal Justice Act 1993, and led to similar disagreement as to the precise meaning of an everyday word. In another case relating to insider dealing, *Hannam v the Financial Conduct Authority* (2014) the Upper Tribunal held, on appeal, that 'precise' information must be such that it is possible to predict the direction of the movement in the share price which would or might occur if the information were made public.

However, subsequently, in March 2015 in *Jean-Bernard Lafonta v Autorité des Marchés Financiers* (Case C-628/13) the CJEU decided to the contrary that 'precise' does not require that a party be able 'to infer from that information, with a sufficient degree of probability, that, once it is made public, its potential effect on the prices of the financial instruments concerned will be in a particular direction'. All that is required is that the holder need know only that the information would affect the price of the shares, rather than knowing whether the share price would go up or down.

Bromley LBC v GLC (1983) may be cited as an instance where the courts arguably took a covert political decision under the guise of applying the literal meaning of a particular word in a piece of legislation.

In *Owens v Dudley Metropolitan Borough Council* (2011) the Court of Appeal confirmed that, where statute does not define a term, it should be given its ordinary meaning. In this case the claimant was employed as a special needs teacher and counsellor. Although her contract of employment described her as a teacher, her employer claimed that she was not in fact a teacher and consequently could not be a member of the Teachers' Pension Scheme. At first instance the High Court held that she was not a teacher as she merely provided services ancillary to teaching. The Court of Appeal held that, as there was no specific definition of 'teacher' in the Teachers' Pension Scheme, the dictionary definitions of the term should be referred to. As the dictionary definition was wide and went beyond people who stand in front of pupils in a classroom, the claimant was held to come within the definition.

2   *The golden rule*

This rule is generally considered to be an extension of the literal rule. In its general expression, it is used in circumstances where the application of the literal rule is likely to result in what appears to the court to be an obviously absurd result. The golden rule was first stated by Lord Wensleydale in *Grey v Pearson* (1857), but its operation is better defined by the words of Lord Blackburn in *River Wear Commissioners v Adamson* (1877) as follows:

> [W]e are to take the whole statute and construe it all together, giving the words their ordinary signification, unless when so applied they produce an inconsistency, or an absurdity or inconvenience so great as to convince the Court that the intention could not have been to use them in their ordinary signification, and to justify the Court in putting them in some other signification, which, though less proper, is one which the Court thinks the words will bear.

It should be emphasised, however, that the court is not at liberty to use the golden rule to ignore, or replace, legislative provisions simply on the basis that it does not agree with them; it must find genuine difficulties before it declines to use the literal rule in favour of the golden one. How one determines or defines genuine difficulty is of course a matter of discretion and, therefore, dispute. As Lord Blackburn's definition makes clear, the use of the rule actually involves the judges in finding what they consider the statute should have said or provided, rather than what it actually did state or provide. As will be seen below, the justification for this judicial activity is based on that extremely wide, amorphous, not to say spurious, legal concept: public policy. However, such a justification immediately raises the questions of the judges' understanding of, and right to determine, public policy, which will be considered in the next section of this chapter.

It is sometimes stated that there are two versions of the golden rule:

(a)   *The narrow meaning.* This is used where there are two apparently contradictory meanings to a particular word used in a legislative provision or the provision is simply ambiguous in its effect. In such a situation, the golden rule operates to ensure that preference is given to the meaning that does not result in the provision being an absurdity. An example of the application of the golden rule in this narrow sense is *Adler v George* (1964). The defendant had been charged, under the Official Secrets Act 1920, with obstruction in the vicinity of a prohibited area, whereas she had actually carried out the obstruction inside the area. The court preferred not to restrict itself to the literal wording of the Act and found the defendant guilty as charged.

(b)   *The wider meaning.* This version of the golden rule is resorted to where, although there is only one possible meaning to a provision, the court is of the opinion that to adopt such a literal interpretation will result in Lord Blackburn's 'inconsistency, absurdity or inconvenience'. The classic example of this approach is to be found in *Re Sigsworth* (1935), in which the court introduced common law rules into legislative provisions, which were silent on the matter, to prevent the estate of a murderer from benefiting from the property of the party he had murdered. Just as it was contrary to public policy to allow a murderer to benefit directly from the proceeds of his offence, so it would equally be contrary to public policy to allow the estate of a murderer to benefit from his offence. However, the public policy issue becomes less certain when one realises that there was actually no question of the murderer benefiting directly in this case, as he had committed suicide. In that light, the decision can be seen as punishing those who would have benefited on his death for an offence that they had nothing to do with – effectively cutting them out from what had been a legitimate expectation before the murder. In October 2003, the Law Commission recommended a change in the rule in *Sigsworth* and proposed a change in the law to allow children to inherit from grandparents who have been murdered by the children's father or mother. As the report states, the law should penalise killers, not their children. Its provisional view was that the law should operate as though the killer had died, allowing the children to inherit the property.

Another example of this approach is found in *R v National Insurance Commissioner ex p Connor* (1981), in which the court held, in spite of silence in the actual legislation, that Connor was not entitled to a widow's pension on the grounds that she had been the actual cause of her widowed status by killing her husband. Once again, when taken at face value, the decision in *Connor* appears perfectly justifiable on the grounds of public policy as the court stated, but appears less so when it is pointed out that Connor was actually found guilty of manslaughter and sentenced merely to a two-year period of probation.

Subsequent to the *Connor* case, the Forfeiture Act 1982 was passed, giving courts the discretionary power to ignore the rule of public policy that precludes a person who has unlawfully killed another from acquiring a benefit as a consequence of the killing. The Act does not apply in relation to murder, but nonetheless it does give the courts discretion to mitigate the effects of the rule applied in *Connor* where they are of the opinion that the circumstances of the case merit it. Thus, in *Dunbar v Plant* (1997), the Court of Appeal held that the forfeiture rule applied to the survivor of a suicide pact who had abetted the death of her partner. The court, however, applied the Forfeiture Act to permit her to benefit from his share in their jointly owned house and to claim against his life insurance policy.

In deciding whether or not to make use of the Forfeiture Act, the courts will look at the behaviour of both the killer and the person killed, so it might be expected that it would be used in relation to cases where the killing has been as a result of long-term abuse or some other mitigating circumstances. However, as the introduction of the public policy rule was itself a product of the common law, so the courts have in any case felt free to distinguish and limit the strict application of the rule in *Connor* (see, for example *Re K (Deceased)* (1985)).

3   *The mischief rule*

At one level, the mischief rule is clearly the most flexible rule of interpretation, but in its traditional expression it is limited by being restricted to using previous common law rules in order to decide the operation of contemporary legislation. It is also, at least somewhat, paradoxical that this most venerable rule, originally set out in *Heydon's Case* (1584), is also the one which most obviously reveals the socio-political nature of judicial decisions.

In *Heydon's Case*, it was stated that in making use of the mischief rule, the court should consider the following four things:

(a)   What was the common law before the passing of the statute?

(b)   What was the mischief in the law which the common law did not adequately deal with?

(c)   What remedy for that mischief had Parliament intended to provide?

(d)   What was the reason for Parliament adopting that remedy?

It has to be remembered that, when *Heydon's Case* was decided, it was the practice to cite in the preamble of legislation the purpose for its enactment, including the mischief at which it was aimed. (An example where the preamble made more sense than the actual body of the legislation is the infamous Bubble Act of 1720.) Judges in this earlier time did not, therefore, have to go beyond the legislative provision itself to implement the mischief rule. With the disappearance of such explanatory preambles, the question arises as to the extent to which judges can make use of the rule in *Heydon's Case* to justify their examination of the policy issues that underlie particular legislative provisions. Contemporary practice is to go beyond the actual body of the legislation. This, however, raises the question as to what courts can legitimately consider in their endeavour to determine the purpose and meaning of legislation, which will be considered separately below.

The example usually cited of the use of the mischief rule is *Corkery v Carpenter* (1950), in which a man was found guilty of being drunk in charge of a 'carriage', although he was in fact only in charge of a bicycle. A much more controversial application of the rule is to be found in *Royal College of Nursing v DHSS* (1981), where the courts had to decide whether the medical induction of premature labour to effect abortion, under the supervision of nursing staff, was lawful. In this particularly sensitive area, whether one agrees with the ultimate majority decision of the House of Lords in favour of the legality of the procedure or not probably depends on one's view of abortion. This fact simply serves to highlight the socio-political nature of the question that was finally determined by the House of Lords under the guise of merely determining the legal meaning of a piece of legislation.

3.4.3.1 The relationship of the rules of interpretation

It is sometimes suggested that the rules of interpretation form a hierarchical order. On that basis, the first rule that should be applied is the literal rule, and that rule only cedes to the golden rule in particular circumstances where ambiguity arises from the application of the literal rule. The third rule, the mischief rule, it is suggested, is only brought into use where there is a perceived failure of the other two rules to deliver an appropriate result. On consideration, however, it becomes obvious that no such hierarchy exists. The literal rule is supposed to be used unless it leads to a manifest absurdity, in which case it will give way to the golden rule. The immediate question this supposition gives rise to is – what is to be considered as an absurdity in any particular case, other than the view of the judge deciding the case? The three rules are contradictory, at least to a degree, and there is no way in which the outsider can determine in advance which of them the courts will make use of to decide the meaning of a particular statute. Many may welcome the fact that the courts have moved towards a more explicitly purposive approach as outlined previously and as was recommended by the Law Commission report in 1969. It has to be recognised, however, that such a shift in approach provides the judiciary with additional power in relation to determining the meaning and effect of legislation. Cynics might say that such change merely makes overt the power that the judiciary always had, but previously exercised in a covert way.

3.4.4 AIDS TO CONSTRUCTION

In addition to the three main rules of interpretation, there are a number of secondary aids to construction. These can be categorised as either intrinsic or extrinsic in nature:

3.4.4.1 Intrinsic assistance

Intrinsic assistance is derived from the statute, which is the object of interpretation; the judge uses the full statute to understand the meaning of a particular part of it. The *title*, either long or short, of the Act under consideration may be referred to for guidance (*Royal College of Nursing v DHSS* (1981)). It should be noted, however, that a general intention derived from the title cannot overrule a clear statement to the contrary in the text of the Act.

It was a feature of older statutes that they contained a *preamble*, which was a statement, preceding the actual provisions of the Act, setting out its purposes in some detail and to which reference could be made for purposes of interpretation. Again, however, any general intention derived from the preamble could not stand in the face of express provision to the contrary within the Act.

Whereas preambles preceded the main body of an Act, schedules appear as additions at the end of the main body of the legislation. They are, however, an essential part of the Act and may be referred to in order to make sense of the main text.

Some statutes contain section headings and yet others contain marginal notes relating to particular sections. The extent to which either of these may be used is uncertain, although *DPP v Schildkamp* (1969) does provide authority for the use of the former as an aid to interpretation.

Finally, in regard to intrinsic aids to interpretation, it is now recognised that punctuation has an effect on the meaning of words and can be taken into account in determining the meaning of a provision.

3.4.4.2 Extrinsic assistance

Extrinsic assistance, that is, reference to sources outside of the Act itself, may on occasion be resorted to in determining the meaning of legislation – but which sources? Some external sources are unproblematic. For example, judges have always been entitled to refer to *dictionaries* in order to find the meaning of non-legal words. They also have been able to look into *textbooks* for guidance in relation to particular points of law, and in using the mischief rule, they have been able to refer to *earlier statutes* to determine the precise mischief at which the statute they are trying to construe is aimed. The Interpretation Act 1978 is also available for consultation with regard to particular difficulties.

Unfortunately, its title is somewhat misleading, in that it does not give general instructions for interpreting legislation, but simply defines particular terms that are found in various statutes.

Other extrinsic sources, however, are more controversial. In 3.3, the various processes involved in the production of legislation were considered. As was seen, there are many distinct stages in the preparation of legislation. Statutes may arise as a result of reports submitted by a variety of commissions. In addition, the preparation of the precise structure of legislation is subject to consideration in working papers, known as *travaux préparatoires*. Nor should it be forgotten that in its progress through Parliament, a Bill is the object of discussion and debate, both on the floor of the Houses of Parliament and in committee. Verbatim accounts of debates are recorded and published in *Hansard*.

Each of these procedures provides a potential source from which a judge might discover the specific purpose of a piece of legislation or the real meaning of any provision within it. The question is, to which of these sources are the courts entitled to have access?

Historically, English courts have adopted a restrictive approach to what they are entitled to take into consideration. This restrictive approach has been gradually relaxed, however, to the extent that judges are allowed to use extrinsic sources to determine the mischief at which particular legislation is aimed. Thus, they have been entitled to look at Law Commission reports, Royal Commission reports and the reports of other official commissions. Until fairly recently, however, *Hansard* literally remained a closed book to the courts, but in the landmark decision in *Pepper v Hart* (1993), the House of Lords decided to overturn the previous rule. The issue in the case was the tax liability owed by teachers at Malvern College, a fee-paying school. Employees were entitled to have their sons educated at the school while paying only 20 per cent of the usual fees. The question was as to the precise level at which this benefit in kind was to be taxed. In a majority decision, it was held that where the precise meaning of legislation was uncertain or ambiguous or where the literal meaning of an Act would lead to a manifest absurdity, the courts could refer to *Hansard*'s reports of parliamentary debates and proceedings as an aid to construing the meaning of the legislation.

The operation of the principle in *Pepper v Hart* was extended in *Three Rivers DC v Bank of England (No 2)* (1996) to cover situations where the legislation under question was not in itself ambiguous but might be ineffective in its intention to give effect to some particular EC directive. Applying the wider purposive powers of interpretation open to it in such circumstances (see above, 3.4.2), the court held that it was permissible to refer to *Hansard* in order to determine the actual purpose of the statute. The *Pepper v Hart* principle only applies to statements made by ministers at the time of the passage of legislation, and the courts have declined to extend it to cover situations where ministers subsequently make some statement as to what they consider the effect of a particular Act to be (*Melluish (Inspector of Taxes) v BMI (No 3) Ltd* (1995)).

It is essential to bear in mind that *Pepper v Hart* was not intended to introduce a general purposive approach to the interpretation of non-European Community legislation. Recourse to *Hansard* is to be made only in the context of the mischief rule, as a further method of finding out the mischief at which the particular legislation is aimed.

In some areas of social concern, however, like traffic accidents or underage drinking, Parliament has seen fit to pass what are known as 'strict liability' offences. These are criminal offences for which it is *not* necessary for the prosecution to prove that the defendant had a particular attitude towards the crime in question, for example, that he intended to commit it, but merely that the relevant conduct took place. The thinking behind such criminalisation of conduct is that because defendants will not be able to escape liability by pleading that they did not intend to produce a particular result or that they did not have relevant knowledge, everyone will be encouraged to be that much more vigilant that they do not offend that particular law.

Sometimes, someone comes before the criminal law courts accused of an offence created by statute, and the courts must decide whether the words of the statute imply that it is necessary for the prosecution to prove the defendant had a mental element. The general rule here is that Parliament will be presumed not to have wanted to create a strict liability criminal offence unless it has been explicit about wanting to do so. There are, though, a number of factors to be taken into account in answering this question, including the nature of the language used, the subject matter of the activity and the overall framework of the Act. In *Sweet v Parsley* (1970), the accused had a house just outside of Oxford, which she rented out and visited only occasionally. She was convicted of being concerned in the management of premises used for the purpose of smoking cannabis, contrary to s 5(b) of the Dangerous Drugs Act 1965; however, she had had no knowledge that the house was being used in this way. The House of Lords held that her conviction should be quashed, since it had to be proved that it was the accused's 'purpose' that the premises were used for smoking cannabis (that is, that she intended the premises to be so used). In the case, Lord Reid said that:

> . . . whenever a section is silent as to *mens rea* there is a presumption that . . . we must read in words appropriate to require *mens rea*.

In *R v Hussain* (1981), the Court of Appeal decided that possessing a firearm without a certificate is, under s 1 of the Firearms Act 1968, an offence of strict liability, so that the prosecution is not required to prove that the accused knew the article he had was a firearm. Similarly, the Court of Appeal decided in *R v Bradish* (1990) that, under s 5(1) of the Firearms Act 1968, the offence of being in possession of a prohibited weapon (a spray canister containing CS gas) is a crime of strict liability. It was therefore not a defence for the accused to argue that because the gas was concealed within the canister, he did not know, and could not reasonably have been expected to know, that the article in his possession was a prohibited weapon. The court's choice in these cases to impose strict liability is in furtherance of the general purpose of the firearms legislation, that is, to put everyone on their guard that so wrong is the possession of firearms that those who have them without the appropriate licence will effectively be deemed automatically to be guilty of an offence.

In another case, the Court of Appeal decided that the offence created by s 11 of the Company Directors (Disqualification) Act 1986 of acting as a director of a company while an undischarged bankrupt, except with the leave of the court, was one of strict liability. Thus, a mistaken but genuinely held belief that the bankruptcy had been discharged was no defence to the crime (*R v Brockley* (1994)). The court took the view that the mischief sought to be tackled by s 11 of the Act was of wide social concern and that, therefore, the creation of strict liability would promote the object of the Act by obliging bankrupts themselves to ensure that their bankruptcy was in fact discharged before they acted again as company directors.

In *R v K* (2001), the defendant was charged with indecently assaulting a 14-year-old girl, who had in fact consented and who had told him she was over 16. Section 14(1) of the Sexual Offences Act 1956 was silent as to *mens rea* so far as knowledge of the girl's age was concerned. On the other hand, s 14(4) expressly stated that genuine belief was to be a defence where an adult woman lacked the mental capacity to consent. Consequently, the Court of Appeal could legitimately infer that Parliament had *not* intended genuine belief to be a defence for s 14(1), otherwise it would have said so. The House of Lords reversed the finding of the Court of Appeal, holding that, as the 1956 Act was a consolidating Act, drawing together provisions from several previous Acts without making any substantive changes to them, the inference suggested by the Court of Appeal was not appropriate and the common law presumption against strict liability should prevail.

- *Against retrospective effect of new law.* The courts operate a presumption of interpretation that statutes will not operate retrospectively. It is one thing for Parliament to legislate that, for example, as from next year all fox-hunting is illegal. It would be quite another thing for Parliament to legislate that not only will fox-hunting be illegal if carried on in future, but that anyone who participated in such an event during the last five years is open to prosecution today. Such a presumption against retrospective effect is important in relation to crimes, but is relevant in other areas too, such as contractual arrangements and taxation. This principle operates not only to stop people whose conduct was innocent at the time from being convicted by a backward-looking Act, but also to stop people whose conduct was guilty at any given time from being free from blame just because an Act decriminalises certain conduct. So, if an Act abolishes an offence by repealing a statutory provision, then the repeal will not affect the punishment of someone who has been convicted of this crime at an earlier stage, nor the continuation of legal proceedings in respect of crimes that were committed before the law was changed. The presumption against retrospective effect was considered by the Court of Appeal in *Home Secretary v Wainwright* (2002). Two relatives visiting a prisoner were strip-searched as a condition of entry to the prison, and subsequently claimed a violation of their right to respect for private life. The court held that since the events in question had happened before the HRA 1998 came into force, s 3 of that Act could not be relied on. As Parliament had expressly made s 22(4) of the Act retroactive, its failure to do the same for s 3 must be taken to have been intentional. See also *R v Lambert* (2001) and *R v Kansal* (2001).

As Parliament is supreme, there being no body with higher constitutional powers, it can pass retrospective legislation if it wishes, but it must do so using express words to achieve this end. The War Damage Act 1965 was passed specifically to overrule the decision of the House of Lords in *Burmah Oil Co Ltd v The Lord Advocate* (1965), and to deprive Burmah Oil of the results of having won that case. The oil company's installations in Burma, which was then a British colony, had been destroyed by the British Forces in 1942 in order to prevent them being captured by Japanese forces. The company, which was registered in Scotland, sued the Crown for compensation. The Crown contended that no compensation was payable when property was destroyed under the royal prerogative. The House of Lords decided that compensation was payable. The Act of Parliament was then passed to override the House of Lords' decision and to prevent the burden of compensation having to be met by the taxpayer. An example of modern legislation which has been made expressly retrospective is the War Crimes Act 1991. This Act allows the Attorney General to authorise criminal proceedings for homicide committed in Germany or German-occupied territory during World War II. The prosecution can be against a person in the UK regardless of his nationality at the time of the alleged offence. The relaxation of the 'double jeopardy' rule by s 75 of the Criminal Justice Act 2003 has retrospective effect (s 75(6)).

Under the Jobseeker's Allowance (Employment, Skills and Enterprise Scheme) Regulations 2011 the unemployed could be required to engage in work or training or lose their benefits. Jamie Wilson, a qualified HGV driver, refused to undertake work for an organisation collecting, renovating and distributing unwanted furniture for six months for 30 hours a week. As a result, he was told that his benefits would be stopped for six months. Cait Reilly, a geology graduate who wanted to work in museums, was required to stop her voluntary work at a local museum and instead work for the retail business Poundland for two weeks. It was accepted that she was working rather than training, although she received no addition to her unemployment benefits.

In the subsequent challenge to how they were treated, *Wilson and Reilly v DWP* (2013), the Court of Appeal held that the Jobseeker's Allowance (Employment, Skills and Enterprise Scheme) Regulations 2011 were invalid because they failed to describe the schemes made under them in sufficient detail and that notices given under the regulations were inadequate. However, in order to save the estimated liability of up to £130 million, the government, in the form of the Secretary of State for Work and Pensions and former leader of the Conservative Party, Ian Duncan Smith, immediately introduced retroactive primary legislation, the Jobseekers (Back to Work Schemes) Act 2013, to counter the consequences of the Court of Appeal decision. The aim of the Act was simply to ensure that claimants who had had their benefits sanctioned unlawfully could not claim a refund on the basis of the Court of Appeal judgment, and that where benefit cuts had not yet been implemented for refusal to engage in the scheme, these could now be applied.

Subsequently, on appeal, the Supreme Court confirmed the reasoning of the Court of Appeal stating that:

> 'were it not for the 2013 Act and the 2013 Regulations, we would have affirmed the order of the Court of Appeal.'

However, the court had to recognise the efficacy of the new legislation in righting the previous procedural wrongs. Whether substantive wrongs were remedied is another question.

- *Against deprivation of liberty.* The law courts work on the assumption that Parliament does not intend to deprive a person of his liberty unless it is explicitly making provision for such a punishment. Thus, Lord Scarman has stated that:

> ... if Parliament intends to exclude effective judicial review of the exercise of a power in restraint of liberty, it must make its meaning crystal clear (*R v Secretary of State for the Home Department ex p Khawaja* (1983)).

The House of Lords ruled that an immigration Act that it was examining did not have the effect of placing the burden of proof on an immigrant to show that the decision of the Home Office to detain him was unjustified. In other words, one could not read the Act in a way that allowed someone to be deprived of their liberty unless and until they proved that such imprisonment was unjustified.

- *Against application to the Crown.* Unless the legislation contains a clear statement to the contrary, it is presumed not to apply to the Crown.

- *Against breaking international law.* Where possible, legislation should be interpreted in such a way as to give effect to existing international legal obligations.

- *In favour of words taking their meaning from the context in which they are used.* This final presumption refers back to, and operates in conjunction with, the major rules for interpreting legislation considered previously. The general presumption appears as three distinct sub-rules, each of which carries a Latin tag. The *noscitur a sociis* rule is applied where statutory provisions include a list of examples of what is covered by the legislation. It is presumed that the words used have a related meaning and are to be interpreted in relation to each other. (See *IRC v Frere* (1969), in which the House of Lords decided which of two possible meanings of the word 'interest' was to be preferred by reference to the word's location within a statute.) The *ejusdem generis* rule applies in situations where general words are appended to the end of a list of specific examples. The presumption is that the general words have to be interpreted in line with the prior restrictive examples. Thus, a provision which referred to a list that included 'horses, cattle, sheep and other animals' would be unlikely to apply to domestic animals such as cats and dogs. (See *Powell v Kempton Park Racecourse* (1899), in which it was held that, because a statute prohibited betting in a specified number of *indoor* places, it could not cover an *outdoor* location.) The *expressio unius exclusio alterius* rule simply means that where a statute seeks to establish a list of what is covered by its provisions, then anything not expressly included in that list is specifically excluded. (See *R v Inhabitants of Sedgley* (1831), where rates expressly stated to be payable on *coal* mines were held not to be payable in relation to *limestone* mines.)

For further examples and resources illustrating the way statutory interpretation is carried out, exercises and technical guidance, please go to: www.routledge.com/cw/slapper where you will find a guide to Using Legislation.

3.5   DELEGATED OR SUBORDINATE LEGISLATION

Delegated legislation is of particular importance. Generally speaking, delegated legislation is law made by some person or body to whom Parliament has delegated its general law-making power. A validly enacted piece of delegated legislation has the same legal force and effect as the Act of Parliament under which it is enacted but, equally, it only has effect to the extent that its enabling Act authorises it.

It should also be recalled that s 10 of the HRA 1998 gives ministers power to amend primary legislation by way of statutory instrument where a court has issued a declaration that the legislation in point is incompatible with the rights provided under the ECHR.

The output of delegated legislation in any year greatly exceeds the output of Acts of Parliament. For example, in the parliamentary year 2013 only 33 UK public general Acts were passed, as against 3,318 statutory instruments.

In statistical terms, therefore, it is at least arguable that delegated legislation is actually more significant than primary Acts of Parliament.

There are various types of delegated legislation:

- *Orders in Council*. Consideration of this type of legislation is confused by the interplay of related and overlapping concepts and the historical process that saw Parliament exercise control over the power of the Crown.

Historically, Orders in Council were the result of the exercise of the royal prerogative in consultation with the Privy Council, the monarch's close advisers. As has already been mentioned, some aspects of these prerogative powers remain and are exercised through the issuing of Orders in Council. Orders in Council made under prerogative powers are primary legislation. However, distinct from such exercise of prerogative powers are the statutory orders which arise from the fact that parliament, through statute, has given the Crown powers to make law through the issuing of Orders in Council. It is this latter type of Orders in Council that is correctly referred to as delegated legislation. The passing of statutory Orders in Council may also involve a parliamentary procedure, depending on the Act from which they stem. Consequently some Orders may need to be laid before Parliament in draft before being made, or after they have been made. Alternatively, the Act may require the Order to be approved by Parliament before it comes into force. The importance of this distinction lies in the fact that, as has already been explained, under the HRA 1998 the courts have greater power in relation to secondary legislation than they do in regard to primary legislation.

The Privy Council is nominally a non-party-political body of eminent parliamentarians, but in effect it is simply a means through which the government, in the form of a committee of ministers, can introduce legislation in the form of Orders in Council, without the need to go through the full parliamentary process. Although it is usual to cite situations of state emergency as exemplifying occasions when the government will resort to the use of Orders in Council, the use of this statutory form is far from uncommon. Perhaps the widest scope for Orders in Council is to be found in relation to EU law, for under s 2(2) of the European Communities Act 1972, ministers can give effect to provisions of Union law which do not have direct effect (see, further, below, 5.2.4).

Ministers may also be given statutory power to make orders to introduce or alter existing provisions, but such orders are not to be confused with Orders in Council. To add further potential confusion, since 1946, under s 1 of the Statutory Instruments Act (SIA) 1946, every power to make an Order in Council conferred by an Act of Parliament passed after 1 January 1948 must be in the form of a statutory instrument. Consequently, most Orders in Council are also statutory instruments, but there still exists the possibility of Orders in Council that are not to be issued as SIs, either being the result of the exercise of prerogative power or deriving from a pre-1948 statute.

- *Statutory instruments* are the means through which government ministers introduce particular regulations under powers delegated to them by parliament in enabling legislation.

- *Bylaws* are the means through which local authorities and other public bodies can make legally binding rules. Bylaws may be made by local authorities under such enabling legislation as the Local Government Act 1972.

- *Court Rule Committees* are empowered to make the rules which govern procedure in the particular courts over which they have delegated authority, under such Acts as the Senior Courts Act 1981 (originally passed as The Supreme Court Act 1981 but changed in name by the Constitutional Reform Act 2005, Sched 11), the County Courts Act 1984 and the Magistrates' Courts Act 1980.

- *Professional regulations* governing particular occupations may be given the force of law under provisions delegating legislative authority to certain professional bodies who are empowered to regulate the conduct of their members. An example is the power given to The Law Society, under the Solicitors' Act 1974, to control the conduct of practising solicitors.

3.5.1   ADVANTAGES IN THE USE OF DELEGATED LEGISLATION

The advantages of delegated legislation include the following:

- *Time saving*

  Delegated legislation can be introduced quickly, where necessary in particular cases, and can permit rules to be changed in response to emergencies or unforeseen problems.

  The use of delegated legislation, however, also saves parliamentary time generally. Given the pressure on debating time in Parliament and the highly detailed nature of typical delegated legislation, not to mention its sheer volume, Parliament would not have time to consider each individual piece of law that is enacted in the form of delegated legislation. It is considered of more benefit for Parliament to spend its time in a thorough consideration of the principles of the enabling Act, leaving the appropriate minister or body to establish the working detail under its authority.

- *Access to particular expertise*

  Related to the first advantage is the fact that the majority of Members of Parliament simply do not have sufficient expertise to consider such provisions effectively. Given the highly specialised and extremely technical nature of many of the regulations that are introduced through delegated legislation, it is necessary that those authorised to introduce the legislation should have access to the necessary external expertise required to formulate such regulations. With regard to bylaws, it practically goes without saying that local and specialist knowledge should give rise to more appropriate rules than reliance on the general enactments of parliament.

- *Flexibility*

  The use of delegated legislation permits ministers to respond on an *ad hoc* basis to particular problems, as and when they arise, and provides greater flexibility in the regulation of activity subject to the minister's overview.

3.5.2 DISADVANTAGES IN THE PREVALENCE OF DELEGATED LEGISLATION

The disadvantages in the use of delegated legislation include the following:

- *Accountability*

  A key issue involved in the use of delegated legislation concerns the question of accountability and erosion of the constitutional role of Parliament. Parliament is presumed to be the source of legislation, but with respect to delegated legislation, the individual members are not the source of the law. Certain people, notably government ministers and the civil servants who work under them to produce the detailed provisions of delegated legislation, are the real source of such regulations. Even allowing for the fact that they are, in effect, operating on powers delegated to them from parliament, it is not beyond questioning whether this procedure does not give them more power than might be thought appropriate, or indeed constitutionally correct, while at the same time disempowering and discrediting parliament as a body.

- *Scrutiny*

  The question of general accountability raises the need for effective scrutiny, but the very form of delegated legislation makes it extremely difficult for ordinary Members of Parliament to fully understand what is being enacted and to monitor it effectively. This difficulty arises in part from the tendency for such regulations to be highly specific, detailed and technical. This problem of comprehension and control is compounded by the fact that regulations appear outside the context of their enabling legislation, but only have any real meaning within that context.

- *Bulk*

  The problem faced by ordinary Members of Parliament in effectively keeping abreast of delegated legislation is further increased by the sheer mass of such legislation. If parliamentarians cannot keep up with the flow of delegated legislation, how can the general public be expected to do so?

3.5.3 THE LEGISLATIVE AND REGULATORY REFORM ACT 2006

In previous editions of this book the authors have, to a greater or lesser degree, focused on the increase in the power of Ministers of State to alter Acts of Parliament by means of statutory instruments in the pursuit of economic, business and regulatory efficiency.

The first of these (dis)empowering Acts of Parliament that brought this situation about was the Deregulation and Contracting Out Act (DCOA) 1994, introduced by the last Conservative government. It was a classic example of the wide-ranging power that enabling legislation can extend to ministers in the attack on such primary legislation as was seen to impose unnecessary burdens on any trade, business or profession. Although the DCOA 1994 imposed the requirement that ministers should consult with interested parties to any proposed alteration, it nonetheless gave them extremely wide powers to alter primary legislation without the necessity of having to follow the same procedure as was required to enact that legislation in the first place. For that reason, deregulation orders were subject to a far more rigorous procedure (sometimes referred to as 'super-affirmative') than ordinary statutory instruments. The powers were extended in its first term in office by the Labour government under the Regulatory Reform Act (RRA) 2001.

It was, however, only with the proposed Legislative and Regulatory Reform Bill 2006 that alarm bells started to ring generally. This critical reaction was based on the proposed power contained in the Act for ministers to create new criminal offences, punishable with less than two years' imprisonment, without the need for a debate in parliament.

The proposals under the Legislative and Regulatory Reform Bill 2006 were constitutionally dangerous to the extent that they gave to the executive powers that should be a function of the legislature.

As a result of opposition, the government amended the legislation to ensure that its powers could only be used in relation to business and regulatory efficiency.

Under s 1 of the Legislative and Regulatory Reform Act (LRRA) 2006, a minister of the Crown can make a legislative reform order for the purpose of removing or reducing any burden to which any person is subject as a result of any legislation. A burden is defined as:

- a financial cost
- an administrative inconvenience
- an obstacle to efficiency, productivity or profitability; or
- a sanction, criminal or otherwise, which affects the carrying on of any lawful activity.

However, it is at least somewhat reassuring that such powers cannot be used:

- to confer or transfer any function of legislation on anyone other than a minister
- to impose, abolish or vary taxation
- to amend or repeal any provision of the Human Rights Act 1998

Nor can the Act be used to amend or repeal any provision of Part 1 of the LRRA, which includes the above prohibitions.

Similar fears were raised in relation to the Public Bodies Act 2011. Although not as wide-ranging as was originally proposed, the Act still gives government ministers wide powers to abolish non-government bodies and agencies, referred to as quangos.

3.5.4 CONTROL OF DELEGATED LEGISLATION

The foregoing difficulties and potential shortcomings in the use of delegated legislation are, at least to a degree, mitigated by the fact that specific controls have been established to oversee it:

3.5.4.1 Parliamentary control over delegated legislation

Power to make delegated legislation is ultimately dependent upon the authority of Parliament and Parliament retains general control over the procedure for enacting such law. New regulations in the form of delegated legislation are required to be laid before Parliament. This procedure takes two forms depending on the provision of the enabling legislation. Some regulations require a positive resolution of one or both of the Houses of Parliament before they become law. Most Acts, however, simply require that regulations made under their auspices be placed before Parliament. They automatically become law after a period of 40 days unless a resolution to annul them is passed.

The problem with the negative resolution procedure is that it relies on Members of Parliament being sufficiently aware of the content, meaning and effect of the detailed provisions laid before them. Given the nature of such statutory legislation, such reliance is unlikely to prove secure.

Since 1973, there has been a *Joint Select Committee on Statutory Instruments* whose function it is to scrutinise all statutory instruments. The Joint Committee is empowered to draw the special attention of both Houses to an instrument on any one of a number of grounds specified in the Standing Orders (No 151 of the House of Commons and No 74 of the House of Lords) under which it operates, or on any other ground *which does not relate to the actual merits of the instrument or the policy it is pursuing.*

The House of Commons has its own *Select Committee on Statutory Instruments*, which is appointed to consider all statutory instruments laid *only* before the House of Commons. This committee is empowered to draw the special attention of the House to an instrument on any one of a number of grounds specified in Standing Order No 151; or on any other ground. However, as with the joint committee, it is not empowered to consider the merits of any statutory instrument or the policy behind it. As an example of its operation, after considering two statutory instruments, namely Personal Equity Plan (Amendment No 2) Regulations 2005 (SI 2005/3348) and Individual Savings Account (Amendment No 3) Regulations 2005 (SI 2005/3350), the Committee considered that they should be drawn to the attention of the House of Commons on the ground that there appeared to be a doubt whether they were *intra vires.*

EU legislation is overseen by a specific committee – as are local authority bylaws. In 2003 the House of Lords established a *Committee on the Merits of Statutory Instruments*, the task of which is to consider the policy implications of statutory instruments. It has wide-ranging remit and is specifically charged with the task of deciding whether the attention of the House should be drawn to a particular statutory instrument on any one of the following grounds:

- that it is politically or legally important or gives rise to issues of public policy likely to be of interest to the House;
- that it is inappropriate in view of the changed circumstances since the passage of the parent Act;
- that it inappropriately implements EU legislation;
- that it imperfectly achieves its policy objectives. (http://www.publications. parliament.uk/pa/ld/ldmerit.htm)

A case study on the passage of statutory instruments:
The Tax Credit Regulations 2015

As part of its continued austerity programme the Conservative government proposed that alterations be made to the regime of tax credits which were paid to people in work but previously thought not to be earning sufficient money to maintain themselves adequately. The treasury proposed significantly to limit people's eligibility for such tax credit payment, using a statutory instrument, the Tax Credits (Income Thresholds and Determination of Rates) (Amendment) Regulations 2015 under powers delegated to it under the Tax Credits Act 2002. The delegated powers required the approval of both Houses of Parliament and had been appropriately approved by the House of Commons. However, in its consideration in the House of Lords the members of that House voted in one motion for the cuts to be postponed pending an independent review of the proposals. On a second motion they also voted to provide transitional financial support for at least three years for those likely to be affected by the proposals.

The votes were not unexpected but nonetheless they did raise some anger and doubt about the constitutionality of the Lords' action.

As has been seen, the Parliament Acts certainly placed limitations on the Lords' powers in relation to ordinary Bills, but as delegated legislation was not a prominent feature of pre-1950 legislation, those Acts remained silent on the Lords' powers in relation to such secondary legislation. As a consequence, it would appear that the House of Lords had a formal veto over delegated legislation, but it was suggested, a suggestion supported by the government in the current issue, that a constitutional convention had emerged that the Lords should not vote on such matters. However, although it was certainly unusual for the Lords to vote on, and certainly vote against, secondary legislation, it has to be admitted that it was not unprecedented. Indeed, at the time when the majority of hereditary peers were removed from the Lords, the sometime Conservative Leader in the House Lord Strathclyde made a bold speech stating that 'I declare this convention dead', before using his voting power to vote down secondary legislation relating to the election of the mayor of London.

The government also questioned the right of the House of Lords to vote against the statutory instrument, as they maintained it was a financial matter and therefore subject to the normal rules under the Parliament Acts.

Where the Lords are concerned about the passage of a particular statutory instrument, they have the choice of two types of motion to vote on: the one most used is the 'non-fatal' motion, which merely expresses 'regret at the government's action', rather than looking to block it. One such motion was before the house in relation to the tax credits issue but was rejected. Also rejected was 'fatal' motion against the passage of the legislation, which would have completely curtailed the legislation in question. Instead the Lords chose the non-fatal options which resulted in the instrument being passed back to the Commons for it to be considered further.

Following the votes in the House of Lords, the government made known its extreme displeasure. Chancellor of the Exchequer, George Osborne, said he would heed the outcome of the vote, but said it raised constitutional issues of 'unelected Labour and Lib Dem lords defying the will of the elected House of Commons'. Somewhat ironically the government announced that Lord Strathclyde would be looking into the implications of the whole issue as it impacted on the future role of the House of Lords.

3.5.4.2 Judicial control of delegated legislation

It is possible for delegated legislation to be challenged through the procedure of judicial review, on the basis that the person or body to whom Parliament has delegated its authority has acted in a way that exceeds the limited powers delegated to them. Any provision outside this authority is *ultra vires* and is void. Additionally, there is a presumption that any power delegated by Parliament is to be used in a reasonable manner, and the courts may on occasion hold particular delegated legislation to be void on the basis that it is unreasonable. The process of judicial review will be considered in more detail in Chapter 13. However, an interesting example of this procedure may illustrate the point. In January 1997, the Lord Chancellor raised court fees and, at the same time, restricted the circumstances in which a litigant could be exempted from paying such fees. In March, a Mr John Witham, who previously would have been exempted from paying court fees, successfully challenged the Lord Chancellor's action. In a judicial review, it was held that Lord Mackay had exceeded the statutory powers given to him by Parliament. One of the judges, Rose LJ, stated that there was nothing to suggest that Parliament ever intended 'a power for the Lord Chancellor to prescribe fees so as to preclude the poor from access to the courts'.

R (Public Law Project) v Secretary of State for Justice (2014) is a recent example of the courts finding the use of delegated legislation to alter primary legislation to be *ultra vires*. As its title indicates, the statutory instrument in questions, the Legal Aid, Sentencing and Punishment of Offenders Act 2012 (Amendment of Schedule 1) Order 2014, sought to amend Schedule 1 to the Legal Aid, Sentencing and Punishment of Offenders Act (LASPO) 2012 by introducing a residence test limiting the provision of legal aid to those who could show 'a meaningful connection' with the UK. The court held that the introduction of the residence test by way of secondary legislation exceeded the power to make delegated legislation conferred on the Secretary of State by the parent statute.

Lord Justice Moses (with whom Mr Justice Collins and Mr Justice Jay agreed) identified the objective of the primary legislation as being the provision of legal aid to those with the greatest need. As the proposed amendment actually had 'nothing to do with need or an order of priority of need . . . [but was], entirely, focused on reducing the cost of legal aid', it violated the principle that subsidiary legislation must serve and promote the object of the primary legislation under which it is made. Consequently it was held to be *ultra vires* and ineffective.

The power of the courts in relation to delegated legislation has been considerably increased by the enactment of the HRA 1998. As has been seen, the courts cannot directly declare primary legislation invalid, but can only issue a declaration of incompatibility. However, no such limitation applies in regard to subordinate legislation, which consequently may be declared invalid as being in conflict with the rights provided under the ECHR. This provision significantly extends the power of the courts in relation to the control of subordinate legislation, in that they are no longer merely restricted to questioning such legislation on the grounds of procedure, but can now assess it on the basis of content, as measured against the rights provided in the ECHR. It should be noted that some Orders in Council, as expressions of the exercise of the royal prerogative, are not open to challenge and control in the same way as other subordinate legislation.

A Case Study on ultra vires: HM Treasury v Mohammed Jabar Ahmed (2010)

In this, the first substantive case heard by the Supreme Court, it quashed fully the Terrorism (United Nations Measures) Order 2006 and quashed parts of the al-Qaida and Taliban (United Nations Measures) Order 2006 as being *ultra vires* the powers extended to the Treasury under the United Nations Act 1946.

Both Orders had been made by the Treasury under power conferred by s 1 of the United Nations Act (UNA) 1946, which was enacted to facilitate the taking of measures to implement decisions of the UN Security Council. In each case the Orders were made to give effect to resolutions of the United Nations Security Council, which were designed to suppress and prevent the financing and preparation of acts of terrorism.

The Orders specifically provided for the freezing of the funds, economic resources and financial services available to individuals who had been included on a United Nations list of associates of Usama Bin-Laden, or were involved in international terrorism, or were reasonably suspected of involvement with international terrorism.

In delivering the leading judgment, Lord Hope (with the agreement of Lord Walker and Lady Hale) emphasised the far-reaching and serious effect of the asset-freezing measures on not just the individuals concerned, but also their families. Using the scope afforded by the rule in *Pepper v Hart*, he concluded that the legislative history of the 1946 Act demonstrated that Parliament 'did not intend that the 1946 Act should be used to introduce coercive measures which interfere with UK citizens' fundamental rights'. The crucial question for the court to consider was whether s 1 of UNA conferred power on the executive, *without any parliamentary scrutiny*, to give effect in this country to decisions of the Security Council, which are targeted against individuals. And the answer to that question was a clear no.

In answering the question in that way, the Supreme Court was at pains to emphasise that it was in no way usurping the role of the legislature. Indeed as Lord Phillips put it:

Nobody should form the impression that in quashing the TO and the operative provision of the AQO the Court displaces the will of Parliament. On the contrary, the Court's judgment vindicates the primacy of Parliament, as opposed to the Executive, in determining in what circumstances fundamental rights may legitimately be restricted.

3.6   LAW REFORM: THE ROLE OF THE LAW COMMISSION

At one level, law reform is either a product of parliamentary or judicial activity. Parliament tends, however, to be concerned with particularities of law reform, and the judiciary are constitutionally and practically disbarred from reforming the law in anything other than an opportunistic and piecemeal way. Therefore, there remains a need for the question of law reform to be considered generally and a requirement that such consideration be conducted in an informed but disinterested manner. Thereafter it is a matter for Parliament to introduce the necessary legislation to bring any proposed reform into effect.

Reference has already been made to the use of consultative Green Papers by the government as a mechanism for gauging the opinions of interested parties to particular reforms. More formal advice may be provided through various advisory standing committees. Among these is the *Law Reform Committee*. The function of this Committee is to consider the desirability of changes to the civil law which the Lord Chancellor may refer to it. The *Criminal Law Revision Committee* performs similar functions in relation to criminal law.

Royal Commissions may be constituted to consider the need for law reform in specific areas. The Commission on Criminal Procedure (1980) led to the enactment of the Police and Criminal Evidence Act 1984, and the recommendation of the 1993 Royal Commission on Criminal Justice (Runciman Commission) informed subsequent reform of the criminal law system.

Committees may be set up in order to review the operation of particular areas of law, the most significant of these being the Woolf review of the operation of the civil justice system. Similarly, Sir Robin Auld conducted a review of the whole criminal justice system and Sir Andrew Leggatt reviewed the tribunal system. Detailed analysis of the consequences flowing from the implementation of the recommendations of these reviews will be considered subsequently.

If a criticism is to be levelled at these Committees and Commissions, it is that they are all *ad hoc* bodies. Their remit is limited and they do not have the power either to widen the ambit of their investigation or to initiate reform proposals.

The *Law Commission* fulfils the need for some institution to concern itself more generally with the question of law reform. It was established under the Law Commissions Act 1965 and its general function is to keep the law as a whole under review and to make recommendations for its systematic reform to ensure that the law is as fair, modern, simple and cost-effective as possible.

As part of its goal to make the law as simple as possible, the Commission has adopted three interrelated approaches: codification, consolidation and revision.

Codification

The Commission looks towards the codification of the law. Codification has already been mentioned in respect of Civil Law in Chapter 1 and the Commission has expressed its view that the law would be more accessible to the citizen, and easier for the courts to understand, if the English system also adopted a series of statutory codes. The Commission has had a long-established aim of working towards a codification of criminal law; however, the tenth programme of law reform signalled a change in approach, reflecting a more realistic recognition of the difficulties involved in such a project and the need to reform the law before it can be successfully codified.

As the Commission stated in its 10th programme:

> The complexity of the common law in 2007 is no less than it was in 1965. Further, the increased pace of legislation, layers of legislation on a topic being placed one on another with bewildering speed, and the influence of European legislation, continue to make codification ever more difficult. The Commission continues to believe that codification is desirable, but considers that it needs to redefine its approach to make codification more achievable. Accordingly the Commission has decided that:
>
> (1) It will continue to use the definition of codification used by Gerald Gardiner in Law Reform Now, that is, 'reducing to one statute, or a small collection of statutes, the whole of the law on any particular subject'.
>
> (2) Consistently with Gardiner's concerns in 1964, the Commission's main priority is first to reform an area of the law sufficiently to enable it to return and codify the law at a subsequent stage. If it can codify at the same time as reforming, it will do so.
>
> The first direct effect of these decisions is that the Commission has removed from this programme, mention of a codification project in relation to criminal law. The duty in reforming the criminal law, as elsewhere, is to identify reform projects that will make the law accessible, remove uncertainties and bring it up to date with the aim that in the future we will return and codify the area if we cannot do so as part of the project. Rather than specifically referring to codification as the intended outcome, we have introduced a new item which seeks to undertake projects to simplify the criminal law. We see this work as the necessary precursor to any attempts to codify the criminal law.

Consolidation

This process brings together all existing statutory provisions, previously located in several different pieces of legislation, under one Act. As explained in Chapter 3 above, under this procedure the law itself remains unchanged, but those who use it are able to find it all in one place. An example, cited by the Commission, is the Powers of Criminal Courts (Sentencing) Act 2000, which brought together in a single piece of legislation sentencing powers which were previously to be found in more than a dozen Acts.

Statute law revision

The Commission continuously keeps under review the need to remove antiquated and/ or anachronistic laws from the statute book, the continued existence of which make it subject to derision, even if they do not bring it into disrepute. As the Commission states, the purpose of its statute law repeals work is to modernise and simplify the statute book, reduce its size and save the time of lawyers and others who use it. Implementation of the repeal proposals is by means of special Statute Law (Repeals) Acts and 18 such Acts have been introduced since 1965, repealing more than 2,000 Acts either completely or partially.

It was as a result of this process, and following a 1995 Law Commission Report (No 230), that the Law Reform (Year and a Day Rule) Act was introduced in 1996. This Act removed the ancient rule which prevented killers being convicted of murder or manslaughter if their victim survived for a year and a day after the original offence. The Statute Law (Repeals) Act 2004 removed a Victorian Act which empowered the Metropolitan Police to license shoeblacks and commissionaires and, in so doing, removed the offence of fraudulently impersonating a shoeblack or commissionaire. The nineteenth, most recent, and biggest ever Statute Law (Repeals) Act (2013) repealed 817 whole Acts and part repealed 50 other Acts. The earliest repeal was from around 1322 (Statutes of the Exchequer) and the latest was part of the Taxation (International and Other Provisions) Act 2010. Repeals in the Act included:

- An 1856 Act passed to help imprisoned debtors secure their early release from prison
- A 1710 Act to raise coal duty to pay for 50 new churches in London
- A 1696 Act to fund the rebuilding of St Paul's Cathedral after the Great Fire 1666
- An 1800 Act to hold a lottery to win the £30,000 Pigot Diamond

The Commission is a purely advisory body and its scope is limited to those areas set out in its current programme of law reform, which has to be approved by the Lord Chancellor. It recommends reform after it has undertaken an extensive process of consultation with informed and/or interested parties. At the conclusion of a project a report is submitted to the Lord Chancellor and Parliament for their consideration and action.

Although the scope of the Commission is limited to those areas set out in its programme of law reform, its ambit is not unduly restricted, as may be seen from the range of matters covered in its twelfth programme set out in July 2014.

In addition to continuing work on 13 ongoing projects from the eleventh programme it lists nine new topic areas as follows:

- *Sentencing procedure*: a law reform project to recommend a single sentencing statute.

- *Mental capacity and detention*: a project to consider how deprivation of liberty should be authorised and supervised in settings other than hospitals and care homes. This follows sharp criticism of the present state of the law by Justices of the Supreme Court.

- *Land registration*: a project that will comprise a wide-ranging review of the Land Registration Act 2002 (itself a Law Commission Act).

- *Wills*: a law reform project to review the law of wills, focusing on mental capacity and will making, formalities that dictate how a will should be written and signed, and how mistakes in wills can be corrected.

- *Bills of sale*: a law reform review of the law relating to bills of sale loans, including logbook loans, which has become a recent area of concern in relation to non-controlled lending.

There are also two scoping exercises designed to see whether detailed proposals for law reform should be developed:

- *Firearms*: a scoping exercise to consider the enactment of a single statute containing modified and simplified versions of all firearms offence.

- *Protecting consumer prepayments on retailer insolvency*: a scoping review to assess the scale of the problem and consider whether to increase protection for consumers.

Finally, there are two wide-ranging topics specific to purposes of the Welsh Government:

- *The form and accessibility of the law applicable in Wales:* an Advice to Government, considering ways in which the existing legislation can be simplified and made more accessible, and how future legislation could reduce problems.

- *Planning and development control in Wales:* a law reform project to recommend a simplified and modernised planning system for Wales.

The Twelfth Programme of Law Reform is available on the Commission's website at: http://lawcommission.justice.gov.uk/areas/12th-programme.htm

In addition to these programme projects, ministers may refer matters of particular importance to the Commission for its consideration. As was noted in Chapter 1, it was just such a referral by the Home Secretary, after the Macpherson Inquiry into the *Stephen Lawrence* case, that gave rise to the Law Commission's recommendation that the rule against double jeopardy be removed in particular circumstances. An extended version of that recommendation was included in the Criminal Justice Act 2003.

Annual reports list all Commission publications. The Law Commission claims that, in the period since its establishment in 1965, over 100 of its law reports have been implemented. Examples of legislation following from Law Commission reports are: the Contracts (Rights of Third Parties) Act 1999, based on the recommendations of the Commission's Report No 180, *Privity of Contract*; and the Trustee Act 2000, based on the Commission's Report No 260. In February 2002 the Land Registration Act was passed, which has had a major impact on the land registration procedure. The Act implemented the draft Bill which was the outcome of the Commission's largest single project.

Current judicial review procedures are very much the consequence of a 1976 Law Commission report, and a review of their operation and proposals for reform were issued in October 1994.

In the area of criminal law, the preparatory work done by the Commission on several aspects of the criminal justice system (bail, double jeopardy and the revelation of an accused person's bad character) was incorporated into the Criminal Justice Act 2003.

In addition, ss 5 and 6 of the Domestic Violence, Crime and Victims Act 2004 reflect the recommendations of an earlier Commission report. The issue investigated related to situations where a child is non-accidentally killed or seriously injured, and it is apparent that one or more of a limited number of defendants must have committed the crime, but there is no evidence that allows the court to identify which of the defendants actually committed the offence. The Domestic Violence, Crime and Victims Act 2004 also contains provisions reflecting the Commission report relating to the prosecution of people charged with multiple offences.

In August 2004 the Commission published its Report on Partial Defences to Murder, recommending the reform of the defence of provocation, with particular reference to murders committed in the context of domestic violence. That report also included a recommendation that the Home Office undertake a wholesale review of the law of murder, including sentencing regimes, and subsequently in December 2005 the Commission published its proposals for reforming the law of murder, *Bringing the Law of Murder into the 21st Century*. Its initial conclusion was that the current law on murder 'is a mess' and in an attempt to remedy that situation it provisionally recommended that there should be three tiers of homicide:

- In the top tier would be cases where there is an intention to kill. This is the worst category and would retain the mandatory life sentence.

- In the second tier would be cases of killing through reckless indifference to causing death and intention to do serious harm but not to kill. This tier would also include revised versions of provocation, diminished responsibility and duress. The sentence would depend on the details of the case.

- In the third tier (manslaughter) would be cases of killing by gross negligence or intention to cause harm but not serious harm.

In November 2006 the Law Commission published its final report setting out recommendations for reform of the law of homicide proposing the adoption of the three-tier structure, comprising first-degree murder, second-degree murder and manslaughter.

Although the recommendations on partial defences were implemented to a substantial extent in the Coroners and Justice Act 2009, in January 2011 the new government let it be known that it would not implement the remainder of the recommendations on the grounds that the time was not right to take forward such a substantial reform of the criminal law.

The Commission's recommendations in relation to the offence of corporate killing were incorporated in the Corporate Manslaughter and Corporate Homicide Act 2007, and its recommendations on inchoate liability for assisting and encouraging crime were enacted in the Serious Crime Act 2007. Finally, the Commission's report and draft Bill on bribery led to the passing of the Bribery Act 2010, which came into force in July 2011, and its 2013 report on juror misconduct and internet publication informed the provisions in Part 3 of the Criminal Justice and Courts Act 2015 (see 14.8).

Having emphasised the role of the Law Commission as a source of new law, it remains a fact that many of its reports recommending reform remain to be implemented, even though a number of them have been accepted by the government (see Part 3 and Appendix A, Law Commission Annual Report 2014–2015 at http://www.lawcom.gov.uk/document/annual-reports/).

In response to such failure of implementation, a former Law Lord, Lord Lloyd of Berwick, introduced the Law Commission Bill 2008–09 in the House of Lords. In support of the Bill, Lord Kingsland pointed out that: 'Over the years . . . [the Law Commission] has been tasked with many seemingly intractable problems, has grappled with them and produced a solution, only to find that solution spurned by the political classes.'

The resultant Act contains provisions to amend the Law Commissions Act 1965 so as to:

- require the Lord Chancellor to prepare an annual report, to be laid before Parliament, on the implementation of Law Commission proposals;

- require the Lord Chancellor to set out plans for dealing with any Law Commission proposals which have not been implemented and provide the reasoning behind decisions not to implement proposals;

- allow the Lord Chancellor and Law Commission to agree a protocol about the Law Commission's work. The protocol would be designed to provide a framework for the relationship between the UK government and the Law Commission, and the Lord Chancellor would have to lay the protocol before Parliament.

The fourth report on the implementation of Law Commission proposals was published in May 2014. It lists the reports that have been implemented or which are in the process of implementation. It also sets out the two reports which the government has decided should not be legislated. As usual there is a long list of reports waiting for a government decision.

It should also be mentioned that in order to expedite the passage of such legislation, in 2008 the House of Lords Constitution Committee adopted a procedure to quicken the passage of non-controversial Law Commission Bills through the House of Lords and the procedure was adopted fully in 2010.

Mention should also be made of the relatively new Civil Justice Council (CJC), established under the Civil Procedure Act 1997. The remit of this Council, which is made up of a variety of judges, lawyers, academics and those representing the interests of consumers and others, under the chair of the Master of the Rolls, currently Lord Dyson, is to:

- keep the civil justice system under review;
- consider how to make the civil justice system more accessible, fair and efficient;
- advise the Lord Chancellor and the judiciary on the development of the civil justice system;
- refer proposals for change to the civil justice system to the Lord Chancellor and the Civil Procedure Rule Committee;
- make proposals for research.

Given the massive upheaval that resulted from the implementation of Lord Woolf's review of the civil justice system, it is to be hoped that the CJC will function effectively to bring about smaller alterations in the system as soon as they become necessary.

Access to Justice for Litigants in Person (or self-represented litigants)

In November 2011 the Civil Justice Council released a critical report entitled: *Access to Justice for Litigants in Person (or self-represented litigants)*. The report followed an examination of how litigants in person are likely to be affected by reductions to public funding for legal advice and representation, and ways in which public and voluntary bodies could best respond to the challenges arising as a result of this cutback in funding. The working party found that the numbers of litigants representing themselves will increase, giving rise to the fear that:

> Many of them will not know how to bring or defend legal proceedings in the absence of legal advice and representation and will either suffer a reduction in the quality of justice or they will entirely abandon their efforts to enforce or defend their rights or will try to take their cases to court but not do so properly.

The CJC report makes 10 recommendations for immediate action:

1   Improving the accessibility, currency and content of existing online resources;
2   Producing a 'nutshell' guide for self-represented litigants (SRLs);
3   Improving judicial and court services for SRLs;
4   Advice for judges on the availability of legal pro bono services;
5   Guidance for court staff when dealing with SRLs;

6   Guidance for legal professionals, and what SRLs can expect from lawyers;

7   Notice of McKenzie Friends (these are people who volunteer to assist unrepresented parties);

8   Introducing a code of conduct for McKenzie Friends;

9   Freeing up in-house lawyers to provide pro bono services; and

10   A call for leadership from major advice and pro bono agencies across England and Wales to drive collaboration.

The report went on to make recommendations to be addressed in the medium term:

(a)   A systematic review should be undertaken of court leaflets, forms and information, involving consultation with experts in the field;

(b)   Making a primary website available that pulls together and maintains the best independent guidance;

(c)   Increasing the number of courts that offer Personal Support Units and information officers to assist SRLs;

(d)   Producing a user-friendly guide to the Small Claims Court;

(e)   Improving access to legal advice;

(f)   Developing LawWorks' early electronic advice for SRLs and agencies;

(g)   Finding new means of funding the administration of pro bono and other voluntary legal services;

(h)   Offering surgeries and after-hours court information sessions for SRLs;

(i)   Keeping records of numbers and circumstances of SRLs, and ensuring court user committees address their needs; and

(j)   Reviewing the question of access to appeals after refusals by a judge on the 'paper' application.

The Council maintained its consideration for the self-represented litigant in its response to the proposed changes to judicial review. As it stated:

> The Council is particularly concerned that reforms do not have an adverse impact on the ability of self-representing litigants (SRLs) to seek effective access to justice through JR. Reforms could potentially have a disproportionate and adverse effect on SRLs due to the particular issues which they face in obtaining access to the courts. SRLs, specifically, face additional barriers to justice as:
>
> > They are generally unfamiliar with court procedure, how to go about obtaining necessary relevant evidence, how to structure their applications and how to comply with the relevant Pre-Action Protocols;

> A disproportionate number of SRLs do not speak English as a first language, have a protected characteristic under the Equality Act or are vulnerable in some other way (such as for reasons of mental health). Any negative impact on effective access to justice can therefore be exacerbated in the case of such litigants.

Subsequent changes in the state funding of litigation have made the position of litigants in person, and the courts, even more problematic (see, further, 15.2.2).

CHAPTER SUMMARY: SOURCES OF LAW: LEGISLATION

LEGISLATION

Legislation is law produced through the parliamentary system. The government is responsible for most Acts, but individual Members of Parliament do have a chance to sponsor Private Member's Bills. The passage of a Bill through each House of Parliament involves five distinct stages: first reading; second reading; committee stage; report stage; and third reading. It is then given Royal Assent. The Supreme Court only has limited scope to delay legislation.

Among the problems of drafting Acts is the need to reconcile such contradictory demands as brevity and precision. Legislation can be split into different categories: public Acts affect the general public; private Acts relate to particular individuals; consolidation Acts bring various provisions together; codification Acts give statutory form to common law principles; amending Acts alter existing laws, and amendments may be textual, which alters the actual wording of a statute, or non-textual, in which case the operation rather than the wording of the existing law is changed.

STATUTORY INTERPRETATION

This refers to, and follows from, the previous consideration that law does not speak for itself and does not have meaning ascribed to it. That function belongs to the judiciary. However, in giving practical effect to legislation, judges may exercise creative power that rightly belongs to the legislature.

In deciding what meaning to ascribe to legislation, judges tend to adopt either a literal or a purposive approach. These two general approaches are traditionally divided into three supposedly distinct rules:

- the literal rule;
- the golden rule; and
- the mischief rule.

It should be recognised that such rules are not necessarily compatible.

In addition, judges make use of a number of presumptions in relation to the application of legislation.

DELEGATED LEGISLATION

Delegated legislation appears in the form of: Orders in Council; statutory instruments; bylaws; and professional regulations.

The main advantages of delegated legislation relate to: speed of implementation; the saving of parliamentary time; access to expertise; and flexibility.

The main disadvantages relate to: the lack of accountability of those making such law; the lack of scrutiny of proposals for such legislation; and the sheer amount of delegated legislation.

Controls over delegated legislation are: in parliament, the Joint Select Committee on Statutory Instruments; and, in the courts, *ultra vires* provisions may be challenged through judicial review.

LAW REFORM

Law reform in particular areas is considered by various standing committees particularly established for that purpose and Royal Commissions may also be established for such purposes. The Law Commission, however, exists to consider the need for the general and systematic reform of the law.

FOOD FOR THOUGHT

1   In relation to the concept of the separation of powers mentioned in Chapter 2, consider the extent to which Parliament as a whole decides on law. The ideal is of the legislature, the actual Members of Parliament, debating issues in order to produce the best possible legislation. However, is that really the case? Consider where most legislation comes from, who proposes it and who ensures that it is enacted. It has been suggested that the executive controls Parliament through its control of party politics. On that basis, the issue to consider is the extent to which the parliamentary process is just a rubber-stamping exercise for party political programmes.

2   Consider the current structure of the Houses of Parliament, an issue of some contemporary and long-standing debate. In particular, consider the function and membership of the House of Lords. What additional function does it perform over that of the House of Commons and how should its membership be decided?

3   Generally, law applies to everyone and ignorance of the law is no excuse for breaking it. Yet, to most new law students, let alone ordinary members of the public, certain pieces of legislation are almost totally incomprehensible. This raises certain issues for consideration as follows:

Why can legislation not be written in ordinary language?

Who is legislation actually written for?

Why do judges have to interpret legislation?

To what extent is interpretation creation?

4   There is a huge amount of law generated every year and lots of it comes in the form of delegated legislation. To what extent is this just a fact of contemporary political life, or is it a matter of concern?

FURTHER READING

Bates, T, 'The contemporary use of legislative history in the United Kingdom' (1995) 54(1) CLJ 127

Bell, J and Engle, G, *Cross: Statutory Interpretation*, 3rd edn, 1995, London: Butterworths

Bennion, F, 'Statute law: obscurity and drafting parameters' (1978) 5 British JLS 235

Bennion F, *Understanding Common Law Legislation: Drafting and Interpretation,* 2009, Oxford: OUP

Boulton, C (ed), *Erskine May's Treatise on the Law, Privileges, Proceedings and Usage of Parliament*, 1989, London: Butterworths

Committee on the Preparation of Legislation, *Renton Committee Report*, Cmnd 6053, 1975, London: HMSO

Cross, R, *Cross and Harris, Precedent in English Law*, 4th edn, 1991, Oxford: Clarendon

Editorial, 'Disability discrimination: tribunal interprets DDA to cover discrimination by association' (2008) 869 IDS Emp L Brief 3–5

Elliot, M and Perreau-Saussine, A, 'Pyrrhic public law: Bancoult and the sources, status and content of common law limitations on prerogative power' [2009] PL 697–722

Eskridge, W, *Dynamic Statutory Interpretation*, 1994, Cambridge, MA: Harvard UP

Friedman, L, 'On interpretation of laws' (1988) 11(3) Ratio Juris 252

Goodhart, A, 'The *ratio decidendi* of a case' (1959) 22 MLR 117

Holdsworth, W, 'Case law' (1934) 50 LQR 180

Jenkins, C, 'Helping the reader of Bills and Acts' (1999) 149 NLJ 798

Jones, O, *Bennion on Statutory Interpretation*, 6th edn, 2013, LexisNexis

MacCormick, N, *Legal Rules and Legal Reasoning*, 1978, Oxford: Clarendon

Manchester, C and Salter, D, *Exploring the Law: The Dynamics of Precedent and Statutory Interpretation*, 4th edn, 2011, London: Sweet & Maxwell

Masterman, R, 'Interpretations, declarations and dialogue: rights protection under the Human Rights Act and Victorian Charter of Human Rights and Responsibilities' [2009] PL 112–31

Mora, PD, 'The compatibility with art. 10 ECHR of the continued publication of a libel on the Internet: *Times Newspapers Ltd (Nos 1 and 2) v The United Kingdom*' (2009) 20(6) Ent LR 226–8

Simpson, A, 'The *ratio decidendi* of a case' (1957) 20 MLR 413; (1958) 21 MLR 155

Stone, J, 'The Ratio of the Ratio Decidendi' (1959) 22 MLR 597

Watson-Brown, A, 'In search of plain English – the Holy Grail or mythical Excalibur of legislative drafting' (2011) 33(1) Stat LR

USEFUL WEBSITES

www.uk-legislation.hmso.gov.uk/acts.htm
An extensive collection of Acts of Parliament.

www.lawcom.gov.uk
The official website of the Law Commission is a valuable resource because it carries scores of reports that provide very useful critical digests of whole areas of law.

www.legislation.gov.uk
The UK Statute Law database.

www.parliament.uk
The official website of Parliament.

www.hmcourts-service.gov.uk
The official website of Her Majesty's Courts Service.

www.supremecourt.uk
The official website of the Supreme Court.

COMPANION WEBSITE

Now visit the companion website to:

- test your understanding of the key terms using our Flashcard Glossary;
- revise and consolidate your knowledge of 'Sources of law: Legislation' using our Multiple Choice Question testbank;
- view all of the links to the Useful Websites above;
- read further about using cases and legislation in the Legal Skills Guide;
- view a sample exam question and answer on sources of law, taken from the authors' latest Questions & Answers book on The English Legal System.

www.routledge.com/cw/slapper

SOURCES OF LAW: CASE LAW

4

4.1 INTRODUCTION

Case law, or common law, refers to the creation and refinement of law in the course of judicial decisions. The preceding chapter has highlighted the increased importance of legislation in its various guises in today's society but, even allowing for this and the fact that case law can be overturned by legislation, the UK is still a common law system and the importance and effectiveness of judicial creativity and common law principles and practices cannot be discounted and should not be underestimated.

4.2 PRECEDENT

The doctrine of binding precedent, or *stare decisis*, lies at the heart of the English legal system. The doctrine refers to the fact that, within the hierarchical structure of the English courts, a decision of a higher court will be binding on a court lower than it in that hierarchy. In general terms, this means that when judges try cases, they will check to see if a similar situation has come before a court previously. If the precedent was set by a court of equal or higher status to the court deciding the new case, then the judge in the present case should follow the rule of law established in the earlier case. Where the precedent is from a lower court in the hierarchy, the judge in the new case may not follow, but will certainly consider, it. (The structure of the civil courts will be considered in detail in Chapter 6 and that of the criminal courts in Chapter 9.)

4.3 LAW REPORTING

It is apparent that the operation of binding precedent is reliant upon the existence of an extensive reporting service to provide access to previous judicial decisions. This section briefly sets out where one might locate case reports on particular areas of the law. This is of particular importance to counsel, who are under a duty to bring all relevant case authority to the attention of the court, whether it advances their case or not.

- Lloyd's Law Reports (Lloyd's Rep);
- Report on Tax Cases (TC or Tax Cas);
- Criminal Appeal Reports (Cr App R).

European Community reports

Although European cases may appear in the reports considered above, there are two specialist reports relating to EC cases:

- *European Court Reports (ECR)*

  These are the official reports produced by the European Court of Justice (ECJ). As such, they are produced in all the official languages of the Community and consequently suffer from delay in reporting.

- *Common Market Law Reports (CMLR)*

  These are unofficial reports published weekly in English by the European Law Centre.

Reports of the European Court of Human Rights in Strasbourg are provided in the European Human Rights Reports (EHRR).

CD-ROMs and internet facilities

As in most other fields, the growth of information technology has revolutionised law reporting and law finding. Many of the law reports mentioned above are available both on CD-ROM and on the internet. See, for example, Justis, Lawtel, LexisNexis and Westlaw UK, among others. Indeed, members of the public can now access law reports directly from their sources in the courts, both domestically and in Europe. The first major electronic cases database was the Lexis system, which gave immediate access to a huge range of case authorities, some unreported elsewhere. The problem for the courts was that lawyers with access to the system could simply cite lists of cases from the database, without the courts having access to paper copies of the decisions. The courts soon expressed their displeasure at this indiscriminate citation of unreported cases trawled from the Lexis database (see *Stanley v International Harvester Co of Great Britain Ltd* (1983)).

The British and Irish Legal Information Institute (Bailii: www.bailii.org) is a charitable institution which provides online access to cases and legislation in the UK, Ireland and Europe.

Neutral citation

In line with the ongoing modernisation of the whole legal system, the way in which cases are to be cited has been changed. Thus, from January 2001, following *Practice Direction (Judgments: Form and Citation)* [2001] 1 WLR 194, a new neutral system was introduced and extended in the following year in a further Practice Direction in April 2002. Cases in the various courts are now cited as follows:

Supreme Court	[year]	UKSC case no
House of Lords	[year]	UKHL case no
Court of Appeal (Civil Division)	[year]	EWCA Civ case no
Court of Appeal (Criminal Division)	[year]	EWCA Crim case no

High Court

Queen's Bench Division	[year]	EWHC case no (QB)
Chancery Division	[year]	EWHC case no (Ch)
Patents Court	[year]	EWHC case no (Pat)
Administrative Court	[year]	EWHC case no (Admin)
Commercial Court	[year]	EWHC case no (Comm)
Admiralty Court	[year]	EWHC case no (Admlty)
Technology and Construction Court	[year]	EWHC case no (TCC)
Family Division	[year]	EWHC case no (Fam)

Tribunal decisions are now also reported using neutral citation. Thus a case decided by the Upper Tribunal (Administrative Appeals Chamber) would be reported in a similar format:

[year]   UKUT case no (AAC)

Those First-tier Tribunal decisions that are reported (e.g. a Health Education and Social Care case) would be cited:

[year]   UKFTT case no (HESC)

Within an individual case, the paragraphs of each judgment are numbered consecutively, and where there is more than one judgment, the numbering of the paragraphs carries on sequentially. Thus, for example, the neutral citation for the House of Lords' decision in *Jackson v HM Attorney General* considered above at 3.3.2 is [2005] UKHL 56 and the citation for the quotation from Lord Bingham in the case is at paragraph 25. The specific law report series within which the case is reported is cited after the neutral citation; thus, the decision may be found at [2005] 3 WLR 733 or [2005] 4 All ER 1253.

Citing authorities in court

In March 2012, Judge LCJ issued a Practice Direction to clarify the practice and procedure governing the citation of authorities in the Senior Courts of England and Wales. Consequently:

● where a judgment is reported in the Official Law Reports (AC, QB, Ch, Fam) published by the Incorporated Council of Law Reporting for England and Wales, that report must be cited. Other series of reports and official transcripts of judgment may only be used when a case is not reported in the Official Law Reports;

- if a judgment is not, or not yet, reported in the Official Law Reports but it is reported in the Weekly Law Reports (WLR) or the All England Law Reports (All ER), that report should be cited. If the case is reported in both the WLR and the All ER, either report may properly be cited;

- if a judgment is not reported in the Official Law Reports, the WLR or the All ER, but it is reported in any of the authoritative specialist series of reports which contain a headnote and are made by individuals holding a Senior Courts qualification, the specialist report should be cited;

- where a judgment is not reported in any of the reports referred to above, but is reported in other reports, they may be cited;

- where a judgment has not been reported, reference may be made to the official transcript if that is available. Handed-down text of the judgment should not be used, as that may have been subject to late revision after the text was handed down. In any event, an unreported case should not usually be cited unless it contains a relevant statement of legal principle not found in reported authority.

4.4   PRECEDENT WITHIN THE HIERARCHY OF THE COURTS

Supreme Court

Perhaps the most significant change to have taken place in the English legal system in recent times is the replacement of the judicial committee of the House of Lords by the Supreme Court. The Supreme Court began its work on 1 October 2009 and was officially opened by the Queen on 16 October 2009. The court will be considered in much more detail in later chapters, but as the replacement for the House of Lords it now clearly sits at the pinnacle of the English court hierarchy and, as such, its future decisions will have the same effect and binding power as those of its predecessor. Given the novelty of the Supreme Court, with the related lack of actual judgments, the decision has been taken that it would be wrong simply to delete references to the House of Lords and tedious to continually refer to the House of Lords as the House of Lords/Supreme Court. Consequently all future, and indeed previous, references to the House of Lords will be assumed to apply to the Supreme Court. However, it is inescapable that what follows will contain a mixture of the two titles as is considered appropriate. It should also be mentioned that the Supreme Court continues the previous alternative existence of the House of Lords as the distinct institution the Privy Council.

Supreme Court decisions

The decisions of the Supreme Court are binding on all other courts in the legal system, except the Supreme Court itself. The House of Lords was bound by its own previous decisions until it changed this practice in 1966. The old practice had been established in the nineteenth century and was reaffirmed in a famous case in 1898 – *London Tramways Co Ltd v London County Council*. The rationale for the old practice was that decisions of the highest court in the land should be final so that there would be certainty in the law and a finality in litigation.

The rule, however, did not appear to create certainty and had become very rigid by the end of the nineteenth century. The practice was eventually changed in July 1966 when Lord Gardiner, the Lord Chancellor, made a statement on behalf of himself and his fellow Law Lords. This *Practice Statement* [1966] 3 All ER 77 runs as follows:

> Their Lordships regard the use of precedent as an indispensable foundation upon which to decide what is the law and its application to individual cases. It provides at least some degree of certainty upon which individuals can rely in the conduct of their affairs as well as a basis for orderly development of legal rules.
>
> Their Lordships nevertheless recognise that too rigid adherence to precedent may lead to injustice in a particular case and also unduly restrict the proper development of the law. They propose, therefore, to modify their present practice and, while treating former decisions of this House as normally binding, to depart from a previous decision when it appears right to do so.
>
> In this connection they will bear in mind the danger of disturbing retrospectively the basis on which contracts, settlements of property, and fiscal arrangements have been entered into and also the special need for certainty as to the criminal law.
>
> This announcement is not intended to affect the use of precedent elsewhere than in this house.

The current practice enables the Supreme Court to adapt English law to meet changing social conditions and to pay attention to the decisions of superior courts in the Commonwealth. It was also regarded as important at the time that the House of Lords' practice be brought into line with that of superior courts in other countries, like the United States Supreme Court and state supreme courts elsewhere, which are not bound by their own previous decisions. It also has the effect of bringing the practice of the UK's highest domestic court into line with the practice of both the ECJ and the European Court of Human Rights (ECtHR), neither of which is bound by a rigid doctrine of precedent, although in practice they do not wilfully ignore previous decisions they have made. The possibility of the Supreme Court changing its previous decisions is a recognition that law, whether expressed in statutes or cases, is a living, and therefore changing, institution that must adapt to the circumstances in which and to which it applies if it is to retain practical relevance.

Any appellant who intends to ask the Supreme Court to depart from its own previous decision must draw special attention to this in the appeal documents (*Practice Direction (House of Lords: Preparation of Case)* [1971] 1 WLR 534). After 1966, the House used this power quite sparingly and no doubt the Supreme Court will continue this reluctance. It will not refuse to follow its earlier decision merely because that decision was wrong. A material change of circumstances will usually have to be shown.

In *Conway v Rimmer* (1968), the House of Lords unanimously overruled *Duncan v Cammell Laird and Co* (1942) on a question of the discovery of documents. *Duncan v Cammell Laird and Co* concerned the question of whether a plaintiff could get the defendant to disclose documents during wartime, which related to the design of a submarine. *Conway v Rimmer* concerned whether a probationary police officer could insist on getting disclosure of reports written about him by his superintendent. In the earlier case, the House of Lords held that an affidavit sworn by a government minister was sufficient to enable the Crown to claim privilege not to disclose documents in civil litigation, without those documents being inspected by the court. In the later case, their Lordships held that the minister's affidavit was not binding on the court. The second decision held that it is for the court to decide whether or not to order disclosure. This involves balancing the possible prejudice to the state if disclosure is ordered against any injustice that might affect the individual litigant if disclosure is withheld. Today, the minister's affidavit will be considered by the court, but it is no longer the sole determinant of the issue.

In *Herrington v British Railway Board* (1972), the House of Lords overruled *Addie and Sons v Dumbreck* (1929). In the earlier case, the House of Lords had decided that an occupier of premises was only liable to a trespassing child if that child was injured by the occupier intentionally or recklessly. In its later decision, the House of Lords changed the law in line with the changed social and physical conditions since 1929. Their Lordships felt that even a trespasser was entitled to some degree of care, which they propounded as a test of 'common humanity'.

In *R v United Railways of the Havana and Regla Warehouses Ltd* (1961), the House of Lords decided that damages awarded in an English civil case could only be awarded in sterling. The issue came up for reconsideration in 1976, by which time there had been significant changes in foreign exchange conditions, and the instability of sterling at the later date was of much greater concern than it had been in 1961. In the second case, *Miliangos v George Frank (Textiles) Ltd* (1976), the House of Lords overruled the earlier decision, stating that damages could be awarded in other currencies.

In *R v Secretary of State for the Home Department ex p Khawaja* (1983), the House of Lords departed from its own previous decision made two years earlier – *R v Secretary of State for the Home Department ex p Zamir* (1980). The earlier case had put the main burden of proof on an alleged illegal immigrant to show that his detention was not justified. In its decision two years later, the House of Lords expressed the view that the power of the courts to review the detention and summary removal of an alleged illegal immigrant had been too narrowly defined in the 1980 decision. It held that continued adherence to the precedent would involve the risk of injustice and would obstruct the proper development of law.

In *Murphy v Brentwood District Council* (1990), the House of Lords overruled its earlier decision in *Anns v Merton London Borough Council* (1978) on the law governing the liability of local authorities for the inspection of building foundations. In the earlier decision, the House of Lords held that a local authority was under a legal duty to take reasonable care to ensure that the foundations of a building complied with building regulations. The duty was owed to the owner and occupier of the building who had a legal action if the duty was broken. This created a very wide and extensive duty of care for local authorities, which was out of kilter with the development of this area of law (negligence) in relation to other property-like goods. There was considerable academic and judicial resistance to the decision in *Anns*. In overruling it, the House of Lords in *Murphy* cited the reluctance of English law to provide a remedy for pure economic loss, that is, loss that is not consequential upon bodily injury or physical damage.

If a person commits a murder or assists someone to do so under duress, that is, while under threat that unless they kill or help, they themselves will be murdered, should this afford them a legal defence? In *DPP for Northern Ireland v Lynch* (1975), the House of Lords decided that duress was available as a defence to a person who had participated in a murder as an aider and abettor. Twelve years later, the House of Lords overruled that decision. It held in *R v Howe* (1987) that the defence of duress is not available to a person charged with murder or as an aider and abettor to murder. Some people might regard it as unjust that a person who kills, or assists in a killing, while under duress should be so severely punished under the criminal law, but in taking away the defence of duress from murderers and those who assist them, the House of Lords founded its decision partly upon considerations of social policy (it made references to a rising tide of crimes of violence and terrorism that needed a strict response from the law) and a recognition that, where people killed others or assisted in such events while under duress, their conviction could be addressed by other mechanisms, such as the availability of parole and the royal prerogative of mercy.

Another significant example of the House of Lords recognising and accommodating changed circumstances can be seen in *Hall v Simons* (2000), in which it declined to follow the previous authority of *Rondel v Worsley* (1969), which had recognised the immunity of barristers against claims for negligence in their presentation of cases (see below, 16.5.1, for an extended analysis of this case).

In *R v G* (2003) the House of Lords disapproved of Lord Diplock's objective explanation of recklessness in relation to criminal law as stated previously in *R v Caldwell* (1982).

Whether or not the Supreme Court is inclined to be more active than the former House of Lords is a moot point, but it certainly is true that 2015 saw it changing precedents in two significant areas.

Thus *Montgomery v Lanarkshire Health Board (Scotland)* [2015] UKSC 11 saw a change in approach to medical negligence. In *Sidaway v Board of Governors of the Bethlem Royal Hospital* (1985) the House of Lords had no doubt reflected a historically more reverential/paternalistic approach to the medical profession in holding that it was generally a matter for doctors to decide how much patients should be told about their

In *Knauer v Ministry of Justice* (2016) a seven-strong panel of the Supreme Court over-turned two previous House of Lords judgments, *Cookson v Knowles* (1979) and *Graham v Dodds* (1983), in ruling that the multiplier in assessing damages for fatal accident claims should be calculated from the date of the trial, not the date of death. Delivering the judgment of the court, Lord Neuberger and Lady Hale stated the reason for the decision was that:

> Calculating damages for loss of dependency upon the deceased from the date of death, rather than from the date of trial, means that the claimant is suffering a discount for early receipt of the money when in fact that money will not be received until after trial (para 7).

This case is of particular interest in that the judge at first instance, in the High Court, was sympathetic to the claimant's case, which was supported by a Law Commission report on the issue, but recognised that he could not simply ignore the clear precedent set in the House of Lords decisions. He did, however, authorise an a 'leapfrog ' appeal straight to the Supreme Court, which itself was very conscious of the issue of precedent, as its judgment made clear:

> . . . it is important not to undermine the role of precedent in the common law. Even though it appears clear that both the reasoning and conclusion on the point at issue in *Cookson v Knowles* and *Graham v Dodds* were flawed, at least in the light of current practice, it is important that litigants and their advisers know, as surely as possible, what the law is. Particularly at a time when the cost of litigating can be very substantial, certainty and consistency are very precious commodities in the law. If it is too easy for lower courts to depart from the reasoning of more senior courts, then certainty of outcome and consistency of treatment will be diminished, which would be detrimen-tal to the rule of law.
> In our view, therefore, the issue is whether this is a case where this Court should apply the 1966 Practice Statement. In that connection, it is well established that this Court should not refuse to follow an earlier deci-sion of this Court or the House of Lords merely because we would have decided it differently . . . More than that is required, not least because of the desirability of certainty in the law, as just discussed. However, as Lord Bingham said in the same passage, while 'former decisions of the House are normally binding . . . too rigid adherence to precedent may lead to injustice in a particular case and unduly restrict the development of the law'.
> This Court should be very circumspect before accepting an invitation to invoke the 1966 Practice Statement. However, we have no hesitation in concluding that we ought to do so in the present case (paras 21–23).

The jurisprudence of ex turpi causa non oritur actio

In *Jetivia SA v Bilta (UK) Ltd* [2015] UKSC 23 the Supreme Court considered the issue of '*ex turpi causa non oritur actio*', otherwise known as the 'illegality defence'. This term refers to the doctrine which holds that a party cannot pursue a legal remedy if it arises as a result of, or in connection with, their own illegal act. In this instance the Supreme Court had no doubt in holding that, where the directors of a company involve their company in a fraudulent transaction, the *ex turpi* doctrine cannot be used to prevent the company from taking action against those directors. In other words, the fraudulent directors cannot rely on their own wrongdoing to escape liability, as those dishonest acts are not attributable to the company.

The Court's decision in *Jetivia* was unanimous, but the same cannot be claimed for the underlying reasoning in the individual judgments as regards the jurisprudential underpinnings of the *ex turpi* doctrine. However, as the actual decision was on the basis of non-attribution, the detailed and differing considerations of the *ex turpi* doctrine were no more than *obiter dicta*. On the basis of the contradictory explanations of the operation of the doctrine, not only in this but also in previous Supreme Court cases, Lord Neuberger concluded in his judgment that the best course of action would be for an expanded Supreme Court panel to specifically address the doctrine of *ex turpi* as soon as possible. Such a hearing will of course depend on a suitable case arising and being argued as far as the Supreme Court.

The whole issue was considered in an interesting internet article by barrister Ryan S. Deane available at http://www.andrewskurth.com/pressroom-publications-1231.html.

Deane's conclusion was:

> As things stand, the safe bet is that the law underpinning the illegality defence remains as stated in *Tinsley v Milligan*. The decision remains binding authority unless and until the Supreme Court expressly departs from its approach. With the prospect of a final battle involving every member of the Supreme Court, however, it is advisable to wait until the dust settles before a victor in this war about illegality can be declared.

It would be advisable to keep an eye open for future developments in this area.

A case study: The House of Lords, the Practice Statement and the Limitation Act 1980

Under s 2 of the Limitation Act 1980, the general rule is that the period of limitation for an action in tort is six years from the date on which the cause of action accrues.

However, ss 11 to 14 establish a different regime for actions for damages for negligence, nuisance or breach of duty where the damages are in respect of personal injuries. In these latter cases, the limitation period is three years from either the date when the cause of action accrued or the 'date of knowledge' as defined in s 14, whichever is the later. In addition, s 33 gives the court discretion to extend the period within which a claim can be lodged when it appears that it would be equitable to do so. It can be seen that the latter regime is much more liberal than the strictly constrained s 2 procedure, and in recent cases the House of Lords has been required to consider the extent to which the more liberal s 11 regime should be applied. In doing so, however, it has had to consider the extent to which its own previous restrictive judgments should continue to apply or whether it should exercise its powers under the 1966 practice statement in order to overrule those previous authorities.

The first such decision, *Horton v Sadler* (2007), concerned the circumstances under which a court might exercise its discretion to allow an out-of-time claim under s 33 of the Act. In *Walkley v Precision Forgings Ltd* (1979) the House had previously decided that the exercise of such discretion was not possible where a writ had been issued before the limitation period expired, but the action had not been pursued to completion. The reasoning of the court appeared to be that, as the action had actually been started within the limitation period, it could not be argued that it was the limitation period as such that prevented its completion. However, in *Horton v Sadler* the House of Lords revealed the flaw in the earlier reasoning in *Horton*, which had focused on the first action to the exclusion of the later action. In the opinion of the House in *Horton* it was the circumstances of the later case, begun after the expiration of the limitation period, that had to be examined in deciding whether or not the s 33 discretion could be exercised. For that reason, the House of Lords overruled its previous ruling in *Walkley v Precision Forgings Ltd*.

The next issue relating to the operation of the Limitation Act 1980 arose in a series of unrelated cases in which six appellants, all of whom alleged that they had been victims of sexual abuse during their childhood, appealed against decisions of lower courts that their claims were statute-barred under s 2 of the Limitation Act 1980. The cases assumed a level of notoriety in the popular press due to the linked case of *A v Hoare* (2008) in which the defendant had been convicted in 1989 of an attempted rape of the claimant, involving a serious and traumatic sexual assault. He was sentenced to life imprisonment, but in 2004, while still serving his sentence, he won £7 million on the UK national lottery. Subsequently the claimant started proceedings for damages in December 2004.

In each of the cases, the respective judges had been constrained by judicial precedent to follow the previous House of Lords' judgment in *Stubbings v Webb* (1993), which had decided unanimously that s 11 of the Limitation Act 1980 did not apply in cases of deliberate assault, including indecent assault. The House clearly considered that an action for an intentional trespass to the person did not amount to an action for 'negligence, nuisance or breach of duty' within the meaning of s 11(1) of the Act. As a consequence of *Stubbings*, such claimants were subject to the three-year limitation period rather than the more generous provisions in ss 11–14 and s 33 which allowed for claims to be brought out of time if the court considered this was equitable.

In *A v Hoare* the House of Lords, again unanimously, held that *Stubbings v Webb* had been wrongly decided and concluded that ss 11 and 33 of the Limitation Act 1980 did extend to claims for damages in tort arising from trespass to the person, including sexual assault. As Baroness Hale pointed out, it is a common feature of claims for sexual abuse that they are instituted many years after the events complained of and thus very often after a limitation period of six years has passed. To subject such claims to the rigours of s 2 limitations effectively would be to deny access to justice to those who had suffered such abuse.

A's case was remitted to the Queen's Bench Division to decide whether the discretion under s 33 should be exercised in her favour and subsequently, and not very surprisingly, in June 2008 Mr Justice Coulson exercised the s 33 discretion in favour of A.

A subsequent appeal by Hoare to the ECtHR was rejected as inadmissible (*Hoare v UK* (2011)). In rejecting Hoare's argument that the House of Lords had effectively changed the law, retrospectively, the court stated that:

> however clearly drafted a legal provision may be, in any system of law, there is always an inevitable element of judicial interpretation. Equally, there will always be a need for elucidation of doubtful points and for adaptation to changing circumstances.

Perhaps the ultimate irony for Hoare lay in the fact that the ECtHR had previously refused to interfere in the original *Stubbings* case (*Stubbings v UK* (1993)).

Precedent, the Supreme Court and the European Court of Human Rights

The effect of the Human Rights Act on the operation of the doctrine of precedent, and in particular the impact of decisions of the ECtHR on the Supreme Court, has already been mentioned in Chapter 2. Reference may well be made to the stark expression of that relationship made by Lord Rodger in *Secretary of State for the Home Department v AF* (2009), one of the last cases to be heard by the House of Lords:

> Even though we are dealing with rights under a United Kingdom statute, in reality, we have no choice . . . Strasbourg has spoken, the case is closed.

However, a more considered, if no less resigned, expression of the relationship, with the ECtHR being clearly the superior court with its judgments overruling those of the domestic English court, may be found in Lord Hoffmann's pragmatic judgment in the same case. As he put it:

> I agree that the judgment of the European Court of Human Rights ('ECtHR') in *A v United Kingdom* (Application No 3455/05) requires these appeals to be allowed. I do so with very considerable regret, because I think that the

decision of the ECtHR was wrong and that it may well destroy the system of control orders which is a significant part of this country's defences against terrorism. Nevertheless, I think that your Lordships have no choice but to submit. It is true that section 2(1)(a) of the Human Rights Act 1998 requires us only to 'take into account' decisions of the ECtHR. As a matter of our domestic law, we could take the decision in *A v United Kingdom* into account but nevertheless prefer our own view. But the United Kingdom is bound by the Convention, as a matter of international law, to accept the decisions of the ECtHR on its interpretation. To reject such a decision would almost certainly put this country in breach of the international obligation which it accepted when it acceded to the Convention. I can see no advantage in your Lordships doing so.

On replacing the House of Lords, the Supreme Court adopted a more open and self-confident approach to the authority of the ECtHR. Thus in *R v Horncastle* (2009) ([2009] UKSC 14 for reference), one of the earliest cases heard by the newly constituted court, Lord Phillips explained the relationship as follows:

The requirement to 'take into account' the Strasbourg jurisprudence will normally result in the domestic court applying principles that are clearly established by the Strasbourg court. There will, however, be rare occasions where the domestic court has concerns as to whether a decision of the Strasbourg court sufficiently appreciates or accommodates particular aspects of our domestic process. In such circumstances it is open to the domestic court to decline to follow the Strasbourg decision, giving reasons for adopting this course. This is likely to give the Strasbourg court the opportunity to reconsider the particular aspect of the decision that is in issue, so that there takes place what may prove to be a valuable dialogue between the domestic court and the Strasbourg court.

Subsequently, in *Manchester City Council v Pinnock* (2011) ([2011] UKSC 6 for reference), before he became president of the Supreme Court, Lord Neuberger went further in stating that:

This Court is not bound to follow every decision of the ECtHR. Not only would it be impractical to do so: it would sometimes be inappropriate, as it would destroy the ability of the Court to engage in the constructive dialogue with the ECtHR which is of value to the development of Convention law (see e g R v Horncastle (2009)). Of course, we should usually follow a clear and constant line of decisions by the ECtHR: R (Ullah) v Special Adjudicator (2004). But we are not actually bound to do so or (in theory, at least) to follow a decision of the Grand Chamber. As Lord Mance pointed out in Doherty v Birmingham (2009), section 2 of the HRA requires our courts to 'take into account' EurCtHR decisions, not necessarily to follow them. Where, however, there is a clear and constant line of decisions whose effect is not inconsistent with some fundamental substantive or procedural aspect of our law, and whose reasoning does not appear to overlook or misunderstand some argument or point of principle, we consider that it would be wrong for this Court not to follow that line.

Then, as president of the Supreme Court, Lord Neuberger considered the role of judges in human rights jurisprudence in a speech delivered to a conference at the Supreme Court of Victoria, Melbourne, Australia. Perhaps rather disingenuously quoting his own passage in *Pinnock* above as the view of the court, he concluded, surely with an edge of irony, that:

Save where we feel that Strasbourg has misunderstood or misappreciated our common law system, we UK judges have, I suspect, sometimes been too ready to assume that a decision, even a single decision of a section of that court, represents the law according to Strasbourg, and accordingly to follow it. That approach is attributable to our common law attitude to precedent . . . I think that we are beginning to see that the traditional common law approach may not be appropriate, at least to the extent that we should be more ready not to follow Strasbourg chamber decisions.

Such comments by Lord Neuberger not only pre-empted the Conservative Party's legislative proposals to remove the authority of the 'Strasbourg court'(see p 63), but revealed them as nugatory in practice and merely ideological in effect. Interestingly in a subsequent lecture at Bangor University in October 2014, Lord Neuberger also suggested the benefits of a written constitution, which also chimed in with Conservative Party proposals.

Mistakes by the Supreme Court

The following tautology may be applied in relation to the Supreme Court: as the ultimate authority on the law, it says what the law is; and as what it says is the law, it cannot be wrong. However, what happens if the Supreme Court subsequently believes that what it said the law was, was wrong? On rare occasions decisions of

person, not that of a brain-damaged person, as was involved in the case. In the minority, Lord Steyn suggested that the particular characteristics possessed by the defendant must be attributed to the reasonable man.

In two later decisions, the Court of Appeal declined to follow the majority in *Luc Thiet Thuan*, holding that, as the majority decision in that case was in conflict with decisions of the Court of Appeal, the doctrine of precedent required the Court of Appeal to follow its own decisions (see *R v Campbell* (1997) and *R v Parker* (1997)). However, in *R v Smith (Morgan)* (2001) a majority of the House of Lords held that *Luc Thiet Thuan* had been wrongly decided and by a majority of 3:2 held that juries could take account of the personal characteristics of defendants that made them particularly susceptible to losing self-control. As with *Anderton v Ryan*, this decision met with concentrated academic attack and it became generally, if certainly not universally, accepted that the House of Lords had got it wrong. The problem, however, was that no immediate opportunity presented itself for the House of Lords to reverse the decision in *Morgan Smith*. Instead, the Law Lords elected to make use of an appeal to the Privy Council in a case from Jersey, which has its own legal jurisdiction, but with a murder law based on English law. The case was *Attorney General for Jersey v Holley* (2005).

More in recognition of the potential consequences of their actions than the importance of the case *per se*, nine of the total of 12 Law Lords sat on the Privy Council hearing and ruled. As Lord Nicholls, in the majority, stated (para 1):

> The decision of the House in *Morgan Smith* is in direct conflict with the decision of their Lordships' board in *Luc Thiet Thuan v the Queen*. And the reasoning of the majority in the *Morgan Smith* case is not easy to reconcile with the reasoning of the House of Lords in *R v Camplin* . . . *This appeal, being heard by an enlarged board of nine members, is concerned to resolve this conflict and clarify definitively the present state of English law*, and hence Jersey law, on this important subject (emphasis added).

Such an intention was also accepted by the minority, who acknowledged the effect of the majority decision was to clarify the state of English law in relation to the partial defence of provocation. The conclusion, by a majority of six to three, was that the *Morgan Smith* case had been wrongly decided. Thus the Privy Council had made its decision; what remained was to consider the impact of that ruling in relation to the operation of the doctrine of precedent within the English court structure. The opportunity to do so came when the joined appeals in *R v James and R v Karimi* came before the Court of Appeal in January 2006.

The issue before the court was simple: was the Court of Appeal bound to follow the House of Lords' decision in *Morgan Smith*, or was the decision of the Privy Council in *Holley* to be preferred? Once again, a strengthened bench of the Court of Appeal, made up of five rather than the usual three members, indicated the importance of the case. In reaching its decision, the Court of Appeal was extremely sensitive to the manner in which *Holley* had been used as a device for subverting the traditional operation of the doctrine of precedent, but in an exercise of judicial realism it both raised, and dealt with, the central issues relating to precedent; thus per Lord Phillips, Chief Justice, paras 41–42:

> it is not this court, but the Lords of Appeal in Ordinary who have altered the established approach to precedent. There are possible constitutional issues in postulating that a Board of the Privy Council, however numerous or distinguished, is in a position on an appeal from Jersey to displace and replace a decision of the Appellate Committee on an issue of English law. Our principles in relation to precedent are, however, common law principles. Putting on one side the position of the European Court of Justice, the Lords of Appeal in Ordinary have never hitherto accepted that any other tribunal could overrule a decision of the Appellate Committee. Uniquely a majority of the Law Lords have on this occasion decided that they could do so and have done so in their capacity as members of the Judicial Committee of the Privy Council. We do not consider that it is for this court to rule that it was beyond their powers to alter the common law rules of precedent in this way.
>
> The rule that this court must always follow a decision of the House of Lords and, indeed, one of its own decisions rather than a decision of the Privy Council is one that was established at a time when no tribunal other than the House of Lords itself could rule that a previous decision of the House of Lords was no longer good law. *Once one postulates that there are circumstances in which a decision of the Judicial Committee of the Privy Council can take precedence over a decision of the House of Lords, it seems to us that this court must be bound in those circumstances to prefer the decision of the Privy Council to the prior decision of the House of Lords.* That, so it seems to us, is the position that has been reached in the case of these appeals (emphasis added).

As a consequence of the preceding cases it is now apparent that the Privy Council can in exceptional circumstances overrule precedents of the House of Lords. According to the Court of Appeal in *James*, those exceptional circumstances arose as a result of the following attributes in the case:

- All nine of the Lords of Appeal in Ordinary sitting in *Holley* agreed in the course of their judgments that the result reached by the majority clarified definitively English law on the issue in question.

- The majority in *Holley* constituted half the Appellate Committee of the House of Lords. We do not know whether there would have been agreement that the result was definitive had the members of the Board divided five/four.

- In the circumstances, the result of any appeal on the issue to the House of Lords is a foregone conclusion.

It might not be over-cynical to suggest that such 'exceptional' circumstances will occur as and when the Justices of the Supreme Court (a) agree with advocates who in a case make such a suggestion, and (b) deem it desirable to change the law in such a case. It certainly cannot be denied that the decisions in *Holley* and *James* fundamentally alter the previous understanding of the way in which the doctrine of precedent operates within the English legal system and affords the Justices of the Supreme Court a second way of altering their previous decisions in addition to the Practice Statement of 1966.

The Court of Appeal

In civil cases, the Court of Appeal is generally bound by previous decisions of the House of Lords. Although the Court of Appeal, notably under the aegis of Lord Denning, attempted on a number of occasions to escape from the constraints of *stare decisis*, the House of Lords repeatedly reasserted the binding nature of its decisions on the Court of Appeal. The House of Lords emphasised the balance between the need for certainty in the law against the need to permit scope for the law to develop, and in so doing, it asserted its function, as the court of last resort at the head of the hierarchy, to undertake necessary reform. The relationship between and functions of the House of Lords and the Court of Appeal was clearly stated by Lord Diplock in *Davis v Johnson* [1978] 1 All ER 1132 at 1137–38:

> In an appellate court of last resort a balance must be struck between the need on the one side for legal certainty resulting from the binding effect of previous decisions and on the other side the avoidance of undue restriction on the proper development of law. In the case of an intermediate appellate court, however, the second desideratum can be taken care of by an appeal to a superior court, if reasonable means of access to it are available; while the risk to the first desideratum, legal certainty, if the court is not bound by its own previous decisions grows ever greater with increasing membership and the number of three-judge divisions in which it sits . . . So the balance does not lie in the same place as the court of last resort.

The decision to be taken by the Court of Appeal when faced with conflicting precedents from the Supreme Court and the Privy Council has been considered previously. The more general relationship between the Court of Appeal and the Privy

Council was clarified by Lord Neuberger MR in *Sinclair Investments (UK) Ltd v Versailles Trade Finance Ltd* (2011). In explaining the situation of the Court of Appeal he stated:

> We should not follow the Privy Council decision . . . in preference to decisions of this court, unless there are domestic authorities which show that the decisions of this court were *per incuriam*, or at least of doubtful reliability. Save where there are powerful reasons to the contrary, the Court of Appeal should follow its own previous decisions . . . It is true that there is a powerful subsequent decision of the Privy Council which goes the other way, but that of itself is not enough to justify departing from the earlier decisions of this court. . . . I do not suggest that it would always be wrong for this court to refuse to follow a decision of the Privy Council in preference to one of its own previous decisions, but the general rule is that we follow our previous decisions, leaving it to the Supreme Court to overrule those decisions if it is appropriate to do so. Two recent cases where this court preferred to follow a decision of the Privy Council rather than an earlier domestic decision which would normally be regarded as binding (in each case a decision of the House of Lords) are *R v James* and *Abou-Rahmah v Abacha*. In each case, the decision was justified, based as it was on the proposition that it was a foregone conclusion that, *if the case had gone to the House of Lords, they would have followed the Privy Council decision* (paras 72–74, emphasis added).

However, as has been seen in section 2.5.1.2 above, the Court of Appeal in *Mendoza v Ghaidan* (2002) used s 4 of the HRA to extend the rights of same-sex partners to inherit a statutory tenancy under the Rent Act 1977. In so doing, it extended the earlier decision of the House of Lords in *Fitzpatrick v Sterling Housing Association Ltd* (1999), which had been decided before the HRA came into force. Thus, it can be seen that the HRA gives the Court of Appeal latitude to effectively overrule decisions of the House of Lords which were decided before the HRA came into effect and in conflict with the ECHR.

See also the reasoning of the Court of Appeal in *D v East Berkshire Community NHS Trust* (2004) in which the Court of Appeal held that the decision of the House of Lords in *X (Minors) v Bedfordshire County Council* (1995) could not be maintained after the introduction of the Human Rights Act 1998, as that Act had undermined the policy consideration that had largely dictated the House of Lords' decision. That approach was directly approved in *Kay v London Borough of Lambeth* (2005) (see below).

Similarly, decisions of the ECJ, which effectively overrule previous decisions of the House of Lords, will also be followed by the Court of Appeal.

The Court of Appeal generally is also bound by its own previous decisions in civil cases. There are, however, a number of exceptions to this general rule. Lord Greene MR listed these exceptions in *Young v Bristol Aeroplane Co Ltd* (1944):

- Where there is a conflict between two previous decisions of the Court of Appeal. In this situation, the later court must decide which decision to follow and, as a corollary, which to overrule. Such a situation arose in *Tiverton Estates Ltd v Wearwell Ltd* (1974). In that case, which dealt with the meaning of s 40 of the Law of Property Act 1925 (subsequently repealed), the court elected to follow older precedents rather than follow the inconsistent decision in *Law v Jones* (1974). The decision in *Tiverton Estates Ltd v Wearwell Ltd* can be justified as the mere working out of the rules of precedent. As *Law v Jones* must have been made in ignorance of, or based on a failure to properly understand, the earlier decisions (see *per incuriam*, below), it could have been ignored on that ground alone. However, this particular exception is wider than that, in that it allows the current Court of Appeal to choose between the previous conflicting authorities. Hence, the Court of Appeal could have decided to follow *Law v Jones* if it preferred.

- Where a previous decision of the Court of Appeal has been overruled, either expressly or impliedly, by the House of Lords. An express overruling would obviously occur where the House of Lords actually considered the Court of Appeal precedent, but it is equally possible that the *ratio* in a precedent from the Court of Appeal could be overruled without the actual case being cited and considered. In this situation, the Court of Appeal, in line with the normal rules of precedent, is required to follow the decision of the House of Lords. Thus, in *Family Housing Association v Jones* (1990), the Court of Appeal felt obliged to ignore its own precedents on the distinction between a licence and a tenancy in property law where, although they had not been expressly overruled, they were implicitly in conflict with later decisions of the House of Lords in *AG Securities Ltd v Vaughan* (1988) and *Street v Mountford* (1985).

- Where the previous decision was given *per incuriam* or, in other words, that previous decision was taken in ignorance of some authority, either statutory or case law, that would have led to a different conclusion. In this situation, the later court can ignore the previous decision in question. It is important to emphasise, however, that the missing authority must be such that it must have led to a different conclusion; the mere possibility is not enough. There are so many case authorities that it is simply not possible to cite all of them. However, the essential authorities, those that lead to a particular decision, must be considered. It is the absence of any such of these authorities that renders a decision *per incuriam*. As will be appreciated, the instances of decisions being ignored on the basis of a ruling of *per incuriam* are 'of the rarest occurrence' (*Morelle Ltd v Wakeling* (1955)). One example, however, may be seen in *Williams v Fawcett* (1985), in which the Court of Appeal did find such exceptional circumstances as would permit it to treat its previous decisions as having been made *per incuriam*. The facts of the case involved an appeal against a decision to commit a person to prison for contempt of court in breaching a non-molestation order. Previous decisions of the Court of Appeal had held that any such committal order had to be signed by the court officer who issued it. However, the present court found that the law as stated in the Criminal Court Rules did not allow for appeal simply on the grounds that the order was not signed by a proper officer as long as the seal of the court was applied. Of crucial importance among the circumstances that led to the finding of *per incuriam* in relation to the earlier decisions was the fact that, given the expense involved, the case would be unlikely to go to the House of Lords for its final determination of the legal situation. It should be noted that this justification can be seen to fit with the previous quotation from Lord Diplock in *Davis v Johnson*, to the extent that the Court of Appeal decided that, in this instance, there was no 'reasonable means of access to' the court of last resort. A similar justification for another finding of *per incuriam* can be found in *Rickards v Rickards* (1989), in which the Court of Appeal held that its previous decision in *Podberry v Peak* (1981) had misunderstood and wrongly applied the House of Lords' decision in *Laine v Eskdale* (1891). In overruling *Podberry*, the court held that it had the power to hear an appeal against a refusal to extend the time limit within which a person could appeal against the award of a lump sum in a clean-break divorce settlement. The court once again held that as the issue involved was so serious, and as it was unlikely to go to the House of Lords, then the Court of Appeal should itself remedy the earlier misunderstanding stated in its own previous decision. An interesting example of the principle can be found in *R (on the Application of W) v Lambeth LBC* (2002), in which the Court of Appeal overruled its earlier judgment of only six months previously in *R (A) v Lambeth LBC* (2001) as regards the interpretation and effect of s 17 of the Children Act 1989. The matter of interest is not so much that the later court held that the earlier one would have reached a different conclusion had the law been fully explained to it, but that one of the judges in the unanimous decision in *R (W) v Lambeth LBC* was Laws LJ, who had delivered a minority judgment to the same effect in *R (A) v Lambeth LBC*.

There used to be a further exception to the general rule that the Court of Appeal was bound by its own earlier decisions and that was in relation to an interlocutory or interim decision made by a panel of only two judges (*Boys v Chaplin* (1968)); even interim decisions by a full panel of three judges were still binding. However, as a consequence of the Woolf reforms and under the Civil Procedure Rules 1998, the distinction between interlocutory and final appeals was removed. Consequently, it was held in *Cave v Robinson, Jarvis and Rolf* (2002) that the decision in *Boys v Chaplin* was no longer sustainable, although the Court of Appeal stated that it might be possible to adjust the reasoning in *Boys v Chaplin* where the later court was satisfied that the earlier decision of the two-person court was 'manifestly wrong'.

Although on the basis *of R v Spencer* (1985) it would appear that there is no difference in principle between the operation of the doctrine of *stare decisis* between the criminal and civil divisions of the Court of Appeal, it is generally accepted that in

His conclusion, with which the other members of the judicial panel concurred, was equally forthright in maintaining the integrity of the existing structure of binding precedent within the domestic hierarchical structure (para 43):

> . . . certainty is best achieved by adhering, even in the Convention context, to our rules of precedent. It will of course be the duty of judges to review Convention arguments addressed to them, and if they consider a binding precedent to be, or possibly to be, inconsistent with Strasbourg authority, they may express their views and give leave to appeal, as the Court of Appeal did here. Leap-frog appeals may be appropriate. In this way, in my opinion, they discharge their duty under the 1998 Act. But they should follow the binding precedent . . .

However, Lord Bingham did allow for one *exceptional* set of circumstances. As previously mentioned, he and the other members of the House of Lords specifically acknowledged that in such circumstances as occurred in *D v East Berkshire Community NHS Trust*, where the previous authority had been set without reference to the Human Rights Act, the Court of Appeal would be at liberty to avoid following the previous decision of the House of Lords.

Subsequently, in its judgment in *McCann v United Kingdom* (2008), the ECtHR disagreed with the majority of the House of Lords in *Kay* (2005), holding that *Connors* (2004) was not confined to cases involving the eviction of travellers, nor was it limited to cases where the applicant was seeking to challenge the law itself rather than its application or procedure in a particular case. However, in *Doherty v Birmingham City Council* the House of Lords decided that the basic rule in this area remained as laid down by the majority in *Qazi v Harrow* (2004) and reaffirmed by the majority in *Kay*. Although in *McCann* the European Court of Human Rights had endorsed the reasoning of the minority in *Kay*, the House of Lords in *Doherty* decided that the approach of the ECtHR could best be implemented by applying and developing the reasoning of the majority, rather than the minority, view expressly supported by the ECtHR.

In September 2010, when the *Kay* case reached the ECtHR, that court followed its own reasoning in *McCann* and reasserted its preference for the minority opinions in the House of Lords' judgments in *Kay*. The ECtHR judgment in *Kay* was handed down while the House of Lords was hearing another case relating to the same issue in *Manchester City Council v Pinnock*. The ECtHR's *Kay* decision was actually handed down after the oral hearing of the *Pinnock* case and the House of Lords asked for written submissions on its effect. The judgment of the House of Lords was delivered by Lord Neuberger, who was still sitting as a member of that court before taking up his position as Master of the Rolls and represents a falling in line, if ever so slightly hesitantly, with the jurisprudence of the ECtHR:

48. This Court is not bound to follow every decision of the ECtHR. Not only would it be impractical to do so: it would sometimes be inappropriate, as it would destroy the ability of the Court to engage in the constructive dialogue with the ECtHR which is of value to the development of Convention law. Of course, we should usually follow a clear and constant line of decisions by the ECtHR. But we are not actually bound to do so or (in theory, at least) to follow a decision of the Grand Chamber. As Lord Mance pointed out in *Doherty v Birmingham* [2009] 1 AC 367, para 126, section 2 of the HRA requires our courts to 'take into account' ECtHR decisions, not necessarily to follow them. Where, however, there is a clear and constant line of decisions whose effect is not inconsistent with some fundamental substantive or procedural aspect of our law, and whose reasoning does not appear to overlook or misunderstand some argument or point of principle, we consider that it would be wrong for this Court not to follow that line.

49. In the present case there is no question of the jurisprudence of the ECtHR failing to take into account some principle or cutting across our domestic substantive or procedural law in some fundamental way. That is clear from the minority opinions in *Harrow v Qazi* [2004] 1 AC 983 and *Kay v Lambeth* [2006] 2 AC 465, and also from the fact that our domestic law was already moving in the direction of the European jurisprudence in *Doherty v Birmingham* [2009] 1 AC 367. *Even before the decision in* Kay v UK *(App no 37341/06), we would, in any event, have been of the opinion that this Court should now accept and apply the minority view of the House of Lords in those cases. In the light of* Kay, *that is clearly the right conclusion.*

Therefore, if our law is to be compatible with Article 8, where a court is asked to make an order for possession of a person's home at the suit of a local authority, the court must have the power to assess the proportionality of making the order, and, in making that assessment, to resolve any relevant dispute of fact (emphasis added).

High Court Divisional Courts

The Divisional Courts, each located within the three divisions of the High Court, hear appeals from courts and tribunals below them in the hierarchy. They are bound by the doctrine of *stare decisis* in the normal way and must follow decisions of Supreme Court and the Court of Appeal. In turn, they bind the courts below them in the hierarchy, including those dealing with ordinary High Court cases. The Divisional Courts are also normally bound by their own previous decisions, although in civil cases, they may make use of the exceptions open to the Court of Appeal in *Young v Bristol Aeroplane Co Ltd* (1944) and, in criminal appeal cases and cases relating to judicial review, the Queen's Bench Divisional Court may refuse to follow its own earlier decisions where it feels the decision to have been made wrongly.

In *R v Greater Manchester Coroner ex p Tal* (1984), the Divisional Court held that it had supervisory jurisdiction in relation to coroners' courts, although this was contrary to its previous decision in *R v Surrey Coroner ex p Campbell* (1982). In so doing, the court stated that its power to depart from its previous decisions was conferred under the Senior Courts Act 1981, but it also held, on the basis of the House of Lords' decision in *O'Reilly v Mackman* (1982), that *Campbell* had wrongly applied *Anisminic v Foreign Compensation Commission* (1969). *Tal*, therefore, may also be seen as an example of the normal exceptions in *Young v Bristol Aeroplane Co Ltd*.

In *R v Stafford Justices ex p Commissioners of Customs and Excise* (1990), the Queen's Bench Divisional Court held that its previous decision in *R v Ealing Justices ex p Dixon* (1990) had been wrongly decided. Both cases related to the rights to undertake prosecutions where individuals had been charged, as required under s 37 of the Police and Criminal Evidence Act (PACE) 1984, by the police. Contrary to the *Ealing Justices* case, the Divisional Court in the *Stafford Justices* case held that merely being charged by the police did not require that the police should pursue the prosecution and that Customs and Excise could undertake the prosecution. In a similar case, although this time relating to the powers of the Inland Revenue to undertake prosecutions on indictment without the consent of the Attorney General, the Divisional Court approved the *Stafford Justices* decision and stated clearly that the *Ealing Justices* case should no longer be followed (*R v Criminal Cases Review Commission ex p Hunt* (2001)).

The House of Lords implicitly approved the Divisional Court's power to overrule its own previous decisions in *DPP v Butterworth* (1994). This case was the culmination of a number of cases relating to the refusal to provide a breath specimen contrary to s 7(6) of the Road Traffic Act 1988. In *DPP v Corcoran* (1993), a Divisional Court held that where a person was not informed for which of two potential offences he was being required to provide a specimen, any prosecution was undermined for duplicity. However, in *DPP v Shaw* (1993), a differently constituted Divisional Court subsequently held that *Corcoran* was wrongly decided and was an example of a *per incuriam* decision. *Shaw* rather than *Corcoran* was followed in the later Divisional Court decision in *DPP v Butterworth*. That decision was expressly approved by the House of Lords.

High Court

The High Court is also bound by the decisions of superior courts. Decisions by individual High Court judges are binding on courts inferior in the hierarchy, but such decisions are not binding on other High Court judges, although they are of strong persuasive authority and tend to be followed in practice. The simple reason for this is that different judgments would lead to confusion in relation to exactly how the particular law in question was to be understood. It is possible, however, for High Court judges to disagree and for them to reach different conclusions as to the law in a particular area. The question then becomes, how is a later High Court judge to select which precedent to follow? It is usually accepted, although it is not a rule of law, that where the later decision has actually considered the previous one and has provided cause for not following it, then that is the judgment which later High Court judges should follow (*Colchester Estates v Carlton Industries plc* (1984)).

Conflicting decisions at the level of the High Court can, of course, be authoritatively decided by reference upwards to the Court of Appeal and then, if necessary, to the Supreme Court, but when the cost of such appeals is borne in mind, it is apparent why, even on economic grounds alone, it is important for High Court judges not to treat their discretion as a licence to destabilise the law in a given area.

In relation to conflicting judgments at the level of the Court of Appeal, the High Court judge is required to follow the later decision.

Crown Courts cannot create precedent and their decisions can never amount to more than persuasive authority.

County Courts and magistrates' courts do not create precedents.

4.5 BINDING PRECEDENT

Not everything in a case report sets a precedent. The contents of a report can be divided into two categories:

- *Ratio decidendi*

  It is important to establish that it is not the actual decision in a case that sets the precedent; that is set by the rule of law on which the decision is founded. This rule, which is an abstraction from the facts of the case, is known as the *ratio decidendi* of the case. The *ratio decidendi* (Latin for 'reason for deciding') of a case may be understood as the statement of the law applied in deciding the legal problem raised by the concrete facts of the case.

- *Obiter dictum*

  This phrase is Latin for 'a statement by the way'. Any statement of law that is not an essential part of the *ratio decidendi* is, strictly speaking, superfluous, and any such statement is referred to as an *obiter dictum* (*obiter dicta* in the plural), that is, said 'by the way'. Although *obiter dicta* do not form part of the binding precedent, they are persuasive authority and can be taken into consideration in later cases if the judge in the later case considers it appropriate to do so.

The division of cases into these two distinct parts is a theoretical procedure. Unfortunately, judges do not actually separate their judgments into the two clearly defined categories, and it is for the person reading the case to determine what the *ratio* is. In some challenge a politically supreme parliament would be unwise to say the least. It is for that reason that the courts on occasion take refuge behind the cloak of a naïve declaratory theory of law.

4.8   THE PRACTICAL IMPORTANCE OF PRECEDENT

The foregoing has set out the doctrine of binding precedent as it operates in theory to control and indeed limit the ambit of judicial discretion. It has to be recognised, however, that the doctrine does not operate as stringently as it appears at first sight and that there are particular shortcomings in the system that have to be addressed in weighing up the undoubted advantages with the equally undoubted disadvantages.

Nonetheless, the practical importance of the doctrine of precedent can be seen in the history of three conjoined cases, *Fairchild v Glenhaven Funeral Services Ltd and Others* (2002).

The cases related to claims for compensation for injury – mesothelioma, a terminal lung disease caused by the exposure of workers to asbestos fibre – during the course of their working lives with more than one employer. Both the High Court and the Court of Appeal held that the claimants' cases could not succeed, as they could not prove which exposure to asbestos fibre had actually caused the resultant disease. As they could not prove which employer was at fault, no employer could be held liable.

Only a matter of days before the House of Lords was due to hear the appeal, a consortium of insurance companies, which would have had to provide any recompense in the final analysis, offered to settle the present cases on a voluntary basis and set up a compensation scheme for the hundreds of other claimants who were waiting for the outcome of those cases. The point, however, was that the payments to be made would have been significantly less than would have been awarded if the claimants won their case in the House of Lords. The insurers decided that they would rather not risk an adverse decision in the House of Lords, and actually told the Lords' judicial office that the settlement had been reached, thus removing the need to hear the final appeal. In reality, no such settlement had been reached.

The representative of the claimants stated that the settlement scheme was a 'sordid attempt to manipulate the judicial process, the whole objective [being] to ensure that the Court of Appeal's decision remains intact'. The representative of the insurers stated that it was 'not cynical – it was practical'. Lord Bingham, the senior judge in the House of Lords, stated that the episode had been 'entirely regrettable'.

When the cases subsequently came before the House of Lords, the fears of the insurance companies were proved justified by that court overruling the decision of the Court of Appeal, thus laying the insurers open to significantly more liability than they would have had to meet under their voluntary scheme.

It has to be admitted, however, that this sort of manoeuvring also occurs in relation to trade union and other civil rights cases, where the specialist lawyers who deal with such issues attempt to ensure that potentially ground-breaking issues are argued in relation to relatively stronger cases rather than very weak ones. The practicality is that once a positive precedent, the legal rule, is established in the strong case, it can be extended into

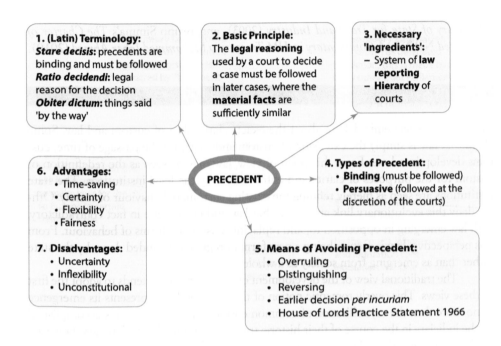

1. **(Latin) Terminology:**
Stare decisis: precedents are binding and must be followed
Ratio decidendi: legal reason for the decision
Obiter dictum: things said 'by the way'

2. **Basic Principle:**
The **legal reasoning** used by a court to decide a case must be followed in later cases, where the **material facts** are sufficiently similar

3. **Necessary 'Ingredients':**
– System of **law reporting**
– **Hierarchy** of courts

PRECEDENT

4. **Types of Precedent:**
• **Binding** (must be followed)
• **Persuasive** (followed at the discretion of the courts)

6. **Advantages:**
• Time-saving
• Certainty
• Flexibility
• Fairness

7. **Disadvantages:**
• Uncertainty
• Inflexibility
• Unconstitutional

5. **Means of Avoiding Precedent:**
• Overruling
• Distinguishing
• Reversing
• Earlier decision *per incuriam*
• House of Lords Practice Statement 1966

FIGURE 4.1 *Precedent: an aide-mémoire.*

a wider area. It would, however, be much more difficult to overturn a contrary precedent handed down in a weak case.

4.9   BOOKS OF AUTHORITY

When a court is unable to locate a precise or analogous precedent, it may refer to legal textbooks for guidance. Such books are subdivided, depending on when they were written. In strict terms, only certain works are actually treated as authoritative sources of law. Among the most important of these works are those by Glanvill from the twelfth century, Bracton from the thirteenth century, Coke from the seventeenth century and Blackstone from the eighteenth century. When cases such as *R v R* are borne in mind, it might be claimed, with justification, that the authority of such ancient texts may be respected more in the breach than in the performance. Given the societal change that has occurred in the intervening time, one can only say that such a refusal to fetishise ancient texts is a positive, and indeed necessary, recognition of the need for law to change in order to keep up with its contemporary sphere of operation. Legal works produced after Blackstone's *Commentaries* of 1765 are considered to be of recent origin, and they cannot be treated as authoritative sources. The courts, however, will look at the most eminent works by accepted experts in particular fields in order to help determine what the law is or should be. See, for example, the citation of Shetreet's *Judges on Trial*, and De Smith, Wolf and Jowell, *Judicial Review of Administrative Action*, in Lord Browne-Wilkinson's decision in *Re Pinochet* (1999), Bennion's *Statutory Interpretation* in *Wilson* the EU as anything other than an economic market and objected to, and resiled from, various provisions aimed at social, as opposed to economic, affairs. Thus, the UK was able to opt out of the Social Chapter of the Treaty of Maastricht. The New Labour administration in the UK had no such reservations and, as a consequence, the Treaty of Amsterdam 1997 incorporated the European Social Charter into the EC Treaty which, of course, applies to the UK (see below).

As the establishment of the single market within the European Community (EC), as the EEC became, progressed, it was suggested that its operation would be greatly facilitated by the adoption of a common currency, or at least a more closely integrated monetary system. Thus, in 1979, the European Monetary System (EMS) was established, under which individual national currencies were valued against a nominal currency called the ECU and allocated a fixed rate within which they were allowed to fluctuate to a limited extent. Britain was a member of the EMS until 1992, when financial speculation against the pound forced its withdrawal. Nonetheless, other members of the EC continued to pursue the policy of monetary union, now entitled European Monetary Union (EMU), and January 1999 saw the installation of the new European currency, the Euro, which has now replaced national currencies within what is now known as the Eurozone. The UK did not join the EMU at its inception and there is little chance that membership will appear on the political agenda for the foreseeable future, especially given the financial crisis that is enveloping many of the EMU states, particularly those on the periphery of the EU. It remains to be seen whether the ongoing financial crisis results in the break-up of the EMU, or its strengthening, as the current members may be forced to seek more economic unity to address its consequences.

Treaty of Nice

In December 2000 the European Council met in Nice in the south of France. The Council consists of the heads of state or government of the member countries of the EU, and is the body charged with the power to make amendments to EU treaties (see below). The purpose of the meeting was to prepare the Union for expansion from its then 15 to 25 members by the year 2004, and so to its current 28 members. New members ranged from the tiny Malta with a population of 370,000 to Poland with its population of almost 39 million people. In order to accommodate this large expansion, it was recognised that significant changes had to be made in the institutions of the current Union, paramount among those being the weighting of the voting power of the Member states. Although parity was to be maintained between Germany, France, Italy and the UK at the new level of 29 votes, Germany and any two of the other largest countries gained a blocking power on further changes, as it was accepted that no changes, even on the basis of a qualified majority vote, could be introduced in the face of opposition from countries constituting 62 per cent of the total population of the Union. The recognition of such veto power was seen as a victory for national as against supranational interests within the Union and a significant defeat for the Commission. However, the number of matters subject to qualified majority voting was increased, although a number of countries, including the UK, refused to give up their veto with regard to the harmonisation of national and corporate tax rates. Nor would the UK, this time supported by Sweden, agree to give up the veto in relation to social security policy. Core immigration was another area in which the UK government retained its ultimate veto (see 5.3.1 for current voting power).

At the same time as these changes were introduced, the members of the Council of Europe also signed a new Charter of Fundamental Rights. Among the rights recognised by the charter are included:

- right to life;
- respect for private and family life;
- protection of family data;
- right to education;
- equality between men and women;
- fair and just working conditions;
- right to collective bargaining and industrial action;
- right not to be dismissed unjustifiably.

It is significant that the charter was not included within the specific Treaty issues at Nice, at the demand of the UK. The UK had also ensured that some of the references, particularly to employment matters, were subject to reference to domestic law.

Lisbon Treaty

Although the Treaty of Nice was difficult and time-consuming in its formation, it looked for some time as though its terms would be replaced before they had actually come into effect. This possibility came about as a result of the conclusions of the *Convention on the Future of Europe*, which was constituted in February 2002 by the then members to consider the establishment of a European Constitution. The Convention, which sat under the presidency of the former President of France, Valéry Giscard d'Estaing, produced a draft constitution, which it was hoped would provide a more simple, streamlined and transparent procedure for internal decision-making within the Union and to enhance its profile on the world stage. Among the proposals for the new constitution were the following:

- the establishment of a new office of President of the European Union;
- the appointment of an EU foreign minister;
- the shift to a two-tier Commission;
- fewer national vetoes;
- increased power for the European Parliament;
- simplified voting power;
- the establishment of an EU defence force by 'core members';
- the establishment of a charter of fundamental rights.

In the months of May and June 2005 the move towards the European Constitution came to a juddering halt when first the French and then the Dutch electorates voted against its implementation. Such a signal failure meant that it was not necessary for the UK government to conduct a referendum on the proposed constitution as it had promised. However, as with most EU initiatives, the new constitution did not disappear and re-emerged as the Treaty of Lisbon, signed by all the members in December 2007. Once again the UK government, together with the Polish one, insisted that a protocol, number 7, be appended to the treaty ensuring that the charter of fundamental rights could not create new rights in the UK. The Lisbon Treaty gave rise to much ill-feeling in many states for the reason that it incorporated most of the proposals originally contained in the previously rejected constitutional proposal. In legal form, the Lisbon Treaty merely amended the existing treaties, rather than replacing them as the previous constitution had proposed. In practical terms, however, all the essential changes that would have been delivered by the constitution were contained in the treaty – a fact widely recognised by some EU leaders, although not the UK's. Thus Angela Merkel, Chancellor of Germany, was quoted in June 2007 in the *Daily Telegraph* as saying, 'The substance of the Constitution is preserved. That is a fact', and Valéry Giscard d'Estaing, Chairman of the Convention on the Future of Europe which drafted the Constitution was quoted, in a European Parliament press release on 17 July 2007, as saying, 'In terms of content, the proposals remain largely unchanged, they are simply presented in a different way . . . This text is, in fact, a rerun of a great part of the substance of the Constitutional Treaty.'

1. The Council of Europe:
– Set up in 1947 by European states following WWII, to protect human rights. It should be emphasised that this body is totally separate from the European Union
– Enacted the **European Convention on Human Rights**, of which the UK is a signatory but which the UK has never fully incorporated into national law
– **This body should not be confused with the European Council or the Council of the European Union**

2. The European Court of Human Rights:
– Established by the Council of Europe to enforce the rights contained in the European Convention on Human Rights
– Following the enactment of the Human Rights Act in the UK, the decisions of this court now have to be considered by our national courts
– **This court should not be confused with the Court of Justice of the European Union (CJEU)**

3. The European Union (EU):
– Originally known as the European Economic Community (EEC) when established by the Treaty of Rome 1957, it was created in order to ensure peace in Europe through economic integration of its Member States
– The EEC was subject to a change of name following the Treaty on European Union, 1992 (TEU or Maastricht Treaty) after which it became known as the European Community (EC)
– The TEU also created the European Union (EU) of which the EC was a component part
– Since the enactment of the Lisbon Treaty in 2009, the EC no longer exists and all references should now be to the EU
– The UK became a member in 1973, after the enactment of the **European Communities Act 1972**

WHO'S WHO IN THE EUROPEAN CONTEXT

FIGURE 5.1 *Who's Who in the European Context.*

As a matter of interest and political significance, most member countries decided to ratify the new treaty through their legislatures rather than by hazarding it in a referendum, a decision that caused much discontent in many countries. In the UK, the government declined to have a referendum on the basis of the, not totally convincing, suggestion that the treaty was simply an amendment and a tidying-up measure and consequently did not need the confirmation of a referendum in the way necessary and promised for the constitution.

The necessary alterations to the fundamental treaties governing the EU, brought about by the Lisbon Treaty, were published at the end of March 2010 in the form of an updated *Treaty on European Union* (TEU), a newly named *Treaty on the Functioning of the European Union* (TFEU) (formerly the *Treaty Establishing the European Community*), together with *the Charter of Fundamental Rights of the European Union* (CFREU).

The Treaty on European Union (TEU)

The text of the treaty is divided into six parts as follows, with reference to some of the most important specific provisions:

1   *Common Provisions*

- Article 1 of this treaty makes it clear that 'The Union shall be founded on the present Treaty and on the Treaty on the Functioning of the European Union (hereinafter referred to as "the Treaties"). Those two Treaties shall have the same legal value. *The Union shall replace and succeed the European Community.*' This provision means that the previous confusion between when it was more appropriate to refer to EC rather than the EU has been removed and that it is now correct under all circumstances to refer to the EU. Article 47 provides further that the EU has legal personality, which means that the EU, as well as its constituent members, will be able to be a full member of the Council of Europe. As yet, the EU has not joined the Council, although an agreement to do so was established in July 2011.

- Article 2 establishes that the EU is 'founded on the values of respect for human dignity, freedom, democracy, equality, the rule of law and respect for human rights, including the rights of persons belonging to minorities'.

- Article 3 then states the aims of the EU in very general terms as follows:

  o   the promotion of peace, its values and the well-being of its peoples; the assurance of freedom of movement of persons without internal frontiers but with controlled external borders;

  o   the creation of an internal market . . . aiming at full employment and social progress, and a high level of protection and improvement of the quality of the environment;

  o   the establishment of an economic and monetary union whose currency is the Euro; the promotion of its values, while contributing to the eradication of poverty and observing human rights and respecting the Charter of the United Nations;

○   the sixth aim requires that the EU pursue its objectives by 'appropriate means'.

● Article 6 binds the EU to the Charter of Fundamental Rights of the European Union and the European Convention on Human Rights.

2   *Provisions on democratic principles*

● Article 9 establishes the equality of EU citizens and that every national of a Member state shall be a citizen of the Union. It makes clear that citizenship of the Union is *additional to* and does *not replace* national citizenship.

3   *Provisions on the institutions*

● Article 13 establishes the institutions in the following order and under the following names (except for the ECB these will be considered in detail below):

○   the European Parliament;

○   the European Council;

○   the Council;

○   the European Commission;

○   the Court of Justice of the European Union;

○   the European Central Bank;

○   the Court of Auditors.

● Article 15 establishes the President of the European Council.

● Articles 15(2) and 18 establish the High Representative of the Union for Foreign Affairs and Security Policy to conduct the Union's common foreign and security policy.

4   *Provisions on enhanced co-operations*

● Article 20 allows a number of Member states to co-operate in furthering integration in a particular area where other members are blocking full integration.

5   *General provisions on the Union's external action and specific provisions on the Common Foreign and Security Policy*

● Articles 21–46 relate to the establishment and operation of a common EU foreign policy including:

○   compliance with the UN charter, promoting global trade, humanitarian support and global governance;

○   establishment of the European External Action Service, which will function as the EU's foreign ministry and diplomatic service;

○   the furtherance of military co-operation including mutual defence.

6   *Final provisions*

- Article 47 establishes the legal personality of the EU.
- Article 48 deals with the method of treaty amendment; either through the ordinary or the simplified revision procedures.
- Articles 49 and 50 deal with applications to join the EU and withdrawal from it.

The Treaty on the Functioning of the European Union (TFEU)

This document, going back through several iterations to the original Treaty of Rome, contains the detail of the structure and operation of the European Union.

Article 2 of this treaty provides that:

> When the Treaties confer on the Union exclusive competence in a specific area, only the Union may legislate and adopt legally binding acts, the Member states being able to do so themselves only if so empowered by the Union or for the implementation of Union acts.

Article 3 specifies that the Union shall have exclusive competence in the following areas:

(a)   customs union;

(b)   the establishing of the competition rules necessary for the functioning of the internal market;

(c)   monetary policy for the Member states whose currency is the Euro;

(d)   the conservation of marine biological resources under the common fisheries policy;

(e)   common commercial policy.

Article 3 provides that the Union shall also have exclusive competence for the conclusion of an international agreement when its conclusion is provided for in a legislative act of the Union or is necessary to enable the Union to exercise its internal competence, or in so far as its conclusion may affect common rules or alter their scope.

The provision of specific articles will be considered below.

The Charter of Fundamental Rights of the European Union (CFREU)

The Charter contains 54 Articles divided into seven titles. The first six titles deal with substantive rights relating to:

- *dignity*, including the right to life and the prohibition of torture and inhuman or degrading treatment or punishment;
- *freedom*, including the right to liberty and security of person, the right to engage in work and the freedom to conduct a business;

within domestic law which was inconsistent with EC/EU law was either abrogated or had to be modified so as to avoid inconsistency.

(ii)   The common law recognised a category of constitutional statutes.

(iii)   The 1972 Act was a constitutional statute which could not be impliedly repealed.

(iv)   The fundamental legal basis of the UK's relationship with the EU rested with domestic rather than European legal powers.

Thus did Laws LJ maintain balance between the supremacy of EU law in matters of substantive law, and the supremacy of the UK Parliament in establishing the legal framework within which EU law operates. Clause 18 of the European Union Bill 2010/11 provides a statutory confirmation of Laws' reasoning.

An example of EU law invalidating the operation of UK legislation can be found in the *Factortame* cases. The Common Fisheries Policy established by the EEC had placed limits on the amount of fish that any member country's fishing fleet was permitted to catch. In order to gain access to British fish stocks and quotas, Spanish fishing boat owners formed British companies and reregistered their boats as British. In order to prevent what it saw as an abuse and an encroachment on the rights of indigenous fishermen, the British government introduced the Merchant Shipping Act 1988, which provided that any fishing company seeking to register as British would have to have its principal place of business in the UK and at least 75 per cent of its shareholders would have to be British nationals. This effectively debarred the Spanish boats from taking up any of the British fishing quota. Some 95 Spanish boat owners applied to the British courts for judicial review of the Merchant Shipping Act 1988 on the basis that it was contrary to Community law.

The High Court decided to refer the question of the legality of the legislation to the ECJ under Art 267 of the Treaty on the Functioning of the European Union (TFEU) (formerly Art 234 and Art 177 of previous versions of the treaty (see below, 5.3.6)), but in the meantime granted interim relief in the form of an injunction disapplying the operation of the legislation to the fishermen. On appeal, the Court of Appeal removed the injunction, a decision that was confirmed by the House of Lords. However, the House of Lords referred the question of the relationship of Community law and contrary domestic law to the ECJ. Effectively, they were asking whether the domestic courts should follow the domestic law or Community law. The ECJ ruled that the Treaty of Rome required domestic courts to give effect to the directly enforceable provisions of Community law and, in doing so, such courts are required to ignore any national law that runs counter to Community law. The House of Lords then renewed the interim injunction. The ECJ later ruled that in relation to the original referral from the High Court, the Merchant Shipping Act 1988 was contrary to Community law and therefore the Spanish fishing companies should be able to sue for compensation in the UK courts. The subsequent claims also went all the way to the House of Lords before it was finally settled in October 2000 that the UK was liable to pay compensation, which was estimated at between £50 million and £100 million.

The foregoing has demonstrated the way in which, and the extent to which, the fundamental constitutional principles of the UK are altered by its membership of the

EU. Both the sovereign power of Parliament to legislate in any way it wishes and the role of the courts in interpreting and applying such legislation are now circumscribed by EU law. There remains one hypothetical question to consider and that relates to the power of Parliament to disapply legislation from the EU. While CJEU jurisprudence might not recognise such a power, it is certain that the UK Parliament retains such a power in UK law. If EU law receives its superiority as the expression of Parliament's will in the form of s 2 of the European Communities Act, as suggested by Lord Denning in *Macarthys*, it would remain open to a later Parliament to remove that recognition by passing new legislation. Such a point was actually made by the former Master of the Rolls in his judgment in that very case:

> If the time should come when our Parliament deliberately passes an Act with the intention of repudiating the Treaty or any provision in it or intentionally of acting inconsistently with it and says so in express terms then I should have thought that it would be the duty of our courts to follow the statute of our Parliament.

Article 10 (formerly 5) requires:

> Member states to take all appropriate measures, whether general or particular, to ensure fulfilment of the obligations arising out of this Treaty or resulting from action taken by the institutions of the Community. They shall facilitate the achievement of the Community's tasks. They shall abstain from any measure which could jeopardise the attainment of the objectives of this Treaty.

This Article effectively means that UK courts are now EU law courts and must be bound by, and give effect to, that law where it is operative. The reasons for the national courts acting in this manner were considered by John Temple Lang, Director in the Competition Directorate General, in an article entitled 'Duties of national courts under Community constitutional law' [1997] EL Rev 22. As he wrote:

> National courts are needed to give companies and individuals remedies which are as prompt, as complete and as immediate as the combined legal system of the Community and of Member states can provide. Only national courts can give injunctions against private parties for breach of Community law rules on, for example, equal pay for men and women, or on restrictive practices. Private parties have no standing to claim injunctions in the Court of Justice against a Member state; they can do so only in a national court. In other words, only a national court could give remedies to individuals and

companies for breach of Community law which are as effective as the remedies for breach of national law.

European Union Act 2011

In September 2011, Parliament passed the European Union Act 2011. The main purpose of the Act was to make provision for the application of the post-Lisbon treaties. However, the Act also amended the European Communities Act (ECA) 1972 to ensure that any proposed future EU treaty, or amendment to the treaties, which purports to transfer competences or areas of power from the UK to the EU will have to be subject to a domestic referendum. Section 18 of the Act, for the first time, places the common law principle of parliamentary sovereignty on a statutory footing and states that all EU law takes effect in the UK only by virtue of the will of Parliament, as provided in the ECA 1972. Such measures were taken in an endeavour to provide clear statutory authority for the superiority of domestic law over EU law and to circumscribe any suggestion that EU law constitutes a new higher autonomous legal order in its own right. It has been suggested that these measures were a sop to the Eurosceptic wing of the Conservative Party within the coalition government and their precise effect remains to be seen.

The UK's position in the EU

It cannot go unnoticed, and uncommented upon, that the UK's relationship with the EU and its constituent members is a matter that raises concerns among some politicians and some members of the public – a concern strengthened by the flow of refugees and asylum seekers towards Europe in the second half of 2015. Prior to the General Election in 2015 the Conservative Party declared that, if elected, it would seek to renegotiate the UK's terms of membership of the EU and put the results of such negotiation to the public in a referendum on the UK's continued membership of the union. Following his party's success in the election, Prime Minister Cameron initiated his campaign of renegotiation towards the end of 2015, with the intention of holding the in/out referendum in June 2016.

5.2   SOURCES OF EUROPEAN UNION LAW

European Union law, depending on its nature and source, may have a direct effect on the domestic laws of its various members; that is, it may be open to individuals to rely on it without the need for their particular state to have enacted the law within its own legal system (see *Factortame*).

There are two types of direct effect. Vertical direct effect means that the individual can rely on EU law in any action in relation to their government, but cannot use it against other individuals. Horizontal direct effect allows the individual to use the EU provision in an action against other individuals. Other EU provisions only take effect when they have been specifically enacted within the various legal systems within the Union.

The sources of EU law are fourfold:

- internal treaties and protocols;
- international agreements;
- secondary legislation;
- decisions of the CJEU.

5.2.1 INTERNAL TREATIES

Internal treaties govern the Member states of the EU, and anything contained therein supersedes domestic legal provisions. Upon the UK joining the then Community, the Treaty of Rome was incorporated into UK law by the ECA 1972. Since that date the UK has been subject to the various iterations of the ruling treaties. As was considered previously, the ruling treaties are now:

- Treaty on European Union (TEU);
- Treaty on the Functioning of the European Union (TFEU);
- Charter of Fundamental Rights of the European Union.

As long as treaties are of a mandatory nature and are stated with sufficient clarity and precision, then they have both vertical and horizontal effect (*Van Gend en Loos* (1963)).

5.2.2 INTERNATIONAL TREATIES

International treaties are negotiated with other nations by the European Commission on behalf of the EU as a whole and are binding on the individual members of the EU.

5.2.3 SECONDARY LEGISLATION

Secondary legislation is provided for under Art 249 (formerly 189) of the Treaty of Rome. It provides for three types of legislation to be introduced by the European Council and Commission:

- *Regulations* apply to, and within, Member states generally, without the need for those states to pass their own legislation. They are binding and enforceable from the time of their creation and individual states do not have to pass any legislation to give effect to regulations. Thus, in *Macarthys Ltd v Smith* (1979), on a referral from the Court of Appeal to the ECJ, it was held that Art 157 (formerly 141) entitled the plaintiff to assert rights that were not available to her under national legislation, the Equal Pay Act 1970, that had been enacted before the UK had joined the EEC. Whereas the national legislation clearly did not include a

The classic area in which these powers can be seen in operation is competition law. Under Arts 101 and 102 (formerly Arts 81 and 82) of the TFEU, the Commission has substantial powers to investigate and control potential monopolies and anti-competitive behaviour, and it has used these powers to levy what, in the case of private individuals, would amount to huge fines where breaches of EU competition law have been discovered. In November 2001, the Commission imposed a record fine of £534 million on a cartel of 13 pharmaceutical companies that had operated a price-fixing scheme within the EU in relation to the market for vitamins. The highest individual fine was against the Swiss company Roche, which had to pay £288 million, while the German company BASF was fined £185 million. The lowest penalty levelled was against Aventis, which was only fined £3 million due to its agreement to provide the Commission with evidence as to the operation of the cartel. Otherwise its fine would have been £70 million. The Commission took two years to investigate the operation of what it classified as a highly organised cartel, holding regular meetings to collude on prices, exchange sales figures and co-ordinate price increases.

In the following month, December 2001, Roche was again fined a further £39 million for engaging in another cartel, this time in the citric acid market. The total fines imposed in this instance amounted to £140 million.

In 2012 the Commission imposed the biggest antitrust penalty in its history, fining six firms including Philips, LG Electronics and Panasonic a total of €1.47 billion (£132 billion) for running two cartels for nearly a decade.

The 2006 Fining Guidelines (http://ec.europa.eu/competition/antitrust/legislation/fines.html) give the Commission the power to increase fines by 100 per cent for repeat offending, even if the infringements took place long before the existence of the cartel in question. Saint-Gobain, the car glass manufacturer, had been the subject of previous Commission decisions relating to similar infringements in 1984 and 1988. In this instance, the Commission increased Saint-Gobain's fine by 60 per cent for the earlier violations, but in March 2014, the General court (see below, 5.3.6) announced its decision to reduce it, from €880 million to €715 million.

In 2004 the then EU Competition Commissioner, Mario Monti, levied an individual record fine of €497 million (£340 million) on Microsoft for abusing its dominant position in the PC operating systems market. In addition, the commissioner required Microsoft to disclose 'complete and accurate' interface documents to allow rival servers to operate with the Microsoft Windows system, or face penalties of €2 million (£1.4 million) for each day of non-compliance. In January 2006 Microsoft offered to make available part of its source code – the basic instructions for the Windows operating system. In an assertion of its complete compliance with Mario Monti's decision, Microsoft insisted it had actually gone beyond the Commission's remedy by opening up part of the source code behind Windows to rivals willing to pay a licence fee.

The offer, however, was dismissed by many as a public relations exercise. As a lawyer for Microsoft's rivals explained, 'Microsoft is offering to dump a huge load of source code on companies that have not asked for source code and cannot use it. Without a road map that says how to use the code, a software engineer will not be able to design inter-operable products.'

In February 2006 Microsoft repeated its claim that it had fully complied with the Commission's requirements. It also announced that it wanted an oral hearing on the allegations before national competition authorities and senior EU officials, a proposal that many saw as merely a delaying tactic postponing the imposition of the threatened penalties until the court of first instance has heard the company's appeal against the original allegation of abuse of its dominant position and, of course, the related €497 million fine. In July 2006, the Commission fined Microsoft an additional €280.5 million, €1.5 million per day from 16 December 2005 to 20 June 2006. On 17 September 2007, Microsoft lost their appeal and in October 2007, it announced that it would comply with the rulings.

However, in February 2008 Microsoft was fined an additional €899 million for failure to comply with the 2004 antitrust decision. In June 2012 Microsoft's appeal was rejected by the General Court of the EU (see below), although the total of the fine for non-compliance was reduced to €860. As a result, Microsoft was fined a total of €1.64 billion.

In May 2009 the Commission levied a new record individual fine against the American computer chip manufacturer Intel for abusing its dominance of the microchip market. Intel was accused of using discounts to squeeze its nearest rival, Advanced Micro Devices (AMD), out of the market. The amount of the fine was €1.06 billion (£950 million, or $1.45 billion). Intel's subsequent appeal was rejected by the General Court in June 2014. The Court said that the fine amounted to 4.15 per cent of Intel's annual revenue, less than half of the maximum 10 per cent fine that the Commission had the power to levy.

The Commission also acts, under instructions from the Council, as the negotiator between the EU and external countries.

In addition to these executive functions, the Commission has a vital part to play in the EU's legislative process. The Council can only act on proposals put before it by the Commission. The Commission therefore has a duty to propose to the Council measures that will advance the achievement of the EU's general policies.

5.3.6   THE COURT OF JUSTICE OF THE EUROPEAN UNION

The CJEU is the judicial arm of the EU, and in the field of EU law its judgments overrule those of national courts. It consists of 28 judges, one from each Member state, assisted by eight Advocates General, and sits in Luxembourg. The Court may sit as a full court, in a Grand Chamber of 13 judges or in Chambers of three or five judges. The role of the Advocate General is to investigate the matter submitted to the Court and to produce a report, together with a recommendation, for the consideration of the Court. The actual Court is free to accept the report or not as it sees fit.

The SEA 1986 provided for a new Court of First Instance to be attached to the existing Court of Justice. Under the Treaty of Lisbon it was renamed the General Court. It has jurisdiction in first instance cases, with appeals going to the CJEU on points of law. The former jurisdiction of the Court of First Instance, in relation to internal claims by EU employees, was transferred to a newly created European Union Civil Service Tribunal in 2004. Together the three distinct courts constitute *the Court of Justice of the European Union*. The aim of introducing the two latter courts was to reduce the burden of work on the CJEU, but there is a right of appeal, on points of law only, to the full CJEU.

The Court of Justice performs two key functions:

(a)   It decides whether any measures adopted, or rights denied, by the Commission, Council or any national government are compatible with Treaty obligations. Such actions may be raised by any EU institution, government or individual. In October 2000, the Court of Justice annulled EU Directive 98/43, which required Member states to impose a ban on advertising and sponsorship relating to tobacco products, because it had been adopted on the basis of the wrong provisions of the EC Treaty. The Directive had been adopted on the basis of the provisions of the Treaty relating to the elimination of obstacles to the completion of the internal market, but the Court decided that under the circumstances, it was difficult to see how a ban on tobacco advertising or sponsorship could facilitate the trade in tobacco products.

Although a partial prohibition on particular types of advertising or sponsorship might legitimately come within the internal market provisions of the Treaty, the Directive was clearly aimed at protecting public health and it was therefore improper to base its adoption on the freedom to provide services (*Germany v European Parliament and EU Council* (Case C-376/98)).

A Member state may fail to comply with its Treaty obligations in a number of ways. It might fail or indeed refuse to comply with a provision of the Treaty or a regulation; alternatively, it might refuse to implement a directive within the allotted time provided for. Under such circumstances, the state in question will be brought before the CJEU, either by the Commission or another Member state, or indeed individuals within the state concerned.

In 1996, following the outbreak of 'mad cow disease' (BSE) in the UK, the European Commission imposed a ban on the export of UK beef. The ban was partially lifted in 1998 and, subject to conditions relating to the documentation of an animal's history prior to slaughter, from 1 August 1999, exports satisfying those conditions were authorised for despatch within the Community. When the French Food Standards Agency continued to raise concerns about the safety of British beef, the Commission issued a protocol agreement, which declared that all meat and meat products from the UK would be distinctively marked as such. However, France continued in its refusal to lift the ban.

Subsequently, the Commission applied to the CJEU for a declaration that France was in breach of Community law for failing to lift the prohibition on the sale of correctly labelled British beef in French territory. In December 2001, in *Commission of the European Communities v France*, the CJEU held that the French government had failed to put forward a ground of defence capable of justifying the failure to implement the relevant Decisions and was therefore in breach of Community law.

France was also fined in July 2005 for breaching EU fishing rules. On that occasion the CJEU imposed the first ever 'combination' penalty, under which a lump-sum fine was payable, but in addition France is liable to a periodic penalty for every six months until it had shown it was fully complying with EU fisheries laws. The CJEU set the lump-sum fine at €20 million and the periodic penalty at €57.8 million.

The Court held that it was possible and appropriate to impose both types of penalty at the same time, in circumstances where the breach of obligations has both continued for a long period and is inclined to persist.

(b)   It provides authoritative rulings, at the request of national courts, under Art 267 (formerly 234) of the TFEU, on the interpretation of points of EU law. When an application is made under Art 267, the national proceedings are suspended until such time as the determination of the point in question is delivered by the CJEU. While the case is being decided by the CJEU, the national court is expected to provide appropriate interim relief, even if this involves going against a domestic legal provision, as in the *Factortame* case.

This procedure can take the form of a preliminary ruling where the request precedes the actual determination of a case by the national court.

Article 267 provides that:

> The Court of Justice shall have jurisdiction to give preliminary rulings concerning:
>
> (a)   the interpretation of treaties;
>
> (b)   the validity and interpretation of acts of the institutions of the Union and of the European Central Bank;
>
> (c)   the interpretation of the statutes of bodies established by an act of the Council, where those statutes so provide.
>
> Where such a question is raised before any court or tribunal of a Member state, that court or tribunal may, if it considers that a decision on the question is necessary to enable it to give judgment, request the Court of Justice to give a ruling thereon.

> Where any such question is raised in a case pending before a court or tribunal of a Member state against whose decision there is no judicial remedy under national law, that court or tribunal shall bring the matter before the Court of Justice.

The question as to the extent of the CJEU's authority arose in *Arsenal Football Club plc v Reed* (2003), which dealt with the sale of football souvenirs and memorabilia bearing the names of the football club and consequently infringing its registered trademarks. On first hearing, the Chancery Division of the High Court referred the question of the interpretation of the Trade Marks Directive (89/104) in relation to the issue of trademark infringement to the CJEU. After the CJEU had made its decision, the case came before Laddie J for application, who declined to follow that decision. The grounds for so doing were that the ambit of the CJEU's powers was clearly set out in Art 234. Consequently, where, as in this case, the CJEU makes a finding of fact that reverses the finding of a national court on those facts, it exceeds its jurisdiction and it follows that its decisions are not binding on the national court. The Court of Appeal later reversed Laddie J's decision on the ground that the CJEU had not disregarded the conclusions of fact made at the original trial and, therefore, he should have followed its ruling and decided the case in Arsenal's favour. Nonetheless, Laddie J's general point as to the CJEU's authority remains valid.

It is clear that it is for the national court and not the individual parties concerned to make the reference. Where the national court or tribunal is not the 'final' court or tribunal, the reference to the CJEU is discretionary. Where the national court or tribunal is the 'final' court, then reference is obligatory. However, there are circumstances under which a 'final' court need not make a reference under Art 267 (formerly 234). These are:

- where the question of EU law is not truly relevant to the decision to be made by the national court;
- where there has been a previous interpretation of the provision in question by the CJEU so that its meaning has been clearly determined;
- where the interpretation of the provision is so obvious as to leave no scope for any reasonable doubt as to its meaning.

This last instance has to be used with caution given the nature of EU law; for example, the fact that it is expressed in several languages using legal terms that might have different connotations within different jurisdictions. However, it is apparent that where the meaning is clear, no reference need be made.

Reference has already been made to cases that have been referred under the Art 267 procedure. Thus, the first case to be referred to the CJEU from the High Court was *Van Duyn v Home Office* (1974), the first case to be referred from the Court of Appeal was *Macarthys Ltd v Smith* (1979), and the first from the House of Lords was *R v Henn* (1982).

Reference has also been made in Chapter 4 to the methods of interpretation used by courts in relation to EU law. It will be recalled that, in undertaking such a task, a purposive and contextual approach is mainly adopted, as against the more restrictive methods of interpretation favoured in relation to UK domestic legislation. The clearest statement of this purposive, contextualist approach adopted by the CJEU is contained in its judgment in the *CILFIT* case:

> Every provision of EU law must be placed in its context and interpreted in the light of the provisions of EU law as a whole, regard being had to the objectives thereof and to its state of evolution at the date on which the provision in question is to be applied.

It can be appreciated that the reservations considered previously in regard to judicial creativity and intervention in policy matters in the UK courts apply *a fortiori* to the decisions of the CJEU.

Another major difference between the CJEU and the courts within the English legal system is that the former is not bound by the doctrine of precedent in the same way as the latter is. It is always open to the CJEU to depart from its previous decisions where it considers it appropriate to do so. Although it will endeavour to maintain consistency, it has, on occasion, ignored its own previous decisions, as in *European Parliament v Council* (1990), where it recognised the right of the Parliament to institute an action against the Council.

The manner in which EU law operates to control sex discrimination through the Equal Treatment Directive is of significant interest and, in *Marshall v Southampton and West Hampshire Area Health Authority* (1993), a number of the points that have been considered above were highlighted. Ms Marshall had originally been required to retire earlier than a man in her situation would have been required to do. She successfully argued before the CJEU that such a practice was discriminatory and contrary to Community Directive 76/207 on the equal treatment of men and women.

The action related to the level of compensation she was entitled to as a consequence of this breach. UK legislation, the Sex Discrimination Act 1975, had set limits on the level of compensation that could be recovered for acts of sex discrimination. Marshall argued that the imposition of such limits was contrary to the Equal Treatment Directive and that, in establishing such limits, the UK had failed to comply with the Directive.

The Court of Appeal referred the case to the ECJ, as it then was, under Art 267 (formerly 234) and the latter determined that the rights set out in relation to compensation under Art 5 of the Directive were directly effective, and that, as the purpose of the Directive was to give effect to the principle of equal treatment, that could only be achieved by either reinstatement or the awarding of adequate compensation. The decision of the ECJ therefore overruled the financial limitations placed on sex discrimination awards and effectively overruled the domestic legislation.

P v S and Cornwall CC (1996) extended the ambit of unlawful sex discrimination under the Directive to cover people who have undergone surgical gender reorientation (sex change). However, in *Grant v South West Trains Ltd* (1998), the ECJ declined to extend the Directive to cover discrimination on the grounds of sexual orientation (homosexuality), even though the Advocate General had initially supported the extension of the Directive to same-sex relationships. While *Grant* was in the process of being decided in the ECJ, a second case, *R v Secretary of State for Defence ex p Perkins (No 2)* (1998), had been brought before the English courts arguing a similar point, that discrimination on grounds of sexual orientation was covered by the Equal Treatment Directive. Initially, the High Court had referred the matter, under Art 267 (formerly 234), to the ECJ for decision, but on the decision in *Grant* being declared, the referral was withdrawn. In withdrawing the reference, Lightman J considered the proposition of counsel for Perkins to the effect that:

> . . . there have been a number of occasions where the ECJ has overruled its previous decisions; that the law is not static; and, accordingly, in a dynamic and developing field such as discrimination in employment there must be a prospect that a differently constituted ECJ may depart from the decision in *Grant* . . . But, to justify a reference, the possibility that the ECJ will depart from its previous decision must be more than theoretical: it must be a realistic possibility. The decision in *Grant* was of the full Court; it is only some four months old; there has been no development in case law or otherwise since the decision which can give cause for the ECJ reconsidering that decision . . . I can see no realistic prospect of any change of mind on the part of the ECJ.

It could be pointed out that there could be no change in case law if judges such as Lightman J refused to send similar cases to the CJEU, but there may well be sense, if not virtue, in his refusal to refer similar cases to the court within such a short timescale.

5.3.7 THE COURT OF AUDITORS

Given the part that the Court of Auditors played in the 1998/99 struggle between the Parliament and the Commission, the role of this body should not be underestimated.

As its name suggests, it is responsible for providing an external audit of the EU's finances. It examines the legality, regularity and soundness of the management of all the EU's revenue and expenditure.

5.4 THE EUROPEAN COURT OF HUMAN RIGHTS

The Convention for the Protection of Human Rights and Fundamental Freedoms, better known as the 'European Convention on Human Rights', was opened for signature in Rome on 4 November 1950; it entered into force on 3 September 1953. The European

Court of Human Rights (ECtHR) was subsequently established to hear cases under the Convention in 1959.

It has to be established and emphasised from the outset that the substance of this section has absolutely nothing to do with the EU as such; the Council of Europe, of which the ECtHR is the adjudicatory institution, is a completely distinct organisation and, although membership of the two organisations overlaps, they are not the same. The Council of Europe has 47 countries as members with a combined population of more than 800 million people and is concerned not with economic matters but with the protection of civil rights and freedoms.

It is gratifying, at least to a degree, to recognise that the ECHR and its Court (the ECtHR) are no longer a matter of mysterious external control, the Human Rights Act (HRA) 1988 having incorporated the ECHR into UK law, making the ECtHR the supreme court in matters related to its jurisdiction. Much attention was paid to the ECHR and the HRA in Chapter 2 (see above, 2.5), so it only remains to consider the structure and operation of the ECtHR. Two points should be emphasised at this juncture. First, although the number of domestic cases relating to the ECHR will continue to increase and consequently domestic human rights jurisprudence will emerge and develop, it should be borne in mind that in relation to these cases, the ultimate court of appeal remains the ECtHR. Second, as has been considered at 2.5, s 2 of the HRA requires previous decisions of the ECtHR to be taken into consideration by domestic courts, and this means *all* decisions of the ECtHR, not just the cases that directly involve the UK. Consequently, it remains imperative that students of the UK legal system be aware of, and take into consideration, the decisions of that court.

The Convention originally established two institutions:

(a) *The European Commission of Human Rights.* This body was charged with the task of examining, and if need be investigating the circumstances of, petitions submitted to it. If the Commission was unable to reach a negotiated solution between the parties concerned, it referred the matter to the Court of Human Rights.

(b) *The ECtHR.* The ECHR provides that the judgment of the Court shall be final and that parties to it will abide by the decisions of the Court. This body, sitting in Strasbourg, was, and remains, responsible for all matters relating to the interpretation and application of the current Convention.

It is frequently stated, and with justification, that the ECHR and the ECtHR have been the victims of their own success, with the number of applications being made to them increasing year upon year. The ever-increasing pressure on the institutions was exacerbated by the break-up of the old Communist Eastern Bloc and the fact that the newly independent countries, in the full sense of the word, became signatories to the Convention. As the workload increased, so the incipient sclerosis of the original structure became apparent in the ever-increasing backlog of applications waiting to be dealt with. As a consequence of such pressure, it became necessary to streamline the procedure by amalgamating the two previous institutions into one Court. In pursuit of this aim, Protocol 11 to the Convention was introduced in 1994. A protocol to the Convention is a text which adds one or more rights to the original Convention or amends certain of its provisions. They are binding only on those states that have signed and ratified them.

The new ECtHR came into operation on 1 November 1998, although the Commission continued to deal with cases that had already been declared admissible for a further year. Nonetheless, it was still accepted that the court needed additional reform to allow it to function effectively under the ever-increasing burden of cases it has to deal with. The following are further suggestions and actions to achieve this necessary reform.

The Woolf Report

In 2005 the former Lord Chief Justice of England, Lord Woolf, led a panel to consider what steps could be taken to deal with the ECtHR's current and projected caseload.

As the review, issued in December 2005, repeated, the Court was a victim of its success. Nonetheless, it was faced with an enormous and ever-growing workload, thus it was quite clear that something had to be done, in the short term, if the Court was not to be overwhelmed by its workload.

Among the Review's main recommendations were the following:

(i)   *The Court should redefine what constitutes an application*

It should deal only with properly completed application forms that contain all the information required for the Court to process the application.

(ii)   *Satellite offices of the Registry should be established*

These would be located in key countries that produce high numbers of inadmissible applications. The satellite offices would provide applicants with information as to the Court's admissibility criteria, and the availability, locally, of ombudsmen and other alternative methods of resolving disputes. This could divert a significant number of cases away from the Court. Satellite offices would also be responsible for the initial processing of applications. They would then send applications, together with short summaries in either French or English, to the relevant division in Strasbourg. This would enable Strasbourg lawyers to prepare draft judgments more quickly.

(iii)   *Ombudsmen and other methods of alternative dispute resolution should be used more*

Not surprisingly, given his championing of alternative dispute resolution (ADR) in the English legal system, Lord Woolf's team recommended the encouragement of greater use of national Ombudsmen and other methods of ADR, thus diverting from the Court a large number of complaints that should never have come to it in the first place. As part of this approach the panel also recommended the establishment of a specialist '*Friendly Settlement Unit*' in the Court Registry, to initiate and pursue proactively a greater number of friendly settlements.

(iv)   *The Court should deliver a greater number of pilot judgments*

Pilot judgments refer to applications concerning similar issues, also known as 'systemic issues', that arise from the non-conformity of a particular country's domestic law with the convention. Following the Woolf recommendations, the Court has adopted the procedure of giving priority to examining one or more specific applications of that kind while adjourning similar cases. Once the pilot case is determined, the Court calls on the government concerned to bring the domestic legislation into line with the convention and indicates the general measures to be taken.

Priority rules

In June 2009 the Rules of Court were changed to alter the order in which cases may be dealt with. Until then, cases had been processed mainly on a chronological basis. As a consequence, however, some extremely serious allegations of human rights violations could take several years to be examined by the Court. This clearly unsatisfactory procedure was amended to allow for the prioritisation of certain applications.

Protocol 14

Protocol 14, although originally adopted in May 2004, was not fully ratified until 2010. The measure was designed to improve the efficiency of the Court through four provisions, which:

- extended the period of judicial service from six to nine years;
- allowed for a single judge, assisted by a non-judicial rapporteur, to reject cases where they are clearly inadmissible from the outset. This replaces the system where, previously, inadmissibility was decided by committees of three judges;
- allowed committees of three judges to give judgments in repetitive cases where the case law of the Court is already well established, where such cases were previously heard by chambers of seven judges;
- introduced a new admissibility criterion to the effect that the applicant must have suffered a 'significant disadvantage' as a result of the breach of their rights. There is the safeguard that the case must have already been duly considered by a domestic tribunal, with the additional proviso that the case raises no general human rights concerns requiring the case to be examined on its merits.

Given the continued delay on the part of the Russian Federation in ratifying Protocol 14, the other members of the European Council decided in May 2009 that the protocol should be adopted by all those countries willing to agree to its immediate implementation. Subsequently, the Russian Federation ratified the protocol in January 2010, and given the fact that Russia remains the major source of applications coming before the ECtHR, this should have a considerable impact on the rate with which the court processes applications and cases.

Council of Europe conferences

Since 2010, three conferences have been convened to consider the future of the Court and to identify methods of guaranteeing long-term effectiveness.

In February 2010 the *Interlaken Declaration* stated that additional measures were urgently required in order to:

(i)   achieve a balance between the number of judgments and decisions delivered by the Court and the number of incoming applications;

(ii)   enable the Court to reduce the backlog of cases and to adjudicate new cases within a reasonable time, particularly those concerning serious violations of human rights;

(iii)   ensure the full and rapid execution of judgments of the Court and the effectiveness of its supervision by the Committee of Ministers.

While recognising and upholding the right of individuals to petition the Court it saw the need to:

● improve the filtering out of inadmissible claims;

● reduce the number of repetitive cases;

● facilitate the adoption of friendly settlements;

● encourage the use of pilot cases to decide general issues.

As for the Court, it was invited to:

● avoid reconsidering questions of fact or national law that have been considered and decided by national authorities;

● apply uniformly and rigorously the criteria concerning admissibility and jurisdiction;

● consider the possibility of applying the principle *de minimis non curat praetor* (to the effect that the court should not bother with petty cases).

Subsequently in April 2011 the *Izmir Declaration* invited Member states to 'ensure that effective domestic remedies exist . . . providing for a decision on an alleged violation of the convention and, where necessary, its redress', thus lessening the pressure on the ECtHR. It more specifically focused on the advisability of introducing 'a procedure allowing the highest national courts to request advisory opinions from the [Strasbourg] Court concerning the interpretation and application of the convention'.

Finally, in April 2012 the *Brighton Declaration* agreed the following measures designed to tackle perceived shortcomings in the operation of the court:

● amending the convention to specifically include the principles of subsidiarity and the margin of appreciation. The declaration emphasised the fundamental importance of the principle of subsidiarity and pointed out that the ECtHR acts as a safeguard for violations that *have not been remedied at a national level*;

● amending the convention to tighten the admissibility criteria in order that trivial cases can be passed over to allow the court to focus on more serious abuses. The declaration recognised the significant steps already undertaken to achieve this end within the framework of Protocol No 14;

● reducing the time limit for applications to the court from six to four months;

● improving the selection process for judges in recognition of their crucial role in deciding cases. It was emphasised that judgments of the court need to be clear and consistent in order to promote legal certainty. This was seen as helping national courts to apply the convention more precisely, and helping potential applicants decide whether they have grounds for making an application. However, it was also stressed that consistency in the application of the convention did not require the implementation of the convention uniformly through all 47 states, thus recognising the need to allow for a margin of appreciation;

- ensuring that state parties to the convention executed judgments of the court expeditiously by requiring the committee of ministers to take effective measures in respect of any state party that failed to comply with its obligations under Art 46 of the convention;

- setting out a roadmap for further reform to anticipate future challenges and develop a vision for the future of the convention, so that future decisions can be taken in a timely and coherent manner.

The conference declarations above led to the adoption of Protocols 15 and 16 to the Convention. Protocol 15, adopted in 2013, inserted references to the principle of subsidiarity and the doctrine of the margin of appreciation into the Convention's preamble, as a means of reducing the number of cases that can be taken to the Court. It also reduces from six to four months the time within which an application must be lodged with the Court after a final national decision.

The same year, 2013, also saw the adoption of Protocol 16, which allows the highest domestic courts and tribunals to request the Court to give advisory opinions on questions of principle relating to the interpretation or application of the rights and freedoms defined in the convention. Not only would this reduce the need for cases to proceed to the Court but it was also designed to foster dialogue between courts and enhance the Court's 'constitutional' role. Any such requests would always be optional, could only be submitted by constitutional courts or courts of last instance, and the opinions given by the Court would not be binding.

Court statistics and further reform

In September 2014 in the course of a presentation to a joint meeting of various committees concerned with the reform of the Court, the Registrar of the Court, Erik Fribergh, presented statistics which he claimed showed the success of previous measures and undercut the need for further reform. As he stated, on 1 July 2014 the Court had 84,515 pending applications – half as many as in 2011. The Registrar presented the case for a temporary extraordinary budget of 30 million over eight years starting in 2015 to process the remaining backlog of cases and that thereafter the Court 'would deal with all incoming cases in a way which would roughly respect the Brighton criteria.'

Fribergh, rather sarcastically, concluded:

> The recent years have seen great success in terms of how the Court has got to grips with its case-load. The Court should be allowed to continue with this steady progress without the distraction of constant and sometimes confused

- limiting the ability to seek interception warrants to the existing nine intercepting authorities and existing three statutory purposes subject to IPC oversight.

- introducing a 'double-lock' on ministerial authorisation of intercept warrants with a panel of seven judicial commissioners given power of veto. Thus, judicial commissioners, as well as government ministers, will be required to approve warrants before they come into force. However, exemptions will apply in 'urgent cases'.

- requiring that applications for targeted interception warrants will need to specify a particular person, premises or operation.

- requiring the Prime Minister to be consulted in all cases involving interception of MPs' communications. It had previously been thought that the Wilson convention (named after the former Prime Minister) ensured that MPs' and peers' phones would not be tapped, and in 1997, the then prime minister, Tony Blair, said the doctrine extended to electronic communication, including emails. However, in October 2015 an Investigatory Powers Tribunal judgment confirmed that MPs' and peers' private communications were not protected from interception by the security services.

- repealing the acquisition of communications under the 1984 Telecommunications Act, under very general powers of which successive governments had secretly allowed security services to access data from communications companies.

- making it a criminal offence to recklessly or knowingly obtain communications data without lawful authority.

CHAPTER SUMMARY: SOURCES OF LAW: THE EUROPEAN CONTEXT

THE EUROPEAN UNION

UK law is now subject to European Union law in particular areas.

In practice, this has led to the curtailment of parliamentary sovereignty in those areas.

SOURCES OF EUROPEAN UNION LAW

The sources of EU law are:

- internal treaties and protocols – the TEU, TFEU, and Charter of Fundamental Rights are examples;

- international agreements;

- secondary legislation; and

- decisions of the Court of Justice of the European Union.

1. The UK Constitutional Principle of Parliamentary Sovereignty
- The UK Parliament is the highest legislative body in the UK
- It may enact any law which it sees fit, providing future Parliaments are not bound by that law
- No other body may overrule its laws

2. The Principle of Supremacy of EU Law
- Provides that where EU law and national law conflict, EU law will be supreme (*Costa v ENEL*)
- Acceptance of this principle in the UK is illustrated by Lord Bridge´s *dicta in Factortame*

3. Maintenance of the UK Doctrine
In theory at least, the doctrine of parliamentary supremacy is maintained by the argument that the UK Parliament may repeal the European Communities Act at any time, thus removing the nee to comply with EU laws

THE PRINCIPLE OF UK PARLIAMENTARY SOVEREIGNTY AND EU LAW

FIGURE 5.3 *The Principle of UK Parliamentary Sovereignty and EU Law.*

1. Why Does the EU Need Institutions?
The EU Institutions (listed in Art 13 TEC) have a variety of functions as they act as the day-to-day 'government' of Europe, taking decisions relating to legislative, executive and judicial functions

2. The Council:
- A peripatetic body, representing the governments of the Member states. Its composition changes according to the subject matter under discussion
- It is an important decision-making body, with decisions normally taken by Qualified Majority Voting (QMV)
- The body is supported by a permanent body of staff known as COREPER

3. The European Parliament:
- A democratically elected body which represents the interests of EU citizens
- It has an important legislative role, which includes agreeing the EU budget
- It also has supervisory functions, primarily in relation to the Commission

THE INSTITUTIONS OF THE EC/EU

6. Other Bodies:
- **The European Council:** an institution composed primarily of the heads of government of the states
- It is responsible for directing EU policy
- **The Court of Auditors:** an institution which ensures EU money is spent in accordance with the EU's budget
- **The European Central Bank:** works to maintain a stable financial system

5. The Court of Justice of the EU (CJEU):
- The CJEU is the judicial arm of the EU and is charged with ensuring that the law of the EU is observed (Art 19 TE)
- It has the important function of interpreting EU law for the benefit of the Member states (Art 267 TFEU)
- It also hears actions relating to compliance with EU law by both the other Institutions (Art 263 TFEU) and the Member states (Art 258 TFEU)

4. The European Commission:
- The Commission represents the interests of the EU as a whole
- The Commission drafts EU legislation
- It also has a function in regard to the supervision of Member states, ensuring that they fulfil their EU obligations

FIGURE 5.4 *The Institutions of the EC/EU.*

Secondary legislation takes three forms:

- regulations that are directly applicable;
- directives that have to be given statutory form; and
- decisions that are directly applicable.

MAJOR INSTITUTIONS

The major institutions of the European Union (EU) are:

- the Council of Ministers;
- the European Parliament;
- the Commission; and
- the European Court of Justice.

THE EUROPEAN COURT OF HUMAN RIGHTS

Refer to Chapter 2 above for a consideration of the effect of the ECHR on United Kingdom law.

The Council of Europe, the European Commission on Human Rights and the European Court of Human Rights are distinct institutions whose purpose is to regulate the potential abuse of human rights. They are not part of the EU structure.

Since the enactment of the Human Rights Act 1998, the European Convention on Human Rights has been incorporated into UK law. It remains to be seen what effect this has on domestic UK law, but it cannot but be significant.

FOOD FOR THOUGHT

1   Among the general public there is confusion between European institutions, their courts and their laws and it is quite common for even politicians to confuse decisions of the Court of Justice of the EU and the European Court of Human Rights. It is essential that the two are not confused, but how can this be achieved?

2   Within the European Union there exists a tension between those countries who would support a more integrationist approach towards a federal state of Europe and those who would prefer to see the Union in purely economic market terms.

3   In the context of national sovereignty, consider whether the United Kingdom could leave the EU, either in theory or in practice.

4   The European Court of Human Rights is threatened with sclerosis if it does not deal with more cases, or deals with those cases differently. What reform is necessary and how is it to be achieved, to ensure that the ECtHR continues to function adequately?

FURTHER READING

Benoetvea, J, *The Legal Reasoning of the European Court of Justice: Towards a European Jurisprudence*, 1993, Oxford: Clarendon

Borgsmit, K, 'The Advocate General at the European Court of Justice: a comparative study' (1988) 13 EL Rev 106

Craig, P and de Búrca, G, *EU Law: Text, Cases and Materials*, 5th edn, 2011, Oxford: OUP

Davies, K, *Understanding EU Law*, 5th edn, 2012, Abingdon: Routledge

Dickson, B, *Human Rights and the European Convention*, 1997, London: Sweet & Maxwell

Foster, N, *EU Treaties and Legislation*, 24th edn, 2013, Oxford: OUP

Gormsen, LL, 'The European Commission's priority guidelines on Article 82 EC' (2009) 14(3) Comms L 83

Kaczorowska, A, *EU Law*, 3rd edn, 2013, Abingdon: Routledge

Ward, I, *A Critical Introduction to European Law*, 3rd edn, 2009, London: Butterworths

USEFUL WEBSITES

http://eur-lex.europa.eu/en/index.htm
This site is the official database for all EU law. It includes the Official Journal, Treaties, recent case law, and legislation.
http://curia.europa.eu
The official website for the Court of Justice of the European Union.
www.echr.coe.int
The official website of the European Court of Human Rights (ECtHR).

COMPANION WEBSITE

Now visit the companion website to:

- test your understanding of the key terms using our Flashcard Glossary;
- revise and consolidate your knowledge of 'Sources of Law: The European context' using our multiple choice question testbank;
- view all of the links to the Useful Websites above.

www.routledge.com/cw/slapper

THE CIVIL COURTS   6

The first part of this chapter looks at the civil court structure and at which type of cases are heard in which trial courts, the rules relating to transfer of cases from one level of court to another, the system of appeals and the criticisms that have been made of the various aspects of these systems.

What is the difference between a criminal and civil case? There are several key distinctions.

Criminal cases are brought by the state against individual or corporate defendants, whereas civil cases are brought by one citizen or body against another such party. The state here involves the police (or possibly Customs and Excise officers or health and safety inspectors), who investigate the crime and collect the evidence, and the Crown Prosecution Service, which prepares the Crown's case. In civil cases, the state is not involved (although it may be a party to the case, such as in a judicial review claim), except in so far as it provides the courts and personnel so that the litigation can be judged. If a party refuses, for example, to be bound by the order a court makes in a civil case, then that party may be found in contempt of court and punished, that is, imprisoned or fined.

The outcomes of civil and criminal cases are different. If a criminal case is successful from the point of view of the person bringing it (*the prosecutor*) because the magistrate or jury finds *the defendant* (sometimes called *the accused*) guilty as charged, then the result will be a sentence. There is a wide range of sentences available, from absolute or conditional discharges (where the convicted defendant is free to go without any conditions or with some requirement, for example, that the defendant undertakes never to visit a particular place) to life imprisonment. Criminal sentences, or 'sanctions', are imposed to mark the state's disapproval of the defendant's crime. There is often a considerable cost in imposing a punishment. The prison population was 85,698 in September 2014, an increase of 1 per cent on the previous year (*Offender Management Statistics Quarterly Bulletin*, Ministry of Justice, October 2014). At an average cost of £102 per prisoner per day (*Hansard*, 27 March 2012, col 1070W), the average cost to the state is £37,000 per prisoner per year. By contrast, fines (the most common sentence or 'disposal') can often bring revenue to the state. In any event, the victim of a crime never

Where such a court is evenly divided, three or five judges must rehear the case before it can be further appealed to the Supreme Court.

There may be four or five divisions of the court sitting on any given day. The court has a heavy workload. In the Court of Appeal Civil Division, a total of 4,291 applications were filed or set down in 2013, its highest level since 2005, and an increase of 12 per cent on 2012. In 2013 3,865 applications were disposed of, an increase of 4.5 per cent on 2012.

6.8   THE APPEAL PROCESS

6.8.1   THE ACCESS TO JUSTICE ACT 1999 (PART IV)

In relation to civil appeals, the Access to Justice Act (AJA) 1999 made several changes. It:

- provided for permission to appeal to be obtained at all levels in the system (s 54);
- provided that, in normal circumstances, there will be only one level of appeal to the courts (s 55);
- introduced an order-making power to enable the Lord Chancellor to vary appeal routes in secondary legislation, with a view to ensuring that appeals generally go to the lowest appropriate level of judge (s 56);
- ensured that cases which merit the consideration of the Court of Appeal reach that court (s 57);
- gave the Civil Division of the Court of Appeal flexibility to exercise its jurisdiction in courts of one, two or more judges (s 59).

Together, these measures are intended to ensure that appeals are heard at the right level, and dealt with in a way which is proportionate to their weight and complexity; that the appeals system can adapt quickly to other developments in the civil justice system; and that existing resources are used efficiently, enabling the Court of Appeal (Civil Division) to tackle its workload more expeditiously. The provisions relating to the High Court (ss 61–65) allow judicial review applications.

6.8.2   RIGHT TO APPEAL

The AJA 1999 provides for rights of appeal to be exercised only with the permission of the court, as prescribed by rules of court. Previously, permission was required for most cases going to the Civil Division of the Court of Appeal, but not elsewhere. Under the Act, with three exceptions, permission to appeal must be obtained in all appeals to the County Court, High Court or Civil Division of the Court of Appeal. The exceptions are appeals against committal to prison, appeals against a refusal to grant *habeas corpus*, and appeals against the making of secure accommodation orders under s 25 of the Children Act 1989 (a form of custodial 'sentence' for recalcitrant children). There is no appeal against a decision of the court to give or refuse permission, but this does not affect any right under rules of court to make a further application for permission to the same or another court.

The Act provides that, where the County Court or High Court has already reached a decision in a case brought on appeal, there is no further possibility of an appeal of that decision to the Court of Appeal, unless (s 55) the Court of Appeal considers that the appeal would raise an important point of principle or practice, or there is some other compelling reason for the court to hear it. This is known as the second appeals test.

6.8.3 DESTINATION OF APPEALS

Section 56 of the AJA 1999 enables the Lord Chancellor to vary, by order, the routes of appeal for appeals to and within the County Courts, the High Court and the Civil Division of the Court of Appeal. Before making an order, the Lord Chancellor will be required to consult the Heads of Division, and any order will be subject to the affirmative resolution procedure. The following appeal routes are specified by order:

- In fast-track cases heard by a district judge, appeals will be to a circuit judge.
- In fast-track cases heard by a circuit judge, appeals will be to a High Court judge.
- In multi-track cases, appeals of interim decisions made at first instance by a district judge will be to a circuit judge, by a master or circuit judge to a High Court judge, and by a High Court judge to the Court of Appeal.
- In multi-track cases, appeals of final orders, regardless of the court of first instance, will be to the Court of Appeal.
- The Heads of Division are the Lord Chief Justice, the Master of the Rolls, the President of the Family Division and the Vice Chancellor.
- A decision is interim where it does not determine the final outcome of the case.

The legislation provides for the Master of the Rolls or a lower court to direct that an appeal that would normally be heard by a lower court be heard instead by the Court of Appeal. This power would be used where the appeal raises an important point of principle or practice, or is a case that, for some other compelling reason, should be considered by the Court of Appeal.

6.8.4 CIVIL DIVISION OF COURT OF APPEAL

The 1999 Act makes flexible provision for the number of judges of which a court must be constituted in order for the Court of Appeal to be able to hear appeals. Section 54 of the Senior Courts Act 1981 provided that the Court of Appeal was constituted to exercise any of its jurisdiction if it consisted of an uneven number of judges not less than three. In limited circumstances, it provided that a court could be properly constituted with two judges. The 1999 Act allows the Master of the Rolls, with the concurrence of the Lord Chancellor, to give directions about the minimum number of judges of which

Scotland

- The Court of Session.

Northern Ireland

- The Court of Appeal in Northern Ireland
- (in some limited cases) the High Court.

As the highest court of appeal in the United Kingdom, the Supreme Court acts as the final arbiter on cases. Occasionally, it will be called upon to interpret European law and the European Convention on Human Rights as they relate to UK domestic laws. Under European law, Member states' courts should always make their rulings according to principles laid down in relevant decisions by the Court of Justice of the European Union (CJEU). If the Supreme Court is considering a case where interpretation of a CJEU decision is unclear, the Justices must refer the question to the CJEU for clarification. They will then base their own decision on this answer.

In cases relating to the European Convention on Human Rights, it is accepted that no national court should 'without strong reason dilute or weaken the effect of the Strasbourg case law' (Lord Bingham of Cornhill in *R (Ullah) v Special Adjudicator* (2004)). If human rights principles appear to have been breached, it may be possible to make a claim to the European Court of Human Rights after all avenues of appeal in the United Kingdom have been exhausted, or if the Supreme Court has no jurisdiction in the particular case.

Lord Phillips of Worth Matravers, first president of the Supreme Court, says of its purpose:

> The object is to give formal effect to an important constitutional principle – the separation of powers, by transferring the function of the [highest] court from technically being a function carried out by Parliament to a function carried out by a court of judges.
>
> (*The Times*, 1 October 2009)

There have been changes to procedure from those adopted by the House of Lords. Lord Phillips favours more sittings of bigger panels (seven or nine justices instead of five commonly collected for House of Lords' cases) and more single or majority judgments rather than each judge giving his or her own. However, the number of appeals upon which seven or nine Justices sat fell to approximately 9 per cent of the total hearings during 2013/14 (as opposed to 11 per cent in 2012/13 and around 24 per cent in both 2011/12 and 2010/11). The current president is Lord Neuberger and the appointment of Lady Hale as deputy president in 2013 represents the highest judicial office achieved by a woman in the UK.

Frances Gibb, legal editor of *The Times*, has noted that:

> Until now, the highest court in the land was a committee of the House of Lords known as the law lords. They were hidden from public view in an obscure corridor in the depths of the Palace of Westminster and the public scarcely knew they existed. So the idea of giving the 12 law lords their own building and distinct identity as Supreme Court justices quite separate from the legislature has constitutional logic.
>
> (*The Times*, 1 October 2009)

6.10 THE COURT OF JUSTICE OF THE EUROPEAN UNION AND THE EUROPEAN COURT OF HUMAN RIGHTS

These distinct courts, although outside of the English legal system as such, have an essential impact on English law. The precise nature of these courts and their impact on the English legal system was considered in detail in Chapter 5.

6.11 JUDICIAL COMMITTEE OF THE PRIVY COUNCIL

The Judicial Committee of the Privy Council was created by the Judicial Committee Act 1833. Under the Act, a special committee of the Privy Council was set up to hear appeals from the Dominions. The cases are heard by the judges (without wigs or robes) in the Supreme Court in London. The Committee's decision is not a judgment but an 'advice' to the monarch, who is counselled that the appeal be allowed or dismissed.

The Committee is the final court of appeal for 23 Commonwealth territories and four independent Republics within the Commonwealth. The Committee comprises Privy Councillors who are Supreme Court Justices. In most cases, which come from places such as the Cayman Islands and Jamaica, the Committee comprises five Justices, sometimes assisted by a judge from the country concerned. The decisions of the Privy Council are very influential in English courts because they concern points of law that are applicable in this jurisdiction and they are pronounced upon by Supreme Court Justices (like their predecessor Lords of Appeal in Ordinary from the House of Lords) in a way which is thus tantamount to a Supreme Court ruling. These decisions, however, are technically of persuasive precedent only, although are likely to be followed in some circumstances by English courts; see, for example, *The Wagon Mound* (1963), a tort case in which the Privy Council ruled, on an appeal from Australia, that in negligence claims, a defendant is liable only for the reasonably foreseeable consequences of his tortious conduct. The Judicial Committee hears the following domestic appeals to Her Majesty in Council:

- from Jersey, Guernsey and the Isle of Man;
- from the Disciplinary Committee of the Royal College of Veterinary Surgeons;
- against certain schemes of the Church Commissioners under the Pastoral Measure 1983.

In 2013, 53 appeals were entered, including 10 each from Trinidad and Tobago and from Mauritius. Twenty-eight cases were dealt with (some of which may have originated from a previous year), 12 were dismissed after hearing and a further 15 were allowed after hearing. There were 56 petitions for special leave to appeal in 2013; of these 20 were granted and 35 refused.

CHAPTER SUMMARY: THE CIVIL COURTS

THE DIFFERENCES BETWEEN CIVIL AND CRIMINAL LAW

There is no such thing as inherently criminal conduct. A crime is whatever the state has forbidden on pain of legal punishment. The conduct that attracts criminal sanctions changes over time and according to different social systems. The terminology and outcomes of the two systems are different. In criminal cases, the *prosecutor prosecutes the defendant* (or *accused*); in civil cases, the *claimant sues the defendant*.

HER MAJESTY'S COURTS AND TRIBUNALS SERVICE

Her Majesty's Courts and Tribunals Service was created in April 2011. It brings together Her Majesty's Courts Service and the Tribunals Service into one integrated agency providing support for the administration of justice in courts and tribunals.

Her Majesty's Courts and Tribunals Service is an agency of the Ministry of Justice. It uniquely operates as a partnership between the Lord Chancellor, the Lord Chief Justice and the Senior President of Tribunals.

The agency is responsible for the administration of the criminal, civil and family courts and tribunals in England and Wales and non-devolved tribunals in Scotland and Northern Ireland. Its aim is to provide for 'a fair, efficient and effective justice system delivered by an independent judiciary'.

MAGISTRATES' COURTS

Magistrates' courts have a civil jurisdiction. They hear some family proceedings and deal with non-payment of council tax.

COUNTY COURT

The County Court deals with various types of civil case, both small claims and fast-track cases. Over two million proceedings are started each year. The main advantage to litigants using the small claims process is the fact that, if sued, they can defend without fear of incurring huge legal costs, since the costs that the winning party can claim are strictly limited.

HIGH COURT

The High Court has three administrative divisions: the Court of Chancery, the Queen's Bench Division (QBD) and the Family Division. High Court judges sit mainly in the Courts of Justice in the Strand, London, although it is possible for the High Court to sit anywhere in England or Wales. Each branch also has a Divisional Court which is an appeal court, mainly for the magistrates' and County Court. The Court of Protection that deals exclusively with matters arising under the Mental Capacity Act 2005 has the same powers as the High Court.

THE COURT OF APPEAL (CIVIL DIVISION)

The court hears appeals from the three divisions of the High Court, the Divisional Courts, the County Court, the Employment Appeal Tribunal, the Asylum and Immigration Upper Tribunal, the Lands Tribunal, the Transport Tribunal and the Court of Protection. The most senior judge is the Master of the Rolls.

RIGHT TO APPEAL

Rights of appeal can be exercised only with the permission of the court, as prescribed by rules of court. There are three exceptions: appeals against committal to prison, appeals against a refusal to grant *habeas corpus* and appeals against the making of secure accommodation orders under s 25 of the Children Act 1989.

THE SUPREME COURT

In 2009 the Supreme Court assumed the jurisdiction of the Appellate Committee of the House of Lords and the devolution jurisdiction of the Judicial Committee of the Privy Council. It is an independent institution, presided over by 12 independently appointed judges, known as Justices of the Supreme Court.

FOOD FOR THOUGHT

1   In 2009, 36 per cent of the UK population were eligible for legal aid. Since 2004, civil legal aid expenditure has decreased by 15 per cent and following the Legal Aid, Sentencing and Punishment of Offenders Act 2012, far fewer people are now eligible for legal aid in social welfare cases. What are the access to justice issues that arise when legal aid is cut? Are there other ways of improving access to justice in times of economic strife?

2   The civil justice system in the UK is adversarial. Should litigants be forced to use mediation before they go to court in order to reduce costs and alleviate the backlog in the court system?

FURTHER READING

Blackstone's Civil Practice, 2015, Oxford: OUP

Robins, J, 'Could do better' (2015) 165 NLJ 7648, p 8

Gold, S, 'Civil way' (2009) 159 NLJ 7378

Millett, T, 'A marked improvement' (2008) 158 NLJ 7321

Ministry of Justice, *Court Statistics Quarterly*, Jan–March 2014

New Law Journal, 'New charter for civil courts' [2007] 138

Parpworth, N, 'The hunt goes on' (2008) 158 NLJ 8118

USEFUL WEBSITES

http://www.justice.gov.uk/about/hmcts

https://www.gov.uk/government/organisations/hm-courts-and-tribunals-service
The official site of Her Majesty's Courts and Tribunals Service.

www.judiciary.gov.uk/about-the-judiciary/advisory-bodies/cjc
The site of the Civil Justice Council.

https://www.supremecourt.uk
The website of the Supreme Court.

COMPANION WEBSITE

Now visit the companion website to:

- test your understanding of the key terms using our Flashcard Glossary;
- revise and consolidate your knowledge of 'The civil courts' using our multiple choice question testbank;
- view all of the links to the Useful Websites above.

www.routledge.com/cw/slapper

THE CIVIL PROCESS 7

Jarndyce [v] Jarndyce drones on. This scarecrow of a suit has, in the course of time, become so complicated that no man alive knows what it means. The parties to it understand it least; but it has been observed that no two Chancery lawyers can talk about it for five minutes without coming to a total disagreement as to all the premises. Innumerable children have been born into the cause; innumerable young people have married into it; innumerable old people have died out of it. Scores of persons have deliriously found themselves made parties in *Jarndyce [v] Jarndyce*, without knowing how or why; whole families have inherited legendary hatreds with the suit. The little plaintiff or defendant, who was promised a new rocking horse when *Jarndyce [v] Jarndyce* should be settled, has grown up, possessed himself of a real horse, and trotted away into the other world. Fair wards of court have faded into grandmothers; a long procession of Chancellors has come in and gone out . . . there are not three Jarndyces left upon the earth perhaps, since old Tom Jarndyce in despair blew his brains out at a coffee-house in Chancery Lane; but *Jarndyce [v] Jarndyce* still drags its dreary length before the Court, perennially hopeless.

(Charles Dickens, *Bleak House*, 1853)

Many critics believe that the adversarial system has run into the sand, in that, today, delay and costs are too often disproportionate to the difficulty of the issue and the amount at stake. The solution now being followed to that problem requires a more interventionist judiciary: the trial judge as the trial manager.

(Henry LJ, *Thermawear v Linton* (1995) CA)

7.1 INTRODUCTION

The extent of delay, complication and therefore expense of civil litigation may have changed since the time of Dickens' observations about the old Court of Chancery, but how far the civil process is as efficient as it might be is a matter of some debate. The civil justice budget was reduced by 25 per cent between 2010 and 2015.

1. The Need for Reform:
The Woolf Inquiry found the civil system to be:
  – complicated
  – costly
  – excessively protracted
This led to reformed civil process under the Civil Procedure Act 1997, which has as its objective to deal with cases justly

2. The Present System:
– Statutory changes effected by the Civil Procedure Rules 1998, supplemented by practice directions and pre-action protocols
– Important changes include increasing the management role of the courts, placing further emphasis on pre-action settlement of disputes and greater brevity in regard to witness statements and expert evidence

THE REFORMED CIVIL PROCESS

3. Court and Track Allocation:
– High Court is limited to personal injury claims over £50,000, other claims over £10,000 and claims required by law to start in that court
– Other claims are to be heard in the County Court
– All cases must be allocated to one of three 'tracks':
 i. Small Claims Track: claims up to £10,000
 ii. Fast Track: claims between £10,000 and £25,000
 iii. Multi-track: claims over £25,000

FIGURE 7.1 *The Reformed Civil Process.*

equity claims where the property is worth at least £350,000; claims where an Act of Parliament requires a claim to start in the High Court; or specialist High Court claims.

Cases are allocated to one of three tracks for a hearing, that is, small claims, fast track or multi-track, depending on the value and complexity of the claim.

The documentation and procedures

Most claims will be begun by a multipurpose form and the provision of a response pack, and the requirement that an allocation questionnaire is completed is intended to simplify and expedite matters.

7.3.1　THE CIVIL PROCEDURE RULES

The CPR are the same for the County Court and the High Court. The vocabulary is more user-friendly, so, for example, what used to be called a 'writ' is a 'claim form' and a *guardian ad litem* is a 'litigation friend'.

Although in some ways all the fuss about the new CPR being so far-reaching creates the impression that the future will see a sharp rise in litigation, the truth may be different. The Queen's Bench Division of the High Court is the court that deals with all substantial claims in personal injury, breach of contract and negligence actions. According to official figures (*Judicial and Court Statistics 2011*, Ministry of Justice, 28 June 2012), 153,624 writs and originating summonses were issued by the court in 1995. By 2013, however, the number of annual actions issued was down to 13,035 (HM Government website of quarterly court statistics). The number of claims issued in the County Courts (which deal with less substantial civil disputes in the law of negligence) has also fallen. In 1998, the number of claims issued nationally was 2,245,324 but in 2014 it was 1,595,441 with 44,804 hearings or trials.

7.3.2 THE OVERRIDING OBJECTIVE (CPR PART 1)

The overriding objective of the CPR is to enable the court to deal justly with cases. It applies to all of the rules, and the parties to a case are required to assist the court in pursuing the overriding objective. Further, when the courts exercise any powers given to them under the CPR, or in interpreting any rules, they must consider and apply the overriding objective. The first rule reads:

> 1.1(1) These rules are a new procedural code with the overriding objective of enabling the court to deal with cases justly and at proportionate cost.

Costs are now fundamental to litigation and all parties, unless unrepresented, must file and exchange costs budgets in form H verified by a statement of truth. Under CPR 3.17, when making any case management decision, the court will have regard to any available budgets of the parties and will take into account the costs involved in each procedural step.

This objective includes ensuring that the parties are on an equal footing and saving expense. When exercising any discretion given by the CPR, the court must, according to r 1.2, have regard to the overriding objective and a checklist of factors, including the amount of money involved, the complexity of the issue, the parties' financial positions, and how the case can be dealt with expeditiously and fairly, and allot an appropriate share of the court's resources while taking into account the needs of others.

7.3.3 PRACTICE DIRECTIONS

Practice directions (official statements of interpretative guidance) play an important role in the new civil process. In general, they supplement the CPR, giving the latter fine detail. They tell parties and their representatives what the court will expect of them in respect of documents to be filed in court for a particular purpose, and how they must co-operate with the other parties to their action. They also tell the parties what they can expect of the court; for example they explain what sort of sanction a court is likely to impose if a particular court order or request is not complied with. Almost every part of the new rules has a corresponding practice direction. They supersede all previous practice directions in relation to the civil process.

Part 36 offers to settle can be made in the following instances:

- in both money (including claims for provisional damages) and non-money claims;
- in respect of the whole or part of the claim or in relation to an issue that arises;
- in respect of liability alone, thus leaving the issue of the amount of any damages to be dealt with later;
- in respect of counterclaims and any additional (Part 20) claim.

Part 36 offers to settle can be made by both a claimant and a defendant in a dispute, at any stage of a dispute before or after proceedings have commenced and in appeal proceedings. Part 36 offers to settle can be made prior to the commencement of court proceedings.

The party making the offer is called the 'offeror' and the party receiving it is called the 'offeree'. Under the revised Part 36 rule, where an offer relates to settlement of a money claim it is no longer possible to accompany the offer with the payment of funds into court. This provision applies irrespective of who the offeror is and whether that party has the means or assets to pay. When a Part 36 offer is accepted by the claimant the defendant must pay the sum offered within 14 days (unless the parties agree to extend the time period), failing which the claimant can enter judgment.

The court will take into account any pre-action offers to settle when making an order for costs. Thus, a side that has refused a reasonable offer to settle will be treated less generously in the issue of how far the court will order their costs to be paid by the other side. For this to happen, the offer must be one which is made to be open to the other side for at least 21 days after the date it was made (to stop any undue pressure being put on someone with the phrase 'take it or leave it, it is only open for one day then I shall withdraw the offer').

If an offer to settle is to be made in accordance with Part 36 it must be made in writing and state that it is intended to have the consequences of Part 36. Where the defendant makes the offer, it must specify a period of not less than 21 days within which the defendant will be liable for the claimant's costs if the offer is accepted. In addition, either party's offer must state whether it relates to the whole or part of the claim, or to an issue which arises in it and if so to which part or issue and whether any counterclaim is taken into account. The revised Part 36 rule allows the parties to withdraw any offer after the expiry of the 'relevant period' as defined in Rule 36.3.1.c without the court's permission. However, before the expiry of the 'relevant period' it is possible for a Part 36 offer to be withdrawn or its terms changed to be less advantageous to the 'offeree' only with the court's permission.

Several aspects of the new rules encourage litigants to settle rather than take risks in order (as a claimant) to hold out for unreasonably large sums of compensation, or try to get away (as a defendant) with paying nothing rather than some compensation. The system of Part 36 payments or offers does not apply to a claim allocated to the small claims track but, for other cases, it seems bound to have a significant effect. Part 36 applies prior to a small claims track allocation and on reallocation from this track to the other two tracks.

Thus, if at the trial a claimant does not get more damages than a sum offered by the defendant, or obtain a judgment more favourable than a Part 36 offer, the court will, unless it considers it unjust to do so, order the claimant to pay any costs incurred by the defendant after the latest date for accepting the payment or offer without requiring the court's permission, together with interest on those costs.

Similarly, where, at trial, a defendant is held liable to the claimant for a sum at least equal to the proposals contained in a claimant's Part 36 offer (that is, where the claimant has made an offer to settle), the court may order the defendant to pay interest on the award at a rate not exceeding 10 per cent above the base rate for some or all of the period, starting with the date on which the defendant could have accepted the offer without requiring the court's permission. In addition, the court may order that the claimant be entitled to his costs on an indemnity basis together with interest on those costs at a rate not exceeding 10 per cent above base rate for the period from the latest date when the defendant could have accepted the offer without requiring the court's permission.

The court has a general and overreaching discretion to make a different order for costs than the normal order under Part 44.

District Judge Frenkel has given the following example:

> Claim, £150,000 – judgment, £51,000 – £50,000 paid into court. The without prejudice correspondence shows that the claimant would consider nothing short of £150,000. The claimant may be in trouble. The defendant will ask the judge to consider overriding principles of Part 1: 'Was it proportional to incur the further costs of trial to secure an additional £1,000?' Part 44.3 confirms the general rule that the loser pays but allows the court to make a different order to take into account offers to settle, payment into court, the parties' conduct including pre-action conduct and exaggeration of the claim ((1999) 149 NLJ 458).

Active case management imposes a duty on the courts to help parties settle their disputes. A 'stay' is a temporary halt in proceedings, and an opportunity for the court to order such a pause. Either party to a case can also make a written request for a stay when filing their completed allocation questionnaire. Where all the parties indicate that they have agreed on a stay to attempt to settle the case, provided the court agrees, they can have an initial period of one month to try to settle the case. If the court grants a stay, the claimant must inform the court if a settlement is reached, otherwise at the expiry of the stay it will effectively be deemed that a settlement has not been reached and the file will be referred to the judge for directions as considered appropriate.

The court will always give the final decision about whether to grant the parties more time to use a mediator or arbitrator or expert to settle, even if the parties are agreed they wish to have more time. A stay will never be granted for an indefinite period.

7.4.4   APPLICATIONS TO BE MADE WHEN CLAIMS COME BEFORE A JUDGE (CPR PART 1)

The overriding objective in Part 1 requires the court to deal with as many aspects of the case as possible on the same occasion. The filing of an allocation questionnaire, which is to enable the court to judge in which track the case should be heard, is one such occasion. Parties should, wherever possible, issue any application they may wish to make, such as an application for summary judgment (CPR Part 24), or to add a third party (CPR Part 20), at the same time as they file their questionnaire. Any hearing set to deal with the application will also serve as an allocation hearing if allocation remains appropriate.

7.4.5   WITNESS STATEMENTS (CPR PART 32)

In the *Final Report on Access to Justice*, Lord Woolf recognised the importance of witness statements in cases, but observed that they had become problematic because lawyers had made them excessively long and detailed in order to protect against leaving out something that later proved to be relevant. He said 'witness statements have ceased to be the authentic account of the lay witness; instead they have become an elaborate, costly branch of legal drafting' (para 55).

Witness statements must contain the evidence that the witness will give at trial. They should be drafted in lay language and should not discuss legal propositions. Witnesses will be allowed to amplify on the statement or deal with matters that have arisen since the report was served, although this is not an automatic right and a 'good reason' for the admission of new evidence will have to be established.

7.4.6   EXPERTS (CPR PART 35)

The rules place a clear duty on the court to ensure that 'expert evidence is restricted to that which is reasonably required to resolve the proceedings'. That is to say that expert evidence will only be allowed either by way of written report, or orally, where the court gives permission. Equally important is the rules' statement about experts' duties. Rule 35.3 states that it is the clear duty of experts to help the *court* on matters within their expertise, bearing in mind that this duty overrides any obligation to the person from whom they have received instructions or by whom they are paid.

There is greater emphasis on using the opinion of a single expert. Experts are only to be called to give oral evidence at a trial or hearing if the court gives permission. Experts' written reports must contain a statement that they understand and have complied with, and will continue to comply with, their duty to the court. Instructions to experts are no longer privileged and their substance, whether written or oral, must be set out in the expert's report. Thus, either side can insist, through the court, on seeing how the other side phrased its request to an expert.

7.5   COURT AND TRACK ALLOCATION (CPR PART 26)

Part 7 of the CPR sets out the rules for starting proceedings. A new restriction is placed on which cases may be begun in the High Court. The County Courts retain an almost unlimited jurisdiction for handling contract and tort claims (that is, negligence cases, nuisance cases but excluding a claim for damages or other remedy for libel or slander unless the parties agree otherwise). Issuing proceedings in the High Court is now limited to:

- personal injury claims with a value of £50,000 or more; other claims with a value of more than £100,000;
- claims where an Act of Parliament requires proceedings to start in the High Court;
- specialist High Court claims which need to go to one of the specialist 'lists', like the Commercial List, the Technology and Construction List; or
- equity claims where the property is worth at least £350,000.

The new civil system works on the basis that the court, upon receipt of the defence, requires the parties to complete 'allocation questionnaires' (giving all the relevant details of the claim, including how much it is for and an indication of its factual and legal complexity). Under Part 26 of the CPR, the case will then be allocated to one of three tracks for a hearing. These are (a) small claims track; (b) fast track; and (c) multi-track. Each of the tracks offers a different degree of case management. The multi-track has, since 6 April 2009, a minimum limit of £25,000.01.

The small claims limit is £10,000, although personal injury (which in 2017 will increase to £5,000 for soft tissue injury and subject to consultation all injury claims) and housing disrepair claims for over £1,000, and illegal eviction and harassment claims are excluded from the small claims procedure. The limit for cases going into the fast-track system is £25,000. Applications to move cases 'up' a track on grounds of complexity will have to be made on the allocation questionnaire (see below). All small claims up to £5,000 will now be dealt with by mediation.

Directions (instructions about what to do to prepare the case for trial or hearing) will be proportionate to the value of the claim, its importance, its complexity and so on. Each track requires a different degree of case monitoring, that is, the more complex the claim, the more milestone events there are likely to be (i.e. important points in the process, like the date by which the allocation questionnaire should be returned). Time for carrying out directions, no matter which track, may be extended or shortened by agreement between parties, but must not, as a result, affect any of the milestones relevant to that track. The time for carrying out directions will be expressed as calendar dates rather than periods of days or weeks. Directions will include the court's directions concerning the use of expert evidence.

7.5.1   THE SMALL CLAIMS TRACK (CPR PART 27)

There is no longer any 'automatic reference' to the small claims track. Claims are allocated to this track in exactly the same way as to the fast track or multi-track. The concept

- a maximum of one day (five hours) for trial;
- trial period must not exceed three weeks and parties must be given 21 days' notice of the date fixed for trial unless in exceptional circumstances the court directs shorter notice;
- normally, no oral expert evidence is to be given at trial, but where allowed, will be limited to one expert per party in any expert field and expert evidence in two expert fields; and
- costs allowed for the trial are fixed depending on the level of advocacy.

Directions given to the parties by the judge will normally include a date by which parties must file a listing questionnaire. As with allocation questionnaires, the procedural judge may impose a sanction where a listing questionnaire is not returned by the due date. Listing questionnaires will include information about witnesses, and confirm the time needed for trial, parties' availability and the level of advocate for the trial.

The milestone events for the fast track are the date for the return of allocation and listing questionnaires and the date for the start of the trial or trial period.

7.5.3   THE MULTI-TRACK (CPR PART 29)

The multi-track is intended to provide a flexible regime for the handling of claims over £25,000, or lower, more complex claims if not appropriate for the fast track.

This track does not provide any standard procedure, such as those for small claims or claims in the fast track. Instead, it offers a range of case management tools – *standard directions*, *case management conferences* and *pre-trial reviews* – which can be used in a 'mix and match' way to suit the needs of individual cases. Whichever of these is used to manage the case, the principle of setting a date for trial, or a trial period at the earliest possible time, no matter that it is some way away, will remain paramount.

Where a trial period is given for a multi-track case, this will be one week. Parties will be told initially that their trial will begin on a day within the given week. The rules and practice direction do not set any time period for giving notice to the parties of the date fixed for trial.

7.6   DOCUMENTATION AND PROCEDURES

One of the main aims of the Woolf reforms is to simplify court forms. Under the old system, there were various forms that needed to be completed at the outset of a claim – different types including summonses, originating applications, writs and petitions. Under the new system, most claims will be begun by using a 'Part 7' claim form.

7.6.1   HOW TO START PROCEEDINGS – THE CLAIM FORM (CPR PART 7)

A Part 7 claim form has been designed for multipurpose use. It can be used if the claim is for a *specified* amount of money (the old term was *liquidated* damages) or an *unspecified* amount (replacing the term *unliquidated* damages). The form can also be used for non-monetary claims, for example, where the claimant just wants a court order, not money. The person issuing the claim form is called a claimant (plaintiff in old vocabulary) and the person at whom it is directed will continue to be known as a defendant.

Under the new rules, the court can grant any remedy to which the claimant is entitled, even if the claimant does not specify which one he wants. It is, though, as Gordon Exall has observed ((1999) SJ 162, 19 February), dangerous to start a claim without having a clear idea of the remedy you want. The defendant might be able to persuade the court not to allow the claimant a certain part of his costs if he (the defendant) finds himself having to consider a remedy that had not been mentioned prior to the trial.

There is now the facility to make a money claim online, which reduces the cost of commencing proceedings. A helpful free guide to starting and defending small claims produced by the Civil Justice Council is available at www.judiciary.gov.uk.

7.6.2   ALTERNATIVE PROCEDURE FOR CLAIMS (CPR PART 8)

Part 8 of the rules introduced the *alternative procedure for claims*. This procedure is commenced by the issue of a Part 8 claim form. It is intended to provide a speedy resolution of claims that are not likely to involve a substantial dispute of fact, for example applications for approval of infant settlements, or for orders enforcing a statutory right such as a right to have access to medical records (under the Access to Health Records Act 1990). The Part 8 procedure is also used where a rule or practice direction requires or permits its use.

The main differences between this and the Part 7 procedure are as follows:

- a hearing may be given on issue or at some later stage if required;
- only an acknowledgement of service is served with the claim form by way of a response document;
- a defendant must file an acknowledgement of service to be able to take part in any hearing;
- a defendant must serve a copy of the acknowledgement on the other parties, as well as filing it with the court;
- no defence is required;
- default judgment is not available to the claimant; the court must hear the case;
- there are automatic directions for the exchange of evidence (in this case, in the form of witness statements);
- Part 8 claims are not formally allocated to a track; they are automatically multi-track cases.

7.6.3   STATEMENT OF CASE – VALUE (CPR PART 16)

The 'value' of a claim is the amount a claimant reasonably expects to recover. Unless the amount being claimed is a specified amount, a claimant will be expected (Part 16) to state the value band into which the claim is likely to fall. The value bands reflect the values for the different tracks (for example, £1 to £10,000 for small claims). Value is calculated as the amount a claimant expects to recover, ignoring any interest, costs, contributory negligence or the fact that a defendant may make a counterclaim or include a set-off in the defence. If a claimant is not able to put a value on the claim, the reasons for this must be given.

7.6.4 STATEMENT OF CASE – PARTICULARS OF CLAIM (CPR PART 16)

Particulars of claim may be included in the claim form, attached to it, or may be served (that is, given or sent to a party by a method allowed by the rules) separately from it. Where they are served separately, they must be served within 14 days of the claim form being served. The time for a defendant to respond begins to run from the time the particulars of claim are served.

Part 16 is entitled *Statements of case* (replacing the term *pleadings*). Statements of case include documents from both sides: claim forms, particulars of claims, defences, counterclaims, replies to defences and counterclaims, Part 20 (third party) claims and any *further information* provided under CPR Part 18 (replacing the term *further and better particulars*). Part 16 also sets out what both particulars of claim and defences should contain.

Part 16 states:

(1)   The claim form must –

    (a)   contain a concise statement of the nature of the claim;

    (b)   specify the remedy which the claimant seeks;

    (c)   where the claimant is making a claim for money, contain a statement of value in accordance with rule 16.3;

    (cc) where the claimant's only claim is for a specified sum, contain a statement of the interest accrued on that sum; and

    (d)   contain such other matters as may be set out in a practice direction.

The Woolf Report was against obliging the claimant to state the legal nature of the claim, as this would prejudice unrepresented defendants. If the nature of the claim is uncertain, then the court can take its own steps to clarify the matter.

Where a claimant is going to rely on the fact that the defendant has been convicted for a crime arising out of the same circumstances for which the claimant is now suing, then the particulars of claim must contain details of the conviction, the court which made it, and exactly how it is relevant to the claimant's arguments.

It is optional for the claimant also to mention any point of law on which the claim is based and the names of any witnesses which he proposes to call. All statements of case must also contain a statement of truth.

7.6.5 STATEMENTS OF TRUTH (CPR PART 22)

A statement of truth is a statement that a party believes that the facts or allegations set out in a document, which they put forward, are true. It is required in statements of case, witness statements and expert reports. Any document that contains a statement of truth may be used in evidence. This will avoid the previous need to swear affidavits in support of various statements made as part of the claim.

Any document with a signed statement of truth that contains false information given deliberately, that is, without an honest belief in its truth, will constitute a contempt of court (a punishable criminal offence) by the person who provided the information. Solicitors may sign statements of truth on behalf of clients, but on the understanding that it is done with the clients' authority, and with clients knowing that the consequences of any false statement will be personal to them.

7.6.6 RESPONSE TO PARTICULARS OF CLAIM (CPR PART 9)

When a claim form is served, it will be served with a response pack. The response pack will contain an acknowledgement of service, a form of admission and a form of defence and counterclaim. The response pack will be served with a claim form containing the particulars of claim, which are attached to it or, where particulars of claim are served after the claim form, with the particulars. A defendant must respond within 14 days of service of the particulars of claim. If a defendant ignores the claim, the claimant may obtain judgment for the defendant to pay the amount claimed. A defendant may:

- pay the claim;
- admit the claim, or partly admit it;
- file an acknowledgement of service; or
- file a defence.

Requirements have also been introduced regarding the content of a defence. A defence that is a simple denial is no longer acceptable and runs the risk of being struck out by the court (that is, deleted so that it may no longer be relied upon). A defendant must state in any defence:

- which of the allegations in the particulars of claim are denied, giving reasons for doing so, and must state their own version of the events if they intend to put forward a different version to that of the claimant;
- which allegations the defendant is not able to admit or deny but which the claimant is required to prove;

- which allegations are admitted; and
- if the defendant disputes the claimant's statement of value, the reasons for doing so and, if possible, stating an alternative value.

These rules mark a significant change of culture from the old civil procedure rules. Under the old rules, a defendant could, in their defence, raise a 'non-admission' or a 'denial'. The first meant that the defendant was putting the plaintiff (now claimant) to proof, that is, challenging them to prove their case on the balance of probabilities. The second meant that the defendant was raising a specific defence, for example, a 'development risks defence' under the Product Liability Act 1988. Defendants were allowed under the old rules to keep as many avenues of defence available for as long as possible. Under the new rules, the defendant must respond according to the choices in the four options above. According to r 16.5(5), if the defendant does not deal specifically with an allegation, then it will be deemed to be admitted. However, where a defendant does not specifically deal with an allegation, but in any event sets out in their defence the nature of their case on that issue, it will be deemed that the matter be proved.

7.6.7   SERVICE (CPR PART 6)

Where the court is to serve any document (not just claim forms), it is for the court to decide the method of service. This will generally be by first-class post. The deemed date of service is two days after the day of posting for all defendants, including limited companies. Where a claim form originally served by post is returned by the Post Office, the court will send a notice of non-service to the claimant stating the method of service attempted. The notice will tell the claimant that the court will not make any further attempts at service. Service therefore becomes a matter for claimants. The court will return the copies of the claim form, response pack and so on, for claimants to amend as necessary and re-serve.

Claimants may serve claim forms, having told the court in writing that they wish to do so, either personally, by post, by fax, by document exchange (a private courier service operated between law firms) or by email or other electronic means. A claimant who serves the claim form must file a certificate of service within seven days of service with a copy of the document served attached.

7.6.8   ADMISSIONS AND PART ADMISSIONS (CPR PART 14)

The possibility of admitting liability for a claim for a specific amount and making an offer to pay by instalments, or at a later date, applies to both County Court and High Court cases. Where the claim is for a specific amount, the admission will be sent direct to the claimant. However, if a claimant objects to the rate of payment offered, there are changes that affect the determination process, that is, the process by which a member of a court's staff or a judge decides the rate of payment.

Cases involving a specific amount where the balance outstanding, including any costs, is less than £50,000, will be determined by a court officer. Those where the balance is £50,000 or more, or for an unspecified amount of any value, must be determined by a Master or district judge. The Master or judge has the option of dealing with the determination on the papers without a hearing or at a hearing.

A defendant in a claim for an unspecified amount of money (damages) will be able to make an offer of a specific sum of money in satisfaction of a claim, which does not have to be supported by a payment into court. A claimant can accept the admission and rate of payment offered as if the claim had originally been for a specific amount. The determination procedure described above will apply where a claimant accepts the amount offered, but not the rate of payment proposed.

If a claimant does not accept the amount offered, a request that judgment be entered for liability on the strength of the defendant's admission may be made to the court. This is referred to as *judgment for an amount and costs to be decided by the court* (replacing *interlocutory judgment for damages to be assessed*). Where judgment is entered in this way, the court will, at the same time, give case management directions for dealing with the case.

Where a request for such a judgment is received, the court file will be passed to a procedural judge. The judge may: allocate the case to the small claims track and give directions if it is of appropriate value; ask that the case be set down for a *disposal* hearing; or where the amount is likely to be heavily disputed, order a trial. Directions will be given as appropriate. A disposal hearing in these circumstances may either be a hearing at which the court gives directions, or at which the amount and costs are decided.

7.6.9   DEFENCE AND AUTOMATIC TRANSFER (CPR PART 26)

Claims for specified amounts will be transferred automatically to the defendant's 'home court' where the defendant is an individual who has filed a defence. The defendant's home court will be the court or district registry, including the Royal Courts of Justice, for the district in which the defendant's address for service as shown on the defence is situated. This means that, where a solicitor represents the defendant, this will be the defendant's solicitor's business address.

Where there is more than one defendant, it is the first defendant to file a defence who dictates whether or not automatic transfer will take place. For example, if there were two defendants to a claim, one an individual and one a limited company, there would be no automatic transfer if the limited company was the first defendant to file a defence.

7.6.10   ALLOCATION QUESTIONNAIRE (FORM N150)

The purpose of this document is to enable the judge to allocate in which track the case should be heard. When a defence is filed, the issuing court will send out a copy of the defence to all other parties to the claim, together with an allocation questionnaire, a notice setting out the date for returning it, and the name and address of the court (or district registry or the Royal Courts of Justice (that is, High Court), as appropriate) to which the completed allocation questionnaire must be returned. A notice of transfer will also be sent if the case is being automatically transferred.

(e)   it is a hearing of an application made without notice and it would be unjust to any respondent for there to be a public hearing;

(f)   it involves uncontentious matters arising in the administration of trusts or in the administration of a deceased person's estate; or

(g)   the court considers this to be necessary, in the interests of justice.

7.8   APPEALS (CPR PART 52)

The appeal system is covered in Chapter 6.

There is generally no automatic right to appeal under the CPR, except as provided for in r 52.3 or statute. The exceptions include situations where the appeal is against:

(i)   a committal order;

(ii)   a refusal to grant *habeas corpus*; or

(iii)   a secure accommodation order.

Generally, parties need permission to appeal and this will be granted only where:

(a)   the court considers that the appeal would have a real prospect of success; or

(b)   where there is some other compelling reason why the appeal should be heard.

Permission to appeal will usually be made to the lower court at the hearing against which it is to be appealed. Alternatively, an appeal can be made to the appeal court in an appeal notice usually within 14 days after the date of the decision to be appealed unless directed otherwise by the lower court.

The important procedural points and the routes to appeal will vary depending on whether the matter involves a final decision.

Generally, an appeal will lie to the next court above. From a district judge of the County Court, appeal lies to a circuit judge; from a Master or district judge of the High Court, or a circuit judge, appeal lies to a High Court judge; and from a High Court judge, appeal lies to the Court of Appeal. In almost all cases, permission is needed in order to appeal.

Paragraph 2A.1 of the Practice Direction to Part 52 provides:

> Where the decision to be appealed is a final decision –
>
> 1   in a Part 7 claim allocated to the multi-track; or
>
> 2   made in specialist proceedings (under the Companies Act 1985 or 1989 or to which sections I, II, or III of Part 57 or any of Parts 58 to 63 apply)
>
> the appeal is to be made to the Court of Appeal (subject to obtaining any necessary permission).

A final decision 'is a decision of a court that would finally determine (subject to any possible appeal or detailed assessment of costs) the entire proceedings whichever way the court decides the issues before it'. A decision will not be deemed a final decision where an order is made on a summary or detailed assessment of costs or on an application to enforce a final decision. In these circumstances the appeal will follow the general appeal route.

If a decision of a circuit judge is in relation to fast-track claims, claims on the multi-track except for final decisions, and Part 8 claims including final decisions but excluding final decisions in specialist proceedings, appeal lies to the High Court. However, a Part 8 claim that is a final decision and is treated as allocated to the multi-track may be sent direct to the Court of Appeal if the court considers appropriate.

Under CPR 52.14 a lower court may order the appeal to be sent directly to the Court of Appeal, where it considers that the appeal would raise an important point of principle or practice or there is some other compelling reason for the Court of Appeal to hear it.

Generally an appeal will be limited to a review of the decision of the lower court unless a practice direction provides otherwise or the court considers that in the circumstances of the particular appeal it would be in the interests of justice to order a rehearing. The appeal court will not hear any oral evidence or new evidence unless it orders otherwise. An appeal will be allowed where the decision in the lower court was wrong, or unjust due to a serious procedural or other irregularity in the lower court's proceedings.

When the court deals with appeals it must have regard to the overriding objective in CPR 1.1. Consequently, the appeal court is only likely to deal with appeals where they are founded on an error of law, against a finding of fact, in respect of the exercise of a discretion, involving new evidence or a change of circumstances or where a serious procedural or other irregularity arises causing injustice.

Appeals from the Court of Appeal lie to the Supreme Court, but the appellant must be granted leave either by the Court of Appeal or by the Supreme Court. The application for leave must first be made to the Court of Appeal, and then if refused, by petition for leave to appeal, which will be heard by the Supreme Court sitting in public. Only cases involving points of public importance reach the Supreme Court and there are usually fewer than 50 civil appeals heard by the Supreme Court each year. It is possible, under the Administration of Justice Act 1969, for the Supreme Court to hear an appeal direct from the High Court, 'leapfrogging' the Court of Appeal. The agreement of both parties and the High Court judge is required. Such cases must concern a point of statutory interpretation (including the construction of a statutory instrument), which has been fully explored by the High Court judge, or concern a point that he or she was bound by precedent to follow.

7.9 REMEDIES

The preceding sections of this chapter have examined the institutional and procedural framework within which individuals pursue civil claims. What it has not addressed is the question why people pursue such claims. Taking a claim to court can be expensive, time-consuming and very stressful, but people accept these costs, both financial and personal, because they have a grievance that they require to be settled. In other words, they are seeking a remedy for some wrong they have suffered, or at least that they believe they have suffered. In practice, it is the actual remedy available that the litigant focuses on, rather than the finer points of law or procedure involved in attaining that remedy; those are matters for the legal professionals. It is appropriate, therefore, to offer a brief explanation of remedies, although students of the law will engage with the details of remedies in the substantive legal subjects, such as contract and tort. As will be seen, it is essential to distinguish between the common law remedy of damages, available as of right, and equitable remedies, which are awarded at the discretion of the court (see above, 1.3.2).

7.10   DAMAGES

As has been said, the whole point of damages is compensatory: to recompense someone for the wrong they have suffered. There are, however, different ways in which someone can be compensated. For example, in contract law, the object of awarding damages is to put the wronged person in the situation they would have been in had the contract been completed as agreed; that is, it places them in the position they would have been in after the event. In tort, however, the object is to compensate the wronged person, to the extent that a monetary award can do so, for injury sustained; that is, to return them to the situation they were in before the event.

7.10.1   TYPES OF DAMAGES

(a)   *Compensatory damages*: these are the standard awards considered above, intended to achieve no more than to recompense the injured party to the extent of the injury suffered. Damages in contract can only be compensatory.

(b)   *Aggravated damages*: these are compensatory in nature, but are additional to ordinary compensatory awards and are awarded in relation to damage suffered to the injured party's dignity and pride. They are, therefore, akin to damages being paid in relation to mental distress. In *Khodaparast v Shad* (2000), the claimant was awarded aggravated damages after the defendant had been found liable for the malicious falsehood of distributing fake pictures of her in a state of undress, which resulted in her losing her job.

(c)   *Exemplary damages*: these are awarded in tort in addition to compensatory damages. They may be awarded where the person who committed the tort intended to make a profit from their tortious action. The most obvious area in which such awards might be made is in libel cases, where the publisher issues the libel to increase sales. Libel awards are considered in more detail at 14.6.1 below, but an example of exemplary awards can be seen in the award of £50,000 (originally £275,000) to Elton John as a result of his action against *The Mirror* newspaper (*John v MGN Ltd* (1996)).

(d) *Nominal damages*: these are awarded in the few cases which really do involve 'a matter of principle', but where no loss or injury to reputation is involved. There is no set figure in relation to nominal damages; it is merely a very small amount.

(e) *Contemptuous damages*: these are extremely small awards made where the claimant wins their case, but has suffered no loss and has failed to impress the court with the standard of their own behaviour or character. In *Reynolds v Times Newspaper Ltd* (1999), the former Prime Minister of Ireland was awarded one penny in his libel action against *The Times* newspaper; this award was actually made by the judge after the jury had awarded Reynolds no damages at all. Such an award can be considered nothing if not contemptuous.

7.10.2   DAMAGES IN CONTRACT

The estimation of what damages are to be paid by a party in breach of contract can be divided into two parts: remoteness and measure.

Remoteness of damage

What kind of damage can the innocent party claim? This involves a consideration of causation, and the remoteness of cause from effect, in order to determine how far down a chain of events a defendant is liable. The rule in *Hadley v Baxendale* (1854) states that damages will only be awarded in respect of losses that arise naturally, that is, in the natural course of things, or which both parties may reasonably be supposed to have contemplated, when the contract was made, as a probable result of its breach.

The effect of the first part of the rule in *Hadley v Baxendale* is that the party in breach is deemed to expect the normal consequences of the breach, whether they actually expected them or not.

Under the second part of the rule, however, the party in breach can only be held liable for abnormal consequences where they have actual knowledge that the abnormal consequences might follow. In *Victoria Laundry Ltd v Newham Industries Ltd* (1949), the defendants contracted to deliver a new boiler to the plaintiffs, but delayed in delivery. The plaintiffs claimed for normal loss of profit during the period of delay, and also for the loss of abnormal profits from a highly lucrative contract, which they could have undertaken had the boiler been delivered on time. In this case, it was decided that damages could be recovered in regard to the normal profits, as that loss was a natural consequence of the delay. The second claim failed, however, on the grounds that the loss was not a normal one, but was a consequence of an especially lucrative contract, about which the defendant knew nothing.

As a result of the test for remoteness, a party may be liable for consequences which, although within the reasonable contemplation of the parties, are much more serious in effect than would be expected.

In *H Parsons (Livestock) Ltd v Uttley Ingham and Co* (1978), the plaintiffs, who were pig farmers, bought a large food hopper from the defendants. While erecting it, the defendants failed to unseal a ventilator on the top of the hopper. Because of lack of ventilation, the pig food stored in the hopper became mouldy. The pigs that ate the mouldy food contracted a rare intestinal disease and died. It was held that the defendants were liable for the loss of the pigs. The food affected by bad storage caused the illness as a natural consequence of the breach, and the death from such illness was not too remote.

Measure of damages

Damages in contract are intended to compensate an injured party for any financial loss sustained as a consequence of another party's breach. The object is not to punish the party in breach, so the amount of damages awarded can never be greater than the actual loss suffered. The aim is to put the injured party in the same position they would have been in had the contract been properly performed. Where the breach relates to a contract for the sale of goods, damages are usually assessed in line with the market rule. This means that, if goods are not delivered under a contract, the buyer is entitled to go into the market and buy similar goods, and pay the market price prevailing at the time. They can then claim the difference in price between what they paid and the original contract price as damages. Conversely, if a buyer refuses to accept goods under a contract, the seller can sell the goods in the market and accept the prevailing market price. Any difference between the price they receive and the contract price can be claimed in damages.

Non-pecuniary loss

At one time, damages could not be recovered where the loss sustained through breach of contract was of a non-financial nature. The modern position is that such non-pecuniary damages can be recovered. In *Jarvis v Swan Tours Ltd* (1973), the defendant's brochure stated that various facilities were available at a particular ski resort. The facilities available were in fact far inferior to those advertised. The plaintiff sued for breach of contract. The court decided that Jarvis was entitled to recover not just the financial loss he suffered, which was not substantial, but also for loss of entertainment and enjoyment. The Court of Appeal stated that damages could be recovered for mental distress in appropriate cases, and this was one of them.

7.10.3   DAMAGES IN TORT

Remoteness of damage

Even where causation is established, the defendant will not necessarily be liable for all of the damage resulting from the breach. The question to be asked in determining the extent of liability is whether the damage is of such a kind as the reasonable person should have foreseen, but this does not mean that the defendant should have foreseen precisely the sequence or nature of the events. The test for remoteness of damage in tort was set out in *The Wagon Mound (No 1)* (1961). The defendants negligently allowed furnace oil to spill from a ship into Sydney Harbour. The oil spread and came to lie beneath a wharf owned by the plaintiffs. The plaintiffs had been carrying out welding operations and, on seeing the oil, they stopped welding in order to find out whether it was safe to continue. They were assured that the oil would not catch fire and resumed welding. However, cotton waste that had fallen into the oil caught fire, which in turn ignited the oil, and the resultant fire spread to the plaintiff's wharf. It was held that the defendants were liable in tort, as they had breached their duty of care. However, they were only held liable for the damage caused to the wharf and slipway through the fouling of the oil. They were not liable for the damage caused by fire because that damage was unforeseeable due to the high ignition point of the oil.

Economic loss

There are two categories of economic loss that may form the basis of a claim in negligence. First, there is economic loss arising out of physical injury or damage to property and, second, there is what is known as 'pure economic loss', which is unconnected with physical damage. Following recent developments, only the former is recoverable unless the claimant can show that there was 'a special relationship' between them and the defendant (*Williams v Natural Life Health Foods Ltd* (1998)).

7.11 EQUITABLE REMEDIES

Equitable remedies are not available as of right and are awarded only at the discretion of the court. They will not be granted where the claimant has not acted properly. There are a number of maxims that relate to the awarding of equitable remedies. Thus, for example, it is frequently stated that '*He who comes to equity must come with clean hands*', which simply means that persons looking for the remedy must have behaved properly themselves (*D & C Builders v Rees* (1966)). The actual remedies are as follows.

Specific performance

It will sometimes suit a party to break their contractual obligations and pay damages; however, through an order for specific performance, the party in breach may be instructed to complete their part of the contract. An order of specific performance will only be granted in cases where the common law remedy of damages is inadequate, and providing the matter does not fall into a category where the courts will not order specific performance. It is not usually applied to contracts concerning the sale of goods where replacements are readily available. It is most commonly granted in cases involving the sale of land, where the subject matter of the contract is unique.

Generally, specific performance will not be available in respect of contracts of employment or personal service. However, in light of *C H Giles & Co Ltd v Morris and others* (1972), it would appear that the courts may be prepared to depart from this principle in certain circumstances.

Specific performance will not be granted if the court has to constantly supervise its enforcement. In *Ryan v Mutual Tontine Westminster Chambers Association* (1893),

the landlords of a flat undertook to provide a porter, who was to be constantly in attendance to provide services such as cleaning the common passages and stairs, and delivering letters. The person appointed spent much of his time working as a chef at a nearby
club. During his absence, his duties were performed by a cleaner or by various boys.
The plaintiff sought to enforce the contractual undertaking. It was held that, although
the landlords were in breach of their contract, the court would not award an order of
specific performance.

The reason given was that to enforce the contract would require constant supervision by the court. In addition, it was held that damages were an adequate remedy and
hence the only available course of action. By comparison, in *Posner and others v Scott-
Lewis and others* (1986) an order for specific performance was granted. In this case,
the landlord had covenanted (so far as it was in his power) with the tenants to employ
a resident porter to carry out certain specified tasks. The court held that the covenant
was specifically enforceable as they could order the landlord to employ a resident porter
within a specified time, as this would not require constant supervision by the court. If
the landlord failed to adhere to the order, the tenants could go back to the court and
take appropriate action.

Injunction

This is the term used in relation to the courts' powers to order someone to either do
something or, alternatively, to refrain from doing something. Injunctions are governed by s 37 of the Senior Courts Act 1981 and they may be granted on an interim
or a permanent basis. Breach of an injunction is a contempt of court. Examples of
specific injunctions are 'freezing orders', formerly known as Mareva injunctions,
which are interim orders that prevent defendants from moving their assets out
of the jurisdiction of the English courts before their case can be heard. Another
well-known order is the search order, formerly known as an Anton Piller order,
which prevents the concealment or disposal of documents that might be required
in evidence at a later time. It can also authorise the searching of premises for such
evidence.

In contrast, an injunction directs a person not to break their contract. It can have
the effect of indirectly enforcing contracts for personal service. In *Warner Bros v Nelson*
(1937), the defendant, the actress Bette Davis, had entered a contract that stipulated that
she was to work exclusively for the plaintiffs for a period of one year. When she came to
England, the plaintiffs applied for an injunction to prevent her from working for someone else. The court granted the order to Warner Bros. In doing so, the court rejected
Nelson's argument that granting it would force her either to work for the plaintiffs or not
to work at all. An injunction will only be granted to enforce negative covenants within
the agreement, and cannot be used to enforce positive obligations (*Whitwood Chemical
Co v Hardman* (1891)).

Rectification

This award allows for the alteration of contractual documents. It is generally assumed
that written contractual documents accurately express the parties' terms, especially

where the document has been signed. There are occasions, however, when the court will allow the written statement to be altered where it does not represent the true agreement (*Joscelyne v Nissen* (1970)).

Rescission

This action sets aside the terms of a contractual agreement and returns the parties to the situation they were in before the contract was entered into. The right to rescind a contract may be available as a result of fraud, misrepresentation of any type or the exercise of undue influence. The right can be lost, however, for a number of reasons, such as it being impossible to return the parties to their original position, affirmation, delay or the intervention of third party rights.

7.12 COSTS (CPR PARTS 44–48)

Fixed costs (CPR Part 45)

There are rates for the fixed costs allowed on issue of a claim and on entry of judgment where a party is represented by a solicitor.

The fee structure is designed so that fees become payable as the various stages of a claim are reached (a 'pay as you go' regime).

Courts are proactive in collecting fees, in particular those that are payable at allocation and listing stages, but *without interrupting* a case's progress. There are sanctions for non-payment of allocation and listing questionnaire fees, which could lead to a party's statement of case being struck out.

Assessment (CPR Part 47)

The terms *taxed* costs and *taxation* (which were previously used to denote that costs a lawyer was claiming had been approved by a senior officer of the court) are now redundant and have been replaced by *assessment*. Costs will either be assessed summarily, that is, there and then, or there will be a *detailed assessment* at some later stage where one party has been ordered to pay another's costs.

Summary assessment

Judges will normally summarily assess costs at the end of hearings, both interim and final, and particularly at the end of fast-track trials. Parties will be expected to bring any necessary documentation to the hearing for this purpose. In this way, the need for detailed assessment of costs is avoided so far as possible.

7.13 WHAT HAS THE NEW SYSTEM ACHIEVED?

The CPR, the most fundamental changes in civil process for over 100 years, have radically altered the operation of civil justice. Since the new rules came into force (26 April 1999), they have been regularly reformed, the latest being the eighty-second update, which came into force in December 2015.

Part of the rationale of the new rules was to expedite the way cases were dealt with and to allow more cases to be settled early through negotiation between the parties or ADR. In this respect, there was some early evidence of success. During the May to August period in 1999, there was a 25 per cent reduction in the number of cases issued in the County Courts compared with the same period the previous year. By the end of January 2000, there was a further fall of 23 per cent. Mr Justice Burton of the QBD presented an interesting assessment of the new rules. Speaking at the City law firm, Kennedys, he outlined five benefits of the reforms, five problems and what he referred to as 'one big question mark' ((2000) Law Soc Gazette, 10 February).

The five problems with the reforms were: the courts' inflexibility in not allowing parties to agree extensions of time between themselves; the danger of the judiciary pushing time guillotines onto parties; the risk that lawyers and clients could exploit 'standard' disclosure to conceal important documents; single joint experts possibly usurping the role of judges; and summary assessments of costs leading to judges making assumptions replacing detailed costs analysis. The benefits were listed as: pre-action protocols; emphasis on encouraging settlement; judicial intervention; Part 24 strike-out provisions; and Part 36 offers to settle.

Mr Justice Burton said there had been three options for reforming appeals:

1   to extend the present system in order to discourage more than one appeal;

2   to refuse appeals without leave; or

3   to abolish the present system, giving no right to re-hearings, only appeals.

He said he regretted that all three had been adopted (in the Access to Justice Act 1999). The consequence will be pressure on judges 'to get it right first time' and higher costs for parties.

The issue of costs is a recurring theme that has been commented upon by many notable people in the legal world. Ted Greeno, a partner at Herbert Smith, believed that the Woolf reforms would result in higher costs for commercial cases. He was of the opinion that the rise in costs has nothing to do with the court's adversarial system but 'is a result of the introduction of pre-action protocols, case management and unnecessary bureaucracy, as well as unrealistic timetables and the unpredictable threat of costs sanctions which cause lawyers to practise "defensively"'.

Sir Anthony Clarke has commented that 'unless you are an extremely rich individual, a corporation or an organ of the state, no one can afford to litigate'. He believes that 'the most important issue that the civil justice system needs to worry about is control over costs' ((2006) Law Soc Gazette, 21 April).

Overall, it could be argued that the Woolf reforms can be seen as a triumphant step in the right direction as they have resulted in a wider proportion of society being able to achieve greater access to justice, especially where the problem is of a relatively small nature and can be dealt with quickly and cheaply in the lower courts. However, the reforms may not be so good where, for example, the problem involves complex commercial issues and/or where a matter goes to appeal, as costs rack up very quickly with the parties requiring the assistance of solicitors, barristers and experts and with the length of time it can take to resolve the more complex case. However, the Woolf reforms have been criticised by Dame Hazel Genn in her Hamlyn lectures (F. Gibb, 'Woolf v Genn: the decline of civil justice', *The Times*, 23 June 2009). Dame Hazel believed that the civil justice reforms were not about greater access or greater justice to society but rather a route to divert litigants away from the courts and instead direct them to mediation. Part of this rationale, she believed, was due to the self-financing of the civil court system and the government's lack of commitment to civil justice in favour of the criminal justice system. Dame Hazel believed that while society had strong views on civil justice, they were not picked up due to 'a lack of solid empirical evidence'. It was noted in this article that Lord Woolf has publicly commented upon Dame Hazel's views and expressed dissatisfaction with her argument that not enough empirical evidence was put forward. This is because Dame Hazel was one of Lord Woolf's review team when he was looking at proposed reforms to the civil justice system. In expressing criticism of Dame Hazel, Lord Woolf acknowledged that one commentator, Professor Michael Zander, was critical of his reforms but remained consistent with his views. Professor Zander did not consider that the government's intention was to utilise the reforms to reduce resources to the civil justice system and his proposed reforms required directly the opposite, namely proper resourcing. While Lord Woolf acknowledged that the civil justice system is not high profile as far as government is concerned compared to the criminal justice system, he emphasised that this has nothing to do with judges. Lord Woolf also believed that mediation is a 'proper functioning part of the justice system that does help in certain cases to achieve justice'.

7.14 ENFORCEMENT OF CIVIL REMEDIES

It is one thing to be awarded a remedy by the court against another party, but it is another thing to actually enforce that remedy. Consequently, an effective enforcement system is essential to providing access to justice.

In March 2003, the LCD issued the White Paper *Effective Enforcement*, in which it claimed to set out a strategy for reforming the current system by:

- improving methods of recovering civil debt; and
- establishing a more rigorous system of controls for enforcement agents, previously known as bailiffs.

On 12 June 2003 the Department for Constitutional Affairs (DCA) was created and took over the LCD's responsibilities for the court system and judiciary. In July 2006, the DCA

THE NEW CIVIL PROCESS

The changes were effected through the Civil Procedure Act 1997 and the CPR 1998. These have been supplemented by new practice directions and pre-action protocols.

THE OVERRIDING OBJECTIVE (CPR PART 1)

The overriding objective of the new CPR is to enable the court to deal justly with cases. The first rule reads:

> 1.1(1) These rules are a new procedural code with the overriding objective of enabling the court to deal with cases justly and at proportionate cost.

PRACTICE DIRECTIONS

Practice directions (official statements of interpretative guidance) play an important role in the new civil process. In general, they supplement the CPR, giving the latter fine detail. They tell parties and their representatives what the court will expect of them in respect of documents to be filed in court for a particular purpose, and how they must co-operate with the other parties to their action. They also tell the parties what they can expect of the court.

THE PRE-ACTION PROTOCOLS

The pre-action protocols (PAPs) are an important feature of the reforms.

They exist for cases of clinical disputes, personal injury, disease and illness, construction and engineering disputes, defamation, professional negligence, housing disrepair, housing possession following rent arrears, housing possession following mortgage arrears, low value personal injury claims in road traffic accidents, low value personal injury (employers' and public liability) claims, dilapidations at end of lease or tenancy of a commercial property and judicial review.

They are likely to be followed, over time, with similar protocols for cases involving other specialisms like debt.

CASE CONTROL (CPR PART 3)

Judges will receive support from court staff in carrying out their case management role. The court will monitor case progress by using a computerised diary monitoring system.

Active case management includes:

(a)   encouraging the parties to co-operate with each other in the conduct of the proceedings;

(b)   identifying the issues at an early stage;

(c)   deciding promptly which issues need full investigation and trial and, accordingly, disposing summarily of the others;

(d)   deciding the order in which issues are to be resolved.

Parties are required to adhere strictly to the timetable set by the courts, and r 3.9 has been strengthened to make it more difficult to obtain relief from sanctions. However, some recent cases have seen the courts not applying the rule so strictly.

CASE MANAGEMENT CONFERENCES

Case management conferences may be regarded as an opportunity to 'take stock'. There is no limit to the number of case management conferences that may be held during the life of a case, although the cost of attendance at such hearings measured against the benefits obtained will always be a consideration in making the decision.

PRE-TRIAL REVIEWS

Pre-trial reviews will normally take place after the filing of listing questionnaires and before the start of the trial. Their main purpose is to decide a timetable for the trial itself (including the evidence to be allowed and whether this should be given orally), to determine instructions about the content of any trial bundles (bundles of documents including evidence such as written statements, for the judge to read) and to confirm a realistic time estimate for the trial itself.

STAYS FOR SETTLEMENT (CPR PART 26) AND SETTLEMENTS (PART 36)

Under the new CPR, there is a greater incentive for parties to settle their differences.

The court will take into account any pre-action offers to settle when making an order for costs. Thus, a side that has refused a reasonable offer to settle will be treated less generously in the issue of how far the court will order their costs to be paid by the other side. For this to happen, the offer, though, must be one that is made open to the other side for at least 21 days after the date it was made (to stop any undue pressure being put on someone with the phrase: 'take it or leave it; it is only open for one day, then I shall withdraw the offer').

WITNESS STATEMENTS (CPR PART 32)

Under the new rules, witness statements must contain the evidence that the witness will give at trial, but they should be briefer than those drafted under the previous rules; they should be drafted in lay language and should not discuss legal propositions. Witnesses will be allowed to amplify on the statement or deal with matters that have arisen since the report was served, although this is not an automatic right and a 'good reason' for the admission of new evidence will have to be established.

EXPERTS (CPR PART 35)

New rules place a clear duty on the court to ensure that 'expert evidence is restricted to that which is reasonably required to resolve the proceedings'. That is to say, expert evidence will only be allowed either by way of written report or orally, where the court gives permission. Equally important is the rules' statement about experts' duties.

COURT AND TRACK ALLOCATION (CPR PART 26)

Part 7 of the CPR sets out the rules for starting proceedings. A new restriction is placed on which cases may be begun in the High Court. County Courts retain an almost unlimited jurisdiction for handling contract and tort claims (that is, negligence cases, nuisance cases, but excluding a claim for damages or other remedy for libel or slander unless the parties agree otherwise). Issuing proceedings in the High Court is now limited to:

- personal injury claims with a value of £50,000 or more;
- other claims with a value of more than £100,000;
- equity claims where the property is worth at least £350,000;
- claims where an Act of Parliament requires an action to start in the High Court; or
- specialist High Court claims that need to go to one of the specialist 'lists', like the Commercial List, and the Technology and Construction List.

The new civil system works on the basis of the court, upon receipt of the claim (accompanied by duly filled-in forms giving all the relevant details of the claim, including how much it is for and an indication of its factual and legal complexity), allocating the case to one of three tracks for a hearing. These are:

- small claims
- fast track
- multi-track.

The new small claims limit is £10,000, although personal injury and housing disrepair claims for over £1,000 and illegal eviction and harassment claims will be excluded from the small claims court. Personal soft tissue injury claims will be increased to £5,000 in 2017 and other injury claims may follow after consultation. The limit for cases going into the fast-track system is £25,000, and only claims for over £100,000 can be issued in the High Court. Applications to move cases 'up' a track on grounds of complexity will have to be made on the new allocation questionnaire.

DOCUMENTATION AND PROCEDURES

HOW TO START PROCEEDINGS – THE CLAIM FORM (CPR PART 7)

Under the new system, most claims will be begun by using a 'Part 7' claim form – a form which has been designed for multipurpose use. It can be used if the claim is for a *specified* amount of money (the old term was *liquidated* damages) or an *unspecified* amount (replacing the term *unliquidated* damages) and for non-monetary claims.

Under the new rules, the court can grant any remedy to which the claimant is entitled, even if the claimant does not specify which one they want.

ALTERNATIVE PROCEDURE FOR CLAIMS (CPR PART 8)

Part 8 of the new rules introduces the alternative procedure for claims. This procedure is commenced by the issue of a Part 8 claim form. It is intended to provide a speedy resolution of claims that are not likely to involve a substantial dispute of fact, for example, applications for approval of infant settlements, or for orders enforcing a statutory right such as a right to have access to medical records (under the Access to Health Records

Act 1990). The Part 8 procedure is also used where a rule or practice direction requires or permits its use.

STATEMENT OF CASE – PARTICULARS OF CLAIM (CPR PART 16)

Particulars of claim may be included in the claim form, attached to it, or may be served (that is, given or sent to a party by a method allowed by the rules) separately from it. Where they are served separately, they must be served within 14 days of the claim form being served. The time for a defendant to respond begins to run from the time the particulars of claim are served.

Part 16 of the CPR is entitled 'statements of case' (replacing the word 'pleadings'). Statements of case include documents from both sides: claim forms, particulars of claims, defences, counterclaims, replies to defences and counterclaims, Part 20 (third party) claims and any further information provided under Part 18 of the CPR (replacing the term 'further and better particulars'). Part 16 of the rules also sets out what both particulars of claim and defences should contain.

STATEMENTS OF TRUTH (CPR PART 22)

A statement of truth is a statement that a party believes that the facts or allegations set out in a document, which they put forward, are true. It is required in statements of case, witness statements and expert reports. Any document that contains a statement of truth may be used in evidence. This will avoid the previous need to swear affidavits in support of various statements made as part of the claim.

DEFENCE AND AUTOMATIC TRANSFER (CPR PART 26)

Claims for specified amounts will be transferred automatically to the defendant's 'home court' where the defendant is an individual who has filed a defence. The defendant's home court will be the court or district registry, including the Royal Courts of Justice, for the district in which the defendant's address for service as shown on the defence is situated. This means that where a solicitor represents the defendant, this will be the defendant's solicitor's business address.

Where there is more than one defendant, it is the first defendant to file a defence who dictates whether or not automatic transfer will take place. For example, if there were two defendants to a claim, one an individual and one a limited company, there would be no automatic transfer if the limited company was the first defendant to file a defence.

ALLOCATION QUESTIONNAIRE (FORM N150)

The purpose of this document is to enable the judge to allocate in which track the case should be heard. When a defence is filed, the issuing court will send out a copy of the defence to all other parties to the claim together with an allocation questionnaire, a notice setting out the date for returning it and the name and address of the court (or district registry or the Royal Courts of Justice – that is, High Court – as appropriate) to which the completed allocation questionnaire must be returned. A notice of transfer will also be sent if the case is being automatically transferred.

The allocation questionnaire will not be served on the parties when a defendant files a defence if r 14.5 or r 15.10 applies or if the court decides to dispense with its service.

When all the parties have filed their allocation questionnaire, or at the end of the period for returning it, whichever is the sooner (providing the questionnaires have not been dispensed with or the case stayed under r 26.4), the court will allocate the claim to a track. If there is sufficient information, the judge will allocate the case to a track and a notice of allocation and directions will be sent out to each party. Where the judge has insufficient information, an order may be made for a party to provide further information.

Where only one party has filed a questionnaire, the judge may allocate the claim to a track providing he or she has enough information or will order that an allocation hearing be listed and that all parties must attend.

DEFAULT JUDGMENT (CPR PART 12)

If a defendant (to a Part 7 claim) files an acknowledgement stating an intention to defend the claim, this extends the period for filing a defence from 14 to 28 days from the date of service of the particulars. Failure to file an acknowledgement or, later, failure to file a defence can result in default judgment, that is, the court will find for the claimant, so the defendant will lose the case.

REMEDIES

It is essential to distinguish between the common law remedy of damages, available as of right, and equitable remedies, which are awarded at the discretion of the court.

DAMAGES

Damages are compensatory, to recompense someone for the wrong they have suffered. There are, however, different ways in which someone can be compensated.

In contract law, the object of awarding damages is to put the wronged person in the situation they would have been in had the contract been completed as agreed: that is, it places them in the position they would have been after the event. In tort, however, the object is to compensate the wronged person, to the extent that a monetary award can do so, for injury sustained: that is, to return them to the situation they were in before the event.

EQUITABLE REMEDIES

Specific performance

This remedy will only be granted in cases where the common law remedy of damages is inadequate. It is not usually applied to contracts concerning the sale of goods where replacements are readily available. It is most commonly granted in cases involving the sale of land, where the subject matter of the contract is unique.

Injunction

This is the term used in relation to the courts' powers to order someone either to do something or, alternatively, to refrain from doing something.

Rectification

This award allows for the alteration of contractual documents.

Rescission

This action sets aside the terms of a contractual agreement and returns the parties to the situation they were in before the contract was entered into.

COURT FEES

A new fee structure takes account of the different procedures, a movement towards a 'pay as you go' fees regime and the need for full cost recovery. 'Pay as you go' means that parties will be expected to contribute more in fees, the more court and judicial time they use, for example, if they do not settle and carry on to trial.

FOOD FOR THOUGHT

1   The English legal system has always been categorised as an adversarial system with the judge sitting as an umpire rather than a participant in cases. As a consequence the conduct of cases was to a large degree in the hands of the lawyers. Consider the consequences of such lack of judicial control for all the parties concerned in the case. Then consider how the Woolf reforms were designed to overcome these problems by instituting a process of greater judicial control.

2   To what extent is it fair to claim that the reforms have been about saving time and money, both clients' and the state's? How exactly have these savings been pursued?

3   Although referred to as the 'new' civil process, the Woolf reforms have been in operation for more than 15 years. Is it not time to assess how successful they have been? How would such an assessment be made?

4   In relation to the small claims procedure, consider why there are different financial limits: £10,000 for the majority of claims but £1,000 for personal injury claims and housing disrepair actions. Why are the latter considered to need more judicial attention, and does this imply anything about possible shortcomings in the fast-track procedure?

5   It is accepted that 'justice delayed is justice denied', but can the same not be said in relation to a failure to provide adequate enforcement of remedies?

FURTHER READING

Blackstone's Civil Procedure (HH Judge William Rose (ed)), 2014, Oxford: OUP

Burns, R, 'A view from the ranks' (2000) 150 NLJ 1829

Genn, H, *Hamlyn Lectures 2008: Judging Civil Justice*, 2009, Cambridge: CUP

Genn, H, *Hard Bargaining: Out of Court Settlements in Personal Injury Claims*, 1987, Oxford: OUP

Gold, S, 'Civil Way' (2008) 158 NLJ 1370

Gold, S, 'Civil Way' (2008) 158 NLJ 1412

Harrison, R, 'Cry Woolf' (1999) 149 NLJ 1011

Kinley, A, 'Preparing the way' (2009) 153(40) SJ 8

Miller, F, 'The adversarial myth' (1995) 145 NLJ 743

New Law Journal, 'Increase in Civil Cases in High Court' [2007] 1628

Sime, S, *A Practical Approach to Civil Procedure*, 2014, Oxford: OUP

Solon, M, 'Selecting the best' (2008) 158 NLJ 1299

Squire, G, 'No more hired guns' (2009) 153(40) SJ 20

Thacker, R, 'The new Supreme Court' (2009) Legal Action 20

Zander, M, 'Are there any clothes for the emperor to wear?' (1995) 145 NLJ 154

Zuckerman, AAS, 'A reform of civil procedure – rationing procedure rather than access to justice' (1995) 22 JLS 156

USEFUL WEBSITES

www.justice.gov.uk/civil/procrules_fin/menus/rules.htm

This site, hosted by the Ministry of Justice, contains all the Civil Procedure Rules, and is regularly updated.

www.judiciary.gov.uk/about-the-judiciary/advisory-bodies/cjc

The official website of the Civil Justice Council.

COMPANION WEBSITE

Now visit the companion website to:

- test your understanding of the key terms using our Flashcard Glossary;
- revise and consolidate your knowledge of 'The civil process' using our multiple choice question testbank;
- view all of the links to the Useful Websites above.

www.routledge.com/cw/slapper

THE FAMILY COURTS AND PROCESS

8

Today, family courts are largely concerned with the law relating to the family unit. They deal with:

- marriage;
- divorce decrees;
- cohabitation;
- some types of domestic violence;
- disputes between parents over the upbringing of their children;
- financial support for children upon divorce or separation;
- local authority intervention where children may need to be protected from abuse or neglect; and
- adoption.

Until 22 April 2014, family cases were dealt with at Family Proceedings Courts (which were part of the magistrates' courts), at County Courts or in the Family Division of the High Court. From 22 April 2014, all family cases are now dealt with in the Single Family Court.

The number of cases that started in family courts in England and Wales in July to September 2015 was 61,449; nearly the same as that for the equivalent quarter of 2014, maintaining a steady flat trend. Nearly half of new cases are divorce cases (*Family Court Statistics Quarterly England and Wales*, July to September 2015, p 6, Ministry of Justice Statistics bulletin, December 2015).

As part of an effort to reform the family justice system, the Single Family Court, or Family Court as it is sometimes called, was created under the Crime and Courts Act 2013; the Family Court can deal with all family proceedings except those which have been exclusively reserved for the High Court. The creation of the Family Court was designed to give family matters their own unique place inside the justice system.

In August 2013, the Children and Family Court Advisory and Support Service (Cafcass), a non-departmental public body set up to safeguard and protect the welfare of children involved in family proceedings, received a total of 4,053 new private law cases (Cafcass Private Law Demand, August 2013 statistics, 9 September 2013). In July 2013, Cafcass received 870 care applications (Cafcass Care Applications, July 2013 statistics, 8 August 2013), a record month for care applications with the second highest number of care applications in a single month.

Adoption rates, too, have soared: the Department for Education reported in 2013 that 3,980 children were adopted between April 2012 and March 2013, up from 3,470 the previous year. This is higher than in any year since 1992, when comparable records began (Statistical First Release, Department for Education, 26 September 2013, SFR36/2013). It has been suggested that the increase in adoption rates is attributable to the government's efforts at finding loving homes for children in care ('Adoptions show "record" increase', *BBC News* online, 26 September 2013), though some argue that the increase is driven by a lucrative business which sees foster carers and the government profit from adoption agreements ('Big money to be made in the adoption trade', *The Telegraph* online, 19 June 2010). In recent times, however, there has been a significant reduction in adoptions. During July to September 2015, there were 1,463 adoption orders issued, down 17 per cent for the equivalent quarter in 2014. In 65 per cent of these, the adopters were a male/female couple, while in 18 per cent the adopter was a sole applicant (*Family Court Statistics Quarterly England and Wales*, July to September 2015, p 22, Ministry of Justice Statistics bulletin, December 2015).

8.3 THE CHILDREN ACT 1989 AND THE PARAMOUNTCY PRINCIPLE

The Children Act 1989 came into force on 14 October 1991 and was designed to

> reform the law relating to children; to provide for local authority services for children in need and others; to amend the law with respect to children's homes, community homes, voluntary homes and voluntary organisations; to make provision with respect to fostering, child minding and day care for young children and adoption; and for connected purposes.
> (the Children Act 1989, introductory text, 18 November 1989)

It is the most important piece of child protection legislation in the United Kingdom.

The Children Act 1989 is designed to make the welfare of every child the primary, or paramount, concern in cases involving children. This is often referred to as the 'paramountcy principle'.

The guiding principles found within the Children Act 1989, which apply to all proceedings concerning children brought under the Act, are:

- the welfare of the child will be the paramount consideration (the paramountcy principle) (s 1(1));
- delay to proceedings is likely to prejudice the welfare of the child and courts must be mindful of this when considering decisions relating to the upbringing of a child (s 1(2));
- the welfare checklist, which includes the consideration of the wishes and feelings of the child, their age, gender and other factors, must be considered by courts in relation to specific decisions (s 1(3));
- a court should not make an order under the Act unless the court considers that doing so would be better for the child than making no order at all (s 1(5)).

Covering a broad range of issues relating to children, and encompassing both private and public family law, the Children Act 1989 deals with:

- child welfare and parental responsibility issues (Part I);
- orders with respect to children in family proceedings (Part II);
- local authority support for children and families (Part III);
- care and supervision (Part IV);
- protection of children (Part V);
- community homes (Part VI);
- voluntary homes and voluntary organisations (Part VII);
- registered children's homes (Part VIII);
- private arrangements for fostering children (Part IX);
- child minding and day care for young children (Part X).

The Act's central principle focuses on the idea that responsibility in the first instance for a child's upbringing rests with that child's family, and that for the majority of children, their interests will be best served within their family unit. When that is no longer the case, the Act allows for government agencies to support the family where necessary, and to protect children where required. It also emphasises the need to ensure that all children and young people going through the family courts are consulted and are as fully informed as possible about decisions relating to them.

8.4 LEGAL AID AND THE FAMILY COURTS

Family legal aid covers both public and private law, and includes matters relating to the Children Act, domestic abuse, financial provision and mediation. As resources in the family justice system become scarce, largely due to ailing economic conditions, legal aid, which offers support through public funding, to families who are unable to pay for legal advice or proceedings, has been drastically reduced for civil cases by the newly enacted Legal Aid, Sentencing and Punishment of Offenders Act (LASPO) which came into effect in April 2013. As a result, only a very narrow set of family cases are now eligible for legal aid, including:

- cases where a victim of domestic violence is divorcing or separating from an abusive partner; and
- cases where a child is at risk of abuse from a partner.

Successful applications are now also dependent upon a further condition: evidence of abuse must be produced before legal aid may be granted.

Providing some relief to the very limited circumstances in which legal aid may now be considered for family matters is the Exceptional Cases Funding Scheme (ECF). The scheme allows cases to be considered if failure to grant legal aid would result in a breach of a client's rights under the European Convention on Human Rights (Lord Chancellor's Guidance on Exceptional Funding (Non-Inquests)).

Legal aid statistics produced for 2014 by the Ministry of Justice highlight a startling decrease in legal aid for family law matters, with a 60 per cent drop compared to figures for 2012. The largest drop was seen within private law Children's Act proceedings (there were 30,000 fewer certificates granted), and is attributed to the implementation of LASPO. Public family law cases were less affected, as they are driven by Local Authority applications to issue proceedings and are non-means and merits tested (Legal Aid Statistics in England and Wales, Legal Aid Agency, Ministry of Justice, 24 June 2014).

In 2015, the key issues of the family justice system include the increased number of litigants in person (21 per cent over one year); the lack of legal aid in family cases was cited as the most substantial problem of the system by 17 per cent of specialist lawyers responding to questions from the accountancy firm Grant Thornton, while the courts generally not being 'fit for purpose' was the main difficulty cited by 14 per cent (*Matrimonial Survey 2015*, Grant Thornton, 1 December 2015).

The National Audit Office has shown that across all family court cases starting there was a 30 per cent increase in those in which neither party had legal representation in 2013–14 compared with 2012–13 (*Implementing reforms to civil legal aid*, Report by the Comptroller and Auditor General Ministry of Justice and Legal Aid Agency, National Audit Office, HC 784 Session, 014–15 20 November, 2014) and in the first quarter of 2015, 76 per cent of private family law cases had at least one party who was not represented (Lord Falconer, *Five years in the death of the British justice system*, New Statesman, 8 September 2015).

The Justice Committee, which is appointed by the House of Commons to examine the expenditure, administration and policy of the Ministry of Justice and its associated public bodies, has also reported on this issue. It noted (Justice – Eighth Report, *Impact of changes to civil legal aid under Part 1 of the Legal Aid, Sentencing and Punishment of Offenders Act 2012*, 4 March 2015, para 92):

The National Audit Office in its report, Implementing the civil legal aid reforms, found the number of cases in which neither party in a family law case had representation had increased by 18,519, around 30 per cent of all cases. In the first quarter of 2014, 80 per cent of all private family law cases had at least one party that was not represented. In contrast, the Minister told us, however, that the number of litigants in person in private family law cases had only risen by a 'small percentage' from 66 per cent of cases in which at least one party was not represented to 74 per cent. An additional complication is that the number of cases in the family courts has dropped since the introduction of the legal aid reforms by around 40 per cent. Whatever the true figure may be, evidence we have received strongly suggests not only a significant increase in parties without legal representation but also that litigants in person may be appearing in more complicated cases or be less able to represent themselves

A steady decrease in public funding has led to an ever-widening gap in the system, leading to a rise in the number of court-goers representing themselves in family proceedings, as they are unable to afford legal representation but do not qualify for legal aid. Once referred to as self-represented litigants (SRLs), members of the public who process their own cases or represent themselves in court are now called Litigants in Person, or LIPs (Terminology for Litigants in Person, Practice guidance issued by the Master of the Rolls, Lord Dyson, 11 March 2013). As early as 2005, and based on an analysis of 1,334 family cases, a study found that 64 per cent of private adoption cases and 60 per cent of divorce cases featured at least one self-represented litigant (R Moorhead and M Sefton, 'Litigants in Person: unrepresented litigants in first instance proceedings', DCA Research Series 2/05, March 2005, Cardiff University (Department for Constitutional Affairs), p 97). In the first quarter of 2014, 74 per cent of private law children's cases featured at least one self-represented party (*Court Statistics Quarterly*, January to March 2014, Table 2.4, Litigants in Person in Private Family Law Cases, Ministry of Justice Analytical Series, 2014).

A Litigant in Person may choose to process their case solely on their own, or sporadically seek out legal assistance, rather than pay for long-term legal representation, which lowers costs and helps the LIP if they are not fully aware of the law surrounding their case. An increase in LIPs in the family courts has led to an increase in the use of lay advocates, known as McKenzie Friends. A McKenzie Friend is able to assist a self-represented litigant by:

- providing moral support;
- taking notes in court;
- helping with case papers;
- giving advice on any aspect of the conduct of the case

(Practice Guidance, McKenzie Friends (Civil
and Family Courts), 12 July 2010).

McKenzie Friends vary in experience and competence, usually charge less for their assistance than solicitors and barristers, and often work for free. The name derives from a case in which the role was first recognised, *McKenzie v McKenzie* (1970). As the demand for McKenzie Friends has steadily increased inside the family justice system, a call to consider regulating their activity was made in April 2014 by the Legal Services Consumer Panel, with a view to protecting litigants in person from poor advice and unreasonable charges (Fee Charging McKenzie Friends, The Legal Services Consumer Panel, April 2014). However, there is a view that regulating the McKenzie sector at this time may deter lay advisers and reduce the level of support that litigants in person so desperately need as they try to navigate the system without conventional representation.

8.5 REFORMATION OF THE FAMILY JUSTICE SYSTEM

Reformation of a system can be viewed as a healthy response to environmental and societal changes, and an increased understanding of what needs to be improved upon. Yet it can also be the result of ongoing difficulties which are not properly addressed in the first instance. The family justice system is continuously trying to adapt to the ever-changing dynamics of society, but a lack of government funds and a slow turn-around time to implement much-needed changes on the ground means that the system continues to find itself subject to review and, ultimately, reform.

The latest series of recommendations for reform stem from the Family Justice Review, a report which focused on examining possible areas for reform with the family justice system, and which was published on 3 November 2011. The government's response to that review was laid before Parliament on 6 February 2012. A judge within the family courts, Mr Justice Ryder, was appointed by the then President of the Family Division, Sir Nicholas Wall, to make judicial proposals for what has been termed 'the modernisation of family justice'. The proposals were designed to make the family courts simpler and easier to use.

The proposals contained two key elements:

- a focus on strong judicial leadership and management; and
- robust case management of proceedings.

The key areas for reform included:

- a Single Family Court, to promote a significant culture change through strong judicial leadership, and focusing on evidence-based good practice;
- the provision of a network of Local Family Court Centres, under the umbrella of the Single Family Court, led by designated Family Judges where all levels of judges and magistrates will sit as judges of the Family Court;
- management of judicial resources to help reduce court delays;
- cultivating a good practice framework, to improve outcomes for children;

- robust case management of public family law cases;
- assisting Litigants in Person with the law and procedure;
- facilitating the voice of the child (the expression, by children where possible, of their wishes and feelings)

(Judicial Proposals for the Modernisation of Family Justice,
Mr Justice Ryder, July 2012).

Areas which remain untouched by the reforms include:

- the High Court, whose unique jurisdiction will be preserved;
- keeping England and Wales divided into geographical areas, judicially led and managed by the Designated Family Judge;
- the day-to-day management and administration of family cases.

Speaking at the national conference of Resolution, an organisation made up of family lawyers who practice a collaborative approach to handling family cases, Mr Justice Ryder said the aim of the reforms was to 'create a new court and better processes that work in the real world', which could only be achieved through a 'revolutionary culture of change' (Resolution National Conference, Stratford-upon-Avon, 12 April 2013). Many of the reforms have now been implemented, but it remains to be seen whether they are improving the quality of, and access to, justice.

8.6   MEDIA REPORTING IN THE FAMILY COURTS

Prior to 2009, only specific courts could be opened up to allow reporting of family matters, and members of the public and the media were often barred from attending family hearings.

However, on 27 April 2009, all levels of the family courts were opened, but only to accredited members of the media: qualified journalists working for authorised news outlets. Courts are still able to restrict access to hearings if they consider it to be in the best interests of any children involved, or to protect parties or witnesses in the case, who are also able to request such a restriction on their own behalf.

Courts also have the power to restrict what can be reported if they feel it would protect the welfare of any child or families involved in the proceedings. The court may also relax reporting restrictions in individual cases if they feel it would be appropriate or in the public interest to do so.

Further clarification on the position of media reporting by the President of the Family Division, Sir Nicholas Wall, consolidated and smoothed out some of the tensions between open justice, the need for justice to be seen to be done, and privacy and confidentiality concerns (A Wolanski and K Wilson, 'The Family Courts: Media Access and Reporting', Resources, Judicial College Office, Guidance, July 2011), but his successor, Sir James Munby, took reformation in this area a step further.

An outspoken advocate for greater transparency within the family courts, Sir James Munby released a draft Practice Guidance on media reporting, which was widely welcomed by the media, the general public and some members of the legal profession. The Practice Guidance, which has been issued for consultation and comment and is designed to be a guide for legal practitioners, recommends that decisions of family courts should always be published, unless there are compelling reasons against publication, and that some judgments should be published in anonymised form, where appropriate ('Transparency in the Family Courts and the Court of Protection, Publication of Judgments', Draft Practice Guidance, Sir James Munby, President of the Family Division, July 2013).

Section 12 of the Administration of Justice Act 1960 currently makes it a contempt of court to publish a judgment in a family court case involving children, unless the judgment has been delivered in public, or the judge has authorised publication. The July 2013 Practice Guidance effectively creates a presumption that all judgments should be published, unless compelling reasons exist to prevent publication and keep them private. The underlying notion of openness in family proceedings stems from a long-standing tenet in English law that any justice system should be transparent in its day-to-day workings, and allow itself to be examined by the very people who use the system.

The presumption of publication is wide and includes:

- cases brought by local authorities;
- cases involving the making or refusal of orders including emergency protection orders, orders involving a deprivation of liberty, or the withholding of significant medical treatment; and
- orders involving the restraint of publication on information relating to the proceedings.

In all other cases not specifically mentioned in the Practice Guidance, the Guidance suggests that a presumption of publication exists where:

- a party or member of the media applies for an order requesting publication of a judgment; and
- the judge is satisfied that, having taken into account any rights arising from relevant provisions within the European Convention on Human Rights (ECHR), the judgment may be published.

The Guidance suggests that reporting of cases and the extent to which a judgment is anonymised should be decided on a case-by-case basis, and places emphasis on ensuring anonymity does not extend beyond protecting the privacy of the families involved, unless there are good reasons to do so. The Draft Guidance also recommends that restrictions on reporting should be limited and that public authorities and expert witnesses should be named unless there are compelling reasons not to, a broad departure from previous reporting restrictions which shielded expert witnesses, for example, from being named in reported judgments. The number of judgments and family cases which explicitly reveal the names of expert witnesses has steadily increased over the last decade, allowing for debate over concerning issues inside the family courts (see for example 'The doctor who took my baby away', *The Telegraph* online, 1 April 2012).

The Practice Guidance is part of an incremental approach to increasing transparency in the family courts. Following a family case over which Mr Justice Munby presided, he said:

> We must have the humility to recognise – and to acknowledge – that public debate, and the jealous vigilance of an informed media, have an important role to play in exposing past miscarriages of justice and in preventing possible future miscarriages of justice . . . The remedy, even if it is probably doomed to only partial success, is . . . more transparency. Putting it bluntly, letting the glare of publicity into the family courts.
>
> (*Daily Telegraph*, 5 September 2013)

8.7   FAMILY LAW AND PHILOSOPHY

Family law affects every area of life and often incites policy-makers and governments to address some very difficult questions, questions which can be highly controversial in nature.

8.7.1   MARRIAGE, COHABITATION AND DIVORCE

The gradual decline in the twentieth century of people getting married, and an increased trend in divorce, has sparked an ongoing national debate about whether society is taking a step back or merely moving towards a way of life which is better suited to the human condition. And as more and more people choose cohabitation (living with a partner rather than being married or in a civil partnership with them, sometimes for many years) as a means of expressing their togetherness, family law has found it challenging to adapt to such choices.

In an attempt to reconcile the gaps in the law between married couples and cohabiting ones, Lord Lester proposed the Cohabitation Bill in 2009. The Bill sought to give cohabiting couples the right to make a claim for financial provision at the end of their relationship, either through separation or death – a right which is currently afforded to married couples. The Bill, although widely welcomed by family lawyers, was also opposed by some academics and peers in the House of Lords. Other dissenters took the view that people who chose to cohabit did so because they were making a conscious

as three who had experienced family proceedings. The report highlighted the need to look at the way proceedings might affect children, to make information more child-friendly and to give children the opportunity to produce a plan detailing how they would like to be supported and have their voice heard ('Do more than listen. Act' – Consultation response to the Family Justice Review undertaken for the Family Justice Council', 27 July 2011).

And in July 2014, at the newly established Voice of the Child Conference, Justice Minister Simon Hughes announced that children inside the family courts would be listened to and heard more effectively, with the government committing to allowing children as young as 10, and younger where appropriate, to have access to judges to make their views and feelings known ('Children will be seen and heard in family courts', government press release, 25 July 2014).

8.8 THE FUTURE OF THE FAMILY COURTS

The future of family law, while uncertain, and for all the controversy it courts, is a hopeful one. As society changes and our understanding of the human condition evolves, the family courts too must keep pace with and react to those changes. The modernisation of the family justice system in the twenty-first century is perhaps one of the most exciting periods in history for the family courts, and for its impact on future generations.

The enactment of the Marriage (Same Sex Couples) Act 2013 made provision, for the first time, for the marriage of same-sex couples in England and Wales. Maria Miller MP, who sponsored the Bill, told the media that the passing of the Bill was 'clear affirmation' that 'respect for each and every person is paramount, regardless of age, religion, gender, ethnicity or sexuality'. However, not everyone backed the Bill; the Conservative MP Sir Gerald Howarth viewed the Bill as having 'absolutely no mandate' (BBC News online, 17 July 2013). The first same-sex marriage ceremonies took place on 29 March 2014.

Other areas of family law, too, are wading into increasingly controversial waters. The Family Drug and Alcohol Court (FDAC), set up in 2008 by a pioneering family judge, District Judge Nicholas Crichton, has been accused of being a violation of judicial power, due to the extent of the interaction between judges in these courts and the families that come before them (BBC Radio 4, *Law In Action*, 15 March 2012). The judiciary did not agree though, and since its inception, FDAC, which uses a different approach from that adopted by mainstream family courts to help families with substance abuse, has won awards for its work and continues to lead the way in effective and humane care of families struggling with drug and alcohol addiction. Statistics for FDAC show that at the time of the final court order, 39 per cent of FDAC mothers were reunited with their children, compared to 21 per cent of mothers from a comparison group in ordinary care proceedings. There was also a marked reduction in costs for local authorities, as children stayed with their parents, care placements were shorter and there were fewer contested cases (Family Drug and Alcohol Court (FDAC), Evaluation Research Study, Brunel University, 2008–10).

CHAPTER SUMMARY: THE FAMILY COURTS AND PROCESS

FAMILY COURTS

Family courts are concerned with the law relating to the family unit. They deal with:

- marriage;
- divorce decrees;
- cohabitation;
- some types of domestic violence;
- disputes between parents over the upbringing of their children;
- financial support for children upon divorce or separation;
- local authority intervention where children may need to be protected from abuse or neglect; and
- adoption.

Jurisdiction to hear these matters is conferred to Family Proceedings Courts, which are specialist magistrates' courts, as well as County Courts and the Family Division of the High Court, through the umbrella of the Single Family Court, which may sit anywhere in England and Wales.

PRIVATE AND PUBLIC FAMILY LAW

Family courts are broadly divided into two areas: private and public family law. These areas are not mutually exclusive, as private family cases can often become public in nature, where for example a concern over a child's living arrangements may reveal more serious concerns about that child's day-to-day care. However, public family law cases must always start in the Family Proceedings Courts, though they can be transferred to County Courts to minimise delay, consolidate proceedings or where the matter is exceptionally serious, complex or important.

Family court judges are charged with handling cases arising from these areas of law, which typically result in a series of directions, or orders, requiring a person to do or not to do something.

Private family law matters are brought by individuals, like parents, spouses and next of kin, usually in connection with a divorce or parents' separation. Judges dealing with these matters can make various orders, for example to control who holds the legal rights and responsibilities for a child.

Public law cases are usually brought by local authorities (although the NSPCC, as an 'authorised person', currently also has powers to bring such cases), and can include issues such as:

- emergency protection orders, removing a child from harm by relocating them to a place of safety, or ensuring they are not removed from a safe environment;

- family assistance orders (s 16 of the Children Act 1989), as in private law proceedings;
- supervision orders, where children are placed under the supervision of their local authority;
- care orders, conferring parental responsibility of a child to the local authority who are applying for an order.

THE CHILDREN ACT 1989 AND THE PARAMOUNTCY PRINCIPLE

The Children Act 1989 is designed to make the welfare of every child the primary, or paramount, concern in cases involving children. This is often referred to as the 'paramountcy principle'. This means the welfare of the child will be the paramount consideration for all decisions made under the Act.

LEGAL AID AND THE FAMILY COURTS

Legal aid has been drastically reduced for civil cases by the Legal Aid, Sentencing and Punishment of Offenders Act (LASPO) 2012. As a result, only a very narrow set of family cases are now eligible for legal aid, and include:

- cases where a victim of domestic violence is divorcing or separating from an abusive partner; and
- cases where a child is at risk of abuse from a partner.

REFORMATION OF THE FAMILY JUSTICE SYSTEM

The latest series of recommendations for reform stem from the Family Justice Review. A judge within the family courts, Mr Justice Ryder, was appointed to make judicial proposals for what has been termed 'the modernisation of family justice'. The proposals were designed to make the family courts simpler and easier to use.

The proposals contained two key elements:

- a focus on strong judicial leadership and management; and
- robust case management of proceedings.

Key areas which have been reformed:

- a single family court, to promote a significant culture change through strong judicial leadership, and focusing on evidence-based good practice;
- the provision of a network of Local Family Court Centres, under the umbrella of the Single Family Court, led by Designated Family Judges where all levels of judges and magistrates will sit as judges of the Family Court.

DOMESTIC VIOLENCE

The definition of domestic violence, which is not a legal formula, was recently extended to include 16- and 17-year-old victims, and is legally defined as:

any incident or pattern of incidents of controlling, coercive or threatening behaviour, violence or abuse between those aged 16 or over who are or have been intimate partners or family members regardless of gender or sexuality. This can encompass but is not limited to the following types of abuse:

- psychological
- physical
- sexual
- financial
- emotional.

This definition came into force on 31 March 2013, and includes female genital mutilation (FGM) in which women and girls are forcibly mutilated in order solely to prevent them from experiencing sexual pleasure, and forced marriage.

FOOD FOR THOUGHT

1   Scandals surrounding child sexual abuse and exploitation have become so acute that the government has now set up an Inquiry to find out the extent to which state and non-state institutions have failed to protect children from abuse. To date, there have been more than 67 inquiries in England alone looking at child protection issues – do you think another inquiry will make a difference? (Independent Panel Inquiry Into Child Sexual Abuse, https://childsexualabuseinquiry. independent.gov.uk)

2   The latest research on Litigants in Person suggests that engaging self-represented parties in the decision-making process would be beneficial to improving case outcomes. Do you agree? (Litigants in Person in Private Family Law Cases, Ministry of Justice Analytical Series 2014)

3   The administration and recording of marriage has steadily moved away from the church to the state. Should people now be able to marry privately without state intervention?

FURTHER READING

Cretney, S, *Family Law in the Twentieth Century: A History*, 2003, Oxford: OUP

Hewitt, L and Hughes, S, 'The changing Face(book) of family law' (2013) NLJ 7555

Ministry of Justice, *Family Court Statistics Quarterly, England and Wales*, July to September 2015, Ministry of Justice Statistics bulletin, December 2015

Moorhead, R and Sefton, M, 'Litigants in Person: unrepresented litigants in first instance proceedings', DCA Research Series 2/05, March 2005, Cardiff University (Department for Constitutional Affairs)
Munby, J, 'Sloppy practice in adoption', 20 September 2013, NLJ online
Wall, N, 'Changing the culture', 29 November 2011, Judiciary of England and Wales
Waller, P, 'Going the distance', 4 May 2012, NLJ online
Wolanski, A and Wilson, K, 'The Family Courts: Media Access and Reporting', Resources, Judicial College Office, Guidance, July 2011

USEFUL WEBSITES

http://unsafespaces.com/
The Not So Big Society Blog.

www.coram.org.uk/supporting-parents/family-drug-and-alcohol-court
The Family Drug and Alcohol Court.

http://familylaw.allpartyparliamentarygroup.org.uk
All Party Parliamentary Group on Family Law and the Court of Protection.

http://researchingreform.net
Researching Reform.

COMPANION WEBSITE

Now visit the companion website to:

- test your understanding of the key terms using our Flashcard Glossary;
- revise and consolidate your knowledge of 'The family courts and process' using our multiple choice question testbank;
- view all of the links to the Useful Websites above.

www.routledge.com/cw/slapper

THE CRIMINAL COURTS 9

9.1 INTRODUCTION

There are over 12,000 different criminal offences in English law, 3,700 of which have been created since 1997. Professors Andrew Ashworth and Lucia Zedner identified that criminalisation is no longer a last resort but has become 'a routine system for management disorder' (A Ashworth and L Zedner (2008) 'Defending the criminal law: reflections on the changing character of crime', 2 *Criminal Law and Philosophy* 21). Criminal offences can be classified in different ways. You could, for example, classify them according to whether they are offences against people or property; you could classify them according to the type of mental element (*mens rea*) required for the offence, for example, 'intention' or 'recklessness'. Another type of classification, and the one that concerns us here, is whether the offence is triable *summarily*, that is, in a magistrates' court (for relatively trivial offences like traffic offences), or is an *indictable* offence (the more serious offences like murder, manslaughter, rape and robbery are *indictable only*), triable in front of a judge and jury in a Crown Court.

From the mid-nineteenth century, magistrates were empowered to hear some indictable cases in certain circumstances. Today, there is still a class of offence that is triable 'either way', that is, summarily or in a jury trial. A typical example would be a potentially serious offence such as theft, but one that has been committed in a minor way, as in the theft of a milk bottle. These offences now account for about 80 per cent of those tried in Crown Courts. Most defendants, however, opt for summary trial. The magistrates' court has the power to refuse jurisdiction – that means to refuse to deal with the matter – if it thinks, having considered the facts of the case, that its powers of sentencing would be insufficient if the case resulted in a conviction.

Where several defendants are charged together with either-way offences, each defendant's choice can be exercised separately. So, if one elects for trial in the Crown Court, the others may still be tried summarily if the magistrates agree (*R v Brentwood Justices ex p Nicholls* (1991)).

Radical reforms to modernise the criminal courts and strip out 500,000 hearings a year were announced by the government in 2015. The chancellor of the exchequer pledged £700 million for an IT revolution in the justice system (*The Times*, 26 November 2015).

s 130(12) gives priority to the issue of a compensation order over a fine. In 2010, the Crown Court and magistrates' courts issued 154,428 compensation orders. The total cost in 2010 was £44,620,426 (*Hansard*, 20 June 2011, col 86W).

Alongside any such compensation order, an offender may also be required to pay prosecution costs, on a scale currently starting at £85, and a so-called Victim Surcharge, currently priced from £15 to £120. This surcharge is statutorily imposed regardless of whether or not there was a victim or victims but goes to the Victims and Witness General Fund. In this way, it can be understood as a tax on the cost of a prosecution. It is also payable on conviction in the Crown Court. Section 54 of the Criminal Justice and Courts Act 2015 introduced the criminal courts charge, a mandatory charge payable on conviction (whether as a result of a plea or after trial) and refusal of an appeal in respect of all offences committed on or after 13 April 2015. The provisions are draconian, as judges and magistrates have no power to refuse to impose the charge or to determine the level of charge. Charges range from £150 for a conviction in the magistrates' court to £1,200 for a conviction after trial on indictment in the Crown Court. The charges raised concerns in a number of quarters about their effect on the poorest and most vulnerable defendants, and on 3 December 2015 the Lord Chancellor, Michael Gove, announced that as of 24 December 2015 they would no longer be imposed.

9.2.2 OFFENCES TRIABLE 'EITHER WAY'

Where the defendant is charged with an offence triable 'either way', the first matter to be established is whether he should be tried summarily (by magistrates) or on indictment (in the Crown Court by a judge and jury). The procedures by which this matter is resolved are known as plea before venue and allocation hearings. There were substantial changes made to this procedure in May 2013 when changes made by Sched 3 to the Criminal Justice Act 2003 to ss 17–21 of the Magistrates' Courts Act 1980 finally came into effect.

In a plea before venue hearing, that is, one where the accused is charged with an either-way offence, they are first asked if they wish to indicate a guilty plea. If they do, the magistrates will hear the facts of the case and see details of any previous convictions. The magistrates retain the power to commit them for sentence to the Crown Court if they feel that their powers of punishment are inadequate (this is dealt with later in more detail). If they feel that they have enough power to deal with the accused, then they proceed to sentence them.

If the defendant pleads not guilty or declines to indicate their plea, then an allocation hearing is held under s 19 Magistrates' Courts Act 1980. In this hearing the prosecution and defence make submissions about whether the case should be heard at the magistrates' or Crown Court. The magistrates then decide whether to agree to hear the case or decline to do so and commit it to the Crown Court. If they agree to hear the case, then the accused can still choose (elect) to have their case heard by a jury and – if they so choose – the case will be committed for Crown Court trial. If they decide in favour of the magistrates' court, then it will fix a date for a summary trial.

Second, if the determination is in favour of trial on indictment (by either method), the case will be sent to the Crown Court under s 51 Crime and Disorder Act (CDA) 1998. The old system of committal proceedings, where magistrates established whether there was a *prima facie* case to be heard before sending the case to the Crown Court, was abolished in May 2013.

Most defendants charged with 'either-way' offences are tried by magistrates: 36,167 cases were committed to the Crown Court in 2013 because the magistrates considered their sentencing powers to be inadequate and on average 4 per cent of cases go to the Crown Court because the defendants elect trial by jury (*Judicial and Court Statistics Quarterly, April–June 2014,* Ministry of Justice, 2014).

The defendant therefore can insist on trial on indictment, but cannot insist on being tried summarily if the magistrates decline jurisdiction. Similarly, the magistrates can decide that the defendant should be tried on indictment, but cannot insist that he or she be tried summarily. Prosecutions conducted by the Attorney General, the Solicitor General or the Director of Public Prosecutions must be tried on indictment if so requested by the prosecutor.

If a defendant charged with a number of related either-way offences pleads guilty to one of them at plea before venue and is sent to the Crown Court to be tried for the rest, the power in s 4 of the PCC(S)A 2000 – to send the offence to which he or she has pleaded guilty to the Crown Court for sentence – still exists.

9.2.3   SENTENCING IN THE MAGISTRATES' COURTS

Concern is often expressed at what sometimes appear to be quite notable discrepancies in sentencing practices employed by different benches of magistrates. It might be that these variations are unavoidable in circumstances where the rigidity of fixed penalties is unacceptable for most offences and regional differences in types of prevalent crime prompt justices to have certain attitudes to particular offences. Media reports from courtrooms are also unlikely to pick out the full detail and nuances of cases; there is clearly a difference between following a case in the press and watching it from the public gallery. There are several research surveys that demonstrate the discrepancies in magistrates' sentencing. Tarling, for example (*Sentencing and Practice in Magistrates' Courts*, 1979, Home Office Study 98), showed that in the 30 courts he surveyed, the use of probation (as it was then called) varied between 1 per cent and 12 per cent, suspended sentences between 4 per cent and 16 per cent, and fines between 46 per cent and 76 per cent. In one study, it was found that custody rates, average custodial sentence lengths (ACSL) and the use of life and Indeterminate Sentences for Public Protection (IPPs) vary significantly across the 42 Criminal Justice Areas (CJAs) in England and Wales. For example, of those CJAs with custody rates in the top five for 2006, three (Essex, Bedfordshire and London) were consistently in the top five for 2003, 2004 and 2005. Similarly, for those CJAs with custody rates in the bottom five for 2006, two (Dyfed–Powys and Lincolnshire) were consistently in the bottom five for 2003, 2004 and 2005 (T Mason, N de Silva, N Sharma, D Brown and G Harper, *Local Variation in Sentencing in England and Wales*, 2007, Ministry of Justice).

9.2.3.1   Committals for sentence

Currently, cases committed to the Crown Court for sentence must be heard in the Crown Court by a bench composed of a High Court judge, circuit judge or recorder sitting with between two and four JPs. The Powers of the Criminal Courts (Sentencing) Act 2000 ss 3–7 states that where, on a summary trial of an offence triable 'either way' a person aged 18 or over is convicted, the magistrates can commit the convicted person to the Crown Court for sentence if the magistrates are of the opinion that the offence was so serious that greater punishment should be inflicted for it than they have power to impose, or, in the case of a violent or sexual offence, that a custodial sentence for a period longer than the magistrates have power to impose is necessary to protect the public from serious harm, or, under s 4, the defendant is being sent to the Crown Court for a trial of related offences.

9.2.3.2   Warrant execution and fine default powers

The police used to be primarily responsible for arresting fine defaulters and those in breach of community sentences. Increasingly, however, some police forces have given this work a low priority. The Courts Act 2003 extended the use of the Department for Work and Pensions' long-standing Third Party Deduction Scheme, which allows deductions from benefits to enforce payment of fines. The level of deductions is contained in the Fines (Deductions from Income Support) (Amendment) Regulations 2004.

Deductions can be applied when the offender is first sentenced, subsequently applied if the offender defaults as part of a resetting of payment terms, or used as a further sanction by the fines officer. Other deductions can include council tax, rent arrears, fuel costs, housing costs and water charges.

9.2.4   YOUTH COURTS

The procedures previously discussed apply only to those aged at least 18. Defendants under 18 years of age will normally be tried by a youth court, no matter what the classification of the offence (summary, either way, indictable only). Section 51A of the Crime and Disorder Act 1998 provides for sending a defendant under 18 to the Crown Court for trial. If the charge is homicide or a firearms offence under either s 51A Firearms Act 1968 or s 29(3) Violent Crime Reduction Act 2006, it must be tried on indictment. Sending the young person to the Crown Court is also mandatory under s 51A(2) where:

- the charge is a specified offence under s 224 CJA 2003 and it appears to the court that the young person, if convicted, may be a 'dangerous' offender under s 226 CJA 2003; or
- the offence charged is a serious one (under s 91 Powers of Criminal Courts (Sentencing) Act 2000) and might attract a lengthy custodial sentence under the circumstances.

A young person may be tried on indictment where the offence in question is related to one which must be sent to the Crown Court under the provisions listed above. The court also has discretion where:

- the offence charged is a 'grave' crime punishable with at least 14 years' imprisonment, or a range of sexual and firearms offences;
- the defendant is jointly charged with an adult who is going to be tried on indictment and the court considers that it is in the interests of justice that both should be tried on indictment.

A defendant under 18 may be tried summarily in an adult magistrates' court where:

- he or she is to be tried jointly with an adult. This is subject to the power to commit both for trial on indictment, and also subject to a power to remit the defendant under 18 for trial to a youth court where the adult pleads guilty, or is discharged or committed for trial on indictment, but the defendant is not.

When defendants under 18 are tried by magistrates in the youth court, there will generally be three justices to hear the case, of whom one must be a man and one a woman. These justices will have had special training to deal with such cases. There are special provisions relating to punishment for this age group. Section 9 of the Criminal Justice and Immigration Act 2008 says a sentencing court must have regard to 'the principal aim of the youth justice system', which is to 'prevent offending (or re-offending) by persons aged under 18'. It identifies the purposes of sentencing as:

(a) the punishment of offenders;
(b) the reform and rehabilitation of offenders;
(c) the protection of the public; and
(d) the making of reparation by offenders to persons affected by their offences.

The current maximum fine for a child (under 14 years of age) is £250, and for a young person (under 18) £1,000. Members of both groups may be made the subject of a variety of orders, including the youth rehabilitation order, which is a generic community order which permits the imposition of a range of requirements for e.g. activity, supervision, a curfew, etc. A sentence of imprisonment may be imposed only on a defendant who is at least 21 years old. A sentence of detention in a young offenders' institution may be imposed only on a defendant who is at least 18 years old (the intention is to bring all those aged at least 18 within the imprisonment regime). For those under 18, the custodial sentence is a detention and training order, which may be imposed only where an adult could have been sentenced to imprisonment. Where the defendant is under 15, a detention and training order can be imposed only if he or she is a 'persistent' offender. In measures under Part III of the PCC(S)A 2000, the youth court will on some occasions be obliged, and on others will have the discretion, to refer the young offender to a youth offender panel, the members of which will agree with the young offender and his or her family a course of action designed to tackle the offending behaviour and its causes. This could involve actions such as making apologies, carrying out reparation, doing community work or taking part in family counselling.

Traditionally, the aim of the youth court system has been to take the young offender out of the normal criminal court environment, and this has involved strict rules about public access to the court. In general, members of the public have not been permitted to attend and reporting restrictions have been very tight. Parents can be required to attend, and must attend in the case of any person under the age of 16, unless such a requirement would be unreasonable in the circumstances. The name or photograph of any person under 18 appearing in a case must not be printed in any newspaper or broadcast without the authority of the court or the Home Secretary. Also the youth justice system has introduced a system of warnings and reprimands (formerly known as cautions) that are issued instead of court proceedings for many offenders in an attempt to divert them from the youth court system.

9.2.5 INDICTABLE OFFENCES – SENDING TO THE CROWN COURT

Under s 51 of the Crime and Disorder Act 1998, where an adult defendant is charged with an indictable-only offence – one which can be tried only by a Crown Court (for example, murder, manslaughter, rape or robbery), the court shall send them directly to the Crown Court for trial. They are 'sent forthwith'. Where they are also charged with an either-way offence or a summary offence, they may be sent directly to the Crown Court for that as well, provided the magistrates believe that it is related to the indictable offence and, in the case of a summary offence, it is punishable with imprisonment or involves obligatory or discretionary disqualification from driving. Under this procedure, the accused may apply to a Crown Court judge for the charge(s) to be dismissed, and the judge should so direct if it appears that the evidence would be insufficient to convict the accused (Sched 3 to the CDA 1998).

9.3 THE CROWN COURT

Until 1971, the main criminal courts were the Assizes and the Quarter Sessions. These courts did not sit continuously and were not held in locations that corresponded with centres of population, as had been the case when they developed. The system was very inefficient as circuit judges wasted much time simply travelling from one town on the circuit to the next, and many defendants spent long periods in gaol awaiting trial.

Change was made following the *Report of the Beeching Royal Commission on Assizes and Quarter Sessions* (1969). The Courts Act 1971 abolished the Assizes and Quarter Sessions. These were replaced by a single Crown Court, a part of the Supreme Court of Judicature. The Crown Court is not a local court like the magistrates' court, but a single court which sits in 77 centres. England and Wales are divided into six circuits, each with its own headquarters and staff. The centres are divided into three tiers. In first-tier centres, High Court judges hear civil and criminal cases, whereas circuit judges and recorders hear only criminal cases. Second-tier centres are served by the same types of judge, but hear criminal cases only. At third-tier centres, recorders and circuit judges hear just criminal cases.

Criminal offences are divided into three classes according to their gravity.

9.3.1 THE JUDGES

High Court judges are usually from the Queen's Bench Division (QBD). Circuit judges are full-time appointments made by the Queen on the advice of the Lord Chancellor. They are drawn from advocates with at least seven years' experience of Crown Court practice (s 71 of the CLSA 1990) or lawyers who have been recorders. Appointment is also possible for someone who has had three years' experience in a number of other judicial offices like that of the district judge (magistrates' courts). Circuit judges retire at the age of 72, or 75 if the Lord Chancellor thinks it in the public interest.

The Courts Act 2003, ss 65–67, introduced greater flexibility in the deployment of judicial resources, allowing district judges (magistrates' courts) to deal with and make orders in relation both to allocation and to other interim issues in cases reserved to the Crown Court. High Court judges, circuit judges and recorders are able to sit as magistrates when exercising their criminal and family jurisdiction.

A circuit judge may be removed from office by the Lord Chancellor on the grounds of incapacity or misbehaviour (s 17(4) of the Courts Act 1971). This right has not been exercised since 1983, when Judge Bruce Campbell, an Old Bailey judge, was removed from office a week after being convicted of two charges of smuggling.

To qualify for appointment as a recorder, a person must have seven years' experience of advocacy in the Crown Court or County Courts. JPs may also sit in the Crown Court, provided they are with one of the types of judge mentioned above. It is mandatory for between two and four JPs to sit when the Crown Court is hearing an appeal or dealing with persons committed for sentence by a magistrates' court.

9.3.2 JURISDICTION

The Crown Court hears all cases involving trial on indictment. It also hears appeals from those convicted summarily in the magistrates' courts. At the conclusion of an appeal hearing, it has the power to confirm, reverse or vary any part of the decision under appeal (s 48(2) of the Senior Courts Act 1981). If the appeal is decided against the accused, the Crown Court has the power to impose any sentence that the magistrates could have imposed, including one that is harsher than the one originally imposed on the defendant.

9.3.3 DELAY AND OTHER CONCERNS REGARDING CROWN COURT PROCEEDINGS

Defendants committed to the Crown Court to be tried might have to wait a long time. The *Judicial and Court Quarterly Statistics, January–March 2014* (Ministry of Justice, June 2014) reports that:

> For cases completing at the Crown Court during Q1 2014, the number of days from offence to completion has remained unchanged at 304 days when compared with the same quarter in the previous year. However, changes can be seen when looking at the time spent in the magistrates' courts and the Crown Court. When comparing Q1 2014 with Q1 2013, the time spent at the magistrates' courts between first hearing and being sent to the Crown Court has fallen from 26 days to 8 days, whereas the time spent at the Crown Court has increased from 139 days to 155 days. This is mainly the result of the national abolition of committal hearings for triable either way cases.

Ever since the Streatfield Committee Report recommended in 1961 that the maximum time a defendant should have to wait after committal for trial should be eight weeks, there have been many schemes to help achieve this aim, but none has been particularly successful. Since 1985, for example, a person charged with an offence triable 'either way' can request the prosecution to furnish them with information (in the form of witness statements, a summary of the case, etc) of the case against them. This was aimed at increasing the number of guilty pleas by showing to the defendant at an early stage the strength of the prosecution's case.

When one remembers that the average time to try a case on a plea of 'not guilty' is about 14 hours, the burden of work on the Crown Court – dealing with over 90,000 trials and almost 120,000 defendants each year – is considerable. The consequent delay has very serious repercussions for the criminal justice system: justice delayed is justice denied. The accuracy of testimony becomes less reliable the longer the gap between the original reception of the data by a witness and his account of it in court. Also important is the stress and pain for those innocent defendants who have to wait so long before their case can be put to a jury.

9.4 MAGISTRATES' COURTS V CROWN COURTS

For offences triable 'either way', there has been much debate about the merits of each venue. The introduction of the 'plea before venue' procedure previously described has significantly reduced the number of cases committed for trial to the Crown Court and significantly increased the number committed for sentence. In 2013, 68 per cent of defendants pleaded guilty to all counts, 30 per cent pleaded not guilty to at least one count, and 2 per cent did not enter a plea. Since 2001, the guilty plea rate has steadily risen from 56 per cent to the current rate of 68 per cent. Initiatives in the Crown Court and other agencies, such as offering an early plea sentencing discount (a more lenient sentence if the defendant pleads guilty early) and providing early charging advice from the Crown Prosecution Service at police stations, have helped to increase the guilty plea rate.

One of the reasons defendants choose to have their cases tried at the Crown Court is that prosecution cases sometimes fall apart during the delay before a Crown Court hearing, allowing the defendant to go free. Another is that juries cannot be compelled to give reasons for convicting, unlike magistrates, who can be required to justify their reasons in writing for review in the High Court, which can overturn convictions or acquittals. Thus, there is a greater chance with jury convictions that an appeal court will regard a conviction (should there be one) as unsafe and unsatisfactory because the jury's reasons for having convicted will not be known. Thus, a defendant who suspects that they might be convicted can reasonably prefer to be convicted by a jury than by a magistrate because the former do not and cannot give reasons for their verdicts and are therefore perhaps easier to appeal. Jury verdicts are arguably more likely to be regarded as unsafe on appeal because it will not be known whether some improper factor (like a judge's misdirection) had entered their deliberation. The reports of the Court of Appeal (Criminal Division) contain many cases where the court states that a conviction should be quashed because a misleading statement from the judge might have influenced the jury. It might be said that a defendant should prefer the magistrates' court as the sentencing is generally lower, but when the defendant's antecedents are known (after a conviction), they can still be committed to the Crown Court for sentence, so the magistrates' courts are not really preferable to a defendant with a criminal record who fears another conviction is likely.

However, it is worth remembering that the Crown Court has more draconian powers of sentence compared to the magistrates' court – for example on a burglary it can sentence a defendant to 14 years' imprisonment whereas a magistrates' court's limit is six months.

9.5   CRIMINAL APPEALS

The process of appeal depends upon how a case was originally tried, whether summarily or on indictment.

9.5.1   APPEALS FROM MAGISTRATES' COURTS

Two routes of appeal are possible. The first route allows only a defendant to appeal. The appeal is to a judge and between two and four magistrates sitting in the Crown Court and can be: (a) against conviction (only if the defendant pleaded not guilty) on points of fact or law; or (b) against sentence. Such an appeal will take the form of a new hearing

testified against him about matters during the marriage. The Court of Appeal allowed his appeal against conviction, but Lord Goddard said: 'Do not think that we are doing this because we think that you are an innocent man. We do not. We think that you are a scoundrel' (*The Times*, 17 November 1953). The idea behind such remarks is that rules are rules, and the rules of evidence must be obeyed in order to ensure justice. Once you start to accept breaches of the rules as being justified by the outcome (ends justifying means), then the whole law of evidence could begin to collapse.

The proposal to include 'or might be unsafe' was rejected for the reason probably best summarised by Lord Taylor, the then Lord Chief Justice, who argued in the Lords that there was no merit in including the words 'or may be unsafe', as the implication of such doubt is already inherent in the word 'unsafe'.

Cases decided since the new formula was introduced have tended to indicate that the Court of Appeal has not adopted an entirely restrictive interpretation. Thus, a conviction was quashed as unsafe in *Smith (Patrick Joseph)* (1999) because of irregularities at trial, even though the accused had admitted his guilt during cross-examination. The Human Rights Act (HRA) 1998, incorporating the European Convention on Human Rights (ECHR), introduced a further significant element into the consideration of this issue. Article 6 ECHR, to which English courts must give effect unless incompatible with an Act of Parliament, gives the defendant a right to a fair trial. Irregularities in a trial, including misdirections by the judge, admission of improperly obtained evidence and so on, might cast doubt on the fairness of the trial without necessarily making the conviction unsafe on a narrow view of that word. In *Davis* (2001), the Court of Appeal suggested that since a conviction might be unsafe even where there was no doubt about guilt, but there were serious irregularities at the trial, English rules on appeals were compatible with Art 6. However, it went on to argue that a violation of Art 6 did not necessarily imply that the conviction must be quashed. Subsequently, Lord Woolf CJ argued in *Togher* (2000) that obligations under the ECHR meant that it was almost inevitable that if the accused had been denied a fair trial, his conviction would have to be regarded as unsafe. Confusingly the European Court of Human Rights itself does not always follow the restrictive approach, appearing to use consequentialist reasoning to justify using evidence obtained in violation of Art 3 ECHR (the prohibition against torture and inhuman and degrading treatment) in a criminal trial in the case of *Gäfgen v Germany* (2011).

The *Davis* decision was appealed to the House of Lords, where the reasoning and approach of the appellate court was confirmed as correct (2008). The *Davis* decision on the compatibility of anonymous witnesses with the demands of Art 6 ECHR should now be read in conjunction with the *Horncastle* decision of the UK Supreme Court ([2009] UKSC 14) and the affirmation of the Supreme Court's decision by the Grand Chamber of the European Court of Human Rights in *Al-Khawaja v United Kingdom* (2012). The upshot of these decisions is that Art 6 will not *automatically* be breached where hearsay statements amount to the 'sole and decisive' evidence in a criminal trial.

The Court is also vigilant about the operation of s 78 of the Police and Criminal Evidence Act (PACE) 1984, which allows a court to exclude unfair evidence or unfairly obtained evidence. Section 78 operates as a so-called exclusionary discretion rule.

The question may arise as to whether the Court of Appeal should receive fresh evidence. There is a discretion under s 23(1) of the CAA 1968 to receive fresh evidence if it is thought necessary or expedient in the interests of justice. Section 23(2) provides a set of criteria which the court must consider. They are:

- whether the evidence appears to the court to be capable of belief;
- whether it appears to the court that the evidence may afford any ground for allowing the appeal;
- whether the evidence would have been admissible at the trial on the issue under appeal; and
- whether there is a reasonable explanation for the failure to adduce the evidence at trial.

9.5.3   APPEALS FROM THE CROWN COURT: PROSECUTION APPEALS AND RELATED PROCEDURES

The prosecution has only limited rights of appeal, which may or may not affect the individual defendant in the case. There is no right of appeal as such against a defendant who has been acquitted, unless s 75 of the Criminal Justice Act 2003 applies (the abolition of the double jeopardy rule, discussed below). The options open to the prosecution if they are dissatisfied with the outcome of Crown Court proceedings are as follows.

The (limited) procedure for either party to apply to the Crown Court for a case to be stated to the High Court is discussed above at 9.5.2.

9.5.3.1   Attorney General's reference on a point of law

Under s 36 of the CJA 1972, the Attorney General can refer a case which has resulted in an acquittal to the Court of Appeal where he or she believes the decision to have been questionably lenient on a point of law. The Court of Appeal deals just with the point of law and the defendant's acquittal is not affected even if the court decides the point against the defendant. It merely clarifies the law for future cases.

9.5.3.2   Attorney General's reference on sentence

Sections 35–36 of the CJA 1988 allow the Attorney General to refer indictable-only cases to the Court of Appeal where the sentence at trial is regarded as unduly lenient. The Court can impose a harsher sentence.

9.5.3.3   Application to quash tainted acquittals

The High Court can quash tainted acquittals under s 54 of the Criminal Procedure and Investigations Act (CPIA) 1996. An acquittal is 'tainted' where someone has since been convicted of conspiring to pervert the course of justice in the case by interfering with the jury.

Part 9 of the Criminal Justice Act (CJA) 2003 provides for prosecution appeals in respect of rulings in Crown Court trials which terminate the case. The right of appeal arises only in trials on indictment and lies to the Court of Appeal (s 57). Under s 57(2) the prosecution are prohibited from appealing rulings on discharge of the jury and those rulings that may be appealed by the prosecution under other legislation, for example, appeals from preparatory hearings against rulings on admissibility of evidence and other points of law.

Section 57(4) provides that the prosecution must obtain leave to appeal, either from the judge or the Court of Appeal.

Section 58 sets out the procedure that must be followed when the prosecution wishes to appeal against a terminating ruling, whether rulings that are formally terminating and those that are *de facto* terminating in the sense that they are so fatal to the prosecution case that, in the absence of a right of appeal, the prosecution would offer no or no further evidence. It applies to rulings made at any time before the start of the judge's summing up to the jury.

Where the prosecution fails to obtain leave to appeal or abandons the appeal, the prosecution must agree that an acquittal follow (s 58(8) and (9)).

Section 59 provides two alternative appeal routes: an expedited (fast) route and a non-expedited (slower) route. The judge must determine which route the appeal will follow (sub-s (1)). In the case of an expedited appeal, the trial may be adjourned (sub-s (2)). If the judge decides that the appeal should follow the non-expedited route, he or she may either adjourn the proceedings or discharge the jury, if one has been sworn (sub-s (3)). Sub-section (4) gives both the judge and the Court of Appeal power to reverse a decision to expedite an appeal, thus transferring the case to the slower non-expedited route. If a decision is reversed under this sub-section, the jury may be discharged.

Section 61 sets out the powers of the Court of Appeal when determining a prosecution appeal (and see s 67).

Section 61(1) authorises the Court of Appeal to confirm, reverse or vary a ruling that has been appealed against. After the Court of Appeal has ordered one or other of these disposals, it must then always make it clear what is to happen next in the case.

When the Court of Appeal confirms a ruling, it must then order the acquittal of the defendant(s) for the offence(s) which are the subject of the appeal (s 61(3) and (7)).

When the Court of Appeal reverses or varies a ruling, it must either order a resumption of the Crown Court proceedings or a fresh trial, or order the acquittal of the defendant(s) for the offence(s) under appeal (s 61(4) and (8)). The Court of Appeal will only order the resumption of the Crown Court proceedings or a fresh trial where it considers it necessary in the interests of justice to do so (s 61(5) and (8)).

The Criminal Justice Act also allows for the retrial of serious offences.

Section 75 sets out the cases that may be retried under the exception to the normal rule against *double jeopardy*. These cases all involve serious offences which in the main carry a maximum sentence of life imprisonment, and which are considered to have a particularly serious impact either on the victim or on society more generally. The offences to which the provisions apply are called 'qualifying offences' and are listed in Sched 5 to the Act. They include murder, manslaughter, rape and arson endangering life.

The cases that may be retried are those in which a person has been acquitted of one of the qualifying offences, either on indictment or following an appeal, or of a lesser qualifying offence of which he could have been convicted at that time. This takes into account cases of 'implied acquittals', in which, under the current law, an acquittal would have prevented a further prosecution being brought for a lower-level offence on the same facts. For example, an acquittal for murder may also imply an acquittal for the lower-level offence of manslaughter, but new evidence may then come to light, which would support a charge of manslaughter. A person may only be retried in respect of a qualifying offence.

In certain circumstances, cases may also be tried where an acquittal for an offence has taken place abroad, so long as the alleged offence also amounted to a qualifying offence and could have been charged as such in the UK. This would include, for example, offences such as war crimes, and murder committed outside the UK, for which the courts in England and Wales have jurisdiction over British citizens abroad. Such cases are likely to be rare. Sub-section (5) recognises that offences may not be described in exactly the same way in the legislation of other jurisdictions.

Prosecutor's application

Section 76 allows a prosecutor to apply to the Court of Appeal for an order that quashes the person's acquittal and orders him or her to be retried for the qualifying offence. A 'prosecutor' means a person or body responsible for bringing public prosecutions, such as the Crown Prosecution Service or HM Customs and Excise. Where a person has been acquitted outside the UK, the court will need to consider whether or not the acquittal would act as a bar to a further trial here and, if it does, the court can order that it must not be a bar.

Applications to the Court of Appeal require the personal written consent of the Director of Public Prosecutions (DPP). This provides a safeguard to ensure that only those cases in which there is sufficient evidence are referred to the Court of Appeal. The DPP will also consider whether it is in the public interest to proceed. This section also recognises any international obligations arising under the Treaty of the European Union, under which negotiations are taking place to support the mutual recognition of the decisions of the courts in other EU Member states.

Applications may also be brought by public prosecuting authorities if new evidence arises in cases that have previously been tried by means of a private prosecution.

Only one application for an acquittal to be quashed may be made in relation to any acquittal. In March 2006, a man accused of a 1989 murder became the first person to have his case referred to the Court of Appeal under this procedure. The body of Julie Hogg, 22, from Teesside, was found hidden behind her bath by her mother, Ann Ming. William Dunlop, 42, was acquitted of Ms Hogg's murder. In April 2005, police said they were to re-examine the case of Ms Hogg. William Dunlop previously faced two murder trials, but each time the jury failed to reach a verdict and he was formally acquitted in 1991. The then Director of Public Prosecutions, Ken Macdonald, said that after looking at submissions from the Chief Crown Prosecutor for Cleveland, Martin Goldman, he was satisfied the Crown Prosecution Service should apply to the Court of Appeal for a retrial. The Court of Appeal heard this application and ordered a retrial of Dunlop under s 75. In October 2006 he pleaded guilty to murdering Ms Hogg and was sentenced to life imprisonment. The Court of Appeal had applied s 75 when the CPS applied for a rehearing of Dunlop's case and felt that: (1) a jury could be selected which would not have any prior knowledge of Dunlop's earlier conviction; (2) any such recollection was outweighed by the fact that Dunlop had repeatedly confessed to Ms Hogg's murder since his acquittals in 1991 and that he had been convicted of perjury in relation to his denial of that offence; (3) the delay did not render a retrial unfair; (4) the new evidence under s 78 was both compelling and overwhelming (it consisted of Dunlop's repeated confessions) and he was in no position to rebut the new evidence; and (5) justice required that he face a retrial.

As the first example of this new procedure these comments by the Court of Appeal are clearly important. This provision was subsequently invoked by the Court of Appeal to quash the acquittal of Gary Dobson for the murder of the black teenager Stephen Lawrence in 1993 (*R v Dobson* (2011)) (see also 1.3.5). Following Dobson's second trial in 2011, he was convicted of murder.

Determination by the Court of Appeal

Section 77 sets out the decisions that the Court of Appeal may make in response to an application for an acquittal to be quashed. The court must make an order quashing an acquittal and ordering a retrial if it considers that the requirements set out in ss 78 and 79 of the Act are satisfied, namely that there is new and compelling evidence in the case, and that it is in the interests of justice for the order to be made. The court must dismiss an application where it is not satisfied as to these two factors.

New and compelling evidence

Section 78 sets out the requirement for there to be new and compelling evidence against the acquitted person in relation to the qualifying offence, and defines evidence which is 'new and compelling'. Evidence is 'new' if it was not adduced at the original trial of the acquitted person. Evidence is 'compelling' if the court considers it to be reliable and substantial and, when considered in the context of the outstanding issues, the evidence appears to be highly probative of the case against the acquitted person. The court is thus required to make a decision on the strength of the new evidence. So, for example, new evidence relating to identification would only be considered 'compelling' if the identity of the offender had been at issue in the original trial. It is not intended that relatively minor evidence, which might appear to strengthen an earlier case, should justify a retrial.

Interests of justice

Section 79 sets out the requirement that in all the circumstances it is in the interests of justice for the court to quash an acquittal and order a retrial. In determining whether it is in the interests of justice, the court will consider in particular: whether there are existing factors that make a fair trial unlikely (for example, the extent of adverse publicity about the case); the length of time since the alleged offence was committed; and whether the police and prosecution acted with due diligence and expedition in relation to both the original trial and any new evidence. The court may take into account any other issues it considers relevant in determining whether a retrial will be in the interests of justice.

The Criminal Justice and Immigration Act 2008 alters the test for ordering a retrial in England and Wales (or that the trial should resume) where the Court of Appeal allows a prosecution appeal against a terminating ruling. The original CJA 2003 provided that a court should not order a resumed or fresh trial unless it considered it necessary in the interests of justice to do so. Now, under s 44 of the 2008 Act, the court may not order that the defendant be acquitted unless it considers that he could not receive a fair trial/retrial.

9.6   CRIMINAL APPEALS TO THE SUPREME COURT

Following the determination of an appeal by the Court of Appeal or by the Divisional Court, either the prosecution or the defence may appeal to the Supreme Court. Leave from the court below or the Supreme Court must be obtained and two other conditions fulfilled according to s 33 of the CAA 1968:

(1)   the court below must certify that a point of law of general public importance is involved; and

(2)   either the court below or the Supreme Court must be satisfied that the point of law is one which ought to be considered by the Supreme Court.

Section 68(1) of the CJA 2003 amends s 33(1) of the Criminal Appeal Act 1968 to give both the prosecution and defence a right of appeal to the Supreme Court from a decision by the Court of Appeal on a prosecution appeal against a ruling made under Part 9 of the Act.

9.7   JUDICIAL COMMITTEE OF THE PRIVY COUNCIL

The Judicial Committee of the Privy Council was created by the Judicial Committee Act 1833. Under the Act, a special committee of the Privy Council was set up to hear appeals from the Dominions. The cases are heard by the judges (without wigs or robes) in a committee room in London. The Committee's decision is not a judgment but an 'advice' to the monarch, who is counselled that the appeal be allowed or dismissed.

The Committee is the final court of appeal for certain Commonwealth countries that have retained this option, and from some independent members and associate members of the Commonwealth. The Committee comprises Privy Councillors who are Justices of the Supreme Court.

Most of the appeals heard by the Committee are civil cases. In the rare criminal cases, it is only on matters involving legal questions that appeals are heard. The Committee does not hear appeals against criminal sentence.

Her Majesty The Queen, in the exercise of the Royal Prerogative of Mercy, granted to Mr Bentley a posthumous pardon limited to sentence.

Following submissions from the applicants' solicitors and the completion of its own inquiries, the CCRC concluded that the Court of Appeal should reconsider Mr Bentley's conviction. The trial was seen as unfair in a number of respects; for example the fact that, although aged 18, Bentley had a mental age of 11 was kept a secret from the jury, and the judge's summing up to the jury was astonishingly biased in favour of the police. In August 1998, on a momentous day in legal history, the Court of Appeal cleared Bentley of the murder for which he was hanged 46 years earlier. In giving judgment, the Lord Chief Justice, Lord Bingham, said: 'the summing up in this case was such as to deny the appellant that fair trial which is the birthright of every British citizen.'

The latest figures (CCRC *Case Statistics*, figures to 30 September 2013) show the following data:

Total applications:	18,153
Cases waiting:	688
Cases under review:	835
Completed:	16,690 (including ineligible), 565 referrals
Heard by Court of Appeal:	543 (374 quashed, 153 upheld)

Taking a global perspective on legal systems, it is unusual for any machinery of justice to provide as many opportunities for appeal and challenge as exist in the English system.

9.9   A MISCARRIAGE OF JUSTICE: SOME LESSONS FOR THE CRIMINAL JUSTICE SYSTEM

One of the English legal system's worst miscarriages of justice cases in recent history was exposed in the Court of Appeal in February 1998. In 1979, Vincent Hickey, Michael Hickey, Jimmy Robertson and Pat Molloy, who became known as the Bridgewater Four, were convicted of the murder of a 13-year-old boy, Carl Bridgewater. Although the men were not angelic characters (and two had serious criminal records), they strenuously protested that they were not guilty of the horrific child murder.

Eighteen years later, and after two earlier failed visits to the Court of Appeal and seven police investigations, three of the men were released on 21 February 1998 on unconditional bail in anticipation of an appeal hearing in April. The fourth defendant, Mr Molloy, died in jail in 1981. The appeal was eventually allowed.

The Crown had conceded that the case against the men was 'flawed' by evidence falsified and fabricated by police officers. There had also come to light significant fingerprint evidence, tending to exonerate the four, which was not disclosed to the defence by the prosecution. Mr Molloy was questioned for 10 days without access to a solicitor, and a fabricated statement from Vincent Hickey was used to persuade Mr Molloy to confess to the crime. Before he died, Mr Molloy claimed he had been beaten by police officers in the course of his interrogation. The former police officers alleged to have falsified the evidence were investigated but not prosecuted.

The case was given extensive coverage in the print and broadcast media in February 1997 and made a significant impact upon public consciousness. It did not reach the Court of Appeal through the Criminal Cases Review Commission, which had only been set up the year before. This major case raises many points germane to the operation of the criminal justice system. The following are of particular importance.

The case was originally investigated in 1978, before PACE 1984 had been passed. The requirements under PACE 1984 for suspects to be given access to legal advice (s 58, Code C) and for interviews to be recorded (s 60, Code E) may have reduced or eliminated the opportunity for police malpractice of the sort which occurred in the *Bridgewater* case.

Although the criminal justice system ultimately corrected an injustice, this result was achieved primarily through the indefatigable efforts of a few dedicated family members, campaigning journalists and Members of Parliament who would not let the issue disappear from the public forum. The case attracted attention because of the terrible nature of the crime – a child murder. It is quite possible that many other unjust convictions in cases with more mundane facts are never propelled into public discussion or overturned.

Miscarriages of justice cases involve two types of insult to notions of legal fairness: (a) the wrongly imprisoned endure years of incarceration; and (b) the real culprits (a child killer in the *Bridgewater* case) are never identified and could well go on to commit other offences.

The men were released due to the discovery of evidence that had been fabricated and falsified; yet the CPIA 1996 restricts defence access to prosecution evidence.

The CCRC was established to re-evaluate alleged cases of miscarriages of justice. One criticism of it has been that it does not have its own independent investigators, but must rely on police officers to re-examine cases.

The jury is only as good as the information and arguments put before it allows it to be. After the prosecution's case had been devastated by the discovery of new scientific evidence in 1993 (a forensic psychiatrist showed that Molloy's 'confession' used language the suspect would not have used), the foreman of the jury from the 1979 trial risked prosecution for contempt of court by issuing a statement to say that he thought that the men were not guilty. He, along with another juror, said they regretted that they had not been given all the evidence that was available at the time of the trial.

9.10 CORONERS' COURTS

The coroners' courts are one of the most ancient parts of the English legal system, dating back to at least 1194. They are not, in modern function, part of the criminal courts, but because of historical associations, it makes more sense to classify them with the courts in this chapter rather than that dealing with civil courts. The coroner was an appointment originally made as *custos placitorum coronae*, keeper of the pleas of the Crown. They had responsibility for criminal cases in which the Crown had an interest, particularly a financial interest.

APPEALS

Criminal appeals from the magistrates go to the Crown Court or to the QBD Divisional Court 'by way of case stated' on a point of law or that the JPs went beyond their proper powers, or by way of judicial review. If the prosecution succeeds on appeal, the court can direct the magistrates to convict and pass the appropriate sentence. There is also an appeal by way of case stated from the Crown Court to the Divisional Court when the Crown Court has heard an appeal from the magistrates' court. From the Crown Court, appeals against conviction and sentence lie to the Court of Appeal (Criminal Division). The High Court has jurisdiction to hear cases stated by the Crown Court for an opinion. The prosecution has some, limited, options to refer or appeal aspects of Crown Court decisions to the Court of Appeal.

The Judicial Committee of the Privy Council hears final appeals from some Commonwealth countries and its decisions are of persuasive precedent in English law.

REVIEW AFTER APPEAL

In an attempt to deal with possible miscarriages of justice, and following the recommendations of the Royal Commission on Criminal Justice in 1993 (the Runciman Commission), the Criminal Appeal Act 1995 established the Criminal Cases Review Commission (CCRC). The CCRC has power to investigate and to refer cases to the Court of Appeal (or, where appropriate, the Crown Court) where it considers that there is a real possibility of an appeal succeeding.

THE CORONERS' COURTS

These are not part of the criminal justice system. Their main function is to decide the cause of unnatural deaths. Verdicts such as unlawful killing might result in other legal processes like criminal prosecutions or human rights claims.

FOOD FOR THOUGHT

1   The age of criminal responsibility in the UK is 10. This is one of the lowest ages of criminal responsibility in the world. Where an adult defendant with the mental age of a 10-year-old could establish a defence of diminished responsibility or insanity, does it make sense for an actual 10-year-old to be tried as an adult?

2   Evidence obtained using oppressive techniques is not admissible in criminal proceedings. But what about the situation where the police believe that a child's life is in immediate danger and so threaten a suspect with physical violence if he does not tell them where the child is? If the suspect confesses and the child is found dead, should that confession be admissible evidence?

FURTHER READING

Bates, T, 'The contemporary use of legislative history in the United Kingdom' (1995) 54(1) CLJ 127

Bell, J and Engle, G (Sir), *Cross: Statutory Interpretation*, 3rd edn, 1995, London: Butterworths

Bennion, F, 'Statute law: obscurity and drafting parameters' (1978) 5 British JLS 235

Bennion, F, *Statutory Interpretation*, 2nd edn, 1992, London: Butterworths

Burrows, D, 'Enforcement matters: Part 1' (2009) 159 NLJ 334; Part II (2009) 159 NLJ 415

Carlen, P, *Magistrates' Justice*, 1976, Oxford: Martin Robertson

Committee on the Preparation of Legislation, *Renton Committee Report*, Cmnd 6053, 1975, London: HMSO

Dugg, A, Farmer, L, Marshall, S and Tadros, V (eds), *The Trial on Trial – Truth and Due Process*, 2004, Oxford: Hart Publishing

Eskridge, W, *Dynamic Statutory Interpretation*, 1994, Cambridge, MA: Harvard UP

Fitzpatrick, B, *Going to Court*, 2006, Oxford: OUP

Friedman, L, 'On interpretation of laws' (1988) 11(3) Ratio Juris 252

Gibb, F, 'The highest court in the land opens its doors to the public', *The Times*, 1 October 2009

Grove, T, *The Magistrates' Tale*, 2002, London: Bloomsbury

Hillman, M, 'For the public good?' (2008) 158 NLJ 661

Manchester, C, *Exploring the Law: The Dynamics of Precedent and Statutory Interpretation*, 2006, London: Sweet & Maxwell

Matthews, P and Foreman, J (eds), *Jervis: On the Office and Duties of Coroners*, 1993, London: Sweet & Maxwell

Moxon, D and Hedderman, C, 'Mode of trial decisions and sentencing differences between courts' (1994) 33(2) Howard J of Criminal Justice 97

New Law Journal, 'Increase in cases to CCRC' [2007] 1060

Richardson, PJ (ed), *Archbold: Criminal Pleading, Evidence and Practice*, 2016, London: Sweet & Maxwell

Stone, J, 'The Ratio of the Ratio Decidendi' (1959) 22 MLR 597

USEFUL WEBSITES

www.justice.gov.uk/about/hmcts/
The official website of Her Majesty's Courts and Tribunals Service.

www.magistrates-association.org.uk
The official website of the Magistrates' Association.

www.justice.gov.uk
The official website of the Criminal Justice System.

COMPANION WEBSITE

Now visit the companion website to:

- test your understanding of the key terms using our Flashcard Glossary;
- revise and consolidate your knowledge of 'The criminal courts' using our multiple choice question testbank;
- view all of the links to the Useful Websites above.

www.routledge.com/cw/slapper

THE CRIMINAL PROCESS: (1) THE INVESTIGATION OF CRIME

10.1 INTRODUCTION

The criminal justice system has unceasingly been the subject of widespread heated debate in Parliament, the broadcast media and the print media, and in academic and professional journals. It has been subject to extensive and continuous statutory change, spanning many areas, including those of criminal evidence, bail, juries and appeals. We examine some of these, where relevant, in this chapter and in Chapters 11 and 14.

The Crime Survey for England and Wales (CSEW) is a face-to-face victimisation survey in which people resident in households in England and Wales are asked about their experiences of a selected number of offences in the 12 months prior to the interview. It covers both children aged 10–15 and adults aged 16 and over, but does not cover those living in group residences (such as care homes, student halls of residence or prisons), or crimes against commercial or public sector bodies. For the population and offence types it covers, the CSEW is a valuable source for providing robust estimates on a consistent basis over time, as it has a consistent methodology and is unaffected by changes in levels of reporting to the police, recording practice or police activity. Respondents to the survey are also asked about their attitudes towards different crime-related issues, such as the police, the criminal justice system, and perceptions of crime and anti-social behaviour. The CSEW provides a better reflection of the true extent of crime because it includes incidents that are not reported to the police and crimes which are not recorded by them.

The CSEW is able to capture all offences experienced by those interviewed, not just those that have been reported to, and recorded by, the police. It covers a broad range of victim-based crimes experienced by the resident household population. However, there are some serious but relatively low-volume offences, such as homicide and sexual offences that are not included in its main estimates.

Figures from the (CSEW) in June 2015 showed that, for the offences it covers, there were in the previous year an estimated 6.5 million incidents of crime against households and resident adults (aged 16 and over). This is an 8 per cent decrease compared with the previous year's survey, and the lowest estimate since the CSEW began in 1981.

The long-running debate over how to deal with the policing and prevention of terrorism is also discussed in detail in Chapter 2 (at 2.3).

10.2.3 THE POLICE AND CRIMINAL EVIDENCE ACT 1984

The Police and Criminal Evidence Act 1984 (PACE) was designed to provide a comprehensive code for policing in response to some of the miscarriages of justice described above. It consists of the Act and accompanying Codes of Practice A–H, issued under s 66 of the Act, and updated at regular intervals. Current versions can be found at https://www.gov.uk/guidance/police-and-criminal-evidence-act-1984-pace-codes-of-practice. The Serious Organised Crime and Police Act 2005 (SOCPA) made major amendments to PACE by revising the framework of arrest and search powers.

10.3 STOP AND SEARCH

PACE 1984 gives the police power to search 'any person or vehicle' and to detain either for the purpose of such a search (s 1(2)). A constable may not conduct such a search 'unless he has reasonable grounds for suspecting that he will find stolen or prohibited articles' (s 1(3)). Any such item found during the search can be seized (s 1(6)). An article is 'prohibited' if it is either an offensive weapon or it is 'made or adapted for use in the course of or in connection with burglary, theft, taking a motor vehicle without authority or obtaining property by deception or is intended by the person having it with him for such use by him or by some other person' (s 1(7)).

Section 1 of PACE was amended by s 1 CJA to include articles made, adapted or intended for use in causing criminal damage, under s 1 of the Criminal Damage Act 1971. The effect is to give police officers power to stop and search where they have reasonable suspicion that a person is carrying, for example, a paint spray can, which they intend to use in producing graffiti.

An offensive weapon is defined as meaning 'any article made or adapted for use for causing injury to persons or intended by the person having it with him for such use by him or by some other person' (s 1(9)). This definition is taken from the Prevention of Crime Act 1953. It has two categories: things that are offensive weapons *per se* (that is, in themselves), like a baton with a nail through the end or knuckle-dusters, and things that are not offensive weapons, like a spanner, but which are intended to be used as such. If the item is in the first category, then the prosecution need prove only that the accused had it with them to put the onus onto the accused to show that they had a lawful excuse.

Stop and search powers can also be exercised under s 8A regarding items covered by s 139 of the CJA 1988. These items are any article that has a blade or is sharply pointed, except folding pocket knives with a blade of less than three inches. It is an offence to possess such items without good reason or lawful authority, the onus of proof being on the defendant. The courts will not accept the carrying of offensive weapons for generalised self-defence unless there is some immediate, identifiable threat.

Under s 2 of PACE 1984, a police officer who proposes to carry out a stop and search must state their name and police station, and the purpose of the search. A plain-clothes officer must also produce documentary evidence that they are a police officer. The officer must also give the grounds for the search. Such street searches must be limited to outer clothing; the searched person cannot be required to remove any article of clothing other than a jacket, outer clothes or gloves. The officer is required to make a record of the search immediately, or as soon as is reasonably practicable afterwards (s 3). The record of the search should include the object of the search, the grounds of the search and its result (s 3). A failure to give grounds as required by s 2(3)(c) will render the search unlawful (*R v Fennelley* (1989)).

Section 1 of the Crime and Security Act 2010 amends s 3 of PACE 1984 to reduce recording requirements where a search is conducted under s 2 (and see revised paras 4.1–4.10). There is no longer a requirement to record the person's name or description, whether anything was found or whether any injury or damage was caused as a result of the search. However, the police are obliged to record:

- ethnicity
- objective of search
- grounds for search
- identity of the officer carrying out the stop and search
- date
- time
- place.

It seems that failure to comply with these conditions will make the search unlawful. See *Fennelley* (1989), a case where the defendant was not told why he was stopped, searched and arrested in the street. Evidence from the search, some jewellery, was excluded at the trial. Evidence of drugs found on him at the police station was also excluded.

10.3.1 THE CODE OF PRACTICE FOR THE EXERCISE OF STATUTORY POWERS OF STOP AND SEARCH

As explained above, the Codes of Practice under PACE clarify how the police should exercise their powers. Code A details how searches under stop and search powers are to be conducted. The admissibility of evidence gained through the use of a dubious stop and search event may be in doubt if there are serious breaches of Code A. Someone charged with obstructing or assaulting a police officer in the exercise of duty may raise breaches of the Code in defence. Unlawful search or seizure may also provide a basis for an application for exclusion of evidence thus obtained under s 78 of PACE 1984.

The primary purpose of stop and search powers is to enable officers to allay or confirm suspicions about individuals without exercising their powers of arrest. The Code applies to powers of stop and search and states at para 2.1(a) that these are 'powers serious violence against a person, serious damage to property, endangering the life of a person other than the 'terrorist'. This must be coupled with creating a serious risk to the health or safety of the public or a section of the public, or designing seriously to interfere with or seriously to disrupt an electronic system. The above action(s) must be designed to influence the government or to intimidate the public or a section of the public, and made for the purpose of advancing a political, religious or ideological cause. However, where the use or threat of action involves the use of firearms or explosives, it need not be designed to influence the government or to intimidate the public or a section of the public.

In *Gillan and Quinton v UK* (2010) the ECtHR held that the requirement on a person to submit to a stop and search under s 44 of the TA 2000 represented a clear interference with the right to respect for private life under Art 8 ECHR, finding that the provisions of the TA 2000 had been neither sufficiently circumscribed nor subject to adequate safeguards against abuse. The court was also influenced by the massive increase in the use of the power since it had been introduced and the fact that it was disproportionately used against ethnic minorities. As a result of the judgment, the coalition government made a remedial order under the Human Rights Act 1998 (the Terrorism Act 2000 (Remedial) Order 2011), which has the effect of repealing ss 44, 45, 46 and most of s 47. The new Protection of Freedoms Act 2012 now provides the police with more circumscribed powers to authorise stop and search of persons and vehicles without reasonable suspicion (s 47A) in exceptional circumstances. This places the powers provided by the Terrorism Act 2000 Remedial Order 2011 on a permanent footing. The Protection of Freedoms Act 2012 also changes stop and search powers in the Terrorism Act 2000 (ss 43 and 43A) which require reasonable suspicion to enable searches of vehicles or their occupants. Codes of practice supporting the new legislation were laid before Parliament in May 2012 in the form of the Terrorism Act 2000 (Codes of Practice for the Exercise of Stop and Search Powers) Order 2012. In addition PACE codes of practice C, G and H have been amended to introduce a new code of practice for the video-recording with sound of interviews carried out under s 41 of, and Sched 7 to, the Terrorism Act 2000 and post-charge questioning of terrorist suspects under the Counter-Terrorism Act 2008.

10.3.5 ENTRY AND SEARCH OF PREMISES

Section 18 of PACE provides powers to enter and search premises. These are further covered by Code B. Paragraph 1.3 states:

> The right to privacy and respect for personal property are key principles of the Human Rights Act 1998. Powers of entry, search and seizure should be fully and clearly justified before use because they may significantly interfere with the occupiers' privacy. Officers should consider if the necessary objectives can be met by less intrusive means.

Paragraph 7.7 states:

> The Criminal Justice and Police Act 2001, Part 2, gives officers limited powers to seize property from premises or persons so that they can sift or examine it elsewhere. Officers must be careful they only exercise these powers when it is essential and they do not remove any more material than necessary. The removal of large quantities of material, much of which may not ultimately be retainable, may have serious implications for the owners . . . Officers must carefully consider if removing copies or images of relevant material or data would be a satisfactory alternative to removing originals.

In 2011, amendments to Code B extended the conditions which must be met in order for a search under s 18 of PACE to be authorised. Under the previous version of the Code, para 4.3 required that the authorising officer (of the rank of inspector or above) be satisfied that the necessary grounds under s 18 existed. This paragraph has now been extended to require the inspector to be satisfied, in addition to the grounds set out in s 18, 'that the premises are occupied or controlled by the arrested person'. This reflects the judgment in *Khan v Commissioner of Police of the Metropolis* (2008). A suspect had falsely provided Mr Khan's address as his own upon arrest. Entry and search of this address was duly authorised and undertaken under s 18. The Commissioner argued that s 18 should be interpreted so as to qualify the requirement of occupation and control by the suspect by reference to the belief of knowledge of the officer. The Court of Appeal rejected this submission and, dismissing the Commissioner's appeal, found that there was no justification for such a reading and that 'the requirement for occupation or control is central and fundamental to the operation of section 18'. The amended Code A was an attempt to achieve what the Metropolitan Police Commissioner failed to do in *Khan*: that is, to circumvent the clear wording of s 18 to protect the police from claims for damages in circumstances where the wrong address is searched in good faith.

10.4   ARREST

According to AV Dicey, 'individual rights are the basis not the result of the law of the constitution' (*Law of the Constitution*, 6th edn, p 203; cited by Judge LJ in *R v Central Criminal Court ex p The Guardian, The Observer and Bright* (2002)). Before considering the rights of the citizen and the law governing arrest and detention, what happens in the police station and what evidence is admissible in court, it is appropriate to look first at what the citizen can do if those rights are violated.

10.4.1   REMEDIES FOR UNLAWFUL ARREST

Like other areas of law where the liberty of the subject is at stake, the law relating to arrest is founded upon the principle of *justification*. If challenged, the person who has no member of the public is present (*McConnell v Chief Constable of Manchester* (1990)). Although mere shouting and swearing alone will not constitute a breach of the peace, it is an offence under s 28 of the Town Police Causes Act 1847. If it causes harassment, alarm or distress to a member of the public, it may constitute an offence under s 5 of the Public Order Act 1986. In either case, it could lead to arrest under the Police and Criminal Evidence Act 1984.

10.4.5 ARREST UNDER LEGISLATION

The right to arrest is generally governed by s 24 of PACE 1984 (as amended by SOCPA 2005 s 110) in respect of arrest by police officers and s 24A in respect of arrest by other people. PACE 1984 preserves an old common law distinction in respect of the powers of constables and private individuals when making such arrests (*Walters v WH Smith & Son Ltd* (1914)). Where an arrest is being made after an offence is thought to have been committed, then PACE 1984 confers narrower rights upon the private individual than on the police officer.

In particular, the changes made by SOCPA provide, in the case of a constable's power of arrest, for all offences to be 'arrestable' subject to a necessity test. This means that someone who has committed a relatively low-order criminal offence, like littering, could, in theory, be arrested if an officer deemed it necessary and was able to satisfy his or her desk sergeant at the police station that this was so. That might occur, for example, if the person being requested to pick up the litter refused to do so, and then refused to give his or her name to the officer.

---

24 Arrest without warrant: Constables

(1)   A constable may arrest without a warrant –

  (a)   anyone who is about to commit an offence;

  (b)   anyone who is in the act of committing an offence;

  (c)   anyone whom he has reasonable grounds for suspecting to be about to commit an offence;

  (d)   anyone whom he has reasonable grounds for suspecting to be committing an offence.

(2)   If a constable has reasonable grounds for suspecting that an offence has been committed, he may arrest without a warrant anyone whom he has reasonable grounds to suspect of being guilty of it.

(3)   If an offence has been committed, a constable may arrest without a warrant –

  (a)   anyone who is guilty of the offence;

  (b)   anyone whom he has reasonable grounds for suspecting to be guilty of it.

(4)   But the power of summary arrest conferred by subsection (1), (2) or (3) is exercisable only if the constable has reasonable grounds for believing that for any of the reasons mentioned in subsection (5) it is necessary to arrest the person in question.

(5)   The reasons are –

(a)   to enable the name of the person in question to be ascertained (in the case where the constable does not know, and cannot readily ascertain, the person's name, or has reasonable grounds for doubting whether a name given by the person as his name is his real name);

(b)   correspondingly as regards the person's address;

(c)   to prevent the person in question –

(i)   causing physical injury to himself or any other person;

(ii)   suffering physical injury;

(iii)   causing loss of or damage to property;

(iv)   committing an offence against public decency (subject to subsection (6)); or

(v)   causing an unlawful obstruction of the highway;

(d)   to protect a child or other vulnerable person from the person in question;

(e)   to allow the prompt and effective investigation of the offence or of the conduct of the person in question;

(f)   to prevent any prosecution for the offence from being hindered by the disappearance of the person in question.

(6)   Subsection (5)(c)(iv) applies only where members of the public going about their normal business cannot reasonably be expected to avoid the person in question.

24A Arrest without warrant: Other persons

(1)   A person other than a constable may arrest without a warrant –

(a)   anyone who is in the act of committing an indictable offence;

(b)   anyone whom he has reasonable grounds for suspecting to be committing an indictable offence.

(2)   Where an indictable offence has been committed, a person other than a constable may arrest without a warrant –

(a)   anyone who is guilty of the offence;

(b)   anyone whom he has reasonable grounds for suspecting to be guilty of it.

(3)   But the power of summary arrest conferred by subsection (1) or (2) is exercisable only if –

(a)   the person making the arrest has reasonable grounds for believing that for any of the reasons mentioned in subsection (4) it is necessary to arrest the person in question; and

(b)   it appears to the person making the arrest that it is not reasonably practicable for a constable to make it instead.

(4)   The reasons are to prevent the person in question –

(a)   causing physical injury to himself or any other person;

(b)   suffering physical injury;

(c)   causing loss of or damage to property; or

(d)   making off before a constable can assume responsibility for him.

SOCPA extended police powers in a highly controversial way. The case to extend powers for the police is built on the idea that those who have done nothing wrong will have nothing to fear from the exercise of the powers. The extension of police powers is also defended on the grounds that any arrest, to be lawful, must be 'necessary' (see s 24(5) of PACE as amended, above, by s 110 of the Serious Organised Crime and Police Act).

There are, however, clear reasons for concern at this development. A society in which the police have unlimited powers can be described as a 'police state', and such tyranny is almost universally disfavoured. That, of course, is very far from the position now in the UK, a country that has what are among the best-protected liberties in the world. However, the closer that law in the UK moves towards giving the police very wide powers to arrest, the greater the need for concern. A society in which people can be arrested for any offence, in which CCTV is ubiquitous (Surveillance UK, *The Independent*, 22 December 2005), and in which police 'success' is progressively measured by how many arrests and crimes are solved, might reduce certain sorts of offending (although many sorts of criminality are not reduced by such policies). But how comfortable a place would it be to live? The inhabitants of many countries in which there are dictatorial governments and no respect for civil liberties do not seem to rejoice in the crime-free streets. At all events, the most desirable balance between freedom not to be interfered with by police officers, and policing that improves society by effectively reducing crime, is ultimately a political question for the public, rather than the small section of the public comprising judges, lawyers and police officers.

10.4.6   WHAT IS THE MEANING OF 'REASONABLE GROUNDS FOR SUSPECTING'?

Many of the powers of the police in relation to arrest, search and seizure are founded upon the presence of reasonable 'suspicion', 'cause' or 'belief' in a state of affairs, usually that a suspect is involved actually or potentially in a crime.

In *Castorina v Chief Constable of Surrey* (1988), detectives reasonably concluded that the burglary of a company's premises was an 'inside job'. The managing director told them that she had recently dismissed someone (the plaintiff), although she did not think it would have been her, and that the documents taken would be useful to someone with a grudge. The detectives interviewed the plaintiff, having found out that she had no criminal record, and arrested her under s 2(4) of the Criminal Law Act (CLA) 1967 (which has now been replaced by s 24 PACE 1984). She was detained at the police station for almost four hours, interrogated and then released without charge. On a claim for damages for wrongful arrest and detention, a jury awarded her £4,500. The trial judge held that the officers had had a *prima facie* case for suspicion, but that the arrest was premature. He had defined 'reasonable cause' (which the officers would have needed to show they had when they arrested the plaintiff) as 'honest belief founded upon reasonable suspicion leading an ordinary cautious man to the conclusion that the person arrested was guilty of the offence'. He said an ordinary man would have sought more information from the suspect, including an explanation for any grudge on her part. In this, he relied on the *dicta* of Scott LJ in *Dumbell v Roberts* (1944) that the principle that every man was presumed innocent until proved guilty also applied to arrests. The Court of Appeal allowed an appeal by the chief constable. The court held that the trial judge had used too severe a test in judging the officers' conduct.

Purchas LJ said that the test of 'reasonable cause' was objective and therefore the trial judge was wrong to have focused attention on whether the officers had had 'an honest belief'. The question was whether the officers had had reasonable grounds to suspect the woman of the offence. There was sufficient evidence that the officers had had sufficient reason to suspect her.

Woolf LJ thought there were three things to consider in cases where an arrest is alleged to be unlawful:

- Did the arresting officer suspect that the person who was arrested had committed the offence? This was a matter of fact about the officer's state of mind.

- If the answer to the first question is yes, then was there reasonable proof of that suspicion? This is a simple objective matter to be determined by the judge.

- If the answers to the first two questions are both yes, then the officer did have a discretion to arrest, and the question then was whether they had exercised their discretion according to *Wednesbury* principles of reasonableness.

This case hinged on the second point and, on the facts, the chief constable should succeed on the appeal.

An arrest, however, becomes lawful once the ground is given. In *Lewis v Chief Constable of the South Wales Constabulary* (1991), the officers had told the plaintiffs of the fact of arrest, but delayed telling them the grounds for 10 minutes in one case and 23 minutes in the other. The Court of Appeal said that arrest was not a legal concept but arose factually from the deprivation of a person's liberty. It was also a continuing act and therefore what had begun as an unlawful arrest could become a lawful arrest. The remedy for the plaintiffs was the damages they had been awarded for the 10 minutes and 23 minutes of illegality: £200 each.

In *Nicholas v Parsonage* (1987), N was seen riding a bicycle without holding the handlebars by two police officers. They told him twice to hold the bars and then he did so. When they drove off, N raised two fingers. They then stopped N and PC Parsonage asked him for his name, telling him it was required as he had been riding his bicycle in a dangerous manner. N refused. P then informed him of his powers under PACE 1984 and requested N's name and address. N again refused. P then arrested him for failing to give his name and address. N attempted to ride off and a struggle ensued. N was subsequently convicted of, *inter alia*, assaulting a police officer in the execution of his duty, contrary to s 51(1) of the Police Act 1964. His appeal was dismissed by the Divisional Court, which held that the arrest under s 25 of PACE 1984 (the law then in force) had been lawful as a constable exercising power under s 25(3) was not required to say why he wanted the suspect's name and address. N had been adequately informed of the ground of arrest under s 28(3) of PACE 1984. N was not arrested for failing to give his name and address; he was arrested because, having committed the minor offence of 'riding in a dangerous manner', it then became necessary to arrest him because the conditions in s 25(3)(a) and (c) were satisfied. These conditions were that an arrest for a minor offence is possible where the officer believes that the service of a summons is impracticable because he has not been given a proper name and address.

Is it necessary for an arrestor to indicate to the arrestee the grounds on which his 'reasonable suspicion' was based? In *Geldberg v Miller* (1961), the appellant parked his car outside a restaurant in London while he had a meal. He was asked by police officers to move the car. He refused, preferring to finish his meal first. On being told that the police would remove the car, he removed the rotor arm from the distributor mechanism. He also refused to give his name and address or show his driving licence and certificate of insurance. He was arrested by one of the officers for 'obstructing him in the execution of his duty by refusing to move his car and refusing his name and address'. There was no power to arrest for obstruction of the police as no actual or apprehended breach of the peace was involved. The court held, however, that the arrest was valid for 'obstructing the thoroughfare', an offence under s 56(6) of the Metropolitan Police Act 1839, an offence the officer had not mentioned. Lord Parker CJ said:

> In my judgment, what the appellant knew and what he was told was ample to fulfil the obligation as to what should be done at the time of an arrest without warrant.

An arrest will be unlawful, however, where the reasons given point to an offence for which there is no power of arrest (or for which there is only qualified power of arrest) and it is clear that no other reasons were present in the mind of the officer (*Edwards v DPP* (1993)). This principle was confirmed in *Mullady v DPP* (1997). A police officer arrested M for 'obstruction', an offence with the power of arrest only if the defendant's conduct amounted to a breach of the peace (for which there is a common law power of arrest) or if one of the general arrest conditions as set out in s 25 is satisfied. The police argued that the officer could have arrested M for a breach of the peace and merely gave the wrong reason. The Divisional Court held that the officer had acted unlawfully and that it would be wrong for the justices to go behind the reason given and infer that the reason for the arrest was another lawful reason.

In some circumstances, the court may infer a lawful reason for an arrest if the circumstantial evidence points clearly to a lawful reason (*Brookman v DPP* (1997)). However, if there is insufficient evidence to determine whether a lawful or unlawful reason was given for the arrest, then the police will fail to show that the arrest was lawful (*Clarke v DPP* (1998)).

10.4.11 THE USE OF FORCE TO EFFECT AN ARREST

The use of force by a member of the public when arresting someone is governed by s 3 of the CLA 1967. This states:

> (1) A person may use such force as is reasonable in the circumstances in the prevention of crime, or in effecting or assisting in the lawful arrest of offenders or suspected offenders or of persons unlawfully at large.

Reasonable force will generally mean the minimum necessary to effect an arrest. The use of force by police officers is governed by s 117 of PACE 1984. This states:

> Where any provision of this Act:
>
> (a) confers a power on a constable; and
>
> (b) does not provide that the power may only be exercised with the consent of some person, other than a police officer, the officer may use reasonable force, if necessary, in the exercise of the power.

10.4.12 DUTIES AFTER ARREST

A person arrested by a constable, or handed over to one, must be taken to a police station as soon as is 'practicable', unless his or her presence elsewhere is 'necessary

in order to carry out such investigations as it is reasonable to carry out immediately'
(s 30(1), (10) of PACE 1984). Where a citizen makes an arrest, he 'must, as soon as he
reasonably can, hand the man over to a constable or take him to the police station or
take him before a magistrate', per Lord Denning in *Dallison v Caffery* (1965). There
is no requirement, however, that this be carried out immediately (*John Lewis & Co v
Tims* (1952)).

10.5   INTERROGATION, CONFESSION AND ADMISSIBILITY OF EVIDENCE

Before moving into the specific provisions of PACE 1984 and the Codes of Practice as
they apply in the police station, it is important to be aware of the general issues at stake
in this area of law. Are the rights of suspects being interrogated by the police sufficiently
protected by law? Is there scope for abuse of power by the police? Are the police bur-
dened by too many legal requirements when trying to induce a suspect to confess to a
crime? What effects are likely to flow from the undermining of the right to silence (see
ss 34–37 of the CJPOA 1994)?

Once again, it is also necessary to bear in mind the significance of the ECHR in this
context. Unless impossible because of conflicting primary legislation, English courts must
interpret rules of law so as to be compatible with obligations under the ECHR. Article 5
guarantees a right to liberty. To justify depriving a person of their liberty before conviction
for an offence, for example, Art 5 requires that there be a lawful arrest or detention for
the purpose of bringing the person before a competent authority on a reasonable suspicion of having committed an offence, or that arrest or detention is considered reasonably
necessary to prevent them from committing an offence. Moreover, every person arrested
shall be informed promptly in a language that they understand of the reasons for their
arrest. The arrested person shall be informed of any charge against them, shall be brought
promptly before a judge and shall be entitled to trial within a reasonable time or to release
pending trial. Clearly, PACE requirements in relation to arrest and detention must be
measured against Art 5. Equally, Art 6 requires a fair trial and declares a presumption
of innocence, matters that bear on the conduct of the trial, the evidence presented, and
the obligation to offer explanations or risk the consequences of adverse inferences being
drawn from silence.

10.5.1   TIME LIMITS ON DETENTION WITHOUT CHARGE

Under s 40 of PACE 1984, the Custody Officer is obliged to review the detention of a
suspect held at the police station as follows:

(a)   the first review shall be not later than six hours after the detention was first
       authorised;

(b)   the second review shall be not later than nine hours after the first;

(c)   subsequent reviews shall be at intervals of not more than nine hours. The purpose of such reviews is to reduce the possibility that the suspect is being held for too long or unnecessarily while the investigation is ongoing. Both the suspect and/ or their solicitor are allowed to make representations about the termination or continuation of the detention.

Section 6 of the CJA 2003 introduced a new innovation – the use of telephones for review of police detention (s 40A PACE). This provision enables reviews of the continuing need for detention without charge carried out under s 40 of PACE 1984 to be conducted over the telephone rather than in person at the police station. Such reviews have to be carried out by an officer of at least inspector rank. PACE 1984 only allows telephone reviews where it is not reasonably practicable for the reviewing officer to be present at the police station.

Under s 41 of PACE 1984, a suspect can be held without being charged for 24 hours before any further authorisation needs to be given. At this point, the situation must be reviewed and further detention must be authorised by an officer of at least the rank of superintendent (s 42). This can only be done if an officer of sufficient rank is satisfied that detention is necessary to secure, preserve or obtain evidence, that the investigation is being conducted diligently and expeditiously, and that the relevant offence was an indictable offence. The period is measured from arrival at the police station. If they are arrested by another force, the time runs from their arrival at the station of the area where they are wanted. If further detention is authorised, this can continue for up to the 36-hour point. After 36 hours from the beginning of the detention, there must be a full hearing in a magistrates' court with the suspect and, if they wish, legal representation (s 43). The magistrates can grant a warrant of further detention for up to a further 60 hours – making a total of 96 hours (ss 43 and 44). However, the police could not be granted the 60-hour period as a whole because the maximum extension that a magistrates' court can grant at one time is 36 hours (ss 43(12) and 44). The magistrates can only grant such extensions if the offence being investigated is an indictable offence and is being investigated diligently and expeditiously. Moreover, it must be shown that the further detention is necessary to secure or preserve evidence relating to an offence for which the suspect is under arrest or to obtain such evidence by questioning them (s 43(4)).

The capacity for extended detention without charge, which has been broadened since the original passage of PACE, assists the police in dealing effectively with a range of offences, for example robbery, where it will sometimes be extremely difficult or impossible to complete the necessary investigatory processes within 24 hours.

Section 38 states that, *after being charged*, the arrested person must be released with or without bail, unless:

- it is necessary to hold them so that their name and address can be obtained; or
- in the case of a person arrested for an imprisonable offence, the custody officer has reasonable grounds for believing that the detention of the person arrested is necessary to prevent them from committing an offence, if they have been arrested for an imprisonable offence; or

- the custody officer reasonably thinks that it is necessary to hold them for their own protection or to prevent them from causing physical injury to anyone or from causing loss of or damage to property; or

- the custody officer reasonably thinks that they need to be held because they would otherwise fail to answer bail or to prevent them from interfering with witnesses or otherwise obstructing the course of justice; or

- the custody officer believes that it is necessary for them to be detained in order that a sample under s 63B can be obtained; or

- they are a juvenile and ought to be held in their 'own interests'.

If the suspect is charged and not released, they will have to be brought before a magistrates' court 'as soon as practicable' – and not later than the first sitting after being charged (s 46(2)).

10.5.2 TREATMENT WHILE DETAINED

Custody officer

Under s 39 PACE, the custody officer has responsibility for ensuring that treatment at the police station complies with PACE and the codes of practice and has some decision-making powers in relation to detention, release and eventual charging (see Chapter 11).

The right to have someone informed

The right to have someone informed after arrest is given to all suspects after arrest (s 56 PACE). It can be delayed for up to 36 hours, however, if the case involves an indictable offence and it must be authorised by an inspector on certain grounds; for example, the arrested person would alert others involved in a crime.

Access to legal advice

Access to legal advice is provided for under s 58 and Code C. The notification must accord with details set out in Code C. Legal advice can be delayed if authorised by a superintendent on various grounds. In certain circumstances, questioning can begin before the detainee's legal adviser arrives.

Basic rights during detention

Code C, paras 8–9 and 12 cover basic rights to food, drink, sleep and an interpreter during detention, including interviews.

Searches at the police station

Searches of people detained at police stations are governed by s 54 PACE 1984 and Code C. Section 54 and Code C, para 4.1 require the custody officer (a particular officer with special responsibilities in police stations) to take charge of the process of searching detainees. He or she must ascertain what the suspect has with them unless they are to be detained for only a short time and not put in a cell. The person detained can be searched to enable this to happen, but the custody officer needs to believe it to be necessary; it is not an automatic right (s 54(6)). Anything the detainee has can be seized and retained, although clothes and personal effects can only be kept if the custody officer *believes* that the detained person *may* use them to escape, interfere with evidence, or cause damage or injury to themselves, to others or to property (s 54(4)). The police are not permitted, however, to retain anything protected by legal professional privilege, that is, private legal communications between the detainee and their legal adviser. The police can also seize things they *reasonably believe* to be evidence of an offence. A search must be carried out by a constable who is the same sex as the person to be searched. Strip searches can only be made where the custody officer thinks it necessary to get some item that the detainee would not be allowed to keep. The officer must make a record of the reason for the search and its result. Section 8 CJA removed the requirement of the custody officer to record or cause to be recorded everything a detained person has with him on entering custody. The custody officer is under a duty to ascertain what the person has with them, but the nature and detail of any recording is at the custody officer's discretion. They also have a discretion as to whether the record is kept as part of the custody record or as a separate record.

Part V of PACE also includes a wide range of powers to take, for example, fingerprints, footwear impressions and both intimate and non-intimate samples, and details when this may be done without consent. The destruction, retention and use of those samples and DNA evidence derived from them has been very controversial given the massive scientific strides in this area. In *S and Marper v UK* (2009) the ECtHR held that, contrary to the House of Lords' earlier decision, holding DNA samples of people who were arrested but later acquitted or had the charges against them dropped was a violation of the right to privacy under Art 8 ECHR. The Protection of Freedoms Act 2012 introduced a new regime to govern this, which has been added to PACE as ss 63D–63U. This is a complex regime. It is fully discussed and its compliance with Art 8 considered in Cape (2013) 'The Protection of Freedoms Act 2012: the retention and use of biometric data provisions' *Crim LR* 23.

10.5.3 ANSWERING POLICE QUESTIONS AND THE RIGHT TO SILENCE

The police are free to ask anyone any questions. The only restriction is that all questioning is supposed to cease once a detainee has been charged. Code C, para 11.6 states that:

> The interview or further interview of a person about an offence with which that person has not been charged or for which they have not been informed they may be prosecuted must cease when the officer in charge of the investigation:
>
> (a) is satisfied all the questions they consider relevant to obtaining accurate and reliable information about the offence have been put

she had already been charged. It followed that in relation to such questions, the suspect did not have to be further cautioned.

Other powers to compel answers on pain of penalties for refusal exist under the Terrorism Act 2000, and refusal to answer certain allegations from the prosecutor can be treated as acceptance of them under the Drug Trafficking Act 1994.

The closest English law comes to creating a duty to give one's name and address is in s 24(5)(a) and (b) of PACE, where the need to ascertain the name and address of a suspect is one of the reasons why an arrest may be lawful.

There is no duty to offer information about crime to the police. However, s 19 of the Terrorism Act 2000 makes it an offence for a person who believes or suspects that another person has committed an offence under any of ss 15–18 (offences involving funding of terrorism), and bases their belief or suspicion on information that comes to their attention in the course of a trade, profession, business or employment to not disclose to an officer as soon as is reasonably practicable their belief or suspicion, and the information on which it is based. Additionally, s 5 of the CLA 1967 creates the offence of accepting money or other consideration for not disclosing information that would lead to the prosecution of a relevant offence.

10.5.5   WHAT CAN BE SAID IN COURT ABOUT SILENCE IN THE FACE OF POLICE QUESTIONING

There is an established common law rule that neither the prosecution nor the judge should make adverse comment on the defendant's silence in the face of questions. The dividing line, however, between proper and improper judicial comment has been a matter of great debate. In Scotland, a trial judge may not comment on a defendant's failure to answer questions. It is suggested that the position in England and Wales, whereby a judge may comment, not only undermines the right to silence but also provides fertile ground for judicial misdirections to the jury, in turn increasing the opportunities for appeal on points that arise simply in default of lack of judicial restraint. There are many reasons why a suspect might remain silent when questioned (for example fear, confusion, reluctance to incriminate another person) and the 'right to silence' enjoyed the status of a long-established general principle in English law. Thus, in *R v Davis* (1959), a judge was ruled on appeal to have misdirected the jury when he told them that 'a man is not obliged to say anything but you are entitled to use your common sense . . . [C]an you imagine an innocent man who had behaved like that not saying anything to the police . . . He said nothing.'

An exception, though, was that some degree of adverse suggestion was permitted where two people were speaking on equal terms and one refused to comment on the accusation made against them by the other. In *R v Parkes* (1974), the Privy Council ruled that a judge could invite the jury to consider the possibility of drawing adverse inferences from silence from a tenant who had been accused by a landlady of murdering her daughter. The landlady and tenant, for the purposes of this encounter, were regarded as having a parity of status, unlike a person faced with questions from the police. It was held in *R v Chandler* (1976) that the suspect was on equal terms with the police officer where the former was in the company of his solicitor. Chandler had refused to answer some of the questions he had been asked by the police officer before the caution. The judge told the jury that they should decide whether the defendant's silence was attributable to his wish to exercise his common law right or because he might incriminate himself. The Court of Appeal quashed Chandler's conviction since the judge had gone too far in suggesting that silence before a caution could be evidence of guilt.

It was proper for the judge to make some comment on a defendant's reticence before being cautioned, provided that the jury were directed that the issue had to be dealt with in two stages: (i) was the defendant's silence an acceptance of the officer's allegations?; and, if so, (ii) could guilt of the offence charged be reasonably inferred from what the defendant had implicitly accepted? The court said that it did not accept that a police officer always had an advantage over a suspect. Everything depended on the circumstances. In an inquiry into local government corruption, for example, a young officer might be at a distinct disadvantage when questioning a local dignitary. That type of interview was very different from a 'tearful housewife' being accused of shoplifting.

The Court of Appeal's decision in *Chandler* asserted that silence might only be taken as acquiescence to police allegations before a caution. The court excluded silence after the caution as being something from which anything adverse can be inferred, because a suspect could not be criticised for remaining silent having been specifically told of that right. This, however, seemed like an irrational dichotomy. If the suspect did, in fact, have a legal right to silence whether or not they had been cautioned, it was very odd that full enjoyment of the right could be effective only from the moment of it being announced by the police. Additionally, any questioning of a suspect at a police station prior to a caution being given was probably in contravention of Code C, para 10, which requires a caution to be given at the beginning of each session of questioning. Violation of the Code affords grounds for an appeal under s 78 of PACE 1984. Cautions need not be given according to para 10.1:

> . . . if questions are for other necessary purposes, eg:
>
> (a)   solely to establish their own identity or ownership of any vehicle;
>
> (b)   to obtain information in accordance with any relevant statutory requirement, see *paragraph 10.9*;
>
> (c)   in furtherance of the proper and effective control of a search, eg, to determine the need to search in the exercise of powers of stop and search or to seek co-operation while carrying out a search . . .

These cases must now all be read in the light of s 34 of the CJPOA 1994.

Except in so far as the new law makes changes, the old law still applies.

In enacting ss 34–37 of the CJPOA 1994, the government was adopting a particular policy. The general purpose of the Act was to assist in the fight against crime. The government took the view that the balance in the criminal justice system had become tilted too far in favour of the criminal and against the public in general, and victims in particular. The alleged advantage of the change in law was that it helped convict criminals who, under the old law, used to be acquitted because they took advantage of the right to keep quiet when questioned without the court or prosecution being able to comment adversely upon that silence. Introducing the legislation, the Home Secretary said that change in law was desirable because 'it is professional criminals, hardened criminals and terrorists who disproportionately take advantage of and abuse the present system'. There was also a feeling that defendants would wait until the last possible moment to formulate their defence, effectively 'ambushing' the prosecution.

Section 34 states that where anyone is questioned under caution by a police officer, or charged with an offence, then a failure to mention a fact at that time which he or she later relies on in his or her defence will allow a court to draw such inferences as appear proper about that failure. Inferences may only be drawn if, in the circumstances, a suspect could reasonably have been expected to mention the fact when he or she was questioned. The inferences that can be drawn can be used in determining whether the accused is guilty as charged. The section, however, permits adverse inferences to be drawn from silence in situations that do not amount to 'interviews' as defined by Code C of PACE 1984, and thus which are not subject to the safeguards of access to legal advice and of contemporaneous recording that exist where a suspect is interviewed at the police station. The caution to be administered by police officers is as follows (with appropriate variants for ss 36 and 37):

> You do not have to say anything. But, it may harm your defence if you do not mention when questioned something which you later rely on in court. Anything you do say may be given in evidence.

Section 58 of the Youth Justice and Criminal Evidence Act (YJCEA) 1999 amended s 34 by adding a new s 34(2A). This restricted the drawing of inferences from silence in an interview at a police station (or similar venue) where the suspect was not allowed an opportunity to consult a solicitor prior to being questioned or charged (see Code D, Annex C). This amendment was intended to meet the ruling of the ECtHR in *Murray v UK* (1996) that delay in access to legal advice, even if lawful, could amount to a breach of Art 6, given the risk of adverse inferences being drawn.

An interesting illustration of the principle at work can be found in *R v Maguire (Glen)* (2008). The appellant offender (M) appealed against his conviction for two offences of wounding contrary to the Offences Against the Person Act 1861 s 20. M was accused, following an argument in a public house, first, of committing an unprovoked attack on a victim in a street with a rice flail, which he had allegedly taken from his pocket, and, second, of emerging from his house with a meat cleaver later the same evening, with which he struck a second victim on the arm. M gave two different accounts of the evening's events, one during a police interview and the other in evidence at the trial. Both versions raised the issue of self-defence. On the Crown's application, the trial judge gave a direction under the Criminal Justice and Public Order Act 1994 s 34 in conventional form, in which he identified two sets of facts on which M had relied at trial but which he had not mentioned in police interview, namely (i) that there had been no real gap between the incidents, that he had been confronted by a mob of people outside his house and that his need to act in self-defence arose at the same time in fending off what was a joint attack by the purported victims, and (ii) that, having emerged from his house, he was naked when obliged to confront the mob. M was convicted but appealed, saying his convictions were unsafe because the judge was wrong to give a direction under s 34 of the 1994 Act.

His appeal was dismissed. The Court of Appeal ruled that:

> With or without such a direction, the Crown's case was plainly going to be that M's evidence had been shown to be untruthful, partly by other contradictory evidence in the case, and also by the way that his account had changed. The judge was virtually certain to refer to it, and he would no doubt have told the jury that it was up to them to say whether the explanation for the change in account might be an innocent one, or whether it was that M's evidence was untruthful. The s 34 direction was a formalised way of saying precisely the same. Section 34 did no more than seek to apply common sense.
>
> Such a direction always raised the question whether the omission to refer to something in interview which appeared later in evidence was or was not an indication that the new material was untruthful. The object of the section and of the direction was to enable the jury to decide that question. In the instant case, the matters identified by the judge were capable of being facts within the meaning of s 34, but even if they were not, the judge's direction would have been substantially the same. The fact that the s 34 direction included the proposition that the jury were entitled to infer some additional support for the Crown from the change of evidence did not alter that. The jury had had the issues which arose in the case properly before them, and the convictions were safe.
>
> The court also said that prosecutors should be cautious about too readily seeking to invite formalised directions under s 34. Anything that over-formalised common sense was to be discouraged.

Section 35 allows a court or jury to infer what appears proper from the refusal of an accused person to testify in his or her own defence, or from a refusal without good cause to answer any question at trial. In para 39.P.2 of the *Criminal Practice Direction* (2013) (EWCA Crim 1631), the Lord Chief Justice indicates that where the accused is legally represented, the following should be said by the judge to the accused's lawyer at the end of the prosecution case if the accused is not to give evidence:

> Have you advised your client that the stage has now been reached at which he may give evidence and, if he chooses not to do so or, having been sworn, without good cause refuses to answer any question, the jury may draw such inferences as appear proper from his failure to do so?

If the lawyer replies to the judge that the accused has been so advised, then the case will proceed. If the accused is not represented, and still chooses not to give evidence or answer a question, the judge must give him a similar warning, ending: ' . . . the jury may draw such inferences as appear proper. That means they may hold it against you.'

Section 36 permits inferences to be drawn from the failure or refusal of a person under arrest to account for any object, substances or mark in their possession, on their person, in or on their clothing or footwear, or in any place at which they are at the time of arrest. Section 37 permits inferences to be drawn from the failure of an arrested person to account for their presence at a particular place where they are found.

Thus, as the late Lord Taylor, the then Lord Chief Justice, observed, the legal changes do not, strictly speaking, abolish the right to silence:

> If a defendant maintains his silence from first till last, and does not rely on any particular fact by way of defence, but simply puts the prosecution to proof, then [ss 34–37] would not bite at all.

The change was widely and strongly opposed by lawyers, judges and legal campaign groups. Liberty, for example, said that drawing adverse inferences from silence undermines the presumption of innocence. Silence is an important safeguard against oppressive questioning by the police, particularly for the weak and vulnerable.

John Alderson, former chief constable of Devon and Cornwall (1973–82) and a respected writer on constitutional aspects of policing, has written of the impending danger when police are able to 'exert legal and psychological pressure on individuals held in the loneliness of their cells'. He stated (*The Independent*, 1 February 1995) that:

> History tells us that, when an individual has to stand up against the entire apparatus of the modern State, he or she is very vulnerable. That is why, in criminal cases, the burden of proof has always rested on the State rather than on the accused. The Founding Fathers of America amended their constitution to that effect in 1791.

An example might be persons detained indefinitely at the Home Secretary's discretion at HMP Belmarsh and HMP Woodhill (see J Cooper, 'Guantanamo Bay, London' (2004) 154 NLJ 41).

Undermining the right to silence may constitute a significant constitutional change in the relationship between the individual and the state. It may be doubted whether the majority of suspects should be put under greater intimidation by the system because of the conduct of a few 'hardened criminals' – the justification for the legislation given by the then Home Secretary when he introduced it.

10.5.8 DIRECTIONS TO THE JURY ON SILENT DEFENDANTS

Following the enactment of the CJPOA 1994, there has been a steady stream of case law about the correct judicial practice when directing the jury about the drawing of adverse inferences under ss 34 and 35.

In *R v Cowan* (1995), the Court of Appeal considered what should be said in the summing up if the defendant decides not to testify. The jury must be directed that (as provided by s 38(3) of the CJPOA 1994) an inference from failure to give evidence could not on its own prove guilt. The jury had to be satisfied (on the basis of the evidence called by the prosecution) that the prosecution had established a case to answer before inferences could be drawn from the accused's silence. The jury could only draw an adverse inference from the accused's silence if that silence could only be sensibly attributed to the accused having no answer to the charge or none that could stand up to cross-examination.

The difficult issue as to correct judicial practice when the accused remains silent during interview on the advice of his or her solicitor was considered in three cases – *R v Beckles* (2004), *R v Hoare & Pierce* (2004) and *R v Howell* (2005). The Court of Appeal arrived at the following position:

- Where an accused gives evidence that they remained silent on the advice of their solicitor, the question for the jury/court is whether – in the situation existing at the time – it is reasonable to expect the accused to have mentioned the relevant fact(s).
- The fact that the court/jury accepts that the accused genuinely relied on legal advice when staying silent and not revealing facts that are subsequently relied

on in court does not mean that the jury are obliged to conclude that it was reasonable for the accused not to mention those facts.

- A court might be more likely to conclude that reliance on legal advice not to put forward facts was reasonable if there was a sound foundation for it – examples being: little or no police disclosure; the case is too complex or too old to expect immediate answers from the accused; the accused has personal problems (for example, mental disability, shock, intoxication).

- A court might be less likely to conclude that reliance on legal advice not to put forward facts was reasonable if the advice was not based on a sound foundation – examples that The Law Society Guidance sets out are: a belief that the detention is unlawful; the victim has not made a written statement; a belief that the victim might withdraw the complaint; a belief that the police will charge anyway, whatever the accused says.

Where, however, a judge concludes that the requirements of s 34 have not been satisfied and therefore that it is not open to him or her to leave to the jury the possibility of drawing adverse inferences, he or she must direct the jury that it should not in any way hold against the accused the fact that they did not answer questions in interview (*R v McGarry* (1998)).

The provisions as to silence must also meet the requirements of Art 6 of the ECHR. The ECtHR held in *Murray v UK* (1996) that this right is not absolute and that a system under which inferences could be drawn from silence did not in itself constitute a breach of Art 6, though particular caution when drawing inferences was necessary. This was reaffirmed in *Condron v UK* (2001), where the Court asserted that though silence could not be the only, or even the main, basis for any conviction, it was right that it should be taken into account in circumstances which clearly called for an explanation from the accused (examples might be having to account for presence at the scene of the crime, or having to account for the presence of fibres on clothing). It should be noted that although the specimen direction issued by the Judicial Studies Board (JSB) and used by judges emphasises that silence cannot be the only basis for a conviction, it does not make any reference to whether it can be the *main basis* for conviction. Thus, there is a possible conflict between the approach under the ECHR and that currently adopted in English courts.

The ECtHR considers that legal advice is of great significance in this system. Thus, both *Murray v UK* and *Condron v UK* stressed the importance of access to legal advice at the time of any interview. As explained earlier, the finding in *Murray v UK* that denial of access to legal advice, in conjunction with the drawing of inferences, amounted to a breach of Art 6 led to the amendment to the CJPOA 1994 contained in s 34(2A). However, access in itself is not the end of the matter. The question which then arises is whether the drawing of inferences may be improper under the ECHR where silence results from legal advice, as discussed above. The ECtHR held in both *Condron v UK* and *Averill v UK* (2000) that legal advice may be a proper reason for declining to answer questions and that it may not be fair to draw adverse inferences in such cases. A solicitor representing a young or otherwise vulnerable person may recognise that the evidence against the client is very weak. Advising such a client to 'say nothing' will often make good sense (see A Keogh, 'The right to silence – revisited again' (2003) 153 NLJ 1352).

The jury should be informed that no adverse inference should be drawn where a defendant 'genuinely and reasonably' relies on a solicitor's advice to remain silent in interview (*R v Beckles* (2004)).

In *R v Robert Webber* (2004), the House of Lords decided that, for the purposes of working out whether a silent defendant in court was 'relying on a fact' used in their defence (and therefore something that could prompt the judge to allow the jury to draw adverse inferences about the defendant's silence), answers given by a witness for the prosecution who was being cross-questioned by the defendant's counsel were facts.

A positive suggestion put to a witness by or on behalf of a defendant could amount to a fact relied on in their defence for the purpose of s 34 of the CJPOA 1994, even if that suggestion was not accepted by a witness.

The defendant (W) appealed from a decision (summarised below) that the trial judge was correct to give a direction under s 34 of the CJPOA 1994. W and two co-defendants had been charged with conspiracy to murder. The prosecution case against W was based on three incidents. When interviewed by police about each incident, W had either denied involvement in any conspiracy or said that he was not present. At trial, W's counsel put it to several prosecution witnesses that their evidence relating to the incidents was wrong. The witnesses rejected counsel's suggestions. The certified question for the House of Lords was whether a suggestion put to a witness by or on behalf of a defendant could amount to a 'fact relied on in his defence' for the purpose of s 34 of the Act, if that suggestion was not adopted by the witness. W submitted that s 34 was directed to evidence and that suggestions of counsel were not evidence unless or until accepted by a witness. The prosecution submitted that such suggestions were matters on which a defendant relied, whether or not they supported them by their own or other evidence, and whether or not prosecution witnesses accepted them.

The court held that a positive suggestion put to a witness by or on behalf of a defendant could amount to a fact relied on in his or her defence for the purpose of s 34 even if that suggestion was not accepted by a witness. The word 'fact' in s 34 covered any alleged fact that was in issue and was put forward as part of the defence case. If the defendant advanced at trial any pure fact or exculpatory explanation or account that, if true, he or she could reasonably have been expected to advance earlier, s 34 was potentially applicable. A defendant relied on a fact or matter in their defence not only when they gave or adduced evidence of it, but also when counsel, acting on their instructions, put a specific and positive case to prosecution witnesses, as opposed to asking questions intended to probe or test the prosecution case. That was so, whether or not the prosecution witness accepted the suggestion put. The appeal was dismissed.

10.5.9 TAPE-RECORDING OF INTERROGATIONS

The police were initially very hostile to the recommendation of the Philips Royal Commission on Criminal Procedure that there should be tape-recording of interviews with suspects. After a while, however, the police became more enthusiastic when it became

The phrase 'anything said or done' means by someone other than the suspect. In *R v Goldenberg* (1988), G, a heroin addict, was arrested on a charge of conspiracy to supply diamorphine. He requested an interview five days after his arrest and during this he gave information about a man who he said had supplied him with heroin. It was argued for G at trial that he had given the statement to get bail and thus to be able to feed his addiction. G contended that the words 'in consequence of anything said or done' included things said or done by the suspect and that the critical things here were the things G had said and done, namely, requested the interview and given any statement that would be likely to get him out of the station. G was convicted and his appeal was dismissed. Neill LJ stated:

> In our judgment, the words 'said or done' in s 76(2)(b) of the 1984 Act do not extend so as to include anything said or done by the person making the confession. It is clear from the wording of the section and the use of the words 'in consequence' that a causal link must be shown between what was said or done and the subsequent confession. In our view, it necessarily follows that 'anything said or done' is limited to something external to the person making the confession and to something which is likely to have some influence on him.

The reasoning in cases like *R v Zavekas* (see above) has now clearly been rejected. This view is confirmed by Code C; if a suspect asks an officer what action will be taken in the event of their answering questions, making a statement or refusing to do either, the officer may inform them what action he or she proposes to take in that event 'provided that the action is itself proper and warranted' (para 11.5).

'Confessions' made to fellow prisoners are particularly controversial. In 1996, Lin, Megan and Josie Russell were attacked while taking their dog for a walk. Lin and Megan were killed; Josie suffered serious injuries. Michael Stone was arrested and charged with the murders. He was then remanded into custody. At his trial in 1998, two fellow inmates, Damien Daley and Harry Thompson, were called as witnesses. Both alleged that Stone had 'confessed' to them. Stone was convicted. The next day, Thompson contacted national newspapers. He said that he had lied in court because of police pressures. In 2001, Stone's convictions were quashed by the Court of Appeal. At his retrial, the prosecution used Daley's evidence and Stone was reconvicted. A strong argument could be made for excluding such dubious evidence under s 78 of PACE. The central problem has been described by Gwyn Morgan in 'Cell confessions' (2002) 152 NLJ 453:

> There may be a strong incentive for 'grasses' to come up with their incriminating stories. Deals may be done with the police as to the withdrawal of charges. Even where this is not the case, those on remand may well feel – even

> if they are wrong – that giving evidence for the prosecution will ease the way when their own cases come up. And where the grasses are already convicted, they may be anxious (again rightly or wrongly) to give a favourable impression to the prison authorities or the parole board. What's more, in contrast to most witnesses, coming to court does not adversely interfere with their lives; it's a day out.

See also 'Cell confessions – no stone left unturned' (2005) 155 NLJ 550.

10.5.13 CAN A SOLICITOR PROVIDE THE 'SOMETHING SAID OR DONE'?

In *R v Wahab* (2003) the accused was arrested on suspicion that he was involved in a conspiracy to supply drugs. He was interviewed in the presence of his solicitor. After the third interview he authorised his solicitor to approach the police to see whether his family, who were also in custody, might be released if he confessed his guilt. In accordance with those express instructions his solicitor approached the police, who made it clear that no promises could be made or guarantees given. The solicitor told W that if he made admissions, the police would look at the whole picture and that if the evidence against the family was 'borderline', they would be released. At a fourth interview W confessed to his involvement in the conspiracy, but only as a middleman.

The accused dismissed his solicitor and employed a different one for his trial, where he sought the exclusion of the fourth interview. The Court of Appeal held that advice properly given to a defendant by his solicitor did not normally provide a basis for excluding a subsequent confession under s 76(2) of the PACE 1984. The Court further held that one of the duties of a legal adviser, whether at a police station, or indeed at a pre-trial conference, or during the trial itself, is to give the client realistic advice. That emphatically did not mean that the advice had to be directed to 'getting the client off', or simply making life difficult for the prosecution; though it had to be sensibly robust considering the advantages that the client might derive from evidence of remorse and a realistic acceptance of guilt, or the corresponding disadvantages of participating in a no-comment interview.

CHAPTER SUMMARY: THE CRIMINAL PROCESS: (1) THE INVESTIGATION OF CRIME

At the beginning of the twenty-first century, we can see governmental recognition of the 'criminal justice system'.

THE CRIMINAL PROCESS (2) THE PROSECUTION

11

The classification of offences and matters relating to transfers for trial, summary trial, and trial on indictment are dealt with in Chapter 9.

Until 1986, England was one of only a few countries that allowed the police to prosecute rather than hand over this task to a state agency such as the office of the district attorney in the United States, or the procurator fiscal in Scotland (an office established in the fifteenth century). The Crown Prosecution Service (CPS) was established by the Prosecution of Offences Act (POA) 1985. As a result the police now play only a limited part in prosecutions beyond the stage of charging the suspect. This chapter examines the workings of the state prosecution service.

The CPS has come under significant criticism in recent times for allegedly poor performance. In December 2015, Alison Saunders, the Director of Public Prosecutions, was accused of living in a bubble after admitting that she goes to court 'every few months, probably' (*The Times*, 16 December 2015). Appearing before the House of Commons' justice select committee, Ms Saunders told MPs: 'I go as much as I can, which is not as often as it should be. I will pop up to court every now and again.' Philip Davies MP said that she was complacent about the state of magistrates' courts. Mr Davies said that in some instances prosecution lawyers were 'literally reading out in court' case files 'they've never even seen before'. Ms Saunders said that despite a 23 per cent cut in resources over three years, the recent public spending round had ensured that the Crown Prosecution Service had received the extra £4.4 million it needed to tackle terrorism cases.

The police have power to take the charging decision in relation to summary offences, retail theft suitable for trial in the magistrates' court and most either-way offences where a guilty plea is anticipated and that are suitable for sentence in the magistrates' court (para 15, DPP's Guidance on Charging 2013 – fifth edition, May 2013 (revised arrangements)). It is a prosecutor who takes the charging decision in more serious or potentially disputed cases. However, the initial decision to divert the suspect from prosecution, charge or refer lies with the police decision-maker, as does the decision to drop a case where there is insufficient evidence. In 2013–14, the CPS took the pre-charge decision in around one-third of cases (Crown Prosecution Service, Annual Report and

Accounts, 2013–14). The basis for charging is fully explained in the DPP's Guidance on Charging 2013.

Before 1986, there were five different forms of prosecution, those by:

- the police, who prosecuted most offences;

- the Attorney General/Solicitor General, whose permission was needed to prosecute for many serious crimes and who could enter a *nolle prosequi* to stop certain prosecutions or give a *fiat* to disallow them from the beginning;

- the Director of Public Prosecutions (DPP), who prosecuted in very serious cases and cases brought to him or her by the government;

- public bodies;

- private prosecutions, which involved having to persuade a magistrate of the propriety in issuing a summons. The Attorney General and the DPP both had the power to take over a private prosecution and then drop it for reasons of public policy. The right to bring private prosecutions was retained by s 6(1) of the POA 1985. Boyce and Gokani suggest that straitened economic times are leading to a substantial increase in private prosecutions from bodies such as Transport for London, the RSPCA (an increasingly active prosecutor) or Virgin or Sky prosecuting those using 'pirate' equipment (W Boyce and R Gokani, 'Private prosecutions' (2014) 111(31) LSG 22).

Today, the first three of the above list are conducted by the CPS. The CPS liaises where necessary with other public bodies which have the power to prosecute offenders: Attorney General's Office; Civil Aviation Authority; Department for Business, Innovation and Skills; Department for Work and Pensions; Environment Agency; Financial Services Agency; Food Standards Agency; Gambling Commission; Health and Safety Executive; Maritime and Coastguard Agency; Office of Fair Trading; Office of Rail Regulation; Serious Fraud Office; and Service Prosecuting Authority.

11.2   THE CROWN PROSECUTION SERVICE

The move to establish a CPS was precipitated by a report from JUSTICE, the British section of the International Commission of Jurists, in its 1970 Report, *The Prosecution Process in England and Wales*. It argued that the police were not best suited to be prosecutors because they would often have a commitment to winning a case even where the evidence was weak, given the investment in a case that its investigation invariably represents. They were also not best placed to consider the public policy aspects of the discretion not to prosecute. The police were firmly opposed to such a change. They argued that statistics showed that the police were not given to pursuing cases in a way that led to a high rate of acquittal. They also showed that in cases involving miscarriages of justice, the decision to prosecute had been taken by a lawyer.

The question was referred to the Philips Royal Commission on Criminal Procedure, which judged the then existing system according to its fairness, openness and accountability. It proposed a new system based on several distinct features, including the following:

- that the initial decision to charge a suspect should rest with the police;
- that thereafter all decisions as to whether to proceed, alter or drop the charges should rest with another state prosecuting agency;
- this agency would provide advocates for all cases in the magistrates' courts apart from guilty pleas by post. It should also provide legal advice to the police and instruct counsel in all cases tried on indictment.

The POA 1985 established a national prosecution service under the general direction of the DPP. The 1985 Act gives to the DPP and the CPS as a whole the right to institute and conduct any criminal proceedings where the importance or difficulty of the case make that appropriate (s 3(2)(b)). This applies to cases that could also be started by the police or other bodies like local authorities. It can also, in appropriate circumstances, take over and then discontinue cases. The CPS relies on the police for the resources and machinery of investigation.

The CPS uses a mixture of employed staff and agents, that is, lawyers in private practice working for the CPS on a fee-for-case basis. In 2013–14, 25.6 per cent of half-day sessions in magistrates' courts were covered by agents.

At the end of March 2014, the CPS employed 6,611 people. It prosecuted 753,743 cases in the magistrates' courts and 94,617 in the Crown Courts, with a conviction rate of 81 per cent in the Crown Court. Over 93 per cent of all staff are engaged in, or support, front-line prosecutions. The CPS has 2,226 prosecutors, including Crown Advocates who take on complex cases in the higher courts, rather than instructing advocates in private practice (*Annual Report and Resource Accounts 2013–2014*, Crown Prosecution Service). In addition, the CPS now includes Advocate Panels, providing lists of quality-assessed advocates. These are the external advocates that CPS will call upon to undertake prosecution advocacy alongside its in-house advocates.

11.2.1 THE DISCRETION TO PROSECUTE

The police have a very significant discretion as to what to do when a crime has possibly been committed. They could turn a blind eye, dispose of the case out of court or, in conjunction with the CPS, charge the suspect, in which case they must decide what is the most appropriate charge or charges commensurate with the facts and seriousness of the alleged conduct. Environmental health officers, the Health and Safety Executive and Environment Agency inspectors, as officers statutorily charged with investigative powers, are in a similar position.

As is very cogently argued by McConville, Sanders and Leng in *The Case for the Prosecution* (1991), prosecution cases are constructed from the evidence and testimony of many people including lay witnesses, victims, the police, CPS lawyers and expert witnesses. Each of these parties is fallible and prone to perceive events in line with their own sorts of experience. The net result of this is that the prosecution case is normally nothing more than designed for low-level offending, they may be used for any offence where it is not in the public interest to prosecute. While the young person must have admitted the offence (and not mentioned anything giving rise to a defence), consent is not required. Parents or other appropriate adults must have been given enough information about the options available and, in the case of sexual offences, the consequences of inclusion on the register of sex offenders must be explained to both the adult and the young person. The caution forms part of the young person's criminal record.

Simple cautions

These are non-statutory and available for any offence. Again, they are designed for low-level offending but may be used for any offence where it is not in the public interest to prosecute. The Crown Prosecution Service must be consulted if the offence is indictable only. The offender must admit the offence and consent and the caution will form part of the criminal record. As with young people, the offender may be placed on the sex offenders register if the offence is one covered by the Sexual Offences Act 2003.

Youth conditional cautions

These are youth cautions with conditions attached, and were introduced by the Crime and Disorder Act 1998. The police may offer these for summary and either-way offences, but a Crown Prosecutor must authorise conditional cautions for indictable-only offences. The conditions may be rehabilitative, reparative or punitive but must be appropriate, proportionate and achievable. Punitive conditions may include unpaid work, but only in respect of youth conditional cautions.

Conditional cautions

These are adult cautions with conditions attached, and their main features are the same as youth conditional cautions (above). In addition, where the offender does not have permission to enter or remain in the UK, the conditions offered may be designed to ensure the offender leaves the UK and does not remain.

11.2.3   THE CODE FOR CROWN PROSECUTORS

The Code for Crown Prosecutors (promulgated on behalf of the DPP) sets out the official criteria governing the discretion to prosecute. It is issued under s 10 of the POA 1985. The seventh edition of the Code was published in January 2013 and can be viewed in full at www.cps.gov.uk/publications/code_for_crown_prosecutors/. The CPS website also includes substantial legal guidance on every aspect of criminal law and procedure.

The Code sets out the basis on which prosecutions may be brought and the underlying principles. It provides two tests: the Threshold Test and the Full Code Test. Prosecution can only start or continue when the Full Code Test is satisfied. The Threshold Test is an exception to the Full Code Test. It may only be applied where the suspect presents a substantial bail risk and not all the evidence is available at the time when he or she must be released from custody unless charged.

The Full Code Test requires two tests to be satisfied before a prosecution is brought: there must be a 'realistic prospect of conviction' (the evidential test); and the prosecution must be 'in the public interest'.

The evidential test requires prosecutors to predict what a jury or bench, properly directed, would be likely to decide. The guidelines require prosecutors to assess the reliability of evidence, not just its admissibility. Glanville Williams ([1985] Crim LR 115) and Andrew Sanders ((1994) 144 NLJ 946) argued that earlier versions of this test, which dealt specifically with reliability in relation to personal characteristics, favoured people who are well respected in society – like police officers and businessmen – in whose favour juries and magistrates might be biased. It disfavoured the sort of victims who are unlikely to make good witnesses. Sanders proposed a better test: whether, on the evidence, a jury or bench ought (on the balance of probabilities) to convict. The Code now says that the test is whether the jury or bench 'is more likely than not to convict the defendant of the charge alleged' (para 4.5).

The public interest must be considered in each case where there is enough evidence to provide a realistic prospect of conviction. In cases of any seriousness, a prosecution will usually take place unless there are public interest factors tending against prosecution which clearly outweigh those tending in favour.

The Code lists some 'public interest factors in favour of prosecution' and some against (para 4.12). Crown Prosecutors and others must balance factors for and against prosecution, carefully and fairly.

In October 2013, a new Code of Practice for Victims of Crime was produced under s 33 Domestic Violence Crime and Victims Act 2004. This Code applies not just to the CPS, but to a wide variety of criminal justice organisations. The CPS is committed to 'championing justice and defending the rights of victims, fairly, firmly and effectively'. The public interest factors in the Full Test Code take into account the circumstances of the victim, for example the effect of a prosecution on the victim's health. If there is evidence that a prosecution is likely to have an adverse impact on the victim's health then it may make a prosecution less likely, taking into account the victim's views.

The Attorney General has commended the Code to prosecutors outside the CPS. This may help to correct inconsistent approaches between the police and CPS on the one hand and, on the other, prosecutors like HMRC and the Health and Safety Executive. As Sanders (see above) has observed, if you illegally gain a fortune or maim someone, you will probably be treated more leniently than ordinary disposals for such offences if the crimes are, technically, tax evasion and operating an unsafe place of work. Local authorities and the Environment Agency seem generally reluctant to prosecute environmental offenders. This can lead to a situation in which environmental crime, for example, makes good business sense. (See M Watson, 'Offences against the environment: the economics of crime and punishment' (2004) 16(4) Environmental Law and Management 2003–04. For the Health and Safety Executive, see G Slapper, *Blood in the Bank* (1999).)

11.2.6 STATE PROSECUTORS IN THE CROWN COURTS

Reference has already been made to the fact that Crown Prosecutors are now able to appear in the higher courts if they are suitably qualified. This has caused a great deal of concern in some quarters. The basis of the worry is that, as full-time salaried lawyers working for an organisation, CPS lawyers will sometimes be tempted to get convictions using dubious tactics or ethics because their own status as employees and prospects of promotion will depend on conviction success rates. Where, as now, barristers from the independent Bar are used by the CPS to prosecute, there is (it is argued) a greater likelihood of the courtroom lawyer dropping a morally unsustainable case.

Section 42 of the Access to Justice Act 1999 tries to overcome any possible difficulties with a provision (amending s 27 of the Courts and Legal Services Act (CLSA) 1990) that every advocate 'has a duty to the court to act with independence in the interests of justice', in other words, a duty that overrides any inconsistent duty that might lie, for example, to an employer. Professor Michael Zander QC has contended, however, that these are 'mere words'. He has said (letter to *The Times*, 29 December 1998) that they are unlikely to exercise much sway over CPS lawyer employees concerned with performance targets set by their line managers, and that:

> The CPS as an organisation is constantly under pressure in regard to the proportion of discontinuances, acquittal and conviction rates. These are factors in the day-to-day work of any CPS lawyer. It is disingenuous to imagine they will not have a powerful effect on decision making.

The Bar was also very wary of this change, an editorial in *Counsel* (the journal of the Bar of England and Wales) saying:

> [W]e are gravely concerned about the extent to which prosecutions will be done in-house by the CPS when the need for independent prosecutors is so well established in our democracy ((1999) *Counsel* 3, February).

It is important to set the arguments in a wider context. What are the social, economic or political debates surrounding this issue of how best to run a system of courtroom prosecutors? The change to having Crown Court prosecutions carried out by salaried CPS lawyers might well be expected to be more efficient, as the whole prosecution can be handled in-house, without engaging the external service of an independent barrister. This assumption has been discredited, however: CPS in-house cases are in fact more expensive to run than instructing chambers-based barristers (see Bar Council, 27 July 2009: 'Independent Study Heavily Criticises CPS Claims about In-House Advocates are Based on "Alice in Wonderland Accounting" '). Some will argue that justice is being sacrificed to the deity of cost-cutting. On the other hand, it could be argued that justice and efficiency are not mutually exclusive phenomena and – as has been shown above – the CPS has been actively recruiting Higher Court Advocates (HCAs) to prosecute in the Crown Court. Keir Starmer QC, the ex-Director of Public Prosecutions, committed himself to the view that 'in-house advocacy is here to stay for the CPS' (9 January 2009). However, the real-term costs of HCAs have been effectively queried, with recent Bar Council meetings discussing the relative expense of independent and in-house barristers. This has culminated in a turf war between in-house CPS advocates and independent practitioners at the Bar. (See the article by Frances Gibb, 'Bar Council says Crown Prosecution Service wasting millions with in-house prosecutions', *The Times*, 27 July 2009.) It remains to be seen what effect the CPS Panel Advocate scheme, which is now up and running, will have on this debate. The most recent report from HM Chief Inspector of the Crown Prosecution Service suggests that the CPS deals well with the most serious and complex casework but that the position is not as good in relation to 'volume' casework (www.justiceinspectorates.gov.uk/hmcpsi/).

<hr>

11.3   BAIL

Bail is the release from custody, pending a criminal trial, of an accused. The relevant statute is the Bail Act (BA) 1976. Bail may be with or without conditions. Conditional bail may be granted, for example, on the promise that an accused will not contact witnesses or co-defendants in a case; that he or she will co-operate with probation or other state agencies; that he or she will report to a police station at specific times; or that he or she will observe a curfew (either a 'doorstop' curfew, where he or she is to present himself or herself to a police officer calling at the curfew address, or one which is electronically monitored via an ankle tag). Other conditions of remand on bail might include the promise that money will be paid to the court by a 'surety' (the person 'standing' the bail money) if he or she absconds, or the deposit of a security, where money is paid into court 'up-front' and is forfeit if the defendant absconds. All decisions on whether to grant bail therefore involve delicate questions of balancing interests, but the exercise begins with the presumption that an accused should be at liberty until proven guilty. The test to be applied is a threshold one. Where there are 'substantial grounds' for believing that the exceptions to bail in the Bail Act 1976 are met, a court may be satisfied that deprivation of the liberty of an accused can be justified.

A person is presumed innocent of a criminal charge unless he or she is proved guilty of it; this implies that no one should ever be detained unless he or she has been found guilty. It follows that there is a presumption of liberty, which the prosecution may oppose only by establishing 'substantial grounds' to overturn that presumption. For several reasons, however, it can be regarded as undesirable to allow some accused people to go back to society before the case against them is tried in a criminal court. Indeed, about 12 per cent of offenders who are bailed to appear in court fail to appear for their trials. In January 2005, the Attorney General called for a crack-down on defendants person has been charged, s 38(1)(a) of the PACE states that a person must be released unless: (a) their name and address are not known; or (b) the custody officer reasonably thinks that their detention is necessary for their own protection; or (c) to prevent them from injuring someone or damaging property, or because they might abscond, or interfere with the course of justice; or (d) the custody officer reasonably believes that the detention of that person is necessary to prevent them from committing any offence.

Sections 38 and 47 of PACE 1984 allow the police to grant conditional bail to persons charged. The conditions can be whatever is required to ensure that the person surrenders to custody, does not commit an offence while on bail, or does not interfere with witnesses or otherwise obstruct the course of justice. The powers of the custody officer, however, do not include a power to impose a requirement to reside in a bail hostel or to attend an interview with a legal adviser, or require the suspect to make him or herself available for inquiries and reports. The police have power to arrest without warrant a person who, having been granted conditional police bail, has failed to attend at a police station at the appointed time (s 46A PACE).

11.3.2 BAIL BY THE COURTS

The Bail Act 1976 created a statutory presumption of bail. It states (s 4) that, subject to Schedule 1, bail shall be granted to a person accused of an offence and brought before a magistrates' court or a Crown Court, and also to people convicted of an offence who are being remanded for reports to be made. The court must therefore grant bail (unless one of the exceptions applies), even if the defendant does not make an application. Schedule 1 provides that a court need not grant bail to a person charged with an offence punishable with imprisonment if it is satisfied that there are 'substantial grounds' (the relevant test) for believing that, if released on bail, the defendant would:

- fail to surrender to custody;
- commit an offence while on bail; or
- interfere with witnesses or otherwise obstruct the course of justice.

The court can also refuse bail if it believes that the defendant ought to stay in custody for his or her own protection, or if it has not been practicable, for want of time, to obtain sufficient information to enable the court to make its decision on bail, or he or she has previously failed to answer to bail (Sched 1, Part I, paras 2–6).

When the court is considering the grounds stated above, all relevant factors must be taken into account. These include: the nature and seriousness of the offence, the character, antecedents, associations and community ties of the defendant, and his or her record for satisfying his or her obligations under previous grants of bail.

Evidence accepted by the Home Office suggests that there is a link between drug addiction and offending. In addition, it is widely accepted that many abusers of drugs fund their misuse through acquisitive crime. There is thus a real concern that, if such offenders who have been charged with an imprisonable offence are placed on bail, they will merely re-offend in order to fund their drug use.

Under s 19 CJA 2003, an alleged offender aged 18 or over, who has been charged with an imprisonable offence, will not be granted bail (unless the court is satisfied that there is no significant risk of his committing an offence while on bail) where the three conditions below exist:

- there is drug test evidence that the person has a specified Class A drug in his or her body (by way of a lawful test obtained under s 63B of PACE or s 161 of this Act); and
- either the offence is a drugs offence associated with a specified Class A drug or the court is satisfied that there are substantial grounds for believing that the misuse of a specified Class A drug caused or contributed to that offence or provided its motivation; and
- the person does not agree to undergo an assessment as to his or her dependency upon or propensity to misuse specified Class A drugs, or has undergone such an assessment but does not agree to participate in any relevant follow-up action offered.

The assessment will be carried out by a suitably qualified person, who will have received training in the assessment of drug problems. If an assessment or follow-up is proposed and agreed to, it will be a condition of bail that it be undertaken. This provision can only apply in areas where appropriate assessment and treatment facilities are in place.

If the defendant is charged with an offence not punishable with imprisonment, Sched 1 provides that bail may be refused only if the court is satisfied that there are substantial grounds for believing that if released on bail (whether subject to conditions or not) he or she would fail to surrender to custody, commit an offence while on bail, or interfere with witnesses or otherwise obstruct the course of justice. Bail may also be refused for the defendant's own protection or there are substantial grounds for believing he or she may cause physical or mental injury (or fear of such) to an associated person.

Section 25 of the CJPOA 1994 provided that, in some circumstances, a person who had been charged with or convicted of murder, attempted murder, manslaughter, rape or attempted rape must not be granted bail. The circumstances were simply that the conviction must have been within the UK, and that, in the case of a manslaughter conviction, it must have been dealt with by way of a custodial sentence. The word 'conviction' is given a wide meaning and includes anyone found 'not guilty by way of insanity'.

There was debate about whether the changes wrought by s 25 were justifiable. A Home Office Minister, defending the section, stated that it would be worth the risk if it prevented just one murder or rape, even though there might be a few 'hard cases', that is, people eventually acquitted of crime, who were remanded in custody pending trial (David Maclean MP, Minister of State, Home Office, HC Committee, col 282, 1994). As Card and Ward remarked in a commentary on the CJPOA 1994, the government, when pushed, was unable to cite a single case where a person released on bail, in the circumstances covered by s 25, re-offended in a similar way. There is no time limit on the previous conviction and there is no requirement of any connection between the previous offence and the one in question. Card and Ward suggest that there is a world of difference between a person who was convicted of manslaughter 30 years ago on the grounds surety or giving a security, curfew, electronic monitoring or contact. This complements the removal by s 17 of the existing High Court power to entertain such appeals.

Section 3 of the BA 1976 allows for an application to vary the conditions of court bail to be made by the person bailed, the prosecutor or a police officer. Application may also be made for the imposition of conditions on unconditional court bail. Section 3 of the BA 1976 allows for the same thing in relation to police bail, although it does not allow the prosecutor to seek reconsideration of the decision to grant bail itself. Under the Bail (Amendment) Act 1993 (as amended), however, the prosecution does have a right to appeal against the grant of bail by a court in all cases of imprisonable offences. When this right of appeal is exercised, the defendant will remain in custody until the appeal is heard by a Crown Court judge, who will decide whether to grant bail or remand the defendant in custody within 48 hours of the magistrates' decision. Parliament was concerned that this power could be abused and has stated that it should be reserved 'for cases of greatest concern, when there is a serious risk of harm to the public' or where there are 'other significant public interest grounds' for an appeal.

Section 240 of the Criminal Justice Act 2003 states that time spent in custody pre-trial or pre-sentence can generally be deducted from the ultimate sentence. No compensation, however, is paid to people who have been remanded in custody but are subsequently found not guilty.

Section 240A of the Criminal Justice Act 2003, as inserted by s 21 of the Criminal Justice and Immigration Act 2008, provides for a deduction from the ultimate sentence if the offender has spent time on bail subject to a curfew of nine hours or more in any given day, coupled with an electronic monitoring condition. The defendant will generally be entitled to an order to the effect that half the number of days spent on bail subject to those conditions should count as time served by the prisoner as part of his or her sentence.

This area of law was subject to a comprehensive revision after a Home Office special working party reported in 1974, and has been legislatively debated and modified twice since the BA 1976. It is, however, still a matter of serious concern, both to those civil libertarians who consider the law too tilted against the accused, and to the police and commentators, who believe it too lenient in many respects. This criticism of the law from both sides of the debate might indicate a desirable state of balance reached by the current regulatory framework

11.4 PLEA BARGAINING AND RELATED ISSUES

'Plea bargaining' has been defined as 'the practice whereby the accused enters a plea of guilty in return for which he will be given some consideration that results in a sentence concession' (Baldwin and McConville, *Negotiated Justice: Pressures on Defendants to Plead Guilty* (1977)). In practice, this can refer to:

●   a situation either where there has been a plea arrangement for the accused to plead guilty to a lesser charge than the one with which he or she is charged (for example, charged with murder, agrees to plead guilty to manslaughter). This is sometimes called 'charge bargaining'; or

- where there is simply a sentencing discount available on a plea of guilty by the accused. This has been given statutory force by s 144 CJA 2003, which requires a court to award a reduced sentence for a timely guilty plea.

  - A form of plea bargaining now also exists in respect of corporate bodies. Deferred Prosecution Agreements (DFAs) were introduced in Schedule 17 of the *Crime and Courts Act 2013*. Under a DPA a prosecutor charges a company with a criminal offence but proceedings are automatically suspended. The company agrees to a number of conditions, such as paying a financial penalty, paying compensation and co-operating with future prosecutions of individuals. If the company does not honour the conditions, the prosecution may resume.

11.4.1   ADVANCE INDICATION OF SENTENCE

Plea bargaining is widespread in some common law countries, for example the United States. It has always been considered impermissible in the English legal system. However, the related issue of whether a judge should give advance indications of sentence has been subject to change since the original leading case of *R v Turner* (1970) was decided. In *Turner* Lord Parker CJ said that the judge should never indicate the sentence which they are minded to impose, nor should they ever indicate that on a plea of guilty they would impose one sentence, but that on a conviction following a plea of not guilty they would impose a more severe sentence. The judge could say what sentence they would impose on a plea of guilty (where, for example, they have read the depositions and antecedents) but without mentioning what they would do if the accused were convicted after pleading not guilty. Even this would be wrong, however, as the accused might take the judge to be intimating that a more severe sentence would follow upon conviction after a guilty plea. The only exception to this rule is where a judge says that the sentence will take a particular form, following conviction, whether there has been a plea of guilty or not guilty.

This aspect of *R v Turner* was overruled in *R v Goodyear (Karl)* (2005), when Lord Woolf, giving the judgment of a specially convened five-judge Court of Appeal, said that a Crown Court judge could give an advance indication of sentence, if, but only if, the defendant requests one. He or she is not obliged to do so and the indication would normally be limited to the maximum sentence likely to be imposed if a plea of guilty were entered at that stage in proceedings (usually the plea and case management hearing). The Criminal Procedure Rules 2014, para 3.23, detail how this process works. In the *Attorney General's Reference (No. 34 of 2010) (R v Simon Roland Langridge)* (2010) the Court of Appeal stressed that it was essential that discussions take place in open court, unless circumstances were exceptionally sensitive.

11.4.2   ACCEPTANCE OF PLEAS BY THE PROSECUTOR

The role of the prosecutor in accepting guilty pleas is governed by the Attorney General's 'Guidelines on the acceptance of pleas and the prosecutor's role in the sentencing exercise (revised 2009)' and s 9 of the Code for Crown Prosecutors. The prosecutor can review, the European Convention on Human Rights (ECHR) and the Human Rights Act 1998 (HRA).

11.5.1 AUTOMATIC LIFE SENTENCE UNDER S 2 OF THE CRIME (SENTENCES) ACT 1997

In 1997, immediately prior to the election of that year, Parliament required the provision of automatic life sentences for those found guilty of a second serious offence. Thus, s 2 of the Crime (Sentences) Act 1997 required judges to pass indeterminate life sentences for those found guilty of a range of offences including attempted murder, rape, manslaughter, wounding, causing grievous bodily harm with intent and robbery with a real or imitation firearm, where the guilty person had been previously convicted of another offence on the list. Given their discontent with the provisions for mandatory sentencing in relation to convictions for murder, it can be appreciated that many of the judiciary, led by the late Lord Justice Taylor, saw the Act as a dangerous party-politicisation of the criminal justice system and an unwarranted interference by the legislature with the scope of judicial power and discretion, and were vociferous in their opposition to it.

However, even when the Act came into force, it still left some scope for judicial discretion whereby they could identify such 'exceptional circumstances' as could justify the non-application of the mandatory sentence. Until the implementation of the HRA, the question was as to what properly constituted such exceptional circumstances, and different courts tended to reach different conclusions of a more or less liberal nature. Thus, in *R v Stephens* (2000), the defendant, who already had a previous serious conviction, was found guilty of grievous bodily harm with intent and was consequently given an automatic life sentence. At his trial, the prosecution had offered, and Stephens had rejected, the opportunity to plead guilty to a lesser charge, which would not have led to the imposition of the automatic life sentence. When it emerged that his counsel had not advised him as to the possible consequences of his decision to defend the more serious charge, the Court of Appeal held that that fact amounted to sufficient exceptional circumstances to quash the life sentence. However, in *R v Turner* (2000), where the defendant was also found guilty of causing grievous bodily harm with intent, the court felt obliged to impose the automatic life sentence, even though a period of some 30 years had elapsed since his previous conviction for manslaughter at the age of 22. The court could find no exceptional circumstances.

This unsatisfactory situation was resolved by reference to the HRA in *R v Offen and Others* (2001), in which the Court of Appeal considered five related claims that the imposition of automatic life sentences was contrary to the ECHR. The facts of Offen's case provide a context for the decision.

Offen had robbed a building society using a toy gun. The cashiers thought the gun was real and placed £960 in his bag. During the robbery, he was nervous and shaking, and apologised to the staff as he left the building. A customer grabbed the bag with the money in it and gave it back to the building society. When he was arrested, Offen admitted the offence, but claimed he had not taken the medication he needed to deal with his schizophrenia. His previous conviction for robbery had been committed in similar circumstances. At his trial, he was subsequently sentenced automatically to life imprisonment.

In delivering its judgment, the Court of Appeal was extremely circumspect in considering its relationship with Parliament and its new powers under the HRA. It was equally firm, however, in its removal of the mandatory element from this aspect of the sentencing process.

As regards its relationship with Parliament, the court stressed that it was of the greatest importance to bear in mind Parliament's intention in establishing the automatic life sentences. In the present instance, it understood that intention as being to protect the public against a person who had committed two serious offences. The Court of Appeal went on, however, to draw the conclusion that, on the basis of that concentration on the importance of protecting the public, it could be assumed that the Act was not intended to apply to anyone who did not pose a future risk.

Focusing on the future danger posed by the offender to the public rather than on the mere fact of their having committed two offences would allow the court to decide each case on the basis of its own particular facts, and if the facts of any particular case showed that the statutory assumption was misplaced, then that would constitute exceptional circumstances for the purposes of s 2 of the 1997 Act. As examples, the committing of different offences, the age of the offender and the lapse of time between the offences could give rise to exceptional circumstances in the context of a particular case that could override the assumption as to the imposition of the mandatory life sentence.

The court's identification of Parliament's intention in passing the Act cannot be doubted. The supposed corollary of this intention is much less certain. However, its process of logic allowed the Court of Appeal to interpret the Act in such a way as to support its own preferred approach, which was effectively to remove the automatic element in the sentencing process and to reintroduce an element of judicial discretion. The foregoing interpretation of the Act was supported by the court's marshalling of the HRA. In their judgments, the three members of the Court of Appeal stated that s 2 of the 1997 Act did not contravene Arts 3 and 5 of the ECHR so long as, and only to the extent that, exceptional circumstances were construed in such a way that it did not result in offenders being sentenced to life imprisonment when they did not constitute a significant risk to the public: that is, as the Court of Appeal had already decided it should be construed. In reaching this conclusion, the Court of Appeal can be seen to be employing s 3 of the HRA, in that it was interpreting the primary legislation of the Crime (Sentences) Act 1997 in such a way as to make it compatible with the ECHR rights. In so doing, the judiciary achieved its preferred end without having to issue a declaration of incompatibility and without having to rely on the government introducing an amendment to its own Powers of Criminal Courts (Sentencing) Act 2000, s 109 of which had re-enacted s 2 of the 1997 Act.

Section 109 of the Powers of Criminal Courts (Sentencing) Act 2000 was itself repealed by s 332 of the Criminal Justice Act 2003, and replaced by ss 224–236, which provide for new sentences for dangerous offences, both indeterminate sentences for public protection and extended sentences. Parliament replaced the relatively simple provision of two serious offences leading to an 'automatic' life sentence with an apparently more flexible concept of dangerousness. By s 229 of the Criminal Justice Act 2003, the courts are obliged to consider whether an offender has fallen into a category of dangerousness by virtue of being convicted of a 'specified offence' and it requires the courts to consider degrees of risks of serious harm from further offences by such an offender. A substantial amount of discretion appears to be given to the sentencing court by s 229:

229 The assessment of dangerousness

(1)   *This section applies where –*

    (a)   a person has been convicted of a specified offence, and

    (b)   it falls to a court to assess under any of sections 225 to 228 whether there is a significant risk to members of the public of serious harm occasioned by the commission by him of further such offences.

(2)   . . . the court in making the assessment referred to in subsection (1)(b) –

    (a)   must take into account all such information as is available to it about the nature and circumstances of the offence,

    [(aa)   may take into account all such information as is available to it about the nature and circumstances of any other offences of which the offender has been convicted by a court anywhere in the world,]

    (b)   may take into account any information which is before it about any pattern of behaviour of which [any of the offences mentioned in paragraph (a) or (aa)] forms part, and

    (c)   may take into account any information about the offender which is before it.

However, when the section is read more closely it can be seen that – when sentencing 18-year-olds and older defendants (the majority of the cases) – the courts will be obliged to make assumptions about the presence of serious risk in sub-s (2). See sub-s (3) – 'the court MUST assume', and so on. Thus the courts are bound by a similar test as under s 109 of the Powers of Criminal Courts (Sentencing) Act 2000.

    The new provisions came into force for offences committed after 4 April 2005. Further changes were made by the Legal Aid, Punishment and Sentencing of Offenders Act 2012, including the abolition of indeterminate sentences for public protection and changes to extended sentences.

11.5.2   MANDATORY LIFE SENTENCES IN RELATION TO MURDER

When the death penalty for murder was removed in 1965, it was replaced by a mandatory life sentence, that is, if an individual is found guilty of murder, the court has no alternative but to sentence them to a period of life imprisonment. By definition, a 'life sentence' is for an indeterminate period, but the procedure is for a period to be specified, which the person must serve before they can be considered for release on parole. The problematic question of who sets this tariff is considered below. The judiciary have been consistently opposed to this fettering of their discretion; a number of leading judges, including the past Lord Chief Justices Bingham and Taylor, have spoken out against it, and in 1993 Lord Chief Justice Lane led a committee that recommended that the mandatory sentence be removed. In 1989, a Select Committee of the House of Lords, appointed to report on murder and life imprisonment, recommended the abolition of the mandatory life sentence. Lord Lane, formerly Lord Chief Justice, chaired a Committee on the Penalty for Homicide, which also produced a critical report in 1993:

> (1) The mandatory life sentence for murder is founded on the assumption that murder is a crime of such unique heinousness that the offender forfeits for the rest of his existence his right to be set free. (2) That assumption is a fallacy. It arises from the divergence between the legal definition of murder and that which the lay public believes to be murder. (3) The common law definition of murder embraces a wide range of offences, some of which are truly heinous, some of which are not. (4) The majority of murder cases, though not those which receive the most publicity, fall into the latter category. (5) It is logically and jurisprudentially wrong to require judges to sentence all categories of murderer in the same way, regardless of the particular circumstances of the case before them. (6) It is logically and constitutionally wrong to require the distinction between the various types of murder to be decided (and decided behind the scenes) by the executive as is, generally speaking, the case at present . . .

As their Lordships correctly pointed out, there can be degrees of heinousness, even in regard to murder, and not all of those convicted deserve to be sentenced to life imprisonment. Mercy killers surely should not be treated in the same way as serial killers. This desire of the judges to remove the restriction in their sentencing power has, however, run up against the wish of politicians to be seen as tough on crime, or at least not soft on crime.

The uncomfortable relationship between criminal justice and party politics can be seen in the conviction for murder of Norfolk farmer Tony Martin in April 2000. Martin had used a shotgun to shoot two people who had broken into his farmhouse. One was injured and the other, 16-year-old Fred Barras, was killed. Martin was charged with murder and, at his trial, evidence was introduced to show that he had lain in wait for his victims, had set traps in his house and had used an illegal pump-action shotgun to shoot Barras in the back as he was attempting to run away. By a majority of 10 to two the jury found him guilty of murder and, as required, the judge sentenced him to life imprisonment. Much of the press considered the sentence to be outrageously severe on a man whom they portrayed as merely protecting his property against the depredations of lawless louts. (It has to be stated that Barras and his accomplice did have 114 previous convictions between them.) In focusing attention on the right of individuals to use

The decision of the House of Lords is, to say the least, somewhat surprising, especially when it is compared with the decision of the Privy Council in *Reyes v the Queen* (2002). In *Reyes*, it was held that a mandatory death sentence, operative in the jurisdiction of Belize, amounted to inhuman and degrading punishment. Among the grounds for that decision was the fact that the mandatory nature of the sentence precluded proper judicial consideration of the appropriate penalty. Although the Privy Council did expressly limit its reasoning to the Belize legal system in *Reyes*, and although the death penalty does stand alone as the harshest of penalties, it is nonetheless arguable that the mandatory life sentence in the United Kingdom achieves a similar, if less severe, consequence in limiting proper judicial consideration of the appropriate sentence to apply in different circumstances. It is apparent in both the *Lichniak* and *Pyrah* cases that the judges deciding the sentences did not really think that life sentences were appropriate, yet they had no choice but to pass such sentences. Can the imposition of an inappropriate sentence be anything other than arbitrary and disproportionate?

As will be considered below, perhaps Lichniak and Pyrah were unfortunate in the timing of their appeals. Those appeals followed a number of highly sensitive decisions in which the courts had used their powers under the HRA to remove the powers of the Home Secretary to set the punitive tariff in mandatory life sentences. Perhaps, given the highly charged, not to say antagonistic, nature of the relationship between the courts and past Home Secretaries, removing the mandatory sentence altogether was a step too far for the courts, or at least a step further than they thought it wise to take under political circumstances at that time.

Juveniles

Just as in the cases of adults sentenced to a mandatory life sentence, so the Home Secretary used to have the power to set the tariff for juveniles sentenced to detention at Her Majesty's pleasure, that is, for an indeterminate period. However, in 1999, the European Court of Human Rights held that the exercise of that power by the Home Secretary was in contravention of the ECHR. The Home Secretary subsequently relinquished the power. The path to such a resolution is traced below.

In 1993, Jon Venables and Robert Thompson, two 10-year-old boys, were found guilty of the murder of two-year-old James Bulger. As juveniles, they were both sentenced, as required under s 53(1) of the Children and Young Persons Act (CYPA) 1933, to be detained at Her Majesty's pleasure. The trial judge recommended a tariff of eight years as an appropriate period for retribution and deterrence, although, on review, Lord Chief Justice Taylor recommended that the tariff should be increased to 10 years. However, the ultimate decision as to the length of the tariff lay with the then Conservative Home Secretary, Michael Howard. Given the particularly brutal manner of the killing, there was very considerable public interest in the case and the sentencing of the two boys. *The Sun* newspaper organised a public petition to the effect that they should be 'locked up for life' or serve at least 25 years. Some 306,000 people signed and submitted petitions to that effect to the Home Secretary, who ultimately decided that the tariff should be set at 15 years. Doubts were raised as to whether, in ignoring the recommendations of the judges in reaching his decision, the Home Secretary had taken a (party) political rather than quasi-judicial decision to assuage the concerns of potential voters by demonstrating a willingness to be tough on crime and criminals.

*R v Secretary of State for the Home Department ex p Venables
and Thompson (1997)*

Lawyers for Venables and Thompson successfully sought judicial review of the Home Secretary's decision. On final appeal to the House of Lords (*Secretary of State for the Home Department v V (A Minor) and T (A Minor)* (1997)), the Home Secretary having lost all the previous cases, it was held that in setting the tariff at 15 years, he had not taken into account the welfare of the children as required by s 44 of the CYPA 1933. Additionally, the House of Lords stated that although the Home Secretary was entitled to take into account considerations of a public character, he must distinguish between legitimate public concern and mere public clamour. The Home Secretary had therefore misdirected himself and his decision was unlawful and should be quashed. The mechanism of judicial review therefore allowed the court to insist that, even if statute permitted the executive, in the form of the Home Secretary, to take sentencing decisions, in reaching any such decision, he must act in a judicial rather than a political manner. As Lord Steyn expressed it ([1997] 3 All ER 97 at 147):

> In fixing a tariff the Home Secretary is carrying out, contrary to the constitutional principle of the separation of powers between the executive and the judiciary, a classic judicial function.

What judicial review could not achieve, however, was either the removal of the Home Secretary's general power or the substitution of the courts' decision for his particular decision. It would still have been for the Home Secretary to take the new decision as to the appropriate tariff, had the Strasbourg Court not intervened before such a decision could be taken.

T v UK; V v UK (1999)

Lawyers for Thompson and Venables had appealed to the ECtHR, claiming that many aspects of their clients' cases had been conducted in a manner that was contrary to the ECHR. In December 1999, the ECtHR delivered its judgment and found that although many of the grounds for appeal were unfounded, the applicants had been denied a fair trial in accordance with Art 6 of the ECHR, as they had not been able to participate effectively in the proceedings. The reason for this finding was that the conduct of the case in the Crown Court must have been at times incomprehensible and frightening to the two boys, and it was not sufficient that they were represented by skilled and experienced lawyers. The Court also held that there had been a violation of Art 6 on the grounds that they had been denied a fair hearing by 'an independent and impartial tribunal'. The fixing of the tariff was tantamount to a sentencing procedure and therefore should have been exercised by an impartial judge, rather than a member of the executive, as the Home Secretary clearly was.

Subsequent to, and consequent upon, this decision, the Home Secretary, by this time the Labour politician Jack Straw, announced in March 2000 that legislation would

UK and *V v UK*, while citing the *Wynne* judgment, the ECtHR reiterated that an adult mandatory life sentence constituted punishment for life. On the face of those authorities, the Court of Appeal in *Anderson and Taylor* declined to challenge the Home Secretary's power in relation to mandatory life sentences.

Perhaps the Court of Appeal's reluctance to challenge the executive's power head-on was based on the realisation that, as the court noted, a decision on the same point was expected within the following year in the ECtHR (*Stafford v UK* (2002)). It is perhaps not overly cynical to suggest that the Court of Appeal adopted its conservative approach in the realisation that, in the context of the prevailing tense relationship between the Home Secretary and the courts, it was perhaps politic to leave the final decision to remove the Home Secretary's power to the ECtHR, which decision their Lordships clearly expected.

Stafford v UK (2002)

Derek Stafford was convicted of murder in 1967 and released on licence in April 1979. His licence required him to remain in the United Kingdom, but he left to live in South Africa. In April 1989 he was arrested in the United Kingdom, having returned from South Africa on a false passport. Although the possession of a false passport only led to a fine, he remained in custody due to the revocation of his life licence. He was released in March 1991, once again on a life licence. In 1994 he was convicted of conspiracy to forge travellers' cheques and passports and sentenced to six years' imprisonment. In 1996 the Parole Board recommended his release on life licence, having reached the conclusion that he did not present a danger of violent re-offending. The Secretary of State rejected the Board's recommendation. But for the revocation of his life licence, the applicant would have been released from prison on the expiry of the sentence for fraud in July 1997, and in June 1997 he sought judicial review of the Secretary of State's decision to reject the Board's recommendation for immediate release. He was successful at first instance, but both the Court of Appeal and the House of Lords denied his claim and upheld the power of the Home Secretary to revoke his licence and thus effectively detain him under ss 39(1) and 35(2) of the Criminal Justice Act 1991 (the latter subsequently replaced by s 29 of the Crime (Sentences) Act 1997), even though there was no prospect of his committing any violent crime in the future. Both courts, however, expressed unease at their decisions. As Lord Bingham CJ stated in the Court of Appeal ([1998] 1 WLR 503 at 518):

> The imposition of what is in effect a substantial term of imprisonment by the exercise of executive discretion, without trial, lies uneasily with ordinary concepts of the Rule of Law. I hope that the Secretary of State may, even now, think it right to give further consideration to the case.

When the case came before the Grand Chamber of the ECtHR in May 2002, and as the Court of Appeal in *Anderson* had expected, it held that it was no longer in the interest of justice to follow its previous decision in *Wynne*. The ECtHR stated that although it was not formally bound to follow any of its previous judgments, it was 'in the interests of legal certainty, foreseeability and equality before the law that it should not depart, without cogent reason, from precedents laid down in previous cases'. However, it felt that the fixing of the tariff for mandatory life sentences was clearly a sentencing exercise, and that it was no longer possible to distinguish between mandatory life prisoners, discretionary life prisoners and juvenile murderers as regards the nature of that sentencing process. The ECtHR also held that the finding in *Wynne* that the mandatory life sentence constituted punishment for life could no longer be maintained. It was therefore open to the court to decide that the Secretary of State's role in fixing the tariff was a sentencing exercise and not merely a matter relating to the administrative implementation of the sentence. As a result, it concluded that the exercise of such power by the Home Secretary was contrary to Art 5(1) and (4) of the ECHR.

When the decision of the ECtHR in *Stafford* was delivered, the UK press immediately returned to the possibility of the imminent release of the child killer Myra Hindley. What they failed to indicate was that the ECtHR itself, in line with previous statements of the UK courts, had actually recognised the validity of 'whole life' tariffs in exceptional circumstances. Its decision was merely that it was for the courts rather than the executive to make such recommendations. In any event, Hindley died in prison in November 2002.

The first person actually to benefit from the *Stafford* decision was Satpal Ram, who was released from prison in June 2002 after having served more than 15 years for a murder he claimed was committed in self-defence in a racial attack. The previous Home Secretary had overturned a Parole Board recommendation to release Mr Ram in 2000. The succeeding Home Secretary preferred to release him rather than contest an action for judicial review of his predecessor's decision, recognising that *Stafford* made any argument to the contrary untenable.

R v Secretary of State for the Home Department ex p Anderson and Taylor (2002)

By November 2002, the appeals in the *Anderson* and *Taylor* cases had reached the House of Lords and were considered by a seven-member panel, indicating their importance. The essential issue under consideration was the effect that the *Stafford* decision in the ECtHR would have on English law, s 35(2) and (3) of the Criminal Justice Act 1991 having been replaced by similar provisions under s 29 of the Crime (Sentences) Act 1997. In the event, the House of Lords followed the decision of the ECtHR and held that the fixing of the tariff for a convicted murderer was legally indistinguishable from the imposition of sentence. Consequently, to ensure compatibility with Art 6(1), any such tariff should be set by an independent and impartial tribunal and not the Home Secretary, who was part of the executive. It was therefore incompatible with Art 6 for the Home Secretary to fix the tariff of a convicted murderer. However, the House of Lords went on to decide that it was not possible to interpret s 29 of the Crime (Sentences) Act 1997 in such a way as to make it compatible with the rights provided under the ECHR. As a result, the House of Lords issued a declaration of incompatibility to the effect that s 29 was contrary to the right under Art 6 to have a sentence imposed by an independent and impartial tribunal.

The above series of cases demonstrates how the implied wishes of the Court of Appeal in *Anderson* could be given express effect in the later House of Lords' decision, without the possibility of any direct accusation of political interference on the part of the judiciary.

The political sensitivity of the preceding cases, and the extent to which they challenge executive power, may go some way to explain the apparent conservatism of the decision of the House of Lords in the *Lichniak* and *Pyrah* cases, considered previously. A close reading of the cases certainly reveals grounds for the House of Lords to overturn those decisions and to remove mandatory life sentences altogether.

The foregoing analysis has used the term 'tariff' to refer to the period that a person sentenced to a life term must serve for the purposes of punishment. It should be noted, however, that, in a Practice Statement issued in May 2002, the Lord Chief Justice accepted the recommendation of the Sentencing Advisory Panel that it should be replaced by the clearer expression 'minimum term'.

The political tension around the issue of sentencing was further heightened when, in May 2003, Home Secretary Blunkett announced his intention to introduce proposals that would introduce a new statutory system in relation to sentencing in murder cases, together with a new Sentencing Guidelines Council to advise judges on appropriate sentencing. The Home Secretary made it clear that he considered that the judges had failed to provide clear and consistent sentencing. Indeed, the proposal can be seen as a direct attack on the Lord Chief Justice, Lord Woolf, whose directive on sentencing, issued in 2002, had indicated that the previous 14-year minimum 'starting point' should be replaced by 16 years for more serious cases and 12 years for lesser crimes such as mercy killings. The Home Secretary was quoted as saying: 'I share public concern that some very serious criminals seem to be serving a relatively short spell in prison . . . It will be Parliament that decides the structure. It will be judges that act within it.' Not surprisingly, the Bar Council described the proposal as 'constitutionally a leap in the dark' and said that the Home Secretary was trying to 'institutionalise the grip of the executive around the neck of the judiciary'.

The proposed scheme was subsequently attacked by Lord Woolf in a speech on the Bill in the House of Lords in June of that year and in the background notes for which he stated that:

> The indirect, knock-on effect of the proposed minimum period is highly undesirable . . . Sentencing, particularly in relation to murder, should be removed from the political arena. The present proposal will have the effect of increasing political involvement.

The Lord Chief Justice also took exception to the proposal to appoint a senior police officer to the Sentencing Council (formerly the Sentencing Guidelines Council) and more generally highlighted the logical contradiction in the Home Secretary's approach. As Lord Woolf stated:

> It is surely extraordinary to propose a council to make guidelines and at the same time include your own guidance in the legislation establishing the council.

Nonetheless, both the Council and the sentencing guidelines in relation to murder were implemented in the Criminal Justice Act 2003, and were the first of its major changes in the criminal justice system to be brought into effect in January 2004.

Section 269 of the Act applies to any murders for which sentence is passed on or after 18 December 2003. It introduces a three-tier system (detailed in Sched 21) and requires the courts to apply the following sentencing principles:

Level 1: Whole life sentences will be the starting point for

- multiple murders, that is, two or more, that show a substantial degree of pre-meditation, involve abduction of the victim prior to the killing or are sexual or sadistic;
- murder of a child following abduction or involving sexual or sadistic conduct;
- murder carried out through acts of terrorism;
- murder where the offender has been previously convicted of murder.

Level 2: Attracting a 30-year minimum sentence for

- murders of police and prison officers in the course of duty;
- murder involving the use of a firearm or explosive;
- killing done for gain (burglary, robbery, etc, including professional or contract killing);
- killing intended to defeat ends of justice (killing of a witness);
- race/religion/sexual orientation motivated murder;
- single sadistic or sexual murder of an adult;
- multiple murders (other than those above).

Level 3: A 15-year minimum sentence will apply for

- other murders by adults and all murders by children under 17.

The whole life recommendation does not apply to offenders below the age of 21, but offenders aged 18 to 20 years of age will be subject to either the 15- or 30-year starting points. Those aged 17 years or under will be subject to a 12-year starting point (House of Commons Briefing Paper, Number 3626, 12 November 2015, *Mandatory life sentences for murder*, Sally Lipscombe and Jacqueline Beard, 2015, London: House of Commons Library).

It should be emphasised that the above recommendations state starting points in sentencing, and once trial judges have determined the starting point by applying the

'specified offence' and it requires the courts to consider degrees of risks of serious harm from further offences by such an offender.

1   Currently one in 10 of the prison population are serving an imprisonment for public protection sentence (see the Prison Reform Trust report *Unjust Deserts: Imprisonment for Public Protection*, 2010). This imprisonment is based on an assessment of 'dangerousness'. In 2010 these indeterminate sentences cost the public purse in excess of £100 million. Are indeterminate sentences ethically and practically justifiable?

2   On 22 November 2013, the prison population in England and Wales was 85,363. When Ken Clarke was Home Secretary for the first time (from 1992 to 1993), the average prison population was 44,628. According to the government, the overall cost of the criminal justice system has risen from 2 per cent of GDP to 2.5 per cent over the last 10 years. That is a higher per capita level than the US or any EU country. Court-ordered community sentences were more effective (by seven percentage points) at reducing one-year proven re-offending rates than custodial sentences of less than 12 months for similar offenders. Prison has a poor record for reducing re-offending – 49 per cent of adults are reconvicted within one year of being released. For those serving sentences of less than 12 months, this increases to 59 per cent. For those who have served more than 10 previous custodial sentences the rate of re-offending rises to 77 per cent (see the *Bromley Briefing*, June 2011). Should short custodial sentences be abolished?

Ashworth, A, *Sentencing and Criminal Justice*, 2010, Cambridge: CUP

Ashworth, A and Redmayne, M, *The Criminal Process*, 2010, Oxford: OUP

Baldwin, J and McConville, M, *Negotiated Justice: Pressures on Defendants to Plead Guilty*, 1977, Oxford: Martin Robertson

Bindaman, D, 'Crown duals' (1999) Law Soc Gazette 22

Buxton, R, 'The private prosecutor as a minister of justice' [2009] 6 Crim LR 427

Carkeek, L, 'Assisted suicide guidance' (2009) 159 NLJ 1391

Cockburn, JS and Green, TA, *Twelve Good Men and True*, 1988, Princeton: Princeton UP

Devlin, P, *Trial by Jury*, 1956, London: Stevens

Findlay, M and Duff, P, *The Jury Under Attack*, 1988, London: Butterworth

Grieve, D, *The Case for the Prosecution: Independence and the Public Interest*, https://www.gov.uk/government/speeches/the-case-for-the-prosecution-independence-and-the-public-interest

Hastie, R, *Inside the Juror: The Psychology of Juror Decision Making*, 1993, Cambridge: CUP

Hucklesby, A and Wahidin, A (eds), *Criminal Justice*, 2013, Oxford: OUP

Lawrence, J, O'Kane, M, Rab, S and Nakhwal, J, 'Hardcore bargains: what could plea bargaining offer in UK criminal cartel cases?' (2008) 7(1) Comp LJ 17

Richardson, J (ed), *Archbold: Criminal Pleading, Evidence and Practice*, 2016, London: Sweet & Maxwell

Rose, D, *In the Name of the Law – The Collapse of Criminal Justice*, 1996, London: Jonathan Cape

Sanders, A, 'Class bias in prosecutions' (1985) 24 Howard J 176

Sanders, A and Young, R, *Criminal Justice*, 2010, Oxford: OUP

Spencer, J, '"Fare-dodging" – strict liability for fraud?' (2014) Arch Rev 5 (on private prosecutions)

Thompson, EP, *Writing by Candlelight*, 1980, London: Merlin

Wurtzel, D, 'Spotlight on the CPS' (2009) *Counsel*, 1 October

USEFUL WEBSITE

www.cps.gov.uk
This is the website of the Crown Prosecution Service.

COMPANION WEBSITE

Now visit the companion website to:

- test your understanding of the key terms using our Flashcard Glossary;
- revise and consolidate your knowledge of 'The criminal process: (2) The prosecution' using our multiple choice question testbank;
- view all of the links to the Useful Websites above.

www.routledge.com/cw/slapper

THE JUDICIARY

12

12.1 INTRODUCTION

The importance of the courts and the judges within the common law has already been considered in previous chapters of this book. It has been suggested that the judges have considerable scope for determining the meaning and effect of law through their marshalling, not to say manipulation, of the rules of precedent and statutory interpretation. The purpose of the present chapter is further to consider those issues but more essentially to consider the actual roles of judges, how they are appointed and how the operation of their judicial functions may raise constitutional issues as to the interests the judiciary represent.

The fairly recent past has seen what can only be described as enormous changes in relation to the judiciary. Not only has the new Supreme Court replaced the House of Lords as the highest court in the United Kingdom, but there has also been a change in the way in which judges are appointed and a reduction in the central role of the Lord Chancellor. Each of these changes has already had an impact on the constitution of the United Kingdom and it is at least arguable that they will have an even greater impact in the future, as will be considered below.

12.2 THE CONSTITUTIONAL ROLE OF THE JUDICIARY

Central to the general idea of the rule of law (see Chapter 2 above) is the specific proposition that it involves the rule of *law* rather than the rule of *people*. Judges hold a position of central importance in relation to the concept of the rule of law. They are expected to deliver judgment in a completely impartial manner through a strict application of the law, without allowing their personal preference, or fear or favour of any of the parties to the action, to affect their decision in any way.

This desire for impartiality is reflected in the constitutional position of the judges. In line with Montesquieu's classic exposition of the separation of powers, the judiciary occupy a situation apart from the legislative and executive arms of the state, and operate independently of them. Prior to the English revolutionary struggles of the seventeenth century between Parliament and the monarch, judges held office at the king's pleasure. Not only did this mean that judges could be dismissed when the monarch so decided, but it highlighted the lack of independence of the law from the state in the form, and person, of the monarch. With the victory of Parliament and the establishment of a state based on popular sovereignty, and limited in its powers, the independence of the judiciary was confirmed in the Act of Settlement 1701. The centrality of the independence of the judges and the legal system from direct control or interference from the state in the newly established constitution was emphasised in the writing of the English philosopher, John Locke, who saw it as one of the essential reasons for, and justifications of, the social contract on which the social structure was assumed to be based.

In order to buttress the independence of the judiciary and remove them from the danger of being subjected to political pressure, it has been made particularly difficult to remove senior judges once they have been appointed. Their independence of thought and opinion is also protected by the doctrine of judicial immunity. Both of these principles will be considered in more detail below, as will the change in the procedure for appointing judges, which cannot but have had an impact on their perceived independence from politics and politicians.

12.2.1   THE CONSTITUTIONAL ROLE OF THE LORD CHANCELLOR

The following brief historical consideration of the constitutional position of the Lord Chancellor and the Appellate Committee of the House of Lords, as the highest court in England was correctly referred to, has to be placed within the immediate context of the changes made by the Constitutional Reform Act (CRA) 2005, which radically altered both institutions. The point of it is to highlight why those changes were, and arguably had to be, made.

The Lord Chancellor always held an anomalous position in respect of the separation of powers in the contemporary state, in that the holder of that position played a key role in each of the three elements of the state. The Lord Chancellor was the most senior judge in the English court structure, sitting as they did in the House of Lords. At the same time, however, the Lord Chancellorship was a party-political appointment, and the occupant of the office owed their preferment to the Prime Minister of the day. Not only was the incumbent a member of the executive, having a seat in the Cabinet, but they were also responsible for the operation of their own government department. In addition to these roles, it should not be overlooked that the Chancellor was also the Speaker of the House of Lords in its general role as a legislative forum.

The party-political role of the Lord Chancellor gave rise to a furore when, in February 2001, Lord Irvine, the then New Labour appointee, personally wrote to lawyers who were known sympathisers of the Labour Party, asking them to donate at least £200 to the party at a fundraising dinner he was to host. His political critics made much of the fact that, as the person ultimately responsible for appointing the judiciary, his soliciting of party funds from those who might apply for such positions in the future could be represented as improper. As such, the press immediately entitled it the 'cash for wigs' affair, echoing the previous 'cash for questions' scandal in the House of Commons and the subsequent 'cash for peerages' scandal. The Lord Chancellor, however, refused to apologise for his action. In a statement to the House of Lords, delivered in his political persona and therefore two paces apart from the woolsack on which he sat when acting as the Speaker of the House of Lords, he stated that:

> I do not believe I have done anything wrong nor do I believe that I have broken any current rules. If I did I would be the first to apologise.

According to Lord Irvine, it was misconceived to claim that the Lord Chancellor was not a party-political post, and that every minister from the Prime Minister down was involved in fundraising. The best that could be said for the Lord Chancellor was that, although he had done nothing unlawful, he had acted in an unwise, politically naïve and injudicious manner, and one that once again brought the anomalous constitutional role of his office to the political foreground and renewed calls for its reformation, if not removal.

In addition to difficulties arising directly from his responsibility for implementing political policies in relation to the legal system, the Lord Chancellor's judicial role also came into question. As a consequence of the fact that the appointment of the Lord Chancellor is a purely political one, there is no requirement that the incumbent should have held any prior judicial office. Indeed, in the case of Lord Irvine, he had never served in any judicial capacity, making his reputation as a highly successful barrister. Nonetheless, as Lord Chancellor, he was the most senior judge and was entitled to sit, as he thought appropriate (see below, 12.2.2, for further observations about the Lord Chancellor's residual powers).

There was, however, a much more fundamental issue relating to the manner in which the Lord Chancellor's former multifunctional role may be seen as having breached the doctrine of the separation of powers. There cannot but be doubts as to the impropriety of a member of the executive functioning as a member of the judiciary and Lord Irvine himself withdrew from sitting in a case in March 1999 in which he recognised the possibility of a conflict of interest. That case involved an action by the family of a man who had died in police custody. The suggestion was made that the Lord Chancellor's participation on the judicial panel raised doubts as to whether the case would be decided by an independent and impartial tribunal. Given his recent guidelines warning the judiciary about the need to be sensitive to issues of conflict of interest, the Lord Chancellor clearly felt himself required to stand down from hearing the case.

In *McGonnell v UK* (2000), the European Court of Human Rights (ECtHR) confirmed the previous decision of the Commission in relation to the judicial function of the Bailiff of the island of Guernsey. It was held that the fact that the Bailiff had acted as the judge in a case in which he had also played an administrative role was in breach of Art 6 of the European Convention on Human Rights (ECHR). In the words of the Commission decision:

> It is incompatible with the requisite appearance of independence and impartiality for a judge to have legislative and executive functions as substantial as those carried out by the Bailiff.

Although those words could apply equally to the Lord Chancellor, the actual court decision was limited to the situation of the Bailiff, and Lord Irvine made it clear that he considered its application to be limited to the particular facts of the Guernsey situation. In any event, the Lord Chancellor continued not to sit on cases where there might appear to be a conflict between his judicial and other roles. In February 2003, the Lord Chancellor's dual role as judge and member of the executive came under attack in the parliamentary assembly of the Council of Europe, which oversees the operation of the ECHR (see Chapter 5). A Dutch member, Erik Jurgens, a vice president of the assembly, tabled a motion that stated that:

> The assembly . . . has repeatedly stressed that judges should be a completely independent branch of government. It is undeniable that combining the function of judge with functions in other branches of government calls that independence seriously into question.

Mr Jurgens was quoted as saying that he was advising eastern European countries seeking entry to the Council of Europe that they would not be admitted unless their judges were totally independent, so it was an anomaly that one of the original members had a figure like the Lord Chancellor, and further that:

> Sooner or later a case is going to come to the European Court of Human Rights at Strasbourg, and I think they will certainly say that this is an unacceptable combination.

In April 2003, Lord Irvine defended the unique position of the Lord Chancellor in an appearance before the parliamentary select committee with oversight of the Lord Chancellor's Department. Questioned on the conflict inherent in his power to make law and still sit as a judge, he responded that he had 'difficulty seeing why this issue is so important', and argued against changing a legal system that had an enviable international reputation, simply for the sake of constitutional purity. As he put it:

> The basic point is that the higher judiciary accept this role – they believe profoundly that it is a superior system to any other.

12.2.1.1   The Constitutional Reform Act 2005

While Lord Irvine preferred to maintain his position rather than bow to constitutional purity, his views were apparently not shared by his colleagues in government and most importantly the Prime Minister, who sacked him in June 2003. As part of a Cabinet reshuffle, which appeared to involve a power struggle between the Home Secretary and the Lord Chancellor, which the former won, Lord Irvine was not only removed from office, but it was announced that his office itself was to disappear. A new ministry, the Department for Constitutional Affairs, was to replace the Lord Chancellor's Department and Lord Falconer was appointed Secretary of State for Constitutional Affairs to replace Lord Irvine as Lord Chancellor. It would appear that the announcement was made without anyone having thought through the constitutional implications, or indeed practicalities, of simply abolishing the position of the Lord Chancellor. Initially, Lord Falconer said he was not the Lord Chancellor and that he would not be assuming all of the functions of his predecessor. However, the realisation soon dawned that it was impossible to eradicate the role of the Lord Chancellor by simple diktat. Lord Falconer had to be Lord Chancellor even if by default, as someone had to perform the constitutional functions attached to the Lord Chancellor's office. So, on the first day in his new role, Lord Falconer was to be seen in wig and tights sitting on the woolsack in the House of Lords, for the simple reason that someone had to do it. As a consequence, Lord Falconer was, at least for the time being, both Secretary of State for Constitutional Affairs and Lord Chancellor, although in the former role he was charged with the duty of abolishing the latter role. It should be noted that from the outset Lord Falconer made it clear that he would not, and never did, sit as a judge. As regards his legislative role in chairing sessions of the House of Lords, the CRA subsequently provided for the election of an independent Lord Speaker and in July 2006 the House of Lords elected Baroness Hayman as the first office-holder.

The proposal of the original Constitutional Reform Bill for the complete abolition of the office of the Lord Chancellor was extremely controversial. Reference has already been made to the concerns of the judiciary as to the abolition of the role of the Lord Chancellor and those concerns were also shared by politicians and social commentators. Many of the latter argued against what they saw as the ditching of hundreds of years of history and practice for the sake of dressing up a Cabinet reshuffle as a matter of constitutional importance.

The government, nonetheless, insisted on pursuing its reforms, and justifying them on the basis of transparency and the recognition that it was no longer appropriate for one person to perform the disparate functions of the Lord Chancellor in clear contradiction of the doctrine of the separation of powers. However, as many correctly pointed out, the constitution of the UK never actually incorporated a strict separation of powers. Nonetheless, that recognition cannot be taken as justifying a situation that, as preceding analysis has shown, was clearly founded on fundamental conflicts of interest and was almost certainly contrary to the European Convention on Human Rights. In this regard, the changes introduced by the Constitutional Reform Act 2005 can be seen to be not only pertinent, but also timely, in their endeavour to address an issue before it became a problem. Nonetheless, as was explained above, the government did submit to the wish to retain the ancient office of Lord Chancellor, although the importance of the role was significantly reduced. Following a Cabinet reshuffle in 2007, which also involved the replacement of the Department of Constitutional Affairs by a new Justice Ministry, the Justice Minister, Jack Straw, became the first member of the House of Commons to assume the role and title of Lord Chancellor. Subsequently, in 2012, Chris Grayling, the Conservative MP, became the first Lord Chancellor to hold no legal qualifications.

As part of the reform of the office of Lord Chancellor, its former judicial functions transferred to the Lord Chief Justice in the role of President of the Courts of England and Wales, who took over responsibility for the training, guidance and deployment of judges. They are also responsible for representing the views of the judiciary of England and Wales to Parliament and ministers (see 12.3).

12.2.2   THE CONSTITUTION AND THE ROLE OF THE HOUSE OF LORDS AND THE SUPREME COURT

As has been mentioned previously, by virtue of the Constitutional Reform Act 2005, the Supreme Court replaced the House of Lords as the highest court in the United Kingdom in October 2009. The Judicial Committee of the Privy Council remains as a distinct entity, but follows the Supreme Court to its new location.

Consequently the Supreme Court is the final court of appeal for all United Kingdom civil cases, and criminal cases from England, Wales and Northern Ireland and hears appeals on arguable points of law of general public importance. However, once again, the explanation for this event requires a brief consideration of its historical and constitutional context. A number of issues came together to raise questions about the operation of the House of Lords as the final court of appeal in the English legal system and the role of the Privy Council. Among these were the devolution of parliamentary power to the Scottish Parliament and Welsh Assembly, the previous and proposed further reform of the House of Lords, the enactment of the Human Rights Act and the role of the House of Lords itself in the *Pinochet* case (see below). However, of far greater significance was the proposal in the Constitutional Reform Act 2005 to replace the currently constituted Appeal Committee of the House of Lords with a new Supreme Court.

The case for the reform of the Lord Chancellor's position and against the location of the most senior judges in the House of Lords was presented to the commission examining the reform of the House of Lords by JUSTICE, the civil rights organisation. Both aspects of the challenges were strongly rejected by the then Lord Chancellor Irvine in a speech to the Third Worldwide Common Law Judiciary Conference in Edinburgh, delivered in July 1999. Nonetheless, spring 2002 saw a spate of speeches and interviews highlighting disagreement, if not actual tension, between the Lord Chancellor and some of the most senior members of the judiciary. In March of that year Lord Steyn, then the second longest serving Law Lord, expressed the view that Lord Irvine's insistence on sitting as a judge in the House of Lords was a major obstacle to the creation of a Supreme Court to replace the House of Lords. In April, the Lord Chancellor's response was reported in the *Financial Times* newspaper. The article stated that 'Lord Irvine may have an impressive intellect, but his lack of diplomacy means he will seldom be short of enemies.' The point of that comment was supported by the Lord Chancellor's reaction to Lord Steyn's previous comments, dismissing them in a tone of effete arrogance as 'rather wearisome . . . he's not a political scientist, he knows nothing about the internal workings of government – or very little'. As reported, he reduced Lord Steyn's argument to a demand for 'a grand new architectural venture', stating that the argument that 'the Lord Chancellor, because of his desire to continue sitting, is preventing the judges from having a new building – that's just nonsense'.

Lord Irvine's views should, however, be contrasted with those of the former senior Law Lord, Lord Bingham, expressed in the Spring Lecture given at the Constitution Unit at University College London in May 2002. In a paper entitled 'A New Supreme Court for the UK', Lord Bingham directly addressed all of the issues raised above, except for the role of the Lord Chancellor, before stating his preference for:

> a supreme court severed from the legislature, established as a court in its own right, re-named and appropriately re-housed, properly equipped and resourced and affording facilities for litigants, judges and staff such as, in most countries of the world, are taken for granted.

As to the views and future role of the Lord Chancellor, the reduction of his direct judicial powers was implicit in the speech. As Lord Bingham concluded, 'inertia . . . is not an option'.

Once again, Lord Irvine's political antennae appear to have lacked acuity, in that not only was he replaced as Lord Chancellor by Lord Falconer, but as has been seen, his successor proposed the establishment of a Supreme Court much along the lines of that suggested by Lord Bingham. Thus Part 2 of the Constitutional Reform Act 2005 contained provisions for the following:

- The establishment of a new, independent Supreme Court, separate from the House of Lords with its own independent appointments system, its own staff and budget and its own building: Middlesex Guildhall. This new Supreme Court should not be confused with the old Supreme Court, which was the title previously given to the High Court and Court of Appeal. In future those courts will be known as the Senior Courts of England and Wales.

- The 12 judges of the Supreme Court will be known as Justices of the Supreme Court and will no longer be allowed to sit as members of the House of Lords. As a matter of fact, all of the present members are life peers and as a result will be able to sit in the House of Lords on their retirement from their judicial office, but this may not always be the case in the future.

- The current Law Lords will become the first 12 Justices of the Supreme Court, and the most senior will be appointed President of the Supreme Court. Lord Phillips, the former Lord Chief Justice, was appointed the first President of the new court and when it actually sat for the first time in October 2009 there were only 11 justices in office.

These measures can be considered in two parts: first, the creation of a Supreme Court, distinct from the House of Lords; and second, the removal of the right of the members of that new Supreme Court to sit as members of the Upper House. Neither of these proposals found favour with a majority of the members of the Law Lords; indeed, in their collective response to the Consultation Paper on constitutional reform, six of the 12 expressed their opposition to the creation of a Supreme Court and eight supported the retention of at least some judicial representation in the House of Lords. The minority supported the complete separation of judicial and legislative activity, as did Lord Falconer, who explained the need for reform thus:

> The present position is no longer sustainable. It is surely not right that those responsible for interpreting the law should be able to have a hand in drafting it. The time has come for the UK's highest court to move out from under the shadow of the legislature.

The relevance of Lord Falconer's argument was given added power by the decision of the Scottish Court of Sessions, the equivalent of the Court of Appeal, in *Davidson v Scottish Ministers (No 2)* (2002). The case involved a challenge to a previous court decision, on the grounds of Art 6 of the ECHR, for the reason that one of the judges in the earlier case, the former Lord Advocate Lord Hardie, had spoken on the issue before the court while a member of the Scottish Assembly. The Court of Sessions held that Lord Hardie should at least have declared his previous interest in the matter and that, in the light of his failure to do so, there was at least the real possibility of bias, and ordered the case to be retried.

In other constitutional systems, both civil, as in France, or common law, as in the United States of America, not only is there a clear separation of powers between the judiciary, the executive and the legislature, there is also a distinct Constitutional Court, with the power to strike down legislation on the grounds of its being unconstitutional. It has to be emphasised that the UK Supreme Court will not be in the nature of these other supreme courts, in that it will not be a constitutional court as such and it will not have the powers to strike down legislation. Consequently, although the proposed alterations clearly increase the appearance of the separation of powers, the doctrine of parliamentary sovereignty remains unchallenged. It was presumably the lack of such power that led Lord Woolf to comment that the new court would effectively replace a first-class appeal court (the House of Lords) with a second-class Supreme Court.

It remains to be seen, however, whether, under the changed circumstances of the contemporary constitution, the Supreme Court, as the highest court in the land, will simply assume the previously limited role of the House of Lords, or whether it will, with the passage of time, assume new functions and increased powers as are consonant with Supreme Courts in other jurisdictions. This issue arose in September 2009 when Lord Neuberger, the current President of the Supreme Court, spoke on a BBC radio programme and expressed the opinion that the advent of the Supreme Court was not unproblematic: as he put it, 'The danger is that you muck around with a constitution like the British constitution at your peril because you do not know what the consequences of any change will be', and he added that there was a real risk of 'judges arrogating to themselves greater power than they have at the moment'. Former Lord Chancellor, Lord Falconer, also expressed the view that the Supreme Court 'will be bolder in vindicating both the freedoms of individuals and, coupled with that, being willing to take on the executive', but Lord Phillips, the first President of the Supreme Court, was more conciliatory towards the executive, expressing the view that, although he could not predict how the court would function in the future, he did not foresee it changing in the way suggested by Lord Neuberger.

It is a commonplace of politics that the devolution of power from the UK Parliament in London, particularly to the Scottish Parliament in Edinburgh, will give rise to disputes as to the relationship between the two bodies. Eventually, such issues will have to be resolved in the courts. Jurisdiction was originally with the Privy Council but has been subsequently transferred to the Supreme Court. During 2010 and 2011 there was considerable tension between the Supreme Court and the Scottish Executive in relation to the court's powers under the Human Rights Act, as a UK rather than a Scottish court, to determine criminal cases in relation to Scots law (see *Cadder v HM Advocate* (2010) and *Fraser v MH Advocate* (2011)). In *AXA General Insurance Limited v The Lord Advocate (Scotland)* (2011) the Supreme Court considered the constitutional position of the Scottish Parliament and concluded, in the words of Lord Hope:

> As a result of the Scotland Act, there are thus two institutions with the power to make laws for Scotland: the Scottish Parliament and, as is recognised in section 28(7), the Parliament of the United Kingdom. The Scottish Parliament is subordinate to the United Kingdom Parliament: its powers can be modified, extended or revoked by an Act of the United Kingdom Parliament. Since its powers are limited, it is also subject to the jurisdiction of the courts.

Lord Hope's judgment in *AXA* is also of general interest with respect to the constitutional relationship between Parliament and the courts.

Nor should it be forgotten that the Human Rights Act has, for the first time, given the courts clear power to declare the UK Parliament's legislative provision contrary to essential human rights (see above, 2.5). Even allowing for the fact that the HRA has been introduced in such a way as to maintain the theory of parliamentary sovereignty, in practice, the courts will inevitably become involved in political/constitutional issues. Once the courts are required to act in constitutional matters, it is surely a mere matter of time before they become Constitutional Courts, as distinct from ordinary courts, with specialist judges with particular expertise in such matters.

12.2.3 JUDICIAL IMPARTIALITY

Re Bow Street Metropolitan Stipendiary Magistrate ex p Pinochet Ugarte (1999)

No consideration of the operation of the judiciary generally, and the House of Lords in particular, can be complete without a detailed consideration of what can only be called the *Pinochet* case (the various cases are actually cited as *R v Bartle* and *R v Evans* (House of Lords' first hearing); *Re Pinochet* (House of Lords' appeal against Lord Hoffmann); *R v Bartle* and *R v Evans* (final House of Lords' decision)).

In September 1973, the democratically elected government of Chile was over-thrown in a violent army coup led by the then General Augusto Pinochet Ugarte; the President, Salvador Allende, and many others were killed in the fighting. Subsequently, in the words of Lord Browne-Wilkinson, in the final House of Lords' hearing ([1999] 2 All ER 97 at 100):

> There is no doubt that, during the period of the Senator Pinochet regime, appalling acts of barbarism were committed in Chile and elsewhere in the world: torture, murder and the unexplained disappearance of individuals on a large scale.

Although it was not suggested that Pinochet had committed these acts personally, it was claimed that he was fully aware of them and conspired to have them undertaken.

In 1998, General Pinochet, by now Senator for life and recipient of a Chilean amnesty for his actions (extracted as the price for his returning his country to democracy), came to England for medical treatment. Although he was initially welcomed, he was subse-quently arrested on an extradition warrant issued in Spain for the crimes of torture, murder and conspiracy to murder allegedly orchestrated by him in Chile during the 1970s. Spain issued the international warrants, but Pinochet was actually arrested on warrants issued by the metropolitan stipendiary magistrate under s 8(1)(b) of the Extradition Act 1989. The legal question for the English courts was whether General Pinochet, as head of state at the time when the crimes were committed, enjoyed diplomatic immunity. In November 1998, the House of Lords rejected Pinochet's claim by a three-to-two majority, Lord Hoffmann voting with the majority but declining to submit a reasoned judgment.

Prior to the hearing in the House of Lords, Amnesty International, which cam-paigns against such things as state mass murder, torture and political imprisonment, and in favour of general civil and political liberties, had been granted leave to intervene in the pro-ceedings, and had made representations through its counsel, Geoffrey Bindman QC. After the *Pinochet* decision, it was revealed, although it was hardly a secret, that Lord Hoffmann was an unpaid director of the Amnesty International Charitable Trust, and that his wife also worked for Amnesty. On that basis, Pinochet's lawyers initiated a very peculiar action: they petitioned the House of Lords about a House of Lords decision; for the first time, the highest court in the land was to be subject to review, but review of itself, only itself differ-ently constituted. So, in January 1999, another panel of Law Lords set aside the decision of the earlier hearing on the basis that Lord Hoffmann's involvement had invalidated the previous hearing. The decision as to whether Pinochet had immunity or not would have to be heard by a new, and differently constituted, committee of Law Lords.

It has to be stated in favour of this decision that the English legal system is famously rigorous in controlling conflicts of interest, which might be seen to affect what should be a neutral decision-making process. The rule, which applies across the board to trustees, company directors and other fiduciaries as well as to judges, is so strict that the mere possibility of a conflict of interest is sufficient to invalidate any decision so made, even if in reality the individual concerned was completely unaffected by their own interest in coming to the decision. In the words of the famous *dictum* of Lord Hewart, it is of fundamental importance that 'justice must not only be done but should manifestly and undoubtedly be seen to be done' (*R v Sussex Justices ex p McCarthy* (1924)). With regard to the judicial process, it has been a long-established rule that no one may be a judge in his or her own cause, that is, they cannot judge a case in which they have an interest. This is sometimes known by the phrase *nemo judex in causa sua*. Thus, for example, judges who are shareholders in a company appearing before the court as a litigant must decline to hear the case (*Dimes v Grand Junction Canal* (1852)). It is therefore astonishing that Lord Hoffmann did not withdraw from the case, or at least declare his interest in Amnesty when it was joined to the proceedings. The only possible justification is that Lord Hoffmann assumed that all of those involved in the case, including the Pinochet team of lawyers, were aware of the connection. Alternatively, he might have thought that his support for a charitable body aimed at promoting civil and political liberties was so worthy in itself as to be unimpeachable: could not, and indeed should not, every English judge subscribe, for example, to cl 3(c) of the Amnesty International Charitable Trust memorandum, which provides that one of its objects is 'to procure the abolition of torture, extra-judicial execution and disappearance'?

In either case, Lord Hoffmann was wrong.

Once it was shown that Lord Hoffmann had a relevant interest in its subject matter, he was disqualified without any investigation into whether there was a likelihood or suspicion of bias. The mere fact of his interest was sufficient to disqualify him unless he had made sufficient disclosure. Hitherto, only pecuniary or proprietary interests had led to automatic disqualification. But, as Lord Browne-Wilkinson stated, Amnesty, and hence Lord Hoffmann, plainly had a non-pecuniary interest sufficient to give rise to an automatic disqualification for those involved with it.

The House of Lords therefore decided that Lord Hoffmann had been wrong, but it remained for the House of Lords to extricate itself, with whatever dignity it could manage, from the situation it had, through Lord Hoffmann, got itself into. This it endeavoured to do by reconstituting the original hearing with a specially extended committee of seven members. Political and legal speculation was rife before the decision of that court. It was suggested that the new committee could hardly go against the decision of the previous one without bringing the whole procedure into disrepute, yet the earlier court had actually contained the most liberal, and civil liberties minded, of the Lords. It was assumed that the new hearing would endorse the earlier decision, if with reluctance, but what was not expected was the way in which it would actually do so.

In reaching the decision that General Pinochet could be extradited, the House of Lords relied on, and established, Pinochet's potential responsibility for the alleged crimes from the date on which the UK incorporated the United Nations Convention on Torture into its domestic law through the Criminal Justice Act 1988 – 29 September 1988. Consequently, he could not be held responsible for any crimes committed before then, but was potentially liable for any offences after that date. Thus, although the later House of Lords' committee provided the same decision as the first one, it did so on significantly different, and much more limited, grounds from those on which Lords

Steyn and Nicholls, with the support of Lord Hoffmann, relied. Such a conclusion is neither satisfactory in law nor in political practice, and did nothing to deflect the unflattering glare of unwanted publicity that had been visited on the House of Lords.

It is important not to overstate what was decided in *Re Pinochet*. The facts of that case were exceptional and it is unlikely that it will lead to a mass withdrawal of judges from cases; however, there might well be other cases in which the judge would be well advised to disclose a possible interest. Finally, with regard to *Re Pinochet*, whatever one's views about the merits, sagacity or neutrality of the current judiciary, there is considerable evidence to support the proposition that, historically, judges have often been biased towards certain causes and social classes. For example, JAG Griffith's book, *The Politics of the Judiciary* (1997) (see 13.7.1), is brimming with concrete examples of judges who have shown distinctly conservative and illiberal opinions in cases involving workers, trade unions, civil liberties, Northern Ireland, police powers, religion and other matters. Lord Hoffmann was wrong, but it is nonetheless ironic that the first senior judge to have action taken against him for possible political bias was someone whose agenda was nothing more than being against torture and unjudicial killings.

Locabail (UK) Ltd v Bayfield Properties Ltd (1999)

Following a number of other cases in which lawyers sought to challenge a judgment on the grounds that through a social interest or remote financial connection the judge was potentially biased, the Court of Appeal delivered authoritative guidance on the matter in *Locabail (UK) Ltd v Bayfield Properties Ltd and Another* (1999).

The Court of Appeal ruled that all legal arbiters were bound to apply the law as they understood it to the facts of individual cases as they found them without fear or favour, affection or ill will: that is, without partiality or prejudice. Any judge, that term embracing every judicial decision-maker, whether judge, lay justice or juror, who allowed any judicial decision to be influenced by partiality or prejudice deprived the litigant of their important right and violated one of the most fundamental principles underlying the administration of justice. The law was settled in England and Wales by the House of Lords in *R v Gough* (1993), establishing that the relevant test was whether there was in relation to any given judge a real danger or possibility of bias. When applying the real danger test, it would often be appropriate to inquire whether the judge knew of the matter relied on as appearing to undermine their impartiality. If it were shown that they did not, the danger of its having influenced their judgment was eliminated and the appearance of possible bias dispelled. It was for the reviewing court, not the judge concerned, to assess the risk that some illegitimate extraneous consideration might have influenced his decision.

There was one situation where, on proof of the requisite facts, the existence of bias was effectively presumed, and in such cases it gave rise to automatic disqualification; namely, where the judge was shown to have an interest in the outcome of the case which they were to decide or had decided (see *Dimes v Proprietors of the Grand Junction Canal* (1852), *R v Rand* (1866) and *R v Camborne Justices ex p Pearce* (1955)). However, it would be dangerous and futile to attempt to define or list factors which might, or alternatively might not, give rise to a real danger of bias, since everything would depend on the particular facts. Nonetheless, the court could not conceive of circumstances in which an objection could be soundly based on the religion, ethnic or national origin, gender, age, class, means or sexual orientation of the judge. Nor, at any rate ordinarily, could an objection be soundly based on his or her social, educational, service or employment background or history; nor that of any member of his or her family; nor previous political associations, membership of social, sporting or charitable bodies; nor Masonic associations; nor previous judicial decisions; nor extracurricular utterances, whether in textbooks, lectures, speeches, articles, interviews, reports or responses to consultation papers; nor previous receipt of instructions to act for or against any party, solicitor or advocate engaged in a case before him or her; nor membership of the same Inn, circuit, local Law Society or chambers.

By contrast, a real danger of bias might well be thought to arise if there existed personal friendship or animosity between the judge and any member of the public involved in the case; or if the judge were closely acquainted with any such member of the public, particularly if that individual's credibility could be significant in the decision of the case; or if in a case where the credibility of any individual were an issue to be decided by the judge, he or she had in a previous case rejected that person's evidence in such outspoken terms as to throw doubt on his or her ability to approach such a person's evidence with an open mind on any later occasion.

It might well be thought that the Court of Appeal was bound to come to this conclusion. Had it ruled that membership of certain societies, or a particular social background, or the previous political associations of a trial judge were grounds for appeal, two consequences would follow. First, there would be a rapid expansion of the use by law firms of special units that monitor and keep files on all aspects of judges' lives. Second, there would be a proliferation of appeals in all departments of the court structure at the very time when there is such a concerted effort to reduce the backlog of appeals. The decision in *Locabail* leaves a question of profound jurisprudential importance: how far can judges judge in an entirely neutral and socially detached manner?

Locabail was decided before the HRA 1998 came into force, but the Court of Appeal soon had the opportunity to assess the rules in *R v Gough* against the requirements of the European Court's approach to bias in relation to Art 6 of the ECHR. *Director General of Fair Trading v Proprietary Association of Great Britain (re Medicaments and Related Classes of Goods (No 2))* (2001) related to a case before the Restrictive Practices Court. Six weeks into the trial, one of the lay members of the panel hearing the case, an economist, disclosed that, since the start of the case, she had applied for a job with one of the main witnesses employed by one of the parties to the case. On learning this, the respondents argued that such behaviour must imply bias on her part and that consequently, the whole panel should stand down, or at least the member in question should stand down. The Restrictive Practices Court rejected the argument. On appeal, the Court of Appeal took the opportunity to refine the common law test as established in *R v Gough*. Previously, the court determining the issue had itself decided whether there had been a real danger of bias in the inferior tribunal. Now, in line with the jurisprudence of the ECtHR, the test was whether a fair-minded observer would conclude that there was a real possibility of bias. In other words, the test moved from being a subjective test on the part of the court to an objective test from the perspective of the fair-minded observer. In the case in question, the Court of Appeal held that there was sufficient evidence for a fair-minded observer to conclude bias on the part of one member of the panel and that consequently, at the stage the trial had reached, her discussions would have contaminated the other two members, who should also have been stood down. The approach adopted by the Court of Appeal in *re Medicaments and Related Classes of Goods (No 2)* was subsequently approved by the House of Lords in *Porter v Magill* (2001), and in the words of Lord Hope the test for bias is 'whether the fair-minded and informed observer, having considered the facts, would conclude that there was a real possibility that the tribunal was biased'.

Subsequently, in *Lawal v Northern Spirit Ltd* (2003), the House of Lords stated that 'public perception of the possibility of unconscious bias is the key' and while not finding it necessary to delve into the characteristics to be attributed to the fair-minded and informed observer, did suggest that such a person would adopt a balanced approach 'neither complacent nor unduly sensitive or suspicious'.

Finally, in *Meerabux v The Attorney General of Belize* (2005), Lord Hope in delivering the report of the Privy Council raised the possibility that had the House of Lords been able to apply the refined version of the test for apparent bias, rather than the test set out in *Gough*, then it is unlikely that it would have found it necessary to find a solution to the problem that it was presented with by applying the automatic disqualification rule. Not a little ironically, Lord Hoffmann himself was a member of this particular Privy Council panel.

12.3 JUDICIAL OFFICES

Although not required to know the names of present incumbents, students should at least be aware of the various titles of judges and equally know which courts they operate in. Much of what follows may be found on the judicial website: www.judiciary.gov.uk.

Lord Chancellor. The history of this particular office has been considered previously and it only remains to state that in its contemporary, reduced state, the office-holder is the current Justice Minister Michael Gove MP.

Lord Chief Justice. The holder of this position is now President of the Courts of England and Wales and the most senior member of the judiciary. As President of the Courts of England and Wales, the Lord Chief Justice is responsible for representing the views of the judiciary of England and Wales to Parliament, the Justice Minister and Ministers of the Crown generally. He or she is also to be responsible, within the resources made available by the Justice Minister, for maintaining appropriate arrangements for the welfare, training and guidance of the judiciary of England and Wales, and for maintaining appropriate arrangements for the deployment of the judiciary of England and Wales and allocating work within courts. The Lord Chief Justice is the President of the Criminal Division of the Court of Appeal and is formally the senior judge in the Queen's Bench Division of the High Court.

President of the Supreme Court and Deputy President of the Supreme Court. These positions are currently held by Lord Neuberger and Lady Hale. They sit on the appointment commission for any new members of the Supreme Court.

Master of the Rolls. The holder of this office is regarded as second in judicial importance to the Lord Chief Justice. He or she is President of the Civil Division of the Court of Appeal and is responsible for the allocation and organisation of the work of the judges of the Division, as well as presiding in one of its courts. At present, this position is held by Lord Dyson, who stood down from the House of Lords to take up this position.

President of the Family Division of the High Court of Justice. This person is the senior judge in the Family Division and is responsible for organising the operation of the Court.

President of the Queen's Bench Division and Judge in Charge of the Administrative Court. This post was instituted by the Constitutional Reform Act 2005 and the functions of the holder are apparent in the title.

Chancellor of the High Court. This post was also created under the CRA 2005 and replaced the former office of Vice Chancellor of the Supreme Court. Although the Lord Chancellor is nominally the head of the Chancery Division of the High Court, the actual function of organising the Chancery Division falls to the Chancellor.

Senior Presiding Judge for England and Wales. The Courts and Legal Services Act (CLSA) 1990 recognised the existing system and required that each of the six separate Crown Court circuits should operate under the administration of two presiding judges appointed from the High Court. In addition, a senior presiding judge is appointed from the Lords Justices of Appeal.

12.3.1 JUDICIAL HIERARCHY

The foregoing are specific judicial offices. In addition, the various judges who function at the various levels within the judicial hierarchy are referred to in the following terms:

Justices of the Supreme Court. When all appointed, these 12 judges now constitute the highest court in the United Kingdom and have been considered in some detail previously. The qualifications and procedure for appointment will be considered below.

Lords of Appeal in Ordinary. These were the people normally referred to as the Law Lords for the simple reason that they were ennobled when they were appointed to their positions and sat in the House of Lords. Historically, they constituted the highest court in the United Kingdom and have been replaced by the Supreme Court as considered above.

Lords Justices of Appeal. This category, of which there are currently 38 incumbents, constitutes the majority of the judges in the Court of Appeal, although the other specific office-holders considered previously may also sit in that court, as may High Court judges specifically requested to do so. They all used to be known as Lord Justice, even if they were female. The first female member of the Court of Appeal, Elizabeth Butler-Sloss, had to be referred to by the male title because the Senior Courts Act 1981 had not considered the possibility of a woman holding such high judicial office. The rules were changed subsequently to allow female judges in the Court of Appeal to be referred to as Lady Justices, and whereas their male counterparts receive knighthoods on their elevation, the women become Dames.

High Court judges. These are sometimes referred to as '*puisne*' (pronounced 'pewnee') judges, in reference to their junior status in relation to those of superior status in the Supreme Court. There is a statutory maximum of 108 such judges appointed. Judges are appointed to particular divisions depending on the amount of work needing to be conducted by that division, although they may be required to hear cases in different divisions and may be transferred from one division to another by the Lord Chancellor. Others, such as former High Court and Court of Appeal judges, or former circuit judges or recorders, may be requested to sit as judges in the High Court. High Court judges are referred to by their name followed by the initial 'J'.

The Lord Chancellor may also appoint deputy judges of the High Court on a purely temporary basis, in order to speed up the hearing of cases and to reduce any backlog that may have built up. The Heilbron Report on the operation of the civil justice system was critical of the use of deputy judges and recommended that more permanent High Court judges should be appointed if necessary. The maximum numbers were subsequently increased to their present level, but the use of deputy judges has continued to provide grounds for criticism of the operation of the legal system, and has led to suggestions that the use of 'second-rate' judges might eventually debase the whole judicial currency.

Circuit judges. Although there is only one Crown Court, it is divided into six distinct circuits, which are serviced, in the main, by circuit judges who also sit as County Court judges to hear civil cases. There are currently some 640 circuit judges, each being addressed as 'Your Honour'.

Recorders are part-time judges appointed to assist circuit judges in their functions in relation to criminal and civil law cases. There are currently over 1,100 recorders in post.

District judges. This category of judge, previously referred to as registrars, is appointed on a full-time and part-time basis to hear civil cases in the County Court. There are currently over 400 district judges.

All judicial statistics are available at https://www.gov.uk/government/collections/criminal-justice-statistics.

The situation of *magistrates* will be considered separately at 12.9 below and the situation of *chairmen of tribunals* and *tribunal judges* will be considered at 12.5.

12.3.2 LEGAL OFFICES

In addition to these judicial positions, there are three legal offices that should be noted:

- The *Attorney General*, like the Lord Chancellor, is a political appointee and a member of the executive, whose role is to act as the legal adviser to the government. For example, in March 2003, the former Attorney General, Lord Goldsmith, controversially advised the government that there was a legal basis for its use of military force against Iraq.

  The Attorney General alone has the authority to prosecute in certain circumstances and appears for the Crown in important cases. As may be recalled from 9.5 above the Attorney General also has powers to appeal against points of law in relation to acquittals under the Criminal Justice Act (CJA) 1972 and can also appeal against unduly lenient sentences under the CJA 1988. The crucially important decision of the House of Lords that DNA evidence, acquired in regard to another investigation and which should have been destroyed under s 64 of the Police and Criminal Evidence Act (PACE) 1984, could nonetheless be used, was taken as the result of a reference by the Attorney General (*Attorney General's Reference (No 3 of 1999)*). The current incumbent is Jeremy Wright MP.

- The *Solicitor General* is the Attorney General's deputy.

- The *Director of Public Prosecutions* (DPP) is the head of the national independent Crown Prosecution Service (CPS) established under the Prosecution of Offences Act 1985 to oversee the prosecution of criminal offences. The decision of the DPP whether to prosecute or not in any particular case is subject to judicial review in the courts. In *R v DPP ex p C* (1994), it was stated that such powers should be used sparingly and only on grounds of unlawful policy, failure to act in accordance with policy and perversity. Nonetheless, successful actions have been taken against the DPP in relation to decisions not to prosecute in *R v DPP ex p Jones* (2000) and in *R v DPP ex p Manning* (2000) (see 11.2 for an examination of the CPS). In November 2013, Alison Saunders was appointed DPP on the resignation of the previous incumbent, Keir Starmer.

12.4 APPOINTMENT OF THE JUDICIARY

The somewhat astonishing fact is that there are approximately 40,000 judicial office-holders in England and Wales if one includes judges, tribunal members and magistrates. This section of this book considers how such a number of people actually come to hold these judicial positions.

In the first of his Hamlyn Lectures of 1993, the then Lord Chancellor, Lord Mackay, stated that the pre-eminent qualities required by a judge are:

> good sound judgment based upon knowledge of the law, a willingness to study all sides of an argument with an acceptable degree of openness, and an ability to reach a firm conclusion and to articulate clearly the reasons for the conclusion.

Although the principal qualification for judicial office was experience of advocacy, Lord Mackay recognised that some people who have not practised advocacy may well have these necessary qualities to a great degree. This was reflected in the appointment of an academic and member of the Law Commission, Professor Brenda Hoggett, to the High Court in December 1993. Professor Hoggett, who sat as Mrs Justice Hale, was the first High Court judge not to have had a career as a practising barrister, although she qualified as a barrister in 1969 and was made a QC in 1989. As Dame Brenda Hale, she sat in the Court of Appeal; as Lady Hale of Richmond, she was the first female member of the Law Lords; and she is now Deputy President of the Supreme Court.

The Courts and Legal Services Act (CLSA) 1990 introduced major changes into the qualifications required for filling the positions of judges. Judicial appointment is still essentially dependent upon the rights of audience in the higher courts, but at the same time as the CLSA 1990 effectively demolished the monopoly of the Bar to rights of audience in such courts, it opened up the possibility of achieving judicial office to legal practitioners other than barristers.

The Tribunals, Courts and Enforcement Act 2007 extended the possibility of holding judicial office to Fellows of the Institute of Legal Executives. This provision came into effect in November 2010.

12.4.1 QUALIFICATIONS

The main qualifications for appointment are as follows (the CLSA 1990 is dealt with in detail at 16.6 below):

- *Lord of Appeal in Ordinary*
  (a)   the holding of high judicial office for two years; or
  (b)   possession of a 15-year Supreme Court qualification under the CLSA 1990.

    The Constitutional Reform Act retained the same qualifications for members of the new Justices of the Supreme Court. There is, however, a new statutory appointments procedure under the proposed legislation, which is considered below.

- *Lord Justice of Appeal*
  (a)   the holding of a post as a High Court judge; or
  (b)   possession of a 10-year High Court qualification under the CLSA 1990.

- *High Court judges*
  (a)   the holding of a post as a circuit judge for two years;
  (b)   possession of a 10-year High Court qualification under the CLSA 1990.

- *Deputy judges* must be qualified in the same way as permanent High Court judges.
- *Circuit judges*
  (a)   the holding of a post as a recorder;
  (b)   possession of either a 10-year Crown Court qualification or a 10-year County Court qualification under the CLSA 1990;
  (c)   the holding of certain offices, such as district judge, Social Security Commissioner, chairman of an industrial tribunal, stipendiary magistrate for three years.

- *Recorders* must possess a 10-year Crown Court or County Court qualification under the CLSA 1990.

- *District judges* require a seven-year general qualification under the CLSA 1990.

12.4.2 SELECTION OF JUDGES

So far, attention has concentrated on the specific requirements for those wishing to fulfil the role of judge, but it remains to consider the more general question relating to the process whereby people are deemed suitable and selected for such office. Although the appointment procedure for judges has changed as a consequence of the Constitutional Reform Act 2005, with the establishment of the Judicial Appointments Commission, it is still necessary briefly to examine the former appointment procedure in order to explain the need for the reforms introduced by that Act.

Senior judicial positions

All judicial appointments remain, theoretically, at the hands of the Crown. Previously, however, the Crown was guided, if not actually dictated to, in regard to its appointment by the government of the day. Thus, as has been seen, the Lord Chancellor was a direct political appointment and the Prime Minister also advised the Crown on the appointment of other senior judicial office-holders such as the Law Lords and Appeal Court judges. Such apparent scope for patronage in the hands of the Prime Minister did not go without criticism.

Also under the previous system judges at the level of the High Court and Circuit Bench were appointed by the Crown on the advice of the Lord Chancellor, and the Lord Chancellor personally appointed district judges, lay magistrates and the members of some tribunals. This system did not go without challenge either, the question being raised as to how the Lord Chancellor actually reached his decision to recommend or appoint individuals to judicial offices.

High Court Bench

In the past, appointment to the High Court Bench was by way of invitation from the Lord Chancellor. However, in 1998, the Lord Chancellor's Department (LCD) issued an advertisement inviting applicants to apply for such positions. However, the Lord Chancellor retained their right to invite individuals to become High Court judges. As regards the system of invitation, the question immediately raised was as to exactly how the Lord Chancellor selected the recipients of their favour. There being no system as such, there could be no transparency and without transparency there had to be doubts as to the fairness of the process. Even where a candidate applied for the post of High Court judge, the procedure was different from applications at a lower level, for the reason that the candidate was not interviewed after the usual consultation process with the senior judiciary and the candidate's own referees. The Lord Chancellor simply decided whom to appoint on the basis of that consultation process. Thus doubts about the secretive nature of the consultancy procedure were compounded as regards applicants for the High Court Bench.

The previous procedure of appointment to the High Court was subject to some sharp criticism in a review conducted for the Bar Council under the chairmanship of the former Appeal Court judge Sir Iain Glidewell. The main review concluded that the system of appointment was not sufficiently transparent. More contentiously, however, it suggested that, given the increased role of the judiciary in matters relating to the review of administrative decisions, devolution issues and human rights, it was no longer constitutionally acceptable for judges to be appointed by the government of the day, of which the Lord Chancellor is a member.

Circuit judges and below

All appointments up to and including circuit judges were made on the basis of open competition but as part of the process comments were solicited from a wide range of judges and lawyers who were approached for assessments on the Lord Chancellor's behalf.

Relying on the recommendations and opinions of the existing judiciary as to the suitability of the potential candidates might appear sensible at first sight. However, it brought with it the allegation, if not the fact, that the system was over-secretive and led to a highly conservative appointment policy. Judges were suspected, perhaps not unnaturally, of favouring those candidates who have not been troublesome in their previous cases and who have shown themselves to share the views and approaches of the existing office-holders.

One of Lord Irvine's earliest actions as Lord Chancellor had been to declare the government's intention to inquire into the merits of establishing a Judicial Appointments Commission. However, rather than carry out that intention, he announced in 1999 that Sir Leonard Peach, the former Commissioner for Public Appointments, would be conducting an independent scrutiny of the way in which the current appointment processes for judges operated. In December of that year, Sir Leonard reported that he had been:

> . . . impressed by the quality of work, the professionalism and the depth of experience of the civil servants involved.

Sir Leonard recommended that a Commission for Judicial Appointments be established, whose role would be to monitor the procedures and act as an Ombudsman for disappointed applicants. However, it was also recommended that the commission should not have any role in the actual appointments, but should merely maintain an independent oversight of the procedure.

Not surprisingly, Lord Irvine was most happy to accept such findings and Sir Leonard's proposals, and the system of appointing the judiciary remained essentially unchanged. The appointment of Sir Colin Campbell, Vice Chancellor of Nottingham University, as the first Commissioner was announced in March 2001. Nonetheless, the work of the Commission proved salutary in relation to the appointments process and its reports did not hold back on providing a constant flow of restrained if sometimes acerbic criticism of the process and indeed the continued role of the Lord Chancellor within that process.

Somewhat surprisingly, in April 2003 Lord Irvine announced – before the select committee with oversight of his department – that he intended to issue three separate consultation documents relating to:

- whether judges and lawyers should continue to wear wigs and gowns in court;
- whether the status of Queen's Counsel should be retained and the related appointment process; and
- the role of the Judicial Appointments Commission.

Once again, Lord Irvine's actions were forestalled by his dismissal from office and his replacement in June 2003 by Lord Falconer, who immediately issued a consultation paper on the establishment of a full-blown Judicial Appointments Commission, which subsequently formed the basis of the proposals in regard to judicial appointments contained in the Constitutional Reform Act 2005.

12.4.3 THE JUDICIAL APPOINTMENTS COMMISSION

Part 4 of the Constitutional Reform Act created a new independent Judicial Appointments Commission (JAC), which was in due course to assume responsibility for the process of selecting all judges for appointment in England and Wales from magistrates to members of the Supreme Court. However, following an agreement between the Lord Chancellor, the Judicial Appointments Commission (JAC), the Lord Chief Justice and the Magistrates' Association, it was decided that the JAC would not take responsibility for the recruitment and selection of magistrates. Consequently that function would remain with the Lord Chancellor's Advisory Committees on Justices of the Peace for the foreseeable future.

The Judicial Appointments Commission makes recommendations to the Lord Chancellor and no one may be appointed whom the Commission has not selected. The Lord Chancellor may reject a candidate, once, and ask the Commission to reconsider, once. However, if the Commission maintains its original recommendation, the Lord Chancellor must appoint or recommend for appointment whichever candidate is selected. The appointments of Lords Justices and above will continue to be made by the Queen formally, after the Commission has made a recommendation to the Lord Chancellor. The Act makes special provision for the appointment of the Lord Chief Justice, Heads of Division and Lords Justices of Appeal. In these cases, the Commission will establish a selection panel of four members, consisting of two senior judges, normally including the Lord Chief Justice, and two lay members of the Commission.

Members of the Judicial Appointments Commission are appointed by the Queen, on the recommendation of the Lord Chancellor. Schedule 12 of the Act sets out the membership of the Judicial Appointments Commission, together with its powers and responsibilities. Of the total of 15 Commissioners:

- six must be lay members;
- five must be members of the judiciary (three judges of the Court of Appeal or High Court, including at least one Lord Justice of Appeal and at least one High Court judge, one circuit judge and one district judge);
- two must be members of the legal profession;
- one must be a tribunal member; and
- one must be a lay magistrate.

Significantly, the Chair of the Commission is one of the lay members. The Act requires that all candidates must be of good character and that selection shall be made strictly on merit. In addition, it gives the Lord Chancellor power to issue guidance to the Commission in regard to what considerations to take into account in assessing merit, which the Commission must have regard to. However, the Act does not prescribe detailed appointments procedures and makes it clear that any such procedures are a matter for the Commission to decide.

It can be seen that although the Lord Chancellor retains the ultimate power to decide whom to appoint, or to recommend to the Queen for appointment, and thus maintains Parliamentary accountability, their discretion has been tightly circumscribed by the provisions of the Act.

The Act also provides for the establishment of a Judicial Appointments and Conduct Ombudsman to whom unsuccessful or disgruntled applicants for judicial office can apply for a consideration of their case. As the full title suggests, the Ombudsman also will have a role to play in relation to matters of a disciplinary nature and s 110 allows complaints to be made to the Judicial Appointments and Conduct Ombudsman about judicial disciplinary cases.

The JAC has identified five core qualities and abilities that are required for any judicial office, although they may be adapted for different posts; thus for example a High Court judge would be expected to display a high level of legal knowledge, whereas a lay tribunal member would be expected to display expertise in their professional field.

1   *Intellectual capacity*
- high level of expertise in your chosen area or profession;
- ability quickly to absorb and analyse information;
- appropriate knowledge of the law and its underlying principles, or the ability to acquire this knowledge where necessary.

2   *Personal qualities*
- integrity and independence of mind;
- sound judgment;

- decisiveness;
- objectivity;
- ability and willingness to learn and develop professionally.

3   *An ability to understand and deal fairly*
- ability to treat everyone with respect and sensitivity whatever their background;
- willingness to listen with patience and courtesy.

4   *Authority and communication skills*
- ability to explain the procedure and any decisions reached clearly and succinctly to all those involved;
- ability to inspire respect and confidence;
- ability to maintain authority when challenged.

5   *Efficiency*
- ability to work at speed and under pressure;
- ability to organise time effectively and produce clear reasoned judgments expeditiously;
- ability to work constructively with others (including leadership and managerial skills where appropriate).

While the JAC is 'committed to widening the range of applicants for judicial appointment and to ensuring that the very best eligible candidates are drawn from a wider range of backgrounds', this goal is to be achieved by encouraging a wider range of applicants and through the provision of a fair and open selection process. That being said, all appointments will be made purely on merit. However, the first appointments of the Commission were subjected to criticism in the newspapers in early 2008 when it was discovered that the first 10 High Court judges appointed under the new system were all men and thus not very different from those appointed under the old system.

The JAC's role in the judicial appointments process begins when they receive a request from Her Majesty's Courts Service (HMCS), the Tribunals Service or on behalf of a tribunal outside the Tribunals Service. It then seeks out the best candidates, using the processes described below as measured against the qualities and abilities relevant to that post. The following sets out the procedures leading to the appointment of judicial office-holders (see also the JAC's website at http://jac.judiciary.gov.uk):

Stage 1: Application

Most positions are advertised widely in the national press, legal publications, the professional press and online. The application form is tailored for each individual selection exercise. Alongside the form, an information pack is available to applicants, which includes details of the eligibility criteria and guidance on the application process. This too is tailored for each exercise. Both documents can be downloaded from the JAC website or are sent out to candidates on request. Once JAC has received a completed application form, it is required under s 63(3) of the Constitutional Reform Act to select people for appointment who are of 'good character' and has established guidance to help people to decide whether there is anything in their past conduct or present circumstances (for example business connections) which might affect their application for judicial appointment. The essential principles in determining good character are:

- the overriding need to maintain public confidence in the standards of the judiciary; and
- that public confidence will only be maintained if judicial office-holders and those who aspire to such office maintain the highest standards of behaviour in their professional, public and private lives.

Stage 2: Assessment

Candidates are asked on their application form to nominate up to three referees normally, or in some cases six. The Commission may also seek references from a list of Commission-nominated referees, which is published for each selection exercise. The time at which references are sought will depend on the assessment method used for shortlisting:

- If a qualifying test is used, references are taken up after the qualifying test and before interviews take place.
- If a paper sift is used, references are taken up before the sift and used to make the shortlisting decisions.

In all cases, references will form part of the information that JAC uses to make final selection recommendations to the Lord Chancellor.

Shortlisting

This may be done on the basis of qualifying tests or paper sift, using the application form and references. For senior appointments, where candidates will usually have an extensive track record, shortlisting will normally be done on information supplied by the candidate and from references.

Interviews and selection days

The next stage of the assessment will vary depending on the nature of the post to be filled. Candidates might be asked to attend a selection day, which may entail a combination of role-plays and an interview. For some specialist and the most senior appointments, there might be only a panel interview.

Panel reports

Panel members assess all the information about each candidate, prepare reports on their findings and agree which candidates best meet the required abilities.

Statutory consultation

As required under ss 88(3) and 94(3) of the CRA, the panel's reports on candidates likely to be considered by the Commission are sent to the Lord Chief Justice and another person who has held the post, or has relevant experience.

Stage 3: Selection and recommendation

Recommendation to the Lord Chancellor

The Commissioners consider all the information gathered on the candidates and select candidates to be recommended to the Lord Chancellor for appointment.

Final checks

For existing judicial office-holders, checks are done with the Office for Judicial Complaints (OJC) that there are no complaints outstanding against them. For all other candidates recommended for appointment, a series of good character checks are done with the police, Her Majesty's Revenue and Customs and relevant professional bodies.

The Lord Chancellor may also require candidates to undergo a medical assessment before their appointment is confirmed. JAC recommends to the Lord Chancellor one candidate for each vacancy. The Lord Chancellor can reject that recommendation but they are required to provide their reasons to the Commission. They cannot select an alternative candidate.

Appointment to the Supreme Court

As regards future appointments to the Supreme Court, s 25 of the Constitutional Reform Act (CRA) sets out three possible routes to qualification. These are:

1   having held high judicial office, for at least two years;

2   having satisfied the judicial-appointment eligibility condition on a 15-year basis;

3   having been a qualifying practitioner for at least 15 years.

Although appointment to office is by the Crown, ss 26, 27, 28, 29, 30 and 31 and Sched 8 CRA 2005 set out the procedure for appointing a member of the Supreme Court. The Lord Chancellor must convene an *ad hoc* selection commission if there is, or is likely to be, a vacancy. Subsequently, the Lord Chancellor will notify the Prime Minister of the identity of the person selected by that commission, and under s 26(4) the Prime Minister *must* recommend the appointment of that person to the Queen.

Schedule 8 contains the rules governing the composition and operation of the selection commission, which will consist of the President of the Supreme Court, who will chair the commission, the Deputy President of the Supreme Court and one member from each of the territorial judicial appointment commissions (see below), one of whom must be a person who is not legally qualified. The next most senior ordinary judge in the Supreme Court will take the unfilled position on the selection commission if either the President or Deputy President is unable to sit.

Section 27 sets out the process that must be followed in the selection of a justice of the Supreme Court. The commission decides the particular selection process to be applied, the criteria or competences against which candidates will be assessed, but in any event the requirement is that any selection must be made solely on merit. However, s 27(8) does require that the commission must take into account the need for the Court to have among its judges generally at least two Scottish judges and usually one from Northern Ireland. The Lord Chancellor, as provided for by s 27(9), may issue non-binding guidance to the commission about the vacancy that has arisen, for example on the jurisdictional requirements of the Court, which the commission must have regard to.

Under s 27(2) and s 27(3) the commission is required to consult:

(i)   senior judges who are neither on the commission nor willing to be considered for selection;

(ii)   the Lord Chancellor;

(iii)   the First Minister in Scotland;

(iv)   the Assembly First Secretary in Wales; and

(v)   the Secretary of State for Northern Ireland.

Sub-section 28(1) provides that after a selection has been made the commission must submit a report nominating one candidate to the Lord Chancellor, who then must also consult the senior judges (or other judges) who were consulted by the commission, the First Minister in Scotland, the Assembly First Secretary in Wales and the Secretary of State for Northern Ireland.

Section 29 sets out the Lord Chancellor's options after they have received a name from the commission and carried out the further consultation under s 28. The procedure may be divided into three possible stages.

1   Stage 1, where a person has been selected and recommended by the appointments commission. At this stage the Lord Chancellor may:

    (i)   accept the nomination and notify the Prime Minister;

    (ii)   reject the selection;

    (iii)   require the commission to reconsider its selection.

2   Stage 2, where a person has been selected following a rejection or reconsideration at stage 1. In this event the Lord Chancellor can:

    (i)   accept the nomination and notify the Prime Minister;

    (ii)   reject the selection but only if it was made following a reconsideration at stage 1;

    (iii)   require the commission to reconsider the selection, but only if it was made following a rejection at stage 1.

3.   Stage 3, where a person has been selected following a rejection or reconsideration at stage 2. At this point, the Lord Chancellor *must* accept the nomination unless they prefer to accept a candidate who had previously been reconsidered but not subsequently recommended for a second time.

In effect this means that the Lord Chancellor's options are as follows. They can:

(i)   accept the recommendation of the commission;

(ii)   ask the commission to reconsider; or

(iii)   reject the recommendation.

Where the Lord Chancellor requires the commission to *reconsider* its original selection, the commission can still put forward the same name with additional justifications for its selection. In such circumstances, the Lord Chancellor will either accept the recommendation or reject it. Alternatively, the commission can recommend another candidate, whom the Lord Chancellor can accept, reject or require reconsideration of.

However, if the Lord Chancellor *rejects* the original name provided by the selection commission, they must submit an alternative candidate giving reasons for their choice.

At this point the Lord Chancellor can either:

(i)   accept the second candidate; or

(ii)   ask the selection commission to reconsider.

On reconsideration the commission can either resubmit the second candidate or propose an alternative candidate. At this point the Lord Chancellor must make a choice. They can either accept the alternative candidate or they can then choose the reconsidered candidate.

Under s 30(1), the Lord Chancellor's right of rejection is only exercisable where in their opinion the person selected is not suitable for the office concerned. The right to require reconsideration is exercisable under three conditions:

(i)   where they feel there is not enough evidence that the person is suitable for office;

(ii)   where they feel there is not enough evidence that that person is the best candidate on merit; or

(iii)   where there is not enough evidence that the judges of the Court will between them have enough knowledge of, and experience in, the laws of each part of the United Kingdom, following the new appointment.

Should the Lord Chancellor exercise either of these options they must provide the commission with their reasons in writing (s 30(3)).

Details of the procedures involved in appointment may be found in the JAC pages of the judiciary website at http://jac.judiciary.gov.uk, together with an interesting collection of essays entitled *Judicial Appointments: Balancing Independence, Accountability and Legitimacy.*

Previous versions of this section have concentrated on an extensive, and admittedly rather dry, examination of available statistics and the pronouncements of various reports, committees and taskforces. While the importance of such evidence is not to be dismissed, perhaps they merely reflect structural underlying attitudes that have to be challenged before change can take place. To that end, and perhaps to better focus on such underlying issues, what follows will preface such consideration by placing it in the context of an apparent disagreement between two members of the current Supreme Court.

Lord Sumption

In an interview with the *Evening Standard* Lord Sumption was reported as offering his opinion on the gender structure of the judiciary. While many of his comments may well have been taken out of context to provide attention-seeking deadlines, such as suggesting that rushing to achieve equal representation for women at the top of the legal profession could inflict 'appalling consequences' on the quality of British justice, nonetheless there are extensive, apparently verbatim, quotations from Lord Sumption that are no less worth comment, not to say concern. Thus he is quoted as expressing the view that it would take decades to have equal representation for women in the judiciary on the basis that:

> These things simply can't be transformed overnight, not without appalling consequence in other directions . . . One has to look at the totality of these problems and not simply at one of them. The lack of diversity is a significant problem, but it isn't the only one . . . It takes time. You've got to be patient. The change in the status and achievements of women in our society, not just in the law but generally, is an enormous cultural change that has happened over the last 50 years or so. It has to happen naturally. It will happen naturally. But in the history of a society like ours, 50 years is a very short time . . . We have got to be very careful not to do things at a speed which will make male candidates feel that the cards are stacked against them. If we do that we will find that male candidates don't apply in the right numbers. 85 per cent of newly appointed judges in France are women because the men stay away. 85 per cent women is just as bad as 85 per cent men . . . What we have in this country is a long cultural tradition which is genuinely based on public service, people feeling that at the end of a successful career at the Bar, that [becoming a judge] it is something that you ought to be willing to do. That's a terrific public asset . . . It's a tradition which you can destroy very easily and never recreate, not without waiting for a very long time. It would be very unfortunate . . . The Bar and the solicitors' profession are incredibly demanding in the hours of work and the working conditions are frankly appalling. There are more women than men who are not prepared to put

up with that. As a lifestyle choice, it's very hard to quarrel with it, but you have to face the consequence which is that the top of the legal profession has fewer women in it than the profession overall does.

Lady Hale
In what may, or may not, have been a rejoinder to Sumption, Baroness Hale of Richmond, Deputy President of the Supreme Court, included the following in a speech delivered at the University of Birmingham:

So how are we doing with appointments to our own Supreme Court? I was sworn in as a 'Lord of Appeal in Ordinary' on 12 January 2004. 15 people have been sworn in as Lords of Appeal in Ordinary or Justices of the Supreme Court of the United Kingdom since then. Even if we leave out the two who were sworn in the day after me, the Court has more than replaced itself since then. One might have hoped that the opportunity would have been taken to achieve a more diverse collegium. It has not happened.

All of those 13 appointments were men. All were white. All but two went to independent fee-paying schools. All but three went to boys' boarding schools. All but two went to Oxford or Cambridge. All were successful QCs in private practice, although one was a solicitor rather than a barrister. All but two had specialised in commercial, property or planning law. None had spent much, if any, time as an employee. I share with them the experience of being white and having been to Cambridge. In every other of those respects I am different: I went to a state day school, my profession was University teacher and then Law Commissioner, my specialism was family and social welfare law. How is it that, despite their very different characters and outlooks, they remain such a homogenous group? . . .

I believe that anyone who is appointing the Justices of the Supreme Court should be able to look at the body of Justices as a whole and ask how they can collectively best serve the needs of the UK justice system. Excellence is important (though I am embarrassed to claim it). But so is diversity of expertise. And so is diversity of background and experience. It really bothers me that there are women, who know or ought to know that they are as good as the men around them, but who won't apply for fear of being thought to be appointed just because they are a woman. We early women believed that we were as good as the men and would certainly not be put

> off in this way. I may well have been appointed because the powers that be realised the need for a woman. I am completely unembarrassed about that, because they were right, and I hope that I have justified their confidence in me. I don't think that all the talk about the best women being deterred is a plot to put them off, but I am sure that they should not be deterred by talk such as this. We owe it to our sex, but also to the future of the law and the legal system, to step up to the plate.

Judicial Diversity Taskforce final annual report, June 2014

This Judicial Diversity Taskforce was set up as the result of the recommendations of a previous Advisory Panel on Judicial Diversity which reported in 2010. It was given the task of overseeing an agreed action plan for change recommended by that panel. In June 2015 it published its final annual progress report, which outlined the progress of the recommendations of the Advisory Panel. The oversight function of the Taskforce will now be the responsibility of the Judicial Diversity Forum, which brings together most of the parties who were in the Taskforce. The Chairman of the JAC, Christopher Stephens, said of the report:

> It is important that the JAC, government, the judiciary and the legal profession continue the work of the Taskforce, including through the Judicial Diversity Forum – it is only through our joint efforts that we will achieve a more diverse judiciary. Since the report was published the JAC has effectively completed all of its 15 allocated recommendations. The final two have been incorporated into our internal change programme, through which we are making improvements to our selection processes. Furthermore the quality of applications remains high and judicial diversity has continued to improve at all levels.
>
> In the last four years (to 31 March 2014) the JAC has recommended 2,890 candidates for judicial office – 44% of them women, 11% Black, Asian and Minority Ethnic candidates and 6% with a self-declared disability. Women made up a third of recommendations for the 2013 High Court exercise and 40% of the previous Chancery Division exercise which has resulted in the highest ever number of women in the High Court. And there is good news for the future as women have shown that if they apply they are often very successful – and even outperform their male colleagues.
>
> Additionally, we now collect and publish data on sexual orientation and religious belief, and are now turning our attention to whether we should monitor social mobility. We all acknowledge there is further work to be done, but the JAC is very encouraged by the results to date. (The report is available on the Ministry of Justice website.)

Judicial Diversity statistics, July 2015 (Introduction from the Lord Chief Justice Thomas)

Together with the Senior President of Tribunals I am pleased to announce the publication of the judicial diversity figures for 2015. Diversity is important to all of us and to the judiciary in particular. It is not just a guarantor of public confidence in justice, it is also a feature of justice itself because it represents both fairness and equality of opportunity.

The figures show a steady improvement in the diversity of the courts and tribunals judiciary. It is encouraging that the numbers of female judges in the High Court and the Court of Appeal are at their highest levels ever. There has been a rise in the number of women on the Circuit Bench, and more than half of all judges in courts and tribunals under 40 years of age are women (55 per cent). On the other hand, it is disappointing that there has been little marked improvement, in either courts or tribunals, in the percentage of judges from a BAME background. However, I believe the percentage of BAME judges under 50 years of age (12 per cent) provides some encouragement for the future.

Clearly there is more to be done. The Judicial Appointments Commission selects candidates for judicial roles on merit irrespective of background, but there is a real need to ensure that there is a level playing field and everyone has a genuine opportunity when applying for judicial appointment. I would like to see a greater number of solicitor, government legal service, CILEx and academic candidates applying. In addition to working with the Judicial Diversity Forum, the judiciary is continuing to engage with students and lawyers from non-traditional backgrounds through outreach events, work-shadowing, mentoring and the work of over 100 Diversity and Community Relations Judges from across England and Wales. These judges work hard to enhance judicial diversity by encouraging engagement by legal professionals, and community groups who are currently under-represented in the judiciary. I very much hope that these efforts will see further improvements in future years.

The headline figures from the latest statistical report show:

- Eight out of 38 Court of Appeal judges are women (21 per cent). In April 2014 the number was seven (18 per cent) it should be noted that that rise of 3 per cent is still only one person.

- The number of High Court judges who are women remains at 21 out of 106, (now 108), (19 per cent).

- The number of female Circuit Judges increased from 131 in April 2014 to 146 in April 2015 (going from 20 per cent to 23 per cent).

- More than half (53 per cent) of the 60 court judges under 40 years of age are women.

- In tribunals, 56 per cent of the 89 judges under 40 are women.

- The overall percentage of female judges has increased in both the courts and tribunals from April 2014 to April 2015 from 24.5 per cent to 25.2 per cent in the courts and 43.0 per cent to 43.8 per cent in the tribunals.

- The percentage of Black and Minority Ethnic (BME) judges across courts and tribunals is unchanged at 7 per cent.

- 12 per cent of judges across courts and tribunals under 50 years of age are from a BME background.

- 36 per cent of courts judges were not barristers by professional background (down from 37 per cent). In tribunals the figure is 67 per cent (down less than 1 per cent).

For further information see https://www.judiciary.gov.uk/about-the-judiciary/who-are-the-judiciary/diversity/judicial-diversity-statistics-2015/.

Case study: Does the gender of the judge matter? Radmacher v Granatino

In *Radmacher (formerly Granatino) v Granatino* (the clue of the substance being in the full title of the case), for the first time the highest court in England was required to consider the issue of prenuptial agreements in which the parties, as a precursor to their marriage, establish a limit on subsequent claims on the event of the marriage breaking up. The question before the court was whether such 'freely entered into' contractual agreements are binding in law to the degree that they override the usual principles of fairness at the time of divorce in such a way as to limit the rights of the parties that the courts would otherwise apply.

There were two particular twists in the case:

- Whereas usually it is the husband looking to protect his interests upon divorce, in this instance it was the ex-wife who was trying to enforce the agreement.

- In recognition of the importance of the case the Supreme Court heard it as a panel of nine justices, including the first and, to date, only woman member of the UK's highest court, Baroness Hale.

In a judgment of 69 pages and 195 paragraphs, the court, by a majority of eight to one, determined that such prenuptial agreements were legal and enforceable. The one dissenting voice was Lady Hale. While seven of the justices produced a single majority judgment of 123 paragraphs, and Lord Mance delivered his own judgment, in essential agreement, in seven paragraphs, Hale delivered her minority judgment in 69 extensive paragraphs. However, the core of her difference may be found in paragraph 137:

> Above all, perhaps, the court hearing a particular case can all too easily lose sight of the fact that, unlike a separation agreement, the object of an antenuptial agreement is to deny the economically weaker spouse the provision

> to which she – it is usually although by no means invariably she – would otherwise be entitled . . . This is amply borne out by the precedents available in recent text-books . . . Would any self-respecting young woman sign up to an agreement which assumed that she would be the only one who might otherwise have a claim, thus placing no limit on the claims that might be made against her, and then limited her claim to a pre-determined sum for each year of marriage regardless of the circumstances, as if her wifely services were being bought by the year? Yet that is what these precedents do. *In short, there is a gender dimension to the issue which some may think ill-suited to decision by a court consisting of eight men and one woman* (emphasis added).

The questions that cannot be avoided in relation to this case are whether Baroness Hale's gender gave her an insight/awareness that was not shared with, or indeed open to, the other eight male judges and, if so, whether this awareness should have been allowed to influence her judgment (this last could of course be rewritten to question the privileging of the assumedly male perspective of the majority of the judges).

As a matter of coincidence, and no doubt one much appreciated by the authors, a book entitled *Feminist Judgments: From Theory to Practice* (Hunter, McGlynn and Rackley) had come out in September 2010 and had set itself the task of reconsidering and 're-judging' several notable cases from a feminist perspective, the application of which, they argued, would have led to very different decisions. Ironically, Baroness Hale's judgments were not found to be beyond criticism.

12.4.5 ALTERNATIVE APPROACHES TO APPOINTING JUDGES

A different approach, following the example of the United States, might be for the holders of the higher judicial offices to be subjected to confirmation hearings by, for example, a select committee of the House of Commons. Lord Mackay dismissed any such possibility as follows:

> The tendency of prior examination . . . is to discover and analyse the previous opinions of the individual in detail. *I question whether the standing of the judiciary in our country, or the public's confidence in it, would be enhanced by such an inquiry*, or whether any wider public interest would be served by it (emphasis added).

It is perhaps unfortunate that the italicised words in the above passage can be interpreted in a way that no doubt Lord Mackay did not intend but which, nonetheless, could suggest a cover-up of the dubious opinions of those appointed to judicial office.

1. Who appoints the judiciary? The Lord Chancellor is responsible for appointing judges based on candidates selected and recommended by the Judicial Appointments Commission (JAC).

2. On what basis are judges selected?
• All candidates for **judicial roles** are selected on merit through *'fair and open competition from the widest range of eligible candidates'* under procedures set out in the **Constitutional Reform Act 2005** (CRA, as amended), and selecting *'only people of good character and having "regard to the need to encourage diversity in the range of persons available for selection for appointments"'*.
• The main provisions relating to eligibility for judicial appointment are set out in the **Tribunals, Courts and Enforcement Act 2007** (TEC Act) which requires candidates to possess relevant qualifications and experience for a minimum period, dependent on the role sought.

The selection and appointment of judges

3. The process of selection up to and including High Court level:
• On notification of a vacancy by the Courts and Tribunals Service, JAC determine the requirements of the position, advertise the vacancy and set up a selection panel which will make its recommendation to the Lord Chancellor.
• Dependent on the post in question, eligibility rules (TCE Act) require that a relevant legal qualification be held for between five and seven years, and that the applicant has been engaged in law-related activity for the same minimum period. Since 2010, posts up to and including that of District Judge are open to ILEX Fellows, as well as to barristers and solicitors.
• **Becoming a magistrate**: no formal qualifications or legal training is required but applicants must be between the ages of 18 and 70, in good health and of good character.

4. The process of senior judicial appointment:
• When a vacancy arises for a senior judicial position (i.e. those above High Court level) the CRA requires that JAC advertise the vacancy and convene a selection panel of five members who consider nominations and make a recommendation to the Lord Chancellor.
• The Lord Chancellor may then accept the recommendation, reject or ask that the panel reconsider their recommendation. If the candidate recommended is not accepted by the Lord Chancellor, reasons must be provided. The Lord Chancellor does not have the authority to select an alternative candidate. (The composition of selection panels is set out by the CRA.)

FIGURE 12.1 *The Judiciary: selection and appointment.*

The 2011 House of Lords Constitution Committee report also expressly rejected the possibility of parliamentarians being involved in pre- or post-appointment hearings of judicial candidates (see immediately above).

An even more radical alternative would be to open judicial office-holding to election as they also do in the United States, although in this case, one might well agree with Lord Mackay that:

> The British people would not feel that this was a very satisfactory method of appointing the professional judiciary.

Alternatively, and following Lord Mackay's emphasis on the professional nature of the judiciary, the UK could follow continental examples and provide the judiciary with a distinct professional career structure as an alternative to legal practice.

As has been seen, the changes made under the Constitutional Reform Act were subjected to many criticisms from the judges to the Commons Committee on Constitutional Affairs, with many social commentators and journalists joining in the attack. It is true that the reforms were an unlooked-for consequence of an ill-thought-out Cabinet reshuffle, and equally true that the proposed alterations provided the possibility of political interference with the independence and operation of the judiciary, especially with the future possibility of a weak Secretary of State for Justice and an overly strong Home Secretary. Nonetheless, it was surely not appropriate, indeed it was inconsistent, for those concerned to resort to an uncritical pragmatic defence of the status quo on the basis that it had worked so far. The system may have worked, but did it do so in an open and transparent manner, and in whose interests did it operate? The opportunity for more radical reforms may not have been taken, but the measures that have been taken surely represent an improvement in the structure and operation of the judicial system.

12.5 TRAINING OF THE JUDICIARY

Following the Constitutional Reform Act 2005, two new judicial institutions were established: the Judicial Office and the Judicial College, both of which operate as independent judicial bodies within the Judicial Office for England and Wales and are funded directly by the Ministry of Justice.

Judicial Office (JO)

This was set up in 2006 to support the judiciary in discharging its responsibilities under the CRA 2005. It reports to the Lord Chief Justice who, as Head of the Judiciary, has the responsibility for:

- representing the views of the judiciary of England and Wales to Parliament, the Lord Chancellor and ministers generally;
- maintaining arrangements for the welfare, training and guidance of the judiciary, within the resources made available by the Lord Chancellor;
- maintaining arrangements for the deployment of judges and the allocation of work within the courts.

The creation of the JO brought together and replaced several units that had previously existed independently, including the Judicial Studies Board (JSB) and the Judicial Communications Office. In 2010 it assumed responsibility for providing secretariat support and sponsorship of the Family and Civil Justice Councils, both of which provide independent advice to government, and in 2011 it assumed responsibility for the work of the Office for Judicial Complaints. Also in 2011 the JO took over responsibility for the Tribunals Judicial Office and for provision of judicial training for the courts' and tribunals' judiciary through a new body, the Judicial College, which replaced the Judicial Studies Board.

The JO provides a broad range of support to the judiciary, including:

- administrative support and advice for training and development for judicial office-holders;
- research, analysis, legal and secretarial support for the senior judiciary and its governance bodies on a wide range of jurisdictional, constitutional and other strategic matters;
- dealing with official complaints against judicial office-holders through the Office for Judicial Complaints;
- human resources and welfare support services;
- communication and media advice and information.

Judicial College

In April 2011, the newly established Judicial College brought together and replaced the Judicial Studies Board and the Tribunals Judicial Training Group and assumed responsibility for training judicial office-holders in the courts and in most tribunals. The Judicial College ensures that high-quality training is provided to enable judicial office-holders to carry out their duties effectively and in a way which preserves judicial independence and supports public confidence in the justice system.

The Judicial College aims to meet the highest professional standards in judicial learning and development.

The College is directly responsible for the development and delivery of training to judges in the Crown, county and higher courts in England and Wales and to tribunals, judges and members who come under the leadership of the Senior President of Tribunals. The Senior President's responsibilities extend to judges and members within reserved tribunals across the UK. The College also provides some direct training to those who exercise judicial functions in the magistrates' courts (in England and Wales), as well as training materials, advice and support to those providing training in the magistrates' courts. In April 2013, the training of all coroners and coroners' officers became part of the Judicial College's responsibilities.

Prior to the establishment of the JSB, now the JC, the training of judges in the UK was almost minimal, especially when considered in the light of the Continental practice where being a judge, rather than practising as an advocate, is a specific and early career choice, which leads to specialist and extensive training.

The Judicial College's activities fall under three main headings (what follows is taken from the publications of the JSB, but remains pertinent to the operation of the JC):

- initial training for new judicial office-holders and those who take on new responsibilities;
- continuing professional education to develop the skills and knowledge of existing judicial office-holders;

- delivering change and modernisation by identifying training needs and providing training programmes to support major changes to legislation and the administration of justice.

The Judicial College provides training and instruction to all part-time and full-time judges in judicial skills. As stated in its strategy document for 2015–17, judicial training has three elements:

- substantive law, evidence and procedure and, where appropriate, expertise in other subjects;
- the acquisition and improvement of judicial skills including, where appropriate, leadership and management skills;
- the social context within which judging occurs, this latter including diversity and equality.

An essential element of the philosophy of the College is that the training is provided by judges for judges.

The Board of the Judicial College is the governing body of the College. It sets the overall strategy for the College, agrees business plans and oversees the delivery of training within the budget allocated to the College.

The Board is supported by a series of committees responsible for the various detailed training programmes as follows:

- *The Tribunals Committee*. It considers the subject expertise required within tribunals as well as considering the overall training needs across the tribunals' judiciary;
- *The Courts' Committee*. It discusses plans and priorities for training across the entire courts' system;
- *The Diversity and Development Committee*. It functions across the entire College to identify issues common to all judiciary and areas of innovation and development for the Judicial College, the dissemination of best practice and ensure that issues of diversity and fair treatment are embedded in all areas of the College;
- *The Wales Training Committee*. It monitors issues that arise from the Welsh Assembly that impact on judicial training;
- *The International Committee*. It implements the College's international strategy to participate in international training projects that strengthen judicial independence, the rule of law and judicial skills.

Judicial training has probably never been of greater public concern or been executed with such rigour since the JSB was established in 1979. For example, the judiciary were subject to thorough retraining in the new civil procedure. This training included residential seminars for all full-time and part-time judges dealing with civil work, local training and conferences held at various national locations. In an interview in October 2009,

the Society of Black Lawyers, Peter Herbert, was quoted as saying that the figures showed 'institutional racism', within the justice system that needed urgent attention. As he said, 'I am not sure what else you can call it. The effect is right across the criminal justice system. From stop and search, to arrest, to charge and to sentencing, every aspect of the process is stacked against defendants from ethnic minority backgrounds. It is not a pretty picture.'

The following are the report's most telling findings:

Victims

> The 2012/13 Crime Survey for England and Wales shows that adults from self-identified Mixed, Black and Asian ethnic groups were more at risk of being a victim of personal crime than adults from the White ethnic group.

Suspects

> **Stop and search**
>
> A person aged ten or older (the age of criminal responsibility), who self-identified as belonging to the black ethnic group was *six times more likely* than a white person to be stopped and searched under section 1 (s1) of the Police and Criminal Evidence Act 1984 and other legislation in England and Wales; persons from the Asian or mixed ethnic group were just *over two times* more likely to be stopped and searched than a white person.

> **Arrest**
>
> For those aged 10 or older, a black person was nearly *three times more likely* to be arrested per 1,000 population than a white person, while a person from the mixed ethnic group was twice as likely to be arrested. There was no difference in the rate of arrests between Asian and white persons.

Defendants

> Black persons were *less likely* to receive an out of court disposal for an indictable offence, and *more likely* to be proceeded against at magistrates' court, than all other ethnic groups. This remained consistent between 2009

and 2012 despite the overall decrease in the proportion of out of court dis-posals of those formally dealt with by the criminal justice system.

Between 2009 and 2012, for indictable offences, there was a decrease across all ethnic groups in the proportion receiving community sentences. In contrast there was *an increase* for most ethnic groups in the proportion receiving an immediate custodial sentence for an indictable offence. The most common sentence outcome for white and mixed ethnic group offend-ers was a community sentence, whilst for black, Asian and Chinese or other offenders the most common sentence outcome was immediate custody.

The average custodial sentence length for indictable offences was *higher* in all years between 2009 and 2012 for offenders from a BAME group compared with those from a white ethnic group. Different types of crime also show sentencing differences. A white person pleading guilty to burglary was sentenced to, on average, 25 months in prison compared with a black person who typically received a 28-month sentence. Of those plead-ing not guilty but convicted by the courts, the sentences were 40 months and 47 months respectively.

Similarly, 76 per cent of white people convicted of production or sup-ply of a class A drug were sentenced to immediate custody compared with 84.8 per cent of black people.

12.6   RETIREMENT OF JUDGES

All judges are now required to retire at 70, although they may continue in office at the discre-tion of the Lord Chief Justice and with the approval of the Lord Chancellor. The Judicial Pensions and Retirement Act 1993 reduced the retirement age from the previous 75 years for High Court judges and 72 years for other judges, although a judge already serving on the implementation of the Act (31 March 1995) retains the pre-existing retirement age. Part-time members of the judiciary were customarily required to retire at 65, but following an initial finding by an employment tribunal in February 2008 that such a policy was discrimina-tory, the Lord Chancellor announced that the retirement age for part-time judges would be increased to bring it into line with the general judicial retirement age of 70. The 2011 House of Lords Constitution Committee, previously considered, recommended that the retirement age for Court of Appeal judges and Supreme Court justices should be raised to 75.

The reduction of the retirement age may have been designed to reduce the aver-age age of the judiciary, but of perhaps even more significance in this respect is the change that was introduced in judicial pensions at the same time. The new provision requires judges to have served for 20 years, rather than the previous 15, before they qualify for full pension rights. This effectively means that if judges are to benefit from full pension rights, they will have to take up their appointments by the time they are 50. Given that judges are predominantly appointed from the ranks of high-earning QCs, this will either reduce their potential earnings at the Bar or reduce their pay package as judges by approximately 7.5 per cent. This measure led to a great deal of resentment within both the Bar and the judiciary, Lord Chief Justice Taylor referring to its unfairness and meanness, and it was one of the issues that fuelled the antagonism between Lord Mackay and the other members of the judiciary.

With regard to compulsory retirement, many people thought it particularly regrettable that Lord Bingham's age meant that he could not assume the role of the first President of the new Supreme Court. That honour passed to Lord Phillips, who was a sprightly 71 when he assumed the office.

Following protracted litigation, including a hearing in the Supreme Court (*O'Brien v Ministry of Justice* [2013] UKSC 6), part-time fee-paid members of the judiciary were held liable to receive pension payments from the state, which increased the extent of the state's liability for judicial pension. However, under the Public Service Pensions Act 2013 future judicial pensions, alongside all other public sector provisions, were converted to a contributory basis with a significant reduction in value for future pensions. The New Judicial Pension Scheme (NJPS) 2015 which came into effect in April of that year, met with angry resistance from judges, many of whom suggested that they would resign rather than accept its terms, which they saw as reducing their remuneration packages to an unacceptable degree.

In the summer of 2005, Sir Hugh Laddie, a High Court Chancery Judge of some 10 years' standing, announced his intention to resign from his position and return to legal practice. He was the first judge to return to private practice for over 30 years and it is reported that his resignation upset the Lord Chancellor by breaking the 'unwritten rule that joining the judiciary is a one-way street'. Sir Hugh compounded the difficulties in the situation when, in February 2006, he delivered a lecture at the University of London, in which he told the audience that although he was an expert in intellectual property law, he was frequently asked to sit on tax and insolvency cases. As he admitted (*Law Society Gazette*, 23 February 2006):

> I knew nothing about tax, except that it came as a nasty shock at the end of the year. I had never studied it or did it at the bar, or insolvency . . . I had colleagues who said that it was marvellous to do cases outside their own field, that it was stimulating. When I resigned, I felt a certain sensitivity about deciding cases about which I had no knowledge. It would have been better to use a roulette wheel.

12.7   JUDICIAL CONDUCT AND DISCIPLINE

In March 2013 a revised *Guide to Judicial Conduct* was published by the Judges' Council after wide consultation with members of the judiciary. The guide:

- offers assistance to judges on issues rather than prescribing a detailed code; and
- sets up principles from which judges can make their own decisions and so maintain their judicial independence.

The guide accepts, as a basis for its more detailed consideration, what are referred to as the Bangalore principles, which were established following a United Nations initiative. The Bangalore principles may be understood as six underlying values with the stated intention of:

> establish[ing] standards for ethical conduct of judges. They are designed to provide guidance to judges and to afford the judiciary a framework for regulating judicial conduct. They are also intended to assist members of the Executive and Legislature, and lawyers and the public in general, to better understand and support the judiciary.

The essential principles are:

(i)   Judicial independence is a prerequisite to the rule of law and a fundamental guarantee of a fair trial. A judge shall therefore uphold and exemplify judicial independence in both its individual and institutional aspects.

(ii)   Impartiality is essential to the proper discharge of the judicial office. It applies not only to the decision itself but also to the process by which the decision is made.

(iii)   Integrity is essential to the proper discharge of the judicial office.

(iv)   Propriety, and the appearance of propriety, are essential to the performance of all of the activities of the judge.

(v)   Ensuring equality of treatment to all before the courts is essential to the due performance of the judicial office.

(vi)   Competence and diligence are prerequisites to the due performance of judicial office.

The worked-out expression of those principles may be seen on the www.judiciary.gov.uk website.

In relation to matters of discipline, the Constitutional Reform Act 2005 gave powers to both the Lord Chancellor and the Lord Chief Justice. Consistent with previous provisions, the position of all senior judicial office-holders is protected, and removal from office of any judge in the High Court or above is only possible following resolutions in both the House of Commons and the House of Lords. Under s 108 CRA, the Lord Chief Justice was given new powers enabling them to:

- advise;
- warn; or
- formally reprimand judicial office-holders.

They may also suspend them in certain circumstances, mainly regarding allegations relating to criminal offences. Such powers are subject to the agreement of the Lord

Chancellor. The Lord Chief Justice may, again with the agreement of the Lord Chancellor, make regulations and rules about the disciplinary process.

The Office for Judicial Complaints/Judicial Conduct Investigation Office

The Constitutional Reform Act 2005 also established the Office for Judicial Complaints (OJC) and gave the Lord Chancellor and the Lord Chief Justice joint responsibility for a new system for dealing with complaints about the personal conduct of all judicial office-holders in England and Wales. The OJC was set up in April 2006 to handle these complaints and provide advice and assistance to the Lord Chancellor and Lord Chief Justice in the performance of their new joint role. In October 2013 the Judicial Conduct Investigations Office (JCIO) took over the functions of the OJC and from 18 August 2014 all complaints became subject to the Judicial Discipline (Prescribed Procedures) Regulations 2014 (http://judicialconduct.judiciary.gov.uk/rules-and-regulations.htm).

In its annual report for the year 2014/15 the JCIO revealed that, over the period, it had received 2,432 separate complaints against judicial office-holders, although 1,570 of these (57 per cent) related to judicial decisions, which are outside its remit. Unless there are elements of misconduct included in the complaint, issues can only be challenged through an appeal process.

The most common complaint, numbering 585 in total, related to inappropriate behaviour or comments. The next most frequent complaint, 63 in total, related to an alleged conflict of interest. There were 51 complaints referring to discrimination. Out of the 75 judicial office-holders subject to disciplinary action, 17 were from the mainstream judiciary, 11 were tribunals' judiciary and 47 were magistrates. This total represents less than 0.2 per cent of the 39,600 judicial office-holders.

As a result of investigation:

- 32 judicial office-holders were removed from office;
- 16 received a reprimand; and
- 26 received formal advice/warning.

In addition, one magistrate was suspended and there were 15 resignations during conduct investigations.

In June 2009, in rejecting an appeal by *The Guardian* newspaper under the Freedom of Information Act 2000, the Information Tribunal decided that the Ministry of Justice does not have to disclose the names of judges disciplined following complaints on the basis that 'Disclosure would risk undermining a judge's authority while carrying out his or her judicial function.'

In October 2013 the Judicial Conduct Investigations Office (JCIO) took over the functions of the Office for Judicial Complaints.

In March 2015 it was announced that three lower-level judges had been removed from office for viewing pornography via their official IT accounts. One other judge resigned before any action could be taken against him.

12.8 JUDICIAL IMMUNITY FROM SUIT

A fundamental measure to ensure the independence of the judiciary is the rule that they cannot be sued in relation to things said or acts done in their judicial capacity in good faith. The effect of this may be seen in *Sirros v Moore* (1975), in which a judge wrongly ordered someone's detention. It was subsequently held by the Court of Appeal that, although the detention had been unlawful, no action could be taken against the judge as he had acted in good faith in his judicial capacity. Although some judges on occasion may be accused of abusing this privilege, it is nonetheless essential if judges are to operate as independent representatives of the law, for it is unlikely that judges would be able to express their honest opinions of the law, and the situations in which it is being applied, if they were to be subject to suits from disgruntled participants.

Given the increased use of the doctrine of *ultra vires* to justify legal action by way of judicial review against members of the executive, it is satisfyingly ironic that at least one judge, Stephen Sedley, who now sits in the Court of Appeal, sees the possibility of a similar *ultra vires* action providing grounds for an action against judges in spite of their previously assumed legal immunity. As he expressed the point in the *London Review of Books* of April 1994:

> Judges have no authority to act maliciously or corruptly. It would be rational to hold that such acts take them outside their jurisdiction and so do not attract judicial immunity.

No doubt such a suggestion would be anathema to the great majority of the judiciary, but the point remains: why should judges be at liberty to abuse their position of authority in a way that no other public servant can?

Before 1991, magistrates could be liable for damages for actions done in excess of their actual authority, but the CLSA 1990 extended the existing immunity from the superior courts to cover the inferior courts, so magistrates now share the same protection as other judges.

It is worth stating at this point that this immunity during court proceedings also extends as far as advocates and witnesses, and of course jurors, although the controls of *perjury* and *contempt of court* are always available to cover what is said or done in the course of court proceedings.

Related to, although distinct from, the principle of immunity from suit is the convention that individual judges should not be subject to criticism in parliamentary debate, unless subject to an address for their removal: legal principles and the law in general can be criticised, but not judges.

12.9 MAGISTRATES

The foregoing has concentrated attention on the professional and legally qualified judges. It should not be forgotten, however, that there are some 22,000 unpaid part-time lay magistrates, 142 full-time professional magistrates (known as district judges (magistrates' courts)) and 125 deputy district judges (magistrates' courts) operating within some 330 or so magistrates' courts in England. These magistrates are empowered to hear and decide a wide variety of legal matters, and the amount and importance of the work they do should not be underestimated: as much as 95 per cent of all criminal cases are dealt with by the magistrates' courts.

Magistrates currently deal with around 500,000 traffic cases each year, which take up a great deal of their time and the time of those whose cases they hear. On average, traffic cases take nearly six months to reach completion, despite the fact that over 90 per cent of cases result in a guilty plea or are proved in the absence of the defendant. In an attempt to speed up the process, specialist traffic courts were established in nine pathfinder areas in England and the government subsequently announced that, from April 2014, there will be a specialist traffic court in each police area (see https://www.gov.uk/government/news/traffic-courts-in-every-area).

The operation of the magistrates' courts and the powers of magistrates have been considered in detail above at 6.3 and 9.2. Since April 2005, magistrates' courts in England and Wales have been administered by Her Majesty's Courts Service (HMCS, now the HMCTS). This amalgamation ended the previously long-standing separation between magistrates' courts, which were administered by a total of 42 independent local committees, and the government-run Court Service that ran the Court of Appeal, the High Court and all Crown and County Courts.

It remains, however, to examine the manner in which magistrates are appointed to their positions.

There is no requirement for lay magistrates to have any legal qualifications. On being accepted onto the bench, however, magistrates undertake a training process, under the auspices of the JC. Magistrates are required to attend training courses, with a special emphasis being placed on Equal Treatment Training. The way in which the training programme seeks to overcome conceptions as to the politically narrow nature of the magistracy is evident in the content of the extensive training materials produced for the magistrates. These include modules on raising awareness and challenging discrimination; discretion and decision-making; prejudice and stereotype; thus, the overall emphasis may be seen to be on equality of people, and equality of treatment. There is, however, a new emphasis on the practical skills involved in performing the duties placed on magistrates, and consequently much of the training will actually be based on sitting as magistrates with the input of specially trained mentors to give guidance and advice on how the new magistrates perform their tasks and fulfil their roles. About 12 to 18 months after appointment the new magistrate is appraised against a set of the competences covering each courtroom role from basic magistrates to chairmen in adult, youth and family courts. Competences include a checklist of observable behaviour and knowledge.

The training course is designed to give new magistrates an understanding of the functions and powers of the bench generally, and to locate that understanding within the context of national practice, particularly with regard to sentencing. On the topic of discretion and sentencing, Lord Irvine provided the magistrates with the following strong advice, not to say warning:

You . . . must exercise your discretion in individual cases with great care within a system that needs to secure continuing public confidence. This is what makes the sentencing guidelines produced by the Magistrates' Association so important. They are guidelines – they do not curtail your independent discretion to impose sentences you think are right, case by case. But the guidelines exist to help you in that process, to give you more information in reaching your decision. And they help to assist the magistracy, to maintain an overall consistency of approach . . . I urge you to follow the guidelines, which are drawn up for your benefit and the magistracy as a whole (Speech to the Council of the Magistrates' Association, March 1999).

One aspect of sentencing that merits attention arises in relation to the increasingly important area of environmental crime. In response to this, and to make magistrates fully aware of its importance, the Magistrates' Association website made available an extremely useful guidance entitled 'Costing the Earth – guidance for sentencers'.

Justices' clerk

Although particular key legal issues may be considered in the course of the training, it is not the intention to provide the magistrate with a complete grasp of substantive law and legal practice. Indeed, to expect such would be to misunderstand both the role of the magistrates and the division of responsibility within the magistrates' court. Every bench of magistrates has a legally qualified justices' clerk, whose function it is to advise the bench on questions of law, practice and procedure, leaving matters of fact to magistrates to decide upon (see above, 9.2). This division of powers raises a further possible area of contention with regard to the operation of magistrates' courts, for in the case of some particularly acquiescent benches, the justices' clerks appear to run the court, and this leads to the suspicion that they actually direct the magistrates as to what decisions they should make. This perception is compounded by the fact that the bench is entitled to invite their clerk to accompany them when they retire to consider their verdicts. A *Practice Direction (Justices: Clerks to the Court)* (2000) set out the role and functions of the clerk to the court. Thus the clerk, or legal adviser who stands in for the clerk, is stated to be responsible for providing the justices with any advice they require to properly perform their functions, whether or not the justices have requested that advice, on the following matters:

- questions of law (including ECHR jurisprudence and those matters set out in s 2(1) of the HRA 1998);
- questions of mixed law and fact;
- matters of practice and procedure;
- the range of penalties available;
- any relevant decisions of the superior courts or other guidelines; other issues relevant to the matter before the court;

- the appropriate decision-making structure to be applied in any given case; and
- in addition to advising the justices, it shall be the legal adviser's responsibility to assist the court, where appropriate, as to the formulation of reasons and the recording of those reasons.

As regards when and where this advice should be given, the *Practice Direction* states that:

> At any time, justices are entitled to receive advice to assist them in discharging their responsibilities. If they are in any doubt as to the evidence which has been given, they should seek the aid of their legal adviser, referring to his/her notes as appropriate. This should ordinarily be done in open court. Where the justices request their adviser to join them in the retiring room, this request should be made in the presence of the parties in court. Any legal advice given to the justices other than in open court should be clearly stated to be provisional and the adviser should subsequently repeat the substance of the advice in open court and give the parties an opportunity to make any representations they wish on that provisional advice.

In October 2007 the senior presiding judge for England and Wales issued new guidelines for the conduct of justices' clerks and assistant justices' clerks. These emphasise the independence and impartiality of clerks.

12.9.1 APPOINTMENT

Under the Justices of the Peace Act 1997, magistrates are appointed to, and indeed removed from, office by the Lord Chancellor on behalf of the Queen, after consultation with local advisory committees. Following the Constitutional Reform Act 2005 it was the intention for the Judicial Appointments Commission eventually to deal with the appointment of magistrates. However, at least for the moment, the Ministry of Justice handles such appointments. In this interim period, recommendations on the appointment of magistrates continue to be made by local advisory committees. These are then passed to the Lord Chief Justice for approval, before being submitted to the Lord Chancellor to make the appointment.

Section 50 of the Employment Rights Act 1996 provides that employers are obliged to release their employees, for such time as is reasonable, to permit them to serve as magistrates. In the event of an employer refusing to sanction absence from work to perform magistrate's duties, the employee can take the matter before an employment tribunal. Understandably, there is no statutory requirement for the employer to pay their employees in their absence, but magistrates are entitled to claim expenses for loss of earnings in the exercise of their office.

Once candidates of a suitable quality have been identified, the local advisory committee is placed under the injunction to have regard to the need to ensure that the composition of the bench broadly reflects the community that it serves in terms of gender, ethnic origin, geographical spread, occupation and political affiliation. It may even be that individuals who are otherwise suitably qualified may not be appointed if their presence would exacerbate a perceived imbalance in the existing bench. Nonetheless, there remains a lingering doubt, at least in the minds of particular constituencies, that the magistracy still represents the values, both moral and political, of a limited section of society. A further significant step towards opening up the whole procedure of appointing magistrates was taken when local advisory committees were granted the power to advertise for people to put themselves forward for selection. As the chairman of the Mid-Staffordshire Magistrates' Bench stated in a local newspaper, although previously rank and social position were the main qualifications, nowadays:

> it is important a bench has a balance of sexes, professions and political allegiances.

In March 1999, the LCD launched a campaign to attract a wider section of candidates to apply to be magistrates. In announcing the campaign, Lord Irvine stated that:

> Magistrates come from a wide range of backgrounds and occupations. We have magistrates who are dinner ladies and scientists, bus drivers and teachers, plumbers and housewives. They have different faiths and come from different ethnic backgrounds, some have disabilities. All are serving their communities, ensuring that local justice is dispensed by local people. The magistracy should reflect the diversity of the community it serves . . . Rest assured appointments are made on merit, regardless of educational background, social class or ethnic background.

The campaign was supported by adverts in some 36 newspapers and magazines, from broadsheets to tabloids, from TV listings to women's magazines. The campaign was particularly aimed at ethnic minorities, its adverts being carried in such publications as the *Caribbean Times*, the *Asian Times* and *Muslim News*. The 1999 campaign was followed in 2001 by a *Judiciary for All* scheme, which aimed to encourage more people from ethnic minority groups to apply to become magistrates. The next initiative to make the bench more reflective of the public was the 'National Strategy for the Recruitment of Lay Magistrates' announced by Lord Falconer in October 2003. As he stated:

> I consider it particularly important that the magistracy is seen to be representative of all sections of our society and that no one group of people should feel that they are under-represented on the magistrates' bench. My Department is already involved with a number of initiatives aimed at encouraging young

> people and minority ethnic groups to become involved in the judicial process and, although the ethnic make-up of the magistracy countrywide is close to the national average for cultural representation per head of population there are still regional variations, both in age and ethnicity, that need to be addressed.

The statistics demonstrate that the gender balance and ethnic mix of the magistracy does not appear to pose a major problem, but the same certainly cannot be said in terms of its class mix. However, in 1998, the LCD issued a consultation paper relating to the political balance in the lay magistracy, which suggested that political affiliation was no longer a major issue, and therefore did not have to be controlled in relation to the make-up of benches of magistrates. As support for its suggestion, the consultancy document made three points. First, that actually ensuring a political balance on the bench raises:

> the danger of creating a perception that politics do play a part in the administration of justice, notwithstanding that it is agreed on all sides that, in a mature democracy, politics have no place in the court room.

Second, that advisory committees:

> have increasingly found that many magistrates have declined to provide the information [relating to their political allegiance] or classed themselves as 'uncommitted'.

Third, it claimed that in any case, 'geodemographic classification schemes', based on an analysis of particular personal attributes such as ethnicity, gender, marital status, occupation, home ownership and car-owning status, are much more sensitive indicators for achieving social balance on benches than stated political allegiance.

Such 'geodemographics' might well represent the emergence of the truly classless society. Alternatively, they might represent a worrying denial of the importance of political attitudes within law generally, and the magistrates' bench in particular.

In any case, in March 2001, Jane Kennedy MP, Parliamentary Secretary to the LCD, announced that, at least for the moment, the Lord Chancellor had reluctantly decided that political balance would have to remain an issue. This statement was made in response to the disclosure that the Magistrates' Advisory Committee in Stoke-on-Trent had sent out a letter to several local organisations, which stated that:

> whilst the overriding criterion for appointment is always the suitability of the candidate, the Advisory Committee is particularly keen to receive

applications from members of ethnic minorities, shop floor workers, the unemployed and Labour Party supporters.

In answering charges that such a letter was politicising the magistracy, Ms Kennedy pointed out that:

Public confidence in lay magistrates is vital. This is achieved, first and fore-most, by individual magistrates discharging their duties effectively. It is also achieved when Benches reflect the diversity of the communities which they serve. In Stoke-on-Trent the Labour vote is significantly under-reflected on the magistrates' Bench. Of those who expressed political affiliation 40 per cent were Labour, compared to 60 per cent who voted Labour in the area at the last General Election. This compares to 47 per cent of the Bench being acknowledged Conservative voters, compared to 27 per cent in the area.

The Advisory Committee was simply and correctly trying to attract more Labour voters to apply to become magistrates, in order that the composition of the bench more broadly reflected the local voting pattern.

The age profile of magistrates

If the class make-up of the magistracy is possibly a problem, then a look at the current statistics will immediately show that the age profile and distribution of the current mag-istrates is certainly a matter for concern: 57 per cent of magistrates are aged 60 or above,

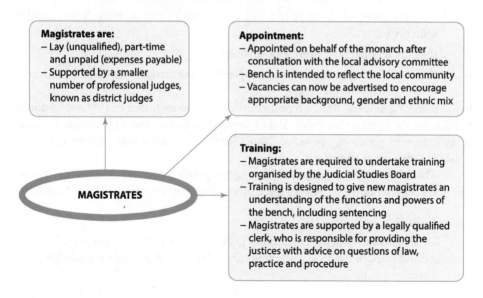

FIGURE 12.2 *Magistrates: an aide-mémoire.*

85 per cent of magistrates are at least 50 and only 0.38 per cent are below the age of 30. Given the strictures that are involved in being a magistrate, it is obvious that the older members of society are more likely to have time to offer their services as magistrates, especially those who have retired. However, the inescapable question arises as to the representative nature of such a body, especially when the core clientele is likely to be a great deal younger than they are. It was an attempt to address this problem, at least of perception if not substance, that the age for service as a magistrate was reduced from 27 to 18 in 2003. Statistics on the magistracy are available at: www.judiciary.gov.uk.

12.9.2   THE FUTURE OF THE MAGISTRATES' COURTS

In December 2000, the results of a report, *The Judiciary in the Magistrates' Courts*, were published. The extensive report was jointly commissioned by the Home Office and the LCD and provided an extremely valuable comparison between the lay magistracy and stipendiaries, now known as District Judges (magistrates' courts). It found as follows.

As regards the lay magistracy

- they are drawn overwhelmingly from professional and managerial ranks;
- 40 per cent of them are retired from full-time employment;
- the cost of an appearance before lay magistrates was £52.10 per hour.

As regards the stipendiaries

- they are younger, but are mostly male and white;
- they hear cases more quickly;
- they are more likely to refuse bail and to make use of immediate custodial sentences;
- they are less likely to need legal advisers;
- the cost of an appearance before stipendiary magistrates was £61.78 per hour.

In the following January, 2001, a report entitled *Community Justice* by Professor Andrew Sanders for the Institute for Public Policy Research called for the replacement of panels of lay justices by panels composed of district judges, the former stipendiary magistrates, assisted by two lay magistrates.

The Magistrates' Association saw the proposals as an attack on what was an extremely representative system of justice. According to its then Chair, Harry Mawdsley:

> Lay magistrates provide community justice: they are ordinary people who live and work in the local community and who have an intimate knowledge of that community.

Although praising the magistracy's gender and ethnic make-up, Mr Mawdsley nevertheless recognised the need to recruit more magistrates from working-class backgrounds.

Magistrates' sentencing power

The Auld Report into the criminal court system, issued in 2001, suggested a compromise between these two positions: the retention of the magistrates' courts as one division in a unified criminal court, with the creation of a new District Division, made up of a district judge and two magistrates, to hear mid-range either-way offences (the third division, the Crown Division, retained the role of the current Crown Court). In the event, the government declined to adopt the Auld recommendations in this regard, but instead proposed to increase the sentencing powers of the magistrates to 12 months in detention in s 154 of the Criminal Justice Act 2003.

However, as yet, the increased sentencing power under s 154 of the Criminal Justice Act 2003 has not been implemented. Under the coalition government, the Justice Ministry had intended to remove this power to increase the sentencing powers of magistrates and included a section to that end in its Legal Aid, Sentencing and Punishment of Offenders Bill. However, following the riots that took place across England in the summer of 2011, the Attorney General, Dominic Grieve, put himself at odds with the then Justice Minister, Ken Clarke, by suggesting that increasing the sentencing powers of magistrates would make the court system more efficient. To the pleasure of the Magistrates' Association, Grieve would appear to have won any argument that took place as the proposal was omitted from the subsequent Legal Aid, Sentencing and Punishment of Offenders Act (LASPO) 2012.

LASPO 2012, however, did increase magistrates' powers in relation to the fines they could impose. Criminal offences are divided into five levels, on an ascending scale of seriousness. Before LASPO 2012, the general maximum fine for a level 5 offence was £5,000, but subsequently magistrates have the power to impose unlimited fines in the most serious cases.

Criminal Justice and Courts Act 2015: Trial by single justice on the papers

The Criminal Justice and Courts Act 2015 (ss. 30, 31) introduced a new single-justice procedure under which proceedings against adults charged with summary-only, non-imprisonable offences can be considered by a single magistrate, on the papers. This means that the trial will take place without the attendance of either prosecutor or defendant, the defendant being able to engage with the court in writing. The stated purpose of this new procedure is to deal more proportionately with straightforward, uncontested cases, involving offences such as road traffic offences. Previously, many defendants either chose not to engage with the process or returned a written guilty plea. In such instances, hearings took place in an empty courtroom with only magistrates, prosecutors and court staff present. The new procedure allows such cases to be dealt with much more efficiently. Cases which prosecutors identify as being suitable for this process will be commenced by a written charge and a new type of document called a 'single justice procedure notice'. This notice will give a defendant a date to respond in writing to the allegation rather than a date to attend court; it will also be accompanied by all the evidence which the prosecutor would be relying on to prove the case. If a defendant pleads guilty and indicates they would like to have the matter dealt with in their absence, or doesn't respond to the notice, then a single magistrate will consider the case on the basis of the evidence submitted in writing by the prosecutor, and any written mitigation from the defendant. They can dismiss the charge, or convict and sentence as appropriate. However, if a defendant wishes to plead not guilty, or otherwise wants to have a hearing in a traditional courtroom, they can indicate their wishes and the current arrangements will apply.

In an article in *Criminal Law & Justice Weekly* in September 2010, entitled 'The future of the magistracy', Noel Cox used some recent changes in New Zealand practice to offer some suggestions as to the way that the role of the magistrates may evolve in England and Wales.

He sees two related processes emerging. First, the jurisdiction of magistrates has expanded in terms of number and complexity over the past few decades as a result of existing crimes being downgraded to summary or offences triable either way, with new offences tending to be categorised in that way from the outset. However, the increased use of fixed penalties for minor summary offences (see below) is a related, if apparently contradictory, development in that it reduces the number of less serious cases coming before the magistrates' courts. It should also be remembered that, to a very large extent, the role of the magistrates' courts as licensing bodies has been removed. Consequently there has been a radical shift of work to magistrates' courts and one that Cox sees as likely to continue. The threat for the lay magistracy is that the increase in the seriousness and complexity of the cases dealt with in their courts will lead, necessarily, to the further professionalisation of the magistracy in the form of increased use of district judges, and their role will be reduced to that of almost lay assessors or jury members, rather than judges.

Cox's conclusion, although not amounting to a death sentence, raised concerns among the magistracy. As he saw it:

> In England and Wales the work of District Judges is currently expanding and their importance is likely to increase, as trial by jury is effectively restricted to the most serious cases. It is also possible that the powers of justices' clerks will continue to expand. They have acquired case management powers that were once reserved to magistrates and the Justices' Clerks Society have argued that its members should sit as chairmen of the bench.
>
> The days of the justice of the peace as an active lay magistrate may be drawing to a close. As a consequence, a long tradition of voluntary community service may be lost. But it would be premature to toll the death knell of the lay magistracy.

12.9.3   MAGISTRATES' COURTS AND OUT-OF-COURT DISPOSAL OF CRIMINAL OFFENCES (OOCDS)

In 2005 the government issued its *Supporting Magistrates' Courts to Provide Justice* initiative, which went out of its way to assure the magistracy of its support. However, in July 2006 a three-department initiative involving the then Constitutional Affairs

Department, the Home Office and the Attorney General announced a new initiative: *Criminal Justice: simple, speedy, summary* or *CJSS*.

- *Simple* – dealing with some specific cases transparently by way of warning, caution or some effective remedy to prevent re-offending without the court process;
- *Speedy* – those cases that need the court process will be dealt with fairly but as quickly as possible;
- *Summary* – a much more proportionate approach still involving due process – dealing with cases during the same week.

The intention was to improve the procedure within the lower courts so that those who pleaded guilty were dealt with as quickly as possible and those who elected to go for trial did not have to wait as long as previously for their hearing. The apparent success of *CJSS* in four pilots led to its rollout to all magistrates' courts.

However, at the same time, the government was pursuing the increased use of non-court procedures for dealing with low-level criminal behaviour and disorder such as fixed penalty notices, penalty notices for disorder, and simple and conditional cautioning.

Fixed penalty notices

Similar to the already common road traffic fixed penalty notices, these generally deal with environmental offences such as litter, graffiti, fly posting and dog fouling. They can be issued to anyone over 10 years old by police, local authority officers and police community support officers.

Penalty notices for disorder

These procedures were introduced to address low-level anti-social behaviour, while also reducing police bureaucracy and paperwork. They can be issued to anyone over 16 years old. The Home Office suggests that such orders may be issued in relation to:

- intentionally harassing or scaring people;
- being drunk and disorderly in public;
- destroying or damaging property;
- petty shoplifting;
- selling alcohol to underage customers;
- selling alcohol to somebody who is obviously drunk;
- using fireworks after curfew.

Although not the same as criminal convictions, failure to pay the penalty may result in higher fines or imprisonment.

Simple cautions

These are used to deal quickly and simply with those who commit less serious crimes, without the need to take them through the court procedure. A caution is not a criminal conviction, but it will be recorded on the police database and may be used in court as evidence of bad character, or as part of an anti-social behaviour application (see above, 1.3.5). Cautions are issued where:

- there is evidence of criminal activity;
- the offender is 18 years of age or over (under the Crime and Disorder Act 1998 younger offenders are given 'reprimands' and 'final warnings' instead of simple cautions);
- the offender admits they committed the crime;
- the offender agrees to be given a caution; if they refuse they may be charged instead.

The use of cautions rather than court proceedings is at the discretion of senior police officers. However, the more serious crimes like robbery or assault must be referred to the Crown Prosecution Service.

Conditional cautions

These were introduced in the Criminal Justice Act 2003 and differ from simple cautions to the extent that the recipient must comply with certain conditions to receive the caution and to avoid prosecution for the offence allegedly committed.

The nature of the conditions that can be attached to a conditional caution must have one or more of the following objectives:

- rehabilitation – such conditions are aimed at helping to change the behaviour of the offender, in order to reduce the likelihood of their re-offending or help to reintegrate the offender into society. They may require attendance at drug or alcohol misuse programmes, or interventions tackling other addictions or personal problems, such as gambling or debt management courses;
- reparation – conditions that aim to repair, or compensate for, the damage done either directly or indirectly by the offender;
- retribution – conditional cautions can include punitive elements, which are designed to penalise the offender for their criminal activity. Such conditions, introduced in the Police and Justice Act 2006, may require the payment of a financial penalty, unpaid work for a period not exceeding 20 hours, or attendance at a specified place for a period not exceeding 20 hours.

The recipient of the caution must admit their guilt or they will be charged and face trial. As with the simple caution, a conditional caution is not a criminal conviction as such. However, it will be recorded on the police database and may be considered in court in the event of another offence. In addition the record will remain on the police database along with photographs, fingerprints and any other samples taken at the time. If the recipient breaches the condition, then they may be arrested and charged with the original offence.

It has been suggested that in the early enthusiasm for the *CJSS* programme, the magistracy had not paid sufficient attention to the 'simple' aspect of *CJSS* as set out above. However, it was not long until the magistrates and their association were complaining about the bypassing of the courts through the use of the non-court procedures.

The suspicion of the magistrates appears to be that the use of alternative mechanisms meant that incidents that should have been heard by them were being dealt with inappropriately and perhaps more leniently than they should have been in order to save police time and state money: it was estimated in October 2009 that only half the 1.4 million offenders dealt with by the justice system each year were actually prosecuted in the courts.

A report published in August 2008 by the Centre for Crime and Justice Studies at King's College London, entitled 'Summary Justice: fast – but fair?', written by Professor Rod Morgan, argued that the government policies aimed at diverting minor offences from court had actually resulted in an extensive widening of the criminal net, with individuals being brought within the ambit of the criminal justice system who would have previously been ignored or dealt with informally.

The report highlighted a rise in the numbers of convictions for violent offences, but much larger rises in the resort to cautions. Thus, convictions for serious indictable violent offences were 11 per cent higher in 2006 compared with 2001, but cautions increased by 92 per cent. The comparable figures for less serious indictable offences included a rise of 19 per cent for convictions but 195 per cent for cautions. Such findings would appear to suggest that cautions have been issued where previously no official sanction would have been applied. It also suggested that regional differences in the use of summary powers, and the fact that decision-making was made in private rather than in open court, resulted in an 'accountability deficit'.

In December 2011, the coalition Minister for Policing, Nick Herbert, addressed the National Council of the Magistrates' Association on the issue of summary justice in which he addressed some of their major concerns. He recognised the need to ask fundamental questions about the system of summary justice in order to reverse the proliferation of administrative disposals that had taken place over the previous few years. He also insisted that the magistracy should have an early role in overseeing how out-of-court sanctions are applied within their locality.

In January 2013, the then chairman of the Magistrates' Association wrote to the then Justice Secretary, Chris Grayling, calling for an inquiry into the police use of cautions, saying that the practice had 'got out of hand'. A subsequent review of simple cautions which were reported in November 2013 recommended that restrictions on their use be introduced and that a wider review of OOCDs be conducted. In response, in November 2014, the government published revised guidance on simple cautions and announced the introduction of a pilot scheme in three areas, to replace cautions with more stringent measures. It was revealed that in the 12 months to the end of March 2014, there had been 391,171 out-of-court disposals comprising 235,323 cautions, 77,933 cannabis warnings and 77,915 penalty notices for disorder.

However, at the start of December 2015, Gove announced that the criminal courts charge would no longer be imposed and that a review would be conducted to consider alternative ways of ensuring that criminals pay their fair share of costs.

Magistrates and the public

In May 2012 the Magistrates' Association published the conclusions of what it described as 'a public engagement programme designed to gain an understanding of people's views on the future of summary justice and the role of magistrates'. The material gathered generated the following conclusions:

- Members of the public believe it is essential that those sitting in judgement on others should be people living or working in the communities they serve but, as judicial office-holders, should be totally independent, impartial, properly trained and competent.
- There is a lack of understanding about the extent of the role of the magistracy, although there does seem to be a belief that magistrates should be involved in all parts of the justice system including out-of-court disposals.
- The magistracy is not yet truly representative of the communities it serves especially in terms of class, age and diversity.
- For most people, and particularly victims, the processes of the justice system are still very difficult to comprehend and access.
- Punishment is expected to be part of a sentence but the priority for the public is for visible action such as community payback to stop re-offending and for magistrates to monitor and review sentences.
- The public wants to know more about the justice system from the practitioners themselves.

In the light of such conclusions, the association recognised the need to build the public's confidence in the magistracy and proposed that it should be the foundation of a community-focused justice system. However, in order to achieve such an objective, it also recognised and adopted the slogan that the magistracy must become more 'active, accessible and engaged' through strengthening and more clearly defining its roles and responsibilities.

CHAPTER SUMMARY: THE JUDICIARY

THE CONSTITUTIONAL ROLE OF THE JUDICIARY

Judges play a central role in the UK constitution. The doctrine of the separation of powers maintains that the judicial function be kept distinct from the legislative and executive functions of the state.

THE CONSTITUTIONAL ROLE OF THE LORD CHANCELLOR

The Lord Chancellor held an anomalous position in respect of the separation of powers within the UK constitution, in that they were at one and the same time: the most senior member of the judiciary and able to hear cases in the House of Lords as a court; a member of the legislature as Speaker of the House of Lords as a legislative assembly; and a member of the executive holding a position in the government. The Constitutional Reform Act 2005 dealt with the problem and subsequently the Lord Chancellor's Department has been replaced by a Ministry of Justice.

JUDICIAL OFFICES

The main judicial offices are the Lord Chancellor, the Lord Chief Justice, the Master of the Rolls, the President of the Family Division, the Vice Chancellor and the Senior Presiding Judge. Law Lords are referred to as Lords of Appeal in Ordinary. Court of Appeal judges are referred to as Lords Justices of Appeal.

APPOINTMENT OF THE JUDICIARY

The Constitutional Reform Act 2005 brought about a Judicial Appointment Commission, to replace the much-maligned previous system based on alleged secret soundings of the judiciary. However, the first appointments of the Commission have themselves been subjected to some criticisms for the conservative nature of the appointments made.

TRAINING OF THE JUDICIARY

Training of English judges is undertaken under the auspices of the Judicial College. Judges from the highest Law Lord to the lowest magistrate are subject to training. It is gratifying to note that anti-discriminatory training is a priority, although some have continued to express doubt about judicial attitudes in this regard. General training focuses on various aspects of discrimination, and special training was undertaken in relation to the Woolf reforms and the introduction of the Human Rights Act. This being said, it remains arguable that the training undergone by UK judges is not as rigorous as the training of judges on the Continent.

REMOVAL OF JUDGES

Senior judges hold office subject to good behaviour. They can be removed by an address by the two Houses of Parliament.

Judges below High Court status can be removed by the Lord Chancellor on grounds of misbehaviour or incapacity and they can remove magistrates without the need to show cause.

JUDICIAL IMMUNITY

To ensure judicial integrity, it is provided that judges cannot be sued for actions done or words said in the course of their judicial function.

This immunity extends to trial lawyers, witnesses and juries.

MAGISTRATES

Magistrates have powers in relation to both criminal and civil law.

District Judges (Magistrates' Courts) are professional and are legally qualified.

Lay magistrates are not paid and they are not legally qualified.

Magistrates are appointed by the Lord Chancellor.

Important issues relate to the representative nature of the magistracy.

THE CONSTITUTIONAL REFORM ACT

The essential features of the Act were designed to inspire transparency, openness and greater public confidence in Britain's constitution. Government ministers are now under a statutory duty to uphold the independence of the judiciary and are specifically barred from trying to influence judicial decisions through any special access to judges. The post of Lord Chancellor has been transformed with transfer of their judicial functions to the President of the Courts of England and Wales, the Lord Chief Justice. He will be responsible for the training, guidance and deployment of judges. He will also be responsible for representing the views of the judiciary of England and Wales to Parliament and ministers.

A new, independent Supreme Court, separate from the House of Lords, was established in 2009.

A new system of appointing judges, independent of the patronage of politicians, has been established. Appointments will be solely on the basis of merit and solely on the recommendation of the newly constituted Judicial Appointments Commission.

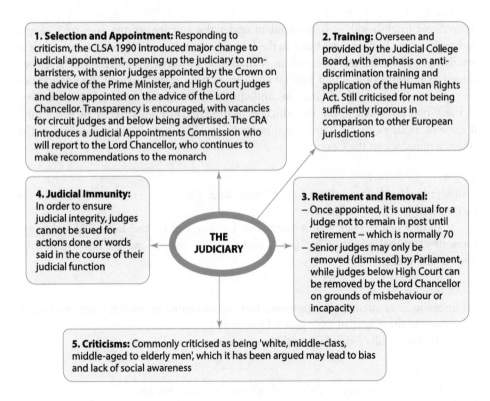

1. Selection and Appointment: Responding to criticism, the CLSA 1990 introduced major change to judicial appointment, opening up the judiciary to non-barristers, with senior judges appointed by the Crown on the advice of the Prime Minister, and High Court judges and below appointed on the advice of the Lord Chancellor. Transparency is encouraged, with vacancies for circuit judges and below being advertised. The CRA introduces a Judicial Appointments Commission who will report to the Lord Chancellor, who continues to make recommendations to the monarch

2. Training: Overseen and provided by the Judicial College Board, with emphasis on anti-discrimination training and application of the Human Rights Act. Still criticised for not being sufficiently rigorous in comparison to other European jurisdictions

4. Judicial Immunity: In order to ensure judicial integrity, judges cannot be sued for actions done or words said in the course of their judicial function

THE JUDICIARY

3. Retirement and Removal:
– Once appointed, it is unusual for a judge not to remain in post until retirement – which is normally 70
– Senior judges may only be removed (dismissed) by Parliament, while judges below High Court can be removed by the Lord Chancellor on grounds of misbehaviour or incapacity

5. Criticisms: Commonly criticised as being 'white, middle-class, middle-aged to elderly men', which it has been argued may lead to bias and lack of social awareness

FIGURE 12.3 *The Judiciary: an aide-mémoire.*

FOOD FOR THOUGHT

1   Much has been made of the creation of a new Supreme Court but the issue to consider is whether, as has been suggested, a first-class Appeal Court has been replaced by a second-class Supreme Court. In particular, what distinguishes the UK Supreme Court from, for example, the Supreme Court of the United States?

2   Consider whether judicial training should be for a profession in its own right, rather than as an adjunct to another profession, such as the Bar.

3   In the context of the magistrates' courts, consider whether there is a place for non-legally qualified judges and whether the age of most magistrates leads to particular problems.

4   Following the English riots of summer 2011, there was some accusation of heavy-handed sentencing policy in the magistrates' courts. This raises questions as to whether magistrates' current sentencing powers should be raised from six to 12 months. Consider the pros and cons of any such change.

FURTHER READING

Bell, J and Engle, G (Sir), *Cross on Statutory Interpretation*, 1995, London: Butterworths

Bennion, F, *Statutory Interpretation*, 1992, London: Butterworths

Bindman, G, 'Lessons of Pinochet' (1999) 149 NLJ 1050

Bindman, G, 'Lessons of history' (2009) 159 NLJ 1110

Blom-Cooper, L, 'Age of judicial responsibility' [2009] PL 429

Cox, N, 'The future of magistracy' (2010) CLJ Weekly, Sept 18

Denning (Lord), *Due Process of Law*, 1980, London: Butterworths

Denning (Lord), *The Discipline of Law*, 1979, London: Butterworths

Dowell, K, 'Neuberger gains political clout after attacking Supreme Court' (2009) 23(35) Lawyer 48

Hunter, R, McGlynn, C and Rackley, E, *Feminist Judgments: From Theory to Practice*, 2010, Oxford: Hart Publishing

Parker, C, 'Judicial decision making' (1999) 149 NLJ 1142

Pearl, D, 'Judging success' (2009) Counsel 13

Pickles, J, *Straight from the Bench*, 1987, London: Hodder and Stoughton

Rackley, E, *Women, Judging and the Judiciary: From Difference to Diversity*, 2014, London: Routledge

Reid (Lord), 'The judge as law maker' (1972) 12 JSPTL 22

Stevens, R, *English Judges: Their Role in the Changing Constitution*, 2005, Oxford: Hart

Weinreb, L, *Legal Reason: The Use of Analogy in Legal Argument*, 2004, Cambridge: CUP

USEFUL WEBSITES

http://webarchive.nationalarchives.gov.uk/+/http://www.dca.gov.uk/judges/diversity.htm

An archived webpage on information regarding the Lord Chancellor's commitment to ensuring 'a judiciary of the highest calibre, with candidates drawn from the widest possible range of available talent'.

www.judiciary.gov.uk
The official website for the Judiciary of England and Wales.

www.justice.gov.uk
Justice Ministry website.

www.supremecourt.uk
Official website of the Supreme Court.

www.gov.uk/government/uploads/system/uploads/attachment_data/file/217354/judicial-diversity-report-2010.pdf
Improving Judicial Diversity: Progress towards delivery of the 'Report of the Advisory Panel on Judicial Diversity 2010', May 2011.

COMPANION WEBSITE

Now visit the companion website to:

- test your understanding of the key terms using our Flashcard Glossary;
- revise and consolidate your knowledge of 'The judiciary' using our multiple choice question testbank;
- view all of the links to the Useful Websites above.

www.routledge.com/cw/slapper

JUDICIAL REASONING AND POLITICS

13

The popular perception of the judicial process is described by David Kairys as government by law, not people, together with the understanding that law is separate from, and superior to, politics, economics, culture and the values and preferences of judges. This perception is based on particular attributes of the decision-making process itself, which Kairys suggests comprises, among other things: the judicial recognition of their subservient role in constitutional theory; their passive role in the operation of the doctrine of precedent; their subordinate role in the determination and interpretation of legislation; and the '*quasi-scientific*, objective nature of legal analysis, and *technical* expertise of judges and lawyers' (*The Politics of Law: A Progressive Critique* (1982)). To the extent that law is generally portrayed as quasi-scientific, the operation of objective, technical and hence supposedly neutral rules, the decisions that judges make are accepted as legitimate by the public. It is necessary, therefore, to consider the nature of reasoning in general and the extent to which judges make use of such reasoning, before considering the social location of the judges. It is only on the basis of the *non-existence* of distinct and strictly applied principles of legal reasoning that the *existence* of judicial creativity and the *possibility* of judicial bias come into consideration.

There is a long-running controversy as to the relationship of law and logic and the actual extent to which legal decisions are the outcome of, and limited by, logical processes. At times, lawyers have sought to reject what is seen as the rigid inflexibility inherent in logical reasoning in favour of flexibility and discretion. As the American Supreme Court Judge, eminent legal writer and proponent of *Legal Realism* Oliver Wendell Holmes expressed it: 'The life of the law has not been logic, it has been experience' (*The Common Law* (1881)).

The implication of this position is that the law is no more than a mechanism for solving particular problems and that judges should operate in such a way as to

13.3.2 INDUCTIVE REASONING

The second classic form of reasoning, *inductive reasoning*, may be described as arguing from the part to the whole; from the particular to the general. Inductive reasoning differs from deductive reasoning in two major respects:

1   It reaches a conclusion that is *not* simply a restatement of what is already contained in the basic premises.
2   It is *less certain* in its conclusions than deductive logic.

An example of this type of reasoning would be:

> The sun has always risen in the east.
> Therefore, the sun will rise in the east tomorrow.

If the premise is true, then the conclusion is probably true, but not 100 per cent necessarily so because the conclusion is not contained in the premise, but is a projection from it. On the basis of past experience, we can reasonably expect the sun to rise in the east tomorrow, but there is the possibility, no matter how remote it might be, that something might happen to the sun, or indeed the earth, to prevent its appearance tomorrow. The point is that we cannot predict with 100 per cent accuracy what will happen in the future just because it happened in the past. Because the inductive argument goes beyond the content of its premises, it provides the power to predict events, but it gives predictive power at the expense of certainty in its conclusion.

An alternative example of this type of inductive reasoning would be:

> John is lying dead with a bullet in his head.
> Jane is standing over him with a smoking gun in her hand.
> Therefore, it can be concluded that Jane shot John.

Now, the conclusion may be reasonable under the circumstances, but there are other possible explanations for the scene. Jane may have simply picked up the gun after someone else had shot John. We cannot actually tell who killed John, but we may reasonably suspect Jane of the crime and she would be the first person to be questioned to confirm either her guilt or innocence. The investigation of this event would use a form of reasoning equivalent to scientific reasoning. From available data, a hypothesis would be formed; in this case, that Jane killed John. Investigations would then be undertaken to test the validity of the hypothesis. Depending on the outcome of the investigation, the original hypothesis would be either accepted, rejected or refined.

13.3.3 REASONING BY ANALOGY

A third type of reasoning is *reasoning by example or analogy*. If deductive reasoning involves reasoning from the whole to the part, and inductive reasoning involves reasoning from the part to the whole, then reasoning by analogy involves reasoning from part to part.

An example of this type of reasoning would be:

Wood floats on water.

Plastic is like wood.

Therefore, plastic floats on water.

Or similarly:

Wood floats on water.

Stone is like wood.

Therefore, stone floats on water.

It can be seen that the truth of the conclusion depends completely on the accuracy of the analogy. The connection between the two objects that are being compared depends on weighing up and assessing their similarities and their differences. Only some characteristics are similar, and the question is whether those are more important than the differences between the two objects. If the analogy is valid, then the conclusion may very well be equally valid, although not necessarily correct, but, if it is not valid, then the conclusion will certainly be wrong, as the above examples demonstrate.

13.4 JUDICIAL REASONING

It is now appropriate to determine whether, or to what extent, judges use logical reasoning in reaching their decisions in particular cases and to determine which forms, if any, they make use of.

13.4.1 THE SYLLOGISM IN LAW

Some statutory provisions and also some common law rules can be expressed in the form of a syllogism. For example, the offence of theft may be reduced into such a formulation:

If A dishonestly appropriates B's property with the intention of permanently depriving B of it, then A is guilty of theft.

A has done this.

Therefore, A is guilty of theft.

This, however, represents an oversimplification of the structure of statute but, more importantly, the effect of concentrating on the logical form of the offence tends to marginalise the key issues in relation to its actual application. As has been stated previously, the great majority of cases are decided on the *truth* of the premises rather than the formal *validity* of the argument used. In other words, argument will concentrate primarily on whether A actually did the act or not and, second, on whether A appropriated the property either 'dishonestly' or 'with the intention of permanently depriving' B of it. Those are questions of fact, not logic.

13.4.2   THE LOGICAL FORM OF PRECEDENT

The operation of the rules of precedent appears, at first sight, to involve a similar operation of deductive logic to that applied in statute law: the judge merely applies the legal principle established in the precedent to the facts in hand to determine the outcome of the case. Thus:

> Precedent: in case X involving particular circumstances, legal principle Y was applied leading to conclusion Z.
>
> *Instant case*: in case W, similar circumstances to those in X have occurred.
>
> Therefore: principle Y must be applied to reach a conclusion similar to Z.

A closer consideration of the actual procedure involved in precedent, however, will reveal that it is not totally accurate to categorise precedent as a form of deductive reasoning.

In looking for a precedent on which to base a decision, judges are faced with a large number of cases from which to select. It is extremely unlikely that judges will find an authority that corresponds precisely to the facts of the case before them. What they have to do is to find an analogous case and use its reasoning to decide the case before them. This use of analogy to decide cases is prone to the same shortcomings as were revealed in the previous consideration of reasoning from analogy in general. The major difficulty is the need to ensure the validity of the analogy made, if the conclusion drawn is to be valid. There is, no doubt, considerable merit in the wish for similar cases to be treated similarly, but given the lack of precision that is inherent in the process of reasoning by analogy, it is not altogether certain that such a wish will be met.

A further reason why the operation of precedent cannot simply be considered as an example of deductive reasoning relates to the process through which the precedent is actually determined once an analogous case has been selected. The binding element in any precedent is the *ratio decidendi* of the decision. In delivering his decision, the judge does not separate the *ratio* of the case from other *obiter* comments. As has been considered previously, the *ratio* is a legal abstraction from the concrete facts of the case in which it appears, and in practice, it is for judges in subsequent cases to determine the *ratio* of any authority. The determination of the *ratio* and thus the precedent in a previous case may be seen as a process of *inductive reasoning*, in that the judge in the present case derives the *general* principle of the *ratio* from the *particular* facts of the previous case. This move from the particular to the general is by its nature inductive. The point to be remembered here is that, as was considered in relation to reasoning in general, the use of inductive reasoning cannot claim the certainty inherent in the use of deductive reasoning. The introduction of this increased element of uncertainty is inescapable and unconscious, but it is also appropriate to note that the determination of precedent by later courts gives the later judges scope to *consciously* manipulate precedents. This is achieved by the later judges formulating the *ratio* of a previous case in the light of their opinion as to what it *should* have been, rather than what it might actually have been. In other words, they have the scope to substitute their version of the *ratio*, even if it contradicts what the original judge thought the *ratio* was.

Thus, the apparent deductive certainty of the use of precedent is revealed to be based on the much less certain use of inductive reasoning and reasoning by analogy, with even the possibility of personal views of the judges playing some part in deciding cases. This latter factor introduces the possibility that judges do not in fact use any form of logical reasoning to decide their cases, but simply deliver decisions on the basis of an intuitive response to the facts of the case and the situation of the parties involved. The suggestion has been made that judges decide the outcome of the case first of all and only then seek some *post hoc* legal justification for their decision; and given the huge number of precedents from which they are able to choose, they have no great difficulty in finding such support as they require. The process of logical reasoning can be compared to the links in a chain, one following the other, but a more fitting metaphor for judicial reasoning would be to compare it with the legs of a chair: forced into place to support the weight of a conclusion reached *a priori*. Some critics have even gone so far as to deny the existence of legal reasoning altogether as a method of determining decisions, and have suggested that references to such are no more than a means of justifying the social and political decisions that judges are called upon to make.

In conclusion, however, it is not suggested that legal reasoning does not employ the use of logic, but neither can it be asserted that it is only a matter of logic. Perhaps the only conclusion that can be reached is that legal reasoning as exercised by the judiciary is an amalgam; part deductive, part inductive, part reasoning by analogy, with an added mixture of personal intuition, not to say personal prejudice.

13.4.3 LEGAL REASONING AND RHETORIC

Following on from the previous questioning of the logical nature of legal reasoning, it might be valuable to consider further the claim that legal decisions are not the outcome of a process of logical reasoning, but are in fact the products of a completely different form of communication. According to Peter Goodrich (*Reading the Law* (1986) at 171):

> the legal art is an art of interpretation; it is concerned not with a necessary or scientific logic, but with probable arguments, with evaluative reasoning and not with absolute certainty. Rhetoric is the discipline which most explicitly studies the techniques relevant to presenting and evaluating, affirming or refuting, such probable arguments . . . rhetoric, here, is defined as the reading of legal texts as acts of communication, as discourse designed to influence, to persuade and to induce action.

the requirements of natural justice and granted a declaration that his dismissal was null and void.

A *prohibiting order*, formerly known as *prohibition*, is similar to *certiorari* in that it relates to invalid acts of public authorities, but it is different to the extent that it is pre-emptive and prescriptive in regard to any such activity and operates to prevent the authority from taking invalid decisions in the first place. An example of the use of the order arose in *R v Telford Justices ex p Badhan* (1991). In this case, an order was issued to stop committal proceedings in relation to an alleged rape that had not been reported until some 14 years after the alleged incident. The delay meant that the defendant would have been unable to prepare a proper defence against the charge.

A *mandatory order*, formerly known as *mandamus*, may be seen as the obverse of a prohibiting order, in that it is an order issued by the High Court instructing an inferior court or some other public authority to carry out a duty laid on them. Such an order is frequently issued in conjunction with an order of *certiorari*, to the effect that a public body is held to be using its powers improperly and is instructed to use them in a proper fashion. In *R v Poplar BC (Nos 1 and 2)* (1922), the court ordered the borough council to pay over money due to the county council and to levy a rate to raise the money if necessary. Failure to comply with the order led to the imprisonment of some of the borough councillors.

In *O'Reilly v Mackman* (1982), however, the House of Lords decided that issues relating to *public* rights could *only* be enforced by means of the judicial review procedure, and that it would be an abuse of process for an applicant to seek a declaration by writ in relation to an alleged breach of a public duty or responsibility by a public authority. In deciding the case in this way, the House of Lords did much to demarcate and emphasise the role of judicial review as the method of challenging public authorities in their performance of their powers and duties in public law.

13.5.3   GROUNDS FOR APPLICATION FOR JUDICIAL REVIEW

Judicial review allows people with a sufficient interest in a decision or action by a public body to ask a judge to review the lawfulness of:

(a)   an enactment; or

(b)   a decision, action or failure to act in relation to the exercise of a public function.

However, it is not an appeal on the merits of a decision. The grounds of application can be considered under two heads: *procedural ultra vires* and *substantive ultra vires*.

Procedural ultra vires, as its name suggests, relates to the failure of a person or body, provided with specific authority, to follow the procedure established for using that power. It also covers instances where a body exercising a judicial function fails to follow the requirements of natural justice by acting as prosecutor and judge in the same case or not permitting the accused person to make representations to the panel deciding the case.

Substantive ultra vires occurs where someone does something that is not actually authorised by the enabling legislation. In *Associated Provincial Picture House v*

Wednesbury Corp (1947), Lord Greene MR established the possibility of challenging discretionary decisions on the basis of unreasonableness.

Lord Greene's approach was endorsed and refined by Lord Diplock in *Council of Civil Service Unions v Minister for the Civil Service* (1984), in which he set out the three recognised grounds for judicial review, namely:

- illegality;
- irrationality;
- procedural impropriety.

Lord Diplock, however, introduced the possibility of a much more wide-ranging reason for challenging administrative decisions: namely, the doctrine of *proportionality*. Behind this doctrine is the requirement that there should be a reasonable relation between a decision and its objectives. It requires the achievement of particular ends by means that are not more oppressive than they need be to attain those ends. The potentially innovative aspect of this doctrine is the extent to which it looks to the substance of the decisions rather than simply focusing on the way in which they are reached.

Lord Diplock's listing of proportionality within the grounds for judicial review was controversial, if not at the very least arguably mistaken. Proportionality, however, is a key principle within the jurisdiction of the ECtHR, and is used frequently to assess the validity of state action which interferes with individual rights protected under the Convention. Consequently, as the HRA has incorporated the European Convention into UK law, proportionality will be a part of UK jurisprudence and legal practice, at least in cases that fall within the scope of the HRA. Although HRA cases and judicial review are different and distinct procedures, nonetheless, it is surely a mere matter of time before the doctrine of proportionality is applied by the judges in judicial review cases unrelated to the Convention.

Indeed, such an approach was supported by Lord Slynn in *R v Secretary of State for the Environment, Transport and the Regions ex p Holding and Barnes* (2001), in which he stated ([2001] 2 All ER 929 at 975):

> The European Court of Justice does of course apply the principle of proportionality when examining such acts and national judges must apply the same principle when dealing with Community law issues. There is a difference between that principle and the approach of the English courts in *Associated Provincial Picture Houses Ltd v Wednesbury Corporation* [1948] 1 KB 223. But the difference in practice is not as great as is sometimes supposed. The cautious approach of the European Court of Justice in applying the principle is shown *inter alia* by the margin of appreciation it accords to the institutions of the Community in making economic assessments. I consider that even without reference to the Human Rights Act the time has come to recognise that this principle is part of English administrative law, not

13.5.4.2   Partial exclusion clauses

Where legislation has provided for a limited time period within which parties have to apply for judicial review, then applications outside of the period will not be successful. In *Smith v East Elloe Rural DC* (1956), the House of Lords, although only by a three-to-two majority, recognised the effectiveness of a six-week limitation clause in the Acquisition of Land (Authorisation Procedure) Act 1946. Although that case was subject to criticism in *Anisminic Ltd v Foreign Compensation Commission* (1969), it was explained and followed in *R v Secretary of State for the Environment ex p Ostler* (1976).

In response to the Franks Committee's recommendation that judicial review should not be subject to exclusion, s 14(1) of the Tribunals and Inquiries Act 1971 was enacted to that end. Unfortunately, it applies only to pre-1958 legislation.

13.5.4.3   The Criminal Justice & Courts Act 2015 and judicial review

In November 2012 the Prime Minister, David Cameron, announced that his government intended to 'get a grip' on people forcing unnecessary delays to government policy by 'cracking down' on the 'massive growth industry' of judicial review.

Following a consultation exercise in 2013, the Justice Ministry announced proposals to reduce the number of judicial review cases, including the following:

- reducing the time limits for bringing a judicial review relating to planning issues from the previous three months to six weeks;

- removing the right to an oral hearing where a judge refuses permission where there has been a prior judicial process, or where the claim was judged to be totally without merit. Consequently any right to appeal to the Court of Appeal would be on the papers;

- the introduction of a new fee for an oral renewal so that fees charged in Judicial Review proceedings better reflected the costs of providing the service. These were increased in line with all court fees under *The Civil Proceedings Fees (Amendment) Order 2014*;

- providing that immigration and asylum judicial review hearings be transferred to the specialist Upper Tier Tribunal rather than the High Court which had previously heard them.

In September 2013 the government's widely imputed antagonism towards judicial review was further evidenced when the Ministry of Justice issued a consultation document entitled *Judicial Review: Proposals For Further Reform*. The consultation exercise sought views on proposals in the following areas:

- a number of measures to rebalance the system of financial incentives so that those involved have a proportionate interest in the costs of the case, including amending payment of legal aid in judicial review cases (subsequently enacted in part 4 of the Criminal Justice and Courts Act (CJ&CA) 2015 below).

- how the courts deal with minor procedural defects that would have made no difference to the final decision. (By virtue of s 84 of the CJ&CA 2015, where the court is of the view that it is 'highly likely' that the result would remain the same, irrespective of the error alleged, it is obliged to refuse the action for judicial review.)

- speeding up appeals to the Supreme Court in important cases. It is apparent from the outset that some cases are going to end up in the Supreme Court and the government wants to reduce the length of time and expense involved by cutting out the need for such cases to go through the Court of Appeal before their inevitable appearance there. (Sections 63–66 of the CJ&CA 2015 allows for this to take place in relation to cases which concern a point of law of general public importance. These provisions apply in all cases, not just those involving judicial review, so mark a considerable extension in relation to the rules relating to 'leapfrog appeals' (see above, 6.6). They also apply to decisions of the Upper Tribunal, the Employment Appeal Tribunal and the Special Immigration Appeals Commission.)

- a new specialist 'planning chamber' for challenges relating to major developments to be taken only by expert judges using streamlined processes. (This court was established in July 2014. In the previous November, immigration and asylum judicial review cases had been transferred from the High Court to the specialist Upper Tier Tribunal.)

- the potential to reform the test for standing, i.e. who is able to bring a judicial review. (This measure was not enacted.)

Such proposals met much opposition, including that of Lord Neuberger, President of the Supreme Court, who spoke out against the attack on judicial review in a speech, in October 2013, in which he expressed the view that:

> The courts have no more important function than that of protecting citizens from the abuses and excesses of the executive-central government, local government or other public bodies. We must look at any proposed changes with particular care . . . bearing in mind that the proposed changes come from the very body which is at the receiving end of judicial reviews.

In spite of such criticism, the government carried on with many substantive reforms. The most significant changes were contained in Part 3, Courts and tribunals, and Part 4, Judicial review, of the Criminal Justice and Courts Act 2015 as cited above.

Among the financial measures in Part 4 of the Act are the following:

- a requirement that applicants for judicial review reveal at the outset how their claim is to be funded and the resources available from others behind the scenes, including, in the case of companies with insufficient resources, their members;

- a requirement on the Court to consider making orders for costs against third parties who are providing financial support to claimants or who are likely to be able to do so;

- a rule that other parties may not be ordered to pay a third party intervener's costs other than in exceptional circumstances;
- a rule that third party interveners in judicial review claims be liable for their own costs and the costs of the other parties that arise from their intervention, other than in exceptional circumstances;
- restriction on the Court's ability to make protective costs orders limiting a claimant's exposure to liability to pay the other side's costs if unsuccessful.

In October 2015 the Bingham Centre, JUSTICE and the Public Law Project jointly published an extremely informative introduction to the judicial review reform provisions in Part 4 of the Criminal Justice and Courts Act 2015. The document was praised by no less an authority than Lord Woolf who, in a foreword to it, wrote: 'It deals with Part 4 of the Act in an exemplary manner. It sets out in clear terms what should be the approach. Its authors are to be congratulated for what they have achieved.' The full title of the document is *Judicial Review and the Rule of Law: An Introduction to the Criminal Justice and Courts Act 2015, Part 4*.

In the same month the Public Law Project also published a wider examination of judicial review under the title The Value and Effects of Judicial Review: The Nature of Claims, their Outcomes and Consequences, written by Varda Bondy, Lucinda Platt and Maurice Sunkin.

The authors preface their summary with the following cautionary comment:

> There are a number of widely held and influential assumptions about the costs and misuse of JR. First, that the past growth in the use of JR has been largely driven by claimants abusing the system, either deliberately or otherwise. Second, that the effect of JR on public administration is largely negative because JR makes it more difficult for public bodies to deliver public services efficiently. Third, that JR litigation tends to be an expensive and time consuming detour concerned with technical matters of procedure that rarely alters decisions of public bodies. These claims have been challenged for their lack of empirical basis and this study provides additional evidence which shows them to be at best misleading and at worst false.

13.6 POLITICS AND THE JUDICIARY

Law is an inherently and inescapably political process. Even assertions as to the substantive autonomy of law (see Chapters 1, 3 and 4) merely disguise the fact that, in making legal decisions, judges decide where the weight of public approval is to be placed and which forms of behaviour are to be sanctioned (see, for example *R v Brown* (1993), where the House of Lords criminalised the sexual activities of consenting sadomasochists, arguably without fully comprehending some aspects of what was going on).

There is, however, an increasingly apparent tendency for contemporary judges to become actively, directly and openly engaged in more overtly political activity. The 1955

Kilmuir rules, named after the Lord Chancellor who introduced them, were designed to control the instances when the judiciary could express opinion in the media. The rules were abrogated in 1987 by Lord Mackay and, since then, the judiciary have been more forthcoming in expressing their views, not just on matters strictly related to their judicial functions but also on wider political matters.

13.6.1   THE POLITICS OF JUDICIAL REVIEW AND THE HUMAN RIGHTS ACT

As has been stated, the HRA merely heightened the potential for conflict between the judges and the executive and Parliament, but the relationship was already subject to some tension as a consequence of the operation of judicial review, as can be seen in a number of cases.

In *M v Home Office* (1993), the House of Lords decided that the court has jurisdiction in judicial review proceedings to grant interim and final injunctions against officers of the Crown, and to make a finding of contempt of court against a government department or a minister of the Crown in either his personal *or his official capacity*.

M v Home Office is of signal importance in establishing the powers of the courts in relation to the executive. It is also interesting to note that in delivering the leading speech, Lord Woolf quoted extensively from, and clearly supported, Dicey's view of the rule of law as involving the subjection of all, including state officials, to the ordinary law of the land (see Chapter 2).

In November 1994, the government suffered two damaging blows from the judiciary. In *R v Secretary of State for Foreign Affairs ex p World Development Movement Ltd* (1995), the Queen's Bench Divisional Court held that the Secretary of State had acted beyond his powers in granting aid to the Malaysian government in relation to the Pergau Dam project. The financial assistance was given, not for the promotion of development *per se*, as authorised by s 1 of the Overseas Development and Co-operation Act 1980, but in order to facilitate certain arms sales. As Rose LJ stated ([1995] 1 All ER 611 at 626):

> Whatever the Secretary of State's intention or purpose may have been, it is, as it seems to me, a matter for the courts and not for the Secretary of State to determine whether, on the evidence before the court, the particular conduct was, or was not, within the statutory purpose.

In *R v Secretary of State for the Home Department ex p Fire Brigades Union* (1995), the Court of Appeal held that the Home Secretary had committed an abuse of power in implementing a scheme designed to cut the level of payments made to the subjects of criminal injuries. The court held that he was under an obligation, under the CJA 1988, to put the previous non-statutory scheme on a statutory basis. It was not open for the Secretary of State to use his prerogative powers to introduce a completely new tariff scheme contrary to the intention of Parliament as expressed in the CJA 1988. The decision of the Court of Appeal was confirmed by a three-to-two majority in the House of Lords in April 1995, the majority holding that the Secretary of State had exceeded or abused powers granted to him by Parliament. It is of interest to note that in his minority judg-ment Lord Keith warned that to dismiss the Home Secretary's appeal would be:

> an unwarrantable intrusion into the political field and a usurpation of the function of Parliament.

In 1997, in *R v Secretary of State for the Home Department ex p Venables and Thompson*, the House of Lords decided that the Home Secretary had misused his powers in relation to two juveniles who had been sentenced to detention during Her Majesty's pleasure.

Even Lord Chancellors have not escaped the unwanted control of judicial review, and in March 1997 John Witham successfully argued that the Lord Chancellor had exceeded his statutory powers in removing exemptions from court fees for those in receipt of state income support (*R v Lord Chancellor ex p Witham* (1997)).

The change of government in 1997 did nothing to stem the flow of judicial review cases, with the occasional embarrassing defeat for the executive. Thus, in *R v Secretary of State for Education and Employment ex p National Union of Teachers* (2000), the Divisional Court held that the Secretary of State for Education had exceeded his statutory powers in seeking to alter teachers' contracts of employment, particularly by introducing threshold standards in relation to a new scheme of performance-related pay. He had sought to introduce the changes in the Education (School Teachers' Pay and Conditions) (No 2) Order 2000 after only four days' consultation with the trade union. The court held that although the Secretary of State had the statutory powers to alter the contracts of employment under the Teachers' Pay and Conditions Act 1991, he had not adopted the correct procedure for doing so as set out in that Act. Consequently, the Education (School Teachers' Pay and Conditions) (No 2) Order was quashed. Although this decision represented a victory for the union and an embarrassment for the Secretary of State, it was only temporary in nature and the new contracts were subsequently introduced following the proper statutory procedure.

Given its centrality in the operation of the criminal justice system and immigration, it is hardly surprising that the Home Department is subject to more claims for judicial review than any other ministry, nor is it surprising that some of them go against it.

In *Alvi v Secretary of State for the Home Department* (2012), the Supreme Court ruled that the Home Secretary could not introduce substantive immigration requirements through policy decisions, guidance or instructions, rather than in the body of the immigration rules themselves. The list of skilled occupations used to assess immigration requests was held not to be part of the Immigration Rules, as the document in which that list was set out had not been laid before Parliament as was required under s 3(2) of the Immigration Act 1971. Although similar to *R v Secretary of State for Education & Employment ex p NUT*, the consequence of the decision had important implications for the operation of immigration policy and was not likely to be so easily remedied. As the Supreme Court acknowledged in reaching its conclusion:

the volume of material that will now have to be laid to give effect to the court's judgment will impose a heavy burden on Parliament and on the Secondary Legislation Scrutiny Committee of the House of Lords in particular.

Although it did offer a possible solution requiring a change in parliamentary procedure:

Methods of communication today are very different from what they were in 1971 when the statutory requirement, which involves laying hard copies of every paper that has to be laid in each House, was introduced. The court questions whether the current system, which is now over forty years old, is still fit for its purpose today. But any changes to it must be a matter for Parliament.

It can be seen from the foregoing that judicial review provided the judiciary with the means for addressing the potential for abuse that followed on from the growth of discretionary power in the hands of the modern State, particularly if it was operated on the basis of the doctrine of proportionality. Alongside the growth in the number of applications, there were also indications that at least some of the higher judiciary saw it as part of their function to exercise such control over the executive. For example, the former Master of the Rolls and former Lord Chief Justice, Lord Bingham, was quoted in *The Observer* newspaper of 9 May 1993 as saying that:

Slowly, the constitutional balance is tilting towards the judiciary. The courts have reacted to the increase in powers claimed by the government by being more active themselves.

Judicial review is a delicate exercise and by necessity draws the judiciary into the political arena, using the word 'political' in its widest, non-party sense. That the judges were aware of this is evident from the words of Lord Woolf in the same article. As he recognised:

Judicial review is all about balance: between the rights of the individual and his need to be treated fairly, and the rights of government at local and national level to do what it has been elected to do. There is a very sensitive and political decision to be made.

However, another former Law Lord, Lord Browne-Wilkinson, observed on a BBC radio programme, admittedly before his elevation to the House of Lords, that a great void was apparent in the political system, deriving from the fact that no government had a true popular majority and yet all governments were able to carry Parliament in support of anything they wanted. He went on to express the view that Parliament was not a place where it was easy to get accountability for abuse or misuse of powers. According to Lord Browne-Wilkinson, while judicial review could not overcome the will of Parliament, judges had a special role because *democracy was defective*. He then asked a rhetorical question as to who else but the judges could ensure that executive action is taken in accordance with law, *and not abused by increasingly polarised political stances*.

Such thinking is also evident in an article by Mr Justice Stephen Sedley (as he was then) in the May 1995 edition of the *London Review of Books*, in which he asserted that, after decades of passivity, there is a new 'culture of judicial assertiveness to compensate for, and in places repair, dysfunctions in the democratic process', and that the last three decades of the twentieth century may have seen the UK constitution being refashioned by judges 'with sufficient popular support to mute political opposition'.

The Impact of the Human Rights Act 1998

As has been seen at 2.5 above, the introduction of the HRA greatly increased judicial power in relation to the other two branches of the constitution.

Initially the judges were reluctant to use their new powers, especially the Court of Appeal and the House of Lords, although the courts below them, and notably Collins J in the SIAC, adopted a much more robust approach.

This initial position was set by Lord Irvine in his inaugural Human Rights Lecture at the University of Durham:

> It is all about balance. The balance between intense judicial scrutiny and reasonable deference to elected decision-makers is a delicate one to strike. But the judiciary have struck it well: and I welcome that. Whilst scrutiny is undoubtedly an important aid to better governance, there are areas in which decisions are best taken by the decision-makers entrusted by Parliament to make them. This may be for reasons of democratic accountability, expertise or complexity.

The former Lord Chancellor may well have been of the view that the judges had got it right, but his views did not sound in harmony with those of his ex-colleague, the former Home Secretary, David Blunkett, who was a consistent source of attack on the judiciary. Perhaps his most severe attack came after Collins J's decision in *R (on the Application of Q) v Secretary of State for the Home Department* (2003), which declared unlawful his power under s 55 of the Nationality, Immigration and Asylum Act 2002 to refuse to provide assistance to those who had not immediately declared their intention to claim asylum when they arrived in the UK. In the press, the then Home Secretary was quoted as saying:

> Frankly, I am fed up with having to deal with a situation where Parliament debates issues and judges then overturn them. We were aware of the circumstances, we did mean what we said and, on behalf of the British people, we are going to implement it.

Of even more concern were the reports that the then Prime Minister was 'prepared for a showdown with the judiciary to stop the courts thwarting government's attempts to curb the record flow of asylum seekers into Britain', and that he was looking into the possibility of enacting legislation to limit the role of judges in the interpretation of international human rights obligations and reassert the primacy of Parliament. There were even reports that the Prime Minister was considering withdrawing completely from the ECHR, rather than merely issuing derogations where it was thought necessary.

Given such pressure, it is perhaps not surprising that when the Court of Appeal heard the *Q* case, while it supported Collins J's decision, it went out of its way to provide the Home Secretary with advice on how to make the Act, and the procedures under it, compatible with ECHR rights.

Critique of judicial activism

The fact that the judges increasingly see it as incumbent upon them to use judicial review and the HRA as the means of questioning and controlling what they see as the abuse of executive power does, at the very least, raise very serious questions in relation to their suitability for such a role. These doubts can be set out in terms of:

Competence

This refers to the question whether the judges are sufficiently competent to participate in deciding the substantive issues that they have been invited to consider under the guise of judicial review, and may be entitled to consider under the HRA. Judges are experts in law; they are not experts in the various and highly specialised areas of policy that by definition tend to be involved in judicial review cases. They may disagree with particular decisions, but it has to be at least doubted that they are qualified to take such policy decisions. A classic example of this difficulty was the 'fares' fair' cases (*Bromley London BC v GLC* (1983) and later, *R v London Transport Executive ex p GLC* (1983)), in which the courts got involved in deciding issues relating to transport policy for London on the pretext that they were judicially defining the meaning of particular words in a statute. The apparently technocratic, and hence neutral, application of rules of interpretation simply serves to disguise a political procedure and, in these cases, the policy issue concerned was certainly beyond the scope of the judges to determine. In *Bellinger v*

Bellinger (2003), the House of Lords, although obviously sympathetic to the case, admitted their incompetence as regards deciding issues relating to the rights of transsexuals. For that reason, they issued a declaration of incompatibility under the HRA 1998 and thus passed the matter to Parliament for review and appropriate reform.

Constitutionality

This refers to the wider point that the separation of powers applies equally to the judiciary as it does to the executive. In interfering with substantive decisions and involving themselves in political matters, albeit on the pretence of merely deciding points of law, the judiciary may be seen to be exceeding their constitutional powers. It has to be remembered that judges are unelected and unaccountable.

Partiality

This refers to the possibility of individual, and indeed corporate, bias within the judiciary, as will be considered at 13.7.1 below.

The foregoing has indicated that the relationship between the state and the courts may, on occasion, involve a measure of tension, with the courts attempting to rein in the activities of the state. The relationship between the judiciary and the executive is well summed up in the words of Lord Justice Farquharson, again taken from an *Observer* article:

> We have to be very careful: the executive is elected. We have a role in the Constitution but, if we go too far, there will be a reaction. The Constitution only works if the different organs trust each other. If the judges start getting too frisky, there would be retaliation, renewed attempts to curb the judiciary.

Although no longer in force, the Kilmuir rules did have a valid point to make:

> the overriding consideration . . . is the importance of keeping the judiciary in this country isolated from the controversies of the day. So long as a judge keeps silent, his reputation for wisdom and impartiality remains unassailable; but every utterance which he makes in public . . . must necessarily bring him within the focus of criticism.

13.7   POLITICS OF THE JUDICIARY

When considering the role which the judiciary play in the process of applying the law, or indeed the process already adverted to in Chapter 4, whereby they actually make the law, criticism is usually levelled at the particular race, class and gender position of the majority of the judges. It is an objective and well-documented fact that the majority of judges are 'white, middle-class, middle-aged to elderly men', but the question that has to be considered is whether this *necessarily* leads to the conclusion that judges reach inherently biased decisions. It is always possible, indeed the newspapers make it relatively easy, to provide anecdotal evidence that apparently confirms either the bias or the lack of social awareness of the judiciary, but the fundamental question remains as to whether these cases are exceptional or whether they represent the norm.

Why should judges' class/race/gender placement make them less objective arbiters of the law? It is worth considering the fact that an *unsupported* general assertion as to the inherently partial approach of the judiciary is itself partial. Simon Lee, not totally fatuously, has highlighted the logical flaw in what he refers to as the 'Tony Benn thesis' (Benn, the former left-wing Labour Party Member of Parliament who created history by being the first hereditary peer to renounce his peerage in order to remain in the House of Commons). Just because judges are old, white, rich, upper middle class, educated at public school and Oxbridge does not mean that they all necessarily think the same way; after all, Benn was a product of the same social circumstances. There is, of course, the point that people from that particular background *generally* tend to be conservative in outlook, and the apparent validity of Lee's argument is clearly the product of logic-chopping that reverses the accepted relationship and uses the exception as the rule, rather than seeing the exception as proving/testing the rule. Nevertheless, Lee's point remains true: that proof of judicial bias is needed.

As previous sections of this book have pointed out, if law were completely beyond the scope of judges to manipulate to their own ends, then the race, class and gender placement of individual judges would be immaterial, as they would not be in any position to influence the operation of the law. As was demonstrated in Chapters 3 and 4, however, the way in which the doctrines that set the limits within which the judiciary operate are by no means as rigid and restrictive as they might at first appear. It was seen that, although judges are supposed merely to apply rather than create law, they possess a large measure of discretion in determining which laws to apply, what those laws mean, and how they should be applied. In the light of this potential capacity to create law, it is essential to ensure that the judiciary satisfactorily represent society at large in relation to which they have so much power, and to ensure further that they do not merely represent the views and attitudes of a self-perpetuating elite.

A Nuffield Foundation-funded report produced in November 1999 by Professor Hazel Genn in conjunction with the National Centre for Social Research, entitled *Paths to Justice*, revealed a truly remarkable lack of general confidence in the judiciary. The research surveyed a random selection of 4,125 people, from which total 1,248 people who had had experience of legal problems were selected for more detailed interview, with a smaller group of 48 being extensively interviewed. The results suggest that two out of three people think that judges are out of touch with ordinary people's lives, but, more worryingly, only 53 per cent thought that they would get a fair hearing if they ever went to court. Disappointingly, at the launch of the report, Lord Woolf claimed that this 'misconception' was due to 'irresponsible media reporting' and stated that:

> It behoves the media to learn from this and recognise the dangers posed to confidence in the judicial system.

Surely, it more behoves the judiciary and the Justice Ministry to do more to redress this negative perception than simply blame the media for focusing on silly judge stories of which, unfortunately, there are still too many.

One of the findings of the report was that judges could improve their image by getting rid of their wigs and gowns. Perish the thought: there are standards and distinctions to be maintained. Thus, in *Practice Direction (Court Dress) (No 3)* (1998), the Lord High Chancellor, Lord Irvine of Lairg, provided:

> Queen's Counsel wear a short wig and silk (or stuff) gown over a court coat; junior counsel wear a short wig and stuff gown with bands; solicitors and other advocates authorised under the Courts and Legal Services Act 1990 wear a black stuff gown, *but no wig*   (emphasis added).

The issue of wigs resurfaced in March 2006 when once again a proposal was put forward to consider getting rid of them. Somewhat surprisingly and counter-intuitively, some supported wigs as a means of benefiting the justice system by protecting the anonymity of counsel and providing suitable gravitas to the less experienced members of the barrister's profession.

In July 2008 the Lord Chief Justice issued a Practice Direction which introduced the wearing of a new civil robe in civil and family law cases together with the announcement that wigs will no longer be worn in such courts. The reforms, which took effect from 1 October 2008, do not apply in criminal cases. Justices of the Supreme Court do not wear wigs or gowns when hearing cases.

13.7.1 CRITICISMS

The treatment of some aspects of potential bias within the judiciary has already been dealt with at 12.2.3 above, but this section addresses a more amorphous form of prejudice, and therefore one that is correspondingly more difficult to recognise or deal with. Given the central position of judges in the operation of law and the legal system, particularly with regard to the growth in judicial review and their new role in relation to giving effect to the HRA, the question these reports raise is whether the social placement of the judiciary leads to any perceptible shortfall in the provision of justice. The pre-eminent critic of the way in which the judiciary permit their shared background, attitudes and prejudices to influence their understanding and statement of the law is Professor JAG Griffith. According to Griffith, bias can occur at two levels:

Personal bias

Personal bias occurs where individual judges permit their own personal prejudices to influence their judgment and thus the effective application of the law. It is relatively easy to cite cases where judges give expression to their own attitudes and in so doing exhibit their own prejudices. As examples of this process, two cases can be cited which consider the rule of natural justice, that a person should not be both the accuser and judge in the same case. In *Hannam v Bradford Corp* (1970), the court held that it was contrary to natural justice for three school governors to sit as members of a local authority education disciplinary committee, charged with deciding whether or not to uphold a previous decision of the governors to dismiss a teacher. This was so even though the three governors had not been present at the meeting where it was decided to dismiss the teacher. On the other hand, in *Ward v Bradford Corp* (1971), the Court of Appeal refused to interfere with a decision by governors of a teacher training college to confirm the expulsion of a student, although they had instituted the disciplinary proceedings and three members of the governors sat on the original disciplinary committee. What possible explanation can there be for this discrepancy? The only tenable explanation is to be found in the latter court's disapproval of the plaintiff's behaviour in that case. The truly reprehensible judgment of Lord Denning concludes that the student lost nothing, as she was not a fit person to teach children in any case. Can such a conclusion be justified on purely legal grounds or is it based on individual morality? Lord Denning did his best to buttress his judgment with spurious legal reasoning, but it could be suggested that, in so doing, he merely brought the process of legal reasoning into disrepute and revealed its fallaciousness.

Courts have also been notoriously unsympathetic to victims of rape and have been guilty of making the most obtuse of sexist comments in relation to such victims. Nor can it be claimed that depreciatory racist remarks have been totally lacking in court cases.

Such cases of bias are serious and reprehensible, but the very fact that the prejudice they demonstrate appears as no more than the outcome of particular judges, who are simply out of touch with current standards of morality or acceptable behaviour, suggests that it might be eradicated by the Lord Chancellor exercising stricter control over such mavericks and appointing more appropriate judges in the first place. Professor Griffith, however, suggests that there is a further type of bias that is actually beyond such relatively easy control.

Corporate bias

Corporate bias involves the assertion that the judges *as a body* decide certain types of cases in a biased way. This accusation of corporate bias is much more serious than that of personal bias, for the reason that it asserts that the problem of bias is *systematic* rather than merely limited to particular maverick judges. As a consequence, if such a claim is justified, it has to be concluded that the problem is not susceptible to treatment at the level of the individual judge, but requires a complete alteration of the whole judicial system. Griffith claims that, as a consequence of their shared educational experience, their shared training and practical experience at the Bar and their shared social situation as members of the Establishment, judges have developed a common outlook. He maintains that they share homogeneous values, attitudes and beliefs as to how the law should operate and be administered. He further suggests that this shared outlook is inherently conservative, if not Conservative in a party-political sense.

   Griffith's argument is that the highest judges in the judicial hierarchy are frequently called upon to decide cases on the basis of a determination of what constitutes the public interest and that, in making that determination, they express their own corporate values, which are in turn a product of their position in society as part of the ruling Establishment. Griffith maintains that judges can be seen to operate in such a way as to maintain the status quo and resist challenges to the established authority. Underlying this argument is the implication that the celebrated independence of the judiciary is, in fact, a myth and that the courts will tend to decide cases in such a way as to buttress the position of the state, especially if it is under the control of a Conservative government.

In an attempt to substantiate his claims, Griffith examines cases relating to trade union law, personal rights, property rights and matters of national security, where he claims to find judges consistently acting to support the interests of the state over the rights of the individual. Some of the concrete examples he cites are the withdrawal of trade union rights from GCHQ at Cheltenham (*Council of Civil Service Unions v Minister for Civil Service* (1984)); the banning of publishing any extracts from the *Spycatcher* book (*AG v Guardian Newspapers Ltd* (1987)); and the treatment of suspected terrorists.

   There certainly have been some overtly right-wing decisions taken by the courts, and the history of trade union cases is replete with them even at the highest level. The greater strength of Griffith's argument, however, would appear to be in the way that the courts have understood and expressed what is to be meant by 'public interest' in such a way as to reflect conservative, but not necessarily illiberal, values. It is surely only from that perspective that the higher judiciary's antagonistic response to some of the electorally driven policy decisions in relation to the legal system by *both* Conservative and New Labour administrations can be reconciled.

As would be expected, Griffith, and other academics associated with the left, have expressed their reservations about the extent to which the HRA will hand power to an unelected, unaccountable, inherently conservative and unreformed body, as they claim the judiciary is.

A notable, if somewhat complacent, response to Griffith's book was provided by Lord Devlin, who pointed out that, in most cases and on most issues, there tended to be plurality rather than unanimity of opinion and decision among judges. He also claimed that it would be just as possible for a more conservatively minded person than Griffith to go through the casebooks to provide a list of examples where the courts had oper- ated in an over-liberal manner. Lord Devlin also adopted a different explanation of the judiciary's perceived reluctance to abandon the status quo. For him, any conservatism on the part of judges was to be seen as a product of age rather than class. In conclusion, he asserted that even if the judiciary were biased, their bias was well known and allowances could be made for it.

The issue of the way in which the criminal appeal procedure dealt with suspected terrorist cases is of particular relevance in the light of the Runciman Commission Report. General dissatisfaction with the trials and appeals involving suspected terrorists such as the Maguire Seven, the Birmingham Six, the Guildford Four, the Tottenham Three, Stefan Kiszko and Judith Ward helped to give rise to the widespread impression that the UK criminal justice system, and in particular the British appeal system, needed to be considered for reform.

In the light of the fact that the appeal system did not seem to be willing to consider the possibility of the accused's innocence once they had been convicted, the Runciman Commission's recommendation that a Criminal Case Review Authority be established, independent of the Home Office, was widely welcomed and resulted in the establish- ment of the CCRC in the Criminal Appeal Act 1995 (see above, 9.9). The question still remains, however, whether those earlier cases reflect an inherently and inescapably con- servative judiciary, or were they simply unfortunate instances of more general errors of the system, which the implementation of the CCRC can overcome? And perhaps more importantly, will the Court of Appeal give a fair hearing to the cases referred to it by the CCRC?

It is apparent from the statistics produced by what was then the Department for Constitutional Affairs (DCA), cited previously, that senior judges were still being appointed from the same limited social and educational elite as they always have been. This gives rise to the suspicion, if not the reality, that the decisions that this elite make merely represent values and interests of a limited and privileged segment of society rather than society as a whole. Even if the accusations levelled by Professor Griffith are inaccurate, it is surely still necessary to remove even the possibility of those accusations.

It is not a little ironic that, in spite of the potential shortcomings that arise from the social composition of the current judicial body, there seems to be a distinct alteration in attitudes to the judiciary among those of a politically left-leaning persuasion. Follow- ing the introduction of the Human Rights Act and especially the decisions of the House of Lords in *A v Secretary of State for the Home Department* (2004) and *A v Secretary of State for the Home Department* (2005), many on the left now apparently see the courts as the bulwark of civilised society, against which beats the persistent tide of authoritarian

- can withhold the costs of any part of an inquiry which strays beyond the terms of reference set by the Minister.

Parliament's role has been reduced to that of the passive recipient of information about inquiries, whereas under the 1921 Act reports of public inquiries were made to Parliament. Now, not only is there no guarantee that any inquiry will be public, but inquiry reports will go to the Minister.

The Minister's role is particularly troubling where the actions of that Minister or those of his or her department, or those of the government, are in question. In effect, the state will be investigating itself. In our view, the Inquiries Act is at odds with the United Nations' updated set of principles for the protection and promotion of human rights through action to combat impunity.

Where Article 2 of the European Convention on Human Rights (which protects the right to life) is engaged, the Inquiries Act is at variance with the United Nations' Principles on the Effective Prevention and Investigation of Extra-legal, Arbitrary and Summary Executions. Indeed, we doubt that the Inquiries Act can deliver an effective investigation in compliance with Article 2. The Minister's powers to interfere in every important aspect of an inquiry robs it of any independence. Even if a Minister were to refrain from exercising those powers that are discretionary, s/he still has absolute power over whether there should be an inquiry at all and over its terms of reference. There is no scope for victims to be involved in or even consulted about the process.

In support of their view, the organisation cited the views of Lord Saville, who chaired one of the most complex public inquiries in UK legal history, the Bloody Sunday Inquiry, who publicly expressed grave reservations about the Act. As they claimed, in a letter to Baroness Ashton at the Department of Constitutional Affairs, dated 26 January 2005, he stated his opinion that:

> I take the view that this provision makes a very serious inroad into the independence of any inquiry and is likely to damage or destroy public confidence in the inquiry and its findings, especially in cases where the conduct of the authorities may be in question.

He added that such ministerial interference with a judge's ability to act impartially and independently of government would be unjustifiable. He further stated that neither he nor his fellow judges on the Bloody Sunday Inquiry would be prepared to be appointed as a member of an inquiry that was subject to a provision of that kind.

The Inquiries Act came under critical attention in July 2008 when the United Nations Human Rights Committee issued its concluding observations on the UK's periodic report under the UN Covenant on Civil and Political Rights. As it stated:

> The Committee remains concerned that, a considerable time after murders (including of human rights defenders) in Northern Ireland have occurred, several inquiries into these murders have still not been established or concluded, and that those responsible for these deaths have not yet been prosecuted. Even where inquiries have been established, *the Committee is concerned that instead of being under the control of an independent judge, several of these inquiries are conducted under the Inquiries Act 2005 which allows the Government minister who is responsible for establishing an inquiry to control important aspects of that inquiry* (Art 6, emphasis added).

In March 2014, a House of Lords select committee published the results of its review of the law and practice relating to public inquiries, *The Inquiries Act 2005: post-legislative scrutiny*.

Its main recommendations were that:

- inquiries into matters of public concern should normally be held under the 2005 Act and ministers should give reasons for any decision to hold an inquiry otherwise than under the act;

- there should be stronger controls on the powers of ministers requiring them to seek the consent of, rather than merely consulting with, the chair of an inquiry before:

  (i) setting or amending terms of reference;

  (ii) adding another member to the inquiry panel or terminating the appointment of a panel member with the minister being required to lay reasons before parliament;

  (iii) except in matters of public security, only allowing the chair, not the minister, to withhold material from publication;

- interested parties, in particular, victims and victims' families, should have an opportunity to make representations about the final terms of reference;

- a central inquiries unit should be created to assist with the practical details of setting up an inquiry, including premises, infrastructure, IT, procurement and staffing;

- Parliament should do more to hold ministers to account following publication of the inquiry report, on responding to recommendations and implementation.

CHAPTER SUMMARY: JUDICIAL REASONING AND POLITICS

REASONING IN GENERAL

Deductive reasoning is reasoning from the whole to the part; from the general to the particular. The syllogism is a form of deductive reasoning. Inductive reasoning is reasoning from the part to the whole; from the particular to the general. Reasoning by analogy is reasoning from part to part.

JUDICIAL REASONING

Laws can be presented in the form of syllogisms but do not actually focus on questions of deductive reasoning. The doctrine of judicial precedent appears at first sight to involve deductive reasoning, but is in fact based on the much less certain use of inductive reasoning and reasoning by analogy.

JUDICIAL REVIEW

Under the constitution of the UK, and within the doctrine of the separation of powers, judges and the executive have distinct but interrelated roles.

Judicial review remedies are the prerogative remedies of *quashing orders, mandatory orders* and *prohibiting orders*, together with the private law remedies of declaration, injunction and damages. Private law remedies cannot be used in relation to public law complaints.

Increased judicial activity in relation to state programmes raises questions about the competence and authority of judges to act, as well as raising doubts as to their political views.

POLITICS OF THE JUDICIARY

Judges have a capacity to make law – the question is, do they exercise this power in a biased way?

Bias can take two forms: personal and corporate.

Accusations of corporate bias suggest that, as a group, judges represent the interest of the status quo and decide certain political cases in line with that interest. However, more recently there has been a reliance on the judiciary as the protectors of human rights.

FOOD FOR THOUGHT

1   Should the membership of the judiciary reflect the underlying social structure? In other words, do the class, race and gender of the judiciary matter, and if so, why?

2   Consider the extent to which the growth of judicial review and human rights actions are increasingly involving the judiciary in political decisions, and whether

or not that is a good thing. In the words of the late Lord Denning, 'Someone must be trusted. Let it be the judges.' Is such an assertion valid in the light of the unrepresentative nature of the judiciary? As Lord Justice Laws has recently asked with regard to the HRA:

'Why should judges decide matters of social policy at all? The political rights, Articles 8–12, with the right set out in the first part and the derogation in the second, create a structure which means that a very large number of legal debates are about how the balance between private right and public interest should be struck. But what authority, expertise, do lawyers have to strike that balance, that is special to them?'

FURTHER READING

Baldwin, J, 'The social composition of magistrates' (1976) 16 British J of Criminology 171

Blom-Cooper, L, 'Bias: malfunction in judicial decision-making' [2009] PL 199

Bondy, V, Platt, L and Sunkin, M, *The Value and Effects of Judicial Review: The Nature of Claims, their Outcomes and Consequences*, 2015, London: The Public Project

Browne-Wilkinson, N (Sir), 'The independence of the judiciary in the 1980s' [1988] PL 4

Clayton, R, 'Decision-making in the Supreme Court: new approaches and new opportunities' [2009] PL 682

Crawford, L, 'Race awareness training and the judges' (1994) Counsel 11

Griffith, JAG, *The Politics of the Judiciary*, 5th edn, 1997, London: Fontana

Hailsham (Lord), 'The office of Lord Chancellor and the separation of powers' (1989) 8 Civil Justice Quarterly 308

Judicial Review and the Rule of Law: An Introduction to the Criminal Justice and Courts Act 2015, Part 4, Bingham Centre for the Rule of Law, JUSTICE and the Public Law Project, London, October 2015

Lee, S, *Judging Judges*, 1988, London: Faber & Faber

MacCormick, N, *Legal Rules and Legal Reasoning*, 1978, Oxford: Clarendon

Mackay (Lord), *The Administration of Justice*, 1994, London: Sweet & Maxwell

Malleson, K, *The New Judiciary: The Effect of Expansion and Activism*, 1999, Aldershot: Ashgate

McLachlin, B, 'The role of judges in modern Commonwealth society' [1994] LQR 260

Murdoch, S, 'Judges use discretion over discharges' (2009) 940 EG 131

Pannick, D, *Judges*, 1987, Oxford: OUP

Parker, H *et al*, *Unmasking the Magistrates*, 1989, Milton Keynes: OUP

Royal Commission on Criminal Justice, *Runciman Report*, Cm 2263, 1995, London: HMSO

Rutherford, A, 'Judicial training and autonomy' (1999) 149 NLJ 1120

Skordaki, E, *Judicial Appointments*, Law Society Research Study No 5, 1991, London: HMSO

Smith, R, 'Judging the judges' (2009) 159 NLJ 1154

Stevens, R, *The Independence of the Judiciary*, 1993, Oxford: OUP

Stevens, R, *The English Judge: Their Role in the Changing Constitution*, 2002, Oxford: Hart Publishing

Of general, as well as specific subject, interest, are the following books, written by two of the most erudite and literary of recent judges.

Bingham, T, *The Business of Judging: Selected Essays and Speeches: 1985–1999* and *Lives of the Law: Selected Essays and Speeches: 2000–2010*, 2011, Oxford: OUP

Sedley S, *Ashes and Sparks: Essays On Law and Justice*, 2011, Cambridge: CUP

USEFUL WEBSITE

www.bailii.org/databases.html
A list of the databases that BAILII holds.

COMPANION WEBSITE

Now visit the companion website to:

- test your understanding of the key terms using our Flashcard Glossary;
- revise and consolidate your knowledge of 'Judicial reasoning and politics' using our multiple choice question testbank;
- view the link to the Useful Website above.

www.routledge.com/cw/slapper

THE JURY

14.1   INTRODUCTION

It is generally accepted that the jury of '12 good men and true' lies at the heart of the British legal system. The implicit assumption is that the presence of 12 ordinary laypersons, randomly introduced into the trial procedure to be the arbiters of the facts of the case, strengthens the legitimacy of the legal system. It supposedly achieves this end by introducing a democratic humanising element into the abstract impersonal trial process, thereby reducing the exclusive power of the legal professionals who would otherwise command the legal stage and control the legal procedure without reference to the opinion of the lay majority.

According to EP Thompson:

> The English common law rests upon a bargain between the law and the people. The jury box is where the people come into the court; the judge watches them and the jury watches back. A jury is the place where the bargain is struck. A jury attends in judgement not only upon the accused but also upon the justice and humanity of the law   (*Writing by Candlelight*).

Few people have taken this traditional view to task but, in a thought-provoking article in the *Criminal Law Review* ([1991] Crim LR 740), Penny Darbyshire did just that. In her view, the jury system has attracted the most praise and the least theoretical analysis of any component of the criminal justice system. As she correctly pointed out, and as will be shown below, juries are far from being either a random or a representative section of the general population. In fact, Darbyshire goes so far as to characterise the jury as 'an antidemocratic, irrational and haphazard legislator, whose erratic and secret decisions run counter to the rule of law'. She concedes that while the twentieth-century lay justices are not representative of the community as a whole, neither is the jury. She points out that jury equity, by which is meant the way in which the jury ignores the law in pursuit of justice, is a double-edged sword which may also convict the innocent; and counters examples such as the *Clive Ponting* case with the series of miscarriages of justice relating to suspected terrorists in which juries were also involved.

Darbyshire is certainly correct in taking to task those who would simply endorse the jury system in an unthinking, purely emotional manner. With equal justification, she criticises those academic writers who focus attention on the mystery of the jury to the exclusion of the hard reality of the magistrates' court. It is arguable, however, that she goes to the other extreme. Underlying her analysis and conclusions is the idea that 'the jury trial is primarily ideological' and that 'its symbolic significance is magnified beyond its practical significance by the media, as well as academics, thus unwittingly misleading the public'. While one might not wish to contradict the suggestion that the jury system operates as a very powerful ideological symbol, supposedly grounding the criminal legal system within a framework of participative democracy and justifying it on that basis, it is simply inadequate to reject the practical operation of the procedure on that basis alone. Ideologies do not exist purely in the realm of ideas; they have real, concrete manifestations and effects – in relation to the jury system, those manifestations operate in such a way as to offer at least a vestige of protection to defendants. In regard to the comparison between juries and the summary procedure of the magistrates' courts, Darbyshire puts two related questions. First, she asks whether the jury system is more likely to do justice and get the verdict right than the magistrates' courts; then she goes on to ask why the majority of defendants are processed through the magistrates' courts. These questions are highly pertinent; it is doubtful, however, whether her response to them is equally pertinent. Her answers would likely be that the jury does not perform any better than the magistrates and, therefore, it is immaterial that the magistrates deal with the bulk of cases. Her whole approach would seem to be concentrated on denigrating the performance of the jury system. A not untypical passage from her article admits that, in relation to the suspect terrorist miscarriages of justice, juries 'were not to blame for these wrongful convictions'. However, she then goes on in the same sentence to accuse the juries of failing 'to remedy the lack of due process at the pre-trial stage', and thus blames them for not providing 'the brake on oppressive State activity claimed for the jury by its defenders'.

Although there is most certainly scope for a less romantic view of how the jury system actually operates in practice, Darbyshire's argument seems to be that the magistrates are not very good but then neither are the juries; and as they only operate in a small minority of cases anyway, the implication would seem to be that their loss would be no great disadvantage. Others, however, would maintain that the jury system does achieve concrete benefits in particular circumstances and would argue further that these benefits should not be readily given up. Among the latter is Michael Mansfield QC who, in an article in response to the Runciman Report, claimed that the jury 'is the most democratic element of our judicial system' and the one that 'poses the biggest threat to the authorities'. (These questions will be considered further in relation to the Report of the Runciman Commission and the Criminal Justice (Mode of Trial) Bills, below, at 14.7.1.)

Having defended the institution of the jury generally, it has to be recognised that there are particular instances that tend to bring the jury system into disrepute. For example, in October 1994, the Court of Appeal ordered the retrial of a man convicted of double murder on the grounds that four of the jurors had attempted to contact the alleged victims using a Ouija board in what was described as a 'drunken experiment' (*R v Young* (1995)). A second convicted murderer appealed against his conviction on the grounds of irregularities in the manner in which the jury performed its functions. Among the allegations levelled at the jury was the claim that they clubbed together and spent £150 on drink when they were sent to a hotel after failing to reach a verdict. It was alleged that some of the jurors discussed the case, against the express instructions of the judge, and that on the following day the jury foreman had to be replaced because she was too hungover to act. One female juror was alleged to have ended up in bed with another hotel guest.

A truly remarkable case came to light in December 2000 when a trial, which had been going on for 10 weeks, was stopped on the grounds that a female juror was conducting what were referred to as 'improper relations' with a male member of the jury protection force who had been allocated to look after the jury during the trial. The relationship had become apparent after the other members of the jury had found out that they were using their mobile phones to send text messages to one another during breaks in the trial. That aborted trial was estimated to have cost £1.5 million, but it emerged that this was the second time the case had had to be stopped on account of inappropriate behaviour on the part of jury members. The first trial had been abandoned after some of the jury were found playing cards when they should have been deliberating on the case.

Another example of the possible criticisms to be levelled against the misuse of juries occurred in Stoke-on-Trent, where the son of a court usher and another six individuals were found to have served on a number of criminal trial juries. While one could praise the public-spirited nature of this dedication to the justice process, especially given the difficulty in getting members of jury panels, it might be more appropriate to condemn the possibility of the emergence of a professional juror system connected to court officials. Certainly, the Court of Appeal was less than happy with the situation, and overturned a conviction when the Stoke practice was revealed to it.

Over the past 15 years, the operation of the jury system has been subject to one Royal Commission (Runciman), one review (Auld) and several statutory attempts to alter it. An examination of these various endeavours will be postponed until the end of this chapter; for the moment, attention will be focused on the jury system as it currently functions.

14.2   THE ROLE OF THE JURY

It is generally accepted that the function of the jury is to decide on matters of fact, and that matters of law are the province of the judge. Such may be the ideal case, but most of the time the jury's decision is based on a consideration of a mixture of fact and law. The jurors determine whether a person is guilty on the basis of their understanding of the law as explained to them by the judge.

The oath taken by each juror states that they 'will faithfully try the defendant and give a true verdict according to the evidence', and it is contempt of court for a juror subsequent to being sworn in to refuse to come to a decision. In 1997, Judge Anura Cooray sentenced two women jurors to 30 days in prison for contempt of court for their failure to deliver a verdict. One of the women, who had been the jury foreman, claimed that the case, involving an allegation of fraud, had been too complicated to understand, and the other

ground that the judge had erred in law in permitting the additional evidence to be put before the jury after it had retired.

In rejecting the appeal the Court of Appeal found that there was no reason in principle why the judge should not have agreed to allow the new evidence to be put before the jury. On the contrary, as they stated:

> [W]e can see every reason why he should have allowed this evidence to go before the jury. The defence invited the judge to do so on the basis that the evidence assisted the appellant's case. It was evidence which trial counsel believed was capable of supporting the appellant's case in an area which both counsel felt the appellant's evidence was weak and required some support. We have no doubt that the appellant agreed to this course of action.

On that basis the court rejected Khan's appeal.

The decision in *Khan* reflects the changed approach of the courts to such situations, as historically the authorities support the view that there was an absolute principle that no further evidence should be given after the judge's summing-up has been concluded and the jury has retired. Thus in *R v Owen* (1952), in which the trial judge allowed a doctor who had already given evidence in the case to be recalled to give evidence in answer to a question raised by the jury after their retirement, the subsequent conviction was quashed. The reason stated by Lord Goddard CJ was that 'once the summing up is concluded, no further evidence ought to be given. The jury can be instructed in reply to any question they may put on any matter on which evidence has been given, but no further evidence should be allowed.'

However, subsequently, in *R v Sanderson* (1953), the Court of Criminal Appeal, including Lord Goddard CJ, held that it was permissible for the evidence of a witness for the defence to be taken after the summing up had been completed, *but before the jury had retired*, and the 'very strict rule' that no evidence whatever must be introduced after the jury had retired was reiterated by Lord Parker CJ in *R v Gearing* (1968).

However, the introduction of the proviso under s 2(1) of the Criminal Appeal Act 1968 (see above, 9.5.2) led to a change in approach and in *R v Davis* (1976) the absolute nature of the rule was questioned and such an approach was approved of in *R v Karakaya* (2005).

More recently in *R v Hallam* (2007) the Court of Appeal actually held that a verdict was unsafe because a judge had refused to permit the jury to see a photograph which could potentially have assisted the appellant's defence, but which had come to light only after the summing-up. In that case the court defined the principle as follows:

> It used to be understood that there was a very firm rule that evidence cannot be admitted after the retirement of the jury, but more recent authorities confirm that there is no absolute rule to that effect. The question is what justice requires.

In criminal cases, even perversity of decision does not provide grounds for appeal against acquittal. There have been occasions where juries have been subjected to the invective of a judge when they have delivered a verdict with which he disagreed. Nonetheless, the fact is that juries collectively, and individual jurors, do not have to justify, explain or even give reasons for their decisions. Indeed, under s 8 of the Contempt of Court Act 1981, it would be a contempt of court to try to elicit such information from a jury member in either a criminal or a civil law case.

In *Attorney General v Associated Newspapers* (1994), the House of Lords held that it was contempt of court for a newspaper to publish disclosures by jurors of what took place in the jury room while they were considering their verdict, unless the publication amounted to no more than a re-publication of facts already known. It was decided that the word 'disclose' in s 8(1) applied not just to jurors, but to any others who published their revelations.

In an interview for *The Times* in January 2001, the Lord Chief Justice, Lord Woolf, expressed himself very strongly in favour of lifting the ban on jury research, though he emphasised that great care was needed in the conduct of any such research.

These factors place juries in a very strong position to take decisions that are 'unjustifiable' in accordance with the law, for the simple reason that they do not have to justify the decisions. Thus, juries have been able to deliver what can only be described as perverse decisions. In *R v Clive Ponting* (1985), the judge made clear beyond doubt that the defendant was guilty, under the Official Secrets Act 1911, of the offence with which he was charged: the jury still returned a not guilty verdict. Similarly, in the case of Pat Pottle and Michael Randall, who had openly admitted their part in the escape of the spy George Blake, the jury reached a not guilty verdict in open defiance of the law.

In *R v Kronlid* (1996), three protestors were charged with committing criminal damage, and another was charged with conspiracy to cause criminal damage, in relation to an attack on Hawk jet aeroplanes that were about to be sent to Indonesia. The damage to the planes allegedly amounted to £1.5 million and they did not deny their responsibility for it. They rested their defence on the fact that the planes were to be delivered to the Indonesian state, to be used in its allegedly genocidal campaign against the people of East Timor. On those grounds, they claimed that they were in fact acting to prevent the crime of genocide. The prosecution cited assurances, given by the Indonesian government, that the planes would not be used against the East Timorese, and pointed out that the UK government had granted an export licence for the planes. As the protestors did not deny what they had done, it was apparently a mere matter of course that they would be convicted as charged. The jury, however, decided that all four of the accused were innocent of the charges laid against them. A government Treasury minister, Michael Jack, subsequently expressed his disbelief at the verdict of the jury. As he stated:

> I, and I am sure many others, find this jury's decision difficult to understand. It would appear there is little question about who did this damage. For whatever reason that damage was done, it was just plain wrong   (*The Independent*, 1 August 1996).

As stated above, jurors swear to return 'a true verdict according to the evidence'. Such verdicts may be politically inconvenient.

It is perhaps just such a lack of understanding, together with the desire to save money on the operation of the legal system, that has motivated the government's expressed wish to replace jury trials in relation to either-way offences (see below, 14.8). In any event, juries continue to reach perverse decisions where they are sympathetic to the causes pursued by the defendants. Thus, in September 2000, 28 Greenpeace volunteers, including its executive director Lord Melchett, were found not guilty of criminal damage after they had destroyed a field containing genetically modified (GM) maize. They had been found not guilty of theft in their original trial in April of that year. Judge David Mellor told the jury:

> It is not about whether GM crops are a good thing for the environment or a bad thing. It is for you to listen to the evidence and reach honest conclusions as to the facts.

However, the jury seemed to have adopted a different approach.

Fear of not achieving a successful conviction also appears to be the reason behind the CPS's belated decision, in February 2004, not to pursue the prosecution of Katherine Gun. Gun was the former GCHQ translator who revealed that the UK and the US were involved in spying on members of the United Nations before a crucial vote on whether the 2003 war on Iraq would be sanctioned by the UN. Although she admitted she was the source of the leak and was consequently, at least *prima facie*, in breach of the Official Secrets Act, her prosecution was dropped after she had put forward the defence of necessity. The decision was apparently taken on the guidance of the Attorney General, who was involved in the Iraq question from the beginning, being the source of the government's advice that the war was legal without the need for a specific resolution to that effect by the United Nations. In September 2008, six Greenpeace climate change activists were cleared of causing £30,000 of criminal damage at a coal-fired power station in Kent. They had admitted trying to shut down the station by occupying the smokestack and painting the word 'Gordon' down the chimney. However, the jury found them not guilty on the basis of their defence, which was that they were justified in their action as they were acting to prevent climate change causing greater damage to property around the world. In his summing-up at the end of an eight-day trial, the judge, David Caddick, said the case centred on whether or not the protestors had a lawful excuse for their actions, and the jury found that they did.

A non-political example of this type of case can be seen in the jury's refusal to find Stephen Owen guilty of any offence after he had discharged a shotgun at the driver of a lorry that had killed his child. And in September 2000, a jury in Carlisle found Lezley Gibson not guilty on a charge of possession of cannabis after she told the court that she needed it to relieve the symptoms of the multiple sclerosis from which she suffered. The tendency of the jury occasionally to ignore legal formality in favour of substantive justice is one of the major points in favour of its retention, according to its proponents.

14.3.1 APPEALS FROM DECISIONS OF THE JURY

In criminal law, it is an absolute rule that there can be no appeal against a jury's decision to acquit a person of the charges laid against him. Although there is no appeal as such against acquittal, there does exist the possibility of the Attorney General referring the case to the Court of Appeal, to seek its advice on points of law raised in criminal cases in which the defendant has been acquitted. This procedure was provided for under s 36 of the Criminal Justice Act (CJA) 1972, although it is not commonly resorted to. It must be stressed that there is no possibility of the actual case being reheard or the acquittal decision being reversed, but the procedure can highlight mistakes in law made in the course of Crown Court trial and permits the Court of Appeal to remedy the defect for the future. (See *Attorney General's Reference (No 1 of 1988)* (1988) for an example of this procedure, in the area of insider dealing in relation to shares on the Stock Exchange. This case is also interesting in relation to statutory interpretation. See also *Attorney General's Reference (No 3 of 1999)*, considered above at 12.3.2.)

In civil law cases, the possibility of the jury's verdict being overturned on appeal does exist, but only in circumstances where the original verdict was perverse; that is, no reasonable jury properly directed could have made such a decision (see *Grobbelaar v NGN Ltd* at 14.6.1).

14.3.2 MAJORITY VERDICTS

The possibility of a jury deciding a case on the basis of a majority decision was introduced by the CJA 1967. Prior to this, the requirement was that jury decisions had to be unanimous. Such decisions are acceptable where there are:

- no fewer than 11 jurors and 10 of them agree; or
- there are 10 jurors and nine of them agree.

Where a jury has reached a guilty verdict on the basis of a majority decision, s 17(3) of the Juries Act (JA) 1974 requires the foreman of the jury to state in open court the number of jurors who agreed and the number who disagreed with the verdict. See *R v Barry* (1975), where failure to declare the details of the voting split resulted in the conviction of the defendant being overturned. In *R v Pigg* (1983), the House of Lords held that it was unnecessary to state the number who voted against where the foreman stated the number in favour of the verdict, and thus the determination of the minority was a matter of simple arithmetic.

However, in *R v Mendy* (1992), when the clerk of the court asked the foreman of the jury how a guilty decision had been reached, he replied that it was 'by the majority of us all'. The ambiguity of the reply is obvious when it is taken out of context and this was relied on in a successful appeal. It was simply not clear whether it referred to a unanimous verdict, as the court at first instance had understood it, or whether it referred to a real majority vote, in which case it failed to comply with the requirement of s 17(3) as applied in *R v Barry*. The Court of Appeal held that in such a situation, the defendant had to be given the benefit of any doubt and he was discharged.

The Court of Appeal adopted a different approach in *R v Millward* (1999). The appellant had been convicted, at Stoke-on-Trent Crown Court, of causing grievous bodily harm. Although the jury actually had reached a majority decision, the foreman in response to the questioning of the clerk of the court mistakenly stated that it was the verdict of them all. The following day, the foreman informed the judge that the verdict had in fact been a majority verdict of 10 for guilty and two against.

The Court of Appeal met the subsequent challenge with the following exercise in sophisticated reasoning. The court at first instance had apparently accepted a unanimous verdict. Therefore, s 17 had not been brought into play at all. And, bearing in mind s 8 of the Contempt of Court Act 1981, discouraging the disclosure of votes cast by jurors in the course of their deliberations, the issue had to be viewed under the policy of the law. It would set a very dangerous precedent if an apparently unanimous verdict of a jury delivered in open court, and not then challenged by any juror, was reopened and subjected to scrutiny. It would be difficult to see how the court could properly investigate a disagreement as to whether jurors had dissented or not. In the instant case, there was a proper majority direction and proper questions asked of the jury and apparently proper and unambiguous answers given without challenge. Therefore, there should be no further inquiry.

There is no requirement for the details of the voting to be declared in a majority decision of not guilty.

14.3.3 DISCHARGE OF JURORS OR THE JURY

The trial judge may discharge the whole jury if certain irregularities occur. These would include the situation where the defendant's previous convictions are revealed inadvertently during the trial. Such a disclosure would be prejudicial to the defendant. In such a case, the trial would be ordered to commence again with a different jury. Individual jurors may be discharged by the judge if they are incapable of continuing to act through illness 'or for any other reason' (s 16(1) of the Juries Act (JA) 1974). Where this happens, the jury must not fall below nine members.

14.4   THE SELECTION OF THE JURY

In theory, jury service is a public duty that citizens should readily undertake. In practice, it is made compulsory, and failure to perform one's civic responsibility is subject to the sanction of a £1,000 fine.

14.4.1 LIABILITY TO SERVE

The JA 1974, as amended by the CJA 1988 and the CJA 2003, sets out the law relating to juries. Prior to the JA 1974, there was a property qualification in respect to jury service that skewed jury membership towards middle-class men. Now, the legislation provides that any person between the ages of 18 and 75, who is on the electoral register and who has lived in the UK for at least five years, is qualified to serve as a juror. The upper age limit was raised to 75 by the Criminal Justice and Courts Act 2015 s 68.

The procedure for establishing a jury is a threefold process:

- An officer of the court summons a randomly selected number of qualified individuals from the electoral register.
- From that group, panels of potential jurors for various cases are drawn up.
- The actual jurors are then randomly selected by means of a ballot in open court.

As has been pointed out, however, even if the selection procedure were truly random, randomness does not equal representation. Random juries, by definition, could be all male, all female, all white, all black, all Conservative or all members of the Monster Raving Loony Party. Such is the nature of the random process; the question that arises from the process is whether such randomness is necessarily a good thing in itself, and whether the summoning officer should take steps to avoid the potential disadvantages that can result from random selection.

As regards the actual random nature of the selection process, a number of problems arise from the use of electoral registers to determine and locate jurors:

- Electoral registers tend to be inaccurate. Generally, they misreport the number of younger people who are in an area simply because younger people tend to move about more than older people and therefore tend not to appear on the electoral roll of the place in which they currently live.
- Electoral registers tend to under-report the number of members of ethnic minorities in a community. The problem is that some members of the ethnic communities, for a variety of reasons, simply do not notify the authorities of their existence.
- The problem of non-registration mentioned above was compounded by the disappearance of a great many people from electoral registers in order to try to avoid payment of the former poll tax. It has been suggested that the alteration of the registration procedure to an individual voluntary process from a compulsory household process will have an even greater impact on the register of voters.

14.4.2 INELIGIBILITY EXCEPTIONS, DISQUALIFICATION AND EXCUSAL

Prior to the CJA 2003, the general qualification for serving as a juror was subject to a number of exceptions.

A variety of people were deemed to be ineligible to serve on juries on the basis of their employment or vocation. Among this category were: judges; Justices of the Peace; members of the legal profession; police and probation officers; and members of the clergy or religious orders. Those suffering from a mental disorder were also deemed to be ineligible. Paragraph 2 of Sched 33 to the CJA 2003 removes the first three groups of persons ineligible – the judiciary, others concerned with the administration of justice, and the clergy – leaving only mentally disordered persons with that status.

This reform came into effect in April 2005. The extent to which 'ordinary' jurors will be influenced by contact with solicitors, barristers and judges remains to be seen (assuming that research into such matters is eventually permitted). In any event the provisions of the CJA 2003 as regards eligibility to serve were challenged, as being contrary to Art 6 of the ECHR, in *R v (1) Abdroikov (2) Green (3) Williamson* (2005), three otherwise unrelated cases. Each of the appellants appealed against their convictions on the grounds that the jury in their respective trials had contained members who were employed in the criminal justice system. The juries in the trials of the first and second appellants had contained serving police officers. The jury in the trial of the third appellant had contained a person employed as a prosecuting solicitor by the CPS. Their proposal was that, as prior to the CJA 2003 there would have been no doubt that the presence of such people on juries would have been unlawful, so their presence in the current cases ran contrary to the need for trials to be free from even the taint of apparent bias.

The Court of Appeal rejected such arguments as spurious, holding that the expectations placed on ordinary citizens in relation to jury service had to be extended to members of the criminal justice system.

However, by a majority of three to two the House of Lords held that the appeals of Green and Williamson should succeed, but that Abdroikov's appeal must fail. Lords Rodger and Carswell, in the minority, held that all the appeals should fail. In reaching its decision the majority looked at the reports of previous committees that had been tasked with examining the operation of juries. Thus they referred to the findings of the 1965 committee chaired by Lord Morris of Borth-y-Gest, which recommended that the police and those professionally concerned in the administration of the law should continue to be ineligible. Then in 2001, Auld LJ reviewed the issue and recommended that everyone should be eligible for jury service save for the mentally ill. He recognised that the risk of bias could not be totally eradicated and envisaged that any question about the risk of bias on the part of any juror could be resolved by the trial judge on the facts of the case. His recommendation was given effect by the Criminal Justice Act 2003 s 321. However, as the House of Lords made clear, Auld LJ's expectation that each doubtful case would be resolved by the trial judge could not be met if neither the judge nor counsel knew that the juror was a police officer or CPS solicitor. The House of Lords recognised that there were situations where police officers and CPS solicitors would meet the tests of impartiality; however, that did not mean they would always do so automatically.

However, according to Lords Rodger and Carswell in the minority, Parliament had endorsed the view that universal eligibility for jury service was to be regarded as appropriate. In reaching that conclusion Parliament had to be taken to have been aware of the test for apparent bias. It must, therefore, be taken to have considered that the risk of bias in the case of serving police officers or CPS solicitors was manageable within the system of jury trial. The consequence of the House of Lords majority decision was pointed out by Lord Rodger in the clearest of terms:

I can see no reason why the fair-minded and informed observer should single out juries with police officers and CPS lawyers as being constitutionally incapable of following the judge's directions and reaching an impartial verdict. It must be assumed, for instance, that the observer considers that there is no real possibility that a jury containing a gay man trying a man accused of a homophobic attack will, for that reason alone, be incapable of reaching an unbiased verdict, even though the juror might readily identify with a fellow gay man. Despite this – if Mr Green's appeal is to be allowed – the observer must be supposed to consider that there is, inevitably, a real possibility that a jury will have been biased in a case involving a significant conflict of evidence between a police witness and the defendant, just because the witness and a police officer juror serve in the same borough or the juror serves in a force which commits its work to the trial court in question. Similarly, if Mr Williamson's appeal is allowed, the observer must be taken to consider that the same applies to any jury containing a CPS lawyer whenever the prosecution is brought by the CPS. In my view, an observer who singled out juries with these two types of members would be applying a different standard from the one that is usually applied. For no good reason, the observer would be virtually ignoring the other 11 jurors . . . your Lordships' decision to allow two of the appeals will drive a coach and horses through Parliament's legislation and will go far to reverse its reform of the law, *even though the statutory provisions themselves are not said to be incompatible with Convention rights*. Moreover, any requirement for police officers and CPS lawyers balloted to serve on a jury to identify themselves routinely to the judge would discriminate against them by introducing a process of vetting for them and them alone. Parliament cannot have considered that such a requirement was necessary since it did not impose it. The rational policy of the legislature is to decide who are eligible to serve as jurors and then to treat them all alike (emphasis added).

The issue of apparent juror bias on account of their occupation was considered further by the Court of Appeal in six conjoined cases in March 2008: *R v Khan* (2008). The occupations involved were those of serving police officers, employees of the CPS – although on this occasion in a prosecution brought by the Department of Trade and Industry – and prison officers. The judgment of the Court of Appeal was delivered by the then Lord Chief Justice, Lord Phillips, in the course of which he explained that, although the CJA 2003 had abolished automatic disqualification from jury service on account of an occupation associated with the administration of justice, it had not made those persons immune to claims of apparent bias and that 'the nature of some occupations is such that there is an obvious danger that the circumstances of a prosecution will give rise to an appearance of bias in relation to those who belong to them'. In its consideration of the issues, the Court of Appeal distinguished between apparent bias towards *a party* in the case and apparent bias towards *a witness* in the case. In the former instance, should it become apparent during a trial that a juror is partial then they should be discharged. If the bias only becomes apparent after the verdict, then the conviction must be quashed. However, the Court held that apparent bias towards *a witness* does not, automatically, have those consequences, and will do so only if it would appear to the fair-minded observer that the juror's apparent bias may affect, or have affected, the outcome of the trial. The fair-minded observer test was established in the House of Lords in *Porter v Magill* (2001).

As regards serving police officers, the Court of Appeal could find no clear principles for identifying apparent bias from the majority judgments in *R v Abdroikov*, but went on to hold that although such jurors may seem likely to favour the evidence of a fellow police officer, that would not automatically lead to the appearance that they favoured the prosecution. For example, if the police evidence was not challenged or was not an important part of the prosecution case, then there would be no reason to suspect bias on the part of the juror. It would only be appropriate to question a conviction for apparent bias if, and only if, the effect of the juror's partiality towards a fellow officer put in doubt the safety of the conviction and thus rendered the trial unfair.

More specifically, the court rejected the proposition that the mere fact that a police officer had taken part in operations involving the type of offence with which a defendant was charged gave rise, of itself, to an appearance of bias on the part of the police officer. As the court pointed out, police officers are likely to have had experience of most of the common types of criminal offence, not least drug dealing. Finally, as regards police jurors, the fact that the jury was told that a defendant had a previous conviction for assaulting a police officer would not of itself raise the issue of apparent bias.

As seen above, in *Abdroikov*, the majority of the House of Lords held that a juror who was a member of the Crown Prosecution Service had the appearance of bias where they acted as a juror in a case prosecuted by their employer. However, the Court of Appeal distinguished the situation under its consideration from that case in holding that there could be no objection to a member of the CPS sitting in a case prosecuted by some other authority, in this particular instance the Department of Trade and Industry.

With regard to the possibility of prison guards acting as jurors, the Court of Appeal made it clear that the mere suspicion that a juror might, by reason of employment in a prison where a defendant had been held, have acquired knowledge of that defendant's bad character could not, of itself, lead an objective observer to conclude that the juror had an appearance of bias. Where the juror had no knowledge of the defendant, there could be no objective basis for imputing bias towards the defendant. Indeed, even actual knowledge of a defendant's bad character would not automatically result in the juror ceasing to qualify as independent and impartial.

In concluding his judgment, Lord Phillips emphasised the court's concern with the need to regularise, and thus avoid appeals from, cases raising the issue of juror bias in relation to particular occupations. As he put it:

> It is undesirable that the apprehension of jury bias should lead to appeals such as those with which this court has been concerned. It is particularly undesirable if such appeals lead to the quashing of convictions so that

re-trials have to take place. In order to avoid this it is desirable that any risk of jury bias, or of unfairness as a result of partiality to witnesses, should be identified before the trial begins. If such a risk may arise, the juror should be stood down . . . It is essential that the trial judge should be aware at the stage of jury selection if any juror in waiting is, or has been, a police officer or a member of the prosecuting authority, or is a serving prison officer. Those called for jury service should be required to record on the appropriate form whether they fall into any of these categories, so that this information can be conveyed to the judge. We invite all of these authorities and Her Majesty's Court Service to consider the implications of this judgment and to issue such directions as they consider appropriate.

In an endeavour to maintain the unquestioned probity of the jury system, certain categories of persons are disqualified from serving as jurors. Among these are anyone who has been sentenced to a term of imprisonment, or youth custody, of five years or more. In addition, anyone who, in the past 10 years, has served a sentence, or has had a suspended sentence imposed on them, or has had a community punishment order made against them, is also disqualified. The CJA 2003 makes a number of amendments to reflect recent and forthcoming developments in sentencing legislation. Thus, juveniles sentenced under s 91 of the Powers of Criminal Courts (Sentencing) Act 2000 to detention for life, or for a term of five years or more, will be disqualified for life from jury service. People sentenced to imprisonment or detention for public protection, or to an extended sentence under ss 227 or 228 of the Act, are also to be disqualified for life from jury service. Anyone who has received a community order (as defined in s 177 of the Act) will be disqualified from jury service for 10 years. Those on bail in criminal proceedings are disqualified from serving as a juror in the Crown Court.

Certain people were excused as of right from serving as jurors on account of their jobs, age or religious views. Among these were members of the medical professions, Members of Parliament and members of the armed forces, together with anyone over 65 years of age. Paragraph 3 of Sched 33 to the CJA 2003 repeals s 9(1) of the JA 1974 and consequently no one will in future be entitled to excusal as of right from jury service.

It has always been the case that if a person who has been summoned to do jury service could show that there was a 'good reason' why their summons should be deferred or excused, s 9 of the JA 1974 provided discretion to defer or excuse service. With the abolition of most of the categories of ineligibility and of the availability of excusal as of right, it is expected that there will be a corresponding increase in applications for excusal or deferral under s 9 being submitted to the Jury Central Summoning Bureau (see below).

Grounds for such excusal or deferral are supposed to be made only on the basis of good reason, but there is at least a measure of doubt as to the rigour with which such rules are applied.

A Practice Note issued in 1988 (now *Practice Direction (Criminal: Consolidated)* [2002] 1 WLR 2870, para 42) stated that applications for excusal should be treated sympathetically and listed the following as good grounds for excusal:

(a)   personal involvement in the case;

(b)   close connection with a party or a witness in the case;

(c)   personal hardship;

(d)   conscientious objection to jury service.

However, a new s 9AA, introduced by the CJA 2003, placed a statutory duty on the Lord Chancellor, in whom current responsibility for jury summoning is vested, to publish and lay before Parliament guidelines relating to the exercise by the Jury Central Summoning Bureau of its functions in relation to discretionary deferral and excusal.

The guidelines, available at www.official-documents.gov.uk/document/other/9 780108508400/9780108508400.pdf, were issued in 2004 and make clear that only in extreme circumstances should a person be excused from jury service. They require summoning officers to refuse requests in the absence of 'good reason'. Even where 'good reason' is shown why the person should not sit on the date they have been summoned, deferral should always be considered in the first instance. Excusal from jury service should be reserved only for those cases where the jury summoning officer is satisfied that it would be unreasonable to require the person to serve at any time within the following 12 months.

The previous, somewhat antiquated procedure for selecting potential jury members, with its accompanying disparity of treatment, was modernised by the introduction of a Central Summoning Bureau based at Blackfriars Crown Court Centre in London. The Bureau uses a computer system to select jurors at random from the electoral registers and issue the summonses, as well as dealing with jurors' questions and requests. The jury summoning system is linked to the national police records system to allow checks to be made against potentially disqualified individuals.

However, severe doubts have been expressed as to the accuracy of the Police National Computer (PNC), which might not only render the checks on juries inaccurate, but might actually contravene the Data Protection Act 1998. When the Metropolitan Police conducted an audit of the PNC in 1999, it was found to have 'wholly unacceptable' levels of inaccuracy, with an overall error rate of 86 per cent. In one case in 2000 at Highbury Corner magistrates' court in north London, a man charged with theft of £2,700 was granted bail on the grounds that the PNC showed that he had no previous convictions. In fact, he was a convicted murderer released from prison on licence.

It has to be stated that, as reported in a parliamentary answer in February 2007, the Secretary of State for the Home Department intimated that later audits carried out in August 2002 had indicated that the general position on data accuracy was far more favourable than had previously been suggested. According to his statement, the exercise found that in 94 per cent of cases, the key information was recorded entirely accurately, and that in the remaining 6 per cent some inaccuracies were found but, in the majority of instances, the inaccuracy was not critical.

TABLE 14.1   *Reproduced from Ministry of Justice Report*

Crown Court
Jury Central Summoning Bureau figures,[1] 2007–2012

	2007	2008	2009	2010	2011	2012
Total number of summons issued[2,3] (r)	388,362	395,503	373,871	373,650	343,949	349,606
Total number of jurors supplied to the court	182,661	183,506	176,351	181,281	170,421	168,914
Deferred to serve at a later date	66,174	66,806	61,892	62,051	57,982	61,252
Number refused deferral	122	103	87	78	54	33
Excused by right having served in past two years	4,518	4,244	3,470	3,881	3,331	3,280
Excused for other reasons[4]	103,064	104,290	96,563	93,782	76,008	76,578
All excused	**107,582**	**108,534**	**100,033**	**97,663**	**79,339**	**79,858**
Number refused excusal	1,641	1,515	1,342	1,485	1,303	1,141
Disqualified – residency, mental disorders, criminality	94,171	96,325	92,704	96,482	89,668	88,836
Disqualified – on selection	58,900	59,017	56,967	56,871	52,115	50,538
Disqualified – failed Police National Computer check	207	225	220	215	239	648
Failed to reply to summons	40,635	45,192	49,086	47,221	43,663	41,925
Summons undelivered	18,325	17,603	13,646	12,916	12,583	13,066
Postponed by Jury Central Summoning Bureau	7,274	9,621	7,439	6,569	4,937	5,427

Source: Jury Central Summoning Bureau
Notes:

[1] Numbers do not add up to the overall total within a given year, as the data reflect rolling 12-month periods with 'carry-over' rules applied to certain rows in the table. For example, the number of disqualifications reported for a given year may include disqualifications for summons that were issued in previous years.

[2] Previously published figures for 2007 to 2009 double-counted summons that were re-issued due to a change in court venue. In this publication, these figures have been revised to remove any double counting.

[3] This figure represents the number of summons that were issued in a year and not the number of people that actually served on a jury in that year. For example, a person summoned for jury service in 2011 may not actually serve until 2012.

[4] Including childcare, work commitments, medical issues, language difficulties, student status, moved from area, travel difficulties and financial hardship.

It is to be hoped that the situation of people with disabilities has been altered for the better by the Criminal Justice and Public Order Act (CJPOA) 1994, which introduced a new s 9B into the JA 1974. Previously, it was all too common for judges to discharge jurors with disabilities, including deafness, on the assumption that they would not be capable of undertaking the duties of a juror.

Under this provision, where it appears doubtful that a person summoned for jury service is capable of serving on account of some physical disability, that person, as previously, may be brought before the judge. The new s 9B, however, introduces a presumption that people should serve and provides that the judge shall affirm the jury summons unless he is of the opinion that the person will not be able to act effectively.

It would appear, however, that the CJPOA 1994 does not improve the situation of profoundly deaf people who could only function as jurors with the aid of a sign language interpreter. That was the outcome of a case decided in November 1999 that profoundly deaf Jeff McWhinney, Chief Executive of the British Deaf Association, could not serve as a juror. For him to do so would have required that he had the assistance of an interpreter in the jury room and that could not be allowed as, at present, only jury members are allowed into the jury room.

Any person who has suffered from 'a disorder or disability of the mind' and, because of that condition, regularly visits a medical practitioner for treatment, is precluded from jury service. As campaigners have pointed out, many people are being excluded from jury service after being treated for conditions such as depression, schizophrenia and bipolar disorder, which are all perfectly manageable through medication. As they also point out, one in four Britons suffers from mental illness at some point in their lives, and one in 10 is prescribed antidepressants.

In 2012 Gavin Barwell MP introduced a Private Member's Bill, the Mental Health (Discrimination) Bill, which looked to outlaw discrimination against people who have experienced mental ill health, including jury service and membership of the House of Commons.

That juries can be 'self-selecting' provides grounds for concern as to the random nature of the jury, but the traditional view of the jury is further and perhaps even more fundamentally undermined by the way in which both prosecution and defence seek to influence its constitution.

Under s 12(6) of the JA 1974, both prosecution and defence have a right to challenge the array where the summoning officer has acted improperly in bringing the whole panel together. Such challenges are rare, although an unsuccessful action was raised in *R v Danvers* (1982), where the defendant tried to challenge the racial composition of the group of potential jurors.

Until the CJA 1988, there were two ways in which the defence could challenge potential jurors:

- *Peremptory challenge*

  The defence could object to any potential jury members, up to a maximum number of three, without having to show any reason or justification for the challenge. Defence counsel used this procedure in an attempt to shape the composition of the jury in a way they thought might best suit their client, although it has to be said that it was an extremely inexact process, and one that could upset or antagonise rejected jurors. In spite of arguments for its retention on a civil liberties basis, the majority of the Roskill Committee on Fraud Trials (January 1986, HMSO) recommended that the right be abolished, and abolition was provided for in the CJA 1988.

- *Challenge for cause*

  The defence retains the power to challenge any number of potential jurors for cause, that is to say that there is a substantial reason why a particular person should not serve on the jury to decide a particular defendant's case. A simple example would be where the potential juror has had previous dealings with the defendant or has been involved in the case in some way. There may be less obvious grounds for objection, however, which may be based on the particular juror's attitudes, or indeed political beliefs. The question arises whether such factors provide grounds for challenge. In what is known as *The Angry Brigade* case in 1972 (see *The Times*, 10–11 December 1971; *The Times*, 12–15 December 1972), a group of people were charged with carrying out a bombing campaign against prominent members of the Conservative government. In the process of empanelling a jury, the judge asked potential jurors to exclude themselves on a variety of socio-political grounds, including active membership of the Conservative Party. As a consequence of the procedure adopted in that case, the Lord Chief Justice issued a practice direction in which he made it clear that potential jurors were not to be excluded on account of race, religion, politics or occupation. Since that practice direction, it is clear that the challenge for cause can only be used within a restricted sphere, and this makes it less useful to the defence than it might otherwise be if it were to operate in a more general way.

It has been argued that the desire of civil libertarians to retain the right of the defence to select a jury that might be more sympathetic to its case is contradictory, because although in theory they usually rely on the random nature of the jury to ensure the appearance of justice, in practice they seek to influence its composition. When, however, the shortcomings in the establishment of panels for juries is recalled, it might be countered that the defence is attempting to do no more than counter the inbuilt bias that ensues from the use of unbalanced electoral registers.

14.4.4.2 Challenge by the prosecution

If the defence attempts to ensure that any jury will not be prejudiced against its case, if not predisposed towards it, the same is true of the prosecution. However, the prosecution has a greater scope to achieve such an aim. While the prosecution has the same right as the defence to challenge for cause, it has the additional option of excluding potential jury members by simply asking them to stand by until a jury has been empanelled. The request for the potential juror to stand by is only a provisional challenge and, in theory, the person stood by can at a later time take their place on the jury if there are no other suitable candidates. In practice, of course, it is unlikely in the extreme for there not to be sufficient alternative candidates to whom the prosecution do not object and prefer to the person stood by.

When the Roskill Committee recommended the removal of the defence's right to pre-emptive challenge, it recognised that, in order to retain an equitable situation, the right of the Crown to ask potential jurors to stand by should also be withdrawn. Unfortunately, although the government of the day saw fit to follow the Committee's recommendation in relation to the curtailment of the defence rights, it did not feel under the same obligation to follow its corresponding recommendation to curtail the rights of the prosecution. Thus, the CJA 1988 made no reference to the procedure and, in failing to do so, established a distinct advantage in favour of the prosecution in regard to selecting what it considered to be suitable juries.

The manifest unreasonableness of this procedure led to the Attorney General issuing a practice note (1988) to the effect that the Crown should only exercise its power to stand by potential jurors in the following two circumstances:

- To prevent the empanelment of a 'manifestly unsuitable' juror, with the agreement of the defence. The example given of 'manifest unsuitability' is an illiterate person asked to sit in a highly complex case. It is reasonable to doubt the ability of such a person to follow the process of the case involving a number of documents, and on that basis they should be stood by.
- In circumstances where the Attorney General has approved the vetting of the potential jury members and that process has revealed that the particular juror in question might be a security risk. In this situation, the Attorney General is also required to approve the use of the 'stand by' procedure.

14.4.4.3 Jury vetting

Jury vetting is the process by which the Crown checks the background of potential jurors to assess their suitability to decide particular cases. The procedure is clearly contrary to the ideal of the jury being based on a random selection of people, but it is justified on the basis that it is necessary to ensure that jury members are not likely to divulge any secrets made open to them in the course of a sensitive trial or, alternatively, on the ground that jurors with extreme political views should not be permitted the opportunity to express those views in a situation where they might influence the outcome of a case.

The practice of vetting potential jurors developed after the *Angry Brigade* trial in 1972, but it did not become public until 1978. In that year, as a result of an Official Secrets Act case, known by the initials of the three defendants as the ABC trial, it became apparent that the list of potential jurors had been checked to establish their 'soundness'.

As a consequence of that case, the Attorney General published the current guidelines for vetting jury panels. Since that date, the guidelines have been updated and the most recent guidelines were published in 1988. These guidelines maintain the general propositions that jury members should normally be selected at random from the panel and should be disqualified only on the grounds set out in the JA 1974. The guidelines do, however, make reference to exceptional cases of public importance where potential jury members might properly be vetted. Such cases are broadly identified as those involving national security, where part of the evidence may be heard *in camera*, and terrorist cases.

Vetting is a twofold process. An initial check into police criminal records and police Special Branch records should be sufficient to reveal whether a further investigation by the security services is required. Any further investigation requires the prior approval of the Attorney General.

In addition to vetting properly so called, the Court of Appeal in *R v Mason* (1980) approved the checking of criminal records to establish whether potential jurors had been convicted of criminal offences in the past and therefore were not eligible to serve as jurors. The Runciman Commission recommended that this process of checking on those who should be disqualified on the basis of previous criminal conviction should be regularised when the collection and storage of criminal records is centralised. This was achieved when the Criminal Records Bureau was established as a result of Part V of the Police Act 1997.

14.4.4.4 The racial mix of the jury

In *R v Danvers* (1982), the defence had sought to challenge the array on the basis that a black defendant could not have complete confidence in the impartiality of an all-white jury. The question of the racial mix of a jury has exercised the courts on a number of occasions. In *R v Ford* (1989), the trial judge's refusal to accept the defendant's application for a racially mixed jury was supported by the Court of Appeal on the grounds that 'fairness is achieved by the principle of random selection' as regards the make-up of a jury, and that to insist on a racially balanced jury would be contrary to that principle, and would be to imply that particular jurors were incapable of impartiality. A similar point was made in *R v Tarrant* (1997), in which a person accused of drug-related offences was convicted by a jury that had been selected from outside the normal catchment area for the court. The aim of the judge had been to minimise potential jury intimidation, but nonetheless, the Court of Appeal overturned the conviction on the grounds that the judge had deprived the defendant of a randomly selected jury.

To deny people the right to have their cases heard by representatives of their own race, on the basis of a refusal to recognise the existence of racial discriminatory attitudes, cannot but give the appearance of a society where such racist attitudes are institutionalised. This has particular resonance given the findings of the Macpherson Inquiry that the police force was 'institutionally racist'. Without suggesting that juries as presently constituted are biased, it remains arguable that if, in order to achieve the undoubted appearance of fairness, jury selection has to be manipulated to ensure a racial mix, then it should at least be considered.

An interesting case study in this respect is the trial in 1994 of Lakhbir Deol, an Asian who was accused of the murder of a white youth in Stoke-on-Trent in 1993. Mr Deol's lawyers sought to have the case moved from Stafford to Birmingham Crown Court on the grounds that Stafford has an almost completely white population, whereas Birmingham has an approximately 25 per cent ethnic minority population. Mr Justice McKinnon repeatedly refused the request and the trial was heard in Stafford as scheduled. Mr Deol was acquitted, so his fears were proved groundless, but surely the worrying fact is that he had those fears in the first place.

In February 2010 the report on empirical research carried out by Professor Cheryl Thomas for the Ministry of Justice stated that:

> While these findings strongly suggest that racially balanced juries are *not needed* to ensure fair decision-making in jury trials with BME (black and minority ethnic) defendants, concerns about *the appearance of fairness* with all-white juries may still remain (emphasis added).

It is heartening to note that the Runciman Commission fully endorsed the views expressed above and recommended that either the prosecution or the defence should be able to insist that up to three jury members be from ethnic minorities, and that at least one of those should be from the same ethnic minority as the accused or the victim. Sir Robin Auld, in his review of the criminal courts, also recommended that provision should be made to enable ethnic minority representation on juries where race is likely to be relevant to an important issue in the case.

In *R v Smith* (2003), the Court of Appeal reaffirmed the traditional view in holding that it had not been unfair for Smith to be tried by a randomly selected all-white jury. In addition, however, the Court held that the selection process had not infringed Smith's rights under Art 6 of the ECHR.

Another case that raised a human rights issue was *R v Mushtaq* (2002), in which the defendant appealed against his conviction for conspiracy to defraud. He had admitted to police that he had played a minor part in the conspiracy, but later claimed that his confession had been obtained by oppression. The judge ruled during the trial that Mushtaq's confession had not been obtained by oppression and was therefore admissible, and in his summing-up to the jury, he emphasised that the confession was central and crucial to the case. Mushtaq claimed that the judge's direction to the jury was in breach of Art 6 of the ECHR and that the jury, *as a separate and distinct public authority*, had a duty to protect his rights. The Court of Appeal dismissed the appeal, holding that the separate functions allocated to the judge and the jury in relation to disputed confessions had significant advantages for ensuring that justice was done. The admissibility of a confession was a matter for the judge and if the prosecution failed to satisfy the judge that a confession was not obtained by oppression, the jury would not hear it. This division of function between judge and jury complied with the requirement to provide an adequate safeguard for a defendant's Art 6 rights, and it could not be said that the jury was a separate public authority having a distinct and separate duty from the judge to protect Mushtaq's rights. In a criminal trial, it was the court acting collectively that had the shared responsibility of ensuring a fair trial.

14.5 RACIAL BIAS IN JURIES

If the law does not allow for the artificial creation of ethnic balance in juries, then it must ensure that ethnically unbalanced juries do not become ethnically biased ones.

In May 2000, the ECtHR held by a majority of four to three that the right of a British Asian to be tried by an impartial tribunal had been violated on the basis of alleged racism within the jury that had convicted him. Kuldip Sander had been charged with conspiracy to commit fraud and was tried at Birmingham Crown Court in March 1995. During the trial, one of the jurors sent a note to the judge stating:

> I have decided I cannot remain silent any longer. For some time during the trial I have been concerned that fellow jurors are not taking their duties seriously. At least two have been making openly racist remarks and jokes and I fear are going to convict the defendants not on the evidence but because they are Asian. My concern is the defendants will not therefore receive a fair verdict. Please could you advise me what I can do in this situation.

The judge adjourned the case, but kept the juror who had written the letter apart from the other jurors while he listened to submission from counsel in open court. The defence asked the judge to dismiss the jury on the ground that there was a real danger of bias. The judge, however, decided to call the jury back into court, at which stage the juror who had written the complaint joined the others. The judge read out the complaint to them and told them the following:

> I am not able to conduct an inquiry into the validity of those contentions and I do not propose to do so. This case has cost an enormous amount of money and I am not anxious to halt it at the moment, but I shall have no compunction in doing so if the situation demands . . . I am going to ask you all to search your conscience overnight and if you feel that you are not able to try this case solely on the evidence and find that you cannot put aside any prejudices you may have will you please indicate that fact by writing a personal note to that effect and giving it to the jury bailiff on your arrival at court tomorrow morning. I will then review the position.

The next morning, the judge received two letters from the jury. The first letter, which was signed by all the jurors including the juror who had sent the complaint, refuted any allegation of racial bias. The second letter was written by a juror who appeared to have thought himself to have been the one who had been making the jokes. The juror in question stated that he was sorry if he had given any offence, that he had many connections with people from ethnic minorities and that he was in no way racially biased.

The judge decided not to discharge the jury and it went on to find the applicant guilty, although it acquitted another Asian defendant. The applicant's appeal, partly on the grounds of bias on the part of the jury, was dismissed by the Court of Appeal.

The majority of the ECtHR, however, held that the trial was conducted contrary to Art 6(1) of the ECHR. The Court considered that the allegations contained in the note were capable of causing the applicant and any objective observer to have legitimate doubts as to the impartiality of the court, which neither the collective letter nor the redirection of the jury by the judge could have dispelled.

In reaching its decision, the Court distinguished the decision in the similar case of *Gregory v UK* (1998). In the *Gregory* judgment, there was no admission by a juror that he had made racist comments, in the form of a joke or otherwise; there was no indication as to who had made the complaint and the complaint was vague and imprecise. Moreover, in the present case, the applicant's counsel had insisted throughout the proceedings that dismissing the jury was the only viable course of action.

The Court accepted that, although discharging the jury might not always be the only means to achieve a fair trial, there were certain circumstances where this was required by Art 6(1) of the ECHR. As the Court stated:

> Given the importance attached by all Contracting States to the need to combat racism, the Court considers that the judge should have reacted in a more robust manner than merely seeking vague assurances that the jurors could set aside their prejudices and try the case solely on the evidence. By failing to do so, the judge did not provide sufficient guarantees to exclude any objectively justified or legitimate doubts as to the impartiality of the court. It follows that the court that condemned the applicant was not impartial from an objective point of view.

The Court, however, refused his claim for compensation of some £458,000, which suggests that it was not convinced that a substitute jury would not have convicted him as well.

It has already been seen that s 8 of the Contempt of Court Act 1981 prevents investigation into what occurs in the privacy of the jury room and such prohibition applies equally to judges. In *R v Qureshi* (2001), the defendant had been convicted of arson and of attempting to attain property by deception. Three days after the verdict, a juror in the trial informed the court that some members of the jury had been racially prejudiced against Qureshi and had decided he was guilty from the outset of the trial. Qureshi's application for permission to appeal against his conviction was rejected by the Court of Appeal on the grounds that the complaint did not arise during the trial, but only after an apparently regular verdict had been delivered. In order to pursue the allegation, the court would have had to investigate what had happened in the jury room and that was precluded by s 8 of the Contempt of Court Act 1981. In reaching this decision, the Court of Appeal distinguished *Sander*, where the complaint arose during the trial, and followed *R v Miah* (1997), where the complaint arose after the event. In the latter case, it was stated that the rule against breaching jury secrecy applied to 'anything said by one juror to another about the case from the moment the jury is empanelled, at least provided what is said is not overheard by anyone who is not a juror'. It has to be asked whether such a rule is acceptable, especially when it conceals possible injustice. For a detailed analysis of these cases, see P Robertshaw, 'Responding to bias amongst jurors' (2002) 66(1) Journal of Criminal Law 84.

In June 2007, the Department of Justice published an extremely illuminating report of the results of a series of four linked empirical studies into the operations of juries in the English and Welsh Crown Courts. The report, entitled 'Diversity and Fairness in the Jury System', was produced by academic Cheryl Thomas, with the assistance of Nigel Balmer.

The four studies had conducted:

- a survey of the socio-economic background of all jurors summoned in England and Wales in one week in 2003 and one week in 2005, involving a total of 15,846 jurors;
- a survey of the socio-economic background of all jurors in jury pools, on jury panels and juries at three Crown Courts over a four-week period, involving 640 jurors;
- a case simulation study with real jurors exploring whether ethnicity affects jury verdicts or juror votes, involving 28 juries with a total of 319 jurors (while this allowed the study to examine whether ethnicity affected jury decision-making, its use of simulation meant that it did not contravene s 8 of the Contempt of Court Act 1981);
- a study of the relationship between jury verdicts, the composition of juries and the ethnicity of defendants in actual cases at three Crown Courts, involving 186 verdicts.

The final report claimed to be the first study to compare the ethnic profile of jurors summoned and serving at each Crown Court in England and Wales with the ethnic population profiles for the areas in which each court operated.

Concern about ethnic minority under-representation on juries implicitly assumes that the ethnic composition of juries may affect jury verdicts, and this is the first research conducted in this country to examine whether the research used case simulation with real jurors, along with a study of jury verdicts in real cases.

Despite its scope and innovation, none of the research required exemption from the current restrictive rules, and illustrates just how much jury research can be conducted in this country within existing restrictions.

The studies set themselves the task of challenging various assumptions about the representative nature of jury service, which have influenced reviews of the jury system and policy development in that area. As the report stated, 'most of these assumptions paint a picture of widespread jury service avoidance and unrepresentative jurors'.

However, somewhat surprisingly, the report claimed to establish that most of those assumptions about jury service were based on myth, rather than reality, as substantiated by the following conclusions it reached: that:

- there was no significant under-representation of black and minority ethnic (BME) groups among those summoned for jury service at virtually all Crown Courts in England and Wales;

- ethnic minorities are summoned in proportion to their representation in the local population in virtually all Crown Courts in England and Wales. However, racially mixed juries are only likely to exist in courts where BME groups make up at least 10 per cent of the entire juror catchment area. The report explained that this was simply the consequence of BME population levels in these catchment areas and the process of random selection;

- while there was some evidence that BME jurors on jury panels appeared to be selected to serve on juries less often than white panel members, the report put this down to 'court clerks inadvertently avoiding reading out juror names that are difficult to pronounce';

- in addition, jury pools were found to closely reflect the local population in terms of gender and age, and the self-employed are represented among serving jurors in direct proportion to their representation in the population;

- the main factor affecting non-responses to summonses is high residential mobility, not ethnicity;

- there was no significant difference between BME and white respondents in their willingness to do jury service or indeed support for the jury system, which was strongly supported by both groups;

- the most significant factors predicting whether a summoned juror will serve or not were not ethnicity but income and employment status (those summoned for jury service who are economically inactive or in lower income brackets are far less likely to serve). Where ethnic minorities did not serve, this was primarily due to ineligibility or disqualification (residency or language);

- there is no mass avoidance of jury service by the British public (85 per cent of those summoned replied to their summonses and the vast majority served);

- the middle classes or 'the important and clever in society' do not avoid jury service. In fact the studies showed the contrary, that the highest rates of jury service are among middle- to high-income earners and higher-status professions. Again, perhaps surprisingly, the employed are over-represented among serving jurors, and the retired and unemployed are under-represented;

- the changes to juror eligibility under the Criminal Justice Act 2003 increased the proportion of those summoned who actually served, from 54 per cent to 64 per cent. Significantly, the proportion of serving jurors between 65 and 69 years of age doubled from 3 per cent in 2003 to 6 per cent in 2005, after their right of excusal was removed.

Perhaps the most controversial study informing the report was the research into the relationship of race and jury decision-making.

As the report recognised, the unstated but underlying assumption for those arguing possible under-representation of ethnic minorities on juries assumes that the ethnic composition of juries can affect jury outcomes.

- The research used case simulation with real jurors, supplemented by a study of jury verdicts in actual cases.
- The simulations were based on a real case, filmed in a real courtroom, with a real judge, barristers, court staff, police and witnesses. Real jurors were the study participants, jury panels were selected by the Court Service random selection programme, all juries included enough jurors to constitute a valid jury (10 to 12 jurors) and they deliberated in a real deliberating room.

All juries saw a film of an identical case where the defendant was charged with causing actual bodily harm (ABH), but where specific case elements were altered for different juries (race of defendant, victim and charges).

In examining the conclusions of the report it is important to distinguish between the decisions of individual jurors and the decision of the jury that they were a member of.

The main finding in relation to juries was that the verdicts of racially mixed *juries* did not discriminate against defendants based on the defendant's race. In the 28 separate jury verdicts, outcomes for the white, black and Asian defendants were remarkably similar.

However, as regards the voting of individual jurors on racially mixed juries, even though the defendant's ethnicity did not have an impact on jury verdicts, the research found that in certain cases ethnicity did have a significant impact on the individual decisions of some jurors. Indeed, the report claimed that 'in certain cases BME jurors were significantly less likely to vote to convict a BME defendant than a white defendant'.

However, any 'same race leniency' among BME jurors was only found when race was not an explicit element of the case, and where the prosecution was racially aggravated actual bodily harm (ABH), BME jurors and white jurors had similar conviction rates for both the white and BME defendants. The report suggested that such leniency among BME jurors reflected their belief that the courts treat ethnic minority defendants more harshly than white defendants. Somewhat disconcertingly, while both black and Asian jurors showed leniency for the black defendant, there was apparently no leniency for the Asian defendant by either Asian or black jurors.

The report also claimed to find evidence of race leniency among white jurors, but again only in cases where race was not an issue in the case. As the report stated: 'In non-race salient cases, white jurors had very low conviction rates for the white defendant, despite consistently stating that they did not believe his evidence and felt he was dishonest.'

Nonetheless, even in the face of these findings the report was confident that any same-race leniency did not have an impact on the verdicts of the juries of which they were members on the basis that '12 jurors must jointly try to reach a decision and that majority verdicts are possible meant that more verdicts were achieved and individual biases did not dictate the decision-making of these racially mixed juries'. However, it was careful to warn that: 'If juries were smaller or if unanimous verdicts were required, then individual juror bias might potentially have a greater impact on jury verdicts.'

In February 2010 a second report for the Ministry of Justice by Professor Thomas entitled 'Are juries fair?' concluded that, in essence, they were, that there was 'little evidence that juries are not fair' and that 'juries overall appear efficient and effective'.

The specific findings concluded that:

- there were no courts with a higher jury acquittal than conviction rate, and this dispels the myth that there are courts where juries rarely convict;
- all-white juries did not discriminate against BME defendants;
- differences in jury conviction rates for different specific offences suggest that juries try defendants on the evidence and the law;
- contrary to popular belief and previous government reports, juries actually convict more often than they acquit in rape cases (55 per cent jury conviction rate);
- while over half of the jurors perceived the judge's directions as easy to understand, only a minority (31 per cent) actually understood the directions fully in the legal terms used by the judge;
- younger jurors were better able than older jurors to comprehend the legal instructions, with comprehension of directions on the law declining as the age of the juror increased.

14.6   THE DECLINE OF THE JURY TRIAL

Many direct attempts have been made in the recent past to reduce the operation of the jury system within the English legal system. These particular endeavours, however, have to be understood in the context of the general historical decline in the use of the jury as the mechanism for determining issues in court cases. Perhaps the heat engendered in the current debate is a consequence of the fact that the continued existence of the jury as it is presently constituted is a matter of political contention.

14.6.1   THE JURY TRIAL IN CIVIL PROCEDURE

There can be no doubt as to the antiquity of the institution of trial by jury, nor can there be much doubt as to its supposed democratising effect on the operation of the legal system. Neither, unfortunately, can there be any grounds for denying the diminishment that has occurred in the fairly recent past in the role of the jury as the means of determining the outcome of trials, nor can the continued existence of the jury as it is presently constituted be taken for granted.

In respect of civil law, the use of juries has diminished considerably and automatic recourse to trial by jury is restricted to a small number of areas and, even in those areas, the continued use of the jury is threatened. Prior to 1854, all cases that came before the common law courts were decided by a judge and jury. The Common Law Procedure Act of that year provided that cases could be settled without a jury where the parties agreed, and since then, the role of the jury has been gradually curtailed until, at present, under s 69 of the Senior Courts Act 1981, the right to a jury trial is limited to only four specific areas: fraud, defamation (i.e. libel and slander), malicious prosecution and false imprisonment. (Similar provisions are contained in the County Courts Act 1984.) Section 11 of the Defamation Act 2013 removes libel land slander from that list, unless the the court decides otherwise. Even in these areas, the right is not absolute and can be denied by a judge under s 69(1) where the case involves 'any prolonged examination of documents or accounts or any scientific or local investigation which cannot conveniently be made with a jury'. (See *Beta Construction Ltd v Channel Four TV Co Ltd* (1990) for an indication of the factors that the judge will take into consideration in deciding whether a case should be decided by a jury or not.)

The question of whether or not juries should be used in libel cases gained wider consideration in the case involving McDonald's, the fast-food empire, and two environmentalists, Dave Morris and Helen Steel. McDonald's claimed that their reputation was damaged by an allegedly libellous leaflet issued by members of an organisation called London Greenpeace including Morris and Steel, which linked McDonald's' products to heart disease and cancer as well as the despoliation of the environment and the exploitation of the Third World. In a preliminary hearing, later confirmed by the Court of Appeal, it was decided that the evidence to be presented would be of such scientific complexity that it would be beyond the understanding of a jury (see *The Times*, 10 June 1997).

The right to jury trial in defamation cases has been the object of particular criticism. In 1975, the Faulks Committee on the Law of Defamation recommended that the availability of jury trial in that area should be subject to the same judicial discretion as all other civil cases. In its conclusions, the Faulks Report shared the uncertainty of the Court of Appeal in *Ward v James* (1965) as to the suitability of juries to determine the level of damages that should be awarded. Support for these views has been provided by a number of defamation cases decided since then, such as *Sutcliffe v Pressdram Ltd* (1990), in which the wife of a convicted serial killer was awarded damages of £600,000. She eventually settled for £60,000 after the Court of Appeal stated that it would reassess the award.

In *Aldington v Watts and Tolstoy* (1990), damages of £1.5 million were awarded. This huge award was subsequently held by the ECtHR to be so disproportionate as to amount to a violation of Tolstoy's right to freedom of expression under Art 10 of the ECHR (*Tolstoy Miloslavsky v UK* (1995)). Domestic law has also sought to deal with what could only be seen as excessive awards of damages in defamation cases, even prior to the Human Rights Act (HRA) 1998, which makes the ECtHR *Tolstoy* decision and Art 10 of the ECHR binding in UK law.

Section 8 of the Courts and Legal Services Act (CLSA) 1990 gave appeal courts the power to alter damages awards made by juries to a level that they felt to be 'proper'.

Nonetheless, the question of what actually constitutes a proper level of damages continued to present problems for juries, which continued to award very large sums. The problem arose from the limited guidance that judges could give juries in making their awards. In *Rantzen v Mirror Group Newspapers* (1993), the Court of Appeal stated that judges should advise juries, in making their awards, to consider the purchasing power of the award and its proportionality to the damage suffered to the reputation of the plaintiff, and should refer to awards made by the courts under s 8 of the CLSA (Rantzen's original award of £250,000 was reduced to £110,000). Still, extremely large awards continued to be made, and in *John v MGN Ltd* (1996), the Court of Appeal stated that past practice should be altered to allow juries to refer to personal injury cases to decide the level of award, and that the judge could indicate what sort of level would be appropriate (John's awards of £350,000 for the libel and £275,000 in exemplary damages were reduced to £75,000 and £50,000, respectively).

In 1996, statute law intervened in the form of the Defamation Act, which was designed to simplify the procedure of defamation cases. The main provisions of the Act are:

(a)   a one-year limitation period for defamation claims;

(b)   a statutory defence based on responsibility for publication. This replaces the common law defence of innocent dissemination;

(c)   an updating of defences in relation to privilege, that is, reporting on the proceedings and publications of, for example, the courts and government;

(d)   a streamlined procedure for dealing with a defendant who has offered to make amends. This would involve paying compensation, assessed by a judge, and publishing an appropriate correction and apology;

(e)   powers for judges to deal with cases without a jury. Under this provision, the judge can dismiss a claim if he considers it has no realistic prospect of success. Alternatively, if he considers there to be no realistic defence to the claim, he can award summary relief. Such relief can take the form of a declaration of the falsity of the statement; an order to print an apology; an order to refrain from repeating the statement; and damages of up to £10,000.

The most significant elements of the Defamation Act came into effect at the end of February 2000, but in January 2001 the Court of Appeal used its common law powers to completely overturn the award of damages in the case of *Grobbelaar v News Group Newspapers Ltd* (2001). Grobbelaar, an ex-football player, had been accused of accepting money to fix football matches. He had been found not guilty in a criminal case and had been awarded £85,000 damages for defamation in a related civil case against *The Sun* newspaper. On appeal, the Court of Appeal held that the newspaper could not rely on the defence of limited qualified privilege, as recently recognised in *Reynolds v Times Newspapers Ltd and Others* (1999), and could be held to account for such defamatory statements as could not be proved true. However, although the Court stated that it would be most reluctant to find perversity in a jury's verdict, it had such jurisdiction and, therefore, duty to consider that ground of appeal. The Court then went on to conclude that no reasonable jury could have failed to be satisfied on the balance of probabilities, and to a relatively high degree of probability, that Grobbelaar had been party to corrupt conspiracies. The court considered that the evidence led inexorably to the view that Grobbelaar's story was 'quite simply incredible. All logic, common sense and reason compelled one to that conclusion'.

As regards overturning the decision of the jury, in the words of Thorpe LJ:

> I recognise and respect the unique function of a jury that heard all of the evidence over some 16 days of trial, nevertheless it would be an injustice to the defendants to allow the outcome to stand.

On further appeal, the House of Lords held that the Court of Appeal was correct in holding that the jury's decision was open to review on the grounds of perversity. However, it found that the Court of Appeal had been wrong to overturn the jury's verdict on the grounds of perversity in this instance, as the verdict could have been explained in such a way that did not necessarily require the imputation of perversity. Grobbelaar's victory, however, was pyrrhic in the extreme; due to his breach of his legal and moral obligations, the damages awarded by the jury were quashed and substituted by the award of nominal damages of £1, with no costs awarded.

The extent of damages and, in particular, exemplary damages awarded against the police in a number of civil actions have also been problematic (see 7.10 for a consideration of types of damages). These actions have arisen from wrongful arrest, false imprisonment, assault and malicious prosecution and usually have involved connotations of racist behaviour on the part of the police. In setting the level of damages, juries have wished signally to demonstrate their disapproval of such police behaviour, but as the courts have correctly pointed out, any payments made come from the public purse, not from the individuals involved. The issue came to a head in *Thompson and Another v Commissioner of Police for the Metropolis* (1997), in which the Court of Appeal considered awards made to two plaintiffs. The first had been assaulted in custody and false evidence was used against her in a criminal trial during which she was held in prison. In a civil action, she was awarded £51,500 damages, of which £50,000 was exemplary damages. The second plaintiff was physically and racially abused by police when they broke into his house and arrested him. In a consequential civil action, he was awarded £220,000 for wrongful arrest, false imprisonment and assault, of which £200,000 was exemplary damages. On appeal, the Court of Appeal stated that in such cases, the judge should direct the jury that:

(i)   damages, save in exceptional circumstances, should be awarded only as compensation and in line with a scale which keeps the damages proportionate with those payable in personal injury cases;

(ii)   where aggravated damages are appropriate, they are unlikely to be less than £1,000, or to be more than twice the basic damages except where those basic damages are modest;

without juries in particular situations. The so-called Diplock courts operate in relation to certain 'scheduled offences', particularly, but not exclusively, ones associated with terrorism.

With regard to the continuation of no-jury trial in Northern Ireland, the United Nations Human Rights Committee, in its concluding observations on the UK's periodic report under the UN Covenant on Civil and Political Rights, stated its concern. In its words:

> The Committee remains concerned that, despite improvements in the secu- rity situation in Northern Ireland, some elements of criminal procedure con- tinue to differ between Northern Ireland and the remainder of the State party's territory. In particular, the Committee is concerned that, under the Justice and Security (Northern Ireland) Act 2007, persons whose cases are cer- tified by the Director of Public Prosecutions for Northern Ireland are tried in the absence of a jury. It is also concerned that there is no right of appeal against the decision made by the Director of Public Prosecutions for North- ern Ireland.

In October 2010 *The Guardian* newspaper reported that The Criminal Cases Review Commission (see above, 9.9) had received applications from more than 200 people who claimed that they had suffered injustices under the Diplock trial system. By that time, the Court of Appeal in Belfast had overturned convictions in 24 of 26 cases referred to it by the Commission. The newspaper alleged that a number of men who served as detec- tives with the Royal Ulster Constabulary (RUC) claimed that senior officers 'encouraged the systematic mistreatment of suspects at Castlereagh interrogation centre in east Bel- fast' after the establishment of the Diplock courts in 1973. The accusation was that the officers took full advantage of the vague wording of emergency legislation in Northern Ireland, which allowed the courts to admit confessions as evidence, *providing there was no evidence* they had been obtained through the use of torture, or inhuman or degrad- ing treatment. This issue clearly links back to the consideration of the use of torture in Chapter 2. A video report of the allegations may be seen at http://www.theguardian. com/uk/2010/oct/11/inside-castlereagh-confessions-torture.

14.6.2.1   Criminal Justice Act 2003: Jury tampering

The term 'jury tampering' covers a range of circumstances in which the jury's indepen- dence is or may appear to be compromised. Such a situation could come about because of actual harm or threats of harm to jury members. It might equally involve intimida- tion or bribery of jury members. Alternatively, it could also include similar improper approaches to a juror's family or friends.

Sections 44 and 46 of the CJA 2003 provide for a trial on indictment in the Crown Court to be conducted without a jury where there is a danger of jury tampering, or continued without a jury where the jury has been discharged because of jury tampering. For an application under s 44 to be granted, the court must be satisfied that there is evidence of a real and present danger that jury tampering would take place. In addition, the court must also be satisfied that the danger of jury tampering is so substantial, notwithstanding any steps that could reasonably be taken to prevent it, as to make it necessary in the interests of justice for the trial to be conducted without a jury. Sub-section (6) sets out examples of what might constitute evidence of a real and present danger of jury tampering, which include:

- a case where the trial is a retrial and the jury in the previous trial was discharged because jury tampering had taken place;
- a case where jury tampering has taken place in previous criminal proceedings involving the defendant or any of the defendants;
- a case where there has been intimidation, or attempted intimidation, of any person who is likely to be a witness in the trial.

Section 46 deals with trials already under way, where jury tampering has or appears to have taken place. In these circumstances, if the judge decides to discharge the jury, as he or she has a right to do in common law, and is satisfied that tampering has occurred, he or she may order that the trial should continue without a jury if he or she is satisfied that this would be fair to the defendant. On the other hand, if the judge considers it necessary in the interests of justice to terminate the trial due to tampering, he or she may order that the retrial should take place without a jury.

In March 2010, after the first non-jury criminal trial for more than 350 years, four members of a gang were convicted of a £1.75 million armed raid on a warehouse near Heathrow Airport in February 2004. Following three previous failed trials, the prosecution had applied for a non-jury trial on the grounds that the third trial had had to be halted because of alleged jury tampering. On subsequent appeal to the ECtHR, *Twomey and Cameron v the United Kingdom* (application no. 67318/09), the court stated that the system of trial by jury was just one example among others of the variety of legal systems existing in Europe, and held that the right to a fair trial did not require that the determination of guilt be made by a jury. On a second issue, that the basis of the evidence of jury tampering had not been fully disclosed to the defence, the court held that the procedure afforded the defence sufficient safeguards, taking into account the important public interest grounds against disclosing the evidence.

In July 2010 Lord Judge CJ, in the Court of Appeal, handed down guidance on how the jury tampering provisions of the CJA 2003 were to be operated in two similar but unrelated cases, *R v J, S, M* (2010) and *R v KS* (2010). In overturning orders for non-jury trials Judge LCJ emphasised that the making of such an order:

remains and must remain the decision of last resort, only to be ordered when the court is sure (not that it entertains doubts, suspicions or reservations) that the statutory conditions are fulfilled. Save in extreme cases,

> *where the necessary protective measures constitute an unreasonable intrusion into the lives of the jurors,* for example, a constant police presence in or near their homes, day and night and at the weekends, or police protection, which means that at all times when they are out of their homes, they are accompanied or overseen by police officers, again day and night and at the weekend, with its consequent impact on the availability of police officers to carry out their ordinary duties, the confident expectation must be that the jury will perform its duties with its customary determination to do justice (emphasis added).

However, in relation to s 46 powers he concluded that:

> If during the course of this, or indeed any trial, attempts are made to tamper with the jury to the extent that the judge feels it necessary to discharge the entire jury, it should be clearly understood that the judge may continue with the trial and deliver a judgment and verdict on his own. The principle of trial by jury is precious, but in the end any defendant who is responsible for abusing this principle by attempting to subvert the process has no justified complaint that he has been deprived of a right which, by his own actions, he himself has spurned.

14.6.2.2 Criminal Justice Act 2003: Complex fraud trials

In 1986, the Roskill Committee on Fraud Trials critically examined the operation of the jury in complex criminal fraud cases. Its report recommended the abolition of trial by jury in such cases. The Roskill Committee did not go as far as to recommend that all fraud cases should be taken away from juries, only the most complex, of which it was estimated that there were about two dozen or so every year. It was suggested that these cases would be better decided by a judge assisted by two laypersons drawn from a panel with specialist expertise. The government declined to implement the recommendations of the Roskill Committee, and instead introduced procedures designed to make it easier to follow the proceedings in complex fraud cases.

After being found not guilty of a £19 million fraud charge, George Walker, the former chief executive of Brent Walker, said: 'Thank God for the jury. It would be madness to lose the jury system.' This enthusiastic endorsement of the jury system is in no little way undercut, however, by the fact that Walker is reported as going on to state that he was sure the jury had not properly understood much of the highly detailed material in the trial, as he admitted: 'I didn't understand a lot of it, so I can't see how they could.'

Mr Walker's enthusiasm perhaps was not shared by his co-accused, Wilfred Aquilina, who was found guilty, on a majority verdict, of false accounting.

The Royal Commission on the Criminal Justice System of 1993 (the Runciman Commission) recognised the particular difficulties faced by jurors in fraud trials but, somewhat surprisingly in the light of its recommendations in relation to offences triable either way, it did not suggest the removal of the jury from such cases. It merely recommended that s 10(3) of the CJA 1988 should be amended to permit judges to put the issues before the jury at the outset of the trial.

In February 1998, the Home Office issued a Green Paper entitled *Juries in Serious Fraud Trials*. The Consultation Paper suggested the need for a new procedure in relation to complex fraud trials, due to the fact that 'the detection, investigation and trial of serious criminal fraud offences have presented certain difficulties not commonly found amongst other types of offences'. A variety of possible alternatives were put forward:

- *Special juries*: these would be made up of qualified people and might be drawn from a special pool of potential jurors. Alternatively, ordinary jurors would have to be assessed as to their competency to sit on the case.
- *Judge-run trials*: specially trained judges, either singly or in a panel, and possibly with the help of lay experts.
- *Fraud tribunals*: following Roskill, these would be made up of a judge and qualified lay members with the power to question witnesses.
- *Verdict-only juries*: in this situation, the judge would hear the evidence and sum up the facts, leaving the jury simply to vote on guilt or innocence.
- *A special juror*: here, 11 of the jury would be selected as normal, but number 12 would be specially qualified in order to be able to assist the others on complex points.

With respect to these alternatives, the government stated that it had no particular preference.

Subsequently, in April 1998, the Home Secretary requested the Law Commission to carry out a review of fraud trials, focusing particularly on whether the existing law was:

- readily comprehensible to juries;
- adequate for effective prosecution;
- fair to defendants; and
- able to cope with changes in technology.

However, in its response in Consultation Paper No 155, *Fraud and Deception* (1999), the Law Commission addressed only the issues of possible criminal offences and did not deal with any procedural issues.

In his extensive *Review of the Criminal Courts* (2001), Sir Robin Auld LJ recommended that in serious and complex frauds, the nominated trial judge should have the power to direct trial by themselves and two lay members drawn from a panel established by the Lord Chancellor for the purpose or, if the defendant requested, by the judge

the case of first offenders, where the consequences of loss of reputation would be signifi-cant. In the words of the Commission:

> Loss of reputation is a different matter, since jury trial has long been regarded as appropriate for cases involving that issue. But, it should only be one of the factors to be taken into account and will often be relevant only to first offenders (see para 6.18 of the Report).

There are two assumptions in this proposal. First, there is the surely objectionable assumption that the reputation of anyone with a previous conviction is not important. But of even more concern is the fact that it is recognised that in the cases of first offend-ers, they should be permitted access to the jury. The question has to be asked: why should this be the case if juries do no more than magistrates do? It appears that in the instance of first offenders, it is recognised that juries do offer more protection than magistrates. Again, this demands the question: why should the extra protection not be open to all?

Criminal Justice (Mode of Trial) Bills

The Runciman Commission Report was produced under the auspices of a Conservative government operating under an economic imperative to reduce costs. If those who were opposed to its findings found comfort in the election of a New Labour government in 1997, they were soon to be disabused when the new (now former) Home Secretary, Jack Straw, announced his intention to reduce the rights to jury trials, essentially to the same end as the Runciman proposals. Thus, the first Criminal Justice (Mode of Trial) Bill was introduced in the parliamentary session of 1999–2000. This Bill sought to amend the MCA 1980 by introducing sections that gave the magistrates, rather than the accused, the power to decide whether a case should be tried summarily or on indictment. As Runciman's Report had been, so the new Bill was solicitous of the protection of those accused whose reputation 'would be seriously damaged as a result of conviction'. The Bill was generally criticised as an illiberal measure by civil liberties organisations and the legal professions, but was particularly attacked for the manner in which it sought to protect the rights of individuals with reputations to protect. Such solicitude for those with reputations to protect, apparently as opposed to the common majority of people, was seen as inherently unjust and dangerously class-based. The opposition to the Bill outside Parliament was matched, and more importantly so in relation to its legisla-tive progress, by equal opposition within the House of Lords, which voted against its passage.

Undaunted by the rejection of his Bill, the Home Secretary reintroduced a reformed version of it in the Criminal Justice (Mode of Trial) (No 2) Bill. In acknowl-edgement of criticisms of the earlier Bill, the (No 2) Bill made it clear that the reputation, or any other personal characteristic, of the accused was not something to be taken into account by the magistrates in deciding on the mode of trial. Nonetheless, the Bill was once again defeated in the House of Lords in 2001.

Although the newly re-elected government insisted that it retained the power to use the Parliament Acts to force a mode of trial Bill through the House of Lords, its approach altered following the publishing of the report on the criminal courts conducted by Sir Robin Auld.

The Auld Review

In his extensive *Review of the Criminal Courts* (2001), Sir Robin Auld LJ included recommendations that were aimed specifically at the current operation of the jury within the criminal justice system. In summary, he recommended the following points:

- Jurors should be more widely representative than they are of the national and local communities from which they are drawn.

- No one in future should be ineligible for, or excusable as of right from, jury service. While those with criminal convictions and mental disorder should continue to be disqualified, any claimed inability to serve should be a matter for discretionary deferral or excusal.

- Provision should be made to enable ethnic minority representation on juries where race is likely to be relevant to an important issue in the case.

- The law should not be amended to permit more intrusive research than is already possible into the workings of juries, though in appropriate cases, trial judges and/or the Court of Appeal should be entitled to examine alleged improprieties in the jury room.

- The law should be declared, by statute if need be, that juries have no right to acquit defendants in defiance of the law or in disregard of the evidence.

- If the jury's verdict appears to be perverse, the prosecution should be entitled to appeal on the grounds that the perversity is indicative that the verdict is likely to be unfair or untrue.

- The defendant should no longer have an elective right to trial by judge and jury in 'either-way' cases.

- Trial by judge and jury should remain the main form of trial of the more serious offences triable on indictment, that is, those that would go to the Crown Division, subject to four exceptions:

  (i) defendants should be entitled, with the court's consent, to opt for trial by judge alone;

  (ii) in serious and complex frauds, the nominated trial judge should have the power to direct trial by themselves and two lay members drawn from a panel established by the Lord Chancellor for the purpose (or, if the defendant requests, by the judge alone);

(iii)   a Youth Court, constituted by a judge of an appropriate level and at least two experienced youth panel magistrates, should be given jurisdiction to hear all grave cases against young defendants;

(iv)   legislation should be introduced to require a judge, not a jury, to determine the issue of fitness to plead.

The Criminal Justice Act 2003

As has been seen, the CJA 2003 introduced significant changes in the role and place of juries in the criminal system, but it did so without addressing the contentious issue of either-way offences. Perhaps this course of action was adopted in the belief that the increase in the sentencing power of the magistrates' courts to 12 months would reduce the pressure on the Crown Courts by cutting down the number of cases sent for sentencing. *It is unlikely, however, that the issue will have gone away for ever.*

How true, but not particularly insightful or prescient, was the previous sentence, because within months of the installation of the coalition government, its 'victims' commissioner', Louise Casey, was calling for jury trial to be removed from petty criminals who were 'clogging up' the courts system and whose cases should be tried by magistrates. In her view, the right to opt for trial by jury in the Crown Court was a 'nicety' of the legal system and was being abused by criminals. As she was quoted as saying:

> In a time of cuts, we need to abandon some of the genteel traditions and niceties of the legal system. How can it be right that a jury can be made to convene to hear arguments about the theft of £20-worth of tea bags, as is the case now, when a magistrate could do the job justly but costing far less?

The simple answer is because it is of *crucial importance* to the person who is charged with the offence, no matter the cost to the state.

14.8   INVESTIGATION OF JURY BEHAVIOUR

The very first recommendation made by the Royal Commission on Criminal Justice was that s 8 of the Contempt of Court Act 1981 should be repealed to enable research to be conducted into juries' reasons for their verdicts. Section 8 makes it an offence to obtain, disclose or solicit any particulars of statements made, opinion expressed, arguments advanced or votes cast by members of a jury in the course of their deliberations in any legal proceedings.

In *Attorney General v Associated Newspapers* (1994), the House of Lords held that it was contempt of court for a newspaper to publish disclosures by jurors of what took place in the jury room while they were considering their verdict, unless the publication amounted to no more than a restatement of facts already known. It was decided that the word 'disclose' in s 8(1) applied not just to jurors, but to any others who published their revelations.

The continued legality of s 8 in the light of Art 6 of the ECHR was considered in *R v Mirza* in January 2004. The appellant Mirza had been convicted on six counts of indecent assault by a majority verdict of 10 to two. He had arrived in the UK from Pakistan in 1988 and, during the trial, he had made use of an interpreter. During the course of the trial, the jury sent a note asking the interpreter whether it was typical of a man with Mirza's background to require an interpreter, despite having lived in the UK for so long. It was explained to the jury that it was usual for people who were not fluent to have an interpreter in complicated and serious cases and, in his summing up, the judge directed the jury not to draw an adverse inference from Mirza's use of an interpreter.

Six days after the case finished, the defence counsel received a letter from one of the jurors claiming that some jurors had, from the beginning of the trial, believed that the use of the interpreter had been a devious ploy. The question of the interpreter was raised early during the jury's deliberations, and the letter writer was 'shouted down' when she objected and sought to remind the other members of the jury of the judge's directions. Members of the jury specifically refused to accept the judge's direction, and some regarded defence counsel's warnings against prejudice in her final speech as 'playing the race card'. The writer concluded that the decision of the jury was that of bigots who considered Mirza guilty because he used an interpreter in court after declining one for his police interviews.

When the case came on appeal to the House of Lords, it was confirmed by a majority of four to one that s 8 of the Contempt of Court Act 1981 prevented any investigation into what had taken place within the confines of the jury room. The majority also relied on a passage in *Gregory v UK* (1998), in which the ECtHR had previously approved the protection of jury secrecy under UK law in deciding that s 8 was not in conflict with Art 6 of the ECHR. In reaching its conclusion, the majority focused on the difficulties involved in assessing and investigating such matters of jury misbehaviour but, as Lord Steyn stated in his minority judgment:

> In my view it would be an astonishing thing for the ECtHR to hold, when the point directly arises before it, that a miscarriage of justice may be ignored in the interest of the general efficiency of the jury system. The terms of Art 6(1) of the ECHR, the rights revolution, and 50 years of development of human rights law and practice, would suggest that such a view would be utterly indefensible.

The issue was further considered by the House of Lords in *R v Smith (Patrick)* in 2005. That case related to a situation where, after a jury had begun its deliberations, the judge received a letter from one of the jurors claiming that some of the other members of the panel were disregarding the judge's directions on the law and were engaging in improper speculation over verdicts. Rather than discharge the jury, the judge, with the approval of

The direction was repeated from time to time throughout the trial.

By 2 August, Sewart had been acquitted of all three charges against her. Knox had been convicted on the conspiracy charge involving Berry, and had been acquitted on one other count. However, verdicts still had to be reached on three other counts. After her acquittal, Sewart continued to attend the ongoing trial of her partner, Knox.

On 4 August, it became apparent to the judge hearing the case that an unknown juror had been in Facebook contact with Sewart, commenting to the effect that she was pleased that Sewart had been acquitted because she was 'with her the whole of the way'. She also suggested that it was a pity that Sewart had not been in court when the verdicts involving Knox were announced because she was not able to see 'the look of delight' on Gary's face when he was acquitted on the remaining charge against him. Sewart had asked her Facebook friend about the conduct of the trial while it was ongoing.

On questioning the jurors individually, the judge established, through her owning up, that the juror in question was Joanne Fraill. Although the judge decided to continue the remainder of the hearings without Fraill's participation, he subsequently decided that the case could not proceed and discharged the rest of the jury.

Both Fraill and Sewart were subsequently found guilty of contempt of court in June 2011. The judgment against Fraill was so stark as to warrant quoting. As Judge LCJ stated (and the structure of what he says is significant):

> 55 . . . it is a feature of this case that when the question of Facebook contact was raised with her in the Crown Court, this woman of good character, immediately and unhesitantly admitted what she had done and apologised for it. During the subsequent investigation she provided evidence against herself of her misuse of the internet throughout the trial. In effect therefore she acknowledged her guilt at the earliest possible opportunity, and for some months now she has been waiting for the present proceedings to take place, and to know what the consequences of her contempt will be. The effect of all these stresses and strains was virtually palpable here in court.
>
> 56 . . . There will be an order for immediate custody for a period of eight months.

Perhaps this is an example of Voltaire's maxim about English justice 'pour encourager les autres'; but it is hardly surprising that this statement was met with overwhelming distress and tears from Fraill. Sewart received a two-month custodial term, suspended for two years.

In November 2011 in *R v Mears*, evidence emerged that a member of the jury had been in mobile phone contact with her fiancé, who had been sitting in the public gallery during a significant part of the trial and had observed proceedings which had taken place in the absence of the jury. A number of texts had been exchanged between them during the trial and the juror admitted receiving texts while in the jury room. One such text sent by the fiancé to the juror during the judge's summing-up read 'guilty'. While the judge at the trial had refused a motion to discharge the jury, the Court of Appeal had no option but to overturn the conviction on the grounds of the risk of prejudice.

Finally, in January 2012, a juror, Dr Theodora Dallas, was gaoled for six months for ignoring instructions to the contrary and conducting internet investigations into the accused person whose trial she was sitting on. When Dallas told the other jurors what she had found – that the accused had been previously accused of rape – they were concerned and informed the presiding judge, who halted the case.

On a related point, following evident breaches of the contempt and libel laws on Twitter, it was announced in December 2013 that the Attorney General would be publishing advisory notes on the gov.uk website and Twitter (@AGO_UK) to help prevent social media users from committing such offences. Advice had previously only been issued to print and broadcast media outlets on a 'not for publication' basis but the new public advice was 'designed to make sure that a fair trial takes place and warn people that comment on a particular case needs to comply with the Contempt of Court Act 1981'.

The change in policy was designed to help inform the public about the legal pitfalls of commenting in a way which could be seen as prejudicial to a court case or those involved. In the words of then Attorney General, Dominic Grieve:

> Blogs and social media sites like Twitter and Facebook mean that individuals can now reach thousands of people with a single tweet or post. This is an exciting prospect, but it can pose certain challenges to the criminal justice system. In days gone by, it was only the mainstream media that had the opportunity to bring information relating to a court case to such a large group of people that it could put a court case at risk. That is no longer the case, and is why I have decided to publish the advisories that I have previously only issued to the media. This is not about telling people what they can or cannot talk about on social media; quite the opposite in fact, it's designed to help facilitate commentary in a lawful way. I hope that by making this information available to the public at large, we can help stop people from inadvertently breaking the law, and make sure that cases are tried on the evidence, not what people have found online.

14.8.2   CRIMINAL JUSTICE AND COURTS ACT 2015: JURIES

As has been stated previously at 3.6, the Law Commission report of December 2013, *Contempt of Court: Juror Misconduct and Internet Publications* (Law Com no 340) provided the basis for the sections in Part 3 of the Criminal Justice and Courts Act 2015, which established new criminal offences in relation to jurors' internet activity.

Under s 47 of the CJ&CA 2015, which amends the Juries Act 1974, it is a criminal offence to undertake any research during the trial period. Research, which is defined as intentionally seeking information which a juror ought reasonably to know is or may be relevant to the case, includes:

(a)   asking a question;

(b)   searching an electronic database, including by means of the internet;

(c)   visiting or inspecting a place or object;

(d)   conducting an experiment; and

(e)   asking another person to seek the information.

Information is relevant if it relates to

(a)   a person involved in events relevant to the case;

(b)   the judge dealing with the issue;

(c)   any other person involved in the trial, whether as a lawyer, a witness or otherwise;

(d)   the law relating to the case;

(e)   the law of evidence; and

(f)   court procedure.

Section 48 creates the related offence of sharing information with a fellow juror, and s 49 criminalises a juror engaging in 'prohibited conduct', defined as '*conduct from which it may reasonably be concluded that the person intends to try the issue otherwise than on the basis of the evidence presented in the proceedings on the issue*'.

Section 50 creates the statutory offence of disclosing details of a jury's deliberation and also extends to non-jurors looking to get information relating to those deliberations. However, there is a public interest defence where such disclosures have been made to a police officer, a judge of the court where the proceedings took place, a judge of the Court of Appeal or the Registrar of Criminal Appeals.

14.9   CONCLUSION

It has been repeatedly suggested by those in favour of abolishing, or at least severely curtailing, the role of the jury in the criminal justice system, that the general perception of the jury is romanticised and has little foundation in reality. Runciman did not actually make this point explicitly, but it is implicit in his assessment of the jury system as against the magistrates' courts. Others have been more explicit; thus, the Roskill Committee expressed the view that:

> Society appears to have an attachment to jury trial which is emotional or sentimental rather than logical (para 8.21).

A similar point had been made previously by the Faulks Committee, but that report also recognised the source of the public's opinion and was careful not to dismiss it as unimportant:

> Much of the support for jury trials is emotional and derives from the undoubted value of juries in serious criminal cases where they stand between the prosecuting authority and the citizen (para 496).

The jury system certainly commands considerable public support. A survey published in January 2004, involving interviews with 361 jurors, found that, for the vast majority of respondents, juries were seen as an essential component of providing a fair and just trial process, and the diversity of the jury was seen as the best way of avoiding bias and arriving at a sound verdict. The major conclusions of the survey were as follows:

- The majority of respondents had a more positive view of the jury trial system after completing their service than they did before. Furthermore, despite the considerable personal inconvenience they may have suffered, virtually all jurors interviewed considered jury trials to be an important part of the criminal justice system.
- Confidence in the jury system was closely associated with the process, fairness, respect for the rights of defendants and ability of all the members of the jury to consider evidence from different perspectives. A jury's representation of a broad spectrum of views was a key factor in jurors' confidence in the Crown Court trial.
- Jurors were very impressed with the professionalism and helpfulness of the court personnel. In particular, they praised the judge's performance, commitment and competence.
- The main impediment to understanding proceedings was the use of legal terminology, although jurors also felt that evidence could sometimes be presented more clearly.
- Over half of the respondents said that they would be happy to do jury service again, while 19 per cent said that they 'would not mind' doing it again. The most positive aspects of engaging in jury service were reported to be having a greater understanding of the criminal court trial, a feeling of having performed an important civic duty and finding the experience personally fulfilling.

The ideological power of the jury system should not be underestimated. It represents the ordinary person's input into the legal system and it is at least arguable that in that way it provides the whole legal system with a sense of legitimacy. It is argued by some civil libertarians that the existence of the non-jury Diplock courts in Northern Ireland brings the whole of the legal system in that province into disrepute.

As Lord Devlin noted (*Trial By Jury*, 1966):

> The first object of any tyrant in Whitehall would be to make Parliament utterly subservient to his will; and the next to overthrow or diminish trial by jury, for no tyrant could afford to leave a subject's freedom in the hands of 12 of his countrymen.

Juror satisfaction

It should also be noted that most jurors seem to be reasonably happy with the system despite the stress and inconvenience it can impose on them. The Justice Ministry carries out an annual survey to measure the expectations, attitudes and experiences of jurors (see www.justice.gov.uk/downloads/publications/statistics-and-data/mojstats/crown-court-jurors-survey-2010.pdf). Jurors are asked to rate the service provided during the pre-court, at court and after court stages of their jury service. Among the findings are that:

- over three-quarters of jurors (77 per cent) said they were satisfied with their overall experience of jury service;
- 87 per cent stated that they were satisfied overall with the treatment they received from the Jury Summoning Bureau before they attended court;
- of those who had been on jury service before, 40 per cent felt their experience this time was better than last, while 14 per cent felt their experience was worse;
- 94 per cent were satisfied with both the politeness and helpfulness of staff, and thought that staff treated jurors fairly and sensitively.

However, only 43 per cent of jurors were satisfied with the time spent waiting to be selected for a trial, so this area clearly constitutes the major source of juror dissatisfaction.

Internet use

Although only a minority of 7 per cent of jurors contacted the Jury Central Summoning Bureau by email, this is a significant increase in numbers compared to 2009 (5 per cent). One in 10 (10 per cent) of those aged 18 to 34 used this method of communication. Nearly two-thirds of jurors were very satisfied with the information they received (65 per cent) and the speed of the response (67 per cent).

THE JURY

The jury has come under close public scrutiny since the Runciman Commission's recommendation to curtail the right to jury trial. It is important to know the standard arguments in favour of the jury and also the arguments showing that it may not be truly random and representative. The detail of the jury's function in a trial and the extent to which its verdict can be appealed against are important. In what ways can the membership of the jury be challenged? Juries lie at the heart of the English criminal justice system but there is debate about whether juries provide any better justice than magistrates' courts or whether the role is purely symbolic.

THE ROLE OF THE JURY

Juries decide matters of fact; judges decide matters of law. Judges can instruct juries to acquit but not to convict. Juries do not have to give reasons for their decision. There is no appeal against an acquittal verdict, although points of law may be clarified by an Attorney General's reference. Civil cases can be overturned if perverse – but not criminal cases. Verdicts can be delivered on the basis of majority decisions. The use of juries has declined in relation to criminal and civil law.

SELECTION OF JURIES

Random in theory – selective in practice. All on the electoral register are liable to serve, but the registers tend to be inaccurate. Service is subject to exemption, excusal and disqualification. Defence and prosecution can challenge for cause. Prosecution can ask jurors to stand by. Jury vetting is checking that jurors are suitable to hear sensitive cases. If Runciman is followed, juries may be required to have a racial mix.

DECLINE IN JURY TRIALS

Under s 69 of the Senior Courts Act 1981, the right to a jury trial is limited to only four specific areas:

- fraud;
- defamation;
- malicious prosecution; and
- false imprisonment.

Even in these areas, the right is not absolute and can be denied by a judge under s 69(1) where the case involves 'any prolonged examination of documents or accounts or any scientific or local investigation which cannot conveniently be made with a jury'.

The Criminal Justice Act 2003 has potentially introduced restriction in jury trials in relation to:

● jury tampering;
● complex fraud cases.

INVESTIGATION OF JURY BEHAVIOUR

Section 8 of the Contempt of Court Act 1981 makes it an offence to obtain, disclose or solicit any particulars of statements made, opinion expressed, arguments advanced or votes cast by members of a jury in the course of their deliberations in any legal proceedings.

FOOD FOR THOUGHT

1   The essential feature of jury selection is randomness, but is that really a value in and of itself? Would an all-male jury be acceptable in a rape trial, even if that were the outcome of a random selection process? If not, why not? Similarly, would an all-black jury be acceptable in a case involving a member of a white supremacist group? However, if these instances are thought to be problematic, why is this the case, and what implications does it have generally for juries' impartiality? Should what goes on in the jury room be sacrosanct, beyond investigation and subject to proceedings for contempt of court, even where the jurors may have engaged in prejudicial behaviour?

2   Some people are concerned that the jury selection process can quite easily result in unsuitable people serving as jurors and, for that reason, suggest that there should be some sort of minimum standard for serving as jurors. Do you agree?

3   In the context of recent development in information technology, should jurors be banned from investigating issues they are deciding about on the internet?

4   In the context of the cost involved, should all jury trials be abolished?

FURTHER READING

Airs, J and Shaw, A, 'Jury Excusal and Deferral' (1999), Home Office Research and Statistics Directorate Research Study No 102, 1999

Arce, R, 'Evidence evaluation in jury decision-making', in Carson, D and Bull, R (eds), *Handbook of Psychology in Legal Contexts*, 2nd edn, 2003, Chichester: John Wiley & Sons

Baldwin, J and McConville, M, *Jury Trials*, 1979, Oxford: Clarendon Press

Barber, JW, 'The jury is still out: the role of jury science in the modern American courtroom' (1994) 31 Am Crim L Rev 1225

Broeder, DW, 'The University of Chicago jury project' (1959) 38 Nebraska LR 744

Carlton, Darbyshire, Harris, Hodgetts and Robbins, in separate articles (1990) 140 NLJ 1264–1276

Chada, R, 'Jury out on justice system' (2009) 106(28) Law Soc Gazette 8

Cornish, WR, *The Jury*, 1970, London: Allen Lane

Corrin, L, '12 heads better than one' (2009) 153(27) SJ 19

Darbyshire, P, 'The lamp that shows that freedom lives: Is it worth the candle?' (1991) Crim LR 740

Devlin, P, *Trial By Jury*, 1956, London: Stevens

Findlay, M and Duff, P, *The Jury Under Attack*, 1988, London: Butterworths

Finkel, NJ, *Common Sense Justice: Jurors' Notions of the Law*, 1995, Cambridge, MA: Harvard UP

Gobert, J, *Justice, Democracy and the Jury*, 1997, Aldershot: Dartmouth

Griffiths, C, 'Jury trial' (1999) Counsel 14

Grove, T, *The Juryman's Tale*, 1998, London: Bloomsbury

Hastie, R, *Inside the Juror: The Psychology of Juror Decision-making*, 1993, Cambridge: CUP

Mathews, R, Hancock, L and Briggs, D, *Jurors' Perceptions: Understanding Confidence and Satisfaction in the Jury System – A Study in Six Courts*, 2004, London: Home Office

Sealy, AP and Cornish, WR, 'Jurors and their verdicts' (1973) 36 MLR 496

Vidmar, N (ed), *World Jury Systems*, 2000, Oxford: OUP

Wolchover, D, 'Twelve good men & true & safe' (2009) Counsel 28

USEFUL WEBSITES

http://4wardeveruk.org/wp-content/uploads/2009/08/p.Diversity-Fairness-in-the-Jury-System.pdf
Diversity and Fairness in the Jury System.

www.justice.gov.uk/downloads/publications/research-and-analysis/moj-research/are-juries-fair-research.pdf
Are juries fair?

COMPANION WEBSITE

Now visit the companion website to:

- test your understanding of the key terms using our Flashcard Glossary;
- revise and consolidate your knowledge of 'The jury' using our multiple choice question testbank;
- view all of the links to the Useful Websites above.

www.routledge.com/cw/slapper

ARBITRATION, TRIBUNAL ADJUDICATION AND ALTERNATIVE DISPUTE RESOLUTION

15

Law is one method of resolving disputes when, as is inevitable, they emerge. All societies have mechanisms for dealing with such problems, but the forms of dispute resolution tend to differ from society to society. In small-scale societies, based on mutual co-operation and interdependency, the means of solving disputes tend to be informal and focus on the need for mutual concessions and compromise to maintain social stability. In some such societies, the whole of the social group may become involved in settling a problem, whereas in others, particular individuals may be recognised as intermediaries, whose function it is to act as a go-between to bring the parties to a mutually recognised solution. The common factor remains the emphasis on solidarity and the need to maintain social cohesion. With social as well as geographical distance, disputes become more difficult to deal with.

It should not be thought that this reference to anthropological material is out of place in a book of this nature. It is sometimes suggested that law itself is a function of the increase in social complexity and the corresponding decrease in social solidarity – the oppositional, adversarial nature of law being seen as a reflection of the atomistic structure of contemporary society. Law as a *formal* dispute resolution mechanism is seen to emerge because *informal* mechanisms no longer exist or no longer have the power to deal with the problems that arise in a highly individualistic and competitive society. That is not to suggest that the types of mechanisms mentioned previously do not have their place in our own society: the bulk of family disputes, for example, are resolved through internal informal mechanisms without recourse to legal formality. It is generally recognised, however, that the very form of law makes it inappropriate to deal adequately with certain areas, family matters being the most obvious example. Equally, it is recognised that the formal and rather intimidatory atmosphere of the ordinary courts is not necessarily the most appropriate one in which to decide such matters, even where the dispute cannot be resolved internally. In recognition of this fact, various alternatives have been developed specifically to avoid the perceived shortcomings of the formal structure of law and court procedure.

consumers about ADR when a dispute cannot be settled directly between the consumer and the trader. The Directive imposes a 90-day time limit for dealing with a dispute and allows consumers to elect to deal with their complaint online or in some other way.

The ODR Regulation

The Regulation requires the establishment by the EU Commission, of an online, inter-active portal (the 'ODR platform') for resolving contractual disputes. The Regulation applies to consumer/trader disputes, domestic and cross-border disputes. Member states must propose an ODR contact to assist with disputes submitted through the ODR platform. Once the EU consumer submits their dispute online, they are linked with national ADR providers who will help to resolve the dispute. According to the Commission the procedure will operate as follows:

- Consumers who encounter a problem with an online purchase will be able to submit a complaint online through the ODR platform, in the language of their choice. The ODR platform will notify the trader that a complaint is lodged against him. The consumer and the trader will then agree on which ADR entity to use to solve their dispute. When they agree, the chosen ADR entity will receive the details of the dispute via the ODR platform.

- The ODR platform will be connected to the national ADR entities set up and notified to the Commission, in line with the new rules of the ADR Directive. The platform will help speed up the resolution of the dispute by allowing ADR entities to conduct the proceedings online and through electronic means. A set of common rules will govern the functioning of the ODR platform. These will include the role of national contact points acting as ODR advisers in their respective countries. Their task will be to provide general information on consumer rights and redress in relation to online purchases, assist with the submission of complaints and facilitate communication between the parties and the competent ADR entity through the ODR platform. For this purpose, ODR advisers will also be linked electronically to the platform.

Proposals for implementation of the Directive for
Consumer ADR in the UK

In November 2014, following a consultation exercise, the Department for Business Innovation and Skills published its proposals for bringing the EU rules into effect within the required time period (*Alternative Dispute Resolution for Consumers*). The document set out the intentions as follows:

> To plug existing gaps and ensure ADR is widely available across all sectors, the Government will assist with the set-up of a residual ADR scheme, which will be available to businesses that are not obliged or committed to using another ADR scheme . . .

> The current UK ADR landscape can also be complex and confusing for consumers. In order to make the system easier for consumers to navigate, to increase awareness of ADR and the process for accessing it and to ensure as seamless a consumer journey as possible, the Government is intending to work with Citizens Advice to create a consumer complaints helpdesk to provide assistance and advice to consumers attempting to resolve a dispute with a trader . . .
>
> The Government will appoint the Trading Standards Institute (TSI) to act as the UK's competent authority covering ADR schemes in the non-regulated sectors. Operating alongside TSI, the Government will appoint the sector regulators as competent authorities for their sectors where appropriate. In order to help traders meet the statutory information requirements concerning the provision of ADR, government will work with the Trading Standards Institute (TSI) to produce appropriate guidance for business.
>
> In relation to the ODR scheme the Government will establish an ODR contact point to help consumers with cross-border disputes submitted via the Commission's ODR platform but will not extend the ODR requirements beyond that.

In April 2015 the government implemented its proposals to comply with the directive and regulation through the Alternative Dispute Resolution for Consumer Disputes (Competent Authorities and Information) Regulations (SI 2015/542). Amendments to the regulations soon followed (ADR for Consumer Disputes (Amendment) Regulations 2015 (2015/1392), to allow for the extension of the time for businesses to comply until 1 October 2015 and allowing non-UK based ADR providers to apply to operate. It should also be mentioned that this change accompanied a major alteration in the law relating to consumer transactions, with the passing of the Consumer Rights Act 2015.

15.2 MEDIATION AND CONCILIATION

A number of alternatives to court proceedings have already been listed, but the two most common, or certainly the two that most immediately spring to mind when the topic of ADR is raised, are mediation and conciliation, and as a consequence, although distinct, they are dealt with together.

15.2.1 MEDIATION

Mediation is the process whereby a third party acts as the conduit through which two disputing parties communicate and negotiate, in an attempt to reach a common resolution to a problem. The mediator may move between the parties, communicating their opinions without their having to meet, or alternatively the mediator may operate in the presence of the parties, but in either situation the emphasis is on the parties themselves working out a shared agreement as to how the dispute in question is to be settled.

Before the Woolf reforms introduced the three-track system, the small claims process was referred to as mediation, due to its much less formal procedural rules and practices. Although the small claims track is still relatively informal in comparison with the other tracks (see above, 7.5), the Court Service introduced a distinct and specific mediation process as an alternative to the court-based procedure. This small claims mediation scheme was funded by HMCS and consequently was free to court users who had a defended small claim.

The scheme was assessed positively after a pilot at Manchester County Court, and in 2007 HMCS began to appoint a number of small claims mediators across England and Wales. By June 2008 each of the 23 HMCS Court Areas in England and Wales had an in-house small claims mediator to deal with appropriate cases. The Ministry of Justice also developed a Mediation Helpline to assist individuals to access mediation. However, in October 2011, an online civil mediation directory replaced the National Mediation Helpline. A spokesperson for the ministry was quoted as saying that 'over recent years calls, mediation referrals and settlements had continued to fall' and 'approximately two-thirds of all calls to the helpline had nothing to do with mediation'. As a result, it was felt not to be worth the £90,000 spent on it annually. Such a statement and action does not fit particularly well with government's supposed commitment to an increased use of ADR.

The new directory has replicated some of the previous functions of the helpline in that it allows individuals to find a mediation provider accredited by the Civil Mediation Council anywhere in England and Wales. The cost of such mediation is based on a fixed fee, depending on the value of the dispute and, although not free, is much cheaper than making use of lawyers and going to court.

The fees for using the National Mediation Scheme are:

Amount claimed	Fees (per party)	Length of session	Extra hours (per party)
£5,000 or less*	£50 + VAT	1 hour	£50 + VAT
	£100 + VAT	Up to 2 hours	
£5,000–£15,000	£300 + VAT	Up to 3 hours	£85 + VAT
£15,000–£50,000**	£425 + VAT	Up to 4 hours	£95 + VAT

Mediation is also available for higher value claims and fees are negotiable.

LawWorks (www.lawworks.org.uk), a legal pro bono charity, offers free civil and commercial mediation to those unable to afford to pay for a commercial provider and without other means of paying. This service is available throughout England and Wales and is free to both parties if one party qualifies for pro bono help. Fee remission is an automatic gateway; in other cases, LawWorks will assess whether the applicant can afford to pay.

In the same year as the Helpline was closed, the Legal Services Commission withdrew funding (£12,000) from the ADRnow website, a resource provided by the Advice

Services Alliance (http://asauk.org.uk) aimed at steering the public towards mediation and other forms of alternative dispute resolution. As a result, ASA had to cease updating its extremely informative and useful ADR material. The Family Mediation Council provides an online service explaining and promoting the advantages of mediation in separation, divorce and other family law issues. It also operates a compulsory accreditation scheme for all family mediators and helps to locate suitable mediators.

The way in which mediation operates will become clear from the cases considered below. However, the mediator may settle the majority of disputes over the telephone without the need for either party to attend a hearing, consequently reducing time and expense. However, if necessary, face-to-face mediation can be arranged, either on court premises or elsewhere as deemed appropriate. In the event of the parties not being able to reach a settlement at the mediation appointment, the case will be listed for a small claims hearing. As the mediation process is confidential, the judge who deals with the subsequent case in court will not be informed of the content of any discussions at any previous mediation proceedings.

15.2.2 MEDIATION IN DIVORCE

Mediation has an important part to play in family matters, where it is felt that the adversarial approach of the traditional legal system has tended to emphasise, if not increase, existing differences of view between individuals and has not been conducive to amicable settlements. Thus, in divorce cases, mediation has traditionally been used to enable the parties themselves to work out an agreed settlement rather than having one imposed upon them by the courts.

This emphasis on mediation was formally strengthened in the Family Law Act 1996. Before receiving legal aid for representation in a divorce case a person was *expected* to have a meeting with a mediator to assess whether mediation was a suitable alternative to court proceedings. The only exception to this requirement was in relation to allegations of domestic abuse. However, excluding those exempted for reasons of domestic abuse, only 20 per cent of people publicly funded in divorce proceedings actually got involved in mediation.

In April 2011 the scheme applying to those making use of legal aid was extended to all parties wishing to go to court to resolve children or property issues following a separation or divorce. Consequently, all applicants to court on family proceedings were *expected* to show that they have already considered mediation and other dispute resolution options by attending a Mediation Information and Assessment Meeting (MIAM). However, the fact was that many applicants did not comply with the expectation.

The expectation that applicants should attend MIAMs became a *requirement* in April 2014 following the enactment of the Children and Families Act 2014 (s 10). The fact that the requirement only applies to applicants and not respondents inevitably reduces the effectiveness of the provision. In November 2014 the Justice Ministry announced that the first mediation session would be funded for both parties, provided at least one of them is already legally aided. Both of these measures may be understood as an attempt to deal with a crisis developing in the recently unified Family Court.

The Legal Aid, Sentencing and Punishment of Offenders Act 2012 introduced reforms, effectively designed to remove legal aid for divorce cases, unless they involve allegations of domestic violence or child abuse. The new Act came into force in April 2013. Among the justifications for cutting legal aid in this particular area was not just the fact that it saved money and reduced pressure on the courts, but that it would also have the additional benefit of reducing antagonism between separating couples as they opted for the, certainly cheaper, but also, unarguably, less confrontational form of mediation. Unfortunately the provisions seem to have had not only an unexpected, but a contrary, outcome. In effect, by removing most access to legal aid in relation to divorce, the government removed the signposts to mediation, which actually led not just to a reduction in the use of mediation, but to a corresponding increase in recourse to the courts and also an increase in self-representation in those courts. In turn, this had the consequence of slowing up of court proceedings as those unused to law and legal procedures attempted to represent themselves.

Following a freedom of information request by family mediator Marc Lopatin, the founder of Lawyer Supported Mediation (now Dialogue First http://dialoguefirst.co.uk/), statistics compiled by the Ministry of Justice revealed a large drop in the number of couples attending family related mediation meetings since the implementation of the legal aid cuts in April 2013. Between April and June 2012, 7,381 couples attended mediation information and assessment meetings in England and Wales, but in the same period in 2013, only 3,854 couples attended such meetings, a drop of 47 per cent.

The irony is that legal aid for mediation was still available; indeed, the government had made an extra £10 million available for such purposes, but no referrals were being made. Couples were avoiding what they saw as the unaffordable expense of funding lawyers through a full divorce hearing, but in so doing they were also avoiding the gatekeepers who could have guided them to a simpler process. Lord McNally, then the Family Justice Minister, was quoted in the press as responding as follows:

> We are aware there has been a recent drop in referrals to mediation and are working closely with the Family Mediation Council and legal profession to address this . . . We are also now changing the law so anyone considering court action over disputes about children or finances will be legally obliged to attend a mediation meeting first.

As stated, making mediation compulsory under the Children and Families Act 2014 would appear to be the response, but whether it is sufficient remains problematic. The underlying tension came to a head in August 2014 when, in a series of linked cases, *Q v Q, Re B* and *Re C* [2014] EWFC 31, president of the Family Court Sir James Munby asked the Justice Ministry to explain how the cases in question could proceed without legal aid. In Munby's words:

> [T]hese are problems which pre-date the implementation in April 2013 of the relevant provisions of the Legal Aid, Sentencing and Punishment of Offenders Act 2012 (LASPO). They are, however, problems which most practitioners and judges with any practical experience of the family justice system would recognise as having been very considerably exacerbated by LASPO . . .

There has been a drastic reduction in the number of represented litigants in private law cases. The number of cases where both parties are represented has fallen very significantly, the number of cases where one party is represented has also fallen significantly and, correspondingly, the number of cases where neither party is represented has risen very significantly.

It is important to realise that there are potential problems with mediation. The assumption that the parties freely negotiate the terms of their final agreement in a less than hostile manner may be deeply flawed, to the extent that it assumes equality of bargaining power and knowledge between the parties to the negotiation. Mediation may well ease pain, but unless the mediation procedure is carefully and critically monitored, it may gloss over and perpetuate a previously exploitative relationship, allowing the more powerful participant to manipulate and dominate the more vulnerable and force an inequitable agreement. Establishing entitlements on the basis of clear legal advice may be preferable to apparently negotiating those entitlements away in the non-confrontational, therapeutic, atmosphere of mediation.

15.2.3 CONCILIATION

Conciliation takes mediation a step further and gives the mediator the power to suggest grounds for compromise and the possible basis for a conclusive agreement. Both mediation and conciliation have been available in relation to industrial disputes under the auspices of the government-funded Advisory, Conciliation and Arbitration Service (ACAS). One of the statutory functions of ACAS is to try to resolve industrial disputes by means of discussion and negotiation or, if the parties agree, the service might take a more active part as arbitrator in relation to a particular dispute.

The essential weakness in the procedures of mediation and conciliation lies in the fact that, although they *may* lead to the resolution of a dispute, they do not *necessarily* achieve that end. Where they operate successfully they are excellent methods of dealing with problems, as the parties to the dispute essentially determine their own solutions and feel committed to the outcome. The problem is that they have no binding power

However, Ward LJ was as emphatic as he was admonitory in his assessment of the present case and his view as to how future cases should be treated. As he put it (paras 41–43):

> *a small building dispute is par excellence the kind of dispute which, as the recorder found, lends itself to ADR.* Secondly, the merits of the case favoured mediation. The defendants behaved unreasonably in believing, if they did, that their case was so watertight that they need not engage in attempts to settle. They were counterclaiming almost as much to remedy *some* defective work as they had contracted to pay for the whole of the stipulated work. There was clearly room for give and take. *The stated reason for refusing mediation, that the matter was too complex for mediation, is plain nonsense.* Thirdly, the costs of ADR would have been a drop in the ocean *compared with the fortune that has been spent on this litigation.* Finally, the way in which the claimant modestly presented his claim and readily admitted many of the defects, allied with the finding that he was transparently honest and more than ready to admit where he was wrong and to shoulder responsibility for it augured well for mediation. The claimant has satisfied me that mediation would have had a reasonable prospect of success. The defendants cannot rely on their own obstinacy to assert that mediation had no reasonable prospect of success . . . *The profession must, however, take no comfort from this conclusion. Halsey has made plain not only the high rate of a successful outcome being achieved by mediation but also its established importance as a track to a just result running parallel with that of the court system.* Both have a proper part to play in the administration of justice. The court has given its stamp of approval to mediation and *it is now the legal profession which must become fully aware of and acknowledge its value.* The profession can no longer with impunity shrug aside reasonable requests to mediate . . . These defendants have escaped the imposition of a costs sanction in this case *but defendants in a like position in the future can expect little sympathy if they blithely battle on regardless of the alternatives* (emphasis added).

In the final analysis, the Court of Appeal directed the defendants to pay 60 per cent of the claimant's costs of the original claim and counterclaim and related proceedings. However, there was still a sting in the tail, for as Ward LJ stated (para 47):

> We have not heard argument on the costs of this appeal. In order that more costs are not wasted, I say that my preliminary view is that costs of the appeal should follow the event. The appellant has been successful and as at present advised and having regard to the checklist of relevant considerations set out in CPR 44.3, I can see no justification for his not having the costs of the appeal.

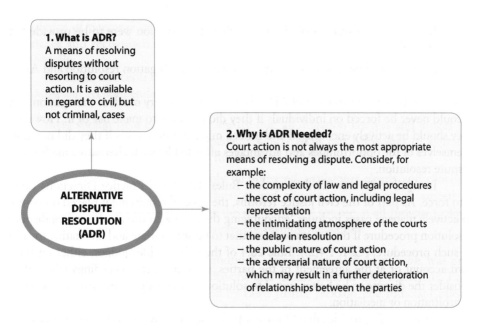

FIGURE 15.1 *Alternative Dispute Resolution (ADR): an aide-mémoire.*

So the Bullards faced even more costs for their failure to take advantage of the earlier offer of mediation. (For another case of money being thrown away in pursuit of a 'matter of principle', and perhaps even more scathing comments by Ward LJ, see *Egan v Motor Services (Bath) Ltd* (2007) in which a claim for about £6,000 damages cost £100,000 in fees.)

15.3   THE COURTS AND ADR

15.3.1 THE WOOLF AND JACKSON REFORMS

Alternative Dispute Resolution mechanisms have assumed an increasingly central place in the English legal system in fairly recent times.

Central to Lord Woolf's review of the civil law system was the perception of the lack of control over the antagonistic process of civil litigation allowing, if not necessarily directly leading to, inherent problems of cost, complexity and delay (see 7.2).

And central to Woolf's solution was the avoidance of litigation and the promotion of early, cost-effective settlement.

In his final report, *Access to Justice,* Woolf prefigured a new landscape for civil justice for the 21st century in which '*litigation will be avoided wherever possible*'. To achieve this end:

● people were to be encouraged to start court proceedings *only as a last resort,* and after using other more appropriate means when these are available;

The judicial development of ADR

The potential consequences of not abiding by a recommendation to use ADR may be seen in *Dunnett v Railtrack plc* (2002). When Dunnett won a right to appeal against a previous court decision, the court granting the appeal recommended that the dispute should be put to arbitration. Railtrack, however, refused Dunnett's offer of arbitration and insisted on the dispute going back to a full court hearing. In the subsequent hearing in the Court of Appeal, Railtrack proved successful. The Court of Appeal, however, held that if a party rejected ADR out of hand when it had been suggested by the court, they would suffer the consequences when costs came to be decided. In the instant case, Railtrack had refused to even contemplate ADR at a stage prior to the costs of the appeal beginning to flow.

The Court of Appeal subsequently applied *Dunnett* in *Leicester Circuits Ltd v Coates Brothers plc* (2003) where, although it found for Coates, it did not award it full costs on the grounds that it had withdrawn from a mediation process. The Court of Appeal also dismissed Coates' claim that there was no realistic prospect of success in the mediation. As Judge LJ stated (para 27):

> We do not for one moment assume that the mediation process would have succeeded, but certainly there is a prospect that it would have done if it had been allowed to proceed. That therefore bears on the issue of costs.

It is possible to refuse to engage in mediation without subsequently suffering in the awards of costs. The test, however, is an objective rather than a subjective one, and a difficult one to sustain, as was shown in *Hurst v Leeming* (2002). Hurst, a solicitor, started legal proceedings against his former partners and instructed Leeming, a barrister, to represent him. When the claim proved unsuccessful, Hurst sued Leeming in professional negligence. When that claim failed, Hurst argued that Leeming should not be awarded costs, as he, Hurst, had offered to mediate the dispute, but Leeming had rejected the offer. Leeming cited five separate justifications for his refusal to mediate. These were:

- the heavy costs he had already incurred in meeting the allegations;
- the seriousness of the allegation made against him;
- the lack of substance in the claim;
- the fact that he had already provided Hurst with a full refutation of his allegation;
- the fact that, given Hurst's obsessive character, there was no real prospect of a successful outcome to the litigation.

Only the fifth justification was accepted by the court, although even in that case it was emphasised that the conclusion had to be supported by an objective evaluation of the situation. However, in the circumstances, given Hurst's behaviour and character, the conclusion that mediation would not have resolved the complaint could be sustained objectively.

In *Halsey v Milton Keynes General NHS Trust* (2004), the Court of Appeal emphasised that the criterion was the reasonableness of the belief. The only ground of appeal in *Halsey* was that the judge at first instance had been wrong to award the defendant, the Milton Keynes General NHS, its costs, since it had refused a number of invitations by the claimant to mediate. As the court emphasised, in deciding whether to deprive a successful party of some or all of their costs on the grounds that they have refused to agree to ADR, it must be borne in mind that such an order is an exception to the general rule that costs should follow the event. In demonstrating such exceptional circumstances, in the view of the Court of Appeal, the burden is to be placed on the unsuccessful party to the substantive action to show why there should be any departure from that general rule. Lord Justice Dyson said (para 28):

> It seems to us that a fair . . . balance is struck if the burden is placed on the unsuccessful party to show that there was a reasonable prospect that mediation would have been successful. This is not an unduly onerous burden to discharge: he does not have to prove that a mediation would *in fact* have succeeded. It is significantly easier for the unsuccessful party to prove that there was a reasonable prospect that a mediation would have succeeded than for the successful party to prove the contrary.

In taking such a stance, the Court of Appeal was sensitive to the possibility, as it implicitly suggested was the case in relation to the claimants in the *Halsey* case, that (para 18):

> . . . there would be considerable scope for a claimant to use the threat of costs sanctions to extract a settlement from the defendant even where the claim is without merit. Courts should be particularly astute to this danger. Large organisations, especially public bodies, are vulnerable to pressure from claimants who, having weak cases, invite mediation as a tactical ploy. They calculate that such a defendant may at least make a nuisance-value offer to buy off the cost of a mediation and the risk of being penalised in costs for refusing a mediation even if ultimately successful . . .

As regards the power of the courts to order mediation, the Court of Appeal declined to accept such a proposition, finding it to be contrary to both domestic and ECHR law. As Dyson LJ stated in delivering the decision of the Court (para 9):

> We heard argument on the question whether the court has power to order parties to submit their disputes to mediation against their will. It is one thing to encourage the parties to agree to mediation, even to encourage them in the strongest terms. It is another to order them to do so. It seems to us that to oblige truly unwilling parties to refer their disputes to mediation would be to impose an unacceptable obstruction on their right of access to the court. The court in Strasbourg has said in relation to Article 6 of the European Convention on Human Rights that the right of access to a court may be waived, for example by means of an arbitration agreement, but such waiver should be subjected to 'particularly careful review' to ensure that the claimant is not subject to constraint . . . If that is the approach of the ECtHR to an *agreement* to arbitrate, it seems to us likely that *compulsion* of ADR would be regarded as an unacceptable constraint on the right of access to the court and, therefore, a violation of Article 6.

It is clear that a party can refuse to accept an offer to participate in mediation, but any such refusal must be reasonable. Unfortunately, what counts as reasonable cannot be defined with certainty, but its centrality is evident in the two cases below.

In *Rolf v De Guerin* (2011) the claimant succeeded to a degree in her claim but only recovered a small proportion of the amount claimed (£2,500 against a claim of £92,515) and failed on a number of her main allegations. On such grounds the court at first instance decided that the costs should *not* 'follow the event' in this case and awarded costs to the unsuccessful defendant.

On appeal, the Court of Appeal took into account Rolf's repeatedly stated willingness to settle the dispute through mediation. The defendant had refused mediation until it was too late to be effective and the Court of Appeal denied the validity of his reasons for refusal. As the reasons for refusal were unreasonable, the Court of Appeal held that each party should bear their own individual costs.

Subsequently, however, in *Swain Mason v Mills & Reeve* (2012), the Court of Appeal reaffirmed the decision in *Halsey* that under certain circumstances parties could refuse to engage in mediation. On the issue of refusal to mediate, the Court of Appeal took a different view from the trial judge in holding that the defendants had not unreasonably refused to mediate. In reaching its decision the Court of Appeal provided a gloss on *Halsey v Milton Keynes General NHS Trust*, holding that it was authority for the following:

- parties should not be compelled to mediate;
- mediation and other ADR processes do not offer a panacea and can have disadvantages as well as advantages and are not appropriate for every case;

- a party's reasonable belief that it has a strong case is a factor in deciding whether it was unreasonable to refuse mediation;
- where a party reasonably believes that it has a watertight case that may well be a sufficient justification for a refusal to mediate;
- account needs to be taken of whether a meditation would succeed, given the parties' stances;
- the court should be astute to the danger of parties being wrongly put under costs pressure as regards mediation.

As Davis LJ put it:

> The fundamental question remains as to whether it had been shown by the unsuccessful party (the claimants) that the successful party (the defendant) had acted *unreasonably* in refusing to agree to a mediation. In my view, that could not be shown here; and I therefore think that the judge was wrong to bring into account, adversely to the defendant, the defendant's attitude to mediation in deciding what costs overall should be awarded.

The Court of Appeal, taking a broad-brush approach, substituted an order that the defendants recover 60 per cent as opposed to the original court decision to award only 50 per cent of its costs.

PGF II SA v OMFS Company 1 Ltd (2013) is significant in that the Court of Appeal clarified the reasoning in *Halsey* by holding that the defendant's refusal even to respond to the claimant's invitations to mediation amounted to unreasonable conduct. In so doing the court accepted the statement of the law as set out in *The Jackson ADR Handbook*. As Briggs LJ stated:

> In my judgment, the time has now come for this court firmly to endorse the advice given in chapter 11.56 of the ADR Handbook, that silence in the face of an invitation to participate in ADR is, as a general rule, of itself unreasonable, regardless whether an outright refusal, or a refusal to engage in the type of ADR requested, or to do so at the time requested, might have been justified by the identification of reasonable grounds.

Although the case had been settled with the last-minute acceptance of the defendant's CPR 36 offer, the trial judge nonetheless penalised the defendant's refusal to mediate by depriving it of costs. The Court of Appeal confirmed that decision, although as his words show, Briggs LJ was aware that the decision was on the cusp of what is appropriate:

> The court's task in encouraging the more proportionate conduct of civil litigation is so important in current economic circumstances that it is appropriate to emphasise that message by a sanction which, *even if a little more vigorous than I would have preferred*, nonetheless operates *pour encourager les autres* (emphasis added).

15.4 ARBITRATION

The first and oldest of these alternative procedures to the courts is arbitration. This is the procedure whereby parties in dispute refer the issue to a third party for resolution, rather than taking the case to the ordinary law courts. Studies have shown a reluctance on the part of commercial undertakings to have recourse to the law to resolve their disputes. At first sight, this appears paradoxical. The development of contract law can, to a great extent, be explained as the law's response to the need for regulation in relation to business activity, yet business declines to make use of its procedures. To some degree, questions of speed and cost explain this peculiar phenomenon, but it can be explained more fully by reference to the introduction to this chapter. It was stated there that informal procedures tend to be most effective where there is a high degree of mutuality and interdependency, and that is precisely the case in most business relationships. Businesses seek to establish and maintain long-term relationships with other concerns. The problem with the law is that the court case tends to terminally rupture such relationships. It is not suggested that, in the final analysis, where the stakes are sufficiently high, recourse will not be had to law, but such action does not represent the first or indeed the preferred option. In contemporary business practice, it is common, if not standard, practice for commercial contracts to contain express clauses referring any future disputes to arbitration. This practice is well established and its legal effectiveness has long been recognised by the law.

Thus in *Cable & Wireless Plc v IBM United Kingdom Ltd* (2002) the two parties had entered into a contractual agreement which provided that in the event of any dispute they:

> shall attempt in good faith to resolve the dispute or claim through an alternative dispute resolution procedure as recommended . . . by the Centre for Dispute Resolution ('CEDR'). However an ADR procedure which is being followed shall not prevent any party . . . from issuing proceedings.

However, when an issue arose the claimant declined to refer its claim to ADR, submitting that the above term was unenforceable because it lacked certainty due to its apparent contradictory wording, which suggested the possibility of both ADR and the issuing of court proceedings. It was suggested that the clause amounted to no more than an agreement to negotiate, which was not enforceable in English law. However, Colman J held that the issuing of proceedings was not inconsistent with the simultaneous conduct of an ADR procedure or with a mutual intention to have the issue finally decided by the courts only if the ADR procedure failed. He also concluded that the fact that the parties had identified a particular procedure from an experienced dispute resolution service provider indicated that they intended to be bound by the ADR provision. As regards the uncertainty issue, Colman J made a wider reference to the applicability of ADR agreements after *Dunnett v Railtrack*, holding that the English courts should not go out of their way to find uncertainty, and therefore unenforceability, in the field of ADR references. As he put it, 'For the courts now to decline to enforce contractual references to ADR on the grounds of intrinsic uncertainty would be to fly in the face of public policy.'

15.4.1 PROCEDURE

Section 1 of the Arbitration Act (AA) 1996 states that it is founded on the following principles:

(a) the object of arbitration is to obtain the fair resolution of disputes by an impartial tribunal without necessary delay or expense;

(b) the parties should be free to agree how their disputes are resolved, subject only to such safeguards as are necessary in the public interest;

(c) in matters governed by this part of the Act, the court should not intervene except as provided by this part.

This provision of general principles, which should inform the reading of the later detailed provisions of the Act, is unusual for UK legislation, but may be seen as reflecting the purposes behind the Act, one major purpose of which was the wish to ensure that London did not lose its place as a leading centre for international arbitration. As a consequence of the demand-driven nature of the legislation, it would seem that court interference in the arbitration process has had to be reduced to a minimum and replaced by party autonomy. Under the 1996 Act, the role of the arbitrator has been increased and that of the court has been reduced to the residual level of intervention where the arbitration process either requires legal assistance or else is seen to be failing to provide a just settlement.

The Act, at least to a degree, follows the Model Arbitration Law adopted in 1985 by the United Nations Commission on International Trade Law (UNCITRAL), although it differs from the model code to the extent that it contains mandatory rules as well as provisions the parties can opt into or out of. For example, the power of the court to remove an arbitrator under s 24 cannot be overridden by the parties to the arbitration.

While it is possible for there to be an oral arbitration agreement at common law, s 5 provides that Part I of the 1996 Act only applies to agreements in writing. What this means in practice, however, has been extended by s 5(3) which provides that, where the parties agree to an arbitration procedure which is in writing, that procedure will be operative, even though the agreement between the parties is not itself in writing. An example of such a situation would be where a salvage operation was negotiated between two vessels on the basis of Lloyd's standard salvage terms. It would be unlikely that the actual agreement would be reduced to written form, but nonetheless, the arbitration element in those terms would be effective.

In analysing the AA 1996, it is useful to consider it in three distinct parts: autonomy of the parties; powers of the arbitrator and the court; and appellate rights:

Autonomy

It is significant that most of the provisions set out in the AA 1996 are not compulsory. As is clearly stated in s 1, it is for the parties to an arbitration agreement to agree what procedures to adopt. The main purpose of the Act is to empower the parties to the dispute and to allow them to choose how it is to be decided. In pursuit of this aim, the mandatory parts of the Act only take effect where the parties involved do not agree otherwise. It is actually possible for the parties to agree that the dispute should not be decided in line with the strict legal rules, but rather in line with commercial fairness, which might be a completely different thing altogether.

In *Jivraj v Hashwani* (2011) the Supreme Court, in overruling the Court of Appeal, held that arbitrators were not employees and consequently the requirement to select arbitrators from a particular religious group (in this case the Ismaili community) did not breach the Employment Equality (Religion or Belief) Regulations 2003.

Powers of the arbitrator

Section 30 provides that, unless the parties agree otherwise, the arbitrator can rule on questions relating to jurisdiction, that is, in relation to:

(a)   whether there actually is a valid arbitration agreement;

(b)   whether the arbitration tribunal is properly constituted;

(c)   what matters have been submitted to arbitration in accordance with the agreement.

Section 32 allows any of the parties to raise preliminary objections to the substantive jurisdiction of the arbitration tribunal in court, but provides that they may only do so on limited grounds which require either: the agreement of the parties concerned; the permission of the arbitration tribunal; or the agreement of the court. Leave to appeal will only be granted where the court is satisfied that the question involves a point of law of general importance.

Section 28 expressly provides that the parties to the proceedings are jointly and severally liable to pay the arbitrators such reasonable fees and expenses as appropriate. Previously, this was only an implied term.

Section 29 provides that arbitrators are not liable for anything done or omitted in the discharge of their functions unless the act or omission was done in bad faith.

Section 33 provides that the tribunal has a general duty:

(a)   to act fairly and impartially between the parties, giving each a reasonable opportunity to state their case; and

(b)   to adopt procedures suitable for the circumstance of the case, avoiding unnecessary delay or expense.

Section 35 provides that, subject to the parties agreeing to the contrary, the tribunal shall have the following powers:

(a)   to order parties to provide security for costs (previously a power reserved to the courts);

(b)   to give directions in relation to property subject to the arbitration;

(c)   to direct that a party or witness be examined on oath, and to administer the oath.

The parties may also empower the arbitrator to make provisional orders (s 39).

Powers of the court

Where one party seeks to start a court action, contrary to a valid arbitration agreement, then the other party may request the court to stay the litigation in favour of the arbitration agreement under ss 9–11 of the AA 1996. Where, however, both parties agree to ignore the arbitration agreement and seek recourse to litigation, then, following the party consensual nature of the Act, the agreement may be ignored.

The courts may order a party to comply with an order of the tribunal and may also order parties and witnesses to attend and to give oral evidence before tribunals (s 43).

The court has power to revoke the appointment of an arbitrator on application of any of the parties where there has been a failure in the appointment procedure under s 18, but it also has powers to revoke authority under s 24. This power comes into play on the application of one of the parties in circumstances where the arbitrator:

(a)   has not acted impartially or there are justifiable doubts as to their impartiality (see *Sierra Fishing Co. v Farran*, 2015);

(b)   does not possess the required qualifications;

(c)   does not have either the physical or mental capacity to deal with the proceedings;

(d)   has refused or failed to properly conduct the proceedings, or has been dilatory in dealing with the proceedings or in making an award, to the extent that it will cause substantial injustice to the party applying for their removal.

Under s 45, the court may, on application by one of the parties, decide any preliminary question of law arising in the course of the proceedings.

Arbitrators

The arbitration tribunal may consist of a single arbitrator or a panel, as the parties decide (s 15). If one party fails to appoint an arbitrator, then the other party's nominee may act as sole arbitrator (s 17). Under s 20(4), where there is a panel and it fails to reach a majority decision, the decision of the chair shall prevail.

The tribunal is required to adopt procedures fairly and impartially, which are suitable to the circumstances of each case. It is also for the tribunal to decide all procedural and evidential matters. Parties may be represented by a lawyer or any other person and the tribunal may appoint experts or legal advisers to report to it.

Arbitrators will be immune from action being taken against them except in situations where they have acted in bad faith.

Appeal

The AA 1950 allowed for either party to the proceedings to have questions of law authoritatively determined by the High Court through the procedure of '*case stated*'. The High Court could also set aside the decision of the arbitrator on grounds of fact, law or procedure. Whereas the arbitration process was supposed to provide a quick and relatively cheap method of deciding disputes, the availability of the appeals procedures meant that parties could delay the final decision and in so doing increase the costs. In such circumstances, arbitration became the precursor to a court case rather than replacing it. The AA 1979 abolished the 'case stated' procedure and curtailed the right to appeal. The AA 1996 has reduced the grounds for appeal to the court system even further.

Once the decision has been made, there are limited grounds for appeal. The first ground arises under s 67 of the AA 1996 in relation to the substantive jurisdiction of the arbitral panel, although the right to appeal on this ground may be lost if the party attempting to make use of it took part in the arbitration proceedings without objecting to the alleged lack of jurisdiction. The second ground for appeal to the courts is on procedural grounds, under s 68, on the basis that some serious irregularity affected the operation of the tribunal. By serious irregularity is meant:

(a)   failure to comply with the general duty to act fairly set out in s 33;

(b)   failure to conduct the tribunal as agreed by the parties;

(c)   uncertainty or ambiguity as to the effect of the award;

(d)   failure to comply with the requirement as to the form of the award.

The threshold for raising an action under s 68 is very restrictive and will succeed 'only if what had occurred was too far removed from what could reasonably be expected from the arbitral process to be justified' (see *ABB Ag v Hochtief Airport GmbH* (2006) EWHC 388 (Comm)). Thus the court will not intervene on the ground that it would have done things differently (see *Lorand Shipping Limited v Davof Trading (Africa) BV MV "Ocean Glory"* (2014) EWHC 3521 (Comm) for an example of a successful claim under s 68.

In *Secretary of State for the Home Department v Raytheon Systems Limited* [2015] EWCH 311 (TCC) the judge, on appeal, held that not only should the original finding of the arbitration panel be set aside on the basis of serious irregularity, but also that the issue should be reconsidered and decided by a different arbitrator panel on the grounds that 'there is a *real* risk, *judged objectively*, that even a competent and respectable arbitral tribunal, whose acts or omissions have been held to amount to serious irregularity causing substantial injustice may sub-consciously be tempted to achieve the same result as before'.

Parties may also appeal on a point of law arising from the award under s 69. However, the parties can agree beforehand to preclude such a possibility, and where they agree to the arbitral panel making a decision without providing a reasoned justification for it, they will also lose the right to appeal.

15.4.2 RELATIONSHIP TO ORDINARY COURTS

The attitude of the courts generally to arbitration may be seen in the words of Mrs Justice Gloster in *Soeximex SAS v Agrocorp International PTE Ltd* [2011] EWHC 2743:

> The Commercial Court is very sensitive to the fact that parties have chosen to have their disputes resolved by an industry or trade arbitral tribunal, rather than by the Courts. As a matter of general approach, it tries to uphold arbitration awards and to read them in a sensible and commercial way. It is very mindful that the Court's role on a s 68 application is not to pick holes in an award, or to indulge in an over-nice analysis of what may be understandably brief reasons given by commercial men in areas with which they are far more familiar than the Court.

However, where, as in the case in question, there are clearly legal issues to be addressed that were not dealt with in the arbitration, the court will allow an appeal and may impose its own, contrary, decision.

In general terms, therefore, the courts have no objection to individuals settling their disputes on a voluntary basis, but at the same time, they are careful to maintain their supervisory role in such procedures. Arbitration agreements are no different from other terms of a contract, and in line with the normal rules of contract law, courts will strike out any attempt to oust their ultimate jurisdiction as being contrary to public policy. Thus, as has been stated previously, arbitration proceedings are open to challenge through judicial review on the grounds that they were not conducted in a judicial manner.

In February 2008 the then Archbishop of Canterbury, Rowan Williams, caused a furore when, in a speech, he suggested that the eventual use of Sharia law to deal with disputes was inevitable in the United Kingdom. His comment was taken out of context, but as some commentators pointed out, it was already possible for Sharia Councils to decide disputes on an informal non-compulsory basis using Sharia principles. Similarly, Jewish people have been able to use their own system of courts, the Beth Din, to decide issues on a voluntary basis. In March 2015, in clear pre-election mode, Home Secretary Theresa May stated that a Conservative government intended to commission an independent figure to complete an investigation into the application of Sharia law in England and Wales on the basis, she claimed, that:

> . . . there is evidence of women being 'divorced' under sharia law and left in penury, wives who are forced to return to abusive relationships because sharia councils say a husband has a right to 'chastise', and sharia councils giving the testimony of a woman only half the weight of the testimony of a man.

Subsequently, in December 2015 the self-styled Commission on Religion and Belief in British Public Life issued a report entitled 'Living with Difference'. The report recognised that many submissions to its inquiry viewed religion-based tribunals negatively, or indeed saw them as having no place in British society. Nonetheless, it did not recommend any immediate action against them; rather, it called for more investigation about the impact that the operation of such tribunals had on women users, and about the impact of state policies on the procedures and substantive rules of these tribunals.

15.4.3 ADVANTAGES

There are numerous advantages to be gained from using arbitration rather than the court system:

Privacy
Arbitration tends to be a private procedure. This has the twofold advantage that outsiders do not get access to any potentially sensitive information and the parties to the arbitration do not run the risk of any damaging publicity arising out of reports of the proceedings.

Informality
The proceedings are less formal than a court case and they can be scheduled more flexibly than court proceedings.

Speed
Arbitration is generally much quicker than taking a case through the courts. Where, however, one of the parties makes use of the available grounds to challenge an arbitration award, the prior costs of the arbitration will have been largely wasted.

Cost

Arbitration is generally a much cheaper procedure than taking a case to the normal courts. Nonetheless, the costs of arbitration and the use of specialist arbitrators should not be underestimated.

Expertise

The use of a specialist arbitrator ensures that the person deciding the case has expert knowledge of the actual practice within the area under consideration, and can form their conclusion in line with accepted practice.

It can be argued that arbitration represents a privatisation of the judicial process. It may be assumed, therefore, that of all its virtues, perhaps the greatest, at least as far as the government is concerned, is the potential reduction in costs for the state in providing the legal framework within which disputes are resolved.

15.5   ADMINISTRATIVE TRIBUNALS

Although attention tends to be focused on the operation of the courts as the forum within which legal decisions are taken, it is no longer the case that the bulk of legal and quasi-legal questions are determined within that court structure. There are, as an alternative to the court system, a large number of tribunals that have been set up under various Acts of Parliament to rule on the operation of the particular schemes established under those Acts.

The generally accepted explanation for the establishment and growth of tribunals in Britain since 1945 was the need to provide a specialist forum to deal with cases involving conflicts between an increasingly interventionist welfare state, its functionaries and the rights of private citizens. It is certainly true that, since 1945, the welfare state has intervened more and more in every aspect of people's lives. The intention may have been to extend various social benefits to a wider constituency, but in so doing, the machinery of the welfare state, and in reality those who operate that machinery, have been granted powers to control access to its benefits, and as a consequence have been given the power to interfere in and control the lives of individual subjects of the state. By its nature, welfare provision tends to be discretionary and dependent upon the particular circumstance of a given case. As a consequence, state functionaries were extended discretionary power over the supply/ withdrawal of welfare benefits. As the interventionist state replaced the completely free market as the source of welfare for many people, so access to the provisions made by the state became a matter of fundamental importance, and a focus for potential contention, especially given the discretionary nature of its provision. At the same time as welfare state provisions were being extended, the view was articulated that such provisions and projects should not be under the purview and control of the ordinary courts. It was felt that the judiciary reflected a culture that tended to favour a more market-centred, individualistic approach to the provision of rights and welfare and that their essentially formalistic approach to the resolution of disputes would not fit with the operation of the new projects.

15.5.1   TRIBUNALS AND COURTS

There is some debate as to whether tribunals are merely part of the machinery of *administration* of particular projects or whether their function is the distinct one of *adjudication*. The Franks Committee (Cmnd 218, 1957) favoured the latter view, but others have disagreed and have emphasised the administrative role of such bodies. Parliament initiated various projects and schemes, and included within those projects specialist tribunals to deal with the problems that they inevitably generated. On that basis, it is suggested that tribunals are merely adjuncts to the parent project and that this therefore defines their role as more administrative than adjudicatory. In *Baker v HMRC* (2013) the First-tier Tribunal expressly stated that it could not grant the relief sought as it was not a court and has no jurisdiction to grant such relief.

If the foregoing has suggested the theoretical possibility of distinguishing courts and tribunals in relation to their administrative or adjudicatory role, in practice it is difficult to implement such a distinction for the reason that the members of tribunals may be, and usually are, acting in a quasi-judicial capacity. Thus, in *Pickering v Liverpool Daily Post and Echo Newspapers* (1991), it was held that a mental health review tribunal was a court whose proceedings were subject to the law of contempt. Although a newspaper was entitled to publish the fact that a named person had made an application to the tribunal, together with the date of the hearing and its decision, it was not allowed to publish the reasons for the decision or any conditions applied.

If the precise distinction between tribunals and courts is a matter of uncertainty, what is certain is that tribunals are inferior to the normal courts. One of the main purposes of the tribunal system is to prevent the ordinary courts of law from being overburdened by cases, but a tribunal is still subject to judicial review on the basis of breach of natural justice, or where it acts in an *ultra vires* manner, or indeed where it goes wrong in relation to the application of the law when deciding cases.

The supervisory body, the Administrative Justice and Tribunals Council, which replaced the previous Council on Tribunals, was itself abolished under the Public Bodies Act 2011 (see 3.5.3). The government declared its intention to abolish the AJTC in a strategy document issued in December 2012 entitled 'Administrative Justice and Tribunals: A Strategic Work Programme 2013–16'. As a result there is now only the Administrative Justice Forum, an independent body sponsored by the MoJ whose function is 'to gauge how the administrative justice and tribunals system is working, and identify any areas of concern or good practice and to provide early, informal, testing of policy initiatives'. However, in spite of the House of Commons Justice Committee expressing doubts about the consequences of getting rid of the AJTC, the Ministry of Justice proceeded to do so on the basis that it 'believe[d] that the independence of the tribunals system administered by HMCTS ensures that tribunal members and their administrative support systems are sufficiently removed from decision makers to diminish the case for a standing body to oversee tribunals. We believe that policy development and oversight of the wider administrative justice system should be led from within the MoJ.'

15.5.2   THE LEGGATT REVIEW OF TRIBUNALS

In May 2000, the then Lord Chancellor, Lord Irvine, appointed Sir Andrew Leggatt to review the operation of the tribunal system, and the attendant Consultation Paper stated that:

> There are signs . . . that the complexity of the system (if indeed it amounts to a system at all), its diversity, and the separateness within it of most tribunals, may be creating problems for the user and an overall lack of coherence.

As Sir Andrew found, there were 70 different administrative tribunals in England and Wales, leaving aside regulatory bodies, and between them they dealt with nearly one million cases a year. However, of those 70 tribunals, only 20 heard more than 500 cases a year and many were, in fact, defunct. Three tribunals still account for over 90 per cent of the caseload dealt with in the tribunal system covering the areas of social security and child support, which deals with around half of the total caseload; employment; and immigration and asylum.

Sir Andrew's task was to rationalise and modernise the tribunal structure, and to that end, he made a number of proposals, including the following:

- *Making the 70 tribunals into one tribunals system*

  He suggested that the existing 'system' did not really merit that title and that combining the administration of the different tribunals was necessary to generate a collective standing to match that of the court system.

- *Ensuring that the tribunals were independent of their sponsoring departments by having them administered by one Tribunals Service*

  He thought that, as happened, where a Department of State may provide the administrative support for a tribunal, pay its fees and expenses, appoint some of its members, provide its IT support and possibly promote legislation prescribing the procedure that the tribunal was to follow, the tribunal neither appeared to be independent, nor was it independent in fact.

- *Providing a coherent appeal system*

  He found the current system to be confusing and some tribunals to have too many appeal stages, leading to long delays in reaching finality.

- *Reconsidering the position of lay members*

  He considered that there was no justification for any members to sit, whether expert or lay, unless they have a particular function to fulfil, as they do in the employment tribunal.

Subsequently, in March 2003, the Lord Chancellor's Office, as it then was, announced its intention to follow the Leggatt recommendation in establishing a new unified Tribunal

Service. The new organisation formally came into being in April 2005 and was launched operationally in April 2006.

On 1 April 2011 Her Majesty's Courts Service and the Tribunals Service were amalgamated into one integrated agency, Her Majesty's Courts and Tribunals Service (HMCTS), providing support for the administration of justice in courts (up to and including the Court of Appeal) and most tribunals, but importantly not Employment Tribunals. The new Service operates as an agency of the Ministry of Justice.

15.5.3   THE TRIBUNALS, COURT AND ENFORCEMENT ACT (TCEA) 2007

In further pursuance of the Leggatt Review, the stated intention of this legislation (TCEA 2007) was the creation of a new, simplified, statutory framework for tribunals, which was to be achieved not just by the bringing together of existing tribunal jurisdictions but by provision of a new structure of jurisdiction and new appeal rights.

- *Unified structure*

  The Act provides for the establishment of a new unified structure to subsume all tribunals, except for the Employment Tribunals, which will remain independent. This unification is to be achieved through the creation of two new tribunals, the First-tier Tribunal and the Upper Tribunal, and in pursuit of that end the Act gives the Lord Chancellor power to transfer the jurisdiction of existing tribunals to the two new tribunals. The Act also provides for the establishment within each tier of 'chambers', so that existing jurisdictions may be grouped together appropriately. Chambers at the first-tier level will hear cases initially and the role of the upper chambers will be mainly, but not exclusively, to hear appeals from the first tier. Each chamber will be headed by a Chamber President, and the tribunals' judiciary, as the legal members of tribunals will now be entitled, will be headed by a Senior President of Tribunals.

- *Appeals*

  The Act specifically recognises and attempts to deal with the previous unclear and unsatisfactory routes of appeal in relation to tribunals' decisions. Under its provisions, in most cases, a decision of the First-tier Tribunal may be appealed to the Upper Tribunal and a decision of the Upper Tribunal may be appealed to the Court of Appeal. However, an appeal will not be allowed if such procedure is excluded by the specific Act or in any order made by the Lord Chancellor. However, it also provides that any such appeal must relate to a point of law and may only be exercised with permission from the tribunal being appealed from or the tribunal or court being appealed to.

- *Administration*

  The Act restated the role of the Tribunals Service, subsequently replaced by the amalgamated HMCTS, in the successful operation of the new unified system.

- *Supervision*

  The Senior President of Tribunals has responsibility for representing the views of the tribunal judiciary to Ministers and Parliament and for training, guidance and welfare. In addition to the powers under the Act, the Lord Chief Justice has delegated to the Senior President some of his powers under the Constitutional Reform Act, particularly in relation to judicial discipline of most tribunal judges and members.

As has been stated, the Administrative Justice and Tribunals Council (AJTC) was abolished by the MoJ in August 2013, and was effectively replaced by the Administrative Justice Advisory Group. The final report of the AJTC contained the following barbed comment:

> The MoJ has attached much weight to the Administrative Justice Advisory Group (AJAG) which it has established to 'play a dynamic role in helping to address issues for users'. The scepticism of the AJTC towards these arrangements has been echoed in Parliament with such descriptions as a 'poorly planned afterthought' and a 'pawn of the Department'. Despite the reservations, this Response acknowledges that AJAG will be the main forum for future identification and discussion of user concerns. We hope that AJAG, especially with an independent chairman, will be able to work robustly.

In April 2014 Jodi Berg was announced as the chair of the newly named Administrative Justice Forum (AJF).

- *Enforcement*

  In relation to enforcement, at present, tribunals have no enforcement powers of their own. Consequently, if a monetary award is not paid then the claimant must register the claim in the County Court before seeking enforcement. Under the TCEA 2007, claimants will be able to go directly to the County Court or High Court for enforcement.

Composition of the First-tier Tribunal

The following seven chambers operate within the First-tier Tribunal. The scope of the tribunal is so extensive that only limited comment can be made in relation to the chambers, but detailed information on each is available on the HMCTS website.

- **General Regulatory Chamber**

  The GRC was established within the First-tier Tribunal on 1 September 2009. The GRC brings together tribunals that heard appeals relating to various regulatory issues. Included among these are the following specific areas:

  - charities
  - claims management services
  - community right to bid
  - copyright licensing
  - electronic communications and postal services
  - environment
  - estate agents
  - exam boards

- food
- gambling
- immigration services
- information rights
- letting and managing agents
- microchipping dogs
- pensions regulation
- professional regulation
- transport.

- **Social Entitlement Chamber**

  The SEC deals with the following areas:

  (a) Asylum Support (it does not deal with asylum claims or other immigration matters)

  (b) Criminal Injuries Compensation

  (c) Social Security and Child Support.

- **Health, Education and Social Care Chamber**

  (a) Care Standards (i.e. appeals from people who have received a decision issued by organisations concerned with children and vulnerable adults, and those which regulate the provision of social, personal and health care)

  (b) Special Education Needs and Disability

  (c) Mental Health Review

  (d) Primary Health Lists: this tribunal hears appeals/applications resulting from decisions made by Primary Care Trusts as part of the local management of such lists, which medical practitioners must be on in order to function.

- **Immigration and Asylum Chamber**

  This chamber deals with appeals against decisions made by the Home Office officials in immigration, asylum and nationality matters. These mainly relate to decisions to:

  - refuse asylum in the UK
  - refuse entry to, or leave to remain in, the UK
  - deport someone already in the UK.

- **Property Chamber**

  This chamber hears appeals and references relating to disputes over property and land including:

  - residential property disputes
  - land registration matters
  - agricultural land and drainage matters.

- **Tax Chamber**

  This chamber has two specific areas of competence:

  (a)   Tax, where it hears appeals against decisions relating to tax made by Her Majesty's Revenue and Customs (HMRC).

  (b)   MPs' expenses, where it hears appeals against certain decisions made by the Compliance Officer. The Compliance Officer is appointed by the Independent Parliamentary Standards Authority (IPSA) and is responsible for determining and paying MPs' expenses. Appeals can be made by MPs under the Parliamentary Standards Act 2009.

- **War Pensions and Armed Forces Compensation Chamber**

  As its title suggests, this chamber hears appeals from ex-servicemen or women who have had their claims for a war pension rejected by the Secretary of State for Defence.

The following is a list of the **Chambers within the Upper Tribunal** already operating:

- **Administrative Appeals Chamber**

  This chamber hears appeals from the present First-tier Tribunals, the General Regulatory Chamber, the Health, Education and Social Care Chamber, Social Entitlement Chamber, and the War Pensions and Armed Forces Compensation Chamber.

- **Tax and Chancery Chamber**

  This chamber hears appeals from the First-tier Tax Chamber Tribunal. This brought together the four existing tax tribunals to hear the full range of direct and indirect tax cases.

- **Lands Chamber (Lands Tribunal)**

  In June 2009 the Lands Tribunal joined the tribunal system established by the TCEA when it became the Lands Chamber of the Upper Tribunal. As its functions have not changed, for the time being the Lands Chamber of the Upper Tribunal is still known as the Lands Tribunal.

- **Immigration and Asylum Chamber**

  In February 2010, immigration and asylum chambers were established in both tiers of the Unified Tribunals framework. The Upper Tribunal is a superior court of record dealing with appeals against decisions made by the First-tier Immigration and Asylum Chamber Tribunal.

The Employment Tribunals

The Employment Tribunal and the Employment Appeal Tribunal continue largely unchanged as a separate 'pillar' of the new system, as do some other specialist tribunals such as Special Immigration Appeals Commission (SIAC) (see 2.5.2). They are subject to the authority of the Senior President for training and welfare purposes and are treated as having the same status as Chambers in the First-tier and Upper Tribunals.

The Employment Tribunals are governed by the Employment Tribunals Act 1996, which sets out their composition, major areas of competence and procedure. They have jurisdiction in relation to a number of statutory provisions relating to employment issues. The majority of issues arise in relation to such matters as disputes over the meaning and operation of particular terms of employment, disputes relating to redundancy payments, disputes involving issues of unfair dismissal and disputes as to the provision of maternity pay.

They also have authority in other areas under different legislation. Thus, they deal with: complaints about racial discrimination in the employment field under the Race Relations Act 1976; complaints about sexual discrimination in employment under the Sex Discrimination Act 1975; complaints about equal pay under the Equal Pay Act 1970, as amended by the Sex Discrimination Act; complaints under the Disability Discrimination Act 1995; complaints about unlawful deductions from wages under the Wages Act 1986; and appeals against the imposition of improvement notices under the Health and Safety at Work Act 1974. There are, in addition, various ancillary matters relating to trade union membership and activities that the Employment Tribunals have to deal with.

The tribunal hearing is relatively informal. As in arbitration hearings, the normal rules of evidence are not applied and parties can represent themselves or be represented by solicitors or barristers. And, as appropriate in an employment context, they may also be represented by trade union officials or representatives, or indeed by any other person they wish to represent them.

Appeal, on a point of law only, is to the Employment Appeal Tribunal.

Although less formal than ordinary courts, the process of taking a case to, or defending a case in, an employment tribunal can be time-consuming and expensive, and employers' representatives have complained about the increased use of tribunals. As an alternative to the formal hearing, the Employment Tribunals offer a Judicial Mediation scheme. This was introduced as a pilot in 2006, and is now available throughout England and Wales. Judicial Mediation involves bringing the parties together for a Mediation Case Management Discussion before an employment judge who remains neutral and tries to assist the parties in resolving their disputes.

In a further attempt to remedy the alleged shortcomings in the Employment Tribunal process, the Advisory, Conciliation and Arbitration Service (ACAS) initiated a voluntary arbitration process for dealing with unfair dismissal claims as an alternative to using the employment tribunals.

However, even before it was introduced, the scheme came under attack from the Industrial Society. In a pamphlet entitled *Courts or Compromise? Routes to Resolving Disputes*, it argued that the new alternative to employment tribunals could well become as rigid, formal and almost as expensive as current tribunal and court processes, and claimed that in any event, the impact on the tribunal system was likely to be slight. While it recognised the advantages in such schemes, that they were faster, cheaper, more informal and flexible than tribunals, it also foresaw inherent risks. The pamphlet argued that ADR does not guarantee fairness or consistency in outcomes. In particular, it highlighted dangers where there is no appeal process, in lack of precedent, and where confidentiality is unjustifiable. It also pointed out the risk that compensation awarded through ADR might be less than in a tribunal or court. In conclusion, it warned that people who opt for ADR need to make sure that they understand the implications, for example, where the decision is binding and leaves no route to appeal.

Employment Tribunal charges

As with the furore over general criminal court charges (see p 490), so there was consternation when the government introduced fees for raising claims in the Employment Tribunal under the Employment Tribunals and the Employment Appeal Tribunal Fees Order 2013 (SI 2013/1893). Under the scheme, claimants were required to pay £160 or £250 to lodge a claim, depending on the type of issue involved, and a further charge of either £230 or £950 if the case was pursued to a hearing. People in receipt of benefits or, on a low income or with only a small amount of savings and investments were eligible to have fees waived or reduced. As detailed in a House of Commons briefing paper, *Employment tribunal fees* (SN07081), following the introduction of fees, the number of single cases *declined by 67 per cent* between October 2013 and June 2015 and the number of cases brought by two or more people *fell by 69 per cent*.

The trade union Unison applied for judicial review of the introduction of tribunal fees on two separate occasions. In February 2014 the first case was rejected by the High Court as insufficient time had passed for the court to assess the impact of the fees order. However, it did allow that, although the fees were not inherently unlawful, they might be deemed so, if they proved discriminatory or rendered it excessively difficult to enforce EU law-derived rights. Consequently, Unison raised a second case in October 2014, and this time included the specific issue that the introduction of fees weighed discriminately more on women, citing statistics that indicated that since the introduction of fees, there had been an 86 per cent drop in sex discrimination claims and an 80 per cent drop in equal pay claims. However, once again the High Court dismissed its action, as did the Court of Appeal, on the basis that the action could not succeed merely on the basis of statistical evidence alone. Unison announced its intention to pursue its case at a later time when specific instances could be used to support the action.

In June 2015 the government announced that it would be conducting a review of the effect of the introduction of fees for the Employment Tribunals. The review will consider how effective fees have been in achieving the objectives of:

- transferring some of the cost from the taxpayer to those who use the employment tribunal service;
- encouraging the use of alternative dispute resolution, such as ACAS;
- improving tribunal efficiency and effectiveness; and
- maintaining access to justice.

It remains to be seen what results from the review, but one would not be accused of being overly cynical to expect not a lot.

Appointment to tribunals is through the Judicial Appointments Commission procedure of application and interview, on the basis of the statutory and non-statutory requirements for the specific post. They are usually made up of three members, only one of whom, the chair, is expected to be legally qualified, although not necessarily a legal practitioner. The other two members are lay representatives. The lack of legal training is not considered a drawback, given the technical and administrative, as opposed to specifically legal, nature

Background to tribunals: Tribunals date back over 200 years and modern, specialist tribunals support the ordinary courts by resolving legal disputes quickly and cheaply within their areas of expertise

The organisation of tribunals: Until recently the organisation of administrative tribunals (i.e. those established by the state) was said to lack coherence. The **Tribunals, Courts and Enforcement Act 2007** (TCEA) was enacted to remedy this, introducing a new system of 'tiers' and 'chambers', each dealing with their own areas of expertise

THE UNIFIED TRIBUNAL STRUCTURE

First Tier: Appeals to First-tier Tribunal against the decisions of government departments and other public bodies. The First-tier Tribunal comprises seven chambers, namely:
- **The General Regulatory Chamber,** covering: Alternative Business Structures, Charity, Claims Management Services, Consumer Credit, Community Right to Bid, Environment, Estate Agents, Examination board, Food, Gambling Appeals, Immigration Services, Information Rights, Local Government Standards in England and Transport
- **The Health, Education and Social Care Chamber,** covering: Care Standards, Mental Health, Special Educational Needs & Disability and Primary Health Lists
- **The Immigration and Asylum Chamber,** covering Immigration and Asylum
- **The Property Chamber,** covering: Land Registration, Agricultural Land & Drainage and Residential Property Tribunal
- **The Social Entitlement Chamber,** covering Asylum Support, Criminal Injuries Compensation, Social Security and Child Support
- **The Tax Chamber,** covering Tax and MP Expenses
- **The War Pensions and Armed Forces Compensation Chamber**, covering War Pensions and Armed Forces Compensation

Upper Tribunal: Hears appeals from the First-tier Tribunal on points of law (i.e. an appeal made over the interpretation of a legal principle or statute). Further appeals may be made, with permission, to the Court of Appeal. The Upper Tribunal comprises four chambers, namely:
- **The Administrative Appeals Chamber**
- **The Immigration and Asylum Chamber**
- **The Lands Chamber**
- **The Tax and Chancery Chamber**

Tribunals which presently remain outside the First/Upper-Tier system: Employment, Employment Appeal, Gangmasters, Licensing Appeals, Gender Recognition Panel, Pathogens Access Appeal Commission, Proscribed Organisations Appeal Commission, Reserve Forces Appeal, Special Immigration Appeals Commission

FIGURE 15.2 *The Unified Tribunal Structure.*

of the provisions the members have to consider. Indeed, the fact of there being two lay representatives on tribunals provides them with one of their perceived advantages over courts. The non-legal members may provide specialist knowledge and thus they may enable the tribunal to base its decision on actual practice as opposed to abstract legal theory or mere legal formalism.

Research into the role of lay members in employment tribunals, conducted in 2010–11, by Corby and Latreille, endorsed the role of lay members and considered that they added value to the operation of tribunals. In particular they found support for the view that unfair dismissal was particularly 'a jurisdiction where lay members added value to decision making, despite a government proposal to enable judges to sit alone in unfair dismissal cases'. Nonetheless, s 4(3) ETA, which details proceedings which may be heard by an Employment Judge sitting alone was extended in 2012 to include actions in relation to unfair dismissal. This is important as, if a judge sitting alone at the Employment Tribunal decides a case, then any appeal hearing at the EAT will normally be decided by a judge sitting alone as well. This may not be as disadvantageous as it seems at first; the EAT only hears appeals on points of law and in any case further research by Susan Corby has found, perhaps somewhat counter-intuitively, that employee appellants have a significantly better chance of success when a decision is made by a judge sitting alone, rather than a judge with lay members.

15.5.5 DOMESTIC TRIBUNALS

The foregoing has focused on public administrative tribunals set up under particular legislative provisions to deal with matters of public relevance. The term 'tribunal', however, is also used in relation to the internal disciplinary procedures of particular institutions. Whether these institutions are created under legislation or not is immaterial; the point is that domestic tribunals relate mainly to matters of private rather than public concern, although at times the two can overlap. Examples of domestic tribunals are the disciplinary committees of professional institutions such as the Bar, The Law Society or the British Medical Association; trade unions; and universities. The power that each of these tribunals has is very great and it is controlled by the ordinary courts through ensuring that the rules of natural justice are complied with and that the tribunal does not act *ultra vires*, that is, beyond its powers. Matters relating to trade union membership and discipline are additionally regulated by the Employment Rights Act 1996.

15.5.6 ADVANTAGES OF TRIBUNALS

Advantages of tribunals over courts relate to such matters as:

- *Speed*

  The ordinary court system is notoriously dilatory in hearing and deciding cases. Tribunals are much quicker to hear cases. A related advantage of the tribunal disadvantage because it has the effect that cases involving issues of general public importance are not given the publicity and consideration that they might merit.

● *The provision of public funding*

It was claimed previously that one of the major advantages of the tribunal system is its lack of formality and non-legal atmosphere. Research has shown, however, that individual complainants fare better where they are represented by lawyers. Additionally, as a consequence of the Franks recommendations, the fact that chairpersons have to be legally qualified has led to an increase in the formality of tribunal proceedings. As a result, non-law experts find it increasingly difficult in practice to represent themselves effectively. This difficulty is compounded when the body that is the object of the complaint is itself legally represented; although the parties to hearings do not have to be legally represented, there is nothing to prevent them from being so represented.

15.6 OMBUDSMAN

As with tribunals, so the institution of the Ombudsman reflects the increased activity of the contemporary state. As the state became more engaged in everyday social activity, it increasingly impinged on, and on occasion conflicted with, the individual citizen. Courts and tribunals were available to deal with substantive breaches of particular rules and procedures, but there remained some disquiet as to the possibility of the adverse effect of the implementation of general state policy on individuals. If tribunals may be categorised as an ADR procedure to the ordinary court system in relation to *decisions taken in breach of rules*, the institution of the Ombudsman represents a procedure for the redress of complaints about *the way in which those decisions have been taken*. It has to be admitted, however, that the two categories overlap to a considerable degree. The Ombudsman procedure, however, is not just an alternative to the court and tribunal system; it is based upon a distinctly different approach to dealing with disputes. Indeed, the Parliamentary Commissioner Act 1967, which established the position of the first Ombudsman, provides that complainants with rights to pursue their complaints in either of those forums will be precluded from making use of the Ombudsman procedure. (Such a prohibition is subject to the discretion of the Ombudsman, who tends to interpret it in a generous manner in favour of the complainant.)

The concept of the Ombudsman is Scandinavian in origin, and the function of the office-holder is to investigate complaints of *maladministration*, that is, situations where the performance of a government department has fallen below acceptable standards of administration. The first Ombudsman, appointed under the 1967 legislation, operated, and the present Ombudsman still operates, under the title of the Parliamentary Commissioner for Administration (PCA), and was empowered to consider central government processes only. The PCA also serves as Health Service Ombudsman, in which capacity they investigate complaints that hardship or injustice has been caused by the National Health Service's failure to provide a service, by a failure in service provided or by maladministration. Since that date, a number of other Ombudsmen have been appointed to oversee the administration of local government in England and Wales, under the Local Government Act 1974. Scotland and Northern Ireland have their own local government Ombudsmen fulfilling the same task. There are also Health Service Commissioners for England, Wales and Scotland, whose duty it is to investigate the administration and provision of services in the health service, and in October 1994 Sir Peter Woodhead was appointed as the first Prisons Ombudsman. This proliferation of Ombudsmen has led to some confusion as to which one any particular complaint should be taken to. This can be especially problematic where the complaint concerns more than one public body. In order to remedy this potential difficulty, a Cabinet Office review recommended in April 2000 that access be made easier through the establishment of one new Commission, bringing together the Ombudsmen for central government, local government and the health service. This initiative moved forward in August 2005 when the Cabinet Office published a *Consultation Paper on the Reform of Public Sector Ombudsmen Services in England*. As yet, the single Commission has not been brought into existence. Following a review of the Local Government Ombudsman Service published in November 2013 the government announced its intention to introduce a single Local Government Ombudsman for England.

The Ombudsman system has also spread beyond the realm of government administration and there are Ombudsmen overseeing the operation of, among other things, legal services (see below, 16.6.7, for details), banking and insurance. Some schemes, such as the legal services scheme, have been established by statute, but many others have been established by industry as a means of self-regulation. It is a peculiarity of the system that reference is always made to the Ombuds*man*, irrespective of the gender of the office-holder. The present Parliamentary Ombudsman is in fact Dame Julie Mellor.

The European Parliament appointed an Ombudsman under the powers extended to it by the Treaty Establishing the European Community (EC Treaty) (Art 195, formerly 138(e)). The European Ombudsman has the function of investigating maladministration in all of the Union institutions, including the non-judicial operation of the Court of Justice of the European Union.

Before going on to consider the work of the Parliamentary Commissioner in some detail, mention should also be made of the various regulatory authorities that were established to control the operation of the privatised former state monopolies such as the water, gas, telephone and railway industries. Thus were Ofcom, Ofgem and Ofwat, and so on, set up, with part of their remit being to deal with particular consumer complaints, as well as the general regulation of the various sectors.

15.6.1 PROCEDURE

Although maladministration is not defined in the Parliamentary Commissioner Act 1967, it has been taken to refer to an error in the way a decision was reached rather than an error in the actual decision itself. Indeed, s 12(3) of the Parliamentary Commissioner Act 1967 expressly precludes the PCA from questioning the merits of particular decisions taken without maladministration. Maladministration therefore can be seen to refer to the procedure used to reach a result rather than the result itself. In an illuminating and much-quoted speech introducing the Act, Richard Crossman, the then Leader of the House of Commons, gave an indicative, if non-definitive, list of what might be included within the term maladministration, and included within it bias, neglect, inattention, delay, incompetence, ineptitude, perversity, turpitude and arbitrariness.

Such a demonstration of solidarity between the PCA and the Committee had the desired effect, leading to the government's climbdown and payments of £5,000 to those property owners who had suffered as a consequence of the housing blight.

On 15 March 2006 the Ombudsman published the above-named report on her investigation into the actions of government bodies in relation to the security of final-salary occupational pensions. She had received more than 200 complaints from MPs relating to the issue, together with 500 direct complaints from members of the public. All of the complaints were against the Department for Work and Pensions, the Treasury, the former Occupational Pensions Regulatory Authority and the National Insurance Contributions Office. However, the claims actually related to some 85,000 people from 400 private pension schemes who had lost part or all of their occupational pensions as a result of their company becoming insolvent between 6 April 1997 and 31 March 2004. Additionally, people whose schemes finished between April 2004 and 31 March 2005 were affected.

The extensive report supported claims that government departments wrongly advised workers that their company pensions were safe and protected by law. In this regard the report focused on leaflets issued by the Department for Work and Pensions advising workers as to the security of their works pensions. Particular weight was placed on one leaflet, issued in January 1996, which proclaimed that the Pensions Act 1995 was introduced specifically because 'the government wanted to remove any worries people had about the safety of their occupational scheme following the "Maxwell affair"'. As a result of such information, many workers who lost out on company pension schemes when their employers went bust felt the government had failed to highlight the risks of occupational pensions.

It was also alleged that on a number of occasions, ministers and officials had ignored relevant evidence when taking policy and other decisions related to the protection of pension rights accrued in such schemes. Thus the government twice reduced the minimum funding requirement (MFR), a formula introduced in 1995 as a result of the Maxwell pensions scandal, designed to make final-salary schemes safer by setting out the level of funding occupational pension schemes were required to have. By reducing the MFR, the government reduced the burden on employers, but in so doing it also decreased the protection offered to members. Although the MFR was never intended to guarantee pensions, the complainants argued that the literature produced by the government agencies implied exactly that. Consequently, many workers thought their pensions were safer than they were.

The investigation uncovered evidence of real suffering, distress and uncertainty about the future among pension scheme members and their families, who had relied on government information when making choices about their future pension provision. Two people had actually committed suicide after learning they would not receive their full pensions.

The report found that official information about the security of final-salary occupational pension schemes provided over many years by the Department for Work and Pensions, the Occupational Pensions Regulatory Authority and other government bodies was *'inaccurate, incomplete, unclear and inconsistent'* and in her conclusion the Ombudsman stated that:

> Government has a unique responsibility in these matters. Government set the pensions policy framework and took upon itself the responsibility of providing information for the public. The maladministration which my investigation has uncovered caused injustice to a large number of people who, as a result, lost the opportunity to make informed choices about their future.

The report made the following five recommendations to the government:

- full restoration of all lost pensions plus any other benefits such as life cover, 'by whichever means is most appropriate, including if necessary by payment from public funds';
- making 'consolatory payments' in recognition of the 'outrage, distress, inconvenience and uncertainty' workers have endured;
- apologising to scheme trustees for the distress they have suffered;
- considering whether to compensate those who are not fully covered by her recommendations;
- reviewing what can be done to reduce the time taken to wind up final-salary schemes.

However, as the report itself revealed that ministers had not accepted the findings of the report and had informed the Ombudsman that they were likely to comply only with the last of her recommendations, she was left to conclude that:

> Therefore, there is no basis on which I can be satisfied that the injustice I have identified will be remedied.

The estimation of costs of compensation was put between £5 billion and £10 billion to be paid over a period of some 40 years, a cost the government refused to meet. While the then pensions minister, Stephen Timms, expressed his sympathy with the workers who lost their pensions, he stated that 'nobody ever said occupational schemes were guaranteed by the taxpayer'. He also claimed that the Ombudsman had made 'an implausible leap' when she suggested literature written by his department backing occupational schemes led to government liability. In his view:

> Responsibility must fall on those companies whose schemes were or are being wound up, and to the trustees who, with the benefit of professional advice, were responsible for protecting members' interests.

Subsequently, the later pensions minister Peter Hain, towards the end of 2007, announced that the government intended to recompense most of the pensioners who had lost out in works schemes.

15.6.2.3   Equitable life: A decade of regulatory failure

This investigation originally took place into the role of the Financial Services Authority (FSA) and other authorities in regulating the conduct of the Equitable Life Assurance Society. In the 1950s the society started selling pension policies with a guaranteed annuity rate (GAR) that allowed policyholders to opt for minimum pension payouts and a bonus when their policy matured. Such policies were sustainable during the high inflation rates of the 1970s, but with current low inflation and interest rates Equitable found it hard to fund its commitments. Consequently, in an attempt to maintain payments to the majority of its customers who did not hold guarantees, it tried to withdraw the guaranteed payouts. However, in July 2000 the House of Lords ruled (in the *Hyman* litigation) that Equitable was required to make good its promises to the 90,000 holders of guaranteed annuity pension policies. As a consequence of this decision, it was apparent that Equitable was not in a position to maintain its payment to its policyholders; in December 2000 it closed its doors to new business and in July 2001 it announced that it was reducing the value of pension policies for with-profits policyholders by about 16 per cent. Later, in September 2001, Equitable published a compromise proposal for policyholders aimed at salvaging the company's finances and meeting its liabilities. This ensured that the existing GAR policyholders would get a 17.5 per cent increase in the value of their policies, but they would have to sign away their guaranteed pension rights. The other policyholders who were not GAR holders were offered a 2.5 per cent increase on the value of their policies, but they were required to sign away their rights to any legal claims. It has been estimated that some 800,000 policyholders have lost money as a result of the actions of Equitable. In August 2001, the government announced the independent Penrose Inquiry into events at Equitable Life; in October 2001, the then Parliamentary Ombudsman, Michael Buckley, announced that he would be carrying out a statutory investigation into the FSA's handling of events at Equitable Life beginning in 1999, when it had assumed responsibility for the prudential regulation of the life insurance industry. The investigation by the Ombudsman took 20 months, and when the report was issued by the Ombudsman in July 2003, it was not met with uniform approval. The Ombudsman 'found no evidence to suggest that the FSA . . . had failed their regulatory responsibilities during the period under investigation'. As she pointed out:

> the responsibility for what individual potential investors were actually told when purchasing new policies or annuities was not a matter for the regulator. Given all the publicity surrounding Equitable's high-profile court case and their subsequent decision to put up the company for sale, I would have expected potential investors to have sought independent advice before investing in Equitable.

However, the investigation had highlighted a specific issue that she wished to draw to Parliament's attention. That was the apparent mismatch between public expectations of the role of the prudential regulator and what the regulator could reasonably be expected to deliver. It was never envisaged by those who framed the legislation establishing the regulatory regime that it would provide complete protection for all policyholders. The emphasis was on a 'light touch' approach to regulation and the avoidance of over-interference in a company's affairs. Referring to calls for her to extend her investigation to an earlier period, the Ombudsman stated that:

> I have the very deepest sympathy for those who have suffered financial loss as a result of events at Equitable. However, given my very limited remit and the conclusions I have drawn from the investigation, I do not believe that anything would be gained from my further intervention, nor do I believe I could meet the expectations of policyholders in terms of the remedies they are seeking. It would be offering policyholders false hope were I to suggest otherwise. I have therefore decided not to investigate further complaints about the prudential regulation of Equitable.

The placing of blame on the management of Equitable rather than on the regulator was confirmed when Lord Penrose issued his report in March 2004. The report laid the blame for the affair at the door of Equitable's management in its finding that 'a culture of manipulation and concealment on the part of some of the company's previous senior management allowed a bonus policy to develop that led to the society's financial weakening – a policy left unchecked by its own board'. However, in July 2004, the

the Administrative Court, quashed the Treasury's decision to reject a number of findings of injustice and maladministration made by the Parliamentary Ombudsman on the basis of the date when state liability should start. Rather than start after 1995, as the Treasury had argued, the High Court held that the commencement date should be pushed back to 1991, thus greatly increasing the number of potential beneficiaries of compensation. The Court gave the Treasury 21 days to respond to the ruling and say what course of action they proposed to take and refused it permission to appeal.

In a subsequent Parliamentary statement the Chief Secretary to the Treasury, Liam Byrne, did not go out of his way to encourage the hopes of those waiting for payments:

> [Sir John Chadwick's] overall task remains the same, namely to advise the Government on those policyholders who have suffered disproportionate impact as a result of those cases of maladministration leading to injustice which the Government now accepts. The Government remains firmly committed to introducing a fair *ex gratia* payment scheme as soon as possible, taking benefit from Sir John's advice on the apportionment of responsibility and practicality of delivery, *and having taken account of the public finances.* Our goal is to introduce a scheme that is administratively quicker and simpler to deliver than that envisaged by the Ombudsman (emphasis added).

One of the first measures announced by the new coalition government in May 2010 was that a scheme would be established to pay the claims in line with the Ombudsman's recommendations. The Equitable Life (Payments) Bill was introduced in July 2010 and was passed in December of that year. It gives the Treasury statutory authority to incur expenditure in making payments to Equitable Life policyholders. It was initially expected that the total could amount to £5 billion. However, following Chadwick's conclusion that even though people had lost £4.8 billion in the debacle, compensation payments should only range between £400 and £500 million, the coalition government was seen to withdraw from its original promise to the Equitable Life claimants. Thus, in October 2010 the Chancellor, George Osborne, announced that reparation of £1.5 billion would be made. In December 2010, Royal Assent was given to the Equitable Life (Payments) Act 2010, which gave effect to the reparation proposals.

15.6.3 EVALUATION

All in all, the system appears to operate fairly well within its restricted sphere of operation, but there are major areas where it could be improved. The more important of the criticisms levelled at the PCA relate to:

- the retention of Members of Parliament as filters of complaints. It is generally accepted that there is no need for such a filter mechanism. At one level, it represents a sop to the idea of parliamentary representation and control. Yet at the practical level, PCAs have referred complaints made to them directly to the constituent's Member of Parliament, in order to have them referred back to them in the appropriate form. It is suggested that there is no longer any need or justification for this farce;

- the restrictive nature of the definition of maladministration. It is possible to argue that any procedure that leads to an unreasonable decision must involve an element of maladministration and that, therefore, the definition as currently stated is not overly restrictive. However, even if such reverse reasoning is valid, it would still be preferable for the definition of the scope of the PCA's investigations to be clearly stated, and be stated in wider terms than at present;

- the jurisdiction of the PCA. This criticism tends to resolve itself into the view that there are many areas that should be covered by the PCA, but which are not. For example, as presently constituted, the Ombudsman can only investigate the *operation* of general law. It could be claimed, and not without some justification, that the process of *making* law in the form of delegated legislation could equally do with investigation;

- the lack of publicity given to complaints. It is sometimes suggested that sufficient publicity is not given either to the existence of the various Ombudsmen or to the results of their investigations. The argument is that if more people were aware of the procedure and what it could achieve, then more people would make use of it, leading to an overall improvement in the administration of governmental policies;

- the reactive role of the Ombudsman. This criticism refers to the fact that the Ombudsmen are dependent upon receiving complaints before they can initiate investigations. It is suggested that a more *proactive* role, under which the Ombudsmen would be empowered to initiate investigation on their own authority, would lead to an improvement in general administration as well as increase the effectiveness of the activity of the Ombudsmen. This criticism is related to the way in which the role of the Ombudsmen is viewed. If they are simply a problem-solving dispute resolution institution, then a *reactive* role is sufficient; if, however, they are seen as the means of improving general administrative performance, then a more *proactive* role is called for.

Following a review of the current ombudsman provision conducted by Robert Gordon in October 2014, the Cabinet Office issued a consultancy paper in March 2015. It was entitled *A Public Service Ombudsman* and sought views about a proposal to establish a single Public Service Ombudsman taking over the functions of:

- The Parliamentary Ombudsman
- The Health Service Ombudsman
- The Local Government Ombudsman
- The Housing Ombudsman.

Now visit the Companion website to:

♥ test your understanding of the key terms using our Flashcard Glossary
● revise and consolidate your knowledge of arbitration, tribunal adjudication and alternative dispute resolution, using our multiple-choice question testbank
● access all of the links to the Useful Websites above.

www.routledge.com/cw/elliott

LEGAL SERVICES 16

We are concerned here with a number of issues related to the provision and organisation of legal services, and issues of public access to legal services. The delivery of legal services today looks very different from the way things were as recently as 1990. The legal profession has undergone a series of major changes as a result of the Courts and Legal Services Act (CLSA) 1990; the provision of public funding, advice and assistance has been drastically altered as a result of changes introduced in 1999; and the Legal Services Act 2007. The introduction of the 'conditional fee arrangement' (no win, no fee) in 1995 was another contentious issue in this area. In the 1950s, only a minute proportion of the population used lawyers to solve problems. Now, in the twenty-first century, a great many individuals, small businesses and organisations are using lawyers often as a matter of course.

The latest Law Society statistics in *Trends in the Solicitors' Profession – Statistical Report 2014* show that as at 31 July 2014 there were 160,394 solicitors 'on the Roll', that is, people qualified to work as solicitors, of whom 130,382 had a current practising certificate (PC). In 2014, there were 15,685 barristers in independent practice in England and Wales. This figure included 1,625 Queen's Counsel (QCs), who are senior and distinguished barristers of at least 10 years' standing who, as a result of outstanding merit, have received a patent as 'one of her Majesty's counsel learned in the law' (Bar Standards Board website, https://www. barstandardsboard.org.uk).

The Legal Services Act 2007

The Legal Services Act 2007 (LSA) heralded major changes in the law. The changes prescribed in this new law are comprehensive and radical. The Act was built around Sir David Clementi's proposals and the key components were:

- Creation of the **Office for Legal Complaints** (OLC), which in turn created the Legal Ombudsman (LO) scheme.
- **Alternative Business Structures** (ABSs), which enable consumers to obtain services from one business entity that brings together lawyers and non-lawyers.

- **Legal Disciplinary Practices** (LDPs), which allow firms to have up to 25 per cent non-lawyer or different kinds of lawyers as partners.
- A new **Legal Services Board** (LSB) to act as a single, independent and publicly accountable regulator with the power to enforce high standards in the legal sector, replacing a variety of regulators with overlapping powers.
- A clear set of **regulatory objectives** for the regulation of legal services.

The possible effects of the Legal Services Act 2007

The Legal Services Board (LSB) permitted ABSs from 6 October 2011. This enabled non-law firms to own legal practices and is commonly called 'Tesco Law' by the media. While Tesco may well offer legal services, other large organisations have already registered an ABS. The Co-operative Society became one of the first to obtain a licence and become an ABS. Direct Line, the insurer, has since acquired a licence to become an ABS. Irwin Mitchell, a large legal practice, and Quindell, an AIM listed company, acquired ABS licences. The Solicitors Regulation Authority (SRA) has issued 340 ABS licences to date (SRA website, www.sra.org.uk, March 2015). Slater and Gordon, the Australian quoted law firm, acquired the legal practice of Russell Jones & Walker in April 2012 following the SRA granting an ABS licence. They have been acquiring more law firms. PricewaterhouseCoopers (PWC), a major international accountancy practice, has acquired an ABS for its legal practice, PwC Legal.

Professor Stephen Mayson of the Legal Services Policy Institute of the University of Law wrote in late 2013:

> We are just at the second anniversary of licences being issued for alternative business structures (ABSs). In the first year, about 40 licences were issued, and progress seemed slow. A year later, there are still only two licensing authorities, but there have been roughly another 200 new licences. A year ago, we were told that there were another 200 applications in the pipeline. And we have had another 200 licences issued in the past twelve months. So it appears to have taken a year just to process the pipeline. There are no indications of how many are in the pipeline at the moment (stephenmayson.com, 6 October 2013).

The Law Society has not ignored the ABS threat to its members and, in autumn 2008, it commissioned a report by Lord Hunt, which was published on 5 October 2009 and titled 'The Hunt Review of the Regulation of Legal Services'. This is a lengthy report, which starts by considering the recent background to the legal profession and then considers various matters including professional regulation, education and training and ABS.

In his report (p 102), Lord Hunt, in considering how ABS might work and be regulated, commented: 'How will the inevitable conflict between economic benefits and ethical concerns be resolved?' An example of this conflict might arise where a firm decided to settle a major piece of litigation, believing that it was in the best interest of the client to do so. The practice's shareholders might suffer a consequential loss of potential profit. Under company law the shareholder may be able to sue the directors for making such a decision. The Australian firm Slater and Gordon, the first legal practice in the Western world to be listed on a stock market, worked with its regulator to solve this conundrum. Its constitution states that 'where an inconsistency or conflict arises between the duties of the company, the company's duty to the court will prevail over all duties'. This position has yet to be tested. As Stephen Mayson has pointed out in his excellent discussion paper on ABS and related issues:

> Experience in other jurisdictions (such as New South Wales) suggests that a focus on ethical behaviour and 'education for compliance' with regulation could pay dividends. Work commissioned by the Department for Constitutional Affairs also suggested that it is not the business structure that should be the principal cause for concern but rather the underlying incentives, and that 'traditional' structures and methods of practice involving only lawyers are just as likely to encourage unethical behaviour.

Slater and Gordon specialise as an insurance complainant practice and, compared with the top English law firms, are very small. Their turnover for the 2015 accounting year was AU$ 627.3 million (£288.8 million) and profit AU$ 114.5 million (£52.7 million), according to their published accounts. The Slater and Gordon business model may well be appropriate for similar practices in the UK, but it is probably less likely to be adopted by the large city corporate law practices.

A new franchise – QualitySolicitors – was founded in 2008 to enable law firms to become members and compete with the changes envisaged by the introduction of ABS. Their objective is to have member law firms across the country in every high street by October 2011. Andrew Holroyd, a former president of The Law Society (and partner in Jackson and Canter, which is now a member of QualitySolicitors), said in the *Law Society Gazette* (7 October 2010): 'The creation of a national legal services brand is essential if we are to compete with the new entrants to the market next year.'

Craig Holt, the chief executive of QualitySolicitors, told the *Law Society Gazette* (7 October 2010) that 'massively increasing our number of fully branded firms will enable us to achieve our goal of becoming the first established household name brand for legal services'. According to their website (www.qualitysolicitors.com, November 2015) they have over 200 branches.

The Institute of Chartered Accountants in England and Wales (ICAEW) was concerned that accountants would not be disadvantaged and in October 2013 applied to the Legal Services Board (LSB) to become an approved regulator and licensing authority for probate under the Legal Services Act 2007. The approval was granted and became effective from 14 August 2014.

In conclusion, the LSA 2007 and its potential effects are beginning to cause both legal and non-legal professions and individual firms to consider how to move forward

Diploma in Law in one year and then proceed as a law graduate. While the Law Society does not require an aptitude test for students wishing to undertake the LPC, the Bar Standards Board requires one. The Bar Course Aptitude Test (BCAT) became compulsory in autumn 2013 and costs £150. After completion of the LPC and traineeship, a trainee solicitor may apply to The Law Society to be 'admitted' to the profession. The Master of the Rolls will add the names of the newly qualified to the roll of officers of the Supreme Court. The requirement for a training contract was changed on 1 July 2014 with the introduction of the SRA Training Regulations 2014 to enable qualification provided that 'a period of recognised training' has been completed. This route is currently controversial as to whether the training will be satisfactory and enable the student to become a solicitor. The SRA has recently proposed a final competency examination at the point of qualification for all new solicitors and has commenced a consultation on the proposal.

In October 2013 the SRA published a policy statement, *Training for Tomorrow*, containing three main proposals:

- competency framework to set out the knowledge, skills and attributes that a solicitor requires at the point of qualification;
- continuing professional development (CPD) to focus on effectiveness of post-qualification training;
- removal of layers of regulation which neither assure quality nor enable excellence.

The *Law Society Gazette* (15 April 2015) reported that a paralegal has become the first solicitor to qualify through the alternative method of 'equivalent means'. The SRA accepted evidence that the paralegal had, while working at a law firm, achieved the same standards as someone qualifying through the traditional training period.

In July 2011 the Legal Education and Training Review was commissioned and published in June 2013 (see below, 16.3.2).

To practise, a solicitor will also require a practising certificate issued by the SRA. The fee comprises four parts as listed below. The SRA's fee structure for 2015 is:

Individual practising fee

A flat fee of £320 for every solicitor seeking a practising certificate.

Firm practising fee

A fee payable by every firm seeking or maintaining authorisation to practise. This is a turnover-based fee as shown in the table below.

Individual Compensation Fund contribution

A flat fee of £32 is payable by each individual.

Firm Compensation Fund contribution

A flat fee of £548 is payable by firms which hold client money.

Firm practising fee calculation of turnover for 2015

Turnover range (A)	Pay per cent of turnover within band (B)	Minimum turnover in band (C)	Minimum fee in band (D)
£0 – £19,999	0.80%	£0	£100
£20,000 – £149,999	0.47%	£20,000	£260
£150,000 – £499,999	0.46%	£150,000	£871
£500,000 – £999,999	0.44%	£500,000	£2,481
£1,000,000 – £2,999,999	0.42%	£1,000,000	£4,681
£3,000,000 – £9,999,999	0.29%	£3,000,000	£13,081
£10,000,000 – £29,999,999	0.24%	£10,000,000	£33,381
£30,000,000 – £69,999,999	0.22%	£30,000,000	£81,381
£70,000,000 – £149,999,999	0.20%	£70,000,000	£169,381
£150,000,000 – £9,999,999,999	0.07%	£150,000,000	£329,381

The firm fee is calculated by following the steps below:

- Identify which band the turnover (T) falls in from column A.
- Take T and subtract the figure in the corresponding column C.
- Multiply this figure by the corresponding percentage in column B.
- Finally, add this figure to the corresponding figure in column D.
- Firm fee then needs to be rounded to the nearest pound (i.e. if less than 50p then round down, and if equal to or more than 50p then round up).

Formula: $(T – C) \times B + D$
Example for turnover of £200,000:
$(£200,000 – £150,000) \times 0.48\% + £918 = £1,158$

Additionally, solicitors have to pay an annual premium for indemnity insurance.

All solicitors must now undergo regular continuing education, known as continuing professional development (CPD), which means attendance at non-examined legal courses designed to update knowledge and improve expertise. Each year, solicitors are required to complete 16 hours of CPD training in the CPD year that currently runs from 1 November to 31 October each year. One CPD point equates to one hour's training. However, the SRA announced a new approach to CPD on 21 May 2014, subject to LSB approval, by removing the 16 hours' compulsory training each year and replacing it with more flexible and appropriate training for an individual's particular needs. It fundamental rules, and a breach could result in sanctions. Rules 2 to 25 are the rules that arise from the core duties and which basically put flesh on the bare bones of rule 1, breach of which may result in sanctions. After each rule there is guidance which is not mandatory and does not form part of the Code of Conduct.

Outcomes-focused regulation (OFR) is the SRA's new approach to regulation. OFR is a move away from a rules-based approach and instead focuses on high-level outcomes governing practice and the quality of outcomes for clients. Version 15 of the Code of Conduct handbook was published on 1 November 2015. The SRA has announced an 18-months process to reduce the size of the Code of Conduct handbook. The objective is to enable firms to have more flexibility in running their practice.

The Legal Ombudsman

The Legal Ombudsman (see also 16.6.7) is an independent, consumer-focused ombudsman scheme set up to resolve complaints about lawyers in England and Wales. The Legal Ombudsman (LO) was established under the Legal Services Act 2007 and began accepting complaints on 6 October 2010. The LO provides a free complaints resolution service to members of the public, very small businesses, charities and trusts.

The LO deals with complaints about solicitors and the following types of professionals (and generally those working for them): barristers, law costs draftsmen, legal executives, licensed conveyancers, notaries, patent attorneys, probate practitioners, registered European lawyers, solicitors, and trademark attorneys.

The LO runs a remuneration scheme for any person dissatisfied with their solicitor's bill. This service is free, providing that the solicitor's bill does not include work for court proceedings. The LO will check the solicitor's bill to ensure that it is fair and reasonable. If the solicitor's work includes court proceedings, then only the court can assess the bill.

The LO can also instruct a solicitor to pay compensation to their client for distress and inconvenience caused by poor service. If a person is dissatisfied with the service they received from their solicitor, they should first lodge a complaint with their solicitor or the solicitor's complaints handling partner. If the aggrieved party fails to receive a response, or a satisfactory response, they can complain to the LO. The LO can make an award of up to £50,000, including any extra expenses and losses. However, the average award is in the region of £450 and most are less than £250. The LO makes awards on the merits of each individual case.

Solicitors' Disciplinary Tribunal (SDT)

The Solicitors' Disciplinary Tribunal is constitutionally independent of The Law Society, although it is funded by them. The SDT's powers arise by virtue of the Solicitors Act 1974. The purpose of the SDT is to consider and determine applications involving allegations of professional misconduct of solicitors or breaches of their professional rules. Such allegations are brought to the attention of the SDT in one of three ways:

- by members of the public;
- on behalf of The Law Society by in-house solicitors/barristers;
- by independent prosecuting solicitors instructed by The Law Society.

In addition, the SRA may refer a case to the SDT if a solicitor's misconduct is likely to lead to a fine, suspension, being struck off or another power given to the SDT.

Whether a referral is made to the SDT depends on two tests being satisfied: the evidential test and the public interest test. The former test requires 'that there is enough evidence to provide a realistic prospect that the solicitor will be found guilty of misconduct' (The Law Society, October 2006). The latter test involves considering the public interest once the evidential test is satisfied. For example, a case may be referred to the SDT if there are grounds for believing the conduct is likely to be continued or repeated, whereas a case may not be referred to the SDT if the misconduct was committed as a genuine mistake or misunderstanding or if the SDT is only likely to impose a small penalty.

The SDT can impose various sanctions which include the following:

- striking off the solicitor from the Roll;
- suspending the solicitor from practice for a fixed or indefinite period;
- ordering the solicitor to pay a penalty (to Her Majesty) for each allegation;
- reprimanding a solicitor.

As mentioned above, the OLC is funded by The Law Society, so there will still be a serious question as to whether this body will be seen as sufficiently independent by the public.

16.3.4   THE CHARTERED INSTITUTE OF LEGAL EXECUTIVES

The Chartered Institute of Legal Executives (CILEx) represents over 10,000 legal executives employed in solicitors' offices. They are legally trained (the Institute runs its own examinations) and carry out much of the routine legal work that is a feature of most practices. The Institute was founded in 1892 and incorporated in 1963 with the support of The Law Society. On 30 January 2012 the former ILEX became incorporated by Royal Charter and its members are now known as Chartered Legal Executives. The Managing Clerks' Association, from which CILEx developed, recognised that many non-solicitor staff employed in fee-earning work, and in the management of firms, needed and wanted a training route that would improve standards and award recognition for knowledge and skills. The education and training facilities CILEx offers have developed in number and diversity so that CILEx is able to provide a route to a career in law, which is open to all.

Legal executives are, in the phrase of the CILEx website (www.cilex.org.uk), qualified lawyers specialising in a particular area of law. They will have passed the CILEx Professional Qualification in Law in an area of legal practice to the same level as that required of solicitors. They will have at least five years' experience of working under the supervision of a solicitor in legal practice or the legal department of a private company or local or national government. Fellows are issued with an annual practising certificate, and only Fellows of CILEx may describe themselves as 'Legal Executives'. Specialising in a particular area of law, their day-to-day work is similar to that of a solicitor.

Legal executives might: handle the legal aspects of a property transfer; assist in the formation of a company; be involved in actions in the High Court or County Courts; draft wills; or advise clients accused of serious or petty crime, families with matrimonial problems, and on many other matters affecting people in their domestic and business affairs. Legal executives are fee earners – in private practice their work is charged directly to clients – making a direct contribution to the income of a law firm. This is an important difference between legal executives and other types of legal support staff who tend to handle work of a more routine nature. In March 2000, six legal executives qualified to become the first legal executive advocates under the CLSA 1990. The advocacy certificates were approved by the then ILEX Rights of Audience Committee. The advocates now have extended rights of audience in civil and matrimonial proceedings in the County Courts and magistrates' courts. In some circumstances, Fellows of CILEx can instruct barristers directly. Public Access (the Bar Council's scheme by which barristers can be directly instructed by some professional and voluntary organisations, rather than by solicitors) enables legal executives to access a wide choice of legal advice and representation for their clients and their employers. In December 2010 the first member of ILEX was appointed a deputy district judge (*Law Society Gazette*, 27 January 2011).

16.4 BARRISTERS

The barrister is often thought of as primarily a court advocate, although many spend more time on drafting, pleadings (now called statements of case) and writing advice for solicitors. Professional barristers are technically competent to perform all advocacy for the prosecution or defence in criminal cases, and for a claimant or defendant in a civil claim. More generally, however, established barristers tend to specialise in particular areas of work. Over 60 per cent of practising barristers work in London.

The Bar had been organised as an association of the members of the Inns of Court by the fourteenth century. Today, there are four Inns of Court (Inner and Middle Temples, Lincoln's Inn and Gray's Inn), although there were originally more, including Inns of Chancery and Sergeants' Inns, the latter being an association of the king's most senior lawyers. Until the CLSA 1990, the barrister had a virtual monopoly on advocacy in all the superior courts (in some cases solicitors could act as advocates in the Crown Court). In most situations, they cannot deal direct with clients but must be engaged by solicitors (but see below, 16.6.2).

16.4.1   TRAINING

Entry to the Bar is now restricted to graduates and mature students. An aspirant barrister must register with one of the four Inns of Court in London. Commonly, a barrister will have a law degree and then undertake professional training (the Bar Practice Training Course (BPTC), formerly known as the Bar Vocation Course) for one year leading to the Bar Examinations. Alternatively, a non-law graduate can study for the Common Professional Examination for one year and, if successful in the examinations, proceed to the Bar Examinations. The Bar Standards Board has imposed an aptitude test since autumn 2013, following approval from the LSB, prior to a student undertaking the BPTC (see 16.3.1). The successful student is then called to the Bar by his or her Inn of Court. It is also a requirement of being called that, during study for the vocational course, the student attends his or her Inn to become familiar with the customs of the Bar. The student then undertakes a pupillage, essentially an apprenticeship to a junior counsel. Note that all barristers, however senior in years and experience, are still 'junior counsel' unless they have 'taken silk' and become Queen's Counsel (QCs). Barristers who do not intend to practise do not have to complete the pupillage. See also the section on the LETR at 16.3.2.

16.4.2   THE INNS OF COURT

The Inns of Court are administered by their senior members (QCs and judges) who are called Benchers. The Inns administer the dining system and are responsible for calling the students to the Bar.

16.4.3   THE GENERAL COUNCIL OF THE BAR

The General Council of the Bar of England and Wales and of the Inns of Court (the Bar Council) is the profession's governing body. It is run by elected officials. It is responsible for the Bar's Code of Conduct, disciplinary matters and representing the interests of the Bar to external bodies like the Lord Chancellor's Department, the government and The Law Society. According to its own literature, this Council:

> fulfils the function of what might be called a 'trade union', pursuing the interests of the Bar and expanding the market for the Bar's services and is also a watchdog regulating its practices and activities.

16.4.4   EDUCATION

The Bar Standards Board (BSB) was established in January 2006 as a result of the Bar Council separating its regulatory and representative functions. That separation was to ensure that there was no conflict of interest between the people whose function was to represent the professional interests of barristers (as trade unions represent the interests of their members) and the people whose function is to regulate standards on behalf of the public and clients. As the independent regulatory board of the Bar Council, the BSB is responsible for regulating barristers called to the Bar in England and Wales. It takes decisions independently and in the public interest, and is not prejudiced by the Bar Council's representative function. The purpose of the BSB is 'to promote and maintain excellence in the quality of legal services provided by barristers to support the rule of law'. It does that by setting standards of entry to the profession and by ensuring that professional practice puts consumers first.

16.4.5   QUEEN'S COUNSEL

Queen's Counsel (QCs) are senior barristers of special merit. In 2014, the Bar had 1,625 QCs in practice. They are given this status (known as 'taking silk' because a part of the robe they are entitled to wear is silk) by the Queen on the advice of the Lord Chancellor. There were, until the suspension of the system in 2003, annual invitations from the Lord Chancellor for barristers to apply for this title. Applicants needed to show at least 10 years of successful practice at the Bar. However, under arrangements announced recently a new independent selection procedure has replaced the widely criticised former system, which relied on secret soundings among senior legal figures. Candidates will be chosen by the Lord Chancellor on the recommendation of an independent panel set up by The Law Society and the Bar Council. If appointed, the barrister will become known as a 'Leader' and he or she will often appear in cases with a junior. The old 'Two Counsel Rule', under which a QC always had to appear with a junior counsel, whether one was really required or not, was abolished in 1977. He or she will be restricted to high-level work (of which there is less available in some types of practice), so appointment can be financially difficult but, in most cases, it has good results for the QC as he or she will be able to considerably increase fee levels.

16.4.6   THE BARRISTER'S CHAMBERS

Barristers were not permitted to form partnerships (except with lawyers from other countries) until April 2010 when the Bar announced new rules following the LSA 2007; they work in sets of offices called chambers. Most chambers are run by barristers' clerks who act as business managers, allocating work to the various barristers and negotiating their fees. Imagine the situation where a solicitor wishes to engage a particular barrister for a case on a certain date and that barrister is already booked to be in another court three days before that date. The clerk cannot be sure whether the first case will have ended in time for the barrister to be free to appear in the second case. The first case might be adjourned after a day or, through unexpected evidential arguments in the early stages in the trial, it might last for four days. If the barrister is detained, then his or her brief for the second case will have to be passed to another barrister in his or her chambers very close to the actual trial. This is known as a late brief. Who will be asked to take the brief and at what point is a matter for the clerk.

The role of the barrister's clerk is thus a most influential one. Since 2003, lay clients have been able to enjoy direct access to barristers under the Public Access scheme (previously known as BarDIRECT); see www.barcouncil.org.uk. It is currently possible for barristers to accept instructions from some licensed organisations as opposed to the normal practice of being briefed by solicitors.

16.5   PROFESSIONAL ETIQUETTE

The CLSA 1990 introduced a statutory committee, the Lord Chancellor's Advisory Committee on Legal Education and Conduct (ACLEC), which, until recently, had responsibilities in the regulation of both branches of the profession.

As part of the government's reforms of legal services generally, and publicly funded legal advice specifically, the Access to Justice Act 1999 (s 35) has replaced the ACLEC (considered by some as slow and ponderous) with the Legal Services Consultative Panel, launched at the beginning of 2000. The Consultative Panel has:

(a)   the duty of assisting in the maintenance and development of standards in the education, training and conduct of persons offering legal services and, where appropriate, making recommendations to the Lord Chancellor; and

(b)   the duty of providing to the Lord Chancellor, at their request, advice about particular matters relating to any aspect of the provision of legal services (including the education, training and conduct of persons offering legal services).

The Law Society (through the Solicitors Regulation Authority) and the Bar Council (through the Bar Standards Board) exercise tight control over the professional conduct of their members. Barristers can meet the client only when the solicitor or his or her representative is present. This is supposed to promote the barrister's detachment from the client and his or her case, and thus lend greater objectivity to counsel's judgment. However, since April 2010 the Bar has relaxed the rules on the work a barrister can undertake (see 16.1). Barristers and solicitors must dress formally for court appearances, although solicitors, when appearing in the Crown, County or High Court, are required to wear robes but not wigs. A barrister not wearing a wig and robe cannot be 'seen' or 'heard' by the judge.

Traditionally, lawyers were not permitted to advertise their services, although this area has been subject to some deregulation in the light of recent trends to expose the provision of legal services to ordinary market forces. Solicitors can, subject to some regulations, advertise their services in print and on broadcast media.

16.5.1   IMMUNITY FROM NEGLIGENCE CLAIMS

Until recently barristers could not be sued by their clients for negligent performance in court or for work that was preparatory to court work (*Rondel v Worsley* (1969)); this immunity had also been extended to solicitors who act as advocates (*Saif Ali v Sidney*

Lords Hope, Hutton and Hobhouse delivered judgments in which they agreed that the immunity from suit was no longer required in relation to civil proceedings, but dissented to the extent of saying that the immunity was still required in the public interest in the administration of justice in relation to criminal proceedings.

Comment

This decision is of major and historic importance in the English legal system for several reasons. It can be seen as a bold attempt by the senior judiciary to drag the legal profession (often a metonymy for the whole legal system) into the twenty-first-century world of accountability and fair business practice. In his judgment, Lord Steyn makes this dramatic observation (*Arthur JS Hall & Co v Simons* [2000] 3 All ER 673 at 684):

> ... public confidence in the legal system is not enhanced by the existence of the immunity. The appearance is created that the law singles out its own for protection no matter how flagrant the breach of the barrister. The world has changed since 1967. The practice of law has become more commercialised: barristers may now advertise. They may now enter into contracts for legal services with their professional clients. They are now obliged to carry insurance. On the other hand, today we live in a consumerist society in which people have a much greater awareness of their rights. If they have suffered a wrong as the result of the provision of negligent professional services, they expect to have the right to claim redress. It tends to erode confidence in the legal system if advocates, alone among professional men, are immune from liability for negligence.

The case raises and explores many key issues of the legal system, including: the proper relationship between lawyers and the courts; the proper relationship between lawyers and clients; the differences between criminal and civil actions; professional ethics; the nature of dispute resolution; and the circumstances under which the courts should make new law. Above all, however, the case has one simple significance: 'It will', in the words of Jonathan Hirst QC, a former Chairman of the Bar Council, 'mean that a claimant who can prove loss, as the result of an advocate's negligence, will no longer be prevented from making a claim. We cannot really say that is wrong' ((2000) *Bar News*, August, p 3).

16.6   THE COURTS AND LEGAL SERVICES ACT 1990

Both branches of the legal profession have traditionally enjoyed monopolies in the provision of certain legal services (for example, advocacy was reserved almost exclusively to barristers, while conveyancing was reserved to solicitors). In the 1980s, Lord Mackay, the then Lord Chancellor, argued that these monopolies did not best serve the users of legal services as they entailed unnecessarily limited choice and artificially high prices. The CLSA 1990 was introduced to reform the provision of legal services along such lines. Today, many of the old monopolies have been broken. Thus, we have solicitor-advocates and non-solicitor licensed conveyancers.

In 1990 in the CLSA, the government broke the solicitors' conveyancing monopoly by allowing licensed conveyancers to practise. There was initially evidence that this increased competition resulted in benefits to the consumer. From 1985, The Law Society had permitted solicitors to sell property, like estate agents, so as to promote 'one-stop' conveyancing. The Consumers' Association estimated that solicitors' conveyancing prices fell by a margin of 25 to 33 per cent before licensed conveyancers actually began to practise.

Under the CLSA 1990, apart from allowing the Bar Council and The Law Society to grant members rights of audience as before, The Law Society is able to seek to widen the category of those who have such rights. Applications are made to the Lord Chancellor, who refers the matter to their Advisory Committee. If the Committee favours the application, it must also be approved by four senior judges (including the Master of the Rolls and the Lord Chief Justice), each of whom can exercise a veto. The Director General of the Office of Fair Trading must also be consulted by the Lord Chancellor. All those who consider applications for extended rights of audience or the right to conduct litigation must act in accordance with the 'general principle' in s 17.

16.6.1 SECTION 17

The principle in s 17 states that the question of whether a person should be granted a right of audience or to conduct litigation is to be determined only by reference to the following four questions:

- Is the applicant properly qualified in accordance with the educational and training requirements appropriate to the court or proceedings?

- Are applicants members of a professional or other body with proper and enforced rules of conduct?

- Do such rules have the necessary equivalent of the Bar's 'cab rank rule', that is, satisfactory provision requiring its members not to withhold their services: on the ground that the nature of the case is objectionable to them or any section of the public; on the ground that the conduct, opinions or beliefs of the prospective client are unacceptable to them or to any section of the public; or on any ground relating to the prospective client's source of financial support (for example, public funding)?

- Are the body's rules of conduct 'appropriate in the interests of the proper and efficient administration of justice'?

Subject to the above, those who consider applications must also abide by s 17's 'statutory objective' of 'new and better ways of providing such services and a wider

choice of persons providing them, while maintaining the proper and efficient administration of justice'.

Successful applications were made by The Law Society, the Head of the Government Legal Service and the Director of Public Prosecutions (DPP). The Advisory Committee, while rejecting the idea of an automatic extension of solicitors' rights of audience
upon qualification (for example, guilty plea cases in Crown Courts), accepted the principle that they should qualify for enlarged rights after a course of advocacy training.
Non-lawyers can also apply for rights of audience in the courts: the Chartered Institute
of Patent Agents successfully applied for rights to conduct litigation in the High Court.
Under s 12 of the CLSA 1990, the Lord Chancellor will use their power to enable lay
representatives to be used in cases involving debt and housing matters in small claims
procedures. Similarly, under ss 28 and 29 of the CLSA 1990, the right to conduct litigation is thrown open to members of any body that can persuade the Advisory Committee,
the Lord Chancellor and the four senior judges that its application should be granted as
the criteria set out in s 17 (above) are satisfied.

The historic monopoly of barristers to appear for clients in the higher courts was
formally ended in 1994 when the Lord Chancellor approved The Law Society's proposals on how to certify its members in private practice as competent advocates. The innovation is likely to generate significant change in the delivery of legal services, especially
in the fields of commercial and criminal cases. The prospective battle between solicitors
and barristers for advocacy work can be simply characterised.

16.6.2   SOLICITORS' RIGHTS OF AUDIENCE

There are now 6,688 solicitors qualified as solicitor-advocates with rights to practise
advocacy in some or most levels of the court structure (SRA website statistics of solicitor
advocates, www.sra.org.uk, October 2015). This development began with changes in the
1990s. In February 1997, the Lord Chancellor, Lord Mackay, and the four designated
judges (Lord Bingham, Lord Woolf, Sir Stephen Brown and Sir Richard Scott; see s 17
of the CLSA 1990) approved The Law Society's application for rights of audience in the
higher courts for employed solicitors, but subject to certain restrictions.

Lord Phillips, the Lord Chief Justice, put forward proposals that will allow solicitor-
advocates to have the same dress code as barristers. The new reforms came into effect
in 2008. Solicitor-advocates finally put on wigs in court (*Law Society Gazette*, 10 January 2008). Solicitor-advocates in criminal cases are allowed to wear wigs, wing collars
and bands. They can also wear stuff gowns. However, in civil and family proceedings the
wigs and other regalia will no longer be worn. The dress code for judges was changed in
2008. The judge's robe, designed by Betty Jackson, received mixed reactions when it was
unveiled in May 2008 ('Thumbs down for designer robe', *The Times*, 15 May 2008).

Under The Law Society's 1998 regulations approved by the Lord Chancellor's
Department, some solicitors (those who are also barristers or part-time judges) are granted
exemption from the new tests of qualification for advocacy. Others need to apply for the
grant of higher courts qualifications, either in civil proceedings, criminal proceedings or in

both. A holder of the higher courts (criminal proceedings) qualification has rights of audience in the Crown Court in all proceedings (including its civil jurisdiction) and in other courts in all criminal proceedings. A holder of the higher courts (civil proceedings) qualification may appear in the High Court in all proceedings and in other courts in all civil proceedings. On 1 April 2010 new rules came into force for solicitors seeking higher rights of audience. The rules were amended on 1 September 2010. On 17 June 2011, The Higher Rights of Audience Regulations 2011 replaced the 2010 regulations with effect from 6 October 2011. Qualification under the new regulations is solely by advocacy assessment based on the SRA's Higher Rights of Audience competence standard, which is run by organisations authorised by the SRA. A detailed summary can be found in the 15th edition of this book.

All solicitors seeking these rights of audience have to pass an advocacy assessment based on higher rights of audience competency standards.

One benefit for law firms is that those that offer advocacy training are likely to attract the best graduates. This is a worry for the commercial Bar, as some graduates will see a training contract with an advocacy element as a better option than the less secure Bar pupillage. The Bar is determined that it will not lose any significant ground in the face of this new competition. Its representatives claim that solicitors will not be able to compete with barristers because of their much higher overheads.

From 2000, there have been three routes to qualification: the 'development' route leading to the all-proceedings qualification; the 'accreditation' route appropriate for solicitors who have significant experience of the higher civil and/or higher criminal courts; and the 'exemption' route which has existed under both the 1992 and 1998 regulations. The accreditation and exemption routes were phased out in 2005, leaving now only the advocacy assessment route as detailed above. Solicitors who obtained Higher Rights of Audience under previous regulations were transferred under the 2010 regulations and retain their existing rights.

Many barristers are very worried about the threat to their traditional work. A potentially significant development is Public Access (originally known as BarDIRECT), a pilot scheme set up in 1999 that enables certain professions and organisations to have direct access to barristers without referral through a solicitor. While this initiative could be one of the keys to the continuing success of the Bar, it is argued that it makes barristers no different from solicitors and could even encroach on the solicitors' market.

16.6.3   THE ACCESS TO JUSTICE ACT 1999 AND RIGHTS OF AUDIENCE

Lawyers' rights of audience before the courts were further addressed in Part III of the Access to Justice Act 1999. It replaces the Lord Chancellor's Advisory Committee on Legal Education and Conduct with a new Legal Services Consultative Panel:

●   It provides that, in principle, all lawyers should have full rights of audience before any court, subject only to meeting reasonable training requirements.

●   It reforms the procedures for authorising further professional bodies to grant rights of audience or rights to conduct litigation to their members; and for approving changes to professional rules of conduct relating to the exercise of these rights.

The Act also contains sections that:

- simplify procedures for approving changes to rules and the designation of new authorised bodies;
- give the Lord Chancellor power, with the approval of Parliament, to change rules that do not meet the statutory criteria set out in the CLSA 1990 as amended by these sections;
- establish the principle that all barristers and solicitors should enjoy full rights of audience; and
- establish the primacy of an advocate's ethical duties over any other civil law obligations.

The legislation enables employed advocates, including Crown Prosecutors, to appear as advocates in the higher courts if otherwise qualified to do so, regardless of any professional rules designed to prevent their doing so because of their status as employed advocates.

16.6.4 PARTNERSHIPS AND TRANSNATIONAL FIRMS

By virtue of s 66 of the CLSA 1990, solicitors are enabled to form partnerships with non-solicitors (multidisciplinary partnerships or MDPs), and the section confirms that barristers are not prevented by the common law from forming such relationships. They are, however, prohibited from doing so (unless with a foreign lawyer) by the Bar. Solicitors are able, under s 89 of the CLSA 1990 (Sched 14), to form multinational partnerships (MNPs). The arrival of MNPs over the coming years will raise particular problems concerning the maintenance of ethical standards by the Solicitors' Regulation Authority over foreign lawyers. MDPs also raise potentially serious problems, as even in arrangements between solicitors and others, it will be likely that certain work (for example, the conduct of litigation) would have to be performed by solicitors.

The business organisation called the limited liability partnership (LLP) was introduced by the Limited Liability Partnership Act 2000. The new business form seeks to amalgamate the advantages of the company's corporate form with the flexibility of the partnership form. Although called a 'partnership', the new form is, in fact, a distinct legal entity that enjoys an existence apart from that of its members. The LLP can enter into agreements in its own name, it can own property, sue and be sued. Traditional partnerships by contrast entail liability for the partners as individuals. Although the LLP enjoys corporate status, it is not taxed as a separate entity from its members. Solicitors do not seem to have been keen to adopt these as their preferred form of firm. The growth in their popularity has been steady. In 2002, fewer than 100 from the then 8,300 law firms had become LPPs. Most were formed because of international constraints in mergers, that is, the foreign firm could not merge with the British one unless the British one became an LLP. By 2012, 13 per cent of law firms in England and Wales were practising as LLPs, and only one firm in the top 50 remained as a traditional partnership (*Law Society Gazette*, 8 May 2012).

Law firms

Another feature of change is the evidently widening gap between the work and income of the top few hundred commercial firms and the 8,000 smaller high-street firms. A series of mergers has created a few relatively huge law firms, and the merger of an English firm with an American one produced the world's first billion-dollar practice. In 1999, partners at Clifford Chance voted to merge with the United States' Rogers & Wells, and Punders in Germany, to form a firm that now employs over 7,000 people in 30 offices worldwide.

The trend of firms merging is continuing. In late 2015, Irwin Mitchell announced that it was taking over Thomas Eggar, which will create a practice with a fee income of approximately £250 million. *The Lawyer*'s UK 200 Annual Report 2014 showed that the top seven law firms all had a turnover in excess of £1 billion, with DLA Piper top at £1.566 billion.

16.6.5   EMPLOYED SOLICITORS

This is a fast-growing area of practice with more than one-fifth of those holding a practising certificate working outside private practice. Employed solicitors are professionals who work for salaries as part of a commercial firm, private or public enterprise, charity or organisation, as opposed to solicitors in private practice who take instructions from various clients.

16.6.6   MONOPOLY CONVEYANCING RIGHTS

Historically, barristers, solicitors, certified notaries and licensed conveyancers enjoyed statutory monopolies, making it an offence for any other persons to draw up or prepare documents connected with the transfer of title to property for payment. The CLSA 1990 broke this monopoly by allowing any person or body not currently authorised to provide conveyancing services to make an application to the Authorised Conveyancing Practitioners' Board (established by s 34) for authorisation under s 37. The Board must be satisfied, before granting authorisation, that the applicant's business is, and will be, carried on by fit and proper persons, and must believe that the applicant will establish or participate in the systems for the protection of the client specified in s 37(7) including, for example, adequate professional indemnity cover and regulations made under s 40 concerning competence and conduct. Banks and building societies were in a privileged position (s 37(8)), since they were already regulated by statute. These institutions did not initially appear enthusiastic to compete with solicitors by establishing in-house lawyers. They have preferred instead to use panels of local practitioners.

The solicitors' monopoly on the grant of probate has also been abolished. Under ss 54–55 of the CLSA 1990, probate services were opened up to be available from approved

1. Solicitors
- Often described as the 'general practitioners' of law, which may be misleading today, as solicitors in larger practices often specialise
- Rights of audience now extend to the senior courts, where a higher court advocacy qualification has been obtained
- In return solicitors have lost their monopoly in areas such as conveyancing
- Training involves a law degree (or GDL/CPE), followed by a Legal Practice Course (LPC) and two years as a trainee
- Supervised by the Solicitors' Regulation Authority, solicitors normally work together in partnerships, while complaints relating to maladministration in the legal profession can be made to the Legal Ombudsman

2. Barristers
- Often thought of as the 'specialists'; the academic stage of training is normally the same as for solicitors, but barristers complete a Bar Vocational Course (BVC), followed by a year's pupillage
- Barristers join one of the Inns of Court, which are responsible for 'calling' members to the Bar
- Supervised by the General Council of the Bar, barristers have rights of audience in all courts
- Senior barristers of merit may 'take silk', becoming Queen's Counsel (QCs)
- Barristers are normally, but not always, self-employed but share offices known as 'Chambers'

3. Legal Executives
The Institute of Legal Executives (ILEX), which was developed from the Managing Clerks Association, represents Legal Executives, who carry out the more routine legal work. Qualified lawyers, such practitioners will be specialists in a particular area of law and now have limited rights of audience in lower courts

THE LEGAL PROFESSION

4. Fusion of the Professions: The ELS is one of only three systems in the world that maintain a divided legal profession. Despite criticism of the present system, the legal professions have argued that fusion would lead to a fall in the quality of advocacy. It has, however, been claimed that there has been 'fusion by the backdoor', as the CLSA 1990 and the AJA 1999 have removed solicitors' monopolies over certain tasks such as conveyancing, as well as barristers' monopoly over advocacy in the senior courts

FIGURE 16.1 *A Breakdown of the Different Legal Professions.*

bodies of non-lawyers. Grant of probate is the legal proof that a will is valid, which is needed for a person to put the will into effect. New probate practitioners directly compete with solicitors for probate work. The grant of probate is only a small part of the probate process, but when it was restricted as business that only a solicitor could perform, it effectively prevented others, except some banks, from being involved in probate. The banks seem best placed to take up work in this area as they already have trustee and executor departments.

16.6.7 THE LEGAL OMBUDSMAN

The Legal Ombudsman (LO) scheme, replacing the previous Legal Services Ombudsman (LSO), was established by the Office for Legal Complaints (OLC) under the Legal Services Act 2007. It began accepting complaints in October 2010. The LO claims to be an independent, consumer-focused ombudsman scheme set up to resolve complaints about lawyers in England and Wales. It provides a free service to all members of the public, very small businesses, charities, clubs and trusts.

It deals with complaints about the following types of lawyers (and generally those working for them):

- barristers;
- solicitors;
- law costs draftsmen;
- legal executives;
- licensed conveyancers;
- notaries;
- patent attorneys;
- probate practitioners;
- registered European lawyers;
- trademark attorneys;

and deals with complaints relating to:

- buying and selling a house or property;
- family law such as divorce;
- wills;
- personal injury;
- intellectual property;
- criminal law;
- civil litigation;
- immigration;
- employment issues.

If the LO decides the service received by the complainant was unsatisfactory, it can require the lawyer to put it right. Although most complaints can be resolved informally, it is empowered to carry out a formal investigation.

CHAPTER SUMMARY: LEGAL SERVICES

The main area of debate on this theme is the best approach to supplying the highest number and widest range of people with legal services appropriate to what citizens need. How can the legal profession become more user-friendly? Have the changes made under the CLSA 1990 to increase competition in the provision of legal services been successful?

Have the restrictive professional monopolies been properly broken and, if so, will the quality of services offered by non-lawyers (for example, conveyancing, probate, litigation) be reduced? Will the exclusion of millions of people from public funding eligibility have any serious consequences?

The impact of the conditional fee arrangements, the 1995 Green Paper on legal aid, and franchising are of special importance, but to deal with these issues properly you need to be familiar with the details of how legal services are delivered in general.

THE LEGAL PROFESSION

The legal profession, although not fused, comprises solicitors and barristers whose work is becoming increasingly similar in many respects. Additionally, the ending of monopolies on litigation, probate and conveyancing has meant that lawyers' traditional work is increasingly becoming blurred with that of other professionals. The liabilities of lawyers for errors and negligence are key issues. Another is the way in which complaints are handled by the professions.

THE COURTS AND LEGAL SERVICES ACT 1990

The CLSA 1990 was passed 'to see that the public has the best possible access to legal services and that those services are of the right quality for the particular needs of the client'. The detail by which the Act sought to do this is very important, especially s 17 (general principle, litigation and rights of audience); s 11 (lay representatives); ss 28–29 (right to conduct litigation); s 66 (multidisciplinary partnerships); s 89 (multinational partnerships); ss 34–37 (conveyancing); ss 21–26 (the Legal Services Ombudsman); and s 58 (conditional fee arrangements).

THE ACCESS TO JUSTICE ACT 1999

The 1999 Act makes many changes that will have an impact upon the professions. It articulates the principle that all lawyers should have full rights of audience before all courts, provided they have passed the relevant examinations. Also, by reforming the procedures for authorising further professional bodies to grant rights of audience, it signals a widening of those rights in the future.

IMMUNITY FROM NEGLIGENCE CLAIMS

Until recently barristers could not be sued by their clients for negligent performance in court or for work that was preparatory to court work (*Rondel v Worsley* (1969)); this immunity had also been extended to solicitors who act as advocates (*Saif Ali v Sidney Mitchell* (1980)). The client of the other side, however, may sue for breach of duty (*Kelly v London Transport Executive* (1982)). This was changed in a major case in 2000, *Arthur JS Hall and Co v Simons and Other Appeals*.

THE LEGAL OMBUDSMAN

An Ombudsman is a person independent of the government or a given field of activity, who investigates complaints of maladministration. The post of Legal Ombudsman is now operated under the LSA 2007 by the Office for Legal Complaints.

OVERVIEW OF CHANGES TO LEGAL PROFESSION

Historically the legal profession was generally considered a safe, conservative and usually profitable business. However, this is starting to change.

The Legal Services Act 2007 received Royal Assent on 30 October 2007 and became fully operational on 6 October 2011 when it allowed the formation of Alternative Business Structures (ABSs).

The Act came into force during a severe and prolonged economic recession, and the latter may also have contributed to the changes in the legal profession.

There have been significant changes during this period with the creation of the QualitySolicitors franchise, mergers of law firms, the newly created ABS structures and Slater and Gordon acquiring English legal practices. The changes are still in their infancy and the ultimate outcome for the legal profession is still unclear.

The *Law Society Gazette* (5 August 2013) reported that a half-yearly report produced by Law Consultancy Network indicated that 38 per cent of firms of fewer than 10 partners thought that there was a good or definite chance of a merger. This trend towards merging is not limited to small firms, as can be seen by the takeover of Thomas Eggar by Irwin Mitchell ('Irwin Mitchell creates £250m firm with Thomas Eggar merger' (2015) *Law Society Gazette*, 26 November). The *Wall Street Journal* (27 October 2013) reported that a number of US law firms were in merger discussions.

The advent of the ABS has been relatively slow, as stated in Stephen Mayson's report dated 6 October 2013 which indicated that in the first two years, only 240 ABS licences had been issued. However, some major developments have taken place under the umbrella of an ABS.

The Co-op Legal Services, which was formed in 2006, was one of the first firms to acquire an ABS. The financial report for the Co-op group for 2014 reported that the legal business made a loss of £4 million in the year, compared with a loss of £9 million in 2013 (Co-operative Group Limited, Annual Report 2014).

The AA has obtained an ABS and from 1 December 2013 commenced a joint venture with law firm Lyons Davidson. Direct Line Insurance has also now obtained an ABS licence.

Russell Jones & Walker acquired an ABS licence and were then acquired by Australian law firm Slater and Gordon (a public quoted company), which has subsequently acquired four more English legal practices.

It is unclear at the present time how the legal market will develop with the current changes and new businesses offering legal services. The largest English law firms that tend to specialise in corporate and related work for major companies appear, at the present time, to be relatively unaffected and still producing turnover in excess of £1 billion and PEP of £1 million. What is becoming clear is the need for the legal profession to adapt to the changes in the legal market. We have already seen a number of law firms of varying size collapse including Halliwells, Cobbetts, Follett Stock, Manches and Dewey & LeBoeuf (a large US firm also operating in the UK). In 2015, Parabis Group, an ABS formed in 2012, was sold off as part of a pre-pack administration.

FOOD FOR THOUGHT

1   Why should the legal profession be divided into two discrete sectors? Whose interests does this really serve?

2   Why do barristers make the best judges, if they do?

3   Much is made of the need for greater access to the legal professions. However, given the increase in the number of law graduates and the restrictions in the number of training contracts and pupillages, is progression not a matter of 'who you know rather than what you know'?

4   In legal firms, attention tends to be focused on the partners/solicitors, but what roles do the legal executives play?

5   Does the introduction of 'Tesco Law' (ABSs) necessarily mean a reduction in standards?

6   Consider the extent to which access to online provision reduces the need for legal professionals.

FURTHER READING

Abel, R, *The Legal Profession in England and Wales*, 1988, Oxford: Basil Blackwell

Baksi, C, 'Solicitor-advocates hit bar' (2008) Law Soc Gazette, 28 March

Browne, D, QC, 'A considered response' (2009) Counsel 3

Bryant, J, 'Proactive regulation will hit solicitors where it hurts' (2009) 23(40) Lawyer 6

Cocks, R, *Foundations of the Modern Bar*, 1983, London: Sweet & Maxwell

Farrow, A and Littler, R, 'Raising the bar' (2009) 153(40) SJ 6

Genn, H and Genn, Y, *The Effectiveness of Representation at Tribunals*, 1989, London: LCD

Guise, T, 'Something for everyone' (2009) 153(41) SJ 19

Holroyd, A, 'Moving with the times' (2008) 105(2) Law Soc Gazette 16

Jackson, R, 'Disappointed litigants and doubtful actions' (1995) Counsel 16

Keogh, A, 'Power sharing' (2008) 158 NLJ 717

Lord Hoffmann, *Arthur JS Hall and Co. v. Simons (A.P.)* (2000) UKHL 38

Money-Kyrle, R, 'Advocates' immunity after *Osman*' (1999) 149 NLJ 945 and 981

Susskind, R, *Tomorrow's Lawyers* (2013) Oxford: OUP

Underwood, K, 'Hope continues' (2007) 151(46) SJ 1542

Williamson, P, 'Open and accountable' (2007) 104(48) Law Soc Gazette 11

USEFUL WEBSITES

www.lawsociety.org.uk
The official site of The Law Society.

www.sra.org.uk
The official site of the Solicitors Regulation Authority.

www.barcouncil.org.uk
The official site of the Bar Council of England and Wales.

http://letr.org.uk
The site of the Legal Education and Training Review.

COMPANION WEBSITE

Now visit the companion website to:

- test your understanding of the key terms using our Flashcard Glossary;
- revise and consolidate your knowledge of 'Legal services' using our multiple choice question testbank;
- read the latest news and updates on the Legal Profession in the Student Law Review;
- view all of the links to the Useful Websites above.

www.routledge.com/cw/slapper

THE FUNDING OF LEGAL SERVICES

17

Legal aid (now called public funding) was introduced after World War II to enable people who could not otherwise afford the services of lawyers to be provided with those services by the state. The system and costs grew enormously over the decades. The system underwent various restrictions and cutbacks during the late 1990s and was replaced by other systems like the Community Legal Service (2000) and the Criminal Defence Service (2001). The term 'legal aid' is still used as a descriptive, non-technical term to refer to state-funded services. It is run by the Legal Services Commission (LSC) and assists over two million people each year. The Legal Aid Agency spent £1.695 billion in 2014–15, compared with £1.9 billion in 2013–14 (Legal Aid Agency Annual Report 2014/15).

The importance of the system was neatly encapsulated by Tim Dutton, QC as Chairman of the Bar Council in 2008. He noted ((2008) NLJ 1031):

> In much the same way that the National Health Service has been held in high regard, we should be proud that our legal aid system has been considered one of the best at providing justice for the most vulnerable and needy in our society.

Following legal aid reforms suggested by Lord Carter in his report, *Legal Aid – A Market-based Approach to Reform*, which was published on 13 July 2006, there were numerous changes made to the legal aid system. This chapter examines all the major elements of state-funded legal services. It also examines the alternative system of funding – conditional fee arrangements – under which payment to lawyers is made dependent on particular results.

In recent times, the extent of the service has been significantly reduced. In a powerful, lucid, and trenchant summary of recent changes, David Pannick QC, a crossbench member of the House of Lords, said this ('Wanted – a legal aid fund that meets needs of ordinary citizens', *The Times*, 10 December 2015):

> When Sir Hartley Shawcross, the attorney-general, opened the second reading debate on the Legal Aid and Advice Bill in December 1948, he said it was a 'charter' for the ordinary citizen. It would 'open the doors of the courts freely to all persons who may wish to avail themselves of British justice without regard to the question of their wealth or ability to pay'. He added that no longer would legal rights be 'luxuries' beyond people's reach. The Legal Aid, Sentencing and Punishment of Offenders Act 2012 (Laspo) undermines those objectives.
>
> Before Laspo, civil legal aid was available for most legal disputes, with specified exceptions, for those who satisfy the means-test criteria. Now civil legal aid is available only for specific types of legal dispute with a narrow (in practice, very narrow) 'exceptional funding' provision for excluded areas. So civil legal aid is no longer available for cases concerning, for example, employment, education (apart from special educational needs), immigration (except for detention), family law (apart from domestic violence and child abuse), and most welfare benefit claims. In addition, the means-test criteria have been tightened so that the 'little man' (or woman) referred to by Sir Hartley is most unlikely to qualify.

Lord Pannick QC concluded that the most promising option for reform is for the Ministry of Justice to promote a legal insurance scheme in which funds are provided for claims that have good prospects of success, to be paid for from the costs awarded in successful cases against the other party, plus a percentage of the sums recovered for claimants.

On 10 December 2015, in a debate in the House of Lords, Lord Lester of Herne Hill QC, a Liberal Democrat, reminded fellow peers that the debate coincided with the UN's human rights day. He then said:

> One fundamental human right is effective access to justice. It is a state's duty to provide a system of legal aid that enables everyone, including the poor and not so rich, to have effective access to courts and tribunals.

In the same debate, Lord Howarth of Newport, a Labour peer who defected from the Conservatives in 1995, made an observation about the recent and substantial reductions in legal aid. He said:

> In 1987, the Conservative government commenced a long attrition of public spending on legal aid. The Labour government more or less carried on the policy after 1997. But it was the coalition government that really took the axe to legal aid. The coalition parties had no mandate for this; their manifestos had not hinted at it.

Without access to legal professional advice and representation, a citizen is, in effect, cut adrift from civil society. Whether it would have been possible substantially to reduce public access to basic education or basic health care without an express mandate, as the coalition government did in respect of legal services, is an open question.

In 2015, 70 per cent of respondents to research conducted by Citizens Advice said they would not be able to afford a lawyer to advise on a problem or dispute. Only about 10 per cent were confident they could afford the cost of legal fees. Fewer than 40 per cent of respondents said the English legal system is working well for the entire population ('Responsive justice: how citizens experience the justice system', Citizens Advice, November 2015).

17.2   BACKGROUND TO RECENT CHANGES

In 2006, the government indicated it was determined to curb the spiralling cost of legal aid expenditure, which was £1.5 billion in 1996–97 and rose to almost £2.1 billion in 2003/04, where it peaked before decreasing slightly over the next few years to around £2 billion a year (Lord Hunt, *Hansard*, 19 February 2008, col 134).

The proposals in a report of a review team under Lord Carter of Coles (*Procurement of Criminal Defence Services: Market-based Reform*, 2006) are being gradually implemented and are set to make substantial changes to the system. The system advocated by Carter is one where lawyers have to bid competitively to win contracts for doing criminal legal aid work. Under this new market-based model, all criminal legal aid lawyers are paid fixed fees – rather than being paid by time spent – and compete for contracts for work in police stations and courts.

The reforms prevent the highest-earning barristers being paid £1 million a year from legal aid, as used to be the case. Such a reorganisation could halve the number of the 2,500 legal aid firms and cause wide-scale mergers.

Most criminal trials are now covered by fixed fees, but fees in the long and most complex criminal trials are still the subject of negotiation between the government and the professional bodies.

There are several state-funded schemes to facilitate the provision of aid and advice. Each scheme has different rules relating to its scope, procedures for application and eligibility. Because of the importance of justice and access to the legal machinery, the idea behind legal aid is to give people who could otherwise not afford professional legal help the same services as more wealthy citizens. This raises important social, political and economic questions. Do poorer people deserve the same quality of legal advice as that which can be afforded by wealthy people? If so, how should such schemes be funded? The LSC, in its strategic plan published in April 2009 for the period 2009 to 2012, had a vision of 'fair access to justice to the people who need it but can least afford it'.

17.3   THE LEGAL AID SCHEME

The Access to Justice Act 1999 set up a new legal aid system and made provisions about rights to supply legal services (see Chapter 16), court procedure (see Chapter 9), magistrates and magistrates' courts (see Chapter 12). The provisions in the Act form part of the wide-ranging programme of reforms to legal services and the courts, described in the government's White Paper, *Modernising Justice*, published on 2 December 1998. Except where noted, the Act only affects England and Wales.

Part I of the 1999 Act established a Legal Services Commission (LSC) to maintain and develop the Community Legal Service (CLS) and the Criminal Defence Service (CDS), which replaced the Civil and Criminal Legal Aid schemes, respectively. The Act also enabled the Lord Chancellor to give the Commission orders, directions and guidance about how it should exercise its functions. The Community Legal Service Fund replaced the legal aid fund in civil and family cases.

On 1 April 2013 the Legal Aid, Sentencing and Punishment of Offenders Act 2012 (LASPO) came into force. This Act introduced the Legal Aid Agency (LAA) following the abolition of the LSC.

The LAA publishes (on the website https://www.gov.uk) full details of all aspects of legal aid for the benefit of both providers and those requiring its services. The information is both detailed and regularly updated, including details of new contracts and application procedures.

Examples are the new 2015 Duty Provider Crime Contract details published on 10 July 2014 and updated on 27 November 2014. The information for applicants extends to 150 pages. Applicants must apply by 29 January 2015 and the contract will commence on 1 October 2015. The LAA announced on 13 November 2015 that because of legal challenges, the existing contract will run from 11 January 2016 to 31 March 2016, with the new contract commencing the following day. However, if because of injunctions, a further extension is required, a backstop date of 10 January 2017 has been set. On 10 June 2015 the *Law Society Gazette* reported that Shailesh Vara, the minister responsible for legal aid, proposed that the number of contracts for providing duty lawyers to advise suspects detained in police stations or defendants at magistrates' courts would be reduced from 1,600 to 527.

17.3.1 CONTROLLED AND LICENSED WORK

As noted at 17.2 above, legal aid funding was granted on a case-by-case basis until the system of franchising was introduced in August 1994, where firms of solicitors meeting certain requirements were able to contract to undertake certain cases without prior approval, and claim funding on a more advantageous basis than previously. This franchise or 'contract' system has formed the basis of the legal aid scheme.

Funded services for all civil contract work fall under the headings of 'controlled work' and 'licensed work'. In non-family cases there are three levels of service for controlled work: legal help, help at court and controlled legal representation, which includes legal representation before a mental health review tribunal or the Asylum and Immigration Tribunal. For controlled work the decision about whether to provide services in a particular case is made by the supplier, who is either a solicitor or a not-for-profit organisation, such as a law centre or Citizens' Advice Bureau (discussed below, 17.9.2). They bid for a contract to provide legal services funded by the LSC to the Regional Legal

Services Committees. Under the contract, the number of cases that may be undertaken by the suppliers is limited.

Licensed work is the equivalent of the case-by-case approval granted for all state-funded legal work prior to 1994 and all non-franchised work prior to the establishment of the LSC. Licensed work is administered through a certification process requiring the Commission's initial approval of the cost, timing and scope of each case. Once the licence is granted, it covers all legal representation before the courts, except for controlled legal representation or services funded by individual case contracts that are managed by the Commission, such as very expensive cases referred to as 'very high cost cases' (VHCCs).

As with all legal aid matters, full details of VHCC contracts are published by the LAA.

17.3.2 CONTRACTING

The work that may be undertaken by a supplier, whether a solicitor or a not-for-profit organisation, covers a wide variety of categories. Civil legal aid work covers family, immigration, social welfare (which covers debt, employment, housing, community care and welfare benefits), mental health, personal injury, clinical negligence, consumer general contract, actions against police, public law and education. Criminal legal aid covers work in police stations, magistrates' courts, Crown Courts, VHCCs and working within the criminal justice system.

The contract for civil work used to be carried out under a General Civil Contract under the CLS. However, this has now been replaced by a new standard contract, which is discussed below, at 17.3.3. Criminal work is now also covered by a new standard contract.

The LAA may terminate the contract for any reason at six months' notice and the providers at three months' notice. Key Performance Indicators (KPIs) are now part of the contract and failure to comply will be a breach of contract.

The coming into force of LASPO introduced new rules from 1 April 2013. An interim contract for Welfare Benefits operated until 31 October 2013. The 2013 Standard Civil Contract (Welfare Benefits) governs the provision of face-to-face Welfare Benefits Services from 1 November 2013.

The 2013 CLA Contract governs the provision of Community Legal Advice from 1 April 2013. CLA services will be provided primarily by telephone and also online and by other 'remote' means.

The 2013 CLA Contract covers remote advice in the categories of Family, Housing and Debt, Education and Discrimination law, as well as face-to-face services in Education and Discrimination law only. Providers may only carry out 'Licensed Work' in the Education and Discrimination categories.

From 1 April 2013, the 2013 Standard Civil Contract governs the provision of face-to-face legal aid services in the categories of Family, Immigration and Asylum, Housing and Debt.

Other categories of law are either not affected by LASPO to the extent that new contracts are required, in which case they will continue to be provided under the 2010

Standard Civil Contract (as amended), or will no longer be within the scope of legal aid provision after 1 April 2013.

The Criminal Legal Aid (Determinations by a Court and Choice of Representative) (Amendment) Regulations 2013 introduced new rules relating to 'Selection of a Queen's Counsel or multiple advocates', which sets out the following conditions:

> 19. (1) A determination that an individual is entitled to select a Queen's Counsel or more than one advocate under regulation 18 may only be made by the following judges –
>
>   (a) subject to paragraph (2), in the course of a trial or a preliminary hearing, pre-trial review or plea and directions hearing, the judge who has been assigned as the trial judge;
>
>   (b) where a trial judge has not been assigned, by –
>
>   (i) a High Court judge; or
>
>   (ii) subject to paragraph (2), a resident judge of the Crown Court or, in the absence of a resident judge, a judge nominated by a resident judge of the Crown Court for the purpose of making such a determination; or
>
>   (c) where the proceedings are in the Court of Appeal, by the Registrar of Criminal Appeals, a High Court judge or a judge of the Court of Appeal.
>
> (2) A determination made by a judge referred to in paragraph (1)(a) or (b)(ii) does not take effect unless it is approved by a presiding judge of the circuit or by a judge nominated by a presiding judge of the circuit for the purpose of giving such approval.

A contract may be awarded to allow a supplier to undertake work within one or more categories. The contract will state the categories and terms under which the supplier may provide legal advice and representation. The purpose of specifying categories in respect of civil contracts is to ensure an appropriate distribution of legal and advice services to meet demand in each region.

In order to assess demand and ensure that the right kind of services are available to meet the needs of a region, Community Legal Service Partnerships (CLSPs) were set up. The purpose of CLSPs was to provide a forum, in each local authority area, for the local authority and the LSC, and if possible other significant funders, to come together to co-ordinate funding and planning of local legal and advice services, to ensure that delivery of services better matches local needs. The LSC no longer facilitates CLSPs, and the LSC has asked each CLSP to consider whether it has a viable role as a provider forum.

17.3.3 CONTRACTS FROM THE LEGAL AID AGENCY

If a law firm is awarded a contract to provide publicly funded legal advice through the LAA, the terms under which it will carry out the work will depend on how it provides the services and the type of legal aid given.

Face-to-face legal aid services for civil cases

Family, immigration and asylum, housing and debt categories of work are governed by the standard civil contract 2013.

Welfare benefits work is governed by the standard civil contract (welfare benefits) contract 2013, except in the north and south-west and Wales, where the welfare benefits contract 2014 applies.

Community care and mental health categories are governed by the standard civil contract 2014.

Actions against the police, public law, clinical negligence, family mediation, and immigration removal centre categories are governed by the standard civil contract 2010.

Remote legal aid services for civil cases

This includes the provision of legal aid by telephone, online and other remote means.

Family, housing and debt, education and discrimination categories of work are governed by the civil legal advice contract 2013.

All legal aid services for criminal cases

All cases that would fall under criminal law are governed by the standard crime contract 2010 or through separate arrangements for Very High Cost Cases (VHCC).

Halted reform

A new set of reforms to criminal legal aid contracts due to be implemented in 2015–16. However, many solicitors firms feared the reforms would entail an unwarranted restriction on who could participate in the duty legal aid rota, and that this would lead to a less diverse and competitive market. Many barristers feared that the commercial model being designed by some solicitors' firms would lead to a diminution in choice and the quality of professional service. In January 2016, faced with 99 separate legal challenges over the prospective procurement process, the Lord Chancellor decided not to introduce the contractual reforms, and to suspend, for a period of 12 months from 1 April 2016 a proposed fee cut for criminal legal aid work (Lord Chancellor and Secretary of State for Justice, Michael Gove MP, Written statement to Parliament Changes to criminal legal aid contracting, 28 January, 2016).

The LAA periodically amends the contract terms of legal aid contracts to deal with changes in legislation or court rulings. The Civil Contract was amended on 17 and 31 July 2015 to reflect new legislation, including Care Act 2014 and Modern Slavery Act 2015. Changes to contract terms and details of any new tenders are available on the LAA website.

A new family contract commenced on 1 February 2012, but this ceased on 31 March 2013 and a new contract commenced the following day. The aim of the Unified Contract is to put not-for-profit advisers on the same footing as solicitors who carry out civil legal aid work and to create greater efficiency when working with providers. It is anticipated that one way this will be achieved is by requiring providers to work with the LAA by means of email to reduce administrative time and costs. In addition, providers will be required to meet certain standards that are contained in KPIs.

Another major change to this new system is the move away from issuing separate contracts to each office of a provider and instead issuing a contract to the whole organisation of the provider with each contract containing a schedule detailing the work that an individual office can undertake. The LAA will be able to stipulate a minimum and maximum number of cases that an individual office may start each year.

17.3.4 QUALITY MARK

In order to be a supplier under either the CLS or the CDS, the solicitor or not-for-profit organisation must achieve the minimum standards under the respective Quality Marks. There are four kinds of Quality Mark and all contract holders must hold the SQM or MQM or LEXCEL. Barristers must hold QMB.

There are four Quality Marks applicable as follows.

SQM: Specialist Quality Mark. This will be for complex matters.

MQM: Family Mediation Quality Mark.

QMB: Quality Mark for the Bar.

LEXCEL: Legal Practice Management standard (owned by Law Society).

17.4 THE LEGAL AID AGENCY

As from 1 April 2013, the Legal Aid Agency (LAA) replaced the Legal Services Commission (s 38 of LASPO).

Legal aid has been one of the fastest growing parts of the public sector over the past 25 years, and expenditure has increased at almost 6 per cent per year in real terms, compared to similar increases in health and education expenditure of approximately 4 per cent and 2 per cent, respectively. At approximately £38 per head of the population, the LSC also spent more in England and Wales than is spent by any other jurisdiction for which comparative data are currently available.

The LAA produces highly detailed quarterly and annual statistics of all the legal aid work undertaken and the related costs. Examples of the information for 2014/15 are:

- Crown Court legal aid granted in 116,183 cases out of 116,820 applications.
- Civil representation costs met by LAA £700.5 million.

17.5   THE COMMUNITY LEGAL SERVICE

Since 1 April 2013, Community Legal Service has been known as Civil Legal Aid (CLA), and Community Legal Advice as Civil Legal Advice (CLAD).

The LAA as successor to the LSC provides both civil and criminal legal aid and advice in England and Wales utilising solicitors, barristers and not-for-profit organisations. The LAA's main objectives are to:

- improve casework to reduce cost, enhance control and give better customer service;
- improve organisational capability to meet the challenges ahead, including developing and engaging their people;
- build and maintain strong partnerships to secure quality provision and contribute fully to wider justice and government aims.

17.5.1   CIVIL LEGAL AID CONTRACT

Civil legal aid is currently carried out mainly under the 2013 Standard Civil Contract and 2010 Standard Civil Contracts. There is also provision for some family work that commenced before April 2013 to be carried out under the provisions of the 2012 Standard Civil Contract (Family and Housing).

17.5.2   FINANCIAL ELIGIBILITY TEST

The Community Legal Service (Financial) (Amendment) Regulations 2007 (which amend the Community Legal Service (Financial) Regulations 2000) set out the thresholds for financial eligibility for all applications for funding made on or after 8 April 2008. The test uses the basic concepts of 'disposable income', that is, income available to a person after deducting essential living expenses; and 'disposable capital', that is, the assets owned by a person after essential items like a home. If a person could sell his or her home, pay off the mortgage and still have more than £100,000 left (called 'equity'), then he or she will not qualify for aid.

Certain services are free, regardless of financial resources, such as services consisting exclusively of the provision of general information about the law, legal system and availability of legal services, legal representation in some cases involving the Children Act 1989 and related proceedings, and representation at a mental health review tribunal. Some services are non-contributory and a client is either eligible or not, whereas others are contributory in accordance with a sliding scale, dependent on how much a client's income or capital exceeds a given threshold. There is a cap amount over which a person is ineligible for legal aid. In summary, the financial eligibility amounts for applications are as follows:

- For all levels of service, there is (as of 1 April 2013) a gross income cap of £2,657 per month. This cap may be increased by £222 per month for each child in excess of four. A client who is directly or indirectly in receipt of Income Support or income-based Jobseeker's Allowance automatically satisfies the gross income test for all levels of service.

•   For the service of Legal Help, Help at Court and Legal Representation before Immigration Adjudicators and the Immigration Appeal Tribunal, the disposable income must not exceed £733 per month.

•   For the service of Family Mediation, Help with Mediation and other Legal Representation (which may be subject to a contribution from income and capital), the disposable income must not exceed £733 per month.

There is a capital limit of £8,000 for all controlled legal representation, except legal representation in respect of immigration matters set out in Regulation 8(3) where it remains £3,000.

When assessing gross income and disposable income, state benefits under the Social Security Contributions and Benefits Act 1992 (Disability Living Allowance, Attendance Allowance, Constant Attendance Allowance, Invalid Care Allowance, Severe Disablement Allowance, Council Tax Benefit, Housing Benefit and any payment out of the social fund), back-to-work bonuses under the Jobseekers Act 1995, war and war widows' pensions and fostering allowances are disregarded. Any person being paid the new Universal Credit will automatically be passported through to legal aid, although capital must be assessed. If a person receives financial support under ss 4 or 95 of the Immigration and Asylum Act 1999 from the National Asylum Support Service (NASS), they are passported through both income and capital tests for controlled work immigration and asylum matters only.

The only level of service assessed by the supplier for which contributions can be sought is Legal Representation in Specified Family Proceedings. However, provided that the client's gross income is below the prescribed limit, clients with a disposable income of £315 or below per month will not need to pay any contributions from income, but may still have to pay a contribution from capital. A client with disposable income in excess of £315 and up to £733 per month will be liable to pay a monthly contribution of a proportion of the excess over £311, assessed in accordance with the following bands:

Band	Monthly disposable income	Monthly contribution
A	£316–£465	Quarter of income in excess of £311
B	£466–£616	£38.50 + third of income in excess of £465
C	£617–£733	£88.85 + half of income in excess of £616

A client whose disposable capital exceeds £3,000 is required to pay a contribution of either the capital exceeding that sum or the likely maximum costs of the funded service, whichever is the lesser.

For example, if disposable income is £480 per month, the contribution will be in Band B, the excess income is £15 (£480 – £465), the monthly contribution would therefore be £43.50 (£38.50 + £5 (a third of the excess income)). The LAA website has an online legal aid eligibility calculator to enable people to check whether they are likely to qualify financially.

Provided it is not disregarded as subject matter of the dispute, a client's main or only dwelling in which he or she resides must be taken into account as capital, subject to the following rules:

(a)   The dwelling should be valued at the amount for which it could be sold on the open market.

(b)   The amount of any mortgage or charge registered on the property must be deducted, but the maximum amount that can be deducted for such a mortgage or charge is £100,000.

(c)   The first £100,000 of the value of the client's interest after making the above mortgage deduction must be disregarded.

17.5.3   THE FUNDING CODE

The basis of funding was governed by s 8 of the Access to Justice Act 1999. This is now governed by LASPO. Under s 4 of the Act the Lord Chancellor can issue guidance and regulations.

The Civil Legal Aid (Merits Criteria) Regulations 2013 replace the previous Funding Code Criteria and the Civil Legal Aid (Procedures) Regulations 2012 replace the previous Funding Code Procedures.

The Lord Chancellor has issued a three-part funding guidance, which replaced the previous Funding Code Guidance. The three parts comprise general guidance, guidance for exceptional funding for inquests and exceptional funding for out-of-scope (non-inquest) cases.

17.5.4   LEGAL SERVICES PROVIDED

Legal services were formerly governed by the Access to Justice Act 1999 Act. This has now been superseded by LASPO. Schedule 1 of LASPO covers civil legal services. These range from the provision of basic information about the law and legal services to providing help towards preventing or resolving disputes and enforcing decisions that have been reached. The scheme encompasses advice, assistance and representation by lawyers (which have long been available under the legal aid scheme), and also the services of non-lawyers. It will extend to other types of service including, for example, mediation in family or civil cases where appropriate.

The Lord Chancellor must designate a civil servant as the Director of Legal Aid Casework. Under s 10 of LASPO the Director can make directions bringing cases that would be excluded within the provisions of the Act in exceptional circumstances.

17.5.5   THE CLA FUND

Unlike the CLS budget, the LAA budget is not established by statute. Instead, the LAA, as a government agency of the Ministry of Justice, submits its budget to the Permanent Secretary (who is the Principal Accounting Officer of the department) and, once it is approved, is required to operate within it. The budget must be approved by a government minister.

17.5.6   EXTENSION OF FINANCIAL CONDITIONS ON AN ASSISTED PARTY

Section 23 of LASPO extends the potential scope of financial conditions imposed on an assisted party in two ways, although there are no immediate plans to use either of these powers:

- It will be possible to make the provision of services in some types of case subject to the assisted person agreeing to repay an amount in excess of the cost of the services provided, in the event that their case is successful (s 23(3)). This might make it possible to fund certain types of case on a self-financing basis, with the additional payments from successful litigants applied to meet the cost of unsuccessful cases. It would also be possible to mix public funding with a private conditional fee arrangement, subject to the same conditions about the uplift to the costs in the event of a successful outcome. The government has suggested that this might be appropriate, for example, where a case could not be taken under a wholly private arrangement, because the solicitors' firm was not large enough to bear the risk of the very high costs likely to be involved.
- It will be possible (s 23(10)) to require the assisted person to repay, over time and with interest, the full cost of the service provided (for example, through continuing contributions from income). This will make it possible to provide services in some categories of case in the form of a loan scheme.

Section 26 of LASPO establishes limits on the liability of the person receiving funded services to pay costs to the unassisted party. The costs he or she must pay cannot go above what is 'reasonable' (s 26(1)), taking into account the financial resources of all parties. It also provides that regulations may specify the principles that are to be applied in determining the amount of any costs awarded against the party receiving funded services, and the circumstances in which a costs order may be enforced against the person receiving funded services.

Today, the regulations that limit the circumstances in which the costs order may be enforced against the person receiving funded services (or the liability of the Agency to meet any costs order on behalf of the person receiving funded services) are made on a more flexible basis. Previously, protection from costs was seen by governments to create too great an advantage in litigation for the person receiving legal aid.

17.5.7   RELATIVE SUCCESS OF THE SCHEME

The 2015 annual report of the LAA shows that the 2014/15 spend was £1.695 million.

Following the introduction of new contracting arrangements, there has been a decline in the number of solicitors' firms providing legal aid services from 4,866 in January 2000 to 2,954 by March 2014, of which there were 1,435 (including 13 telephone providers) for civil work and 1,519 (including three telephone providers) for criminal (LAA Annual Report 2014). Hugh Barrett, executive director for commissioning at the LAA, speaking to the Legal Aid Practitioners Group in October 2015, said the number of firms carrying out criminal legal aid work had fallen from 2,600 to 1,800. The reduction in the supplier base is partly a deliberate move away from reliance on a large number of generalist support firms towards a smaller number of specialist quality-assured providers. However, the reduction also reflects concern among some firms about the level of remuneration offered on civil legal aid work.

17.6   THE CRIMINAL DEFENCE SERVICE

The Criminal Defence Service (CDS), known as Criminal Legal Aid (CRLA) from 1 April 2013, uses criminal legal aid to help people who are under investigation or facing criminal charges. By ensuring that people accused of crimes have access to legal advice and representation, the CRLA also helps the police and courts operate fairly and efficiently.

Criminal legal aid can offer:

- advice and assistance from a solicitor on criminal matters;

- free legal advice from a solicitor at the police station during questioning;

- the cost of a solicitor preparing a case and initial representation for certain proceedings at a magistrates' or Crown Court;

- full legal representation for defence in criminal cases at all court levels;

- a duty solicitor to provide free legal advice and representation at magistrates' court.

The Criminal Defence Service Act 2006 changed the arrangements for the grant of public funding for representation in criminal proceedings in England and Wales. It provides for the power to grant rights to representation to be conferred on the Legal Services Commission (LSC), and now under the direction of the Legal Aid Agency (LAA) instead of that being done by a court. It introduces a test of financial eligibility for the grant of such funding and, in cases where eligibility exists, contributions based on means.

The creation of the Criminal Defence Service (CDS) was part of the government's fundamental reform of the legal aid system, as set out in the Access to Justice Act 1999. The purpose of the CDS is to ensure access for individuals involved in criminal investigations or criminal proceedings to such advice, assistance and representation as the interests of justice require. The CDS was implemented and managed by the LSC, which was also created by the Access to Justice Act 1999. Solicitors are required to work within quality-assured contracts to perform CDS functions.

The LSC was responsible for funding legal representation under the Criminal Defence Service. This is now the responsibility of the LAA. However, under the old structure, it was the courts – and not the LSC – which were responsible for granting the right to have funding. Now the applications for funding are made centrally, not to a court.

The LSC awarded CDS contracts to quality-assured providers. At 31 March 2014, 1,516 solicitors' offices and three telephone providers operated under a CDS contract (LAA Annual Report 2014), a net decrease of 4.78 per cent on 2012/13.

The interests of justice test

The 'interests of justice' test determines whether an applicant is entitled to a Representation Order based on the merits of the case. This is also known as the 'Widgery Criteria' (after the name of the judge in whose 1966 government report on legal aid they were originally formulated).

The applicant must indicate which of the following criteria they believe apply to their case:

- It is likely that I will lose my liberty.
- I have been given a sentence that is suspended or non-custodial. If I break this, the court may be able to deal with me for the original offence.
- It is likely that I will lose my livelihood.
- It is likely that I will suffer serious damage to my reputation.
- A substantial question of law may be involved.
- I may not be able to understand the court proceedings or present my own case.
- I may need witnesses to be traced or interviewed on my behalf.
- The proceedings may involve expert cross-examination of a prosecution witness.
- It is in the interests of another person that I am represented.
- Any other reasons.

If the applicant passes the 'interests of justice' test, he or she must also pass the means test to qualify for legal aid. The aid will be granted to an applicant who does not have the financial means to fund their own representation in a magistrates' court.

The means test in the magistrates' court establishes whether an applicant is financially eligible for legal aid. It only considers income and expenses – capital is not included.

Her Majesty's Courts and Tribunals Service (HMCTS) staff apply the test once they receive a correctly completed application form.

So-called passported applicants are those individuals who automatically pass the means test (for example because of the state benefits they are on). These applicants will still need to pass the interests of justice test to qualify for legal aid. The initial means test assesses the applicant's income and how this is spread between any partners and children.

A full means test is carried out if, through the initial means test, the applicant's adjusted income is calculated (after April 2008) to be more than £12,475 and less than £22,325. It works out an applicant's disposable income after deducting tax, maintenance and other annual costs from the gross annual income. There is also a complex means test for those who have complex financial circumstances. Hardship reviews can be carried out if an applicant can show they are genuinely unable to fund their own representation. A person may qualify for criminal legal aid if their annual disposable income exceeds £3,398 (£283.17 per month), but does not exceed £37,500, subject to making a contribution. This would be refunded if found not guilty. If found guilty and their capital exceeds £30,000, a contribution may be required.

In 2013/14, the public expenditure on the Criminal Defence Service was £908.6 million (LAA Annual Report 2014).

17.7 PUBLIC DEFENDER SERVICE

The Public Defender Service (PDS) was operated by the LSC and since 1 April 2013 has been run by the LAA. The LAA directly employs the PDS staff of solicitors, accredited representatives and administrators. The PDS provides independent advice, assistance and representation on criminal matters.

PDS lawyers are available 24 hours a day, seven days a week to:

- give advice to people in custody;
- represent clients in magistrates', Crown and higher courts where necessary.

All PDS employees must observe the code made under s 29 of LASPO.

The Public Defender Service aims to:

- provide independent, high-quality, value-for-money criminal defence services to the public;
- provide examples of excellence in the provision of criminal defence services nationally and locally;
- provide benchmarking information to be used to improve the performance of the contracting regime for private practice suppliers;
- raise the level of understanding within government and all levels and areas of the Agency of the issues facing criminal defence lawyers in providing high-quality services to the public;
- provide an additional option for ensuring the provision of quality criminal defence services in geographical areas where existing provision is low or of a poor standard;
- recruit, train and develop people to provide high-quality criminal defence services, in accordance with the PDS's own business needs, which will add to the body of such people available to provide criminal defence services generally; and

- share with private practice suppliers best practice in terms of forms, systems and so on, developed within the PDS to assist in the overall improvement of CRLA provision locally.

The Public Defender Service (PDS) is the first salaried criminal provider in England and Wales. There are currently four PDS offices: Cheltenham, Darlington, Pontypridd and Swansea.

17.8   THE MAGEE REVIEW 2009

In October 2009 the Ministry of Justice announced a review of the way the £2 billion legal aid budget was delivered. The resultant conclusions could see separate civil and criminal funds run by different bodies (C Baksi, *Law Society Gazette*, 14 October 2009). The review was established while legal aid lawyers warned that firms providing social welfare legal services were at risk of collapse because of the 'artificial' way work was being distributed by the Legal Services Commission. Lord Bach, the minister for legal aid, appointed Sir Ian Magee, a former permanent secretary at the Department for Constitutional Affairs, to explore ways of optimising value for money in the way legal aid was administered.

Bach told the *Gazette* he was 'ruling nothing out and nothing in'. He said he would be surprised if the LSC ceased to exist, but said it could work alongside another body, with one administering the criminal budget and the other the civil budget. The two budgets could be ring-fenced.

The Law Society had warned that the LSC's policy of capping the number of new social welfare cases or 'matter starts' that a firm can take on could cause some firms to collapse. Nicola Mackintosh of legal aid firm Mackintosh Duncan questioned why the LSC was 'artificially limiting the number of clients who can get access to justice' by allocating firms only a set number of new cases (*Law Society Gazette*, 14 October 2009, p 1).

On 1 April 2013 the LSC was replaced by the LAA.

17.9   THE VOLUNTARY SECTOR

There are over 1,500 not-for-profit advice agencies in England and Wales. They receive their funding – over £150 million a year in total – from many different sources, mainly local authorities, but also charities including the Big Lottery Fund, central government and the LAA. The provision of advice services is not spread consistently across the country. Some areas appear to have relatively high levels of both legal practitioners and voluntary outlets, while others have few or none. For example, the former LSC's South East Area has one Citizens' Advice Bureau per 46,000 people, but, in the East Midlands, 138,000 people share a Citizens' Advice Bureau. The government believes that the fragmented nature of the advice sector obstructs effective planning and prevents local needs for legal advice and help from being met as rationally and fully as possible.

There are currently 43 Law Centres in England and Wales listed on the Law Centres Network's website as at November 2015. These centres are staffed by salaried solicitors, trainee solicitors and non-lawyer experts in other areas like debt management. They are funded by local and central government and charity. They have 'shop-front' access and aim to be user-friendly and unintimidating. They are managed by committees and represented by the Law Centres' Federation (LCF).

Law Centres take on individual cases, providing, for example advice on landlord and tenant matters and representing people at tribunals. Some centres also take on group work since quite often the problems of one client are part of a wider problem. This sort of work is controversial.

Since the introduction of LASPO, the Law Centres' budgets have been cut and sometimes they are now forced to either turn people away or charge for services.

The Citizens Advice Bureaux (CABs) have been assisting people since 1939 and there are now 343 CABs in England and Wales providing free, independent and impartial information and advice from over 3,500 locations. They deal with a high number of cases (over six million a year) and a very wide range of problems of which between a third and a half are legal problems. During 2014/15, bureaux advised 2.5 million clients on almost 6.2 million new problems (www.citizensadvice.org.uk, 25 November 2015). There are, however, very few trained lawyers working for the CABs, but over 20,000 volunteer helpers. In keeping with the changing technology of the modern world, the CABs now offers an online help service through its website, providing independent advice on a range of topics such as money, family, consumer matters and civil rights.

In April 2012 the CABs took over Consumer Direct and in its first year dealt with 837,000 matters.

The CLS launched CLS Direct in July 2004, a website providing free advice on a range of matters similar to the CABs. The website offers topics of the month on the home page such as redundancy rights. It also contains an online calculator to assist people to determine whether they qualify for legal aid. Legal information leaflets and factsheets are also available on this site.

The Bar Council supports a Free Representation Unit for clients at a variety of tribunals for which legal aid is not available. Most of the representation is carried out by Bar students supported and advised by full-time caseworkers. A special Bar unit based in London was formed in 1996 through which more senior barristers provide representation. Some colleges and universities also offer advice. For example, the College of Law in London operates a free advice service in which vocational students give advice on such matters as personal injury cases and employment law.

Both barristers and solicitors operate 'pro bono' (from the Latin phrase *pro bono publico*, meaning 'for the public good') schemes under which legal work is done without charge or at reduced cost for members of the public ineligible for legal aid from the LSC but with limited means, or charitable and other non-profit-making organisations. Examples of pro bono activities include: solicitors attending advice sessions at Citizens Advice Bureaux or other free services; free advice to members of organisations, for example, trade union general advice schemes; secondment to Law Centres; and free advice to charitable organisations.

17.10   CONDITIONAL FEE ARRANGEMENTS

These are sometimes known as 'no win, no fee' agreements. They are not used for family or criminal matters, but can be used in many types of civil action. In a 'no win, no fee' agreement, a litigant's solicitor will only be paid if the claim is successful. If so, the solicitor will also be entitled to an extra fee (known as a success fee). Both the basic fee and this extra fee are normally paid in whole or part by the losing party.

There are other incurred costs (such as court fees or the fee for a medical report). These are normally known as disbursements. Again, the losing party should pay all or part of these costs. A litigant is liable to pay his or her solicitor for any costs that the losing party is not ordered to pay.

If, under such an arrangement, a litigant's claim fails, they will not have to pay their own solicitor, but they will still probably have to pay the costs of the successful party – the other side. That is something, however, against which they can take out insurance. They will also have to pay any other incurred costs (such as court fees or the fee for a medical report). These are normally known as disbursements. The insurance in these circumstances is known as 'after the event' insurance. The client may have to pay the insurance premium.

Background

As part of the scheme to expose the provision of legal services to the full rigour of market forces, the then Lord Chancellor chose to devote an entire Green Paper in 1989 to *Contingency Fees*. Following a recommendation from the Civil Justice Review, the Paper had sought opinion on the funding of litigation on a contingent fee basis. This provides that litigation is funded by the claimant only if he or she wins, in which event the lawyer claims fees as a portion of the damages payable to the claimant. The response to this idea was largely hostile.

The traditional opposition to contingency fees in the English legal system was that they were 'maintenance' (the financial support of another's litigation) and 'champerty' (taking a financial interest in another's litigation). Champerty occurs when the person maintaining another takes as his reward a portion of the property in dispute. It taints an agreement with illegality and renders it void (for a discussion of the principle, see *Grovewood Holding plc v James Capel & Co Ltd* (1995)). Section 14 of the Criminal Justice Act 1967 abolished maintenance and champerty as crimes and torts, but kept the rules making such arrangements improper for solicitors.

English litigation uses the Indemnity Rule, by which the loser pays the costs of the winner and thus puts him or her, more or less, in the position he or she enjoyed before the damage was done. Objectors to contingency fee agreements pointed out that such things were incompatible with the Indemnity Rule because, although the winner's costs would be paid for them by the other side, they would still have to pay for their lawyer from their damages (calculated to put them in the position they would have enjoyed if no wrong had been done to them) so they would not really be 'made whole' by their award. The position is different in the United States, where contingency agreements are common in personal injury cases, because there each side bears its own costs.

It was further contended by objectors to the contingency fee that the legal aid system adequately catered for those who were too poor to afford an ordinary private action. Even if there were people who were just above the legal aid financial thresholds but still too poor to pay for an action, this should be dealt with simply by changing the threshold.

Section 58 of the Courts and Legal Services Act (CLSA) 1990 permitted the Lord Chancellor to introduce conditional fee arrangements, although these cannot apply to criminal cases, family cases or those involving children (s 58(10)). However, there are a number of different arrangements for conditional fees, so one issue to be addressed was the type of conditional fee system that should be applied in England and Wales. The Scottish model, for which initially there was reasonable support, is that of the 'speculative fee', whereby the solicitor can agree with their client that they would be paid their ordinary taxed costs only if they won the case. Two other forms of contingency fee were rejected during the consultation period as being unsuitable. The first was a restricted contingency fee system in which the fee payable in the event of a successful action would be a *percentage of the damages*, but where the actual levels of recovery would be governed by rules. The second was an unrestricted contingency arrangement, similarly based on a percentage of damages, but at uncontrolled levels. These plans were rejected because it was thought that to give the lawyer a stake in the claimant's damages would be likely to create unacceptable temptations for the lawyer to behave unprofessionally in order to secure their fee.

The system eventually adopted is that where conditional fees are based on an 'uplift' from the level of fee the lawyer would normally charge for the sort of work in question. Originally, the maximum uplift was to be 20 per cent in order to induce lawyers to take on potentially difficult cases and to help finance lawyers' unsuccessful conditional fee cases. This would have meant they could charge the fee that they would normally charge for a given type of case, plus an additional fifth.

In August 1993, after a long process of negotiation with the profession, Lord Mackay, the then Lord Chancellor, finally announced that he would allow the conditional fee to operate on a 100 per cent uplift. Thus, solicitors receive no fee if they lose a case, but double what they would normally charge if they win the case. The Law Society had campaigned vigorously against the proposed 20 per cent uplift, arguing that such risks as the 'no win, no fee' arrangement entailed would not be regarded as worth taking by many solicitors simply on the incentive that their fee for winning the case would be 20 per cent more than they would normally charge for such a case. The LCD originally decided to restrict the scheme to cases involving personal injury, insolvency and the European Court of Human Rights.

The system came into effect in June 1995. Such agreements are now legal, provided that they comply with any requirements imposed by the Lord Chancellor and are not 'contentious business agreements'. These are defined under s 59 of the Solicitors Act 1974 as agreements between a solicitor and his or her client made in writing by which the solicitor is to be remunerated by a gross sum, or a salary, at agreed hourly rates or otherwise, and whether higher or lower than that at which he or she would normally be remunerated. A valid CFA must comply with the LCD requirements, be in writing, stating the percentage uplift payable if successful (and 'must not exceed the percentage specified in relation to the description of proceedings to which the agreement relates by order made by the Lord Chancellor' – s 58(4)(c) CLSA 1990 as amended by s 27 of the Access to Justice Act 1999). A CFA cannot be used if proceedings do not allow an enforceable CFA.

The right to use 'no win, no fee' agreements to pursue civil law claims was extended by the Conditional Fee Agreements Order 1998. The Order allowed lawyers to offer conditional fee agreements to their clients in all civil cases excluding family cases. Speaking in the House of Lords on 23 July 1988, the then Lord Chancellor, Lord Irvine, said:

> These agreements will result in a huge expansion of access to justice. Today, only the very rich or the very poor can afford to litigate. In future, everyone with a really strong case will be able to secure his rights free of the fear of ruin if he loses. They will bring the majority of our people into access to justice.

Conditional fees have been the means by which at least several hundred thousand personal injury cases have been brought, and many, in all likelihood, would not have been brought but for the existence of conditional fees. The Order retains the old rule that the maximum uplift on the fees lawyers can charge is 100 per cent. Thus, a lawyer may take on a claim against an allegedly negligent employer whose carelessness has resulted in the client being injured. The lawyer, who might normally charge £2,000 for such a case, can say 'I shall do this work for nothing if we lose, but £3,000 if we win'. In fact, as the price uplift can be up to 100 per cent of the normal fee, he or she can stipulate for up to £4,000 in this example. The Law Society has recommended an additional voluntary cap of 25 per cent of damages, and this has been widely accepted in practice.

The real problems continued to be:

(a)   that the new system, designed really to help the millions who have been regulated out of the legal aid system, does not help people whose cases stand only a limited chance of success, as lawyers will not take their cases; and

(b)   the difficulties of a claimant getting insurance to cover the costs that he or she will have to pay, if he or she loses the claim, for the other side's lawyers. Where a personal injury claim arises from a road traffic incident, it is almost always clear to a solicitor where blame and legal liability probably lie. Risks are therefore calculable by insurance companies, so one can presently insure against having to pay the other side's costs in the event of losing an action on a personal injury case for about £100 in a 'no win, no fee' arrangement. There are, however, many areas, and medical negligence cases are good examples, where the chances of success are notoriously difficult to predict. Thus, insurance against having to pay the other side's costs is prohibitively high, running into many thousands of pounds in some cases. It is quite unrealistic to assume that all such cases, arising often from highly distressing circumstances, will be dealt with in future on a 'no win, no fee' basis. Lawyers will generally not want to take on such cases on such a basis, and even where they do, clients will often not be able to afford the necessary insurance. As insurance to cover client costs in medical 'no win, no fee' cases has proven so expensive, legal aid continues to cover clinical negligence cases.

17.10.1 THE ACCESS TO JUSTICE ACT 1999

The Access to Justice Act 1999 (ss 27–31), together with the Conditional Fee Arrangements Regulations 2000 and the Collective Conditional Fee Agreements Regulations 2000, reformed the law relating to conditional fees to enable the court to order a losing party to pay, in addition to the other party's normal legal costs, the uplift on the successful party's lawyers' fees and, in any case where a litigant has insured against facing an order for the other side's costs, any premium paid by the successful party for that insurance. The intention was to:

- ensure that the compensation awarded to a successful party is not eroded by any uplift or premium. The party in the wrong will bear the full burden of costs;
- make conditional fees more attractive, in particular to defendants and to claimants seeking non-monetary redress (these litigants can rarely use conditional fees now, because they cannot rely on the prospect of recovering damages to meet the cost of the uplift and premium);
- discourage weak cases and encourage settlements;
- provide a mechanism for regulating the uplifts that solicitors charge. In future, unsuccessful litigants will be able to challenge unreasonably high uplifts when the court comes to assess costs.

In the first version of conditional fee arrangements, only people who expected to win money from their case could benefit from conditional fees. This was the only way that most people could afford to pay the success fee. There were also available insurance policies that could be taken out by someone contemplating litigation to cover the costs of the other party and the client's own costs (including, if not a conditional fee case, a client's solicitor's fees) if the case was lost. However, it meant that a successful litigant would not receive all the money he or she was awarded, so the government made provision in the Access to Justice Act 1999 to make it possible for the winning party to recover the success fee and any insurance premium from the losing party.

The rules, which had become very complex for all using them, were simplified in 2005. The Conditional Fee Agreements Regulations 2000 and the Collective Conditional Fee Agreements Regulations 2000 were revoked by the Conditional Fee Agreement (Revocation) Regulations 2005 (SI 2005/2305). The Access to Justice (Membership Organisation) Regulations 2000 were revoked and replaced by the simpler Access to Justice (Membership Organisation) Regulations 2005 (SI 2005/2306).

The removal of the unnecessary regulation was applied to all CFAs across the range of civil cases, including commercial, insolvency, environmental, intellectual property, human rights, privacy, defamation and injury.

Announcing the simplified arrangements, Parliamentary Under Secretary of State Baroness Ashton of Upholland said (10 August 2005):

> Conditional fee agreements play a valuable role in helping people with valid claims obtain access to justice. For many consumers and businesses this provides the only means of obtaining appropriate redress. A regime that is complex and opaque puts the consumer at a disadvantage. Revoking the existing regulations will help make CFA agreements a simpler product and in particular will help consumers to better understand the agreements they enter into and the risks they could face in contemplating litigation. Consumer safeguards will be improved as responsibility for proper advice falls on the solicitor.

Regulation of solicitors involved in CFA cases is the responsibility of the Solicitors' Regulation Authority. It is required to ensure that clients are fully informed about the strength of their case and prospects of success in clear, simple terms. This is designed to help to ensure that only well-founded claims proceed and benefit both claimants and defendants who will be spared the stress of avoidable court hearings.

Collective conditional fee arrangements

Collective conditional fee agreements are designed specifically for mass providers and purchasers of legal services, such as trade unions, insurers or commercial organisations. A collective conditional fee agreement enables a trade union to enter into a single agreement with solicitors to govern the way in which cases for its members will be run and paid for; by simplifying the standard individual process, it reduces the cost of pursuing separate individual cases. The scheme also benefits commercial organisations which are able to enter collective conditional fee agreements to pursue or defend claims arising in the course of business.

17.10.2 THE ADVANTAGES OF CONDITIONAL FEE ARRANGEMENTS

For claimants, the advantages can be summarised as being:

- that lawyers acting in any case will be confident (they will have had to weigh carefully the chances of success before taking the case as their fee depends on winning) and determined;

- there will be freedom from the anxiety of having to pay huge fees;
- there will be no need to pay fees in advance; and
- there will be no delays or worries with legal aid applications.

For defendants there will be advantages too, as the contingency fee system will probably reduce the number of spurious claims. In a period where legal aid is being cut back so drastically, preventing so many people from going to law, this system can be seen as a way of preserving at least some limited access to the legal process. Losing parties will still be liable to pay the other side's costs, so it will be unlikely that people will take action unless they consider they have a good chance of success.

The taxpayer can also be given the advantage in the form of a significant reduction in the funding of the legal aid system. Furthermore, practitioners who are competent to assess and willing to take the risks of litigation will arguably enjoy a better fee-paying basis, increased fee income and overall business, fewer reasons for delay and more satisfied clients with fewer complaints.

Consider two examples. First, a middle-class couple consult their solicitor about injuries received in a road accident. Their joint income and savings put them outside the legal aid scheme. The proposed litigation is beset with uncertainties as the other driver's insurers have denied liability. The couple have to worry about their own expenses and the possibility under the Indemnity Rule of paying for the defendant's costs. Second, a young man who has been injured at work wants to sue his employer. The case will turn on some difficult health and safety law on which there are currently conflicting decisions. He is eligible for legal aid, but he will have to make substantial contributions because of his level of income, and if his claim fails, he will have to pay the same sum again towards the expenses of his employers. In both cases, the prospective litigants might well drop any plan to litigate. Both cases, however, might proceed expeditiously if they found a lawyer to act on a no win, no fee basis.

17.10.3 THE DISADVANTAGES OF CONDITIONAL FEE ARRANGEMENTS

Critics of the system argue that it encourages the sort of speculative actions that occur frequently in the United States, taken up by so-called ambulance-chasing lawyers. It can be argued that the system of contingency fees creates a conflict of interest between the lay client and the lawyer, with a consequential risk of exploitation of the client. Where a lawyer's fee depends on the outcome of a case, there is a greater temptation for him to act unethically. When the Royal Commission on Legal Services (1979) rejected the idea of contingent fees, it stated that such a scheme might lead to undesirable practices by lawyers including:

> the construction of evidence, the improper coaching of witnesses, the use of professionally partisan expert witnesses, especially medical witnesses, improper examination and cross-examination, groundless legal arguments designed to lead the courts into error and competitive touting.

If the case was won, the lawyer claimed a significant part of the damages, but there was also a real danger that lawyers would be pressured to settle too readily to avoid the costs of preparing for a trial that could be lost and therewith the fee. An example would be where an insurance company admits liability but contests the level of damages. The claimant might stand to get substantially higher compensation by contesting the case. Under the new system, however, their solicitor will have a strong interest in advising them to settle. A settlement would guarantee the solicitor's costs and the agreed 'mark-up' (up to 100 per cent more than a normal fee for such work), both of which would be completely lost if the case was fought and lost. This would not occur outside of a conditional fee arrangement. Although the conventional system of payment was not without problems, as Walter Merricks, then of The Law Society, has stated:

> when a lawyer is being paid by the hour, he may have a financial interest in encouraging his client to go on with an open-and-shut case, increasing his own fees.

The Law Society has argued that the system, if not properly regulated, could promote the sort of 'ambulance chasing' practised by American lawyers in the wake of the 1984 Bhopal disaster, in which over 2,500 people were killed by escaping gas from a US company (Union Carbide Corporation) plant in India. American lawyers flew out to act for victims and their relatives and some were reported to be taking fees of 50 per cent of the claimants' damages.

It was argued by some that by allowing lawyers to *double* their normal fee for certain cases, the Lord Chancellor risked eliminating any benefit speculative fees might bring. If the successful client was not to be able to recover the *uplift* from the other side, they would have to fund it themselves out of the damages they had been awarded. In effect, this often resulted in their damages being halved. The uplift can now be recovered, subject to taxation (that is, court official approval), following changes made by the Access to Justice Act 1999.

It is not even clear that the main claim made for the system – that it increases access to the courts – is correct. The Scottish experience is that speculative cases do not exceed 1 per cent of the cases in the caseload of the Faculty of Advocates. One firm opponent of the system is Lord Justice Auld. He has argued that the system will eventually endanger the esteem in which lawyers are held by the public. He has doubted whether the scheme will produce greater commitment by lawyers to their cases: 'There is a distinction to be drawn between the lawyer's commitment to the case and his anxiety to recover his fees. The two do not always correspond.'

Since 1 April 2013, a successful client using a CFA has been obliged to pay any success fee and After-the-Event (ATE) insurance under ss 44 and 46 LASPO.

17.11   RECENT CHALLENGES TO LEGAL AID CUTS

During 2014, the government's schemes and policies to reduce legal aid provision were successfully challenged in the courts on a number of occasions. The latest was in December 2014 when the Court of Appeal ruled that people appealing against deportation had been unlawfully denied legal aid under too-restrictive government guidelines (*R (on the application of) Gudanaviciene and others v The Director of Legal Aid Casework and others* (2014)).

In the ruling, against Chris Grayling, the Lord Chancellor, three appeal judges upheld a High Court decision that the guidance he had issued was 'unlawful and too restrictive'. As Justice Secretary or Lord Chancellor, Mr Grayling had lost seven such challenges in seven months by the end of 2014.

A High Court judge had ruled that the guidance 'sets too high a threshold' and 'produces unfairness' by denying publicly funded legal advice to applicants in 'exceptional cases'. The Court of Appeal decision entailed that six cases in which legal aid had been refused would need to be reconsidered. The High Court had quashed refusals of civil legal aid by the director of legal aid casework, relying on the Lord Chancellor's guidance, to grant legal aid to the six claimants, and the Court of Appeal upheld the decision of the High Court.

All the cases concerned the availability of legal aid in immigration cases under s 10 of the Legal Aid, Sentencing and Punishment of Offenders Act 2012 (LASPO), which deals with exceptional funding applications. Mr Justice Collins said the cases involved EU nationals appealing against decisions that they should be deported following criminal convictions, an alleged victim of trafficking from Nigeria, and other cases involving the right to enter and remain in the UK.

Announcing the court's decision, Lord Dyson said:

> As is well known, the effect of LASPO was to limit the circumstances in which civil legal aid can be granted. Legal aid was withdrawn in a large number of types of case. But provision was made for exceptional case funding by section 10. The Lord Chancellor has issued guidance to which those responsible for deciding whether to grant exceptional case funding must have regard. The aim of section 10 and of the guidance is that legal aid should be provided where it is necessary to ensure that litigants have effective access to justice as required by the Convention on Human Rights and the EU Charter of Fundamental Freedoms
>
> (Frances Gibb, 'Legal aid guidance on deportation cases ruled unlawful by appeal court', *The Times*, 15 December 2014).

Lord Dyson said the court concluded that the guidance 'is unlawful because it mis-states the effect of the relevant jurisprudence'.

While the guidance identified correctly factors to be taken into account in deciding whether to grant exceptional funding, it neutralised their effect by wrongly stating that the threshold for funding was very high and that legal aid is required only in rare and extreme cases.

Lord Dyson stated:

> It is also unlawful because – as is conceded by the Lord Chancellor – it wrongly states that there is nothing in the current case law which says that Article 8 of the convention requires the provision of legal aid in immigration proceedings.

The Court of Appeal ruled (para 45):

> In our judgment, the cumulative effect of [the Lord Chancellor's guidelines] is to misstate the effect of the ECtHR jurisprudence. As we have seen, the Guidance correctly identifies many of the particular factors that should be taken into account in deciding whether to make an exceptional case determination, but their effect is substantially neutralised by the strong steer given in the passages that we have highlighted. These passages send a clear signal to the caseworkers and the Director that the refusal of legal aid will amount to a breach of Article 6(1) only in rare and extreme cases. In our judgment, there are no statements in the case-law which support this signal.

It has been said by some critics of the Court of Appeal's decision (see comments from lawyers under *The Times* article cited above) that the judges, in ruling the Lord Chancellor's guidance unlawful, are acting merely to protect the economic interests of the legal firmament from which they arise. Notably, however, no clear legal reasoning is advanced to refute that of the Court of Appeal.

CHAPTER SUMMARY: THE FUNDING OF LEGAL SERVICES

On 1 April 2013 the Legal Aid, Sentencing and Punishment of Offenders Act 2012 (LASPO) came into force. This introduced the Legal Aid Agency (LAA) and abolished the LSC.

To many people the funding of legal services means legal aid. This effectively relates to two parties, the purchaser (being the person who requires legal assistance) and the seller (being the person who gives the legal advice). Both parties to the transaction have been seriously affected by the government's progressive cutbacks. The person receiving the legal aid is faced with the qualifying earnings limits being frozen since April 2011. In addition, the areas of legal assistance a person can obtain have been reduced since April 2013. The solicitor or other legal professional is affected by reductions in fees payable by the LAA.

On 5 September 2013 the Justice Secretary, Chris Grayling MP, announced in the House of Commons concessions to the government's legal aid Consultation. This consultation received over 1,600 responses from interested legal parties. The main concessions agreed with The Law Society were the creation of two criminal contracts, one for own client work and one for duty solicitor work, and the scrapping of price competitive tendering. These concessions followed the earlier one announced in July reinstating the ability for a client to choose his own solicitor.

Legal aid fees have been cut by 17.5 per cent across the board in two stages – the first 8.75 per cent in 2014 and the second in July 2015. Barrister and solicitor advocates in the most serious criminal cases – very high costs cases – had their fees cut by 30 per cent. To mitigate the effect of some of the cuts, the ministry will introduce interim payments during long-running cases.

In response to a spokesperson for the Ministry of Justice regarding changes to legal aid, Andrew Langdon QC, writing in *The Guardian* (4 October 2013), challenged the assertion that at approximately £2 billion per annum England has one of the most expensive legal aid systems in the world.

He went on to state that:

Spending on our Criminal Justice System has *fallen* for a number of years. In the last five years it's fallen from £1.12bn to £975m and the cost of the most expensive category of cases has halved (from £124m to £67m). As for our system being expensive compared to other countries – this line has been peddled before, though the Ministry knows it's wrong. It's wrong because our system is different from other countries – it's 'adversarial'. So our legal aid budget pays for things that in other countries are transferred to other budgets. The true and fair way of making the comparison – don't take it from me, take it from the 2012 EC report on 'Efficiency of Justice' – shows that out of 14 European legal systems, we are *tenth* when you look at legal spend per inhabitant. Behind amongst others, Spain, Norway, Austria and Belgium. Behind Luxembourg and Switzerland – which is twice as expensive. This is not news to the Ministry. They know that. So why the spin? What's wrong with telling it how it is?

This article concluded that it 'was supported by Alistair MacDonald QC, Leader North Eastern Circuit; Gregory Bull QC, Leader Wales and Chester Circuit; Mark Wall QC, Leader Midlands Circuit; Andrew Langdon QC, Leader Western Circuit; Rick Pratt QC, Leader Northern Circuit; Sarah Forshaw QC, Leader South Eastern Circuit'.

1   Are legal services really akin to health and social services? In any case, should there be a limit to the funds that are expended on the provision of such services?

2   To what extent can voluntary services fill the gap left by professional legal advisers?

3   Anyone who has a phone has received a call from some ambulance-chasing claim firm. To what extent are such people providing a useful service?

4   Conditional fees were once seen as a way of reducing fees and costs, but are now attacked as having the opposite effect. Which version is true and why?

FURTHER READING

Butler, J, 'The funding drought' (2009) 63 Litigation Funding 16–17

Dutton, T, 'A public–private partnership' (2008) 158 NLJ 1013

Gilg, J-Y, 'Carolyn Regan: legal aid is the fourth plank of the welfare state' (2009) 153(29) SJ 10

Morris, A, 'Spiralling or stabilising? – the compensation culture and our propensity to claim damages for personal injury' (2007) 70(3) MLR 349

Morris, P et al, Social Needs and Legal Action, 1973, Oxford: Martin Robertson

Prior, S, 'Clinical negligence: the cost of claims' (2007) 52 Personal Injury Law Journal 11

Rhode, D, Access to Justice, 2004, Oxford: OUP

Robins, J, 'Are accident victims ill-served by "no win, no fee" agreements?' (2008) 158 NLJ 1125

Rothwell, R, 'Litigation funders face new complaints' (2014) 4(3) Law Soc Gazette, 17 February

Smith, R, 'Time to adjust' (2009) 159 NLJ 1271

Underhill, N et al, 'Law for free' (2003) Counsel 14

https://www.gov.uk/government/organisations/legal-aid-agency
The Legal Aid Agency.

Now visit the companion website to:

● test your understanding of the key terms using our Flashcard Glossary;

● revise and consolidate your knowledge of 'The funding of legal services' using our multiple choice question testbank;

● view both the links to the Useful Websites above.

www.routledge.com/cw/slapper

GENERAL LEGAL WEBSITES FOR THE ENGLISH LEGAL SYSTEM

www.bbc.co.uk
For general stories about the law, legal cases, political issues and current affairs, the BBC site is an excellent source of information.

www.bailii.org
The British and Irish Legal Information Institute (BAILII) offers the most comprehensive set of primary legal materials that are available free and in one place on the internet. It includes 46 databases covering seven jurisdictions.

www.bailii.org/uk/cases/UKHL
This includes all the House of Lords' decisions since 1838.

www.supremecourt.uk
The Supreme Court is the final court of appeal in the UK for civil cases. It hears appeals in criminal cases from England, Wales and Northern Ireland. It hears cases of the greatest public or constitutional importance affecting the whole population.

www.parliament.uk
Provides access to Parliament and all parliamentary business. Bills can be followed as they make their way through the legislative procedure.

www.legislation.gov.uk
Provides access to all legislation. This site also houses Explanatory Notes for important legislation, and information about which sections of Acts have been brought into force.

www.gov.uk
All government departments are now accessed through this one site. For example, the Justice Ministry is available at:

www.gov.uk/government/organisations/ministry-of-justice

www.theguardian.com/law/series/guardian-legal-network
The *Guardian* Legal Network brings together the best blogs and sites that cover legal affairs and developments from around the world. The network connects sites that provide high-quality news, comment, analysis, blogs and multimedia.

www.thetimes.co.uk/tto/law (paywall)
The legal site of *The Times*. It is updated continuously every day, and contains a wide range of legal stories, analyses and commentaries. Gary Slapper writes a weekly column for *Times online*. There are also over 600 of his articles in *The Times* online archive.

http://ukhumanrightsblog.com
Barristers from 1 Crown Office Row offer balanced analysis of human rights legal issues.

GENERAL READING

Ashworth, A, *Sentencing and Criminal Justice*, 2010, Cambridge: CUP

Bailey, SH, Gunn, MJ and Ormerod, D, *Smith & Bailey on The Modern English Legal System*, 5th edn, 2007, London: Sweet & Maxwell

Baldwin, J, 'Police interview techniques: establishing truth or proof?' (1993) 33 British J of Criminology 3

Baldwin, J, 'Power and police interviews' (1993) 143 NLJ 1194

Baldwin, J and Hill, S, *The Operation of the Green Form Scheme in England and Wales*, 1988, London: LCD

Baldwin, J and McConville, M, *Negotiated Justice: Pressures on Defendants to Plead Guilty*, 1977, London: Martin Robertson

Baldwin, J and McConville, M, *Negotiated Justice: A Closer Look at the Implications of Plea Bargaining*, 1993, London: Martin Robertson

Barnard, M, 'All bar none' (1999) 96/26 Law Soc Gazette 20

Barnett, H, *Constitutional and Administrative Law*, 11th edn, 2015, Abingdon: Routledge

Bennett, WL and Feldman, MS, *Reconstructing Reality in the Courtroom: Justice and Judgment in American Culture*, 1984, New Jersey: Rutgers UP

Bennion, F, 'Statute law obscurity and drafting parameters' (1978) British JLS 235

Bennion, F, 'A naked usurpation?' (1999) 149 NLJ 421

Bennion, F, *Statutory Interpretation*, 5th edn, 2008, London: Butterworths

Bindaman, D, 'Crown duals' (1999) Law Soc Gazette, 31 March

Bindman, G, 'Lessons of *Pinochet*' (1999) 149 NLJ 1050

Bingham, T, *The Rule of Law*, 2011, London: Penguin

Black, J, Bridge, J, Bond, T and Gribbin L, *A Practical Approach to Family Law*, 2013, Oxford: OUP

Blackstone's Civil Procedure (Plant, C (ed)), 2010, Oxford: OUP

Blake, S, Browne, J and Sime, S, *A Practical Approach to Alternative Dispute Resolution*, 2nd edn, 2012, Oxford: OUP.

Blom-Cooper, L (ed), *The Law as Literature*, 1961, London: The Bodley Head

Broadbent, G, 'Offensive weapons and the Criminal Justice Act' (1989) Law Soc Gazette, 12 July

Burns, R, 'A view from the ranks' (2000) 150 NLJ 1829

Burrow, J, 'Pre-committal custody time limits' (1999) 149 NLJ 330

Cane, P (ed), *Atiyah's Accidents, Compensation and the Law*, 6th edn, 2006, Cambridge: CUP

Cape, E, 'Police interrogation and interruption' (1994) 144 NLJ 120

Card, R and Ward, R, *The Criminal Justice and Public Order Act 1994*, 1994, Bristol: Jordans

Clayton, R and Tomlinson, H, 'Arrest and reasonable grounds for suspicion' (1988) 32 Law Soc Gazette 22

Cragg, S, 'Stop and search powers: research and extension' (1999) Legal Action 3

Craig, P and de Búrca, G, *EU Law: Text, Cases and Materials*, 3rd edn, 2003, Oxford: OUP

Crawford, L, 'Race awareness training and the judges' (1994) Counsel 11

Croall, H, *Crime and Society in Britain*, 2008, London: Longman

Darbyshire, P, 'The lamp that shows that freedom lives – is it worth the candle?' [1991] Crim LR 740

De Sousa Santos, B, *Toward a New Common Sense*, 2002, London: Butterworths

Devlin (Lord), *Trial by Jury*, 1966, London: Stevens

Diamond, D, 'Woolf reforms hike costs' (1999) The Lawyer 2

Dicey, AV, *An Introduction to the Study of the Law of the Constitution* (1885), 10th edn, 1959, London: Macmillan

Dixon, D, Coleman, C and Bottomley, K, 'Consent and legal regulation of policing' (1990) 17 JLS 345

Eekelaar, J and Maclean, M, *Family Justice: The Work of Family Judges in Uncertain Times*, 2013, Oxford: OUP

Exall, G, 'Civil litigation brief' (1999) SJ 32

Flemming, J, 'Judge airs concerns over Woolf reforms' (2000) Law Soc Gazette, 10 February

Freeman, M, *Law and Popular Culture*, 2005, Oxford: OUP

Frenkel, J, 'On the road to reform' (1998) Law Soc Gazette, 16 December

Frenkel, J, 'Offers to settle and payments into court' (1999) 149 NLJ 458

Genn, H, *Hard Bargaining: Out of Court Settlement in Personal Injury Claims*, 1987, Oxford: OUP

Genn, H and Genn, Y, *The Effectiveness of Representation at Tribunals*, 1989, London: LCD

Gibb, F, 'Rude judges must mind their language' (1999) *The Times*, 29 June

Gibb, F, 'Thatcher furious at "vindictive" Pinochet decision' (1999) *The Times*, 16 April

Gibb, F, 'Child killer Bell granted anonymity for life' (2003) *The Times*, 22 May

Gibb, F, 'Falconer takes an axe to legal tradition' (2003) *The Times*, 16 September

Gibb, F, 'Fee cuts prompt barristers to reject legal aid work' (2004) *The Times*, 5 April

Gibb, F, 'Commonwealth and common law: our imperial legacies' (2005) *The Times*, 13 September

Gibb, F, 'Price is important, but quality can't be sacrificed' (2006) *The Times*, 14 February

Gibb, F, 'Some of the EU countries are hypocritical about human rights' (2006) *The Times*, 25 April

Gibb, F, 'Legal profession set for historic reforms' (2009) *The Times*, 20 November

Gibb, F, 'Chilcot and legal advice' (2010) *The Times*, 3 February

Gibb, F, 'Divorce courts may be thing of the past under radical overhaul of family justice' (2010) *The Times*, 21 January

Gibb, F, 'First criminal trial with no jury for 400 years starts' (2010) *The Times*, 13 January

Gibb, F, 'Gilderdale case prompts fresh calls to clarify the law on assisted dying' (2010) *The Times*, 26 January

Gibb, F, 'No win, no fee' deals cost taxpayers and insurers millions' (2010) *The Times*, 15 January

Gibson, B, 'Why Bournemouth?' (1987) 151 JP 520

Glasser, C, 'Legal aid and eligibility' (1988) Law Soc Gazette, 9 March

Glasser, C, 'Legal services and the Green Papers' (1989) Law Soc Gazette, 5 April

Gold, S, 'Woolf watch' (1999) 149 NLJ 718

Goodhart, A, 'The *ratio decidendi* of a case' (1959) 22 MLR 117

Goodrich, P, *Reading the Law*, 1986, Oxford: Basil Blackwell

Grainger, I and Fealy, M, *An Introduction to the New Civil Procedure Rules*, 1999, London: Cavendish Publishing

Griffith, JAG, *The Politics of the Judiciary*, 5th edn, 1997, London: Fontana

Griffiths, C, 'Jury trial' (1999) Counsel 14

Hamer, P, 'Complaints: a new strategy' (1999) 149 NLJ 959

Hanson, S, *Legal Method, Skills and Reasoning*, 3rd edn, 2010, Abingdon: Routledge

Harris, D *et al*, *Compensation and Support for Illness and Injury*, 1984, Oxford: Clarendon

Harrison, R, 'Cry Woolf' (1999) 149 NLJ 1011

Harrison, R, 'Why have two types of civil court?' (1999) 149 NLJ 65

Harrison, R, 'Appealing prospects' (2000) NLJ 1175

Hart, H, *The Concept of Law*, 1961, Oxford: OUP

Hayek, FA von, *The Road to Serfdom* (1971), 1994, London: Routledge and Kegan Paul

Hedderman, C and Moxon, C, *Magistrates' Court or Crown Court? Mode of Trial Decisions and Sentenc-ing*, Home Office Study No 125, 1992, London: HMSO

HM Courts and Tribunals Service, *Annual Report and Accounts 2014–15*, 2015, London: House of Commons.

Holdsworth, W, *A History of English Law*, 1924, London: Methuen

Holland, T, 'Cut price conveyancing' (1994) 144 NLJ 192

Horne, A, Drewry, G and Oliver, D (eds), *Parliament and the Law*, 2013, Oxford: Hart

Hucklesby, A and Wahidin, A, *Criminal Justice*, 2013, Oxford: OUP

Hutchinson, A, *Evolution and the Common Law*, 2005, Cambridge: CUP

Irvine (Lord), 'Community vision under fire' (1999) Law Soc Gazette, 26 May

Jason-Lloyd, L, 'Section 60 of the Criminal Justice and Public Order Act 1994' (1998) 162 JP 836

JUSTICE, *Professional Negligence and the Quality of Legal Services – An Economic Perspective*, 1983, London: JUSTICE

Kadri, S, *The Trial: a History from Socrates to OJ Simpson*, 2005, London: HarperCollins

Kairys, D, *The Politics of Law: A Progressive Critique*, 1982, New York: Pantheon

Keating, D, 'Upholding the Rule of Law' (1999) 149 NLJ 533

Khan, S and Ryder, M, 'Police and the law' (1998) Legal Action 16

Law Society Civil Litigation Committee, 'Unravelling the enigma of *Thai Trading*' (2000) Law Soc Gazette, 9 June

Lee, S, *Judging Judges*, 1988, London: Faber & Faber

Legal Services Ombudsman, *Demanding Progress*, 1999–2000 Annual Report, London: HMSO

Lidstone, K (ed), *Prosecutions by Private Individuals and Non-Police Agencies*, 1980, London: HMSO

Lidstone, K, 'Entry, search and seizure' (1989) 40 NILQ 333

Lidstone, K and Palmer, C, *The Investigation of Crime*, 1996, London: Butterworths

Loughlin, M, *Sword and Scales*, 2000, Oxford: Hart

MacCallum, V, 'Learning lessons' (2001) Law Soc Gazette, 10 January

MacCormick, N, *Legal Rules and Legal Reasoning*, 1978, Oxford: Clarendon

Mackay (Lord), *The Administration of Justice*, 1994, Hamlyn Lectures, London: Sweet & Maxwell

Malleson, K, *The New Judiciary – The Effect of Expansion and Activism*, 1999, Aldershot: Ashgate

Malleson, K and Roberts, S, 'Streamlining and clarifying the appellate process' (2002) Crim LR 272

Mansell, W, Meteyard, B and Thomson, A, *A Critical Introduction to Law*, 3rd edn, 2004, London: Cavendish Publishing

Mayhew, L and Reiss, A, 'The social organisation of legal contacts' (1969) 34 American Sociological Rev 311

McConville, M, Sanders, A and Leng, R, *The Case for the Prosecution*, 1991, London: Routledge

McGrath, P, 'Appeals against small claims track decisions' (1999) 149 NLJ 748

McLaughlin, E and Muncie, J, *Controlling Crime*, 2001, London: Sage and the Open University

Money-Kyrle, R, 'Advocates' immunity after *Osman*' (1999) 149 NLJ 945 and 981

Montesquieu, C, *De l'Esprit des Lois* (1748), 1989, Cambridge: CUP

Morris, P, White, R and Lewis, P, *Social Needs and Legal Action*, 1973, London: Robertson

Motson, S, Stephenson, G and Williamson, T, 'The effects of case characteristics on suspect behaviour during police questioning' (1992) 32 British J of Criminology 23

Murphy, M, 'Civil legal aid eligibility' (1989) Legal Action 4

Napier, M, 'Conditional fees' (1995) 92(16) Law Soc Gazette 1626

News, 'The legal profession and the Community Legal Service' (1999) 149 NLJ 1195

News in Brief, 'Cheap conveyancing' (1998) 148 NLJ 8

Nobles, R, 'The Criminal Case Review Commission' (2005) Crim LR 173

Pannick, D, *Judges*, 1987, Oxford: OUP

Pannick, D, *Advocates*, 1992, Oxford: OUP

Parker, C, 'Judicial decision making' (1999) 149 NLJ 1142

Parpworth, N, 'Breach of the peace: breach of human rights?' (1998) 152 JP 6

Payne, R, 'To counsel, not confront: the law on ADR' (1999) Counsel 30

Popplewell, O, *Benchmark: life, laughter, and the law*, 2003, London: Tauris

Purchas, F (Sir), 'What is happening to judicial independence' (1994) 144 NLJ 1306

Raz, J, 'The Rule of Law and its virtue' (1977) 93 LQR 195

Reid (Lord), 'The judge as law maker' (1972) 12 JSPTL 22

Reiner, R, 'Responsibilities and reforms' (1993) 143 NLJ 1096

Reiner, R, *Crime, Order and Policing*, 1994, London: Routledge

Reiner, R, *The Politics of the Police*, 2nd edn, 2000, Oxford: OUP

Richardson, J (ed), *Archbold: Criminal Pleading, Evidence and Practice*, 2016, London: Sweet & Maxwell

Robertshaw, P, *Rethinking Legal Need: The Case of Criminal Justice*, 1991, Aldershot: Dartmouth

Robertson, G, 'The Downey Report: MPs must realise they are not above the law' (1997) *The Guardian*, 4 July

Rutherford, A, 'Judicial training and autonomy' (1999) 149 NLJ 1120

Rutherford, A, 'Preserving a robust independence' (1999) 149 NLJ 908

Sanders, A, 'Class bias in prosecutions' (1985) 24 Howard J 17

Sanders, A, 'The silent code' (1994) 144 NLJ 946

Sanders, A and Young, R, 'Plea bargaining and the next Criminal Justice Bill' (1994) 144 NLJ 1200

Sanders, A and Young, R, *Criminal Justice*, 1995, London: Butterworths

Sanders, A *et al*, *Advice and Assistance at Police Stations and the 24 Hour Duty Solicitor Scheme*, 1989, London: LCD

Scrivener, A, 'The birth of a new language in the court room: English' (1999) *The Independent*, 26 April

Sedley, S (Sir), 'Human rights: a 21st century agenda' [1995] PL 386

Sidebottom, A, Belur, J, Bowers, K, Tompson, L and Johnson, SD, 'Theft in price-volatile markets: on the relationship between copper price and copper theft' (2011) 48(3) Journal of Research in Crime and Delinquency 396

Sime, S, *A Practical Approach to Civil Procedure*, 16th edn, 2013, Oxford: OUP

Simpson, A, 'The *ratio decidendi* of a case' (1957) 20 MLR 413

Slapper, G, *Blood in the Bank*, 1999, Aldershot: Ashgate

Slapper, G, 'English legal system' (1999) 26 SLR 31

Slapper, G, *Organisational Prosecutions*, 2001, Aldershot: Ashgate

Slapper, G, *How the Law Works*, 4th edn, 2016, Abingdon: Routledge

Slapper, G and Kelly, D, *English Law*, 3rd edn, 2010, Abingdon: Routledge

Smith, JC, 'Criminal appeals and the Criminal Cases Review Commission' (1995) 145 NLJ 534

Smith, R, 'Politics and the judiciary' (1993) 143 NLJ 1486

Smith, R, 'Judicial statistics: questions and answers' (1994) 144 NLJ 1088

Smith, R (ed), *Shaping the Future: New Directions in Legal Services*, 1995, London: LAG

Smith, R (ed), *Achieving Civil Justice*, 1996, London: LAG

St Luce, S, 'Cutting the lifeline' (1999) 149 NLJ 398

Stone, R, *Textbook on Civil Liberties and Human Rights*, 9th edn, 2012, Oxford: OUP

Steyn (Lord), 'The weakest and least dangerous department of government' [1997] PL 84

Susskind, R, *Tomorrow's Lawyers: An Introduction to Your Future*, 2013, Oxford: OUP

Temple Lang, J, 'The duties of national courts under Community constitutional law' [1997] EL Rev 22

Thomas, DA (ed), *Current Sentencing Practice*, 1999, London: Sweet & Maxwell

Thompson, E, *Whigs and Hunters*, 1977, Harmondsworth: Penguin

Thompson, P (ed), *The Civil Court Practice*, 1999, London: Butterworths

Trent, M, 'ADR and the new Civil Procedure Rules' (1999) 149 NLJ 410

Turner, AJ, 'Inferences under s 34 of the Criminal Justice and Public Order Act 1994: Part One' (1999) 163 JP, 27 March

Turner, AJ, 'Inferences under s 34 of the Criminal Justice and Public Order Act 1994: Part Two' (1999) 163 JP, 24 April

Twining, W, *Globalisation and Legal Theory*, 2000, Cambridge: CUP

Twining, W, *Rethinking Evidence: Exploratory Essays*, 2nd edn, 2006, Cambridge: CUP

Twining, W and Meirs, D, *How To Do Things With Rules*, 5th edn, 2010, Cambridge: CUP

Unger, R, *In Law and Modern Society*, 1976, New York: Free Press

Verkaik, R, 'Opinions on counsel' (1998) 95/04 Law Soc Gazette 22

Vignaendra, S, *Social Class and entry into the Solicitors' Profession: Research Study 41*, 2001, London: The Law Society

Wadham, J and Arkinstall, J, 'Human rights and crime' (1999) 149 NLJ 703

Watson, A, 'The right to elect trial by jury: the issue reappears' (1998) 163 JP 636

Weber, M, *Economy and Society (Wirtschaft und Gesellschaft)*, 1968, Roth, G and Widttich, C (trans), Berkeley: California UP

Wendell Holmes, O, *The Common Law* (1881), 1968, London: Macmillan

Williams, G, 'Letting off the guilty and prosecuting the innocent' [1985] Crim LR 115

Wolchover, D and Heaton-Armstrong, A, 'Jailing psychopaths and prison cell confessions' (1999) 149 NLJ 285

Woolf (Lord), 'Judicial review – the tensions between the executive and the judiciary' (1998) 114 LQR 579

Yarrow, S, *The Price of Success*, 1997, Grantham: Grantham

Yarrow, S and Abrams, P, *Nothing to Lose? Clients' Experiences of Using Conditional Fees*, Summary Report, 1999, London: University of Westminster

Zander, M, 'Who goes to solicitors?' (1969) 66 Law Soc Gazette 174

Zander, M, 'Costs of litigation – a study in the Queen's Bench Division' (1975) Law Soc Gazette, 25 June

Zander, M, *Legal Services for the Community*, 1978, London: Temple Smith

Zander, M, 'Investigation of crime' [1979] Crim LR 211

Zander, M, *A Matter of Justice*, 1989, Oxford: OUP

Zander, M and Henderson, P, *The Crown Court Study*, Royal Commission on Criminal Justice Research Study 19, 145, 1993, London: HMSO

Zander, M, 'How does judicial case management work?' (1997) 147 NLJ 353

Zander, M, 'The trouble with fast track fixed costs' (1997) 147 NLJ 1125

Zander, M, 'The Woolf Report: forwards or backwards for the new Lord Chancellor' (1997) 16 Civil Justice Quarterly 208

Zander, M, 'Woolf on Zander' (1997) 147 NLJ 768

Zander, M, *Cases and Materials on the English Legal System*, 10th edn, 2007, Cambridge: CUP

INDEX